ALSO BY WILLIAM O'SHAUGHNESSY

AirWAVES
A Collection of Radio Editorials from the Golden Apple

IT ALL COMES BACK TO ME NOW
Character Portraits from the Golden Apple

MORE RIFFS, RANTS, AND RAVES

VOX POPULI
The O'Shaughnessy Files

MARIO CUOMO
Remembrances of a Remarkable Man

RADIO ACTIVE

WITH STEVE WARLEY and JOSEPH REILLY

SERVING THEIR COMMUNITIES
A History of the New York State Broadcasters Association

RADIO ACTIVE

Radio Active

WILLIAM O'SHAUGHNESSY

WHITNEY GLOBAL MEDIA
PUBLISHING GROUP

New Rochelle, New York 2019

Whitney Media has no responsibility for the persistence or
accuracy of URLs for external or third-party Internet websites referred
to in this publication and does not guarantee that any content on such
websites is, or will remain, accurate or appropriate.

Some content that appears in the print edition of this book
may not be available in the electronic version.

Library of Congress Control Number: 2019906012

Printed in the United States of America

21 20 19   5 4 3 2 1

First edition

For My Children:
Matthew Thayer
David Tucker
Kate Wharton

My Grandchildren:
Tucker Thomas
Isabel Grace
Flynn Thayer
Lily Anna
Amelia Jane

And for the people of Westchester and New York State
who have indulged my enthusiasms and supported our
community radio stations for more than 60 years.

CONTENTS

Foreword by Mario M. Cuomo *xv*

Introduction *1*

PART I. THE FIRST AMENDMENT

"Forty-five Simple Words" by Jack Valenti *5*

Bill O'Reilly's "Character Assassination": A WVOX Commentary *8*

The Silencing of Imus *12*

Bob Grant on the Imus Controversy *15*

"Don't Hush Rush . . . " *18*

Missing in Action by Patrick D. Maines *21*

The Real Obscenity *24*

Floyd Abrams: Notes and Observations on the First Amendment *26*

Free Speech on the Airwaves: Confab with Mario Cuomo *32*

Ambassador Ogden Rogers Reid *43*

Nancy Pelosi v. James Madison *46*

Civil Liberties in an Age of Terrorism *57*

Obsequious Acquiescence by William O'Shaughnessy *62*

Issue Advertising Is the Issue *69*

Re: Corporate Censorship *71*

First Amendment Warriors by William O'Shaughnessy *72*

A Towering Triumvirate *77*

PART II. OPEN MIC RADIO INTERVIEWS

Chris Ruddy, Chairman of Newsmax *85*

Interview with Dan Rather on his Book *What Unites Us* *90*

Bill Mohl, President, Entergy Wholesale Commodities *93*

[vii]

Roger Stone on *The Man Who Killed Kennedy*,
the Cuomos, and More *105*

Richard Norton Smith, Historian and Biographer *115*

Angelo Martinelli, Publisher *137*

"The Mendicant," Father Paul Lostritto, O.F.M. *147*

Bishop Joseph Sullivan *161*

Timothy Cardinal Dolan, Archbishop of New York *170*

Dr. Christopher Comfort, Medical Director, Calvary Hospital *174*

Frank Gifford: "#16" *185*

William O'Shaughnessy on the Fred Dicker Radio Show *188*

Alfred F. Kelly Jr. *191*

Gerald Shargel, Esq. *204*

John Cahill *212*

PART III. OF AN EVENING . . .
A Little Night Music *231*

The Best Interpreters of the Great American Songbook *234*

"A Real New York Evening . . . " Review *236*

On the Occasion of Sirio Maccioni's Eightieth Birthday *237*

Sirio Maccioni of Le Cirque *238*

Saloon Songs from Toots Shor to Sirio Maccioni *249*

More "Saloon Songs" (an Update) *257*

"The Numbers" *264*

The One Night Stand of Charles Osgood *268*

PART IV. IN PRAISE OF "VIVID SOULS"
The Unforgettables *273*

A Different Kind of List *289*

Vivid Women in Every Season *293*

Notes for the Four Seasons Tribute Evening *296*

CONTENTS

Westchester County Press Ninetieth Anniversary *299*

Richard Clark's Eightieth Birthday *301*

Judge Samuel Fredman's Ninetieth-Birthday Celebration *304*

HOPE Community Services Gala: Honoring Frank Endress *311*

Celebrating the 200th Anniversary of the Christian Brothers *314*

A Community Celebration Honoring
Commissioner Patrick J. Carroll *316*

PART V. EULOGIES: THE LAST WORD

Eulogy for John S. Pritchard III *323*

Henry Kissinger's Tribute to John McCain *326*

Philip Roth, Out and About of an Evening *329*

Governor Andrew Cuomo's Eulogy for Jimmy Breslin *333*

A Personal Tribute to Jimmy Breslin *336*

Our Neighbor Ruby Dee *344*

Tribute to Ruby Dee by Harry Belafonte *346*

"A Death in the Family": Tim Russert *349*

Don Rickles and the Focaccia Kid at Le Cirque! *354*

Frances W. Preston, "The Lady from Nashville" *355*

Kate O'Shaughnessy Nulty's Tribute to Mary Jane Wharton,
Her Grandmother *357*

Nelson: A Child of the Neighborhood *359*

William O'Shaughnessy's Tribute to Martin Beck *365*

Tribute to Paul Hutton *368*

Tribute to Peter Mustich, Townie *370*

Another Beloved Townie Open Line Caller *372*

Tribute to Rick Buckley, Beloved Broadcaster *376*

Tribute to Stu Olds, Beloved Broadcast Exec *379*

Tribute to Ward Quaal, Broadcasting's Greatest Statesman *382*

William B. Williams's Hall of Fame Induction *384*

Tribute to Dawson B. "Tack" Nail *387*

The Passing of Peggy Burton *390*

Diane Gagliardi Collins Passes Away at Ninety *392*

John Mara's Eulogy for Ann T. Mara *393*

Eulogy for Joseph A. Anastasi, "The Captain" *398*

Eulogy for the Hon. Salvatore T. Generoso, "The Last Legend" *401*

Caryl Donnelly Plunkett: An Appreciation *404*

An Appreciation of Jim Delmonico (1920–2012) *408*

The Incomparable "Joe Slick": An Appreciation *410*

John Scully: A Sailor and a Gentleman *414*

A Tribute to "Colonel" Marty Rochelle *417*

Tribute to Ambassador Edward Noonan Ney *420*

Tribute to Bob Grant *421*

"The Amazin'" Bill Mazer *422*

Tribute to Governor Brendan Byrne *423*

Page Morton Black, the "Chock full o'Nuts" Lady *424*

Brother Driscoll of Iona, Great Educator and More *427*

Rush Limbaugh III Tribute to Ed McLaughlin *430*

**PART VI. THE OBLIGATORY MARIO M. CUOMO
SECTION IN EVERY BILL O'SHAUGHNESSY BOOK**

"The Morning After": A Stunningly Candid Interview
with Governor Andrew M. Cuomo *441*

Remarks of Gov. Andrew M. Cuomo
at Central Synagogue Interfaith Service *455*

Mario Cuomo: A Dream *460*

Matilda Cuomo *461*

William O'Shaughnessy Interview with Mario Cuomo Re:
Andy O'Rourke *472*

Interview with Mario M. Cuomo *476*

Dutch Treat Club Annual Dinner Presentation
of the Gold Medal for Lifetime Achievement
in the Arts for Governor Mario M. Cuomo *484*

Dutch Treat Club Luncheon *486*

An Evanescent Supreme Court Nomination:
The Gov. Mario M. Cuomo Story *497*

Andrew Cuomo's Eulogy for Mario Cuomo *500*

Mario: This Is Personal *513*

"Quotable Quotes"—Reviews of *Mario Cuomo:
Remembrances of a Remarkable Man* *523*

A Note on Mario Cuomo and Teilhard de Chardin *532*

Mario Cuomo's Omega Society Speech:
A Meditation on Ultimate Values *533*

PART VII. THE EXTRAORDINARY BUSH FAMILY

George W. Bush's Eulogy for His Father,
President George H.W. Bush *541*

Whitney Global Media Endorsement:
George H.W. Bush for President, 1992 *546*

Thank You Letter from "41" *551*

George W. Bush for President, 2000 *552*

Billy Bush Deserves a Second Chance *555*

Phil Reisman: In Defense of Billy Bush *557*

"Great on Imus": A Letter from Jonathan Bush *559*

Jonathan Bush's Letter on Imus to CBS Radio *560*

PART VIII. AIRBORNE ENDORSEMENTS

Governor Andrew Cuomo for Governor *565*

Alessandra Biaggi for State Senate *569*

Julie Killian for State Senate *571*

George Latimer for Westchester County Executive *576*

Rob Astorino for County Executive *580*

Judge Daniel Angiolillo *584*

Ernie Davis for Mayor *587*

Stay the Course with Mayor Bradley *589*

PART IX. A MAN OF LETTERS

Letter to Rush Limbaugh (March 1, 2018) *593*

Letter to Rush Limbaugh (March 26, 2018) *594*

Letter from Rush Limbaugh to William O'Shaughnessy *596*

Letter to Rush Limbaugh (April 23, 2018) *597*

The Holy Roman Catholic Church:
Letter to Michael "Lionel" Lebron *598*

A Note from Dan Rather *600*

Facebook Note from Kate O'Shaughnessy Nulty *601*

In Defense of Le Cirque: Letter to Pete Wells *602*

Letter to Pete Wells Regarding the new Four Seasons *605*

Admiring John Sterling: Letter to Scott Herman *607*

"A Westchester Legend": Letter from Samuel G. Fredman *609*

Re: William B. Williams and Rick Buckley:
Letter from Dick Robinson *611*

Letter to William O'Shaughnessy from Ralph Graves *613*

PART X. THE GREAT ISSUES. ABORTION AND

THE DEATH PENALTY: LIFE IN EVERY INSTANCE

Timothy Cardinal Dolan: Reclaim the Truth
of the Human Person *617*

The Greatest Issue, Abortion: A WVOX Commentary *624*

The Death Penalty (Pope Francis's view) *625*

The Death Penalty (Gov. Mario M. Cuomo's view) *626*

Las Vegas Shooting: Another "Thoughts and Prayers" Day *631*

CONTENTS

The New Killing Season *634*

Comments from "The Deplorables" *636*

The 137 Real Reasons Why Hillary Lost and Trump Won *639*

"Those People" *644*

Down-Home Democracy in the Land of Thomas Paine *646*

Fifty Years after President Kennedy Was Assassinated *647*

Acknowledgments *649*

Index *657*

Photographs follow pages 200 and 424

FOREWORD

I'm grateful to Mario Cuomo for many things and for his countless expressions of friendship during the thirty-eight years I was privileged to know him. Among his many beneficences were the Introductions he wrote for my four previous anthologies for Fordham University Press. As I've so often acknowledged, I am not at all deserving of his blessing, imprimatur, or generous friendship, especially when it comes to anything associated with scholarship, writing, or the mother tongue, the English language.

Almost five years after the governor left us, we still remember him as a deeply religious figure of insight, creativity, passion, and moral courage. As a lawyer, scholar, author, and governor of dazzlingly facile mind, he taught us how to think, how to write, how to feel, how to argue, and how to love.

I was flattered beyond words to have received the following wholly undeserved piece, which was intended as a Foreword to this future book, destined to be yet another anthology of interviews, editorials, musings, eulogies, and commentaries, my fifth such effort for Fordham University Press.

But now that Mario has departed for what Malcolm Wilson, the great Fordham orator (who also served as governor), once called "another and, we are sure, a better world," I'm reminded that the governor spoke at several book parties that launched the publication of my earlier anthologies at the Maccioni family's iconic New York restaurant Le Cirque. At each star-studded event, several hundred showed up, including some *real* writers: Gay Talese, Peter Maas, Stephen Schlesinger, Ken Auletta, Barbara Taylor Bradford, Richard Johnson, Liz Smith, Phil Reisman, Emily Smith, Walter Cronkite, Cindy Adams, and Dan Rather. They came not to hear me but to be with Mario Cuomo—except at the gathering for my most recent book, at which his wonderful and luminous daughter Maria Cuomo Cole filled in for her ailing dad. No one was disappointed as the graceful

Maria read a lovely tribute penned by her illustrious father for my poor literary work.

And with the publication of this new anthology I expect we'll have yet another lovely evening—probably at the new Four Seasons in Manhattan. My only regret, of course, is that Mario himself won't be physically present as we had hoped for this one.

The following Foreword, then, was written by Mario Cuomo himself for my "next book," as yet another expression of that extraordinary friendship I treasure. It was his last gift to me. I'm only sorry my writing and scholarship are not worthy of his friendship. Or of the great man himself.

—W.O.

BROTHER BILL
Mario M. Cuomo

Bill O'Shaughnessy's previous books were so good, I couldn't put them down.

His personal commentaries, written with casually elegant language, make you wish the whole country were hearing and reading his work. Actually, the whole world can now savor his genius thanks to the Internet and WVOX.com. He is a journalist, commentator, connoisseur, a strong political presence, and a forceful advocate of great causes.

During his remarkable fifty-year run as the permittee of WVOX and WVIP, O'Shaughnessy has used his great Gaelic gift of words, a sharp mind, deep conviction, and the capacity for powerful advocacy to inspire the fainthearted, guide the eager, and charm almost everyone he meets. As a broadcaster and author, he has written and spoken simple truths and powerful political arguments with a good and generous heart.

As an interviewer, Bill O'Shaughnessy is a magic miner of fascinating nuggets coaxed from a host of extraordinarily interesting people, some of them celebrities and others previously undiscovered neighborhood gems. O'Shaughnessy is among a select few who create magic with their words. He always brings us a rich flow of genuine American opinions and sentiment.

Few people have as rich a talent for "writing for the ear"—Charles Kuralt and Charles Osgood, certainly. Also the late, legendary Paul Harvey. And Bill O'Shaughnessy.

He can't describe a scene as well as Jimmy Breslin. He's not as "easy" a writer as Pete Hamill. But when he's on his game, Brother Bill is better than anyone on the air or in print.

We didn't always agree politically. But O'Shaughnessy has never lost his instinct for the underdog. He is a constant reminder of a Republican Party that was much better for this country.

He's also an elegant, entertaining, and spellbinding speaker. He might have taken all these gifts and made himself a great political leader or a very rich captain of history. Instead, fifty years ago, he devoted himself to what then was a small and struggling radio station, and ever since then, thanks to his brilliance and dedication, he's created what has become his much-praised WVOX/Worldwide and the highly successful and innovative WVIP, where many different and emerging new voices are heard in the land.

Somebody said to me about his previous four books, "That's quite a body of good work O'Shaughnessy has put together, all while we were dazzled by his high style and glittering persona." I guess that's right. But it is not the body of work; it's the *soul* of the work that I have always been more attracted to.

And that's what O'Shaughnessy does. He doesn't deliver homilies about it. Maybe he doesn't even know it fully. But he is a lover. He loves people. He loves understanding them. He loves not just the big shots, but he loves all the little people too. And you can see it, you can read it, you can feel it, and you can hear it on the radio.

The man is a lover. He uses one word few people in our society use regularly (unless they are in the apparel business!): sweet. The highest compliment he can give you is not to tell you this guy is bright, successful, dazzling in his language or ability, but that he's sweet, or that she's sweet, or that it's sweet. Well, that, in the end, is what I like about him. He understands life, he understands love, and he knows how to portray it.

And always—if you push the discussion with him—you find, not far from the surface, a profound yearning to use his own great gift of life to find more sweetness in the world or perhaps even to create some himself. I know him. And he will find a way, or he will spend the rest of his life trying.

So it's all here: O'Shaughnessy the businessman, reporter, broadcaster, commentator, friend of politicians of all stripes, religious leaders of all stripes—and even an occasional politician "in stripes"!

So I've given you no new knowledge of Bill in this Foreword to his new book. But custom requires that I repeat the obvious, if only to remind ourselves why we are so pleased he was persuaded to put together another work.

One of his great passions is the First Amendment, that nearly sacred guarantee of our unique American freedom of speech and expression, which is being challenged at the moment by government agents seeking to make themselves the dictators of public tastes and attitudes. And Bill O'Shaughnessy is one of the few respected authorities on the subject who have spoken out against these powerful and dangerous political forces, even at the risk of reprisal.

His speech "Obsequious Acquiescence" has been widely read and admired by some of the best legal minds in America, including the estimable Floyd Abrams, the distinguished national First Amendment expert. Indeed, for his lifetime of work on free speech issues, Bill was called "The Conscience of the Broadcasting Industry" by the prestigious Media Institute think tank in Washington.

He's also a philanthropist and humanitarian. And the down-and-out in the broadcasting profession have been the beneficiaries of his dynamic and creative fundraising efforts for the Broadcasters Foundation of America, which he presently serves as chairman of its Guardian Fund to assist the less fortunate in what Brother Bill calls his "tribe."

In *The Screwtape Letters* the great C. S. Lewis wrote that what the Devil wants is for a man to finish his life having to say he spent his life not doing either what is *right* or what he *enjoyed*. For the many years I've known him, Bill O'Shaughnessy has spent most of his time doing things he ought to have been doing and enjoying them immensely.

I have myself been blessed with a glittering array of loyal friends from every phase of my already long life, people willing to weigh my many inadequacies less diligently than they assess what they find commendable. None of these friends has tried harder than Bill O'Shaughnessy to give me a chance to be useful. He is a man of his words. But I'll never have the words I need to express my gratitude adequately to him.

Everyone in our family calls him "Brother Bill." By any name, he is very special.

—*Mario M. Cuomo*

RADIO ACTIVE

INTRODUCTION

Radio Active is William O'Shaughnessy's fifth collection of essays, on-air interviews, tributes and eulogies, endorsements, recollections of an evening, and much more from the lustrous universe of the media mogul declared "perhaps the finest broadcaster in America" by the once-glorious *Litchfield County Times* and knighted as "world-class" and "legendary" by the industry's most distinguished arbiters.

No less a giant of international affairs than former Secretary of State Henry Kissinger likens O'Shaughnessy's essays and other stylish turns to "potato chips," because "you can't stop with only one."

Fortunately for O'Shaughnessy's devoted readers and listeners, who range from Westchester "Townies" to the *cognoscenti* of the eastern establishment and far beyond, this new compendium is voluptuous and catholic in scope across its hundreds of pages, pulsing with brilliant, insightful prose encompassing a life-affirming reverence for luminous people, places, and events from all stations of life, past and present.

Radio Active reprises classic pieces from previous volumes—probing discussions with priests and cardinals, healers, politicians, media influencers, impresarios of dining and entertainment—while debuting thought-provoking new works on great issues of the day, correspondences with O'Shaughnessy's heroes and "villains," and moving elegies brimming with refined lyricism as they pay tribute to beloved figures in American life.

Purposely the book opens with a section on the First Amendment, now and always, it seems, under attack—broadly, and with a bull's-eye on broadcasters who deliver bold, heartfelt opinions that crackle across our land on what remains the purest medium for sound, radio, like pure poetry unchained by the beat of the hip hop generation. Patrick Maines, president of The Media Institute, calls O'Shaughnessy "the conscience of broadcasting," and in these pages broadcasting's "national champion" and "voluptuary" of the First Amendment joins with others to defend free speech on the airwaves and rail against attempts to silence the likes of Don Imus and Howard Stern, as well as that "magnificent bastard" of generosity toward broadcasters who helped pave his path, Rush Hudson Limbaugh III.

As always, there's a special section dedicated to O'Shaughnessy's great friend, former New York Governor Mario M. Cuomo, of sainted memory, and his family—and new is a section devoted to the estimable Bush family, including George W. Bush's powerful eulogy for his father, former President George H.W. Bush.

O'Shaughnessy is widely praised for coaxing from his subjects "provocative and candid revelations" that are "often evaded" in conversations with lesser interlocutors—and he does it with sharp wit, humor, compassion, and his Irishman's gift for taking the full measure of humanity with knowing grace rather than with judgment.

What is the end sum of O'Shaughnessy's literary, lifestyle, and on-air calculus? It is, as Cuomo perfectly described, "a profound impulse to use his own great gift of life to find more fairness, justice and, yes, 'sweetness' in the world . . . or perhaps even to create some himself, if he hasn't found enough."

All true to our great benefit—and all wonderfully, magically poised to come to life as you read *Radio Active*. Enjoy!

William O'Shaughnessy is president and editorial director of Whitney Global Media, parent company of Westchester community stations WVOX and WVIP, both known nationally for excellence and influence. A former president of the New York State Broadcasters Association, O'Shaughnessy has been the Broadcasters champion on First Amendment and free speech issues and is presently chairman of the Guardian Fund of the Broadcasters Foundation of America.

In addition to *Radio Active*, he is the author of *AirWAVES* (1999); *It All Comes Back to Me Now* (2001); *More Riffs, Rants, and Raves*; *VOX POPULI: The O'Shaughnessy Files* (2011); and *Mario Cuomo: Remembrances of a Remarkable Man* (2017).

—*D. Paul Clement,*
Litchfield, January 2019

PART I
THE FIRST AMENDMENT

We've always had terrible things to defend . . .
Lawrence B. Taishoff, chairman,
Broadcasting Magazine

I've devoted a great deal of my professional life to advocacy for the First Amendment and free speech matters. So much so that I've been referred to over the years as a First Amendment voluptuary. I wear the designation as a badge of honor. Thus, I thought it appropriate to devote the first part to the aptly named First Amendment and how it has often been ignored in my own profession.

"Forty-five Simple Words"

by Jack Valenti

I carry around these notes that have sustained me over the years—especially during those moments when I wonder why my colleagues in the broadcasting profession always seem to let others speak for us on these fundamental issues.

These wise men and philosophers and others, so much wiser than Bill O'Shaughnessy, have spoken far more eloquently than I am able. Their counsel instructs us.

Actually, Jack Valenti, the diminutive, brilliant advisor to President Lyndon Johnson, who for many years led the Motion Picture Association of America, had the loveliest paean to the First Amendment: "It's the greatest document ever struck off by the hand and brain of man."

The most important lesson of all has to do with forty-five simple words. These words, bound together in spare, unadorned prose, are indispensable to the nation's security, the wisest and most valuable design for democracy ever put to paper. We call it the First Amendment.

Of all the clauses in the Constitution, it is the one clause that guarantees everything else in the greatest document ever struck off by the hand and brain of man. Listen to these forty-five words, for they are freedom's music: "Congress shall make no law respecting an establishment of religion, or prohibiting the free exercise thereof; or abridging the freedom of speech, or the press; or of the right of the people peaceably to assemble, and to petition the government for a redress of grievances."

In our world where ambiguity infects almost everything, this is the loveliest example of non-ambiguity to be found anywhere. Concise, compact, marching in serried ranks, there is about these words the delicious taste of pure wisdom unsoiled by hesitancy. They don't say "maybe a law" or "possibly a law" or "it depends on the circumstances." What it says is *no* law, which is as clear as the mother tongue can make it. What that glorious amendment means is that no matter how fiery the rhetoric, or frenzied the debate, or how calamitous the cry, government cannot interrupt nor intervene in the speech of its citizens. We are the only nation on this wracked and weary planet with a First Amendment in the very entrails of our democratic process. Which is the prime reason why this republic has endured and prospered for so long.

It's not easy to be a First Amendment advocate. You must allow that which you may judge to be meretricious, squalid, and without redeeming value to enter the marketplace. Often you become so irate at what is invading the culture of the community, particularly words and ideas from which some of us recoil, you want to call your congressional representative to urge him or her to pass a law and protect you from these blasphemous intrusions.

But before you make that call, be wary; be cautious, for throughout history whenever a tyrant first appears, he always comes as your protector. Never let your guard down. Never be beguiled by delusive enticements offered as cures for a disabled culture.

There is no right more crucial to the sustenance of liberty than the right to speak up, to speak out, to tell a story, compose a song, write a book, paint a picture, create a television program, make a movie, the way the creative artist chooses.

I do not quarrel with the passionate sincerity of some public officials and others who are vexed over what they judge to be a breakdown in the civic compact that governs the daily conduct of citizens. I can understand how they feel. But what we are all confronting is the new millennium of communications. It is a daunting confrontation. Through wire, cable, and fiber optic, over the air, underground, and through the ether, we are bombarded with felicities, an avalanche of information, overwhelmed by a tapestry of fragments, buried under data, chat rooms, millions of websites, hundreds of channels, all conveyed to our homes and computers by radio, cable, satellite, the Internet, TV networks and stations, DVDs, and podcasts.

To many of us it's an invasion unlike anything we have ever known or read about. No wonder our anxieties are increased and our insecurities enlarged. Moreover, many parents fret about what this visual and audio sweep is doing to children. But as it was from the birth year of these United States to this hour, there are three citadels that build within children a moral shield that teaches the child what is right and what is plainly wrong. Once that shield is in place, it will rarely be penetrated by unruly intrusions or the blandishments of peers. These three citadels are home, church, and school.

If parents, clerics, or teachers treat their responsibilities casually, if the construction of that moral shield is feebly attended, then no law, no directive, no amount of handwringing will salvage that child's conduct. But that's the way it has always been and always will be.

As for me, I have but one objective. It is to fortify the right of artists to create what they choose, without fear of government intervention of any kind, at any level, for any reason. I want to stand with all other Americans who believe it is their solemn duty to preserve, protect, and defend forty-five simple words, to lay claim for generations of Americans yet unborn that the First Amendment means for them what it means for us, the rostrum from which spring the ornaments and the essentials of this free and loving land.

So wrote Jack Valenti, the Washington, D.C., insider who conjured up this towering and stunning appreciation of the seminal instrument we know as the First Amendment.

Bill O'Reilly's "Character Assassination": A WVOX Commentary

April 20, 2017

Some have called it a "firing," others a "resignation," and *Politico* elegantly and accurately referred to his downfall as a "defenestration," which means an *assassination* by act of throwing someone out a window, or, in more polite discourse, "dismissing someone from a position of power."

We'd call it a "lynching." Granted that leverage may now be The New American Way. But the O'Reilly ouster also reeks of censorship by *organized* corporate intimidation.

"The old order shatters. We slayed the dragon. Never forget this is what we're capable of," bragged Lisa Bloom, attorney for a woman who launched a sexual harassment allegation.

"He was a mouthpiece for Trump . . . and we got him," said another attacker, a U.S. congresswoman!

Marc E. Kasowitz, an O'Reilly lawyer, properly called it "A brutal campaign of character assassination unprecedented in post-McCarthy America. The smear campaign is being orchestrated by far-left organizations bent on destroying O'Reilly for political and financial reasons." Bingo.

The Murdochs, *père et fils*, brought in Paul, Weiss, Rifkind, Wharton and Garrison to "investigate and report." But the atmosphere at white shoe law firms is altogether different from the atmosphere at a television network where sharks swim and poseurs parade—behind and in front of the camera.

We can't shake the notion that ultimately this is a free speech issue, although my friend Judge Jeffrey Bernbach cautions, "Sexual harassment is illegal. That's not free speech."

But who is to blame for the atmosphere, the milieu, the culture where most of the on-camera stars display pulchritude, low-cut *décolletage*, and fine legs abetted by rising hemlines.

Most performers on TV these days are talking airheads who if the teleprompter froze would also instantly become immobile. Most are not serious journalists.

There is something in the jargon of the law profession known as a BFOQ (Bona Fide Occupational Qualification), which means a woman or man can be hired and retained by a television network if he or she is comely or attractive. Thus, there is no question that female performers in this field are looking to get "noticed."

Those prowling the corridors and posing in front of the cameras in this day and age are not exactly Mother Teresas. Or Janet Renos. Nor are they naïve.

When you look at some of O'Reilly's female accusers and detractors, one wonders, Just who is the real predator?

Bill O'Reilly is a performer, a social commentator no different from Howard Stern or Don Imus or Rush Limbaugh, all of whom we defended when the roof fell in.

He was clearly done in by pressure groups and hostile public relations campaigns eagerly embraced by his envious competitors in the public press.

Although there appeared to be multiple allegations of misconduct, there are no reports that O'Reilly ever *touched* anybody. He just *said* stuff. Another interesting player in all this is Megyn Kelly, who turned on O'Reilly perhaps to facilitate her own highly orchestrated and well-publicized exit, and she has been called "that cyborg-like individual who wants to be the next Oprah" by the marvelous contrarian commentator Michael "Lionel" Lebron.

Suspicion exists abroad in the land that O'Reilly was accused by women who would do anything to get ahead in the Fox News milieu. But quality, educated, well-brought-up women know how to handle and deflect offensive moves and untoward and awkward, even predacious, compliments in most workplaces or social situations, which is not to say vulgar behavior is acceptable.

On the current Fox on-air roster of comely females is one Jeanine Pirro, well known to all of us and her neighbors here in Westchester. Few of her Fox female colleagues can match Her Honor Judge Jeanine in displaying pulchritude. And, as her former colleagues on the Westchester bench will readily—and admiringly—confirm, she can also swear like a trooper through those puffed-up, reconstructed lips. Certainly none wear shorter skirts. But could you see any guy taking a verbal shot at "Judge Jeanine"? At their own peril. Forget about it!

In the O'Reilly affair, the allegations against him did not seem to involve violent or even "nonconsensual" physical activity.

As an example, the *New York Times* cited *this* juicy vignette and ribald conversation: "O'Reilly stepped aside and let her off the elevator first (like a gentleman) and said: 'Lookin' good, gal!'" How altogether terrible! How insulting! How abusive! How sexist! How ribald! How injurious! How disgusting!

Many/most of the cant-filled attacks on O'Reilly were dripping with hypocritical or sanctimonious blather. The commentator Lionel also said this week: "This isn't about sexual harassment. This is about sponsors and money." We agree that the fault also resides among many holier-than-thou (spineless) sponsors who abandoned O'Reilly and collapsed in the face of organized, politically correct pressure fueled by envy and by contrary political (anti-Trump) views. That, we're afraid, is *really* what's behind this contretemps. And everyone knows it.

Despite any "findings" of the mighty Paul, Weiss, Rifkind, Wharton and Garrison white shoe law firm, O'Reilly should not have been fired or denied his platform.

To be sure, in this whole dreary matter, we're confronted by a *civility* issue, which is valid, necessary, and altogether appropriate, even in a charged-up, behind-the-scenes office setting populated by bimbos—male and female—lacking in any solid journalistic credentials.

The organized opposition to O'Reilly—and thus to Fox News, and ultimately to President Trump—for the most part, used salacious accusations as weapons to knock him off the air and further drive their own agendas.

There are thousands of show-biz types and feminist lawyers just waiting to cash in on sexual discrimination and sexual harassment suits. But much of this resembles a witch hunt replete with character assassination. Among which was a ten-year-old allegation from an anonymous individual, part of a campaign orchestrated by activist lawyers and Trump haters to destroy O'Reilly.

I've discovered, just this morning, a humorless woman named Letitia James, the "Public Advocate" for New York City, who took to the MSNBC airwaves to attack Bill O'Reilly in harsh, unforgiving tones and a voice dripping with venom that made even Andrea Mitchell and some of her other guests uncomfortable. I'd love to see a debate between this Letitia James and Elizabeth Warren (the former is now attorney general of New York state and the latter aspires to the presidency).

Judge Bernbach doesn't see this as a free speech issue. But censorship from corporate intimidation in the face of politically driven economic boycotts is just as dangerous as the stifling of creative and artistic expression by government fiat, decree, sanction, or regulation.

That's just as treacherous as any racism, misogyny, sexism, or bigotry.

We agree with the president of the United States: "He should not have 'resigned.' He did nothing wrong."

We agree and we also wonder if some of Bill O'Reilly's opponents aren't kith and kin to the mob that ganged up on our protégé and former colleague William "Billy" Bush.

—*William O'Shaughnessy*

The Silencing of Imus

Commentary by William O'Shaughnessy, April 16, 2007. Censorship from corporate timidity in the face of economic boycotts is just as dangerous as the stifling of creative and artistic expression by government fiat, decree, sanction or regulation.

Howard Stern, Opie and Anthony, Bob Grant, Bill Maher, Chris Rock, George Lopez, and even—God forbid!—Rosie. We've always had terrible examples to defend. I got that instruction from the late publisher Larry Taishoff of sainted memory (son of Sol and father of Rob—three generations of First Amendment advocates via their seminal publication, *Broadcasting Magazine*, for decades our sentinel on the Potomac). And Don Imus has given us another terrible example. But defend it we must.

Not the hateful and discomfiting words. But the right of the social commentator to be heard, and the right of the people to decide.

Don Imus is a performer, a disc jockey, a humorist, and a provocateur with a rapier-sharp wit. Unlike many of our colleagues, he avoids raucous vulgarity or incendiary right-wing rhetoric directed at immigrants, illegal aliens, and other familiar targets of our tribe.

Throughout his brilliant career, Imus has been an equal opportunity offender, poking fun at the high and mighty as well as the rest of us for our foibles and pomposity.

He may have occasionally gone too far during a remarkable thirty-year career. Were his comments about the Rutgers basketball team racist or mean-spirited? Only Imus knows for sure, but we doubt it. Were they funny? No.

His mea culpa and apologies seemed sincere. We had thus hoped his sponsors and the executives at CBS, WFAN, MSNBC, and all those local affiliates across the country would stand up to the pressure and continue to carry the I-Man.

So many successful performers take and put nothing back. Imus has been extravagantly generous to a number of worthy causes, often without fanfare.

Imus claims he's been active in our profession for 30 years—actually, it's closer to 40 since he came roaring out of Cleveland. By our calculation, that's about 8,000 broadcasts, with some 2,400,000 ad libs. Admittedly, none as insensitive as his reference to the Rutgers team.

This was a misfire. And it was to be hoped the executives at CBS and NBC would act accordingly.

Here's a baseball analogy. Suppose you had a pitcher, with remarkable stamina, who threw 8,000 innings: Many of his pitches will miss the strike zone. A few may even hit the poor batter. And, during those 8,000 innings, spanning 30 or 40 seasons, he may even bean the umpire! But he's still a great pitcher.

With the possible exception of overnight broadcasting, from dusk until dawn, morning drive is the toughest shift in radio. And when Imus plops those well-traveled bones into a chair, straps on his earphones, and throws his voice out into another morning, armed only with his humor, wit, and irreverence, he may even be compared to a Franciscan priest dragging himself up into a pulpit after thirty or forty years to pronounce the Good News before a sparse, sleepy congregation at an early Mass.

But Imus strives only to make us laugh or think. That's a pretty good way to make a living. And he should thus be protected from those unforgiving critics who heaped scorn and derision upon him as a result of this controversy.

Bob Grant, the dean of radio talk show hosts in the New York area, was a fiery, crusty, take-no-prisoners broadcaster for several decades. He said some terrible things about my cherished friend Mario Cuomo.

But I liked the old guy . . . not alone because he let me run barefoot on his WOR shows and allowed me to plug each of my poor previous books.

During the Imus contretemps I turned the tables and had Bob Grant on *my* show.

Imus misfired. But he should not have been fired.

Censorship from corporate timidity in the face of economic boycotts is just as dangerous as the stifling of creative and artistic expression by government fiat, decree, sanction, or regulation.

That's just as treacherous as any racism, sexism, or bigotry.

Bob Grant on the Imus Controversy

Broadcast April 20, 2007.

WILLIAM O'SHAUGHNESSY: In our profession, the Imus controversy
lingers. The I-Man is silenced. For how long? Nobody knows. And
we're going to switch now to New Jersey for the dean of talk show
hosts, the great Bob Grant. We are all your students, sir. How do you
see this controversy with Imus?

BOB GRANT: Well actually, after reflecting on it, I'm not really
surprised. That doesn't mean I approve of what happened. But Don
has lived on the edge for a long time. And, of course, when I heard
about all this, I immediately thought about what happened to me
eleven years ago.

  Naturally, I understood when he said he was shocked because I
was, too. Neither of us ever intended to get people so angry they
would want us fired.

W.O.: Bob Grant, you, too, have been the victim of intimidation and
coercion.

B.G.: Well, yes indeed. [laughter] So many things were broadcast
with humor and then perceived to be very serious. I remember
asking a program director, a very nice, sympathetic guy, "What
are they taking this all so seriously for?" He replied, "Hey, wait a
minute! That means you've achieved your goal!" And as far as
Don is concerned, I believe certain people have taken him way
too seriously.

W.O.: Should they have fired Don Imus, Bob Grant? MSNBC and CBS?
Should they have thrown him off the air?

B.G.: Well, I thought they would suspend him. Matter of fact, I
predicted, "Well, one week, maybe two." But, apparently, the
pressure was so intense, sponsors were dropping like flies, and

[15]

that's what did it. Purely economic. I'm sure the honchos at NBC and CBS weren't that offended in the beginning.

W.O.: What do you think about the heat he took from Jesse Jackson and Al Sharpton?

B.G.: Well, I've talked to people who say these guys didn't really care about the sensitivity of the Rutgers basketball team. But it's a great opportunity to insert themselves into a controversial issue and ride to the rescue of the damsels in distress.

W.O.: Bob Grant, it's so wonderful to hear your strong voice. Do you miss being on the radio?

B.G.: Yes. [laughter]

W.O.: Well, what does the lion do in the winter? Is there really a famous diner where you're the king?

B.G.: No. [laughter] As a matter of fact, it's not that close to where I live now.

W.O.: We're speaking to you from the Jersey shore?

B.G.: That's right. And I spend a lot of time at my new home in Florida. I love to travel, and I'm having fun just doing things I postponed for all those years.

W.O.: But, Bob Grant, if WABC or WOR called, would you saddle up again, strap on the earphones, and go back to a regular gig?

B.G.: I don't know about that. But maybe a part-time thing, once or twice a week. [He reappeared, for almost a year, on WABC. But the fire was gone.]

W.O.: Are you going to tell us how old you are? Or how young you are?

B.G.: I'll say it indirectly. I made my entrance into the world on March 14, 1929, the birthday of Albert Einstein.

W.O.: Bob Grant, you graced our airways for a long, long time. You got some people mad at you. You made us all think. Has it changed over the years? I remember the great WNEW, and you were at WMCA, the Ellen and Peter Straus station. Do you still listen to the radio?

B.G.: I'm a little embarrassed to tell you, hardly at all. If I jump in the car, maybe I'll put something on.

W.O.: What do you watch on television in your Florida home or on the Jersey shore?

B.G.: Well, naturally, I watch CNN, MSNBC, and Fox News channel. I'm addicted to the news channels. [laughter]

W.O.: Mario Cuomo, your old nemesis, I guess he's about seventy-four now. Did you ever make up?

B.G.: Well, no, we never did, and it's kind of sad in a way because at one time, I felt a great fondness for him, and he was a good friend. And when I say "good friend," you know they throw that word around loosely, but one time, he really was.

   The man has a great sense of humor. We had lunch together a couple of times. Then, I started kidding around, and over time, some people thought it was a shootout at the OK Corral. But I really bear him no malice whatsoever, and he would probably be surprised if he heard that. No, in many respects, he's a remarkable man.

W.O.: Bob Grant, I won't keep you long from your sojourn on the Jersey shore. I get a flash of *déjà vu* when you used to take callers, and I'm a little nervous interviewing the legendary Bob Grant. But it drove you nuts when they'd say, "Hi, Mr. Grant. How are you?" You couldn't stand small talk. Remember that?

B.G.: Well, that was only on the air. In real life, I'd give them a traditional response. But many times on the air, in the beginning of my career on the West Coast, they would start off by saying, "How are you?" and the next thing you know, they're attacking me! So my attitude was, "Let's dispense with the formalities," and my stock reply was, "What's on your mind, pal?"

W.O.: Bob Grant, I just want to hear you say it one more time for the record, "Get off my phone!"

B.G.: I'd be happy to! I might be out of practice, but I'll give it a shot. "Get off my phone, you creep!"

W.O.: Bravo! You still got your fastball! The great Bob Grant. Thank you, sir.

"Don't Hush Rush . . ."

*I don't want to blow his cover . . . but Rush Hudson Limbaugh III
is one of the most generous guys in our broadcasting tribe.
(See my notes to this spectacularly generous man in Part IX.)
The next time somebody takes a shot at El Rushbo, he's going
to have to answer to Yours Truly. (March 14, 2012)*

———————

Howard Stern . . . Don Imus . . . Opie and Anthony . . . Lisa Lampanelli
. . . Chris Rock . . . George Lopez . . . Kathy Griffin . . . Bill Maher . . .
Roseanne Barr . . . Sarah Silverman . . . and George Carlin, of sainted
memory.

We've always had terrible examples to defend. And Rush Limbaugh
has given us another stellar specimen of vulgar discourse. But defend it
we must.

Not the hateful, demeaning, and discomfiting words. But the right of
our colleague—the social commentator—to be heard. And the right of
the people to decide.

Rush misfired. But he should not be fired or denied his platform.

Rush Limbaugh forgot that the young woman from Georgetown—
no shrinking violet she, who bemoaned the fact, for all the world to
hear, that contraception costs some $1,300.00 annually—was some-
one's daughter.

Her candid and sincere congressional testimony thus provoked
Limbaugh's unfortunate, regrettable, and completely inappropriate
attack, which was all too personal and mean-spirited.

Rush Limbaugh is a performer, an entertainer, a provocateur, a
social commentator, and, in his worst moments, a carnival barker for
the hard right. But the sanctimonious holier-than-thou campaign to
destroy and silence him has an agenda that transcends the hurt feelings of one individual.

Phil Reisman, the brilliant and astute Gannett feature columnist, says it's entirely appropriate to remind Rush that chivalry, respectful discourse, and gentlemanly behavior still matter. And I would sign up for that.

To be sure, in this whole dreary matter we're confronted by a *civility* issue, which is valid, necessary, and altogether appropriate. But the mission of the liberal sharks and other windbags who smell blood in the water is not to address the wrong but to drive Limbaugh off the air.

In other words, when you separate the *civility,* or lack thereof, from the *politics*, it's all too clear that Limbaugh's enemies are using this contretemps as a weapon to knock him off his platform—permanently.

It drives them—and us—crazy that Limbaugh represents a significant chunk of the Republican Party. So, as Rockefeller Republicans, he's not at all our cup of tea. Over the years I've listened only very occasionally to his ranting and raving since the great Ed McLaughlin plucked Limbaugh from an obscure broadcasting station in Sacramento, California, and gave him a national platform.

Truth to tell, if my friends at the *New York Post* had not already dubbed Alec Baldwin "The Bloviator," I would suggest that appellation might be more appropriately applied to Mr. Limbaugh.

Like I said, Rush misfired. He missed like a pitcher; he may have hit the poor umpire this time, or some poor bastard behind home plate. (Actually, he hit someone's daughter!) But he should not be fired, even if the whole canon of his work is filled with raucous vulgarity and incendiary right-wing rhetoric directed at immigrants, illegal aliens, and even presidents of the United States.

We broadcasters are ever alert to incursions against free speech from government bureaucrats. But censorship from corporate timidity in the face of economic boycotts, as I've often said, is just as dangerous as the stifling of creative and artistic expression by government fiat, decree, sanction, or regulation.

You don't have to be a First Amendment voluptuary to realize this is just as treacherous as any racism, sexism, bigotry, or vulgarity.

Let the S.O.B. be heard. And trust only the *people* to censure him with a flick of the wrist and a changing of the dial.

I'm uncomfortable as hell about it. But I'm with Limbaugh.
He makes his living with words.

FYI: Full disclosure. A few years after I broadcast this commentary I discovered a whole new, wonderful side to Rush Hudson Limbaugh III. It turns out he is a very generous fellow. As chairman of the Guardian Fund of the Broadcasters Foundation of America, our profession's preeminent national charity which functions as a "Foul Weather Friend" and safety net for our down-and-out colleagues, I thus know who are the generous souls in our tribe (and also the cheap bastards!). Limbaugh has been spectacularly generous to our hurting and almost forgotten brethren.

Missing in Action

By Patrick D. Maines

As the longtime president of the Media Institute, a Washington think tank, Patrick Maines has been a relentless champion of the First Amendment and a defender of free speech in our profession. Here's a thoughtful and scholarly pronouncement from him that resonates still as a cri de coeur to our profession and journalists everywhere.

———————

Politically speaking, freedom of speech in the United States is in tatters. We are beleaguered by "progressives" on the left, "social conservatives" on the right, and policymakers of all stripes, and our ability to freely express ourselves would already be greatly diminished but for the federal courts.

Consider the landscape. The chairman of the FCC and large majorities in Congress favor content controls on indecent and/or violent TV programming. A leading candidate for president co-wrote legislation that would criminalize even certain kinds of political speech when broadcast close to the date of federal elections. Left-leaning activist groups, unwilling to tolerate conservative opinion on talk radio and the Fox News channel, openly advocate a return of the so-called Fairness Doctrine.

Bad as the situation is within policymaking circles, it is little better in academia and even in mainstream journalism, both of which, with a few exceptions, operate in the grip of a kind of political correctness that is the very antithesis of free speech, if not of freedom itself.

Examples of both can be found on campuses in the preponderance of college speech "codes," and among journalists in the rush to abandon and fire Don Imus for what was, after all, a cruelly unfunny joke for which he apologized. Further evidence was recently provided by much of the media coverage of, and the preposterous role of a large number of professors in, the Duke University lacrosse farce.

Given the stakes, one might think that the media are working diligently to preserve at least that part of the First Amendment which guarantees freedom of the press. But in fact they are not.

From media and entertainment companies, and their related charitable and educational foundations, what passes for First Amendment advocacy is a mix of informational initiatives, like Sunshine Week, that are important in their own right but have little or nothing to do with the First Amendment; "education" programs, like the Illinois Press Association's First Amendment Center coloring book for grades K–4; and activities that amount to corporate brand promotion, like the purchase of "naming rights" to attractions at the Newseum in Washington.

And this is the profile of those who are actually *doing* something! Most are doing *nothing*, either because (1) they don't have any real understanding of the issue; (2) they trust that, in the end, they'll be saved by the courts; or (3) they don't really care so long as whatever speech controls are enacted are applied to everyone.

The beginning of wisdom lies in understanding that free speech isn't imperiled because educated people don't know what it is. It's imperiled because educated people subordinate this knowledge to their political and cultural preferences. Whether you call it inconsistency, hypocrisy, or willfulness, it is at the heart of the present danger.

And what a danger it is! Perhaps because of factors like consolidation within elements of the "old media," the ubiquity of pornography, and the rise of conservative opinion within certain parts of the media, virtually every political and ideological group in the United States (save, perhaps, for libertarians) is now in favor of some kind of speech-controlling law or regulation. Taken together, and if enacted, they would amount to restrictions on nearly every kind of speech—from entertainment to news and print to electronic journalism.

That this has not happened, because of strong federal case law, is hardly a cause for complacency. Both parties in Congress have shown a knack for coercing "voluntarism" (and thereby steering clear of the case law) when they have media companies over any kind of barrel.

And even the Supreme Court is by no means impervious to opinion in the larger society.

As direct beneficiaries of the speech clause of the First Amendment, media companies have an obligation to act as the people's sentinels on this issue. As such, they need to see that they are not adding to the problem by acts of omission or commission, and to practice what they preach.

Though it's not widely appreciated, the truth is that the First Amendment is indivisible. We don't have one First Amendment for newspapers and another for the Internet. Nor do we have one for the media and another for individuals, or one for news and one for entertainment.

We have only *one* First Amendment and, such being the ways of precedent, if it is weakened anywhere it's weakened everywhere. Which is why it is incumbent on media companies to act rigorously and selflessly to protect it.

Freedom of speech in the United States is at risk of dying a death of a thousand cuts. For the sake of the nation, as well as the health of their profession, it is to be profoundly hoped that the media, old and new, will rethink and redouble their efforts to safeguard this cornerstone of our constitutional rights.

The Real Obscenity

This piece by Howard Goldfluss, a retired justice of the New York State Supreme Court, originally appeared June 3, 2004, in the Riverdale Review. Judge Goldfluss had a weekly program for many years on WVOX . . . and was a beloved presence at the Friars Club in Manhattan.

It all started with the exposure of Janet Jackson's breast. To say that the FCC overreacted would be a gross understatement—suddenly, an agency of the government seized the opportunity to exercise a fanatic power of censorship that was never contemplated under the First Amendment.

William O'Shaughnessy is the president and editorial director of Whitney Radio—the most influential AM and FM outlets in Westchester County. For years he has warned against unreasonable governmental intrusion into what we can hear or see.

In a commentary prepared for the National Association of Broadcasters in Washington, he hit the nail on the head when he wrote, "There is a runaway freight train heading straight for us—and the First Amendment."

That train has left the station.

Yes, the Supreme Court has ruled that obscenity is not protected under the First Amendment. But how do you define obscenity? The best the court could come up with is: "Whether to the average person, applying contemporary community standards, the dominant theme of the material taken as a whole appeals to the prurient interest."

Wow! What a mouthful! But what does it mean? If we could get past dreaming up a definition of "community standards," then what community are we talking about? Do we apply the standards of Topeka, Kansas, here in New York? Do they apply ours? The Court has never been successful in defining the undefinable, and the proof lies in the wisdom of Justice Potter Stewart when he declared that he could not define obscenity but he knew it when he saw it.

That is about as precise as you can get.

But the FCC is precise in seeking to boost fines for indecency in broadcasting from the current $27,500 ceiling to half a million a pop. It has also asked Congress for the power to revoke broadcasting licenses if a station is cited three times for indecency.

In the interest of full disclosure, I must confess that in hosting a WVOX talk show I have, under the present climate of intimidation, erred on the side of caution in uttering or permitting an utterance that would place Whitney Broadcasting in jeopardy. To his credit, Bill O'Shaughnessy has never even suggested a prior restraint on me or, to my knowledge, any other broadcaster. On the contrary, he continues to speak out against the subjective standard of the FCC which gives a governmental agency the unchallenged right to decide what is obscene, offensive, or immoral. It is what they say it is. Case closed!

There is no limit to the hypocrisy here. Case in point, the rock singer Bono appeared at the 2003 Golden Globe Awards. On national television, he modified the word "brilliant" with an expletive.

But that was pre–Janet Jackson, and at that time the FCC staff ruled that Bono had not violated decency standards. Because his utterance was an isolated use of the word, they changed their minds quickly after Janet's mammary exposure, finding then that his remarks were "indecent and profane."

So much for the integrity and the moral purpose of the Federal Communications Commission.

Floyd Abrams: Notes and Observations on the First Amendment

Here's our July 9, 2014, interview with the great Floyd Abrams. The estimable New York lawyer Floyd Abrams is a glorious First Amendment advocate and champion. Over the years we have sought his wise counsel on free speech matters.

WILLIAM O'SHAUGHNESSY: This is Bill O'Shaughnessy. For the next few minutes while we're in your care and keeping, we're going to visit with one of the most famous constitutional lawyers in the history of the republic. He is a relentless champion of the First Amendment to the Constitution of the United States. It is such a fundamental thing, and he's devoted his whole life to it. His name is Floyd Abrams, Esq. He's a partner in the big white shoe law firm Cahill Gordon in New York. He's taught at Yale; he's taught at Harvard; he's taught everywhere. And he instructs us now. Should I call you Professor Abrams?

FLOYD ABRAMS: Well, how about Floyd, Bill?

W.O.: Floyd Abrams, broadcasters and journalists think all our prerogatives and privileges proceed from the First Amendment. So it's very important, certainly, to all of us, everyone in my tribe. First of all, what's the First Amendment? What does it say for us today?

F.A.: Basically, it was adopted in 1791, two years after the Constitution was adopted. Thomas Jefferson and others made clear they wouldn't agree to the Constitution unless there was a Bill of Rights attached, and the Bill of Rights starts out with the First Amendment, which starts out first by providing that people should have freedom of religion—free exercise of religion—and freedom from the government's intruding into religious beliefs. It then says Congress may make no law abridging the freedom of speech or of the press, which is the part of the First Amendment I've been active with respect to. And then it provides protection for freedom of assembly, the freedom for people peacefully to assemble to seek redress of their grievances. And so in those few lines the Framers laid out their view that Congress—and it was later interpreted to be not just Congress but the states as well—had to really keep "hands off" certain fundamental areas, including religion, speech, and assembly.

W.O.: We're talking with Floyd Abrams, the great First Amendment lawyer who has written a book that has become, in just a few short months, almost like a bible on the subject. It's called *Friend of the Court: On the Front Lines with the First Amendment.* Floyd Abrams, what does it say about this country that you've had to devote so many years to defending the First Amendment? Do we even understand it?

F.A.: Well, look, we have some basic problems in the country. But one of them is we haven't done a very good job educating our children and our people in general in what used to be called civics courses, and a part of that was the Constitution, and a central part of that was the First Amendment. Now, that said, we do have more in the way of free speech rights and free press rights than anyone in the world. That's still true. But it takes sort of constant pressure to keep that true, and constant litigation of one sort or another to assure that people won't too easily be deprived of free speech and free press rights in the interest of other causes, which are very important but which can be served in different ways.

W.O.: Floyd Abrams, on the back of your book *Friend of the Court* for Yale University Press, one of your fellow academics, a professor, compares you with Learned Hand and Oliver Wendell Holmes and Justice Brandeis. Why did these guys get it and a lot of people don't get it?

F.A.: Well, these "guys," Bill, are, of course, the ultimate heavyweights in American constitutional law—maybe you can say American law or maybe even American philosophy. These are people who are brilliant, thoughtful, and passionate in their defense of fundamental rights.

W.O.: Who among these judges—these great jurists—has given you the most underpinning, the most to work with on First Amendment issues? Who is the strongest guy on the subject?

F.A.: Well, it all really begins with the combination of Justice Brandeis and Justice Holmes, who wrote opinions back during World War I and then right after World War I, really establishing for the first time that the First Amendment has a very great breadth to it, a very wide scope in terms of its coverage. And that it can't be overcome by saying, Well, look there are other interests too. I mean, it's really got to be special. It's got to be shown with special force and a sense of special assuredness that other interests must trump the First Amendment for there to even be a close call in the reading of the Constitution. That's one of the great things about it. It's not that it's always easy to know who wins what cases. That's why we have courts and everything. But it's very important to know that certainly, presumptively, we start out with a notion that the government can't come into play in eliminating, let alone prohibiting, or even jailing someone for expressing his or her views on public policy or what the government ought to do or who ought to be elected or anything like that.

W.O.: Constitutional lawyer Floyd Abrams, let me ask you about the current Supreme Court, the high court of the land. The so-called Roberts Court. Do they get it? Are they friendly to you?

F.A.: I think they do. The Roberts Court is a controversial Court because, in many of its opinions, it's obviously been on the conservative side. But I really don't think that's the right way to view it in terms of the First Amendment. The First Amendment question is not who is liberal or progressive or who is conservative or the like. I mean, it's really, Are you willing to defend the expression of views you disagree with and that you might even think might be sort of dangerous? Are you willing to tolerate offensive speech, deeply offensive speech? On those sort of levels, the Roberts Court has been a very strong First Amendment Court. And I think it deserves more credit than it has received.

W.O.: Lawyer and author of *Friend of the Court: On the Front Lines with the First Amendment*, how much should we tolerate? How much is too much? We've heard the argument you can't falsely yell, "Fire!" in a crowded theater forever. But how much is enough? Or too much?

F.A.: First of all, let's talk legally about it. There's a lot of free speech that we allow and that we protect and that we think appalling. That comes with the territory of living in a country that has a First Amendment. But the basic rule has got to be that speech is allowed, and the government can't punish speech as a general matter because of its content, because of what it says, because of what it conveys, because of concerns of damage it may do. And while there are some areas of exceptions—look, we do have libel laws in America—it is still more protective of free speech than anywhere else in the world, but we certainly recognize and enforce libel law, and we enforce privacy law, et cetera. The real issue you hear again and again is what's the rule and what's the exception? And the rule in America, because of the First Amendment, is that people can pretty well say just about anything they want without being subject to any sort of governmental control or sanction or anything of the sort.

W.O.: Floyd Abrams, who was the Supreme Court justice who famously said, "I know it's bad, or obscene or vulgar, when I hear it or when I see it"?

F.A.: Yes, that was Judge Potter Stewart. Justice Stewart was a conservative jurist. Right now one would call him "moderate," I guess. But a very protective judge in terms of the First Amendment. And he had an obscenity case in front of him, and he was trying to express—maybe inarticulately, but maybe really capturing something very well—he was trying to say at the same time it's really hard for me to explain why *this* is obscene and that's *not*. He said I *know* it when I *see* it. And he always, I'm told, was unhappy about having said it just that way. But that became the line by which he is best known through American history now, because on the one hand it captures the thought—we do know some things when we see them or hear them. And we know that some things are over some sort of line we draw in the sand. But obviously it doesn't help a lot analytically because it doesn't tell you how to *tell* what's over the line and what is not.

W.O.: Professor Abrams, counselor Floyd Abrams, author Floyd Abrams, what made these Founders so all-knowing, and who says their wisdom should prevail for these many years? These two hundred–plus years? Are you a strict constitutional . . . ?

F.A.: Well, I'm not what is called an "originalist" in the sense that I ask myself every time there's a new case: What would Thomas Jefferson have said, or John Adams or James Madison have said? They said what they meant to say. The First Amendment reads very broadly. No law abridging the freedom of speech or of the press. And while it is useful to know what they had in mind in the sense of what was before them, I don't think it should be dispositive. Each generation has got to take the language and make sense of it in their own terms. And so to me, the question is not: If I put myself in their position and read the books they had, what would they say? The truth is, we often have no idea. The Supreme Court decided a few weeks ago in the *Aereo* case [*American Broadcasting Cos. v. Aereo, Inc.*] about television transmission and how the copyright law intersects with a particular way of sending a signal. The Founders didn't know anything about signals, not to say television. So it can't look to them except to say they really did want broad—sweepingly broad—protection of free expression. And so we start with that, and then we see where the law takes us. That case was a copyright case. Well, copyright was around at the same time the First Amendment was written. Copyright was written in the Constitution two years before the First Amendment was even adopted. So it's not a little thing. It can't just be sort of tossed over. My basic answer is, I think we have to be careful not to think that juridical wisdom begins and ends with trying to ask the question "What would James Madison say about this?" We don't know. We rarely know. What we know is he wrote the Constitution. And he wrote the Bill of Rights. He's the principal author, and he deliberately left these words open to interpretation, and it's worth going through the process of interpreting them.

w.o.: In my tribe—broadcasting—they say, "What would *Floyd Abrams* say about this?" We're grateful to you, sir. I've admired you for many, many years. We are all your students on these issues. But I have to ask: You've defended networks, you've defended a lot of foul potty-mouths. Did you ever defend Howard Stern?

F.A.: No, although I do say a good word for him in my new book. I do say we ought to let up on him and let him have his say.

w.o.: So you don't think the republic is in any danger from foul or vulgar language? Or from our friend Howard Stern?

F.A.: No, I don't. No, I don't!

w.o.: The book is called *Friend of the Court.* His name is Floyd Abrams. He is the best at what he does, without a doubt the preeminent free speech and free press advocate of our time. Maybe of any time. That's what Yale University said about Floyd Abrams. That's what I say. The book is called *Friend of the Court: On the Front Lines with the First Amendment.* Do you think you're going to outsell Hillary Clinton?

F.A.: Of course!

Free Speech on the Airwaves:
Confab with Mario Cuomo

William O'Shaughnessy interview with David Rehr, president, National Association of Broadcasters; Ambassador Ogden Rogers Reid, president, Council of American Ambassadors; Gov. Mario M. Cuomo of Willkie Farr & Gallagher and Gordon Hastings, president, Broadcasters Foundation of America. Broadcast June 19, 2006.

WILLIAM O'SHAUGHNESSY: It's a pleasure once again to have the privilege of your hearth and home. This is a busy political season abroad in the land and we have a special guest for you this Monday afternoon in the Golden Apple. He's up from the nation's capital, Washington, D.C. We are honored to have him visit WVOX, our community station, which pulses and throbs with some 500 mighty watts of power! He is president of the National Association of Broadcasters in Washington . . . the chief lobbyist, drumbeater, and advocate for every radio and television station in America: David Rehr. Welcome to Westchester, sir.

DAVID REHR: Thank you, Bill . . . I appreciate being here and experiencing, in your station, the very best of local radio.

W.O.: You represent . . . the National Association of Broadcasters . . . about 8,300 members, of which 1,200 are television affiliates and the other 7,000-plus are radio stations all across America.

You're gonna have 7,000 guys mad at you for choosing our airwaves. Not that the word would get out. . . . I don't much like publicity. We won't tell anybody you're here. [laughter]

D.R.: I'll read about it tomorrow and I'll probably see it on all the major TV networks, knowing you, O'Shaughnessy. [laughter]

W.O.: David Rehr, you have so much on your agenda. You're a big Washington-insider lobbyist. I hear you raised millions for George W. Bush . . .

D.R.: Well, I raised a lot of money for the president in his last re-election . . . because at the time I believed him to be very pro-small business, but millions is an overstatement.

W.O.: These proceedings are also greatly enhanced by the presence of the president of the Broadcasters Foundation of America. He's come down from his headquarters in Greenwich: Gordon Hastings. Listen to *this* voice; he's a *real* radio man.

GORDON HASTINGS: Bill, it is always nice to see you. . . . the last time I was behind a microphone was at my own WSRK up in Oneonta, New York. What a pleasure it is to be back at a truly great local station.

W.O.: Well, you're one of us, Gordon. And you are doing the best work of your life with the Broadcasters Foundation of America. The chairman lives over in the next heath, Phil Lombardo, in Bronxville. Gordon and David, we have a great American on the phone: Ambassador Ogden Rogers Reid. Ogden Reid is a man who needs no introduction to our audience here in the heart of the eastern establishment. He represented Westchester in Congress. He was the first ambassador to the infant nation of Israel. His family owned the *Herald Tribune*, a great newspaper of sainted memory, which was founded by Horace Greeley. He is now doing some of the best work of *his* life as president of the Council of American Ambassadors. "Brownie" Reid is a great defender of free speech, and he took on a man named Harley O. Staggers on the floor of the House of Representatives when Frank Stanton and Walter Cronkite were in trouble and looking even at a jail cell. Ambassador Reid, you honor us.

AMBASSADOR OGDEN REID: Well, I thank Bill O'Shaughnessy for his leadership of WVOX and the Broadcasters Foundation and for all the help he has given to the First Amendment.

W.O.: David Rehr, you are a lobbyist . . . not such a great thing to be in this day in age.

D.R.: I remember my mother . . . when she was alive . . . asked me
what I wanted to be . . . and I told her I was going to be a lobbyist.
She said, "Why don't you become a *lawyer*?" I said, "But Mom, you
hate lawyers." She said, "Yeah, but at least I can tell my neighbors
what you *do*!" [laughter] Being a lobbyist in this era of the Jack
Abramoff scandals and some of the other things going on in
Washington gets a lot of bad PR. But when you're standing in the
halls of Congress next to a young person who has juvenile diabetes
and they're trying to be a lobbyist asking the government for funds
to solve juvenile diabetes in this country, you can look at them and
say, "That's what's *great* about America." Everybody's opinion can
be heard and everyone can say what they freely want to say and get
the attention of their member of Congress on behalf of whatever
they believe in.

W.O.: Ogden Reid, how long did you serve in the Congress?

O.R.: I served for twelve years, Bill, and I was concerned with
corruption along with your friend John Lindsay. I agree with what
President Rehr just said. One of the things we were dealing with
were the "private" bills members were putting in to bring an *au pair*
or a nanny from Europe without benefit of committee consideration
or even consideration by Immigration. A member of Congress can
get five or ten thousand dollars every time he puts in one of those
bills. I remember testifying before Charlie Halleck and I said those
communications should be a matter of public record. Halleck
leaned over the bench and said "Reid, what are you trying to do—
depopulate the place?" [laughter] I am all for bringing home the
bacon and doing it fairly and having appropriate lobbying—but with
scrutiny and transparency.

W.O.: Ambassador Reid, I haven't had a chance to ask David Rehr
about "indecency." My mind drifts back to those desperate days
when Mr. Staggers, had you not prevailed, wanted to throw Cronkite
and Dr. Stanton in the slammer.

O.R.: This was all over outtakes, if you recall.

W.O.: Today David Rehr has his hands full because if someone drops
the "F" bomb on these airwaves, it's going to cost about $350,000 . . .

if we are lucky. What advice would you, Ambassador Reid, give to lobbyist and NAB President David Rehr on this thing?

O.R.: I don't like to see speech circumscribed in any way, shape, or form. I suppose there are cases where there have been very blatant, repeated obscenity. Just because a play or show has a mention of it . . . that's a reflection of life. I spent a little bit of time in Paris with the *Herald Tribune* and the French don't understand our trying to control the presentation of speech the way some in the Congress are trying to do. I think it's a mistake . . . and I'd rather have free speech up or down with a little obscenity, than lose free speech altogether.

W.O.: David Rehr, I know you've had a lot of time to think about this big, tough issue. You've got the FCC raising hell, parents raising all kinds of hell, and the Congress just rolled right over on this.

D.R.: The Senate passed the Indecency Fines bill by unanimous consent, which means not *one* senator stood against it. The bill then moved on to the House and passed with all but 35 members voting "No," which is about 401 members voting "Yes." It's an election year and people want to be on the side of "protecting children." I do think we need to take a serious and hard look. It's easy to pick on a few words and a few people who may say some things, but I think the ambassador makes a good point; it isn't too much of a jump from that to starting to control *what* people can *say, when* they can *say* it . . . and *how* they can say it. I think what's made America such a great country is for people to *say* what they *want.*

W.O.: Thank you, Ambassador, for joining us.

O.R.: It's great to be on the air with these distinguished gentlemen . . . and you, Bill, whom I have admired for so long.

W.O.: It's 2:24 on this beautiful, summer-like day. Next . . . do you remember the "Fairness" Doctrine, David Rehr? We would have had a "Fairness" Doctrine. And Rupert Murdoch wouldn't have had his Boston newspapers . . . but for the intercession and great wisdom of our next guest. Please welcome to this important discussion . . . the fifty-second governor of New York: Mario Matthew Cuomo. How are you, sir?

GOVERNOR MARIO CUOMO: Well, I'm disbelieving at the moment, Bill. You've talked about my helping Rupert Murdoch keep his newspapers as "an act of wisdom." It elected me a *public citizen* . . . *that's* what happened, actually. [laughter]

W.O.: Oh, that's right. Murdoch *forgot*. He studied Latin, but was absent the day they taught "Quid Pro Quo."

M.C.: No, he *remembered*! [laughter] He was nice enough to call up and say, "I'm sorry I'm going to have to beat you in this campaign, Mario, because you really did help me out in keeping my papers aloft . . . any way I can help you in the private world, I will . . . good luck to you!" And I've been in the *private* world ever since! Mr. President Rehr, it's a privilege to say hello to you.

I'm in the "me too" category, having listened to Ambassador Reid and having spoken to him only days ago on this very subject. I'm very much where "Brown" Reid is. And you can just put me down as an echo of the Reid sentiments. The Fairness Doctrine *sounded* right—sounded "fair"—but in the long run, I thought it was more dangerous than it was fair.

And there is a certain degree of palpable hypocrisy by the Congress when they make these fine moral judgments about obscenity. First of all, obscenity is such an elusive subject, that the best a Supreme Court justice could do in trying to define it was: "You *know* it when you see it or hear it," I guess. That's a hell of a thing to try to regulate—when you have to have it *happen* to plead guilty.

Apart from that . . . if you want to talk about obscenity in communications . . . how about the billions of dollars they pass every year in invisible bills nobody gets a chance to see? How about all these moments of silence? If they wanted to deal with honesty in communications and morality in communications . . . they should start *there*. We're never going to pass a bill that hasn't been of full exposure. And we know that doesn't happen. We know how they tack on bills for friends at the last moment, et cetera. So it comes with ill grace from any Congress like the ones we've had recently to start talking about how we're terribly worried about the children, et cetera. The parents' jobs are at *home*. There are threats to children coming from all directions and being proliferated. They carry threats at the palms of their hands with all the mechanisms that are out there.

Unless you teach them morality at home or at your school— unless you give them principles they can understand—*they* have to be able to define obscenity, *they* have to be able to say it's wrong on this basis. And when they say it's wrong—they will stop listening to it. But to try to do it in a statute—it just doesn't work.

W.O.: Governor, a lot of people are still mad at you that you didn't run for the presidency.

M.C.: Rupert's not! [laughter]

W.O.: A lot of people were also astonished and disappointed when you hung up on Bill Clinton and wouldn't let him put you on the Supreme Court. First of all, how would you decide this if *you* were a Supreme Court justice? Or a better question is . . . on this obscenity and indecency thing . . . would you have signed it—like President Bush, our hero—if you were *president*?

M.C.: No, I wouldn't have. You can't do it that way, Bill. That's the whole *point*. That was Potter Stewart's point. You *know* it when you *see* it. It was very hard. It gets easier when you're dealing with children. But even then it gets hard. How do you define obscenity? Different generations have defined it differently. But in the end, you're not going to define it for people with a law, with a statute. You're not able to *enforce* it . . . not just the problem of trying to find the words to describe it. Then you have to enforce it. *How* do you enforce it? How many people do you use listening in? It just doesn't work. It's not manageable.

These are *cultural* problems. Not *legislative* problems. The rule has to be self-imposed by your *culture*. Your culture has to decide. I said once to the broadcasters—as a matter of fact, Bill, I think it was out in California with you, in Los Angeles. I gave a speech in which I said we are a people that *desires* what we *disdain* and *disdains* what we *desire*. If it weren't for people who are buying the obscene and even pornographic products, we would not have this problem.

But we have this problem because the *culture* wants it . . . and you are not going to change the culture with a law . . . especially when the public finds the lawmakers to be hypocritical.

w.o.: Governor, let me ask David Rehr . . . do you think your television and radio stations are entirely blameless in all this, as witness the "Opie and Anthony" stunt in the cathedral?

D.R.: I think there are some that are a little . . . edgy.

w.o.: Is "edgy" a new word for vulgar?

D.R.: Yes, but I think another problem in America is that we focus on the 1 or 2 percent that is edgy or vulgar rather than focusing on the 98 percent that is decent, local, and wholesome.

GORDON HASTINGS: There is a term we have all grown up with in the broadcasting business and it hasn't been thrown around these microphones today and that is the *responsibility* of the local broadcaster as a "*gatekeeper*." I've traveled around to many television and radio markets throughout the nation and talked to many broadcasters—general managers, owners—who look at themselves as a "gatekeeper" as to what goes out to their audience. A lot of those people in charge of broadcast stations would have "self-policed" Opie and Anthony. They would not have gotten out of the studio after pulling that kind of a performance at the late S.G. Persons' television or radio station in Alabama. It simply would not have happened because of a "self-policing situation."

w.o.: Governor, is there any way out of this "unholy" mess?

M.C.: If you mean . . . is there a *perfect solution* that will perfectly define what society should find objectionable in references to sex . . . of course not. Society is constantly shifting and evolving.

The "F" word . . . I mean, I have lived long enough . . . probably we all have . . . to be shocked at how freely that word is thrown around in movies, of all kinds, "PG" movies! I went all through that when I was hired by the Weinsteins, with Michael Moore's movie. I had big discussions with people there who were on their way out as the rule makers.

The question was: What's a "PG" rating . . . how do you determine a "PG"? Well, if you use a certain word *twice*, you know, and then we drop it down a class. I said," You're kidding!" These are basically arbitrary rules. It's just the "F" word. Matilda and I were shocked. We had a movie and it was "PG" and the language was just stunning to me.

W.O.: What did Matilda Cuomo say?

M.C.: Tsk, tsk, change the channel, Mario. Stop sweating and change the channel. [aughter] Incidentally, that *is* the solution. Gordon says the broadcasters are "gatekeepers." But let's be candid. You appeal to a certain audience. You know what your audience will tolerate and not tolerate. Some audiences will not tolerate the hip hop language . . . and now that's music in today's definition. It doesn't sell for you. People are offended and they don't like it and you don't show it. Yes, they *are* gatekeepers, but they are not producing through their gatekeepers any predictable universal *standard*. It's the standard that Bill wants for his two radio stations. It's either a good one or not a good one, depending upon the people who listen. When you know you're not going to get enough people tuning in . . . you change your standard or you go out of the business. There is no way to come up with a perfect solution. I think you have to do this with a generalization.

Free speech is so valuable that I will pay even a big price for it . . . even if my sensitivities have to be offended from time to time.

I'll pay that price in the interest of free speech.

W.O.: David Rehr, you have four children, ages three to seven . . . and Governor, you have how many grand*daughters*?

M.C.: Twelve, O'Shaughnessy. And I have *a* grandson, five months old, Bill. Incidentally, I'm working on standards for him. [laughter]

W.O.: Were you shocked when you heard it was a boy? What did your son Christopher Cuomo, who is with ABC News, say . . . "Dad, you're not going to believe this . . ."?

M.C.: Well . . . now, you see . . . as we are defining obscenity, this is a good *example*. Christopher is a television person. He is doing well, thank you, and his wife, Cristina, is a very astute, learned person . . . and they asked Christopher . . . well, this is a *male* . . . and so you named him *Mario* . . . *why*? I think it is easy enough to say "I am very proud of my *father* . . . and *his* name happens to be *Mario*." He didn't say that. He said the baby was born with an unusually large *nose* and I saw it as soon as Cristina saw it . . . we looked at one another and said: "*This* is a *Mario* if I ever saw one!" Now to me *that* is virtual obscenity! [laughter]

W.O.: Let me ask you, "Grandfather" Cuomo and "Father" Rehr . . . When you see this stuff come on television or hear it on the radio, do you get a little crazy?

M.C.: Let me jump in, Bill. We do that all the time. We are alone in the apartment in Manhattan and the grandkids are there all the time and a lot of them stay over—a nine-year-old, a ten-year-old, and I have a twenty-one-year-old . . . we won't count her. We have this problem with them *all the time.*

W.O.: They don't watch cartoons . . .

M.C.: No, they do watch Disney . . . but they want to watch movies too. You have to go to the video store and you have to be very careful. You can't just assume that "PG" does it. You have to *work* at it. You have to let them see what you wish for them to see. Not just because someone told you it is this or that. I agree with the Europeans, who feel we don't put enough of our prohibitory instinct on the subject of violence. If we are going to overdo things, we should overdo the restrictions on *violence.*

I'm as offended at having the kids see so much violence that they take it for granted in what is already a tremendously violent society—the American society—which still has the death penalty when others do not. *That's* violence. It still reveres the gun . . . and has large numbers of people holding semi-automatic weapons over their heads saying, "This is my *flag.*" My God! Talk about violence. We were born in violence, in gunshot and flames, we expanded in violence, we invented the atom bomb, we are a violent people and that bothers me. And so, that kind of stuff I won't let my grandchildren look at if I can get to it first.

W.O.: Remember that line "sticks and stones . . ."? Is there an eloquent way to say that, Mario Cuomo? "Sticks and stones may break my bones . . . but names will never hurt me"?

M.C.: I don't know, Bill. I have a book by A. J. Parkinson, my favorite philosopher and writer. I'll look at it and see what he says. [laughter]

W.O.: We are public *trustees* . . .

G.H.: Thank you for using that term. Because when you are a trustee, all these issues come into play. They come into play as a prudent business decision, and as this whole concept of gatekeeper and what is the prudent thing to do. I don't believe in censorship and we all believe in the First Amendment, but we are also responsible for the maintenance of certain standards as over-the-air broadcasters.

W.O.: Before you leave, Mr. Rehr, is local radio going to be around for a while? Is local-yokel radio going to survive?

D.R.: That's a very good question. I'm moving across the country, I'm leaving here and going to Minnesota and Orlando, and then back to Washington. When I'm out meeting with radio broadcasters, I remind them, in the case of satellite radio . . . that both XM and Sirius have about 10 million subscribers. Every week between 260 and 280 million Americans listen to local radio!

W.O.: I've got twelve people in Mamaroneck myself! [laughter]

D.R.: I think *local radio*, the thing that gets me all fired up every day to represent you and the 8,300 members of the NAB all across the country, is all about *community*. It's about the *community*. Think of what the world would be like if the world had no local radio.

G.H.: There would be only *express* trains! No *local* stops . . . you could take the train from here to Los Angeles and not be able to get off in Norwalk! [laughter]

D.R.: The *Wall Street Journal* has said this radio station is "the quintessential local radio station in America."

W.O.: I don't even *read* the *Journal*!

D.R.: I read it religiously and I needed to come and find out for myself. I have been so impressed with the diversity of viewpoint and the interesting people I meet in the hallways . . . the interns who are getting an education on what local radio is all about.

W.O.: President Rehr, when he returns to D.C., will assemble his high council and advisors and say, "'They don't pay me enough to listen to *O'Shaughnessy!*" [laughter]

D.R.: Radio and television will adapt and we will change and we will evolve. But that's what's great about our industry. We are fiercely entrepreneurial and tremendously competitive, and all of those

[41]

juices and energy will be put in the right direction to serve the
people who are listening.

w.o.: I'm going to give you a new word for what we do: *profession.*
Forget "industry."

d.r.: Profession. Yes, I agree.

w.o.: David, your presence honors us. Thank you, Gordon. And a
special thanks to the great governor of New York, whose wisdom
again instructs us.

Ambassador Ogden Rogers Reid

On the occasion of his ninetieth birthday, June 24, 2015.

WILLIAM O'SHAUGHNESSY: Today we'll visit with an iconic figure on a very significant day, an historic one. The next voice you hear coming from his redoubt in Waccabuc in the rolling hills of northern Westchester will be that of the *first* United States ambassador to the infant state of Israel. He was also publisher of the dearly departed and much-missed *New York Herald Tribune* newspaper, founded by Horace Greeley and sustained by his family—the Reid family—for many years, decades in fact. He was an environmental commissioner of the state of New York and a legendary liberal Republican congressman with a glorious record on First Amendment issues and free speech in the Congress of the United States: Ogden Rogers Reid. Mr. Ambassador, happy birthday! You're ninety years old this very day.

AMBASSADOR OGDEN REID: That's right, Bill. Thank you for calling. You're an old and dear friend.

W.O.: Ambassador Reid, how does it feel to be ninety?

O.R.: Well, it's not much different from being sixty, to tell you the truth.

W.O.: Well, we all hope to achieve that significant milestone. Mrs. Reid, Mary Louise Reid, your spectacular wife of so many years—whom we certainly remember fondly here in southern Westchester—said you celebrated at the famous "21" Club in Manhattan. Did you make a speech?

O.R.: Well, for the occasion, I offered a few remarks, Bill . . . just a few remarks. I thanked people for coming, and that was about it. Most of the folks there have been listening to me for a good long time. [laughter] w.o.: Ambassador Reid, of all the chapters of your life—publisher, politician, ambassador, commissioner, candidate for governor— what gave you the most pleasure? What was the most satisfying, Ambassador "Brown" or "Brownie" Reid, as so many call you by your nickname?

o.r.: I think being ambassador to Israel, Bill.

w.o.: Do you remember those days? Tell us about it? Israel was brand new, an infant state and struggling as it is now.

o.r.: I don't know if there's anything I can summon up from those perilous days. But we did work to strengthen the relations among Israel's neighbors and also keep the peace in the Near East, generally.

w.o.: Ambassador Ogden Reid, what do you think about the future in the Middle East? Is it ever going to be peaceful over there?

o.r.: Yes, I think it will be. Just when, I don't know, Bill.

w.o.: Are *we* doing the right thing, Ambassador Reid? America?

o.r.: I don't exactly know what we're doing between the countries via their present ambassadors with the various intergovernmental relationships, but the test will be only whether we keep the peace and whether progress is made toward that.

w.o.: Sir, I almost forgot in my intro, among your other titles and appellations you were also president of the Council of American Ambassadors. Do you still keep in touch in that rarefied fraternity?

o.r.: Yes, I do. And I'm still chairman—or president—of the Council of Ambassadors.

w.o.: What the hell do ambassadors talk about when you get together?

o.r.: Oh, when we get together, of course, we talk about the urgent current issues that seem to be relevant and who is doing what to try to solve them.

w.o.: Ambassador Reid, I have admired you in every season of your life, never more so than when you took on a man named Harley Orrin Staggers. He was a right-of-way agent from Mineral County, West Virginia, many years ago. And on a free speech matter he wanted to throw Frank Stanton and the legendary Bill Paley of CBS in the damn clunker; he wanted to put them in jail. Early on, when the contretemps began, you didn't have the votes in the House. He was a powerful committee chairman, as I remember it. But you, sir, had your genius and your wits and your conviction and the example of the Founders—plus something called the First Amendment—and you beat the hell out of Harley Staggers on the floor of the House as you rounded up the votes. Do you remember those days?

o.r.: I sure do! It was a difficult and dangerous time. Mr. Staggers also wanted to lock up Walter Cronkite.

w.o.: Does the First Amendment still mean something in our lives, Ogden Reid?

o.r.: Oh, absolutely! It sure does!

w.o.: What does it mean?

o.r.: Freedom. Freedom, Bill.

w.o.: What do you mean, sir?

o.r.: The First Amendment—and the right to speak one's mind—is an important and essential part of the process of maintaining and enhancing and enlarging freedom, wherever it is. In every issue. In every circumstance.

w.o.: Mr. Ambassador Ogden Rogers Reid, I know your family has been feting you and celebrating your ninetieth birthday. Are you getting ready for one hundred?

o.r.: No, I'm getting ready for 110, Bill!

w.o.: Sir, you honor us with your presence on the radio this morning, and as always, with your entire life, and with your shining and courageous example. Congratulations on the ninetieth anniversary of your natal day.

o.r.: Thank you, Bill. I've always admired you and WVOX. We fought a lot of battles together, old friend. You—and that singular radio station—were always with me.

Nancy Pelosi v. James Madison

William O'Shaughnessy commentary re: The "Unfairness"
Doctrine, July 25, 2008.

An influential communications blog recently called for the re-imposition of the so-called Fairness Doctrine, suggesting that House Speaker Nancy Pelosi might favor the effort.

> It will not surprise us if the Fairness Doctrine returns and we wouldn't get all that upset about it. Speaker Nancy Pelosi wants it back on the books. It could be good for broadcasting.

I'm absolutely opposed to this, and just to make myself clear, we'll refer to it henceforth as the *Un*fairness Doctrine.

The misnamed doctrine was struck down on August 4, 1987, by an enlightened FCC of its day. And although the damn thing sometimes resembles Lazarus in the Bible in that it keeps jumping up again and again, I hope we won't associate ourselves with any recurring assault on the First Amendment rights of broadcasters, no matter how agreeably and deceptively named.

It's very simple and very fundamental: The Federal Communications Commission and the Congress should not be allowed to dictate our agenda or shape our priorities. Our opposition to any unfairness doctrine is based, in every season, on the bedrock fundamental wisdom of the Founders: "*Congress shall make no law . . .*" You know the rest.

The bloggers may have Nancy Pelosi on their side. I'm afraid I have only James Madison.

In our best moments we are electronic journalists at the people's business. And clearly, it (any doctrine by government fiat or decree) would be an impermissible intrusion into the editorial process and an inhibitor rather than promoter of controversial expression. It would unquestionably inhibit the presentation of controversy. So much for "balance."

I don't think we want to be among those who would intensify the chill an Unfairness Doctrine would induce. We either believe in the principle that broadcasting is entitled to the full freedom of the press that the First Amendment guarantees. Or we do not.

MARIO CUOMO

Governor Mario Cuomo instructs us:

> You can't get at bad taste and destructive communication through regulation. That's just substituting one evil for another. The ceding of authority, on a basic principle, has to come back to haunt us.

The great Cuomo (whom the *Boston Globe* calls "the pre-eminent philosopher-statesman of the American nation") is saying that maybe this generation of broadcasters, buffeted by new technology and competition (and consolidation), can survive by what I've called our "obsequious acquiescence" and by pulling our punches on free speech and content issues like an Unfairness Doctrine, but our kids won't—the people we leave our businesses to.

BARGAINING CHIP

I'm afraid *broadcasters* are not united in pushing for our long-overdue independence from content regulation. In every season, it seems, structural, so-called pocketbook issues take precedence among the speculators and investors, and even some broadcasters—those "market managers" who operate out of airport lounges with their iPhones and Blackberrys beholden to corporate masters a whole continent away. They'll beat their breasts about ownership caps, newspaper-broadcast cross ownership, multicast must-carry, dual-carriage, retransmission consent, *à la carte* pricing, fin-sin rules, performance taxes, the DTV spectrum and those white spaces in the DTV band, low-power FM, satellite radio, SDARS repeaters, copyright royalties, main studio location, competition from telcos and iPods, etc.

But the broadcasting establishment and the NAB board, sadly, have always viewed the First Amendment as a stepchild among our priorities and even, occasionally, as a bargaining chip.

So before anyone attempts to bestow their imprimatur it would be wise to give this some thought lest a lot of owners, people who make profits in this business (again, read: profession), will sell freedom for a reduction in governmental fees and levies or accommodation on structural, competitive issues. They will make deals with Speaker Pelosi and Congress. They will accept regulation we shouldn't be accepting— all in exchange for an opportunity to make more money, thus adding their weight to a destructive principle.

And what's more (and worse), they will flee from any controversial or meaningful programming and throw radio back to its "jukebox era." That is the real danger. And I don't think we want to encourage that.

UNITED EFFORT

Why not instead use our resources and energy to revive our own flagging spirits and lack of attention to these fundamental issues? All elements of today's modern media would be better served by a united effort by broadcasters, podcasters, bloggers, Internet entrepreneurs, cable operators, et al.—all those now firmly fixed—and those just entering, the Information Age to develop a consolidated, joint resolve against government intrusion into content and free expression.

Fairness? Balance? No matter how comforting it would be for the Congress and the Commission to wrap themselves around "fairness," a concept not explicitly or penumbrally protected by the Constitution as free *speech* and free *press* expressly are, I am confident the Supreme Court will one day be compelled to concentrate on the clear, certain, elegant, unvarnished language in the First Amendment of the Bill of Rights should we ever again be confronted by the siren song of "fairness" by government fiat, decree, or doctrine.

No one disputes what has been called the "coarsening" of our culture. And yet the quest for "fairness" and "balance," while understandable and even commendable, is every much a fool's errand as the crusade to install "decency" on the nation's airwaves. And perhaps even more dangerous.

EYE OF THE BEHOLDER

Can't one just hear a Capitol Hill solon opining: "I *know* fairness when I *hear* it . . . and I also know *balance* when I see it"? Again, it's all in the eye of the beholder. And the same self-appointed censors who would seek to identify and define indecency, vulgarity, or obscenity should not be given the opportunity to determine fairness. Or balance. That should always be left to the journalist and his or her audience, which is the only permissible censor. Turn it off if you don't like it. Don't listen or watch if you find it offensive.

Programming should be based only on our judgment as journalists and the dictates of our audiences in whom we should ultimately place our trust. For the people, in their collective wisdom, are infinitely wiser than any government-appointed regulatory agency's idea of what the public should be allowed to hear and see.

INTELLECTUALS

Thirty-two years ago Eric Sevareid said:

> The Washington intellectuals have always hated anything that the generality of people liked: They must, to preserve their distinctiveness, their eliteness, even (especially) those who claim they love humanity and who want to control the product of our labors. As Eric Hoffer once said, "The businessman just wants your money; the military man wants you to obey. But the intellectual (and the censor) wants your soul. He wants people to get down on their knees and love what they hate and hate what they love."

But more than 200 years ago the Founders saw to it that:

> *Congress shall make no law* respecting an establishment of religion, or prohibiting the free exercise thereof, or *abridging the freedom of speech; or the press*, or of the right of the people peaceably to assemble, and to petition the government for a redress of grievances.

And the diminutive Washington hand Jack Valenti again reminds us:

Those forty-five simple words bound together in spare, unadorned prose are the wisest and most valuable design for democracy ever put to paper. Of all the clauses in the Constitution, it is the one passage that guarantees everything else in the greatest document ever struck off by the hand and mind of man.

In our world where ambiguity infects almost everything, this is the loveliest example of non-ambiguity to be found anywhere. Concise, compact, marching in serried ranks, there is about these immortal words the taste of pure wisdom unsoiled by hesitancy.

What that glorious amendment means is that no matter how fiery the rhetoric, or frenzied the debate, or how calamitous the cry, government cannot interrupt or intervene in the speech of its citizens.

It's not easy to be a First Amendment advocate. You must allow that which you may judge to be meretricious, squalid, smarmy and without so-called "redeeming value" to enter the market-place. Often we become irate ourselves at what is invading the culture of the community, particularly awful words and terrible, even dangerous ideas from which we want to recoil.

ENLIGHTENED REGULATORS

Thankfully not all regulators are immune to the lovely music and instruction of the First Amendment. Listen to these powerful (and courageous) findings announced some twenty years ago by the then-chairman and also the chief general counsel of the FCC as they struck a blow for freedom. Our freedom.

The First Amendment does not guarantee a fair press, only a free press. The fairness doctrine chills free speech, is not narrowly tailored to achieve any substantial government interest, and therefore contravenes the First Amendment and the public interest. As a consequence, we can no longer impose fairness doctrine obligations on broadcasting and simultaneously honor our oath of office.

—FCC Chairman Dennis Patrick

August 4, 1987

The framers had it right. No matter how good the intention, there is no way for government to restrict freedom of speech or the press and foster a robust and unfettered exchange of ideas. If we must choose whether editorial decisions are to be made in the free judgment of individual broadcasters or imposed by bureaucratic fiat, the choice must be for freedom.

—FCC General Counsel Diane Killory

WASHINGTON SAGE

Patrick Maines, the erudite president of the Media Institute, the prestigious Washington think tank, has been trying to drag us kicking and screaming onto the battlefield to confront government intrusion into our creative processes. Said the brainy and quite brave Mr. Maines:

Politically speaking, freedom of speech in the United States is in tatters. We are beleaguered by "progressives" on the left, "social conservatives" on the right, and policymakers and bureaucrats of all stripes, and our ability to freely express ourselves would already be greatly diminished but for the federal courts.

Bad as the situation is within policymaking circles, it is little better in academia and even in mainstream journalism, both of which, with a few exceptions, operate in the grip of a kind of political correctness that is the very antithesis of free speech, if not of freedom itself.

The beginning of wisdom lies in understanding that free speech isn't imperiled because educated people don't know what it is. It's imperiled because educated people subordinate this knowledge to their political and cultural preferences.

Whether you call it inconsistency, hypocrisy, or willfulness, it is at the heart of the present danger.

As direct beneficiaries of the free speech clause of the First Amendment, media companies have an obligation to act as the people's sentinels on this issue. As such, they need to see that

[51]

they are not adding to the problem by acts of omission or commission, and to practice what they preach.

Though it's not widely appreciated, the truth is that the First Amendment is indivisible. We don't have one First Amendment for newspapers and another for the Internet. Nor do we have one for the media and another for individuals, or one for news and one for entertainment, or one for radio and another for television.

We have only *one* First Amendment and, such being the ways of precedent, if it is weakened anywhere it's weakened everywhere. Which is why it is incumbent on media companies to act rigorously and selflessly to protect it.

Freedom of speech in the United States is at risk of dying a death of a thousand cuts. For the sake of the nation, as well as the health of their profession, it is to be profoundly hoped that the media, old and new, will rethink and redouble their efforts to safeguard this cornerstone or our constitutional rights.

OPPOSITE EFFECT

There are also *practical* reasons to oppose Pelosi and friends. A government doctrine would have an *opposite* effect by exerting a chilling restraint of speech because of the cost in time, money, and controversy on already beleaguered broadcasters, who as ordinary, practical businesspeople, however privileged their calling and high estate, often prefer to pull their punches on free speech issues or stay out of the ring entirely on government intrusions into content.

They (the NAB board) would rather save their gunpowder for assaults on the brick and mortar—the structural integrity—of our "industry" that threatens our purses and bottom lines. "Pocketbook" issues we can understand.

I'm afraid that station or network owners (or those market managers) unwilling to fight for full constitutional freedoms ought not to be in the business (read: profession).

During my service at NAB, time and again, I would remind our colleagues that we are not John Deere dealers or holders of a Budweiser franchise!

INDUSTRY OR PROFESSION?

The minutes of NAB's high councils for the past several decades contain thousands of references to our "industry" (some southerners called it an "in-*dust*-ry"). Mr. Sevareid, however, referred to what we do, our electronic journalism, as "a *profession* . . . a *trade* . . . or *calling*." I think that has a better ring to it.

As I finally and mercifully yield, let me point out that I'm not exactly alone in the general tone and tenor of my views. In an attempt to be glib, I said, somewhere earlier that they had Mrs. Pelosi, while I had only Mr. Madison.

FRIENDS OF THE FIRST

But I'm reminded that opposition and revulsion to any so-called fairness doctrine can be found in the writings and pronouncements over the years of some of the brightest thinkers and public servants of our time: William Proxmire, Father Robert Drinan, Fred Friendly, Lionel Van Deerlin, Bob Packwood, Sol and Larry Taishoff, David Bazelon, Roman Hruska, Rush Limbaugh, Louis Boccardi, Nat Hentoff, Floyd Abrams, Jim Quello, Ward Quaal, Rick Kaplar, Rachelle Chong, Dennis R. Patrick, Eric Sevareid, William S. Paley, Julian Goodman, Jacob K. Javits, Joe Reilly, Bob Grant, Mel Karmazin, Bill McElveen, David Hinckley, Eric Rhoads, Ronald Reagan, Dennis Jackson, John Harper, Walter Nelson Thayer, Ossie Davis, Ruby Dee, John Hay Whitney, A. M. Rosenthal, Neal Travis, Arthur O. Sulzberger, Ogden Rogers Reid, Dan Rather, Howard Stern, Sean Hannity, Jeffrey Bernbach, Michael Harrison, Bill Clark, Carl Marcucci, Les Brown, Steve Knoll, Jack Messmer, Fred Danzig, Daniel Patrick Moynihan, Martin Stone, Rainer K. Kraus, John Van Buren Sullivan, Lawrence Winer, Robert McNeil, Mimi Weyforth Dawson, George Carlin, Patricia Diaz Dennis, Charles Barton, Chuck Castleberry, Potter Stewart, Diane Killory, Patrick Maines, Don West, Harry Jessell, John Eggerton, Jim Carnegie, Jay Mitchell, Bob Doll, Tom Taylor, Frank Saxe, Frank Stanton, Walter May, Don Stevens, Robert Corn-Revere, Erwin Krasnow, John Crigler, Walter Cronkite, Bruce Sanford, Patrick Leahy, John Wells King, Judge Joseph Bellacosa, Justice William O. Douglas, and Mr. Cuomo himself. And so many others.

MR. PALEY

The incomparable CBS founder William S. Paley, an iconic figure of our tribe, once said the Fairness Doctrine is like the Holy Roman Empire—only it is neither holy . . . nor Roman . . . and it's not an empire! This occurred at about the same time Mr. Paley took on the Honorable Harley O. Staggers, a right-of-way agent from Mineral County, West Virginia.

It is recalled that Mr. Staggers, who was also chairman of a powerful House subcommittee, wanted to find "contemptible" Paley's associates Frank Stanton and Walter Cronkite and slam their backsides right into a federal jail cell concerning a most controversial television program of the day, "The Selling of the Pentagon."

Chairman Staggers, however, did not reckon with Bill Paley's vision and resolve or with the fierce opposition of a brilliant patrician congressman from Westchester named Ogden Rogers Reid, who raised holy hell about all this on the floor of the Congress, all in very gentlemanly fashion, of course.

"Brown" Reid, as he was known when he published the *New York Herald Tribune,* a newspaper of sainted memory that was founded by Horace Greeley, was on his feet prowling the aisles to line up votes against the powerful chairman bent on censorship.

As the battle joined, Reid, who is now president of the Council of American Ambassadors (he had been our first ambassador to Israel), began to quote the legendary Tito Gainza Paz, the brave South American publisher who stood up to Juan Perón: "You either have a free press, Mr. Reid . . . or you don't."

And then Reid took to the well of the House to do a slow, steady recitation of those forty-five timeless words from the Founders of the republic. Staggers was finished, and his motion for a contempt citation against the CBS elders was defeated.

It really happened not so long ago. And one wonders . . . where are all the William S. Paleys of today who will stand up to coercion and intimidation? And where are the Ogden Reids who find no difference between print and broadcast journalism?

I thus hope those yearning for a new/old fairness doctrine will rethink their position re: "fairness." If nothing else, the history of the doctrine, in its various manifestations, suggests that rather than protecting free speech, it has been used as a cudgel by both liberals and conservatives (and even a few presidents) to stem criticism and stifle dissent.

THE FOUNDERS

The Founding Fathers, in their wisdom, sought to ensure vigorous debate by guaranteeing free speech and a free press, and by restraining the government from interfering. They had faith that the people could distinguish truth from fiction and that the people's interest would best be served by the unrestricted debate that would follow. Any policy or doctrine to regulate fairness assumes that the people's interests would be better served by a *restricted* debate in which the government would serve as a "Papa knows best" referee.

Justice Potter Stewart wrote:

Fairness is far too fragile to be left for a government bureaucracy to accomplish.

DUMP *PACIFICA* AND *RED LION V. FCC*

I also pray that one day soon the courts will overturn *Pacifica*, which held that broadcasting was "uniquely pervasive" . . . and *Red Lion v. FCC*, which upheld content regulation on the grounds that spectrum was a scarce commodity. Both need to fall to the First Amendment in the highest courts in our land. Sooner rather than later. Until then we must hold grimly and tenaciously to every freedom the law now allows and fight for more.

WORDS, DAMN WORDS

Free speech? Some of it ain't so pretty . . . but *all* of it needs to be protected.

Words that are sweet, awkward, horrific, barely audible, meretricious, smarmy, smart-ass, obscene, political, clumsy, uncomfortable, sexy, crude, inarticulate, cutting, just plain silly, X-rated, excessive, dangerous, insulting, serious, scintillating, disappointing, discursive, provocative, disgusting, vulgar, disjointed, unfair, dismissive, inappropriate, stupid, uninhibited, risqué, droll, suggestive, dull, soothing, exhilarating, tormented, slanted, ferocious, coarse, halting, anti-religious, harmful to the community, revolting, humorous, improper, amoral, oneiric, dreary, dolorous, noble, brave, ignoble, resolute, doughty, biased, alliterative, inappropriate, immoral, sacrilegious, un-American, anarchistic, in error, sexual, inane, cutting-edge, incendiary, not serious, appropriate, incorrect, lusty, offensive, insane, passionate, inspiring, beyond the pale, jumbled, florid, long-winded, loud, blunt, lyrical, meaningless, chaste, suggestive, charming, scary, moral, nutty, desperate, out of bounds, over-the-top, overblown, pedantic, pointed, pointless, popular, prurient, pungent, rambling, raucous, religious, ribald, dissonant, rough, serene, sloppy, inartful, soaring, sublime, bawdy, subtle, thoughtful, indecent, truthful, unclear, nasty, unpleasant, unpopular, vague, witty . . . are all part of the essential language of America.

The language of America must be protected. *All* of it. By all of us.

MADAME SPEAKER

Full disclosure: I have considerable regard for Nancy Pelosi. She and I were "unindicted co-conspirators" and collaborators in the effort to persuade Mario Cuomo to mount a bid for the presidency. We spent many hours on the phone discussing and framing the importunings that we hoped might persuade the "Hamlet on the Hudson" to set aside his responsibilities in Albany and enter the presidential sweepstakes. She is one very bright woman. But she is ill-advised on the "fairness" matter.

Civil Liberties in an Age of Terrorism

These remarks were delivered in 2002 at a forum sponsored by the American Civil Liberties Union and the League of Women Voters at Saint Paul's Church on the Eastchester Village Green, a national historic site in Mount Vernon, New York.

Please allow me to acknowledge our admiration for the League of Women Voters. Some think they're just a bunch of damn do-gooders— and they are a bunch of damn do-gooders. They keep all politicians everywhere honest. They try to eliminate personality and BS from the political process—and they neutralize all the glitz and glamour and render it harmless. And this unique and invaluable organization forces politicians—and they literally *drag* the voters—into confronting the real issues.

So I come in gratitude for the League of Women Voters and also for Stanley Shear. I think you have no idea, but those of us in the public press do, of all the good things he does in our lives, to arrange for bridge loans for people whose purse is not so well endowed, so they can buy houses. He's been a glorious champion of the First Amendment, which this historic Saint Paul's National Historic Site celebrates.

As for the American Civil Liberties Union: We have disagreed with them so often. But *they* are usually right. And we, in our comfort and smugness, and affluence, often cannot see the wisdom and courage they bring to the great issues. We could not imagine—or care for—an America without the ACLU. They *unsettle* us. They *challenge* us. They *confront* us. And they *sustain* us.

Here in this hallowed place they talk about a governor of New York and his contretemps with the itinerant printer John Peter Zenger. I spoke with another governor of New York within the hour. And Mario Cuomo, a most wise and intelligent man, said, "Don't go down there,

[57]

O'Shaughnessy! Michael Myers and Stanley Shear and Norman Siegel are too bright for you! They will murder you, and it too will be an historic occasion! Don't go near these two guys because they've devoted their whole lives to this" [laughter].

Actually, I've been here before. I stood outside this lovely church on the village green on a summer day long ago in 1974. How do I remember that far back? I know because Fordham University Press put it in a book. We celebrate and revere the Constitution and the Declaration of Independence. I'm not quite like Senator Robert Byrd from West Virginia, who carries it in his pocket, but I do carry it in my briefcase. This is what I said about the First Amendment, which we are about to discuss, and about this place we're sitting in right now: "It is the peculiar glory of this spot that it witnessed the dawn of civil liberty in America. We do not honor this so-called shrine of the Bill of Rights. This lovely old church is but a monument. Thus, it is perishable and will not last forever."

Although, thanks to the good people who preserved this old church and made it a national landmark, we hope it will go on forever.

So this is what I said that summer day with the bands playing and the flags flying on the Fourth of July almost thirty years ago. (I'm reminded that my New Rochelle neighbor Ossie Davis wiped me out the next year. *He* gave the speech that everybody quotes to this day.)

But my poor effort said: "The principle of freedom of thought, which was affirmed here and went forth from this spot and spread throughout America and England, is worthy of our tribute. On this glorious summer day, that idea, that glorious principle, is still not secure, is still under attack and in need of your patronage and protection."

And I could not resist again reminding those who came with their families, of the words of John Stuart Mill, who said: "We can never be sure that the opinion we are endeavoring to stifle is a false opinion. And if we were sure, stifling it would be an evil still."

So we're talking about freedom of the press and the Bill of Rights. And it means everything to me, and to my profession. It's our dominant characteristic. There's no question about that. We fought wars to protect it. The rights of free speech against oppression, and against search and seizure and invasions of privacy, are very, very strong with us.

But, historically, when you're in a war situation—and I think this is what today is about—whether it was the Civil War or the First World War or the Second World War, you see that our presidents and our governments put a greater emphasis on fighting the war than on protecting liberties.

I'm not so sure that is such a bad thing. And traditionally, even if you look at the courts, they have relaxed a little bit in First Amendment protections in the name of protecting everything—the whole nation.

It was true in every war. Abraham Lincoln, our greatest president, gave up the writ of *habeas corpus*. He ignored the civil rights to preserve the Union. Franklin Roosevelt, who, as the great Cuomo describes him, rose from his wheelchair to lift this nation up against oppression in the war and the evil known as Nazism and totalitarianism, had encampments and locked people up.

On our radio station, just up the road a piece, on September 11th—I'm a great believer that all wisdom resides, ultimately, with the people, so we opened up our phone lines. A lady called and said, "I think you should lock up every Muslim you can get your hands on!" The host said, "That's a brilliant God-damned idea because we're still paying reparations to the *Japanese!*"

In every war, including this one, there's some temporizing of the Bill of Rights, I'm afraid. Some adjustments. And, always, you seek a *balance*, which is my point.

The question is, in creating that balance are you putting too heavy a thumb on the scale, Mr. Attorney General? Are you putting too heavy a thumb on the scale or do you just "adjust the weights" in a war? It's always an argument over *degree*.

I'm an advocate for the First Amendment. But none of these rights are limitless, I suggest. Not free speech, not search and seizure, not even religion. For instance, if your religion says, "You can't treat a child who's ill" (and some religions do), we will take that child from you in this country to save that child's life.

We're not going to give up our essential liberties. The Supreme Court will always be there. It may lean a little, depending on who appoints the justices. But it will always be there and it should "lean" a little. Because the same principle that says you should protect the individual also says, obviously, that you must protect the rights of all, that 280 million, from a bomb that will blow you all up. You don't have to be a liberal or a conservative to believe in intelligence, reasonableness, and balance.

As I listen to Michael Meyers, great columnist, First Amendment champion, and Arlene Popkin, she and Norman Siegel are on the side of the *angels*. The ghosts in this fabled church, through all the years, are rooting for them and for their point of view. I would have been over there because I fought against Tipper Gore, who, with Susan Baker, wanted to label all the rock lyrics as good or bad. And every time they censure Howard Stem and our own tribe turns against him, they drag me out. So 1 would have been over there before 9/11.

I think you have to be clear. The Fourteenth Amendment, as my colleague Cari Robinson, a former assistant U.S. attorney, points out, extends these things only to United States *citizens*. In Afghanistan right now we have FBI agents over there in battle fatigues dragging people out of their beds. And I have no problem with that.

People say, "What about Pearl Harbor?" Pearl Harbor was an attack on a *military installation*. Sure, people died in the hulls of those battleships. Sure, it was a blow to our national ego. And sure, lives were lost. But now this is a new time. They are attacking *civilians*. You can say, "Well, the World Trade Center was a *symbol* of American power and finance and commerce." But real mothers and fathers and children died in those staircases, in the ashes. And they're there still, in the silence.

I'm reminded that Senator Jack Javits, the towering senator from New York who was the father of the War Powers Act, once said, "You either *believe* in the genius of the free enterprise system or you do not." So can we try *another* form of government? No. Don't even think about it. What we've got to do is make this one *better*. As far as the pursuit of money goes, you're right. And the selfishness. And greed. We see it on Wall Street. We see it all around us with the yuppies in Westchester, who have no manners and no inclination of giving. They don't understand charity unless it can help them get ahead at the office.

I think it comes, ultimately, to the Golden Rule. The Jews have a word for it: *tzedakah*; and *tikkun olam*. And, the Christians, who stole it whole from the Jews, have those words of the itinerant rabbi, the

Founder of the Christian religion, To Love Your Neighbor as Yourself. *That's* what we've got to do—not change the damn government.

Miss Martinez asked the best question, and it still lingers: Would you come down on Timothy McVeigh? (She called him a WASP.) I think your suggestion is if it had been a Timothy McVeigh–type, we'd lock up every trailer-trash guy from upstate New York with a gun rack and a pickup truck! So maybe I'm creeping over on the civil liberties side. But we've always had discrimination, and I think it's up to you to make sure that discrimination in our own lives and in our own neighborhoods doesn't go too far.

You hear it on our radio station. Every day my Irish grandmother used to call them "*Eye*-talians." The Eye-talians from the Fourth Ward complain about the Mexicans. There are too many of them out there on the street looking for a day's work. The Mexicans took the place of the Portuguese, who took the place of the Italians. Now the worst, I tell you, are the *Irish*. The Irish get a little money and they move to Pound Ridge and become Congregationalists! [applause] Incidentally, the Irish don't blow up *buildings*. They blow up the *English!* [laughter] So, these things are always shifting. I think it's up to you to always ask these tough questions of your teachers.

You've asked tough questions here today. And I salute you. I admire your intelligence and passion. And I'm persuaded that, with your encouragement, our nation will find that delicate balance between individual liberty and the common good. Even in these desperate days as our nation is poised on the brink of war.

Obsequious Acquiescence by William O'Shaughnessy: A Runaway Freight Train Heading Straight for the First Amendment

This speech was prepared for the NAB Summit on Responsible Programming in Washington, D.C., April 7, 2004.

A runaway train is headed straight for our profession, with a head of steam from the FCC and Congress. The passenger list includes misguided regulators, legislators, concerned citizens, and even some broadcasters. We have to stop this train to preserve our politics, governance, economy, and culture.

The people, our ultimate authority, must have freedom of expression. This extraordinary gift, the right to speak, to advocate, to describe, to entertain, to perform, to dissent—to sing—is more than a wonderful privilege; it makes this democracy a miracle.

The Founding Fathers gave us freedom of expression without nuance or conditions, but plainly and purely.

Some broadcasters, through excessive bad taste, reckless reporting, pervasively biased opinions and analysis, yes, palpable unfairness, have invited laws and rulings the Founding Fathers would have abhorred.

Still, we must stop this train.

We must continue to protect the broadest possible freedom of expression for the press. All of it, written and electronic. It is the coin of our democratic realm. But the flip side of that coin is responsibility.

As editors, as broadcasters, as permittees of the instruments of communication which are in our care and keeping, we should monitor ourselves to avoid retaliation. We have the power to transform our audience of millions and make them fuller, surer, sweeter per Mario Cuomo.

[62]

As long as we treat our power and our privilege with the respect it deserves, we'll preserve for ourselves, and our posterity, the freedom to develop the richest and wisest culture ever.

In an election-year frenzy, Congress may crack down on broadcast "indecency" with scant regard for the robust tradition of free speech at the core of American values. If vulgar, outrageous, and tasteless speech isn't protected by the First Amendment, then the amendment has lost its meaning.

The prohibition against "indecent" speech does not apply to newspapers, magazines, books, or pamphlets. It does not apply to the Internet. It does not apply to satellite television, or cable or satellite radio. At least not yet.

Traditional terrestrial broadcasting is currently exempted from equal protection. A lot of people think that is right and proper. They are wrong. In an age when all media are "electronic," it's increasingly difficult to justify this approach.

Does that mean radio and television will become as free as newspapers? Not likely. In today's climate, it could be the other way around. Will those who cheer as Congress clamps down on broadcasting have second thoughts when their favorite newspaper columnist is muzzled? It could happen.

As the revered Supreme Court Justice William O. Douglas once observed, "The fear that Madison and Jefferson had of government intrusion . . . was founded not only on the specter of a lawless government but [on the specter] of government under the control of a faction foisting *its* views of the common good on the people."

The First Amendment was enacted to prevent that. Yet an FCC policy against "indecent" speech, already dangerously vague, is expanding to include "profane" speech, with strict enforcement.

It has happened before. The Nixon FCC in 1971 declared that a broadcaster should carefully listen to, and understand, all the lyrics in a song before playing it, or else it would "raise . . . serious questions as to whether continued operation of the station is in the public interest."

In response, as Professor Lucas A. Powell Jr. noted in his book *American Broadcasting and the First Amendment*, station WNTN in Newton,

Massachusetts simply eliminated *all* Bob Dylan songs "because management could not interpret the lyrics"!

The FCC should not be the national arbiter of indecency and obscenity. With its inherent power to browbeat industry executives by bestowing, renewing, and revoking licenses, and to grant waivers of ownership rules, the FCC used to regulate by "raised eyebrow," but today, a more apt characterization might be by "sledgehammer."

These issues should be decided by the courts, applying the wisdom of the First Amendment, instead of the FCC, a politically appointed body. Indeed, the courts are the forum for obscenity and indecency regulation on cable, satellite, film, and the print media.

You can tell a lot about a nation, and the world, from what you hear on the radio. The current "indecency" campaign is led by some of the brightest and most capable leaders on the commission and in Congress. I admire their passion to heal an ailing world. But I disagree with their remedy.

"Indecency" should not be the subject of government regulation. If the central concept of our Constitution is liberty, its most important working principle is freedom of expression.

The Founding Fathers knew that, certainly. With a blunt and fundamental clarity, they wrote, "Congress shall make no law respecting an establishment of religion, or prohibiting the free exercise thereof; or abridging the freedom of speech, or of the press."

They understood that an oppressive government could not stifle the truth, or distort it, with a boldly free press. People could say what they wanted, when they wanted. Accurate or not. In good taste or bad. To give two sides of an issue, or only one. All in the name of freedom.

Over the years, the government dared to impose a standard of "right conduct" on broadcasters unthinkable for the print media and other forms of expression.

The reason the Founding Fathers left the balancing and filtering to the people, instead of to the politicians, applies perfectly to electronic broadcasting as well.

Censoring electronic speech seizes an important sector of our freedom and delivers it to a government we already distrust. It substitutes the opinions of faceless and unaccountable bureaucrats for our own.

As Mario Cuomo constantly reminds us, when we seek more civility in our lives, we embody an extraordinary contradiction: a desire for what disgusts us, a disgust for what we desire.

Every age struggles with its own disorder, crises, and calamities, but the world we live in now is so disorienting, it frightens even the historians. This urgent desire to wrestle our society back to the good old days is occurring among inherently liberal officials. Thus, our fear has transcended our political opinions.

The American people are so traumatized by the terrible syndrome of drugs, guns, and violence, they are desperate for bold action. In their anxiety, they confuse displaying this chaos with encouraging and disseminating it.

As radio broadcasters, we must acknowledge our failures. We've done some really stupid things. The Opie and Anthony copulation stunt in St. Patrick's Cathedral is just one episode we'd like to forget. But our radio tribe has also been tarnished by its association with the medium of television.

For at least a generation, ever since the advent of deregulation and the birth of cable, television has become a vessel of escalating narcissism, exhibitionism, prurience, degradation, humiliation, and sexual dysfunction.

With greed and lust in the lead, the seven deadly sins are on parade morning, noon, and night. Viewers all across the land encounter a dreary cavalcade of unwed, jilted mothers on *Maury*; geriatric strippers on *Jerry*; and a long chorus line of promiscuous midgets, cross-dressing male prostitutes, and toothless, white-trash, trailer-park hags at all hours of the day and night.

And it's not just the tawdry Jerry Springer freak shows. It's the mean-spirited sitcoms, the suggestive commercials, and the ever-expanding, mind-blowing realm of "reality TV," the boiled-down essence of experiments in sadomasochism by half-crazed psych majors.

In this sad age of rapidly diminishing cultural standards, television reflects who we are and where we stand in our history. It shows a nation of tortured souls filled with anger and self-loathing.

[65]

But if radio broadcasters seek the protection of the First Amendment for our shock jocks, then our television colleagues are entitled to its embrace for their "reality TV."

Of only this can we be sure: We've always had terrible examples to defend. The great Sol Taishoff's son and heir Lawrence told me that very wise thing when, as founders of *Broadcasting* magazine, they were our sentinels on the Potomac against government intrusion. But, even now, the government must acknowledge freedom of speech and expression.

Even now . . .

A lot of us would like to limit the sex and profanity, as well as disrespect, cynicism, and emptiness. But in any society, the fine line of taste constantly changes. The populace redraws it every season, and we can't stop it.

Imagine if the FCC of the 1950s had tried to codify indecency according to the mores of that era. Television might be restricted to endless reruns of *Ozzie and Harriet* and *Leave It to Beaver*.

For many years, Puritan America banned the word "hell" on radio. Indeed, and somewhat ironically, the word "virgin" was also considered taboo.

Listen again to Noel Coward's "Don't Put Your Daughter on the Stage, Mrs. Worthington." Listen again to the great Cole Porter, "Some get a kick from cocaine," and listen to the orgasmic suggestion and pulsating rhythm as the airplane goes higher and higher. Or the girl in "Kiss Me Kate" who is "always true to you darling, in my fashion." Or "Love for Sale." Or "Let's Do It." And that lovely song, "Bewitched, Bothered and Bewildered." "He's a joke, but I love him . . . because the joke's on me."

William Shakespeare, the Bard of Stratford-on-Avon, called someone "a hoarsome bitch." Benjamin Franklin wrote songs that would shock FCC bureaucrats and senators.

And so did Ogden Nash.

And "The Ballad of the Joking Jesus" was written not by Michael Jackson or Prince, but by James Joyce.

Restricting language works only in a totalitarian atmosphere where one mode of communication predominates. So, no, you can't sing an off-color song in Bulgaria, and yet, even without such songs, they have drunkenness, adultery, and suicide, but not on the radio.

Commissioner Copps, Senator Brownback, Congressman Upton, and their colleagues, with my considerable admiration, want the atmosphere and the milieu of their homes to prevail in society at large. They are of good heart and motive.

We all want our ideas to predominate, to be the ideas of the marketplace. But that wonderful, warm, stable, secure atmosphere in the Copps home, or the Brownback and Upton residences, is different from the atmosphere confronting a ghetto kid in Harlem, or a farm boy in Bismarck, or a beach boy in Berkeley, or even an oil-rig worker in Houston or Alaska.

The commissioner and Congress want an uncomplicated world for their children, without pain, obscenity, or profanity. But their children, *our* children, are finding those very influences in the real world we are trying to shield them from. Indeed, if you've ever listened to a child returning from summer camp, you will realize they make up their own songs, a lot worse than those on the radio!

We are concerned about our children, our most precious possession. We can only hope what we teach them at home will prevail and carry them through life.

If parents give their children the right kind of vehicle, their kids will float on any kind of debris. The censors and the bluenoses can't, however, get rid of the debris. It's part of the landscape. It's called *Life*.

I respect and admire Michael Copps and his formidable intellect. But really, commissioner, should the FCC judge and punish "utterances"?

Once, Richard Nixon established a "Presidential Commission on Pornography." And when its report stated that pornography provided an outlet for passions and prevented violence, the president, the story is told, used some unprintable words himself.

Well, we survived Richard Nixon's colorful language, and we will survive Janet Jackson's breast and Bono's curse word.

However you may feel about Howard Stern, you must acknowledge he is more than a vulgarian. He entertains, performs, and provides cutting-edge comedy and social commentary. If you succeed in silencing him, you silence all of that.

To many, Stern's "trash mouth" is not worth defending. But freedom of speech is. This election year's crusade against "shock jocks" and talk show hosts can have far-reaching consequences.

Some people enjoy confronting the broadcast establishment as it seeks to renew its licenses via "obsequious acquiescence." But it may prove to be incredibly expensive entertainment. Once freedom is eroded, it will be difficult, if not impossible, to restore it. And America will never be the same.

America is wandering a little. Now, we, the people, on our own, without a censor's sharp prod, must choose the right course. That's our hope toward a perfect world, or even a world free to be just a little imperfect.

With all the talent our industry possesses, surely we can help stop this train and set it on the right track.

Issue Advertising Is the Issue

The Mobil Oil Corporation and its brilliant public affairs chief Herb Schmertz advanced the notion years ago that even big corporations have a right and even an obligation to speak out on the great issues. The battle is being fought, to this day, by enlightened advocates such as Arthur Shapiro and Seagram. This commentary by William O'Shaughnessy is from January 16, 1979.

———————

I want to share with you some thoughts—which are my own—about idea advertising. Some have called it "issue advertising," while others refer to it as "advocacy advertising" or "editorial advertising."

I believe a corporation or an individual should have the opportunity to purchase airtime to espouse thoughts or views that may be favorable to the corporation or the individual—or at least in their best interests. Thus, I'm greatly concerned about the reluctance—or outright refusal— of many broadcasters, and especially the networks and many large stations, to accept idea advertising. Advocacy advertising needs some advocacy from the broadcasting industry.

For too long now, many of my fellow broadcasters have been working both sides of the street on free speech matters. Although broadcasters, for the most part, wax eloquent about the glories of the First Amendment, and most of us are instantly capable of a brilliant defense of the genius of the free enterprise system, some of us hesitate to extend those benefits and protections to corporations (or individuals) trying to express and expose ideas.

As Justice Oliver Wendell Holmes put it: "The ultimate good desired is better reached by free trade in ideas—that the best test of truth is the power of the thought to get itself accepted in the competition of the market. That, at any rate, is the theory of our Constitution." And it has always been a cardinal principle that this marketplace of ideas will function best if it is left unencumbered with restraints on expression.

In the *Red Lion* case, the U.S. Supreme Court reiterated that: "It is the purpose of the First Amendment to preserve an uninhibited marketplace of ideas in which truth can ultimately prevail." And the Supreme Court, in *First National Bank of Boston v. Bellotti*, ruled that "free discussion of governmental affairs is the type of speech indispensable to decision making in a democracy." Wrote one justice, "This is not less true because the speech comes from a corporation rather than an individual."

The history of broadcast editorializing is shot through chronologically with contradictions. First the Federal Communications Commission (FCC) forbade such practices, saying that "the broadcaster may not be an advocate" for an idea or person with his federally granted franchise of the airwaves. Then the commission reversed itself and even demanded that broadcasters do some editorializing. When we finally did get the right, many of us gradually let it erode by limp, irrelevant, innocuous statements of general piety—with some notable exceptions.

So, a gut question in all this revolves around our own sense of seriousness, of integrity, of courage, and of conviction about free press/free speech and truly free airwaves. If generally listless, "safe," predictable airborne editorials (contrasted with newspaper editorials) reflect our current industry mentality, then I suspect broadcasters will be even more timorous in this matter of issue advertising.

Clearly, our pluralistic society works best when all points of view are heard and seen. We must take a strong stand in support of freedom of speech in all areas of public life.

Re: Corporate Censorship

May 25, 2017

Organized coercion and intimidation of corporations, networks, news media, and educational institutions, which is often clandestinely and stealthily subsidized, is just as dangerous and chilling to free speech as censorship by government fiat, directive, decree, mandate, or dictum.

And it matters not if it's directed at Bill O'Reilly, Don Imus, Rush Limbaugh, Opie and Anthony, Howard Stern, Glenn Beck, Sean Hannity, Ann Coulter, Billy Bush . . . or Donald J. Trump, president of the United States. It is wrong. All of it.

—*W.O.*

First Amendment Warriors
by William O'Shaughnessy

The First Amendment is aptly named. It has been called the "Crown Jewel" of America's Constitution.

I've been accused, among other unflattering appellations, of being a First Amendment voluptuary. It's a moniker I proudly wear. I've come to believe that a radio station achieves its highest calling when it resembles a platform or forum for the expression of many different viewpoints.

Thus at WVOX and WVIP our mantra has always been "Where Many Different Voices Are Heard in the Land." Mario Cuomo once instructed that if we do it right, a broadcaster can use the public franchise that is in his care and keeping "to build up the community, to make it stronger and—sweeter—than it is."

Governor Cuomo also urged us to amplify *all* the voices in a community—even the raucous and disagreeable ones whose contributions to the language of America are often far from "sweet."

I've tried to do my bit on this vital and essential subject. But I haven't done nearly enough. My own meager and sporadic efforts pale in comparison to the valuable, unrelenting work of these First Amendment warriors I've always admired. I'm not worthy to loosen the strap of their sandals.

Preeminent among them is Floyd Abrams. The estimable Daniel Patrick Moynihan called him "the leading First Amendment advocate of our age." And as I prepared to interview the great lawyer about his new book *Friend of the Court*, my mind also drifted back to the courageous example of some others who have also done yeoman work in the vineyard of free and unfettered public discourse.

We are all students of Ward Quaal, the legendary midwestern icon who presided over the fabled WGN in Chicago during its glory years. (The station's presence in that Toddlin' Town is, to this day, heralded by a huge "Studios of WGN" exit sign on a federal highway leading into town.)

The great journalist Nat Hentoff, who also raged about abortion on demand, will be remembered for his passionate writings on the First Amendment.

Erwin Krasnow, Esq., one of the mandarins of the Washington communications bar who was a chief general counsel of the National Association of Broadcasters in Washington, D.C.

Jerry Gillman, a real First Amendment voluptuary who, with his wife, Sasha, ran a little station at Woodstock in the Catskills mountains.

Patrick Maines, the erudite chief of the Media Institute, the valuable First Amendment think tank in the nation's capital.

The Taishoff family, which began with the late Sol Taishoff and his son Larry, of sainted memory, an incomparable father–son duo who created the altogether essential *Broadcasting & Cable* magazine (now *B & C*), which has been so good to the Broadcasters Foundation of America. By the pen and remarkable intelligence of its Washington bureau chief, John Eggerton, the magazine still functions as our "Sentinel on the Potomac."

The seminal First Amendment work begun by Sol and Larry Taishoff (Sol had White House press pass #1) continues to this day by the grace and wisdom of Larry's son and heir Captain Rob Taishoff, who heads the Taishoff Family Foundation. One of their greatest editors was the articulate and graceful Donald V. West, who also ran the Library of American Broadcasting at the University of Maryland.

New York Times scribes Jack Gould and John J. O'Connor, and Les Brown of *Variety*, who often used their powerful pulpits in support of free and unfettered speech.

Al Neuharth, visionary and founder of *USA Today*, and his Gannett colleague Ken Paulson, who were among those journalists who established the Newseum in Washington, D.C., as a shrine to free speech.

The late John Seigenthauler, legendary editor of the *Nashville Tennessean*.

David Hinckley, the gifted critic-at-large of the *New York Daily News*.

Harry Jessell, another thoughtful and scholarly *B & C* alum who today edits the influential newsletter *TV Newscheck*.

Dennis Jackson, the country squire, New England broadcaster, blogger, and savant.

Michael Harrison of *Talkers* magazine, the influential Internet magazine that promotes the interests of talk show hosts all across the country and annually bestows a First Amendment Award.

Joseph Reilly, whose splendid thirty-year run as president of the New York State Broadcasters Association showed him to be an ardent promulgator of free, unfettered speech. And his successor, David Donovan, who hears the music of the Founders too, loud and clear.

Lionel Van Deerlin, a journalist and broadcaster, who served eight terms in Congress back in the 1960s and 1970s and, as chairman of the House Committee on Communications, supported a broad interpretation of First Amendment rights for broadcasters.

Bob Packwood, a brilliant and articulate Republican moderate from Oregon with a somewhat checkered career in the U.S. Senate. He was pro-abortion but was the first senator to support Nixon's impeachment, and he killed Bill Clinton's 1993 healthcare bill. Packwood was also a staunch supporter of Israel. That recommends him, as do his exemplary and enlightened positions on First Amendment matters.

Norman Siegel, the fiery and feisty fighter for the American Civil Liberties Union and for all of us.

The liberal eastern establishment triumvirate: John Hay "Jock" Whitney, Walter Nelson Thayer, and William S. Paley used their influence, purses, and reputations on free speech matters. Mr. Whitney, a former ambassador to the Court of Saint James's, tried mightily to resurrect and save the *New York Herald Tribune* (founded by Horace Greeley), along with my estimable former father-in-law, Walter Nelson Thayer, and their friend the incomparable Bill Paley, the founder of CBS. Whitney, Thayer, and Paley were hugely influential in national politics and ardent supporters of a free press.

U.S. District Court Judge Charles Brieant, whose name adorns the Federal District Courthouse in White Plains, never needed any encouragement about freedom of expression.

Ken Norwick, one of America's preeminent defenders of free speech and a ranking expert on the laws of libel and slander.

Jane Mago, who headed Legal Affairs for the National Association of Broadcasters in Washington, D.C.

Bruce Sanford, the wise and all-knowing counsel to the Society of Professional Journalists.

The Gannett Company, which has always been strong in this fundamental area. As have Lowry Mays, the billionaire founder of Clear Channel, and the fabled Hubbard family of Minneapolis, led by their towering, if self-effacing, and generous patriarch Stanley S. Hubbard.

Arthur Ochs "Punch" Sulzberger and his son and heir Arthur O. Sulzberger Jr. deserve our everlasting gratitude for protecting and sustaining our beloved *New York Times* as an irreplaceable national resource and staunch defender of robust expression and a free press.

Acknowledgment is also due, in great measure, to the communications trade press over the years who keep our feet to the fire. In addition to the Taishoffs and their acolytes Eggerton, West, and Jessell, we also owe a great debt to the late Dawson "Tack" Nail, Jay Mitchell, B. Eric Rhoads, Carl Marcucci, Mark Miller, Reed Bunzell, Jack Messmer, Ed Ryan, Tom Taylor, Frank Saxe, Jerry DelColliano, Mike Kinosian, and Kevin Casey.

In the political and legislative realm, there has been no greater champion than Ogden Rogers Reid. The former ambassador to Israel and publisher of the much-loved *Herald Tribune* of sainted memory did some of his best work in the halls of Congress when he beat back a move by Representative Harley O. Staggers, chairman of the powerful House Commerce Committee, who was hell bent to actually throw Walter Cronkite and CBS elders William S. Paley and Frank Stanton in the slammer for not giving up news sources and notes. Ogden Reid once casually remarked to Tito Gainza Paz, the great South American publisher, that the press actually enjoyed "partial" press freedom in Argentina. Dr. Paz said, "Mr. Reid, you either *have* freedom of the press, or you do *not*."

And I dare not overlook the entertainers—and social commentators—George Carlin, Howard Stern, Don Imus, Scott Shannon, Dick Gregory, Bob Grant, and our magnificent Westchester neighbor Ossie Davis, who fought the good fight for free speech on a number of battlefields, including our own backyard, right here in Westchester.

And though it's not exactly his legal "specialty," the nationally known Westchester job-discrimination lawyer Jeffrey Bernbach has used his genius, dynamism, and brilliance to keep our own WVOX and WVIP as independent voices in the highly competitive and roiling New York radio market for the good part of fifty years.

Louis Boccardi, the soft-spoken former Associated Press president who moved heaven and hell (with help from a few unmentionable and "interesting" characters) to spring hostage Terry Anderson from his many years of captivity in the Middle East.

My admiration also resides with Michael Assaf, a brilliant New York state attorney, who is wise and knowing on these and many other important issues.

And, as always, our gratitude is boundless and profound for Governor Mario M. Cuomo, who in every season used his unique brilliance and powers of articulation to encourage a society where many different voices are heard in the land. Mario's stunning rhetorical gifts were often engaged in battles to protect and defend freedom of speech.

A Towering Triumvirate

A final word on free speech.

Of all the justices of the Supreme Court, the most persistent and reliable defenders of freedom of speech have been those three towering jurists Louis Brandeis, William Brennan, and William O. Douglas.

In 1973 Justice Douglas thundered, "The Fairness Doctrine has no place in our First Amendment regime. It puts the head of the camel inside the tent and enables administration after administration to toy with TV or radio in order to serve its sordid or its benevolent ends."

President Reagan, at the behest of the great midwestern broadcast legend Ward Quaal, vetoed a bill to restore the Fairness Doctrine in 1987 because, said the president, it was "antagonistic to the freedom of expression guaranteed by the First Amendment."

The brilliant and venerable writer Nat Hentoff in 2005 told a conference of media scholars at Hillsdale College, "The term 'Fairness Doctrine' exemplifies what George Orwell called 'Newspeak': language to mask the deleterious effects of its purported meaning."

James Madison did not have bifurcation of free speech in mind when he submitted his draft of the First Amendment. His words were clear, stark, and unadorned.

Mr. Justice Oliver Wendell Holmes wrote in 1929 (*United States of America v. Schwimmer*): "If there is any principle of the Constitution that more imperatively calls for attachment than any other it is the principle of free thought—not free thought for those who agree with us but freedom for the thought that we hate."

Just for a moment suppose the Brits had advised our impertinent New Rochelle neighbor Thomas Paine that he could just go right ahead and publish all his incendiary rants and ravings—but *only* if he also included, cheek by jowl, in the very same pamphlet, the views of the

Royal Colonial Governor. I'm afraid that beguiling but flawed and dangerous invitation to Mr. Paine (or, indeed, rendered to another pesky, annoying neighbor of the day—John Peter Zenger), far from being an implementation of free speech, would have had just the *opposite* effect. It is surely a restriction of speech if, in order to have the privilege of expressing your own views, you have to accede to government dictums that you also have to root around and drag up someone arguing an opposing view.

At its heart, the First Amendment is another of the checking mechanisms the Founders so intelligently promulgated to ensure that our worst instincts would be tempered by our better values. And speaking of "checking mechanisms"—should the government take on that mantle, we've got a real problem.

Despite the mounting evidence of the harm it causes, political correctness in our nation has so far escaped the opprobrium it deserves. Far from being the language of the enlightened, political correctness is the *lingua franca* of those who believe in control rather than debate. That control, of course, is the very essence of totalitarianism.

The First Amendment protects and serves rich and poor, liberals and conservatives, secularists and believers, and all those privileged to call themselves Americans.

Ambassador Ogden Rogers Reid: "I don't like to see speech circumscribed in any way, shape or form. . . . I'd rather have free speech up or down with a little obscenity, than lose free speech altogether."

"The security of the Nation is not at the ramparts alone. Security also lies in the value of our free institutions. A cantankerous press, an obstinate press, a ubiquitous, a pain in the ass press, must be suffered by those in authority in order to preserve the even greater values of freedom of expression and the right of the people to know." So wrote federal Judge Murray Gurfein.

When James Madison wrote the phrase "Congress shall make no law . . ." across the foolscap in his quarters, he spoke for all Americans of every age. And for every broadcaster.

In 1736, John Peter Zenger wrote, "The itinerant printer who took on the Colonial Governor reminds us that no nation, ancient or modern, ever lost the liberty of speaking freely, writing, or publishing their sentiments, but forthwith lost their liberty in general and became slaves."

In the words of Albert Camus, "A free press can of course be good or bad, but, most certainly, without freedom it will never be anything but bad. Freedom is nothing else but a chance to be better, whereas enslavement is a certainty of the worse."

"Censorship abroad was justified in euphemistic language. Terms like 'responsibility' and 'accountability,' 'values' and 'honor' and even 'democracy' itself were used to support the suppression of speech not only in ruthlessly totalitarian states such as Nazi Germany and the Soviet Union but in far less authoritarian nations as well." So wrote Floyd Abrams.

Alexander Hamilton argued against adding a Bill of Rights to the new Constitution. It was Hamilton's view that it was "unnecessary," even "dangerous," to even suggest that the delegates at the Constitutional Convention in 1787 never even give Congress the power to restrain the liberty of the press.

Mr. Jefferson, however, was deeply suspicious about the new powers being granted to the federal government by the Framers, and the squire of Monticello made it known that he and his followers would not support any Constitution that did not include a crystal-clear Bill of Rights setting forth in direct, unadorned language those liberties upon which Congress could not infringe.

"What I do not like" about the new Constitution, the Virginian sent word to Madison from France, was "the omission of a bill of rights providing clearly, and without the aid of sophisms, for freedom of religion and freedom of the press."

As the Supreme Court later observed, adoption of the Bill of Rights was the *sine qua non* for the adoption of the Constitution itself.

As for the First Amendment, the extraordinary breadth of its language—"*no* law abridging"—is unmistakable.

In *New York Times Co. v. Sullivan*, the crown jewel of First Amendment law, Justice William J. Brennan's memorable voice gave support to the core First Amendment proposition "that debate on public issues should be uninhibited, robust and wide open and that it may well include vehement, caustic, and sometimes unpleasantly sharp attacks." Justice Brennan also found that "uninhibited, robust and wide open" speech should outweigh all but the most vital competing societal interests, and even then only in the narrowest of circumstances.

You don't have to be a First Amendment voluptuary to believe that the Framers would have extended First Amendment protections to the electronic press, what Sol Taishoff called "The Fifth Estate."

An unfettered marketplace of ideas is not only desirable, it's essential.

Floyd Abrams, the magnificent First Amendment champion and advocate, was described by Daniel Patrick Moynihan as "the most significant First Amendment lawyer of our age." He is a senior partner at Cahill Gordon and Reindel LLP and the William J. Brennan Visiting Professor at the Columbia University Graduate School of Journalism. This is what he has said about the First Amendment:

> While my work has led me to the view that sweeping First Amendment protections are essential to protect us against efforts—in bad faith or good—to limit speech, that does not mean I believe that the institutional press or the multitude of speakers that now fill the Internet with information are free from error or that what is published, broadcast and otherwise communicated does no harm. *A free press is not necessarily an accurate or wise one.* Precisely because speech matters so much, it can do great harm, and in fact sometimes does so. Our approach under the First Amendment has wisely, I think, generally been to risk suffering the harm that speech may do in order to avoid the greater harm that suppression of speech has often caused.
>
> The First Amendment protects all who wish to speak—do I really have to say this?—from *governmental* decision-making about what and how much they may say. It is rooted in distrust of government, concern about historic misuse of governmental power. It is *not*—in fact, it is the *opposite* of—granting power to the government to decide who may speak about what.

And even back at the very dawn of our republic, the graceful Virginian Thomas Jefferson wrote:

I know of no safe repository of the ultimate powers of our society but the People themselves; and if we think them not enlightened enough to exercise their control with a wholesome discretion, the remedy is not to take it from them, but to inform their discretion by education.

The spirit of resistance to government is so valuable on certain occasions, I wish it to be always kept alive. The People are the only sure reliance for the preservation of our liberty.

Before becoming president, in 1858, Abraham Lincoln wrote from Edwardsville, Illinois, "What constitutes the bulwark our own liberty and independence? It is not our frowning battlements, our bristling sea coasts, our army and navy. These are not our reliance against tyranny. . . . Our reliance is the love of liberty. . . . Destroy this spirit and you have planted the seeds of despotism at your door."

Turning again to the words of Floyd Abrams: "The latest bunch of proponents of the fairness doctrine are totally unaware of its history of misuse by partisans on all sides ranging from President Kennedy to Accuracy in Media. Worse yet, they want it not because they want 'fairness' but simply to stifle speech of which they disapprove—Fox and Rush today, heaven knows who tomorrow. And many of the folks on the 'other side' who urge the FCC to impose $500,000 fines on broadcasters for the broadcast of 'fleeting expletives' only to discover the First Amendment when it's used against those with whom they agree."

Dan Rather said it succinctly: "A free and truly independent press, fiercely independent when necessary, is the red beating heart of freedom and democracy."

PART II
OPEN MIC INTERVIEWS

Chris Ruddy, Chairman of Newsmax

*Christopher Ruddy, the conservative media mogul,
is Chairman of Newsmax and a confidant of President Donald J.
Trump. In this May 18, 2017, interview he discusses Roger Ailes,
President Trump, the media, and cable news. . . .*

———————

WILLIAM O'SHAUGHNESSY: The world of news and network television
lost a luminous figure this morning with the announcement that
Roger Ailes, formerly of Fox News, has gone to another and, we are
sure, a better world. As he departs, let's go now to Palm Beach to one
of his neighbors, also a network president, the founder of Newsmax.
Can I accurately describe that as somewhat "conservative"? His
name is Christopher Ruddy. Chris: Roger Ailes—did you know him?

CHRIS RUDDY: Bill, I knew him *very* well. I've known him for about
twenty years. He was a genius on television, an incredible giant in
the news business. We once had a cover of Roger Ailes we did for
our magazines. Most people know us for our network and website.
The cover said, "The Most Powerful Man in News!" Roger told me a
few weeks later he met Obama, and Obama said to him, "Oh, the
man Newsmax says is the most powerful man in news!" He was a
giant. He changed the landscape of news and cable news forever.
He changed the country. I don't think Donald Trump would ever
have been elected if it wasn't for Roger.

W.O.: Chris Ruddy, what's going to happen now to Fox News? Are
there opportunities for you, for Newsmax?

C.R.: Well, Bill, we've already been out there on Newsmax TV. We're
now on Verizon FIOS channel 615. We expect to be in another 30
million homes over this summer. People can call their cable
operators and ask for Newsmax TV. We're building a very powerful
lineup. We think we're, in some ways, better than Fox. We give

opportunities for people to call in, to become part of the programming. And we have a lot of good newsmakers coming on all the time. Alan Dershowitz was on yesterday, for example. Fox opened the door for networks like Newsmax. Roger was a pathfinder and broke the media monopoly. For years, you know, the media was largely liberal and left-wing.

w.o.: And now?

c.r.: And now the media, I think, is more open to other points of view. I think CNN, for example, has become more centrist because of Fox. It used to be very left-wing in the day. I know Donald Trump doesn't like the media, but if they didn't have Fox as the counterweight, Donald Trump would have gotten very little airtime on the major networks. I think the country benefits from multiple voices. This idea that we should only have one point of view—back in the day when there were three networks led by Cronkite, let's say, as the preeminent anchor, there was generally an Establishment view on things. Now we have multiple views. Even MSNBC—I watch that too. I don't *agree* with most of their programming, but I think it's good, interesting stuff. I think Ailes would applaud that. That said, I think the guy was—you know, in this business, the difference between genius and insanity is a very thin line! Roger had a lot of quirks. There's been a lot of allegations about him and Fox News and sexual harassment issues. It's not my job to judge that, other than to say that the situation there seems pretty darn messy. As you may know, in the ratings MSNBC is beating Fox in a lot of the key demos now. It's not good for Fox. And I think with Roger not being there, they don't really have an organizing principle any more.

w.o.: Christopher Ruddy, another network said that Roger sold his home up the road apiece in Garrison. And another place he had in Cresskill, New Jersey, and moved to Palm Beach where you are, at the moment. What is it about Palm Beach that all you network chiefs repair to the damn place?

c.r.: Well, it's *Shangri-La* down here. It's an incredibly beautiful area. It's got a lot of people from New York and New Jersey, so there's a cultural mix that's pretty accommodating, let's put it that way. A lot of amenities. The tax environment—we have no state income tax, so a lot of people love that. Roger was also facing a lot of litigation, and a lot of people think the reason he bought a $36 million home on the ocean very quickly was that he was hoping to shield assets in some of the litigation he was going through. I don't know if that's true or not, but it is a smart idea for a lot of people. I love New York. Newsmax has an office in New York. I think New York is still the epicenter of the media world, for instance, and for business and commerce. But Florida is a great state. C'mon down if you haven't been down here yet.

W.O.: Christopher Ruddy, Roger Ailes, in recent years, took a lot of shots. But he happened to have been a very generous man. There's a group called the Broadcasters Foundation of America, and at the risk of embarrassing you, you also are very generous to that national charity. Is there a side to Roger Ailes that maybe people didn't know about? You know a lot about a lot of things.

C.R.: Well, I think he would not have risen to the success he did if there weren't a lot of good attributes. I think he was intensely loyal to his friends. I'm sure he had a charitable side, as you point out. I think he had a lot of empathy for people. We're hearing a lot of dark stuff about what happened there. Again, I don't know if it's true. But I think there was probably a lot of good stuff there. I think he deeply loved America. He really strongly believed in a secure nation. I would talk to him often about the sovereignty of the United States. Before Donald Trump was talking about these issues in any serious way, Roger Ailes was. He was the guy that got everybody worried about the border. Ten years ago, nobody was talking about the border. Now, it's a major issue. And Roger started that. Donald Trump carried the flag. And has done a good job raising that flag.

W.O.: While we have you live this morning from Palm Beach, I want to beg another minute to ask you about your friend, and you were accused in the *New York Times* of being a *very* good friend of the president. I understand there's a photo going around that shows *you* sitting behind the desk in the Oval Office, and he's standing there with his hand on your shoulder. What the hell do you talk about, Chris Ruddy and Donald John Trump? What do you guys schmooze about?

C.R.: Bill, I think that somebody Photoshopped that photo! [laughter] I don't think it's an accurate photo.

W.O.: I don't believe it.

C.R.: I think the CIA or the Russians or Putin or somebody did that, and I'm going to need to launch a full investigation. I will appoint a special counsel to find out why my photo with the president was Photoshopped! [laughter]

W.O.: But you do go to Mar-a-Lago, Chris Ruddy, and you *do* know the guy.

C.R.: I've known him for twenty years. I've known him well, I'd say, for ten years. I am a member of Mar-a-Lago, although I knew him before I was a member. I've known him from the media. I've been with him in Scotland, at the opening of his Scottish club. So I've gotten to really know the president. On his personal side, he's a great guy. He's not what the media is depicting him as. I think he's a businessman, Bill. He's not a politician. And there are good attributes to that, and there are bad attributes to that. So we're finding out he doesn't know that you can't tell the FBI director, "I think you're pushing too hard on my guy." Donald Trump would talk very candidly and openly to people. Nobody told him that's obstruction of justice if you mention this to the FBI. And I don't think he intended that, if he said it at all. So I think they're out to get him. They don't like him.

W.O.: Christopher Ruddy, can he survive, President Trump? Tell us.

C.R.: I think he can. There's a book I've been recommending to everyone. It's called *Big Agenda* by David Horowitz. David has sort of a game plan. He wrote it before Trump became president, and then so much of it became true: the *Big Agenda*. He sort of lays out a way for Trump to survive all this. David predicted a likely impeachment hearing. They were talking about this *before* he even took the oath of office. I think he can. But I do think he needs a strong team of advisors around him that are experienced and better in political matters. I think what we're seeing with the firing of the director of the FBI is that he did not have an experienced team. The very fact that they thought that it would be widely accepted as a good idea and that the way they did it would be accepted as a good idea—it was a very strange situation which has led to this catastrophic situation he potentially faces now.

w.o.: Can Mueller hurt the president?

c.r.: Immensely. But it also will take time. He doesn't have time.

w.o.: Summer has come to New York, Chris. You're not the only one with good weather today. Thank you, Mr. founder of Newsmax. We're glad we can get you now in Westchester on FIOS.

c.r.: Thank you, Bill. You are a legend and a beacon of hope for all of us in the media world.

w.o.: Chris Ruddy, wonderful stuff.

Interview with Dan Rather
on his Book *What Unites Us*

January 25, 2018, Barnes & Noble, Eastchester, New York.

———————

WILLIAM O'SHAUGHNESSY: Dan Rather, you dazzled in Eastchester tonight. What's so damn special about this new book? You've got that catch in the throat.

DAN RATHER: Well, Bill, it's a very *personal* book. I love this country. I love it with a deep, abiding love, and I have no apology that I'm emotional about it. And I'm very much concerned about the country. I'm concerned about what's happening to the country. And in my own small, even microscopic, way, I thought if I can write the book and make even a smidgen of difference, I'll do so. But I don't have any apology. You know, I owe this country so much. I love this country so much that I want to contribute and I want to help her if I can.

W.O.: Tonight you told everyone here assembled that you weren't a priest or a preacher.

D.R.: I said I was *neither* a priest nor a preacher.

W.O.: Or a philosopher.

D.R.: Or a political scientist.

W.O.: But you sounded like one tonight.

D.R.: Well, no, I'm just a reporter who got lucky! Very lucky! I can be evangelical about my country. That's true, so maybe that's what you were picking up on.

W.O.: Dan Rather, we're well aware you are one of the legends of our tribe: radio and television. But it's changed. You talked a lot about change. You've got young kids being anchor people today. Muir on ABC and Glor on CBS.

D.R.: Well, everything changes. When I tend to get down about what's happening about the press and what's happened to radio and television *and* broadcasting, I think, what hasn't changed in the last fifty years? The thing I worry about most is the *authenticity* of reporters. The most valuable thing a reporter can have is the *trust* of the audience, which you have, Bill. But to get that trust, you have to be authentic. And to have authenticity, you have to have covered stories. And so often now, people who are on television who are reporters have never covered a story.

W.O.: They asked you a lot of questions about Trump here at Barnes & Noble, where you had a standing-room-only crowd. But you sort of pulled your punches about President Trump.

D.R.: Well, I'd never admit that. You know, I play no favorites, and I pull no punches. But it is true that what I'm trying very hard to do is be open-minded about the Trump administration—with no illusions, but to say to myself, I want to judge each act and each thing he says on its own. Now I'd have to say, up to and including now, it's pretty bleak, which says, he is doing things as president and saying things as president that are not normal! And we're better than this. I will tell you that we are better than this. And the people of this country know we're better than this and want us to be better than this.

W.O.: But Dan Rather, you told about 1,000 people assembled to hear you in Eastchester tonight that you didn't think he was going to get impeached.

D.R.: And I don't, based on what we know now. My best judgment is, if you're saying to yourself, I think he's going to be impeached, I don't agree. Could it change overnight? On the basis of what we know now, I don't see him being impeached, and one of the main reasons is as long as the Republicans are in control of both houses of Congress, I don't see them voting impeachment on a Republican president.

W.O.: Dan Rather, in your new book, *What Unites Us* by Dan Rather, you don't mention Trump once.

D.R.: No, because I wanted the book to be something broader and deeper. I didn't start out saying I wasn't going to mention Trump.

He's referred to inferentially in the book. I wanted the book, and I think it does, to say, look, Trump is Trump, and we have these problems, but let's keep our eye on the *values* that unite us because Trump and others are trying to exploit our differences and our divisions.

W.O.: Dan Rather: *What Unites Us: Reflections on Patriotism.* You said it's your most personal book yet.

D.R.: It is. Any time you're going to talk about patriotism, it's got to be a personal book. But what I tried to do is tell stories—true stories—out of my own youth and growing up. And from those stories, try to extrapolate from that what I've learned that is of value. Whether people are Republican, Democrats, these are values that have always united us. Such values as empathy, courage, books, and education, the rule of law, these are the things that unite us.

W.O.: Dan Rather, is it all right if I like President Trump and am also a great admirer of Dan Rather?

D.R.: Sure, I welcome it. But we'll have another conversation maybe over an adult beverage, to see whether that is true! Look, with Donald Trump there are policies that he's brought to the presidency that decent people who disagree with him on other things can get behind. He hurts himself and he hurts the country when he tries to give some false equivalency with Nazis, with the Ku Klux Klan. Those aren't policies in of themselves. They are what he indicates he believes, and insofar as they influence policy, it has to be: Stand up, look him in the eye, and say No!

W.O.: Thank you, sir, you honor us with your presence. Mr. Riggio of Barnes & Noble, the great Leonard Riggio, has got to be pleased with this crowd tonight in Eastchester!

D.R.: Thank you, my friend. And I've never forgotten when the heat was on me, you stood by me, and I appreciate that!

W.O.: Well, you've been to every one of my book parties! *And* birthdays! *You* honor us, Dan. You honor our profession. And you honor our country with your abiding love for it.

Bill Mohl, President,
Entergy Wholesale Commodities

Bill Mohl, the former president of Entergy, is a statesman
of the nuclear industry. He ran the Indian Point nuclear plant
in Westchester for several years. An interview from February 21, 2017.

———————

WILLIAM O'SHAUGHNESSY: This is an aptly named "very special"
hour. For the next sixty minutes, while we're in your care and
keeping, a very timely and important program. We're going to talk
about power, nuclear power. We're going to talk about Indian Point.
And we're going to talk about the future of Westchester *after* Indian
Point. With us today in our Westchester studios is a statesman of
his profession. His name is Bill Mohl, and he's president of Entergy
Wholesale Commodities. We had the privilege of doing his very
first sit-down interview when he assumed his important portfolio a
couple of years ago. Bill Mohl, why are you retiring?

BILL MOHL: Great question, Bill, and it's great to be here on WVOX.
You know, I have spent the last four years working the EWC
portfolio and doing everything we can to salvage that portfolio in a
very challenging business environment.

W.O.: EWC?

B.M.: EWC is Entergy Wholesale Commodities. You are well aware of
what happened to the price of natural gas.

W.O.: It's gone down!

B.M.: It's gone way down! In fact, if you look at the energy prices we
see in the market today and let's compare them to ten years ago,
they are about half of what they were ten years ago largely due to
reduction in the price of natural gas. What that has done for our
business, the Entergy Wholesale Commodities, a merchant nuclear
business, is really created extreme financial pressures on that

[93]

business; and so, as a result, we've, over the course of the last four years, made the decision to announce the shutdown of every single plant in the portfolio, most recently including Indian Point.

W.O.: Bill Mohl, Entergy Wholesale Commodities is a lot of words. You own Indian Point?

B.M.: That's correct.

W.O.: And you're going to shut it down? When?

B.M.: We'll be shutting that plant down. There are two units at that site, Bill, so the first unit will shut down in 2020—by April 30th—and the second one will shut down by April 30th of 2021. The only exception to that, Bill, would be if those plants would be needed for reliability; and under the settlement with New York, then that's an option we would both have to agree upon to continue the operation for a maximum of up to four additional years.

W.O.: Do you think Indian Point will keep going somehow?

B.M.: You know, right now that's really up to the state of New York. So the New York Independent System Operator will be performing the evaluation on the reliability needs across the state of New York and specifically in the lower Hudson Valley. So they will be performing a study, probably later this year. As it stands right now, their most recent study says that Indian Point is needed for reliability into the future. Now what they'll take into consideration will be new resources that may be added to the portfolio to offset the loss of the capacity of Indian Point.

W.O.: Why are you closing? I ask you in the intimacy of this room. First of all, before I let you answer that question, Mr. President—I am a *believer* in nuclear power. I also am a believer that Indian Point and Entergy has been—and *is*—the best corporate citizen our home heath, Westchester, has ever had. The best, the most enlightened, and the most generous. You've also been very good to our community radio stations. Thus, will you trust me to conduct myself properly in this interview?

B.M.: Absolutely!

W.O.: All right, *why* are you closing this, besides the prices?

B.M.: So, really, the key factors—number one, to be perfectly frank, as I said: It's low commodity prices. The second is higher operating costs. What we've seen with the cost of operating nuclear plants, it's higher than it was originally expected when we made the investment to buy these plants a number of years ago, and it's escalated well above the rate of inflation. And so higher operating costs obviously have contributed to a significantly reduced margin. So you've got revenues going down, you've got costs going up. And in addition to that, Bill, as a corporation we've been very challenged in this business—this Entergy Wholesale Commodities business—and we've made a strategic decision to focus on the growth of our utilities down South where we can earn a much more reasonable rate of return on our investment. So it's really all of those issues taken into consideration, and we decided to exit this business.

W.O.: Mr. Mohl, you have the governor of New York state—Andrew Mark Cuomo—kind of taking a victory lap. Did Andrew Cuomo close it down?

B.M.: No, absolutely not. The decision was based on the financial viability of the facility. It's no different than the decisions we made at Vermont Yankee, Pilgrim, and Fitzpatrick. Now, with Fitzpatrick upstate, we were fortunate enough to have a third party come on in and want to buy that plant—Exelon. And we also recently made the announcement of our intent to shut down the Palisades plant in Michigan. And all of those were because those facilities were not economically viable not only now—but as we looked into the future.

W.O.: Which reminds me: You think somebody might want to buy Indian Point?

B.M.: You never say never; you always look at every opportunity that comes across the table. However, we think that you look again at what the forward commodity prices are. When you look at energy policy, we do not see a solid federal energy policy in the near future that would place a value on the carbon-free attributes of nuclear. As we look at all of that combined, our point of view is that these plants are going to remain challenged. Now somebody could have a different point of view than we do and want to come on in and take a look at it. We would certainly consider that.

w.o.: Bill Mohl, you've been accused in every telling of being one of the brightest guys in your tribe, in the profession. You once were an associate of the famous, legendary Koch brothers. They were very active in energy and power and still are. What's your guess for the future of Indian Point? Look ahead. They say you're quite the visionary. I'm going to put you to the test.

b.m.: Sure. You know what I see, Bill, is I think it's going to depend on what happens in the very short term with New York. Can they identify clear replacement resources to replace the Indian Point capacity? If they don't have a very robust, executable plan, then I think there could be a high likelihood that Indian Point could run for additional periods up until the four-year extension. But it really lies in the hands of the New York ISO and the New York Public Service Commission.

w.o.: What's that ISO again?

b.m.: It's the New York Independent System Operator, and they've got responsibility for reliability across the entire state of New York.

w.o.: Do Mr. Jones and his colleagues know what kind of impact the closing of Indian Point is going to have on Westchester? I know you know.

b.m.: I don't know if Mr. Jones has a good perspective on that. But clearly, we know that the people in the *local area* understand that and are very concerned. So one of the things—as we entered into the settlement, there were a couple of things we took into consideration: One, we are very confident that that plant needs to run until at least '20 and '21. We also made a commitment that we would provide up to $15 million in benefits to the local communities to make sure it's a smooth transition as we move from an operating plant to a shut-down to decommissioning process.

w.o.: What's the future of your profession? If you had your druthers, where would you go?

b.m.: I think there are a lot of different things. The utility business is changing dramatically, really, with the implementation of new technologies. So I think there's a huge opportunity to work in utility and really have a very positive impact on what customers lives' are—how they receive their power—and providing them different options, providing them different information. The other side of the coin would be working on a policy perspective. I happen to believe that the so-called competitive markets we see up here in the Northeast and in other parts of the country have some flaws. And if we want those markets to survive, we're going to have to change some of the policies surrounding those markets.

w.o.: What about the employees? How many employees have you got now?

b.m.: So, Bill, we've got about 1,000 employees up at Indian Point.

w.o.: What happens to those people?

b.m.: First and foremost, we're going to need each and every one of those employees until the shutdown of the last unit. And so depending on when that is, we'll need those employees, and we've actually provided retention agreements to make sure we keep those employees in place.

w.o.: So they're OK for how long?

b.m.: So right now, they're OK at least until 2021, when we have the current planned shutdown. If that would have to be extended because of reliability needs, we would do whatever we would need to do to make sure we can run that plant safely and reliably and retain those employees. The next thing we've done is make a commitment to our employees that once that plant shuts down and if they want to continue to work with Entergy and are willing to relocate, we will provide them opportunities in other parts of the company—whether that be at other nuclear plants, whether that be within the utility, those type of things. So I feel like we have really gone out of our way to make sure to take care of those people. And, Bill, frankly, they deserve it. It's got to be one of the most resilient workforces of any plant I've ever seen when you consider the scrutiny they've operated under and how well they have operated that plant over the fifteen years that we've owned it.

w.o.: Mr. Mohl, how many of those 1,000 do you think will take you up and go on the road?

b.m.: It's hard to say; it's hard to predict what the future holds. But I'll give you an example. I think at Vermont Yankee when we made an announcement to shut down in 2013, we saw probably maybe seventy-five to a hundred of those folks take us up on opportunities to go to other facilities. And so who knows what that looks like going down the road? But it really depends on what happens in the industry, what resources rise to the top and what skill sets are needed to support those resources.

W.O.: Sir, I've got to ask you, what about the people who depended on Indian Point, the municipalities and the local government and the school boards and hospitals?

B.M.: Bill, we've spend over $30 million a year just in taxes—our property taxes. And if you follow, there's a move afoot in the legislature to really start to talk about what happens when Indian Point shuts down. That's a process that we will make sure we are a key contributor to. The governor will also play a role there as well as the legislature. But that's something that's yet to be determined. In fact, I think they've had some of the local officials from the Westchester area go visit the folks in Vermont so that they really start to understand what the impact is of losing a facility like that, because it's substantial.

W.O.: What do you mean "substantial"?

B.M.: You've got 1,000 employees supporting a local economy. You've got a Fortune 500 company that's paying $30 million–plus a year in property taxes. There's no simple solution to what happens when that goes away. And it has a negative impact on the schools; it has a negative impact on the local economies. So the key is, how do you work together to mitigate some of those issues so that it's a smoother transition and not just an abrupt change?

W.O.: Let me ask you this, Mr. President of Entergy Wholesale Commodities. If Andrew Cuomo changes his mind, would you stick around? You said it's the market. Is there anything *he* could do to change your mind, market aside?

B.M.: Well, not that I can think of, Bill, that you can say is a practical solution. One of the things that happened with the Fitzpatrick Plant was they put in the Clean Energy Standard. And that Clean Energy Standard placed a value on the carbon-free attributes of the plants in upstate New York.

W.O.: Did it make it tougher to operate a plant?

B.M.: No. What it actually did was—the intent there was—they recognized the value of that nuclear generation in terms of meeting the environmental goals of the state of New York. And so they placed a value on the attributes associated with zero carbon emissions. What that did was for a defined period of time actually make those plants at least break even. And so that allowed those plants to continue to operate. Now, with Indian Point, we have the ability to apply for that Clean Energy Standard, effective 2019. The challenge that we're faced with is that would just allow you to break even. In our utility, we have the ability to earn a 9 to 10 percent return on our capital investment. So if you look at the alternatives you face from a broader Entergy business perspective—Entergy Company perspective—you would say I would rather deploy that capital where I could earn a return.

W.O.: President Bill Mohl, we're covering a lot of ground here about the closing of Indian Point. My colleagues in the public press, Mr. President, say that 25 percent of the power for the New York area comes from you—Indian Point. What the hell is going to happen now?

B.M.: Well, one of the things that is going to happen when you lose Indian Point is you're going to lose the value of fuel diversity. Bill, think of your investment portfolio. They say diversity is important in an investment portfolio. Why is that? So that if one part of your portfolio loses money, maybe you have another part that makes money, and it provides a much more balanced return on your investment. Well, it's no different when you have a portfolio of generation resources. You don't want to be overreliant on a single fuel or a single technology. You would like to have a diverse set of resources, and that provides two things: It provides improved reliability, and it also provides a much more stable customer bill. So if there's fluctuation in one, it doesn't take over the whole portfolio. So what is likely going to happen with Indian Point? It will be replaced by natural gas. And that natural-gas portfolio will continue to increase, which means now you're more reliant on a single fuel source, now you're more susceptible to price swings because you have overreliance on a single commodity. If you look at what happened in New England, with the loss of Vermont Yankee, you're also seeing the impacts of that there. And you're also seeing emissions grow because you took out a zero-carbon-emitting resource.

W.O.: Sir, you mention natural gas. In the intimacy of this studio, I have to tell you I'm not a big fan of "fracking." I don't like it. How do you feel about fracking?

B.M.: You know, you have to look at every case, on a case-by-case basis. I personally don't think fracking in general is bad. I think you have to assess what the local impacts will be. And you have to make the right decisions. Obviously, the advent of fracking and the advent of shale gas has really changed the whole picture in terms of the energy availability and energy security of the United States. And so what you have to deal with is if there are areas where perhaps it's unsafe, and obviously you have to make a decision that's prudent. But to say that fracking overall is bad, I don't think is the right answer.

W.O.: You're the president of the damn thing. Who is going to run it now until 2021?

B.M.: Bill, what we've done from a corporate perspective is my role will go away. And we've now got this down to a set of projects. We've got Indian Point. We've got Vermont Yankee where we're trying to do a license-transfer transaction. We've got Pilgrim, which will be shutting down in 2019. We've got to complete the sale of Fitzpatrick to Exelon at the end of this quarter. And then we're working on a transaction in Michigan with Palisades. So we have got a very capable team of people who will make sure that those projects are appropriately managed and that we bring them to closure over time.

W.O.: Am I hearing—hello, hello—that nuclear power is *over*?

B.M.: Absolutely not! Bill, remember that this is only one part of Entergy's business. We have got a utility business down South where we have five different units that operate and are a key contributor to our utility business down South. We are absolutely committed to running those units and keeping them in our portfolio, and by no means are we exiting the nuclear business.

W.O.: Mr. Mohl, Mr. President, why are you exiting New England and New York? Why is all well down South, down there?

B.M.: It's really a different structure. Up here, I told you that we have to compete with everybody else in the market. We have to sell our power directly to other parties. In our southern utilities, it's really the more traditional utility structure where you get cost recovery of your prudently invested costs. And those costs are passed on to your customers. And you're allowed to raise a reasonable rate of return. So it's really the difference in the structure that we're operating under, whereas in the South, we have much more certainty of cost recovery.

W.O.: So, you're saying there's no way you can operate Indian Point and make a buck or two.

B.M.: That's right.

W.O.: You're absolutely sure of that?

B.M.: Yes, sir. We've run a lot of different scenarios. And again, remember, that's our point of view. Somebody else might think differently. But we're not the only ones who are challenged. We've seen a number of these units that have made decisions to shut down over recent years, and frankly, I think there's more to come.

W.O.: How so?

B.M.: Well, they'll be facing the same challenges. If you can't make a reasonable return on your investment, that's just simply unsustainable—some people may be able to stretch that over a period of time, for example, if they believe the price of natural gas was going to go up. Or if they were going to get some other kind of compensation for operating those facilities, which has happened as we saw in upstate New York and we've seen in Illinois. But without that point of view, it's a real challenge to get to the point where you don't have negative margins in this business.

W.O.: Aren't you going to make a lot of Canadians rich? Aren't they going to bring power over the border and that pipeline that nobody likes?

B.M.: There certainly is a lot of discussion about that, Bill. And there are a number of different projects they're talking about where they want to import power from Canada. The question that has to be addressed is, Can you actually put in the infrastructure to facilitate the delivery of that power? And so that means you have to potentially put in new transmission lines. Some of those transmission lines may have to cross or go under the Hudson River. You're pretty familiar with what people think about putting in that kind of infrastructure, and that's going to be a real challenge. There's a lot of talk about that. I haven't seen a plan that I would have confidence in that can be executed to actually import that power from Canada. It's an option.

w.o.: Bill Mohl, another smart guy—you're not the only smart guy we talk to around here—said you're going to make a lot of Canadians rich. The jobs are going up to Canada.

b.m.: And again, when they say that, that is a potential option. I wouldn't exactly describe it as *us* making them rich. We did the best we could in the market that we were provided, based on the energy policies that are in place. And if those energy policies actually end up incentivizing people to import power, that's something that folks just have to deal with. That wasn't our intended outcome of this decision, that's for sure.

w.o.: Bill Mohl, thank you for indulging me once again. As you take you leave, sir, has Westchester treated you all right?

b.m.: Westchester has been great to us. We have a lot of supporters up there, and many of them are somewhat disappointed, obviously, in the decision we've made. But we're committed to working with them to try to make this transition as smooth as possible.

w.o.: You are a gentleman and a statesman of your profession, Mr. Mohl. You've been very good to our county, our home heath, and very good to the people of Westchester. Just before you take your leave—how long is it going to take them to wind down Indian Point? And isn't that going to be a project in itself?

b.m.: You're exactly right, Bill. We talk about an operating plant. We will quickly transition to a shut-down facility, and then we'll have to evaluate what it takes to decommission that plant. So that's something we're currently studying right now. To understand: One, what do we think the *total costs* are associated with that decommissioning? Two, how much money do we have in the Nuclear Decommissioning Trust, and what type of plan can be put in place to start to provide people some perspective on what that's going to look like?

W.O.: Here's a brilliant idea: What if you found it costs more to shut it down than to keep it going?

B.M.: You've got to remember, you've got a cost estimate to shut it down. When you decide to keep it going, that means you're suffering losses every year, and so it really is kind of two different scenarios. I don't think we'll be stuck in that situation, but we do need to study it to determine what we think the future looks like as it relates to decommissioning.

W.O.: Our guest has been Mr. Bill Mohl. He's president—until the end of the month—of Entergy Wholesale Commodities. Sir, I hope you don't mind me accusing you of presiding over the *best corporate citizen Westchester has ever had* during your stewardship.

B.M.: We appreciate that. Entergy is a great company, as you suggest. And they are committed to the communities they serve. The other thing, Bill, if you don't mind, I would like to just specifically thank all the employees at the site. I don't think people appreciate what they've been through, and the angst and the issues they faced as it relates to their families. I hope as people talk about that plant— first and foremost—they remember our employees because they are a very dedicated, hardworking group who have run that plant on a world-class basis over the fifteen years we have operated it. *There's never been a single event at that site which put the public in jeopardy.* I can't tell you how much I appreciate each and every one of those employees for how they've handled the very difficult situation, and furthermore, I'm confident that they will finish strong.

W.O.: I'll give you the last word, sir. You *are* the statesman and nice man I've accused you of being, now and in the past. Good luck to you, sir. That rumble and roar that you hear in the background— they're cutting trees outside. We've got a lot of firewood. You don't deal in firewood, do you? [laughter]

B.M.: Someone might take it off your hands and turn it into wood
pellets or something!

W.O.: Mr. President, thank you. We hope we'll see you again. A
wonderful visit.

B.M.: Thank *you* so much, and thank you always for your support of
Entergy.

Roger Stone on *The Man Who Killed Kennedy,* the Cuomos, and More

Roger Stone is a most colorful character who shakes up the Washington establishment with his books and pronouncements, some of them quite outrageous. We spoke with him about one of his books, The Man Who Killed Kennedy: The Case Against LBJ, *in an interview including reflections on President Obama, Nelson Rockefeller, Mario Cuomo, Andrew Cuomo, Chris Christie, and Richard Nixon. December 10, 2013.*

———————

WILLIAM O'SHAUGHNESSY: As the snow falls here in the heart of the eastern establishment, our first snowstorm of the year, we have with us this morning, for the next several minutes while we're in your care and keeping, a man of politics, and he's also a man of letters. You've seen him on cable television many, many times. He's been an advisor to presidents of the United States. His name is Roger Stone. His new book is controversial, for sure. That's no surprise. Roger Stone, your book is called *The Man Who Killed Kennedy: The Case Against LBJ.* Do you really believe in your heart of hearts that Lyndon Johnson whacked Jack Kennedy?

ROGER STONE: I really do. Not only do I believe it, but my book goes far beyond theory or conjecture. I make the kind of case you could take to court. I make the kind of case that uses fingerprint evidence, eyewitness evidence to tie a man—Malcolm Wallace, who I demonstrate is a hit man for Lyndon Baines Johnson—I take him right to the sixth floor of the Texas Schoolbook Depository building. I don't argue that Johnson did it alone; I do think there was a—I hate this word—"conspiracy" to kill JFK. I do think the Central Intelligence Agency, organized crime, and big Texas oil were in it. Indeed, I just named all the key allies of Lyndon Baines Johnson.

Johnson is the missing piece of the puzzle that's been sitting in plain sight for fifty years.

w.o.: Roger Stone, you even suggest Jack Ruby was an LBJ guy.

R.S.: Yes. The Warren Commission tells us Jack Ruby has no known connection to organized crime. That's an absurdity. He's a soldier for Carlos Marcello. Carlos Marcello is the mobster who runs the mob in both Texas and Louisiana. Marcello's ties to Johnson are indelible. Indeed, Marcello paid Johnson $55,000 a month in a bribe to protect his illegal gambling operations in Dallas, Houston, and San Antonio. In fact, within days of Lyndon Johnson becoming president, the wiretaps that Attorney General Robert Kennedy put on organized-crime figures are immediately terminated. So, yes, I argue that Ruby had a long relationship with Marcello, and Marcello has a long relationship with LBJ.

w.o.: You counseled presidents, among them Richard Nixon and Ronald Reagan. You have some fabulous quotes from Nixon. Do you think Nixon really believed LBJ was the bad guy?

R.S.: I don't think he believed it initially. I think he originally believed the story that the FBI Director J. Edgar Hoover told him, which was that Lee Harvey Oswald committed this crime, that he was a communist, and that he acted alone. Once Nixon saw Ruby blow Oswald away on national TV, as millions of others did—Bill, I'm sure you remember that horrible day—he immediately recognized Ruby as a man who had been introduced to him in 1947 as a protégé of Lyndon Johnson. And, indeed, Richard Nixon had put Jack Ruby—then known as "Jacob Rubenstein"—on the House Un-American Activities Committee payroll as a part-time informant at the behest of his colleague Congressman Lyndon Johnson. The most telling quote, though, is Nixon—when I finally asked him, point-blank, and he said, "That was the thing about Lyndon and me. We both wanted to be president, but I wasn't willing to kill for it."

w.o.: Roger Stone, JFK—television has been awash with reminiscences of that awful day. The problem with all of them is they all end with a caisson and a riderless horse going down Pennsylvania Avenue. Does it really matter who pulled the damn trigger, who shot him? Does it matter?

R.S.: Sure it does. The American people have been falsely led to believe that, firstly, it was Lee Harvey Oswald acting alone, and then that fell apart. There are so many questions about the Warren Commission's conclusions. I don't see how any person with any objectivity or intelligence can believe them. Well then, the government falls back to the idea that it was an "international conspiracy" and that JFK was somehow killed by the Russians or Cubans, of which there is not one iota of evidence. John Kennedy was killed by a *domestic* conspiracy. He was killed because he was trying to lead this country toward the exit in Vietnam. He was killed because he refused to invade Cuba again. He was killed because he refused to assassinate Castro. He was killed because he was making certain monetary changes in our money policy. He was killed because he repealed the oil-depletion allowance, the sweetheart tax breaks oil millionaires get. I don't think there is any question he was removed in a *coup d'état*. And as the Latins say: The person who derives the greatest benefit from the crime is the person who committed it. That would be Lyndon Baines Johnson.

W.O.: Roger Stone, tell us about this so-called LBJ hit man. What's the story on this cat?

R.S.: Malcolm "Mac" Wallace is a person who worked for Lyndon Johnson throughout his whole life in a series of political patronage jobs. He is an "expert marksman," the highest honor the U.S. Marine Corps awards. Whereas Oswald was merely a "marksman," which is the lowest rating they provide. I tie Wallace and LBJ in my book to a series of eight murders in Texas. Murders to cover up corruption. Murders to cover up embezzlement. Murders to cover up vote stealing. Lyndon Johnson could order up a murder the way you and I could order up a ham sandwich. Wallace is indelibly tied to Johnson again and again. When he gets indicted for one of these murders—for first-degree murder—he is bailed out by two of Johnson's biggest fundraising fellows, and he is defended at trial by Johnson's personal attorney John Cofer. He actually gets convicted— Wallace this is—of first-degree murder, but he gets a five-year suspended sentence. And I trace him to murders involving the

Billy Sol Estes case, where government informants who were
squealing on Johnson's corruption were murdered—at least
three of them. Henry Marshall, an Agriculture agent who was
looking into Johnson's relationship with Billy Sol Estes, the
flamboyant Texas wheeler-dealer, was found murdered. That's
another of Mac Wallace's victims. So I think this is the absolute
key point people forget. In November of 1963, John Kennedy was
not just going to dump LBJ from the ticket, Johnson was a man
staring into the abyss. He was facing federal prosecution in two
gigantic scandals of the time. The Bobby Baker scandal—Baker
was the secretary of the Senate and essentially had accepted
millions in bribes for Johnson. But more importantly: the Billy
Sol Estes scandal, where Robert Kennedy and the Justice
Department are aggressively pursuing Johnson, and they had
leaked a package to *Life* magazine. *Life* magazine has nine full-
time reporters on the ground in Texas digging into Johnson's
corruption for a December 1st cover issue. That's the end for
LBJ. He's not just facing political oblivion, he's facing federal
prosecution and the penitentiary. And in November of 1963 it
makes him a very, very desperate man.

w.o.: The book is called *The Man Who Killed Kennedy: The Case
Against LBJ*. We're speaking to the author, Roger Stone. Roger, we
want to ask you about some presidents you've known. But I've also
got to ask you: LBJ has some relatives around. Have you heard from
any of them?

R.S.: I understand that the Johnson Library Board, where his two
daughters serve, is not very happy. I was booked by CNN to be on
with Erin Burnett on their *Crossfire* program until Tom Johnson, the
former chairman of CNN, who also happens to be a member of the
LBJ Library Board, spiked the segment. I find that disappointing
because that's Soviet-style censorship. I don't ask you to believe my
book. I just ask you to consider it. Read it and see what you think
for yourself. But for CNN or the *Huffington Post*, for that matter, or
the *Washington Post* or the *New York Times* to come along and say,
"Don't read that, you shouldn't read that"—that's censorship. And
it's really very sad. I'm happy to say that thanks to the interest of

programs like this one, Bill, and talk radio and the Internet—and thank God for Fox Television in this case—my book has gotten more than enough exposure. It is a *New York Times* bestseller. It was number nineteen last week in the nation out of the top one hundred. It's a *USA Today* bestseller. It reads like a crime novel. It is a story of ambition and greed and politics and power and intrigue and murder and cover-up. It's kind of a fast-moving thriller in a way. And the political connections, I think, will astound people.

W.O.: It is a fast-moving thriller, all right. Who the hell knew you could write? You've counseled presidents; you're a man of politics. You've got a lot of pretty good research in here.

R.S.: I've got a great research partner, Mike Colapietro. But the truth is: I've always been able to read. The problem is to write. I've always been spending my time writing advertising copy for the various clients and causes I work for. And, of course, as you know, it's a lot easier to write a book without limitation than it is to write, say, a thirty-second radio ad. Or a sixty-second radio ad. It's tough to get it into sixty seconds sometimes. I have a book coming out in September, which is really the sequel. It's called *Nixon's Secret.* It will explain the connection between the Bay of Pigs and the Kennedy assassination and Watergate. They all are interrelated. More importantly, it will explain the Nixon pardon by Ford, and it will also explain the eighteen-and-a-half-minute gap. So I think history has often wanted to know why were these guys breaking into the Watergate. Nixon was 25 points ahead of his opponent. Why did he need to do that? Why in the world did Ford sacrifice his reelection and pardon Nixon? That's the next topic I intend to tackle.

W.O.: Roger, I hope this doesn't sound like a silly question, but are you looking over your shoulder? Are you concerned someone is going to whack *you*?

R.S.: That was a concern of my wife and my family when the book was finished. But in all honesty, what I generally found when I went to Texas is that LBJ was a man who ruled by fear rather than by affection. Now it's very easy to find people who love Jack and Bobby Kennedy. It's very hard to find anybody who loved Lyndon

Johnson. People were for him because they feared him. They feared his retribution. Indeed, one was with Billy Sol Estes, one of his closest associates who went to prison and kept his mouth shut. Sol Estes went to a Texas grand jury, and he laid out the details of eight murders before the grand jury, including the murder of John F. Kennedy. Billy Sol Estes writes to the Justice Department in detail, accusing Johnson of the murder of John Kennedy. Why? Because Johnson was dead, and there was no more retribution to be let out.

W.O.: Roger, we've followed you for years. How old are you?

R.S.: Sixty-one. A spry sixty-one.

W.O.: You've counseled presidents. You shuttle between Washington, New York, Miami. Give us your read on Barack Hussein Obama.

R.S.: Well, I think he's the worst president in my lifetime. I am not surprised because his record in the U.S. Senate did not indicate great achievement. No great legislative achievements. No great accomplishments. He wrote two biographies. But he didn't write any major legislation. I frankly think, now we're into a lame-duck situation where he's got three whole years, but his public credibility is destroyed. These are the lowest unfavorable ratings since Richard Nixon, and that was at the height of a national scandal. So I don't have the highest regard for him, and as you know, many, many times the most able men do not become president. I always thought Nelson Rockefeller would have been one of our greatest presidents.

W.O.: Agreed!

R.S.: He had the talent. He had the capability. He had the "big picture" knowledge. But he could never get there. I think that's tragic that a country would elect somebody like Barack Obama. But a man like Nelson Rockefeller—for example—would never become president. I think Robert Kennedy would have been a great president.

W.O.: Speaking of which, what about Mario Cuomo?

R.S.: Mario Cuomo would have been a *great* president! These are big men. Big men who think big thoughts. Mario had the "size" for the office. Nelson Rockefeller had the "size" for the office. Instead, we've elected some men whom I believe to be midgets when it comes to stature and kind of a "big picture" instinct when it comes to where they want to take the country.

w.o.: Roger Stone, is there anyone abroad in the land today, 2013, that you admire who is fighting the good fight? A good politician?

r.s.: I'll tell you a guy who is very, very underrated is Scott Walker, the governor of Wisconsin. Not only did he implement some serious, serious reforms to government, and brought the government back into surplus from having enormous deficits, but he's got a job boom going on. He's made really serious changes in the state's public-employee pension system to make it more affordable for the taxpayers. He's the one guy I think might be able to hold together the moderate wing and the Tea Party wing of his party, or I should say the regular wing and the Tea Party wing. Don't get me wrong. I like Chris Christie. I like his "in your face Jersey style." I know it works in New York. I know it works in Jersey. I don't know if it will work in Iowa. I don't know if it will work in New Hampshire. I think it may be a regional thing. He's a very able man, but it remains to be seen whether he can put it together. I like Rand Paul from the point of view I like the things he stands for. I don't think he's very attractive as a candidate. He looks like he slept in his clothes. He needs a haircut. Ted Cruz. No thanks—*no* thank you!

w.o.: Roger, I can't let you go without asking you point blank who is going to be the next president after Obama?

r.s.: You know, I've been in this business long enough to know that in politics a year is a lifetime. Never mind three years. This is wide open. Unlike previous presidential elections, where there was a front-runner based on the fact they had run before. So McCain runs and loses and then four years later he comes back and wins the nomination. Romney runs and loses then four years later he comes back and wins the nomination. It's almost like you have to have a warm-up run before you can get there. It helps you become well known enough in the country and helps you build a core of supporters around the country to help you get there. There is no such candidate this time. Everyone being talked about on the Republican side certainly is a first-time candidate. It is not apparent to me that Hillary Clinton is going to run. I don't think she's made up her mind. Should she run, she'll be very, very formidable. But those who say, oh, she'll walk right in, there'll be no contest—that's what they said about her the last time. It doesn't *work* that way.

w.o.: How about the son of Mario Cuomo, Andrew, the governor? I've watched him grow in wisdom and age.

r.s.: I have very high regard for Andrew Cuomo. I think Andrew Cuomo has tried to take New York in a different and more moderate direction. I am glad to see that the Moreland Commission is beginning to take on the legislature on full disclosure. If Hillary Clinton does not run, then the only giant left in the Democratic primary is Andrew Cuomo. I don't see anybody else in that field. I think that Andrew Cuomo has grown as a politician so dramatically since his losing the race for governor. He's a man who understands power and authority and how to use it. He's a man who understands politics. He avoids overexposure. He speaks when he has something to say, but he's not out "hot-dogging" for the media every day just to get his name in print. I had many fundamental disagreements with him besides the fact that he's a friend of mine. But he's a tremendously able man.

w.o.: Roger Stone, we've roamed far and wide. You remain a fascinating character after sixty-one years. Are you still doing the best-dressed list for *Esquire*?

r.s.: Yes, this year's best *and* worst dressed. I try to compile the ten best- and worst-dressed in the world. It comes out on New Year's Day. And it's retrospective. So in other words, I will have to produce the list of the best- and worst-dressed people in the world for the year 2013. And if you have any suggestions on either side of that, please shoot me an e-mail.

w.o.: Do you still wear a tie, Roger Stone?

r.s.: You know, I'm the last guy in the entire state of Florida who actually still wears a necktie. And I wear one every day, as I have every day since I was in the first grade. I think I was born in a suit!

w.o.: When you go out for supper, do you wear a jacket? A sport coat?

r.s.: Sure, I wouldn't go out for supper without wearing one.

w.o.: You don't do dress-down Fridays in Florida?

R.S.: That whole philosophy to me is a mistake. There's an appropriate way to dress in the workplace. And I think "dress good, look good, feel good" is one of my basic rules. I can go the Bermuda look once in a while when it gets really hot. I will wear a blue blazer and Bermuda shorts and knee shorts. But by and large I'm not a very informal guy. I didn't own a pair of blue jeans until I was in my forties and my first wife bought them for me.

W.O.: So you're still a spiff at sixty-one. And a hell of a writer. It's called *The Man Who Killed Kennedy: The Case Against LBJ.* And, as I mercifully yield, you're absolutely *certain* he was behind it?

R.S.: I think anyone who reads the book will put it down and say, "Guilty. Guilty as hell." There's no doubt in my mind that he plays a significant role. Let's take the final piece of evidence. When his car goes into Dealey Plaza, three car lanes behind the president of the United States as it makes the 120-degree turn, Lyndon Johnson *before* the first bullet has been fired—and that's the key— hits the deck. He's on the floor. How do we know this? Photographic evidence. We've got the exact time the photograph was taken because it's a news photograph. And, therefore, we've got the time of the first shot. It's clear Johnson hits the deck before the first shot. There's also the memoir of Senator Ralph Yarborough; he was in the car with Johnson. He notes that Johnson abruptly hits the ground before the first shot. And then there is Secret Service member Rufus Youngblood, who tells the Warren Commission that he heard the first shot and pushed Johnson to the floor. But then after Johnson's death, he recanted and said—well, having been shown the news photograph that contradicts that—"I really only said that because the president told me to." So Johnson is on the floor, fiddling with a walkie-talkie in the middle of a motorcade where both sides of the street are filled with friendly people. What does he know that we don't know? Why is he hitting the deck?

W.O.: Questions. They're all in the new book called *The Man Who Killed Kennedy: The Case Against LBJ.* We'll look forward to your new book coming out all about Richard Nixon and the Cubans. What's the name of that?

R.S.: *Nixon's Secret.* It is the secret that not only allowed him to make the greatest comeback of all time in American history but also brought him low in Watergate. And at the same time allowed him to avoid prison through a full presidential pardon.

W.O.: I want to let you in on a little secret; you may know this. But late in life Richard Nixon and Mario Cuomo became pen pals. Did you know they had a mutual-admiration society?

R.S.: I did know that because Nixon always said there were politicians of *poetry* and there were politicians of *prose*. Mario was a politician of poetry. He was an orator. Nixon admired his capability as a speaker and as an orator. And I think Mario Cuomo admired Richard Nixon's intellect, big-picture intellect about China and Russia and international affairs. I find that men who are enormously talented in politics are always attracted to each other despite the fact that they might be in different parties.

W.O.: Roger Stone, thank you. What a tour you've taken us on.

Richard Norton Smith,
Historian and Biographer

The noted historian Richard Norton Smith gave us the very first interview about his long-awaited book on Nelson Rockefeller: On His Own Terms: A Life of Nelson Rockefeller. *October 22, 2014.*

———————————

The great historian Richard Norton Smith worked for more than a decade on a monumental biography of our incomparable Westchester neighbor Nelson Rockefeller.

As I read through *On His Own Terms: A Life of Nelson Rockefeller*, my mind drifted back over the years to many encounters with this unique and colorful individual who was absolutely *sui generis*.

We traveled with Westchester's "Favorite Son" on his Gulfstream, in helicopters, and even golf carts and *Air Force Two*. And arriving at Westchester Airport, even late at night, he would always head straight for the WVOX microphone. Indeed, in all his years as governor and vice president, Nelson never shook off or declined an interview with his hometown radio station.

I've been widely quoted as suggesting that, as a rich man's son, NAR could have been quite a glorious bum had he not entered the arena to devote himself so relentlessly and zestfully to public service.

Professor Smith has captured all of this—and a lot more—from Rockefeller's amazing life in an extraordinary biography of our dynamic and unforgettable neighbor. I hope, if you can find a copy, it will commend itself to a place in your personal library.

We were with NAR at the beginning of his political exploits in the Empire State and at the conclusion of his time in Albany. He actually finished his first campaign for governor in the back seat of one of our WVOX mobile units as we careened around lower Manhattan late on election eve. (As I recall, he insisted on stopping at an Automat for a "refreshment"—and to pump a few more hands.)

And almost fifteen years later, the governor gave us the very last question at his farewell press conference in the state capitol. We asked our Westchester neighbor which of his predecessors whose portraits hung in the fabled Red Room had most "inspired" him. He thought for a moment and said, "I think Teddy Roosevelt. I remember he visited Pocantico when I was a youngster, and I asked him how the giraffes fit into the cars on a circus train."

Nelson Rockefeller, in his own famous and oft-used appellation, was "faibulous!" And even now—thirty-five years after he left us—Nelson remains fabulous.

WILLIAM O'SHAUGHNESSY: Good morning, ladies and gentlemen. For the next several minutes while we're in your care and keeping, a very special guest and a very interesting program—I promise you in advance—you can make book on it. We're here in "Rockefeller country." And among our neighbors are the Rockefellers, and the most vivid and dazzling among them was Nelson Aldrich Rockefeller. He was governor of New York for four terms. He was vice president of the United States. He built Rockefeller Center and the United Nations. Across the microphone this day is his biographer, the legendary historian Richard Norton Smith. Mr. Smith, we welcome you again to Rockefeller country. Your brand-new book is called *On His Own Terms: A Life of Nelson Rockefeller*. But I've got to tell you, I thought I would never live long enough to see it *finally* published. How did you do it?

RICHARD NORTON SMITH: Well, you know, Bill, all good things come to those who wait, right? Fourteen years in the making! I'd like to think it took fourteen years to get it right. It is a huge story, a huge life. Colorful. Controversial. Relevant. One of the things that practically anyone who has ever done research will appreciate—I was writing the story even as the Rockefeller Archives were opening up, and I promptly tore up the first seventy pages of my original manuscript.

W.O.: Why?

R.N.S.: Well, the keepers of the family archives opened up 120 boxes of a collection *within* the collection marked "Family and Friends." Well, you can imagine, that's the gold! For example, there were over 100 letters from Nelson's first wife exchanged with Nelson during their courtship. And among other things it allows us, I think for the first time, to know Mary Todhunter Clark Rockefeller as a three-dimensional figure, a young woman who harbored real doubts about whether she wanted to marry Nelson, whether Nelson wanted to marry her. I've often said if it was a Hitchcock movie and you're in the audience, you'd be shouting at the screen, "Don't go in that room!" because, unfortunately, we know how it turned out. Good history is all about humanizing the past. It isn't simply immersing yourself into the past—that's part of it. But it's also about putting a human face on people and events who are otherwise frozen in textbooks. That takes time. And Nelson was a very elusive figure. Nelson Rockefeller was an incredibly complex man who made it his business to appear simple. One of his children was quoted as saying, "We only wish we knew him as well as the people of New York." The people of New York thought they knew him. This blintz-eating, back-slapping, tax-raising force of nature who was, as you say, the governor for fifteen years, much as Franklin Roosevelt was the president for twelve years. There's still a whole generation of New Yorkers who equate this man with the office.

W.O.: Professor Richard Norton Smith, historian Richard Norton Smith, these proceedings, as we welcome you back to Westchester— Rockefeller country—are greatly enhanced by the presence of the star feature-columnist of the Gannett papers—the *Journal News*—it would be a bowling alley without him! His name is Phil Reisman. And also we welcome the familiar voice of our talk-show host Michael Dandry, who is also quite influential with the *Westchester County Press*, the county's only black-owned newspaper; and some think—although they've never admitted it—that he actually writes the "Snoopy Allgood" column that terrorizes all the local politicians. Also, at my left, across from you in our studio in Westchester this morning, is Nancy King, the editor of the *Westchester Guardian* weekly newspaper. And we're to be joined shortly by Dan Murphy, the editor-in-chief of Mr. Sprayregan's *The Rising* weekly publications.

    Phil Reisman, you've written a lot about local politicians. Do you ever see anything like Nelson Rockefeller around today?

PHIL REISMAN: Well, I was going to ask Richard that question because we have a debate tonight between two—three—gubernatorial candidates, including the Green Party guy. What would Rockefeller make of modern-day elections, including, perhaps, this one going on right now?

R.N.S.: It's a fair question. Unfortunately, it's a question I can't answer, obviously, because I have enough trouble trying to make sense out of the past without projecting into the future. One thing I *am* pretty confident in though: He would still be the optimist to end all optimists. I mean, the contrast between his brand of politics—forget ideology for a moment—just the way he approached problem-solving. He would be the first to tell you he's a pragmatist. He was not an ideologue. But more important than that, he believed every problem had a solution. And the contrast between then and now, when there's such pervasive cynicism, much of it masked as apathy, because it's a notion that government—forget ideology again—isn't working. It isn't even talking about the problems. I mean, there's a consensus out there about a lot of the major issues we confront, and there's this dichotomy between that kind of unarticulated public consensus and the seeming total inability of government—right, left, liberal, conservative—to address those issues. There'd be none of that with Rockefeller.

P.R.: There was an interesting story today about the American public's lack of faith in institutions. He was a *creator* of institutions.

R.N.S.: He was a "Roosevelt Republican." And I mean both Theodore *and* Franklin. It's no secret he got his start, ironically, at the age of thirty-two when Franklin Roosevelt—obviously the leading Democrat in America—plucked the scion of the leading Republican family in America to run Latin America for him.

W.O.: We're talking about Nelson Aldrich Rockefeller. The book is called *On His Own Terms: A Life of Nelson Rockefeller* by Richard

Norton Smith. He spent fourteen years of his life. Professor Smith, do you think you got him?

R.N.S.: I think I came closer than anyone has. I think that's an honest answer to you. Again, as I say—I'll tell you a eureka moment when I thought, "I've got him!" There's a pattern. If you remember, when everyone thought he was going to run in '60 against Nixon, and Nelson surprised everyone at the last minute by *not* running. And then in March of '68, everybody thought he was going to jump in when [George] Romney pulled out, and he surprised everyone by not going. Now, he got back in a month later—urged on, by the way, by Lyndon Johnson. But in any event, there is the famous incident where he didn't go to Attica. Now, on the face of it, all of those incidents run counter to everything else we know about Nelson Rockefeller, who was the most assertive, involved, you name it. . . .

W.O.: Dynamic . . .

R.N.S.: Yes, dynamic, problem-solving. And it was interesting: The one subject the Rockefeller people didn't want to talk about—and I talked to 150 people for this book—was, overwhelmingly, Attica. And it wasn't because they necessarily condemned what he did or didn't do; they didn't understand. They didn't understand what it was. OK, so I started looking for—is there any kind of theory? Is there something that unites all of these seemingly inexplicable lapses about what we think we know about Rockefeller? One of the things I found amazing was that Nelson in his last years was $10 million in hock to his trust.

M.D.: That bears repeating. It's encouraging to *me* personally. He was in debt!

R.N.S.: He decided he would write a memoir. The book never got written, but he wrote over 500 pages of oral history with his great friend Hugh Morrow, his very trusted communications director. So what you got was this very intimate, revealing autobiographical sketch. At one point, there was a quote that absolutely jumped off the page at me in which he—apropos of nothing in particular—said, "When I got to a point I didn't feel confident of being in control, I was never reluctant to step back and wait until a time when I thought I could be in control." "Control" and "creativity" are the two buzzwords you want to keep in mind. He was not a politician who collected art. He was a frustrated artist for whom government—not politics—but *government* afforded him the opportunity to create and control his environment. That's what the South Mall is all about.

W.O.: Does that not sound a little bit like our current governor, Phil Reisman? Nancy King?

NANCY KING: It does sound a little like our current governor. But, again, *control* should be Andy Cuomo's middle name. With that being said, I do understand the complexity. What I take away from the story of Nelson Rockefeller was that with his complexity and in his need to control and to coordinate and to build and solve problems, there was always an inner doubt of himself. I don't know whether it was his dyslexia, his disabilities, or where he fit in the family hierarchy, but I always found he was striving for something he couldn't inherently reach.

R.N.S.: And this is what humanizes Nelson Rockefeller. The last word in the world most people would apply to him is "vulnerable." And he was sure of that. But the fact of the matter is George Hinman, his great political advisor from Binghamton and sort of his ambassador to the Republican Party, explained it once to Ann Whitman, who was his executive assistant—she had been Dwight Eisenhower's secretary. Hinman had a theory—and it's as good as any—and that is he never got over his exposure to Franklin Roosevelt. He wasn't running against John Kennedy or Richard Nixon. It was the ghost of Franklin Roosevelt.

N.K.: Who was a tortured soul in and of himself.

R.N.S.: But he was this larger-than-life, defining figure.

M.D.: Didn't he go so far as to create a think tank around him to help solve problems? That's the big difference between Andrew Cuomo and Rob Astorino. Andrew Cuomo still has Larry Schwartz as *his* think tank. Is that fair?

R.N.S.: He was a moving think tank!

M.D.: He hired people, and he didn't care whether they were Republican or Democrat, conservative or liberal, to actually scientifically solve problems.

R.N.S.: Part of that goes back to the dyslexia. He never heard the word "dyslexia" until he was fifty years old. He went through life thinking he had a deficient IQ. And his mother said, "Surround yourself with people who are smarter than you are"—which helps to explain the think tank and the gurus.

W.O.: You know what's interesting? Here it is 2014. We're sitting here on this Wednesday in Westchester, talking about Nelson Rockefeller—a man who left us how many years ago?

R.N.S.: 1979.

W.O.: 1979. He would have been 106! And he's still relevant. Why, professor?

R.N.S.: He's still relevant for a number of reasons. Some of it is nostalgia for "The Man Who Gets Things Done." How many times during the rebuilding of the World Trade Center site did you hear people say, "Oh, gosh, maybe Robert Moses wasn't so bad after all!" Or "Nelson Rockefeller would have gotten this done." And you know what? He probably would have. It's kind of a posthumous triumph, because Nelson really, genuinely, passionately believed solving problems took precedence over ideological purity. There are millions and millions of Americans who would not use the phrase—either because they're not familiar with it or because they'd be uncomfortable with it—but who are in fact "Rockefeller Republicans." The great Meade Esposito explained in a nutshell the reason he never became president was because he was too liberal for the Republicans and too conservative for the Democrats. Nelson himself said he had a Republican head and a Democratic heart. Guess what? That's not a bad reflection of where the middle of the road is—and there is still a middle of the road—in this country.

W.O.: His name is Richard Norton Smith, the great historian. Random House calls his new book *On His Own Terms* "magisterial." I call it monumental. How many pages is it?

R.N.S.: Well, the text is 721 pages. And then there are 101 pages of footnotes and sources.

W.O.: Phil Reisman, you ask the tough questions, and I ask the good ones.

P.R.: I have a million questions about Nelson Rockefeller. But you alluded to the "rosebud" of Governor Cuomo, which we often discuss: his complicated relationship with his father. How did Nelson get along with *his* father, and how did that shape him?

R.N.S.: It's fascinating. He was his *mother's* son. Abby Aldrich Rockefeller today would have been the candidate. She was the daughter of Senator Nelson Aldrich, the Republican leader of the United States Senate from Rhode Island. But more than that, she was this larger-than-life, ebullient life force. I said she combined the better qualities of Mabel Dodge, Margaret Sanger, and Auntie Mame! The Museum of Modern Art is her creation, handed off to Nelson, in many ways. She handed a lot off to Nelson. She told him as a boy that he can be president of the United States. His ebullience—his openness to new ideas and new people, his curiosity about how ordinary people lived—he got all of that from Abby. His father—he was more like his father than he knew or let on. His father used to say, "Never show more surface than necessary."

W.O.: Professor Smith, you've got almost 900 pages. Did you have to be a little diplomatic? Did you do a little discreet "editing"?

R.N.S.: You always edit. I suspect what you're referring to are some of the more "scandalous"—I don't think that's too strong a word—parts of the story. Particularly the private life. Look . . .

M.D.: The psychosexual chapters?

R.N.S.: You don't spend fourteen years of your life unless you want to do an honest, comprehensive account.

W.O.: Did you find out in those fourteen years a lot of things people don't generally know?

R.N.S.: Oh, sure. Two weeks after he was dumped from the ticket in 1976 by Gerald Ford, he was on the phone to Hubert Humphrey and George Meade. They were on the phone to him, asking if he would consider changing parties and be the Democratic nominee for president in 1976. That's *one* for instance. And another: John Lindsay and Nelson Rockefeller were put on this planet to piss each other off.

N.K.: They sure were.

R.N.S.: The results were historic! And colorful! It's easy to say a plague on both your houses. Lindsay used to refer to Nelson's apartment on Fifth Avenue as Berchtesgaden.

W.O.: Why did he call it that, Professor?

R.N.S.: Well, because of the dominance Nelson had. It was famously said that Nelson *owned* one political party and *leased* the other. But as I said, the rental was not very high.

W.O.: Richard Norton Smith, what did Rockefeller call Lindsay?

R.N.S.: He called Lindsay a lot of things. He used to repeat the story to one of his commissioners that if Lindsay wasn't so tall and good-looking, he'd be pushing a mop and broom somewhere. The dichotomy between these two. John Lindsay was the perfect television pol. He was the epitome of charisma. Nelson was a policy wonk before the term was invented. He said, "I wish John would stick to the stage and leave the governance to me." That in a nutshell sums up how he viewed Lindsay.

W.O.: But, Professor, they were both great with people. Late in life I walked through the town—about twenty blocks—with John Lindsay, and still the bums in the street, the people, the crossing guards—he was like a rock star late in life.

R.N.S.: They had so much in common. They were both extraordinarily gifted, natural street campaigners. I mean, you go back to October 1, 1958, the birth of a legend. It was Louis Lefkowitz's idea.

W.O.: Louis Lefkowitz was . . . ?

R.N.S.: He was the "People's Lawyer," the attorney general in New York. It was entering the last month of Nelson's first campaign for governor against Averell Harriman, who was an admirable stiff—let's be honest.

P.R.: And a rich one.

M.D.: From a comparable side of society.

R.N.S.: Absolutely. In fact, there was a great line. One of the joys of this book was reading seven or eight daily newspapers from those days. They had wonderful columnists. One of them came up with a great line. He suggested that Averell Harriman's campaign slogan should be "Don't switch multi-millionaires in mid-stream!"

[123]

It was Louis Lefkowitz who suggested, "Let's go down to the lower East Side and eat some blintzes." And the rest is history. No one knew it was going to take off the way it did. But everyone who noticed—including even Nelson Rockefeller—saw what a natural campaigner he turned out to be.

w.o.: Was it genuine? Did he really like it?

R.N.S.: It was genuine. He did like it. He was fascinated by how real people lived their lives. He had enormous curiosity, which is the first thing any successful pol is going to have. You can fake sincerity, but you can't fake curiosity.

w.o.: This book *On His Own Terms* just came out yesterday. We're grateful to the elders of Random House for giving us Professor Norton Smith on the very next day. Boy, they've got some schedule for you. You're going to need a Joe Canzeri, who was Rockefeller's colorful advance man, to organize your life for the next several months. Professor, tell us, it's on everyone's mind, so let's get it out of the way. The night he met his Maker. The night he departed for "another and, we are sure, a better world," to quote Malcolm Wilson of sainted memory.

R.N.S.: Well, I decided first of all, that the real story—and I get it; I'm a historian. I think there are two significant historical questions, if you will. The first, of course, is could he have been saved? Could anything different have happened? Did he die needlessly? And I concluded, having done a lot of new interviews, a lot of archival research, that the answer to that is *No*.

w.o.: Set the scene for us.

R.N.S.: One of the things people do not know is that Nelson Rockefeller's health had seriously deteriorated, that he himself believed he was about to die.

M.D.: It brought on some depression also.

R.N.S.: Yes, but he had a very serious heart condition. There was evidence of that for several months. He tried to keep it basically to himself. He couldn't keep it from Happy. He couldn't keep it from people like Joe Canzeri. I personally—and I'm not a doctor—believe he would have died that night wherever he was. He was that close. He had talked to, for example, one of Happy's children just a couple of nights before he died—out of the blue, he was having dinner with her. He said that he wasn't afraid to die, but he was sorry to have to leave everyone. I mean, he was clearly putting his house in order.

W.O.: You have a haunting line in your book: "It won't be long now!"

R.N.S.: I talked to Mrs. Rockefeller, I talked to Happy about that night, and he had gone to the Buckley School. There was a fundraiser; Henry Kissinger spoke. The Buckley School, attended by both of his sons.

Then they went home and had dinner. After which he called Megan [Marshack] to meet him. They were finishing up work on a modern-art book. He told Happy, "The boys are fine. I love you, and I won't be long." Was that a foreshadowing? Who knows?

W.O.: Professor, then he went off to his townhouse . . .

R.N.S.: Right, which is several blocks away on 54th Street.

W.O.: Can you tell us for certain what happened that night?

R.N.S.: The story I tell begins with the 911 call because the story—in my estimation—is of the cover-up, which was hastily improvised and very quickly unraveled. And the significance of that is this: In my view, that's the night the press's attitude permanently changed about what was *public* and what was *private*.

W.O.: What do you mean?

R.N.S.: In the old days, however defined, a potentially embarrassing, essentially private situation would have been treated as such. The fact of the matter is . . .

M.D.: Roosevelt and Kennedy!

R.N.S.: Even then, frankly, had Megan Marshack not climbed into the ambulance and gone to the hospital, she would have been lost to history, and the story would have been whatever the family wished it to be. But the late Al Marshall, who was one of Nelson's deputy governors, told me he got a call from someone very high up in the *New York Times*—who shall remain for the moment nameless—who was quite angry because Hugh Morrow had gone out from the hospital, thinking he would spare the family embarrassment.

W.O.: This is the P.R. man?

R.N.S.: The P.R. man, the communications director. And he basically
concocted the story that Nelson had died at Rockefeller Center.
The *New York Times* was so outraged at being out-and-out lied to,
they saw to it that the 911 call was subjected to electronic analysis.
And if you remember—no reason for you to remember—but the
story is there were in fact *two* transcripts of the 911 call, and
gradually it surfaced that there were other people involved. The
mystery deepened. There was clearly some internal debate going
on within the family as to how much we should reveal. Then the
will was revealed, and it indicated he had forgiven Miss Marshack
a significant loan that she used to buy her condo apartment just
down the street from his townhouse. Anyway, the whole thing, in
effect, unraveled. What no one ever knew was the preexisting
medical condition. And in some ways, had they been more open,
had they been more forthcoming at the time, then the urban
legend might not have taken hold. The sad thing was that for a
generation, for several years at least, it defined him. That's terribly
unfair. No one deserves to be remembered for the worst hour of
their lives.

M.D.: It sure canceled out the Rockefeller Mall in Albany.

P.R.: Is Megan Marshack still around, and does she talk about this
ever?

R.N.S.: As you can imagine, I wrote to her and got no response, which
doesn't surprise me. My understanding is she is married and living
in California. She'd be about sixty now.

W.O.: My mind drifts back, Professor Richard Norton Smith, when as a
young man, I was a great admirer—still am—of Nelson Aldrich
Rockefeller, and *Newsweek* published a letter from me suggesting
that the incidental details of a man's passing are meaningless and
irrelevant. Happy sent me a note: "Good friends rally 'round when
life turns sad and difficult." Where is Happy with all this?

R.N.S.: I don't know. You know I talked with her. She was very gracious
at the onset. I spent a day with her. I'll tell you a wonderful story. It
goes to the heart of who *he* was. She gave me a tour of Kykuit and
then took me down to the Japanese house, the house he had built
for their retirement. And I had been told by someone in a position to

know that Nelson kept his mother's ashes in the house, in Kykuit. And I thought, "Well, what have I got to lose?" Every Rockefeller house is built with the same floor plan. When you walk in on the right, it's mother's room. And on the left is father's room. And sure enough, there's an urn in one corner that looks suspiciously like a funeral urn. So I ask Mrs. Rockefeller, and she said, "Oh, that's true." I said, "Really? How can that be?" Because, obviously, there was a funeral, and they had Abby's ashes interred in the family cemetery on the estate. "Oh, Nelson just reached in and grabbed a handful." Now, that tells me two things: It tells me there was an almost childlike impulsiveness, lack of self-consciousness—which among other things helped to explain why he was such an incredible campaigner in any situation he found himself in. But it also told me there was a sense of entitlement that borders on the bizarre. Could be arrogant. Could be however you want to characterize it. But those qualities coexisted. And it helped me to begin to understand how much I didn't know about Nelson Rockefeller. But let me tell you this, Nelson loved Happy until the day he died, loved her and admired her and had enormous respect for Happy's judgment about people and especially her very good instincts about the people on the streets, which to Nelson was priceless.

w.o.: His name is Richard Norton Smith. We're here in our Westchester studios with Michael Dandry of the *Westchester County Press*, Nancy King of the *Westchester Guardian*, and the great Phil Reisman of Gannett's *Journal News*. Should we take a couple of calls? They're lining up, for an interesting guest. You're on the air with Professor Richard Norton Smith, the great historian.

CALLER: Good morning. The conversation this morning is fascinating. And I'm a fan of Richard Norton Smith. I've been watching you for many years on C-SPAN and PBS. Can we just go back, like fourteen years ago? You could have written about anybody, researched anyone. Why Nelson Rockefeller, of all people?

R.N.S.: It's a great question. If you've ever heard—it sounds so presumptuous—but once in a while there is the book you are born to write. The book opens with that amazing scene at the Cow Palace in July of 1964 where Rockefeller is almost booed off the stage. Well, I was ten years old and a very odd child. An oddly precocious child . . .

w.o.: How so?

R.N.S.: At the age of ten, Nelson Rockefeller was my political hero, and then four years later in '68, at fourteen, I was actually *in* the convention, on the floor, carrying my Rockefeller sign, knowing we were going to lose to Richard Nixon. And then years later, look at what I went on to do. I worked in the Ford White House when Rockefeller was vice president. I worked for a number of years for Bob Dole, who replaced him on the ticket and who, in fact, employed Nelson Rockefeller Jr.

w.o.: Didn't you also run the Abraham Lincoln Museum and Library?

R.N.S.: Yes, I've run several presidential libraries. But before I got into the library business, my career traced the decline of liberal Republicans. I worked for Ed Brooke for a couple of years. Ed Brooke was the senator from Massachusetts. The first popularly elected African American senator and a classic Rockefeller Republican. So the answer to the question is—and I guess this is a subject that had bewitched me for most of my life, and it was also an opportunity to tell a history of the Republican Party over the last fifty years. If you want to explain the origins of the Tea Party, go back to that night in the Cow Palace when Nelson was up there denouncing extremism and in particular the John Birch Society. And, quite frankly, it's not a long stretch from the Birchers to the Birthers. The modern Republican Party arguably was born that night. The next morning, it was a different party. It was Barry Goldwater's party.

w.o.: Didn't Nelson also create the Conservative Party?

R.N.S.: Yes. In many ways the Conservative Party was created by those who didn't originally see themselves as taking over the Republican Party. They were themselves on the right, playing the role the Liberal Party traditionally played on the left, which was moving the center of gravity in their direction and exerting influence and patronage to them. They had no idea they'd be electing a United States senator in less than a decade: James Buckley.

w.o.: Professor Norton Smith, didn't Rockefeller and Barry Goldwater make up toward the end?

r.n.s.: They did. First of all, they had more in common, always. Militant anti-communists. Rockefeller became more conservative in his later years. There's no doubt about it. And, of course, Goldwater, who would go on to become sort of every Democrat's favorite conservative, particularly on issues like gay rights. Barry Goldwater became the classic libertarian who had very little truck with the religious right in the Republican and conservative coalition. So each man had his own odyssey. But it is true that before Nelson died—when Chiang Kai-shek died, Nelson, as vice president, was condemned to go to the funeral. Barry Goldwater went with him. And after about six Dubonnets, crossing the Pacific, they discovered they had a whole lot more in common than they realized.

w.o.: And didn't Barry Goldwater sit in the very last row at Riverside Church?

r.n.s.: One of the more poignant scenes at the memorial service: Barry Goldwater slipped in unseen, unrecognized, and sat in the back pew. But even more poignant than that, the one person Happy Rockefeller saw that week: Richard Nixon was in town to visit his daughter Tricia, who was about to have her child, and he detoured and went up to Pocantico. He spent two hours telling Happy what a great man Nelson was. Wouldn't you have loved to be a fly on that wall?

m.d.: I'm trying to put this in a big historical perspective with parameters around it. We're really talking about Nelson Rockefeller and Ed Michaelian and Bill O'Shaughnessy's Republicans for Cuomo. These were Main Street Republicans in Brooks Brothers suits—is that fair to say?—that don't exist anymore. The elite of the Republican Party? Attorneys, bankers, broadcasters?

r.n.s.: One line that you'll never hear. It goes to what kind of Republican he was. Nelson Rockefeller said, "I believe if you don't have a good education and good health, then society has let you down." You don't hear that from many Republicans today.

N.K.: And if they were to say that, they would be automatically branded at this point a socialist or a "RINO—a Republican in Name Only."

P.R.: It's also different from the New Democrat. They don't talk that language either.

R.N.S.: The irony is Barack Obama is probably to the right—operationally—of Nelson Rockefeller. The center of gravity in this country has moved so far to the right.

P.R.: What was his attitude in terms of tax policy to the richest New Yorkers?

R.N.S.: He is a Theodore Roosevelt Republican. You might say he's a Disraeli Republican. Because what Disraeli did in Britain, and TR—what F.D.R.—did in this country, Nelson explained once. There was someone who noticed he had an autographed picture of F.D.R. on his desk, and he said, "He was a great man." And he explained *why* he was a great man. "He understood you have to give people hope. And beyond that, you have to give people a stake in the private economy. It's great to have a robust private economy. But if that economy is bursting at the seams with social inequities. . . ."—sound familiar? sound contemporary?—"then you're risking revolution." And the genius of Theodore Roosevelt and F.D.R.—they may have been from different parties, but they had the same instincts. They were wealthy men who understood you had to share the wealth. And everyone had to credibly believe they could succeed in this society. That the rules were not stacked against them, et cetera, et cetera, et cetera. And then and only then—in some ways, you could call him the original compassionate conservative.

W.O.: I would call this fabulously (to use Nelson's favorite word) interesting program "Where Once *Giants* Walked the Land."

P.R.: Yes. I was just curious, again in terms of state income tax and things like that, was he in favor of a progressive tax? Today our governor doesn't really want. . . .

R.N.S.: Here's the thing. People use the term "Rockefeller Republican" as though it's monolithic. *Business Week* praised him for having the courage to raise taxes, to close the gap left by Averell Harriman. That was the definition of fiscal responsibility. By the end of his first term, people were beginning to notice and rethink the term "fiscal responsibility." And yet, you know what? Every four years the voters of New York had an opportunity to change hands. He starts out 30 points behind. What did he do? In that campaign he convinced New Yorkers that taxes were well spent. Can you imagine doing that? He created SUNY.

N.K.: With his frustrated architectural designs.

M.D.: Yes, and the MTA.

R.N.S.: New York state spent more money fighting water pollution in the mid-60s than the federal government did in '49. People saw results. And they equated their taxes with the Long Island Railroad. It was easy to laugh, but the fact is he took a terrible railroad and he made it a decent railroad.

N.K.: And that's exactly how you go back to how he solved a problem. It was always through development, and he couldn't stay on budget. And so he said, "Let's build it. Let's fix it. We'll build it."

R.N.S.: He looked into the future. SUNY was all about—down the road we're going to need not only this *many* graduates but this *kind* of graduates. We are today suffering from a deficit in the sciences and math, and there's not a Rockefeller. It was *preventive* government. It was not *reactive* government.

W.O.: I get a flash of *déjàvu*, Richard Norton Smith. Take us to Binghamton and Bob Dole. Did Nelson really give somebody the finger?

R.N.S.: Yes. Malcolm Wilson, who had a very dry sense of humor, said, "Oh, I'm sure he got his fingers mixed up. I'm sure he intended to give him a *thumbs up!*"

W.O.: But did he really give someone the finger?

P.R.: There's a photograph of it!

R.N.S.: Oh, yes, he did it. You can see Dole in the background.

M.D.: Well, by then the whole world was liberated.

W.O.: But that was scandalous. Was he vice president then?

R.N.S.: He was vice president. And not only that, but he was inundated with copies of the picture. Someone on the staff told me they went in and found him one day signing pictures. And they said, "Mr. Vice President, you can't sign those pictures." He said,

"Why not?" He said he got more mail, more *positive* mail, after that than anything since that night in the Cow Palace!

P.R.: Don't you wonder what one of those autographed pictures would go for today?

W.O.: Richard Norton Smith, how old are you now, Professor?

R.N.S.: I'm sixty-one.

W.O.: You told us that Nelson Aldrich Rockefeller, about whom you've written in *On His Own Terms* so beautifully for Random House—it just came out yesterday—was your hero when you were ten. You put fourteen years of your life into it. Is Nelson still your hero?

R.N.S.: It's like marriage. Can you imagine after fourteen years of marriage, would you emerge from that with the same views? I would put it a little differently. I would say he has not lost any of his fascination. If anything, he is more complex. More nuanced. More significant. That's how I would put it.

W.O.: He can also almost still light up a damn room! When you were coming in today, there was a buzz here at the radio station I used to call his "hometown" station. It was almost like *Nelson* was going to walk in the damn place. He dedicated this building a long time ago. And he finished his last night campaigning for governor in the back seat of our mobile unit careening around in Lower Manhattan. I remember we stopped at an Automat. He was hungry down in Chinatown someplace. I miss those days. I miss him.

R.N.S.: It's curious. I think people sensed, paradoxically perhaps, a sense of authenticity about the guy.

W.O.: What do you mean?

R.N.S.: They thought he was *real*. Cab drivers and bartenders. He was "Rocky!" You know?

N.K.: And I also think there was a fascination with the Rockefellers, the Standard Oil history. They were fascinated with the wealth of that gilded era. And I think that's also what drew people to him. Was the fascination only to find he was only "amiable"?

R.N.S.: He knew that. He knew the fourth multiplier that the name had. That the legend had. But he also knew he really liked people. And by simply being himself. . . .

W.O.: We ask you this as a historian, Professor Smith. Is there anybody around today, abroad in the land in the body politic, that they'll be writing about when they're 106? Anybody? Where once giants . . . ?

R.N.S.: In the American political universe?

W.O.: Yes.

R.N.S.: No.

W.O.: Do you think anybody will write of Barack Obama?

R.N.S.: You know, it's impossible to say about a sitting president. He's certainly a historic figure. And, of course, we don't know what the next two years hold. Or beyond. Because, as Jimmy Carter has demonstrated, there are presidents whose greatest contributions come after they leave office. Who knows?

M.D.: And Gerald Ford is in a brand-new light the last few years.

R.N.S.: History does have a way of . . .

P.R.: Somebody just wrote about Calvin Coolidge.

R.N.S.: You know why? You could take Coolidge seriously after you'd had Reagan. It's that kind of small government—Jeffersonian small government. In other words—Arthur Schlesinger, are you listening?—there is more than one model of presidential success than the one Arthur Schlesinger told us about.

W.O.: Professor Richard Norton Smith, what is your next project? Your next gig? You put fourteen years into Nelson Aldrich Rockefeller.

R.N.S.: Well, logically in many ways, I think logically enough!

W.O.: You're not going to run another dumb museum, are you?

R.N.S.: I'm going to take the next six years—someone has very generously put aside sufficient funds to allow me to concentrate on a biography of Gerald Ford, which has not really been done. I mean a full-scale bio, particularly since his passing. And I think people better be prepared for some surprises.

W.O.: He really didn't trip coming out of that airplane?

R.N.S.: Well, he tripped for the best of reasons, you know. He was holding an umbrella over his wife. And the sole of his shoe came undone.

W.O.: What are you going to call your biography of Gerald Ford?

R.N.S.: Don't know. I will tell you—it's funny. Before I wrote word one, I had a title for this book about Nelson. And in all the years I've been writing, this is the first time I ever got the title I wanted. *On His Own Terms.* Because, I think, in a nutshell, it goes to the heart—for better and worse—on how Nelson Rockefeller approached life.

W.O.: Professor, *you* have an amazing life. You're a teacher. Do you miss the classroom?

R.N.S.: No, no. I get to teach on C-SPAN. Writing a book is another form of instruction.

W.O.: Do you write every day?

R.N.S.: No, but I write in longhand. And I have a long-suffering typist. No portion of this book went through less than fifty drafts, which is one reason it took fourteen years.

P.R.: You must have great handwriting.

R.N.S.: She's the only one that can read it. She's amazing!

M.D.: He's too young to have the Palmer method I had, and Bill had.

W.O.: His name is Richard Norton Smith, historian. And his new book—it came out just yesterday—I know it's on Amazon already, and Barnes & Noble, and it's in the bookstores as well: *On His Own Terms.* Like I said, Random House—I guess there's no better publishing house—called it a "magisterial" book. O'Shaughnessy called it a "monumental" book. But like I said at the beginning, with you having these detours to take over museums, Richard, I really thought I'd never live long enough to see it.

R.N.S.: Well, we both reached our goal, Bill O'Shaughnessy.

W.O.: Phil Reisman, I'll give you the last question.

P.R.: Now you're putting pressure on me for the last question! Did Rockefeller have a sense of humor about himself?

R.N.S.: He did.

P.R.: What about all those impressionists who did those marvelous "Rocky" impressions of him because he had that nasal, gravelly, distinct voice?

R.N.S.: He had a sense of political theater. He understood. The whole blintz-eating thing was pure theater. He was Rocky! That was a public persona. There was a whole lot more than that. You have to have a sense of humor to play that role.

M.D.: And yet he hid a lot of his personality in the sense—I don't think people understood the depth of his love of modern art and everything about his personal possessions. He wasn't just a traditional, very wealthy man with Chippendale furniture.

R.N.S.: Dubonnet and Oreo cookies. That was his idea of gourmet dining.

W.O.: Michael speaks of his love of art. Don't you have a thing in your book about Nelson keeping the pope waiting one day while in Rome?

R.N.S.: Actually, he kept the British prime minister *and* the pope waiting because he was in art museums.

W.O.: Did he apologize?

R.N.S.: I don't think so. He had his priorities. The late, great R. W. Apple—Johnny Apple—told me the story about most candidates out on the road: They'll stay up, they'll drink, some will chase skirts. Nelson would get up at six in the morning and have the local art museum opened up so he could go through it. That was *his* idea of an "excursion."

W.O.: We've shared a lot of stories in the last hour while we're in your care and keeping, ladies and gentlemen. This has been an historic program about an historic Westchester neighbor. Professor, you honor us with your presence. We'll have you back in six years to talk about the Gerald Ford book. It's a wonderful book, this Rockefeller book, the one you were born to write. There's a lot of *you* in this book, and we've just touched on it. There are so many more wonderful stories.

R.N.S.: Can I tell you a last, quick one? I'll give you an idea of the relationship between him and Don Rumsfeld, which was hostile, to put it mildly. So hostile—you said he had a sense of humor—well, Nelson, in the early morning, when he was vice president, would walk by Rumsfeld's office and open the doors and shout, "Rummy, you're never going to be vice president!"

W.O.: They say Cheney and Rumsfeld hated him. They tried to thwart him in every way.

R.N.S.: They were not "allies," to put it mildly.

W.O.: But why?

R.N.S.: Some of it was ideological. Gerald Ford came into office under a unique set of circumstances. The right wing never really trusted him. His selection of Nelson Rockefeller alienated them further. And Rumsfeld believed—not surprisingly—that part of his job was to reconcile the right wing of the party, and that would not be advanced by doing what the vice president wanted.

W.O.: Did you talk to Rumsfeld or Cheney for the book?

R.N.S.: Yes, I talked to both of them. Yes. They're friends. I've known them for a number of years because of my Ford connections.

W.O.: Do they still hold it against him?

R.N.S.: Well, a rather poignant moment happened before Laurance Rockefeller died. He gave the ranch out in Jackson Hole to the people of the United States. And who accepted on behalf of the people of the United States? Vice President Dick Cheney.

W.O.: There's a lot more. It's called *On His own Terms: A Life of Nelson Rockefeller*. The author is Richard Norton Smith. The publisher is Random House. I was up half the night last night, and I'll be up again tonight. Thank you, sir. Thank you, Phil Reisman, Michael Dandry, and Nancy King. And Dan Murphy of the rising chain of weeklies awaits in the next studio.

Damn, but I still miss Nelson. Especially every day when I walk by the plaque at our front door, which went up in the '70s to commemorate the day he dedicated the new WVOX building from which we now broadcast.

Like I said, Professor Richard Norton Smith, I thought I'd never see the book that took you fourteen years to gather and compile.

It was worth the wait, for the book you were born to write.

Angelo Martinelli, Publisher

Angelo Martinelli, a former mayor of Yonkers, was a power in the Republican Party for many years. He easily answered to the name Mr. Yonkers. August 24, 2015.

WILLIAM O'SHAUGHNESSY: The legends are out today at our community station. We just saw Mr. Justice Samuel George Fredman. He is all of ninety-three, and he's just now heading down the hall into a studio. I'm in Studio 1A with another certifiable Westchester legend. You know the name for years and years and years. He was the legendary lord mayor of Yonkers, where true love conquers; and you ask anybody on the streets of Yonkers, and they think he's *still* the mayor. He's a multimillionaire publisher, and I just found out he was also a broadcaster. His name is Angelo Martinelli. Mr. Mayor, they're making a new career for you on television—on HBO—with a miniseries.

ANGELO MARTINELLI: This is my last hoorah! They regurgitated the whole desegregation thing in Lisa Belkin's book *Show Me a Hero*. In that book I play a very small role. But they expanded it in the series, and they have Jim Belushi—the actor—playing me. I sent him an e-mail: "You're a better Angelo Martinelli than *I* was!"

W.O.: You've been a larger than life figure in Westchester for years. How old are you now, Angelo?

A.M.: Eighty-seven years old!

W.O.: Do you *feel* eighty-seven?

A.M.: No, I feel about thirty-seven! I don't feel eighty-seven. You look in the mirror, and you're eighty-seven years old. That's an old guy! But I really don't feel that old.

W.O.: Mr. Mayor Angelo Martinelli, your son and heir Ralph Martinelli—publisher of one of your magazines; actually, all of them—he tells me you have holdings in the state of Delaware—in Joe Biden country—and you drive down there all by your lonesome!

A.M.: Oh, sure. Not only do I drive to Delaware, I drive to Florida for three months every year. I drive to Florida in my own car! My wife passed away last November, and she would drive with me. Actually, she never drove. She slept. But God bless her.

W.O.: Do you miss her?

A.M.: I miss her terribly. But do you know something, Bill? God was good to me—he's always been good to me—and he gave me sixty-five wonderful years with a woman that was "the wind beneath my sails."

W.O.: What was Mrs. Martinelli's first name?

A.M.: Carol.

W.O.: I hear she was almost as vivid a personality as you are.

A.M.: She was in the background. She was never out front. But she did a lot. She raised six sons, and we have thirteen grandchildren and four great-grandchildren and more on the way! But she was the matriarch of the family, and she did a fantastic job. When she passed away, there were tributes paid to her at the wake. So many people came I was shocked. So many people said nice things about her because she was a nice person. Maybe I wasn't so nice at times, but *she* was a nice person.

W.O.: What's the secret of sixty-five years together with the same woman?

A.M.: You've got to love each other. And I mean you've really got to love each other. The secret of it is that she was always there for the family, because I was out all the time, doing my thing. My thing was the mayor and the owner of Gazette Press and then starting my magazines. All the magazines I started. I did a lot of it, and she was home taking care of the family; and I think we knew our roles, and we were very, very compatible. We had our arguments, there's no doubt about it. That's the fun of it all, getting over the argument. So I was blessed. I was honestly blessed to have had sixty-five years. And some people say you must feel bad. I say no, I don't feel bad. I feel thankful to God that He gave me that time with her.

W.O.: Are you pretty religious?

A.M.: I'm *very* religious, Bill. Very, very religious, and I'm not ashamed to say it.

W.O.: Mario Cuomo used to say he prays for "sureness." Are you *sure* about all the Church teachings and an afterlife?

A.M.: I have full faith in the Church teachings and an afterlife and everything. I am fully committed. I believe in God. I say my prayers every day. People don't think I do. But I have a prayer book, and I say it every day.

W.O.: What's the most powerful prayer?

A.M.: Do you know what the most powerful prayer has been? Here's what it is. I'm not ashamed to tell you. "Dear Lord, thank you for giving me the strength and health to carry on." That's the first thing. Then I say, "Thank you for giving me sixty-five years with a wonderful woman. And thank you for the family you gave me through that woman. And thank you for the graces and blessings you have bestowed upon me and my family." That's basically the start of my prayer.

W.O.: We're talking today—a great privilege for us—just walking in the door we could feel your energy even at the age of eighty-seven. But you know, I almost called you *Ralph* Martinelli.

A.M.: My brother!

W.O.: Tell us about him.

A.M.: Ralph was one in a million.

W.O.: You're Angelo, and he's Ralph.

A.M.: My brother Ralph. He was one in a million. He really fought hard. You know, we disagreed because he attacked many of my friends.

W.O.: He was a little more "conservative," shall we say?

A.M.: Well, it's often been said he was very much like Genghis Khan! We disagreed because he attacked my friends. And after he died, I got called up by the newspaper asking if I was ever embarrassed by my brother. I say yes. I was embarrassed when his newspapers attacked my friends. A *lot* of my friends: Governor Pataki and others. I said to them that didn't mean I didn't love him. I loved him with a passion.

W.O.: Your brother Ralph Martinelli was publisher of a string of weekly newspapers, and my favorite was *The Eastchester Record*. Do you remember Vinny Bellew?

A.M.: Absolutely! A banker, a former banker.

W.O.: He used to write fabulous, graceful, passionate articles. And as I recall, he was also the recreation superintendent in the town. Has Westchester changed, Angelo Martinelli? From when were you mayor?

A.M.: I was mayor from 1974 to 1987, except for two years.

W.O.: Those were also the days of Malcolm Wilson, of sainted memory.

A.M.: Malcolm was my mentor! Malcolm Wilson did something for me in 1974 when I got elected as mayor outside City Hall, on the steps: Governor Malcolm Wilson swore me in. Now you have to understand, on New Year's Day, the custom of the new governor— because Rocky had left and Malcolm became governor for one year—and on New Year's Day the governors open their home, the Mansion, up in Albany, to the public. He had to forgo that and came down and swore me in. I was on the front page of the *New York Times* only because Malcolm swore me in. Otherwise, if he didn't come down, maybe I would have been on the front page of the *Herald Statesman*, the local paper.

W.O.: They called Malcolm Wilson the greatest orator Fordham ever graduated. Mario Cuomo used to say, "In a debate, Malcolm would defeat you in English—and then finish you off in *Latin*!"

A.M.: Absolutely. He was a champion debater, the greatest I had ever heard. And there was another one from Fordham, Bill Mulligan.

W.O.: William Hughes Mulligan, a federal judge and great after-dinner speaker.

A.M.: Judge Mulligan is in *Show Me a Hero* because there was an incident that happened after I lost the election to Wasicsko and before he took office—between November and January—these four people, Wasicsko, Longo, Spallone, and Chema, and maybe Fagan—

W.O.: Those are legendary Yonkers names.

A.M.: They wanted to hire a new attorney. We were wasting money. We wasted already $15 to 20 million on attorneys. And I said, "Why should we waste any more money?"

W.O.: Why were you hiring all these lawyers?

A.M.: Because they thought they could get a lawyer to win the desegregation case. And so they hired Bill Mulligan because he was a constitutional attorney. There was a little break in the meeting because they were going to vote—I said, "Bill, I came here not to vote for a new attorney because it's just a waste of time and money." But I said I can't ever vote against Bill Mulligan. I just can't. If you tell me there's a constitutional chance we can win this case, I will vote for you. He said there might be a constitutional way to do it. So I said I'm going to vote for you. But I'm not as old as you are and not as learned as you are. But I'm going to give you a little advice. I said, "There's an old saying that if you lay down with dogs you're going to come out with fleas." I said, "You're going to be laying down with the worst dogs you ever saw when you take on this case because I will be out of office January 1st. But you're going to have to be here." He said, "Why do you say that?" "Well, I'm just telling you." And let me tell you about another event. There's a portion in *Show Me a Hero* where the cardinal—Cardinal O'Connor—actually says he would give a piece of the seminary property at Dunwoodie for low-income housing. He told that to Bill Mulligan, who was a trustee of Saint Patrick's Cathedral. And Bill Mulligan referred that to Judge Leonard Sand, and Judge Sand called up—in the show—Cardinal O'Connor and asked him, "Did you really tell him this?" And he said, "For poor people I will do it." Now what happened is the people from Saint John's Church—which is right around the seminary on Yonkers Avenue—they said, "We're not going to give any more money in the basket, and we're not going to give to the cardinal's appeal, and we're going to go to other churches because what the cardinal is doing is wrong—giving this piece of property." The cardinal—after this pressure on him—then said he was "misled," and he backs off. In fact, he calls Bill Mulligan a liar and insists that he never said that. But he said it. And I believe Bill Mulligan.

[141]

w.o.: Is that all in the movie?

a.m.: That's in the movie.

w.o.: I just felt Saint Patrick's Cathedral shake, rumble as you're telling that story. That's where His Eminence John O'Connor is buried.

a.m.: I'm just saying that was not good. And then Spallone became mayor, and they owed Mulligan's firm a lot of money—maybe $600,000 to 700,000. He told Mulligan, "I will never pay you." And he made Mulligan's firm drag. They finally did get paid after a while. But he gave them ulcers. I met Bill Mulligan after that. He said to me, "Boy, were you right about laying down with dogs."

w.o.: William Hughes Mulligan was a huge name around here and in the judiciary. Mr. Mayor Angelo Martinelli, it's so wonderful to revisit these things. You can see a lot of this on television these summer nights, on the HBO *Show Me a Hero*. You're played by Jim Belushi.

a.m.: Yes, a great actor.

w.o.: Did he do right by you?

a.m.: He did. As a matter of fact, he called me from London a while back. He said, "I'm coming in tomorrow, and maybe we can get together." I said, "Why don't you come up to Yonkers, and I'll take you to Peter Kelly's X2O, and we'll have lunch?" He brought his brother Billy with him. He was dressed very casually. I have to tell you right now, when you meet Jim Belushi, it's like meeting a member of the family. He's just a down-to-earth guy. And we got along. We spoke for two-and-a-half hours. And what he wanted to find out is my feelings during the time this happened. He wanted to get into me so he could play me. And I have to tell you something, from what I see portrayed, he's playing me even better than I am!

w.o.: Yonkers, where true love conquers. It seems like you had your share—more than your share—of colorful characters over the years. You come from a time—Angelo Martinelli—we put you back with Nelson Rockefeller and, as I've said, with Malcolm Wilson, with Edwin Gilbert Michaelian and Bill Luddy, the Democrat warlord, and Ogden Reid, and Herman Geist, and Sam Fredman.

a.m.: And don't forget Sal Prezioso, who became my city manager. I brought him in. What a wonderful man. And he did something for me that as a politician nobody else did. I was known in Yonkers as something of a bull in a china shop—a pit bull, at that—and, I have to tell you right now, I had all that energy. And so what happened is when I brought Sal Prezioso in as city manager, he opened up Westchester County to me. He knew everybody in Westchester County. And people who had said, "Oh, that Martinelli, he's just going off the deep end." But he said to them, "Martinelli is a great guy." And he made me better than I am. He made me better known and better liked all around Westchester County because that's how strong and respected Sal Prezioso was.

w.o.: It's no surprise that you're a Republican, Mr. Mayor. Tell me, what's going on in your party now nationally? Trump and company, Jeb Bush, Ted Cruz, Chris Christie, George Pataki (I like him a lot!). You've still got a lot of juice in the GOP tribe, so predict for us.

a.m.: Well, let me tell you something. I think Trump is saying things people want to hear. You can get elected—like in Yonkers—if I told people what they wanted to hear—that I was going to fight this case—I probably would have gotten reelected. But if you tell them the truth of how things are really going to happen, you're not going to get elected. Trump is telling people what they want to hear. Some of the stuff he says is true. But he is killing himself with other things he says. Things I think are not good for him as a politician.

w.o.: Like what?

a.m.: When he criticized John McCain; when he criticized that woman, the moderator Megyn Kelly, at the debate. If you criticize him, he's going to come back at you, and you don't know what he's going to say because he can say the most awful things that should not come out of the mouth of a politician. While he says some good things about immigration and all that, he says other things that really knock him down. He doesn't become viable to me even though he's getting the vote from people. I don't think he's a viable candidate. And remember something. You have like twenty people in there. He's got 20 percent. What's 20 percent of 100 percent? It's very small. So when you start to narrow the other people down, if he keeps his 20 percent, somebody is going to get 80 percent.

[143]

Somebody else is going to get 80 percent. I don't think he's going to be around.

w.o.: You still know how to count votes, Angelo.

a.m.: That's the secret of it. One time when I was mayor—as a Republican—Conservative—early on in my administration I got to support the tenants, and I had a lot of landlords who were good friends of mine.

They said to me, "Angelo, you're a Republican-Conservative. That's a 'Democratic view' you're supporting, with the tenants and the Tenants' Protection Act." They said, "Why?" I said, "I learned how to *count*. There are 80,000 tenants. There's four landlords. Where am I going to get my votes from? Tell me where I'm going to get my votes!" But, in truth, I didn't do it just because of that. I supported the tenants, and I actually became the champion of the tenants. I was the first one to have a tenant advocate in my office as mayor.

w.o.: At the age of eighty-seven, Angelo Martinelli, Mr. Mayor, you're quite entitled to pick the next president for us, because you're also to this day a baron of the Republican Party. Who do *you* want?

a.m.: I can't pick anybody right now, Bill. I like Marco Rubio. I think he's good. I like Jeb Bush, to tell you the truth. I know a lot of people don't like him. I thought he was a good governor of Florida. And I like Carly Fiorina, from California.

w.o.: What about George Elmer Pataki?

a.m.: George Pataki is a great guy. I don't think he's going to get anywhere. I like George Pataki. He's got a good message out there. This is not like the time he ran against Mario Cuomo. Do you understand? I know Mario Cuomo was very close to you, and he was close to me too. I loved him too. But when Pataki ran against Mario Cuomo, people voted against Mario Cuomo, they didn't vote for George Pataki. He didn't realize that the first time when he got elected. Now he got elected again. This isn't going to be a time when they are voting against somebody that George Pataki has an opportunity. I don't think he's got the support generally throughout the country.

w.o.: I think he'd make a great vice president.

A.M.: I think he would. Yes. But I don't think he'll ever be president. He may never be vice president.

W.O.: Forgive me, but there's a Democrat I kind of like named Joe Biden.

A.M.: I shouldn't say this to you on the radio, but I always thought Hillary is going to implode before she gets the nomination. I think something is going to happen.

W.O.: When did you say it?

A.M.: Months ago, when all this came up about the e-mails and all that. I think they're going to go after her. And if Joe Biden gets into this election, I think you're going to see Obama really step up against Hillary—*against* Hillary. And I think Joe's a good guy. I know Joe from the Delaware magazines we own, and he's very close to my son Rob down in Delaware. He comes to all the Delaware magazine things. I think he's a very, very good guy.

W.O.: Angelo Martinelli, we've taxed our friendship of many years too much today. You're a popular figure on every street in Yonkers and beloved on some. Every talk-show host is trying to grab you. And I've kept you too long.

A.M.: I said this is my last hoorah!

W.O.: At eighty-seven. I'm fascinated. Before I let you go, tell me again, you drive to Florida *alone*! Do you take vitamins? What are you on?

A.M.: I came back from Florida, and they found I'm anemic. They started giving me iron pills. I'm taking iron pills. I'm being checked up on pretty well. Most everything seems to be running well!

W.O.: Mr. Mayor, do you ever get stopped by the troopers between here and Florida? That's a long drive.

A.M.: No, I got one ticket in all the time I've done this. And I've done it many, many years. I got one ticket. I was going eighty miles an hour coming back, and they stopped me. I paid it, and that was the end of it. Most of the time I'm going around seventy or seventy-five, and they leave me alone.

W.O.: Don't you have your old badge as mayor?

A.M.: I've got my old badge, but I don't use it. I have a little sticker that I support the police. I haven't been stopped since, so that's good.

W.O.: You're a delight, sir. You've perked us up and given us hope that maybe Yonkers will make it after all, and that maybe this county of Westchester will make it.

A.M.: Yonkers is a great city. It's a great city. It has all the ingredients. And I think Mike Spano is doing a great job as the mayor.

W.O.: You do?

A.M.: Yes, I do. I think he's doing a good job as mayor of Yonkers. He's really bringing people together.

W.O.: The Spanos and Martinellis—ever any tension there? These are the two big political families in your home heath.

A.M.: Well, I think the father of that other family—Lenny—and I get along very well. And my wife and Josephine Spano were honored by the Exchange Club together. And to honor my Carol and Josephine Spano together was very nice for both of them. But I don't think we've ever gotten into anything difficult or unpleasant.

W.O.: You've never bumped up against the Spanos?

A.M.: No, never bumped up against them. No.

W.O.: Sir, you honor us with your presence and with your entire life of eighty-seven years. If Mario Cuomo were here, he'd tell you to *"keep going!"*

A.M.: Mario Cuomo did some great favors for me, Bill. And he was a good guy, a really good guy. I met him when he was secretary of state, and he was on the Control Board with me back in the 1970s. And we became friends. He was a good man. A good *honest* man. That's what he was. A good honest man. I liked him for that. Now there are a lot of people who didn't like his liberal leanings, you might say, and things like that. But he told it like it was, I thought. And because he told it like it was, he lost the election. I told it as it was, and I too lost an election. So there are actually some similarities between us.

W.O.: You're eighty-seven. Do you know what Mario would say to you right now? *"Per cent'anni."*

A.M.: Yes, for one hundred years. That's right! Live for a hundred years.

"The Mendicant," Father Paul Lostritto, O.F.M.

I've been a longtime admirer of the Franciscan Friars, based at St. Francis of Assisi on 31st Street in Manhattan. Mario Cuomo admired them too. He said, "They're three Hail Mary's for a homicide priest." One of the best-known Friars was Father Mychal Judge, a fire department chaplain who was one of the first to perish in the rubble of the World Trade Center on 9/11. I'm also a great admirer of several of the other "Friars Minor," as they call themselves: Father Michael Carnevale, Father Kevin Mackin, and a longtime friend, Father Joe Cavoto. The Friars also run the St. Francis bread line, run by Father Paul Lostritto. December, 2012.

———————————

Three months after we broadcast this interview with Father Paul Lostritto, a Franciscan street priest from Manhattan, an Argentinean prelate—a Jesuit no less—born of Italian parents, stepped out on a cold, windy balcony overlooking Saint Peter's Square in the Eternal City on the 13th of March, 2013, and proclaimed into the night air that he, Jorge Mario Bergoglio, having just been chosen by his brother cardinals and the Holy Spirit to be bishop of Rome, would now like to be known for all time to come as Francis, a name taken from an Italian saint who loved the poor, the hurting, and the forgotten.

Standing on that balcony with stunning simplicity and stark humility, Bergoglio thus took the name of a spoiled young aristocrat of wealth and means who renounced the standing and stature and high estate of his prominent family to become Francis of Assisi, perhaps the greatest saint of an ancient religion founded by a carpenter's son more than 2,000 years ago. The pope from Argentina had once said, "Saint Francis brought to Christianity an idea of poverty against the luxury, pride and vanity of the ecclesiastical powers of the time."

And so now this new Pope Francis, the Jesuit, would stand amidst the ornate pomp, ritual, and ceremonia of a damaged, fading Church by reaching beyond the gilt and trappings for the example of the first Franciscan who spoke to animals and the birds of the air while ministering to the poor, the wretched.

I have long admired the work of today's Franciscan priests at Saint Francis of Assisi Church on 31st Street in Manhattan. It is where suburban Catholics, sinners like me, often repair for Confession loaded with guilt. Mario Cuomo once said, "They forgive us gently and generously."

It seems no one is ever turned away or denied the love and healing of the Franciscans. They have many names, these marvelous friars: Carnevale, McGrath, Cavoto, Carrozzo, Jordan, Judge, Mackin . . . urban street priests who all hear the same music of service to the least fortunate, the lost and the hopeless.

The Saint Francis Breadline, which feeds hungry New Yorkers, has been around for a hundred years. And sometimes even Cardinal Timothy Dolan helps out in the early morning hours.

We invited one of the Friars—Father Paul Lostritto—to tell us about a new program to take the Breadline right into the homes of shut-ins. But in a far-ranging broadcast we covered much more than temporal "bread and butter"(no pun intended) issues.

Surely the gritty, lovely music of the Franciscans on 31st Street would commend them to the favorable judgment of Francis. The one now in Rome. And the one from the hill town of Assisi . . . a mendicant who spoke to the animals and the birds while ministering to the poor.

WILLIAM O'SHAUGHNESSY: I'm a poor, struggling, faltering, weak, uncertain Christian. But there's something very special about the individual we'll visit with for the next hour while we're in your care and keeping. His name is Father Paul Lostritto. He's a Friar, a Franciscan. The Order of Friars Minor is what they call them. And he's based in Manhattan where there's a church called the Church of Saint Francis of Assisi named for the founder of the whole damn thing, the Order. It's down on 31st Street. Today's guest is a very special Friar. Some colleagues, some brothers of his, Joe Cavoto and others, tell me he is one of the craziest of the "monks," as they are sometimes lovingly called. Saint Francis, himself, as you may have heard, was a real nut job—and today's studio guest may be one of the craziest of his inheritors. His name is Father Paul. He's a Franciscan. And he wants to tell us today about *Franciscans Deliver.*

FATHER PAUL LOSTRITTO: It's a new project. At our church we started a breadline in 1930, and it is the oldest running breadline in the United States. Every morning—every day—we hand out between 250 to 350 sandwiches, juices, and coffee to people who line up out in front. Every morning. 365 days a year. Since 1930. The only day we ever closed was for Hurricane Sandy.

W.O.: Father Paul, are you a regular priest? I know you're a Friar . . .

F.P.L.: I guess I'm regular . . . I don't know. Yes . . . I am a Franciscan Friar. What that means is I'm a Roman Catholic priest. But—it's an Order—a Religious Order—so we follow Francis of Assisi's philosophy and teaching, which basically is working with the poor.

W.O.: Saint Francis was—I hope I don't get struck by lightning for saying he was crazy.

F.P.L.: He was . . .

W.O.: He used to talk to birds and animals?

F.P.L.: Yes . . . and they supposedly talked back!

W.O.: Tell me about Francis.

F.P.L.: He lived in the Middle Ages in Italy. His father was what you would call in those days wealthy . . . a clothing merchant and did a lot of traveling. Francis was this young rich kid. A little spoiled. His mother spoiled him. He was kind of a "mama's boy." He had a good time in life. In those days, the thing that made you really cool was if you became a knight. And so that was one of the big things he wanted to do. He became a knight. And he fought the war with this town nearby—Perugia. He was taken prisoner. I believe in prison he began to have second thoughts about what the hell life was all about. But eventually he had a major conversion in which he believes Jesus spoke to him and said . . . "Francis, rebuild my Church." And at the time the Catholic Church was pretty much in even more disarray than it is now.

And so he thought the message from the Cross—this message to "rebuild my Church"—was to physically get stones and mortar and rebuild this chapel that was falling apart. Until he realized that by rebuilding the Church—what Jesus was asking him to do was rebuild the spiritual life of the Church. So here's this little guy—he wanted to live with the poor like Jesus did. He takes the Gospel very literally in terms of having no clothes—no anything other than what's on his back. He went around as a mendicant begging for his food, and people were very attracted to his way of life because he was so filled with joy. He was always singing. He was always happy . . .

w.o.: But they thought he was nuts.

F.P.L.: They did . . . they really thought he was crazy!

w.o.: Francis of Assisi. Have you ever been there? Assisi?

F.P.L.: Oh yes . . . a couple of times. It's a beautiful place . . . it's a pilgrimage destination. Many people love Saint Francis even if they're not really into Catholicism. Everybody knows him because he's the patron saint of animals and ecology. People love him.

w.o.: Father Paul . . . why do they call him the greatest saint of the Church? Do you know how many saints would love to be called the greatest?

F.P.L.: He really . . . revived the Church. Many people say he was like a second Christ, really. He even had the wounds of Christ.

w.o.: Now that's almost blasphemy.

F.P.L.: He had the "stigmata," the actual wounds of Christ. A very holy man.

w.o.: Do you believe that?

F.P.L.: Yes . . . yes, I do. I used to be a skeptic about a lot of things. I'm not anymore. I've come to believe that a lot of the stuff we thought was sort of mythological . . . there's some factual basis to a lot of these things. So, yes. I do believe it.

w.o.: Father Paul Lostritto . . . was recommended to our ear by Father Joe Cavoto and some of his friars down on 31st Street. Again, what's the difference between a Friar and a priest?

F.P.L.: Well, we're all Friars. The word "Friar"—it's like brother. We're brothers. We're a fraternity . . . brothers. Some of us—like myself and Joe Cavoto—went on for Ordination. Other brothers do not. They can go on for other things. Many different things. Some are social workers, or even nurses. We even have some lawyers, artists

... things like that. We're all the same too. We don't make any kind of distinction between he's a "brother" ... and he's a "priest." Brother. We're all brothers. It's a brotherhood.

w.o.: Father Paul ... you came down from Boston recently, and your fellow Friars are very excited about Franciscans Deliver. Do you also hear Confessions? You know a lot of suburban Catholics loaded with guilt, change their voice, and go to Confession at Saint Francis.

f.p.l.: Yes, I do know that. I often hear Confessions down there. A lot of times. In fact I have two hours this evening. Notice the word "have" to. It's nonstop.

w.o.: You seem like a nice guy. Do you get very stern in the Confessional?

f.p.l.: No ... the whole purpose is for people to be freed up and to know they're forgiven. We all make mistakes and we try to learn from it as best as you can. But you've got to move forward. If you're feeling guilty and stuck in the past, you can't move forward. So the whole Sacrament is to help you feel "freed up." You know you're forgiven. You're human. And so now go forward. Free. And do better with your life.

w.o.: That's a great power. The power to forgive sins.

f.p.l.: Yes ... it is not mine. I speak in the Confessional as the priest. I am the voice of the Church. And—not to get too theological— the Church is Christ. And by that—People. You know who we are, we are the Church. And so I represent the People. For example, if you were in the Confessional and you harmed someone, I am the person who forgives you in their name, so to speak. Does that make sense?

w.o.: It does. Mario Cuomo is a great admirer of the work of the Franciscans down on 31st Street. He says you guys are great for Confession. He says you're "three Hail Mary's for a homicide" guys.

f.p.l.: We're kind of easy. That's what people tell us. A lot of priests from all over the city—and from Westchester and the Bronx—come to us for Confession.

w.o.: Priests come to you for Confession?

f.p.l.: Yes ... sometimes we'll get five or six priests in a row.

w.o.: Do they have to say I'm a priest?

F.P.L.: I can tell immediately. But they usually do say I'm a priest.

W.O.: Do they sin?

F.P.L.: They do . . . yes, definitely. I sin. I won't speak for them . . . I'll speak for me. I'm a sinner. You know, we all are. We're all struggling together to make sense of this crazy world.

W.O.: The great Mario Cuomo says we all sin seven times, seven times a day. Where did that come from?

F.P.L.: That comes from the Scriptures. Somebody said something to me the other day that people who are very aware of wanting to do good with their lives—people who are on the right track with life—are very aware of their sinfulness. They're very aware of their faults. Great saints were very aware. Saint Francis would speak about what a great sinner he was. So I think when you're on the right track, you're very aware of what needs to change in your life. You're not always successful. We always make the same freakin' mistakes every day a lot of times. But we're aware . . . we sort of have a goal. We're on the right road, so to speak. Moving in the right direction, even if we fall off the road or get lost.

W.O.: I can't seem to reconcile . . . you're kind of a street priest. You come in with clogs . . . you're a little scruffy. I don't put you in with the . . . pomp and the "ceremonia," as Governor Cuomo call it . . . the miter and the gold and the gilt and the hierarchy.

F.P.L.: Well, Mr. O'Shaughnessy . . . maybe you're going to get me in trouble, but let me tell you I don't relate to it at all either. Not just because I'm a Franciscan . . . we take a vow of poverty and we live it differently. We vow to a different way of life than perhaps the pomp of the other church. But I do feel sometimes disheartened with what seems to be a chasm or a divide between the reality of the world in terms of what's going on and the needs of the poor, for example. Even some of the stances the Church takes in terms of people of God . . . seem to be out of touch very often with what's going on. So, that can be a little disheartening, but I also believe that most of the Church—when I think of the Church—are very vibrant men and women, even in religious orders, who really make a difference. They are making a difference and are out working with the poor. And are out doing things to help people and take their life and their commitment to the Gospel very seriously. But you don't hear about them that often. You don't see them that often. I had a couple of sisters—nuns—at the Breadline this morning and they bought a bunch of students to work the Breadline with me this morning. You don't hear about people like that. You wouldn't even know they are sisters. But . . . you'll hear about the guys in the pomp and circumstance and all that stuff. And when they say stupid things, which often happens, it kind of reverberates down because they are the hierarchy, so people think they are the only voice of the Church.

W.O.: Would you take some calls from our listeners? I don't know if they want to go to Confession. Can you give a General Absolution to all our listeners?

F.P.L.: I could . . . I don't know if it will work . . .

CALLER: Father, earlier you mentioned you used to be more of a skeptic in life. Did that come about when you became a Friar? Was it before that? What exactly did you mean by that?

F.P.L.: I grew up in a Catholic family. A pretty secular family. We went to church on Sundays. I don't come from this "Joe Religious" family. I had some personal experiences in which I really encountered stuff that made me stop and think what life was all about. For example, I was in a coma. I actually died . . . a number of times . . . when I was young. I had a blood clot that went to my lung. The experiences abound—what that did to the people around me. I don't know if I'm making sense. But it was a profound experience that made me re-think what life was all about . . . the importance of life. But also I have had experiences in which it does seem as if God is really there. I've had experiences where I know Christ has been right there to guide me, to help me. Personal stuff like that. I don't know if that makes sense.

W.O.: Father, God speaks in whispers. Why isn't God a little clearer? Or a little louder?

F.P.L.: You're asking me hard questions. I think—I won't say I think, I believe that if you look at the world and the way it is, I'm not so sure God is speaking in whispers. I think there are some profound things we're either addressing or not addressing that are part of our human condition. God gives us free will. And so we have to make our choices. If you ever really loved somebody, you don't tell them what to do. So . . . we're kind of in this to experience God and to be moved and motivated by God. But ultimately we have the choice. I believe that. Look at this recent hurricane.

w.o.: Was that the product of a vengeful God?

f.p.l.: No . . . that's a product of us human beings not paying attention to our environment.

w.o.: Do you really think so?

f.p.l.: I do . . . I think these giant storms are a result of global warming.

w.o.: What are you, an Al Gore?

f.p.l.: Not really . . . but there's something going on if you look at pieces of glaciers over the last twenty or thirty years. Something is definitely happening. Like these storms. This was a pretty big storm. Yes . . . I do think we contribute to these things and we're not listening. I think God is kind of shaking us and saying, look, you've got to get your act together and pull it together. And, of course, as human nature is, we don't usually pay attention. That's just the way we are. We give it a little nod and a little shake and then move on and hope it won't happen again—which is already happening.

w.o.: What do you do when you have doubt?

f.p.l.: Well, when you have doubts oftentimes you don't want to pray or you don't pray. So you can't even say you turned to prayer.

w.o.: Are you talking about Our Father's and Hail Mary's?

f.p.l.: Yes . . . or just even talking to God. I think there are times in our life and my life when I've kind of said Enough! You know, I'm not really interested in listening or talking right now.

w.o.: You said that to God?

f.p.l.: Yes . . . I know . . . but I'm being honest. And I think most of us do feel like that at some point in our lives. I find my way back, Bill. I find my way on the road to Damascus very often through the words and things going on around me through other people. That's often where I will get back on track . . . or something will happen that will jar a memory and remind me . . . Oh, yes . . . *this* is what it's all about. It gets me kind of back on track!

W.O.: His name is Father Paul Lostritto, a Friar of the Roman Church. A Franciscan monk. They also call you "monks" as well as Friars.

F.P.L.: Yes . . . that's kind of a word everybody uses, but we're really not monks. We're mendicants. Monks live in private. They live quiet lives in solitude away from the world. And the mendicant, the Franciscan movement, is all about being *in* the world. It's all about being amongst the poor. That's what Saint Francis's early followers started and what we continue.

W.O.: Everybody loves Cardinal Timothy Dolan. He's a jolly, charismatic, and articulate guy. He's very attentive to his correspondence. Every time I shoot my mouth off, I get a note. The guy may even be the next pope. . . .

F.P.L.: I wish we would also be a little more in dialogue with people who perhaps don't fit into the mainstream. For example, gay people. I mean, they often feel as if they want to belong to church. There are good men and women who love God. But they feel like when they go to church somehow they don't fit into the group. And so they feel ostracized. And that's wrong. No matter how you look at it. And I know Jesus would feel that way. Everybody is welcome. Everybody has a place at His table. And I think we need to sit down and talk about these things rather than pass judgments or decrees about these things. And that's another thing that drives people nuts.

CALLER: Another quick question. Do you think if priests were allowed to marry . . . that would that get them to join?

F.P.L.: I think that would be a wonderful thing. I think that would attract a lot more men to the priesthood. Absolutely. Let's face it. Marriage and sex are all very normal parts of life. You know . . . priests in the Roman Church were married for the first thousand years. It's something that would definitely be a boost to the priesthood.

W.O.: Father Paul, you mentioned the gays. Your particular branch of the Franciscans has done a lot of work in that area. At Saint Francis you have meetings . . . and didn't you have a famous Friar who died at 9/11? Father . . .

F.P.L.: Mychal Judge.

W.O.: Mychal Judge. A legendary Friar. Did you know him?

F.P.L.: I used to go to him for Confession, actually. He was a great priest. He was wonderful to confess to just because he was so normal and he was a sinner. He didn't judge. Like all of us. That's the thing. I think he was very compassionate. Very kind. A very kind man.

W.O.: Do you Friars still remember him? He lived with you. You still think about him?

F.P.L.: Yes . . .

W.O.: Do you pray to him?

F.P.L.: I don't. I know people who do. But he certainly was one of the greats . . .

W.O.: M-Y-C-H-A-L . . . like the Irish! Did he speak with a brogue? He was chaplain of the Fire Department . . .

F.P.L.: No . . . not with a brogue. But he was a chaplain. His room, on 31st Street, at the Friary, is directly across from the firehouse. His room is right on the second floor overlooking it and he was constantly involved with the firehouse and he used to bring me over there when I was younger and a student. He was a hoot! He really was.

W.O.: What can you tell me about a *charism* that attracts . . . ?

F.P.L.: A way of living . . . a philosophy . . . of life and how we approach it and the people that come to church. Like I'm doing the ribbon cutting next weekend for this Franciscans Deliver. I do yoga. So a lot of my yogi friends are coming. A lot of them are fallen-away Catholics. A lot of them are Jewish. A lot of them are Hindus. So they're all excited. It will be great to see them in church. And I know when they come, they'll all feel welcome. The Church of Saint Francis of Assisi is right near Madison Square Garden.

W.O.: Where do you get the food that you give out?

F.P.L.: That's a good question. Right now I have each of the groups that come to Saint Francis—the young adults, the LGBT groups, the secular Franciscans—they're all bringing different food items and they're all responsible for different things. I also have some donors who donate food. People have been very generous and I'm going to have to rely on that generosity to continue to do this work. It's not coming from anywhere else but our own ingenuity to find people and raise the money. This will help us reach out to people who can't get to the Breadline in the neighborhood. Elderly people or shut-ins. The idea is to bring them groceries once a week.

w.o.: You talk about Saint Francis being the greatest saint. What about Mary Magdalene? She was pretty cool. All the sinners like me . . . they like her!

F.P.L.: Oh yes . . . she was pretty cool! I went to her church. There is a church dedicated to her in France in Vezelay where supposedly she ended up and her bones are in the church. Very cool place. And, of course, the Franciscans are there. It's their church. We love Mary Magdalene.

w.o.: Don't you also have a church, Father Paul, in Venice? There is a cool priest there . . .

F.P.L.: Yes . . . I stayed there. I studied art and art history.

w.o.: Who is your favorite artist?

F.P.L.: I would have to say probably Michelangelo . . . perhaps Bellini. In the chapel was this little Madonna painting and it was by Bellini. I said oh my God! Just kind of sitting there! That's so typically Italian because there's so much art in Italy that you do find these little gems kind of squirreled away in these places. Unbelievable! Maybe I shouldn't say this. I hope nobody robs it now.

w.o.: His name is Paul Lostritto . . . a Friar . . . he's founder of Franciscans Deliver. Aren't you having a big "do" this weekend?

F.P.L.: Well . . . we open. People can come in. Next to the church. It's in our old school. The pantry. We used to have a bookstore. It's in the old bookstore. Right next door to the church.

There will be an open house, refreshments. People come in to look around. And then I'm going to have a ribbon-cutting ceremony at the Mass. And once that's done, we'll start bringing the food to people.

w.o.: Do you also preach . . . give sermons, homilies?

F.P.L.: Oh yes!

w.o.: Do you get nervous when you get up there in front of people?

F.P.L.: I do . . . but I love it. I love getting up and preaching. I never thought I would ever enjoy it as much as I do. I like preaching a lot.

w.o.: How can you tell when you're getting across?

F.P.L.: Oh . . . you can tell. You know how that is, Mr. O'Shaughnessy. You're there . . . you can hear a pin drop and they're all looking at you. And there's something about the energy in the room.

W.O.: Well, we've all had moments, but I've got to ask you, do you ever get up there and say, I'm not getting across like happens to me? You look out there and they're blank! Bored! I get that a lot.

F.P.L.: Yes . . . that happens sometimes at weddings and funerals. But weddings even more. Let's face it, people aren't at weddings a lot of times because they want to be at church. They're at weddings because they want to have drinks and have fun. So they're not really paying attention. They're more interested in what they look like and which girl they are going to dance with or sleep with or whatever. That's what they're thinking about!

W.O.: Father Paul Lostritto . . . if someone wants to help your *ministry* . . . initiative . . . scam? What is it?

F.P.L.: Ministry . . . it's a *ministry*. An *outreach* ministry!

W.O.: It's called Franciscans Deliver. If someone wanted to send you a check . . . what would they do?

F.P.L.: Yes . . . Franciscans Deliver and then just write underneath it, "The Saint Francis Breadline" because it's part of the Saint Francis Breadline. You can send it 135 West 31st Street, New York, New York 10001.

W.O.: You say you're mendicants. If somebody gives you, say, five dollars, do you have to turn it over to the other Friars?

F.P.L.: We do . . . but not five dollars. You know . . . I wouldn't think that even makes much of a difference today.

W.O.: If someone gives you $5,000?

F.P.L.: That's totally different. Even $50. You turn it in. We get a stipend every month. And it's adequate. We have our health insurance. We have a few cars if we need them. We have a lot so it's not hard to turn the money in to contribute to the life we have.

W.O.: You're a Lostritto. A lot of vowels there. And there's a Cavoto, our friend. There's another one, Carrozzo. What does he do?

F.P.L.: Carrozzo was our provincial, which is our "head guy." We elect our head person for a period of time and he is . . .

W.O.: Do you think you'll ever get to be provincial?

F.P.L.: Oh . . . I hope not. I hope not.

W.O.: Let this cup pass . . . ?

F.P.L.: Yes . . . exactly.

W.O.: It sounds like you're having too much fun!

F.P.L.: I have a lot of fun. I also have a studio. I'm a painter. So I paint a lot. I do a lot of portrait painting. I have a good life. I have a great life. I really do. Some of my paintings are going to be on prayer cards and they are going to be out and printed soon. That's kind of exciting.

W.O.: But then you'll go down and hear Confessions today?

F.P.L.: Yes . . . 4:00 to 6:00.

W.O.: What do you give out to real bad guys like me?

F.P.L.: You know . . . I don't usually do the penance thing that much. I would say things to people more practical . . . if somebody is fighting with their wife a lot I would say, for your penance go buy her some flowers or tell her you love her.

W.O.: Father . . . we've admired your Franciscan colleagues for many years. A lot of friends of this station—Mario Cuomo and others, Peter Johnson Jr., the famous lawyer and Fox News host, among them—have great regard for what you do. I was educated by the Jesuits. What's the difference between the Jesuits and the Franciscans?

F.P.L.: Oh, there's a lot. We don't have enough time, Mr. O'Shaughnessy. The Jesuits are wonderful. I love the Jesuits too! Let's just say they're "brainy."

W.O.: I was just going to use that word. They teach the kings and princes.

F.P.L.: Exactly.

W.O.: Look what became of me thanks to a Jesuit high school! Were you insulted when I said the Franciscans were a little crazy?

F.P.L.: We're kind of known for being crazy! No . . . that's true. And for having fun. The Franciscans are kind of gettin' down with the people and having *fun*.

W.O.: Like Francis, I guess. You even have your own prayer, don't you?

F.P.L.: Yes, we do:

Lord, make me an instrument of your peace,
Where there is hatred, let me sow love;
Where there is injury, pardon;
Where there is doubt, faith;
Where there is despair, hope;
Where there is darkness, light;
Where there is sadness, joy.
O Divine Master,
grant that I may not so much seek to be consoled,
as to console;
to be understood, as to understand;
to be loved, as to love.
For it is in giving that we receive.
It is in pardoning that we are pardoned,
and it is in dying that we are born to Eternal Life.
Amen.

It is kind of in that idea that we find God . . . not so much in seeking for ourselves, but doing for *others* . . . which is basically the hope and prayer and counsel of Saint Francis.

Bishop Joseph Sullivan

Jimmy Breslin and Mario Cuomo talked about this guy for years. Bishop Joe Sullivan was a streetwise pastor based in Brooklyn and was revered by the denizens of that borough. He was also universally respected by his fellow bishops. But the conventional wisdom was that the outspoken prelate would never make cardinal. I'm sure that pleased him. Bishop Sullivan was a street prelate. I think he was a marvelous man. February 14, 2003.

WILLIAM O'SHAUGHNESSY: Ladies and gentlemen, on this winter day, storm clouds loom on the horizon, the nation hovers on the brink of war, and we're fortunate to have with us a legendary bishop from a neighboring diocese. I've heard about this man for years. My colleagues in the public press don't merely admire him; they revere him. He is an outspoken auxiliary bishop and head of their "trade association." He's actually president of the Auxiliary Bishops Group. Let's welcome, from the diocese of Brooklyn, Bishop Joseph Sullivan. I come recommended to your door, Excellency, by Mario Cuomo and the great Jimmy Breslin himself. You hang out with some very unsavory types, bishop.

BISHOP JOSEPH SULLIVAN: Well, we had the opportunity to meet Mario a long time ago, when he was governor of New York state. He was always an articulate, bright defender of justice. To me, he moved the Church, and the government, in the direction of what Catholics should be concerned about: the poorest in society, the disenfranchised. And I always felt Mario Cuomo tried to make government serve the needs of all the people, especially the ones left out.

w.o.: Bishop Sullivan, Governor Cuomo accused you of being maybe not the best politician in the hierarchy but a splendid "working" priest and a great administrator.

j.s.: I certainly don't want to be a politician, Bill. I don't aspire to that, because I don't think I have the skills for it. I do happen to have an admiration for people in public service, and I personally believe, and have often said this to many elected officials—many not of our own faith—that the politician's role is very much like that of a parish priest. You're there at the first line with people—you're in between people, you get hit from both sides, but you have the experience of knowing the needs of people, articulated not solely by statistics and data but by the experience of people who are trying to live a decent life. While we don't always agree with certain positions of politicians, nevertheless I believe their calling is noble. And most of the people I know work as hard as or harder than anybody else I know.

w.o.: Bishop, another fan of yours is Bishop James McCarthy, who is beloved in my home heath, and respected, and greatly missed.

j.s.: Well, we love him, too. Bishop McCarthy is what you really look for in a priest: a man of great empathy and great sympathy, with personal skills and a caring and capacity for people. He served Cardinal O'Connor in New York City. It's tragic, his situation. But to me, he's a dear friend.

w.o.: Bishop, what of the future of your Church, founded by that carpenter's son from Nazareth? It isn't going through a good patch right now.

j.s.: From history, the Church has gone through a lot of tough times, and some of it of their own making. We've obviously had some people at the highest offices of the Church who did not live up to the Church's ethics or values. We've had outside critics who have pointed out our faults. And the Second Vatican Council made very clear that the *Ecclesia Semper Reformanda* said the Church was always in the process of being reformed and renewed. So yeah, we're going through a hard time, a time, quite frankly, that doesn't come from outside, but inside. And these are always the most difficult things for any organization, particularly a religious organization, when the very standards of ethics that we uphold have been violated by our most trusted members, the clergy. So we have done terrible damage to the image. Even though the percentages are small, the numbers of abused are large, relatively speaking. And for my money, it's going to take a long time to get through this. I don't think the hurt or humiliation we've got at the present time ought to deter us from staying the course, speaking up for the right issues, and advocating for the right causes. If we're going to really broadcast who we are and what our mission is, we have to be like Jesus, who went out among the poor and tried to bring them in. I think we will work through this, and I don't think we should try and get over it and put it behind us. I think in some ways we should be chastened by what happened so that we understand that we are held to a high standard—and we have to live up to that standard. If we don't, we damage what I think is one of the strongest and most powerful presences: the people of God in the Church, trying to live the Christian life and having a profound influence on making this a better society and a better world. So yes, we are having a hard time, and we don't deny it, and we have done wrong and we have to admit it and make our penitence. But I think it should not deter us from speaking out on the war or the death penalty or the unborn. I think the Church still has to be a voice that strives for more credibility because of our behavior, but we should not give up the commitment to the values and the ideals of Jesus.

w.o.: Bishop Joe Sullivan, has your Church really been damaged?

j.s.: Enormously. And I think we know that ourselves. People don't say that very directly. I've got a lot of sympathy, sitting in the subway, from people, not necessarily Catholic people, who tell me they have hope. Jesus said, "Let he who is without sin cast the first stone." I don't think we are without sin, and we're not looking to blame other people for our problems.

w.o.: Did I hear you say you ride the subway? I thought bishops rode around in big cars.

j.s.: To me, the best way to get around in New York is on the subways. I even have a senior pass! The subways are remarkable. We couldn't exist in this city without them.

w.o.: Didn't you suggest, in a weak moment, that some of your bishops should resign? And didn't you get clobbered for it?

j.s.: It wasn't a weak moment, Bill. I met with a group of honest, faithful Catholics, about fifty people, and they said that without some resignations, the Dallas meeting would be a failure. I happen to believe that's true. We have one resignation of a senior cardinal, and I believe Cardinal Law felt he had a responsibility to turn things around. He felt he was the cause of much of the problem. I wrote to the president of the Bishops' Conference that there should have been a number of resignations, as symbolic of the fact that we understood that we all share the problem. Most bishops tried to do the best they could to improve the situation. There is no group of men where there's greater charity, even though we have serious differences among ourselves at times on issues and how to handle them. I think they did wrong, but I think the wrong was not malevolent. For the most part they are bright, they're good—and they did wrong. The ironic thing is that, having come out, the greatest scandal was not that there were delinquencies but that we didn't act appropriately.

w.o.: You have suggested there's no quick fix to this, and the Church shouldn't try to find one. How, then, can it be dealt with so that the lay public thinks you're handling it well?

j.s.: This is a crisis, but it's also an opportunity to be a more open Church, a more transparent Church. We ought to look for better ways to be inclusive of lay leadership and allow participation in the decision-making of the Church. We shouldn't be afraid of that. That's what the council talked about when it was suggested that we have parish councils. We have a Catholic constituency that is better educated than any Catholic community in the world.

w.o.: I hear the sounds of the city behind you in Brooklyn this morning. Mario Cuomo, your admirer, the former governor, says we all sin seven times, seven times, seven times a day. Have you used up your seven today?

j.s.: Well, it's still early, Bill! I got a long time to go and I'm not sure it would only be seven by the end of the day.

w.o.: War clouds are on the horizon. Mario Cuomo was here in Westchester last night saying we ought to buy them off and cut a deal with Saddam. What is your opinion of the president of the United States? How is *he* handling this?

J.S.: I'm not sure we should reveal who we voted for, but I'm a Democrat. And it's not that I vote straight party lines, but I think in many ways I see an admirable performance by President Bush. The three speeches he's given were masterful in the articulation of where he stands. My concern is he is playing the hard game. He wants to put what he calls "spine" into the UN resolutions. In my mind, war should always be only a last resort. And while I'd love to believe the president is really playing the hard policeman as a way of bringing them to the table and bringing about reform, my suspicion is that if he's successful and we never have to go to war, he will have done an admirable job. If it really is only a matter of posturing—and the issue is no longer a matter of *if* but *when*, and we're going to go to war—then I'm unhappy with that kind of direction. Today the Holy Father is meeting with Tariq Aziz from Iraq. And the Holy Father, I think, in his weakened condition physically but with his spiritual and moral condition at the height of his powers, has a voice and a soundness. War should always be a last resort, and my hope is that we never go to war and that we find a way. I am not as clever as Mario Cuomo to figure out what deal you're trying to make. But for my money, there is no way we want to see unleashed biological weapons or nuclear weapons from Iraq and North Korea. It's a very dangerous time, and I have great sensitivity to the incredible power and pressure placed on the president at this moment in history. I am personally an admirer of Colin Powell. Any time I've heard him speak, I find his voice to be one of sanity and reason, and I think in some ways he's brought the administration along in trying to prevent war.

W.O.: Do I hear the street bishop, the bishop of the poor, the idol of types like Breslin, saying nice things about this pope who is supposed to have appointed a lot of conservative guys?

J.S.: Anyone who has a major responsibility, like the president of the United States or the pope—one the spiritual leader and the other with the most powerful position in the world—to have all the gifts is, to me, unrealistic. And so a good administrator tries to place around him the kind of people who balance their certain weaknesses. This pope, to me, is the great teacher, the great spiritual leader of the Church. He is a theologian and a philosopher.

W.O.: What would you change about him, Bishop?

J.S.: I would change the way some of the appointments have come, both at the Vatican itself—and I would also have perhaps looked for different criteria in who you will select as bishop.

W.O.: What about the whole notion of the gold and the gilt and pomp and circumstance and the rings? Do you wear a bishop's ring?

J.S.: Oh, yes, it's a symbol of the office. The ring I have is the design of the Cross, and it has on the top Alpha and Omega, which is the beginning and the end. It has the Baptismal, and the other is the Heart with the Scales of Justice: to live a life of charity and justice. For me the role of the bishop is to be a man who, in his office, is fully conscious of the call of his own baptism: to live a life of love and justice.

W.O.: Does it make you feel uncomfortable when I call you "Your Excellency"?

J.S.: I don't go for foreign titles, Bill! All my Jewish friends here in the city of New York still call me "Father Joe," because they feel comfortable with that.

W.O.: Do the teachings of your Jesus have any relevance now, in 2003, to all the chaos and mess in the world? It seems that families are under siege, nations, big corporations, the Holy Roman Church itself. How do the teachings of Jesus break through?

J.S.: The teachings are totally relevant. I heard Bernard Haring, the great Redemptionist theologian, say that Jesus was not a revolutionary. He was a *pro*-volutionary, meaning He meant to change the world going into the future in the most radical way: not by power, but by love.

W.O.: Bishop Sullivan, who prefers "Father Joe Sullivan," what about the new cardinal in the archdiocese of New York? Edward Cardinal Egan has replaced the beloved John Cardinal O'Connor. It seems the O'Connor people haven't quite accepted him yet.

J.S.: Every man is different, and he's been given an enormous responsibility. He faced unusual challenges, very serious financial problems in the archdiocese. He has his own style and his own way of doing things. He's trying in his own way, according to his own life and his own personality. He's not John O'Connor in terms of being in the public forum, and I don't think he intends to be. He's a bright and gifted man, and a good man and he's trying. None of us are going to win everyone's approval. I think Cardinal Egan is sincerely doing what he thinks is best.

w.o.: Very respectfully, do bishops ever get confused? And if so, what is your killer prayer—say, in the middle of the night? Who better to ask than you?

J.S.: When I pray, it's basically: "Praise, honor, and glory to God the Father, the Son, and the Holy Spirit. Praise and thanksgiving to God, the Father and Creator. Praise and thanksgiving to the Son, the Redeemer, the Son of Mary. For your life, teaching, death, and resurrection. Praise and thanksgiving to the Holy Spirit. Sanctify us, source of light and love. Mother Mary, Father Joseph, and all you holy saints and angels, pray. And all of you holy saints and angels, pray that I may faithfully follow Jesus this day." That's personally what I say every day. You can't substitute for the Our Father and the Hail Mary, but that's the prayer I pray to be faithful.

w.o.: Do you think Jesus listens to all that, or are those just words?

J.S.: I think God hears all sinners, and I love the thing in the Divine Office which says, "God looks upon all as sinners that He may have mercy on them."

w.o.: But most of us are still a little uneasy and confused. People go to church and sometimes they don't feel there's anything happening there. The Church, we know, is flawed. In fact, what kind of God would pick as the first pope a guy he knew would betray him three times?

J.S.: When Jesus picked Peter—that actually should make us very conscious today. When we look at even the concept of zero tolerance in the Church, I understand with deep compassion, I think we've done terrible harm to many victims. But the notion of zero tolerance is a political idea—it's not a religious one. Seventy times seven, that's how often you should forgive.

[167]

w.o.: On the issue that so divides the Church and society—abortion. Where is Bishop Sullivan on that?

j.s.: To me, life is the great gift of God. To the believer, to a person of faith, life is a gift. And from the point of view of Church doctrine, we believe that life begins at the very beginning of the fertilization of the egg, so that's the process of human life. No, we cannot discover when human life actually begins. But we do know that the genetic code is placed at the very fertilization, the very implantation. But the reality, to me, is that abortion is a horrendous act. The whole Christian way of life is that you live for others. The whole thing about abortion is that you live for yourself, and you're willing to take the life of another. I would think that at least we should be able to get into public dialogue this realization and that we would agree that when the signs of humanity exist, that's probably as far as we'll ever be able to get— there is human life there. Just as we do when we test for signs of death—the respiratory system fails, or the heart no longer beats— that, to me, is a sign of death. We should be able to protect people from that point on in a pluralistic culture where there are differences. I'm happy that abortion is such a contentious issue in this society. I think it basically is around the fundamental issue of what's really important.

w.o.: Bishop Sullivan, finally—and you've been so generous with us on this winter day—one of your colleagues across the river in New Jersey said, "No more eulogies! They're not funny, they're embarrassing , we'll handle it!" How do you feel about eulogies?

j.s.: I happen to like John Meyer, the bishop. I was with him on retreat this past January. But there are obviously differences on that. I've been to some of the 9/11 funerals and I was subjected to nine or ten different eulogies. I think that's too much. But with the tragedy, why would you want to limit that? People should be prepared. It should be well done and people shouldn't do that just off the top of their head. But I would never stop eulogies. On the occasions that are most sacred to people, on their weddings, on their day of death when they're mourning a loved one, you should make every accommodation to try to help. I think there are some disciplines required, but I could never see banning a eulogy.

w.o.: When someone climbs up there for Joseph Sullivan, bishop of the Roman Church, what do you want them to say?

j.s.: "God have mercy on his soul! He was a sinner like the rest of us, and he asked forgiveness for all of it."

Timothy Cardinal Dolan, Archbishop of New York

New York's Timothy Cardinal Dolan is a sheer, pure, natural force. I love the guy and interviewed him on February 22, 2016.

WILLIAM O'SHAUGHNESSY: Timothy Cardinal Dolan, Eminence, you honor us with your presence.

CARDINAL DOLAN: Bill, you honor me with the invitation. And it's good to be with you. You are a legend, you know. Although this is my first visit to your beautiful, modern station. I know you were close to Cardinal O'Connor—he was here some years ago—and you've written about him and would introduce him to your friends and at dinners very often. I mean, you're like Georgie Jessel! And you were kind enough when I got to New York to send me some of your excellent books. I'm kind of awed to be with you.

W.O.: Thank you, Eminence. Your imprimatur means a great deal to me. Speaking of which—you know, *you're* like a rock star, if you'll forgive me, the way you walked into the station only to be met with photographers, microphones, and television cameras.

C.D.: I thank you for saying that. I've never been called that before. Now you know Saint Peter was called "The Rock." Are you comparing me to Saint Peter, then? I don't mind being compared to a saint, but I don't know about a rock star.

W.O.: Eminence, we read in the paper and we know you give many eulogies. You pray over people who go to another and, we're sure, a better world. But you're always in a great mood! How the hell do you do it?

C.D.: Have you ever heard of Guinness Stout? [laughter] No, it's your faith, it's your hope, right? It's especially *hope*, Bill.

Look what hope means: that we believe everything is in God's hands and that everything, *ultimately*, is going to work out for the good for those who believe. So even in moments of trial and adversity, tears and sorrows—yes, we don't want to deny them. But you know this isn't the last word. God has the last word, and God's last word is always life and light and goodness and eternal life. So why would you get down? Why would you get depressed? Maybe every once in a while, momentarily. But life's attitude would always be, be upbeat and hopeful.

w.o.: Cardinal Dolan, a friend of yours of sainted memory—one Mario Matthew Cuomo—said he prayed for "sureness." You seem pretty sure of things.

c.d.: Well, I hope there's a confidence there. But you know what, Bill, there's also a wisdom—especially in our Catholic belief—that sometimes confidence comes in knowing that an absolute sureness and certainty you're not always going to have. And sometimes there's an ambivalence, sometimes there are reasons to be afraid, and you stare them in the eyes and you just say, "I know they are out there, but darn it, I am confident!" Be silent, be calm, be confident. The Bible tells us, "Be not afraid, I'm with you!" If you believe that, Bill, think of what we can do. There's nothing we *can't* do with Him.

w.o.: Cardinal Dolan, Your Eminence, you're not only possessed of a great personality but, if you'll allow me, you're also a hell of a writer! You write these gorgeous columns in *Catholic New York*. And what's your slogan, your motto, right across the top of the column?

c.d.: Oh, you know what it is: *To Whom Should We Go?* See, Bill, we bishops—when you're made a bishop they say to you—and you don't have much time to decide—what will your *motto* be? And you've got to choose a Latin phrase—a phrase in the Bible in Latin. And I said, "What do you mean?" to the cardinal who told me the Holy Father wanted me to be bishop.

He said, "What's one of your favorite phrases in the Bible?" And I had to think for but a minute and said, "Well, when Saint Peter said to Jesus, 'Lord, to whom shall we go? You have the words of everlasting life.' To whom shall we go? *Ad quem ibimus*? Can we use that?" He said, "You bet!" And I got it as my motto.

W.O.: Eminence, speaking of a rock star—the pope, the bishop of Rome, you guys had a wonderful visit.

C.D.: Did we ever!

W.O.: Tell us something we haven't heard—that we don't know about him.

C.D.: First of all, he was happy to admit he didn't know too much about New York. So the whole time we're stuck in the back of that tiny Fiat, he's asking me questions—as he's waving to the people— about New York. And what fascinates people about Manhattan, except the huge skyscrapers, right? So as we're driving down one of the streets, he says, "Timothy"—he and my mom can call me by my first name!—"look at that! What is that monument?" I said, "Holy Father, that's an apartment building!" [laughter] He said, "Oh my!" and it dawned on him that's maybe the way New Yorkers live!

W.O.: So you had a good time?

C.D.: We did, indeed, you bet!

W.O.: Do you think his trip was successful?

C.D.: Well, I know *he* thought it was successful, and I sure do. And when I saw him later—I had to spend three weeks in Rome for the Synod on Marriage and Family—and when we had a couple of minutes to chat, he said, "You Americans are so friendly."

And he said he was "overwhelmed by the enthusiasm of my reception." Now, Bill, at first, I was startled by that, but then it dawned on me, what's the caricature of us Americans beyond our shores? The rest of the world thinks we're pagans, we're materialists. We hate religion; we don't like God. We know different. Americans are deeply religious and believers. There are churches all over. But a European or South American has this caricature, and when he came here and saw this exuberant reception and welcome, it moved him very much. And he said, "My Lord, this is America, and they're open to the Word; they're open to the Message. They're open to the Gospel. They're open to me!" And I think that moved him.

W.O.: Your Eminence, thank you for being with us today.

C.D.: Invite me back, will you, Bill? And don't forget, I hope I can have *you* on *my* radio program on Sirius XM to talk about that book on Mario Cuomo, which we all await.

W.O.: Sir, here's one more—and this is the one where I probably shouldn't do another thirty seconds, but as I mercifully yield—what about the *political* scene here? Will I lose you forever if I ask you to comment on the Republicans and Democrats? You haven't got a horse in the race, have you?

C.D.: No, I don't. [laughter] But I am *really* interested in politics. I don't know if you knew that I did my graduate work in American history, so I'm a historian of politics. I follow it closely. But I don't allow myself to get tangled up in the details. Let me just say that every morning I've been lighting a candle in front of Saint Jude [laughter] at Saint Patrick's! There would seem to be a lot of political uncertainty, and I pray we'll soon bring about some type of "clarity" in the political scene.

W.O.: Mario Cuomo, Eminence, would have been crazy—over the moon—about this pope. But I'm going to reveal something you may not know. He was rooting for *you* for that job!

C.D.: You're kidding?

W.O.: No, I'm not kidding.

C.D.: Well, how did he win *three* terms, and I didn't get *one*! [laughter]

W.O.: Sir, you honor us.

C.D.: You honor us, Bill. God bless you and your radio stations and their listeners, particularly those who are struggling. Know that the Lord is with you, and may these beautiful airwaves carry the Lord's blessing through all who are privileged to work for this station—especially Father Chris Monturo, your newest talk-show host.

Dr. Christopher Comfort,
Medical Director, Calvary Hospital

Calvary Hospital in the Bronx, which is run by Frank Calamari,
a highly regarded healthcare executive, does the Lord's work
in the Bronx when life turns sad and difficult and the end is near.
We spoke with Calvary's brilliant medical director, Dr. Christopher
Comfort. December 11, 2012.

"Dying is something you have to do all by yourself. There are no cohorts, no accomplices, no *compadres* . . . it's a solo act."

WILLIAM O'SHAUGHNESSY: For the next fifty minutes while we're in your keeping . . . a very tricky subject. I'm not sure it's the cheeriest, happy-go-lucky topic to be talking about in the countdown to Christmas, but it's to be dealt with—sooner or later for all of us, I expect. Our special guest is the medical director of Calvary Hospital in the Bronx. His name . . . listen to this . . . is Dr. Christopher Comfort. You're aptly named, sir.

DR. CHRISTOPHER COMFORT: Mr. O'Shaughnessy, thanks for having us. I guess it's unusual, the work I do, working at a place that takes care of loved ones who are dying and they do come to us, I guess, for comfort.

W.O.: Doctor Comfort, we've heard about Calvary over the years . . . a palliative care place. And what does the word "palliative" mean?

C.C.: Calvary is fairly unusual. It is the only place quite like it in the country. It's a hospital . . . a place where people come very, very ill . . . usually at the end of life requiring very sophisticated kind of care, not with the intent of cure, but with the intent of keeping them comfortable until their very last days. And I think in some ways that defines what "palliative" is all about. It's a new term in medicine—"palliative" comes from a strange derivation of Latin . . . meaning to cover or shadow. The thinking is that no longer is there the possibility of a cure of illness or disease, but what we do is cover up those symptoms that are distressing to individuals. We deal with the suffering individuals go through, either during the last stages of their illness or perhaps even before that. It's a new discipline because it also says in addition to symptom control or taking care of difficult, egregious symptoms, we also include loved ones in the care.

w.o.: Doctor . . . you've been at this for seventeen years. Do you ever go home drained? You're a Westchester guy. You were in the Bronx as a regular general practitioner. How did you get over to Calvary full time? You're now the medical director. . . .

c.c.: I was involved with Calvary while in practice. I used the facility for the excellent care of some of my patients and slowly made the migration to work at the institution including directing the medical program. I had the honor of working with some wonderful people . . . Frank Calamari who is the president of the hospital . . . Dr. Michael Brescia, who began this work some fifty years ago, a real pioneer in the concept and implementation of palliative care. So for me it was a transition that really was an honor not only for the patients I've been able to work with, but the professionals I've been able to associate with.

w.o.: And what about Dr. Brescia . . . he's a legendary guy . . . been there for a hundred years.

c.c.: He's an amazing individual. In fact, the history is almost a Bronx/Westchester story in terms of Dr. Brescia. His beginnings were actually in the Bronx VA program. And, in fact, his real claim to fame is not starting a world-famous program in terms of palliation. He and Jack Cimino, who was a compatriot of his, actually developed and implemented the arteriovenous shunt, which is the access device used by every individual on dialysis. Fifty years ago he and Jack developed the technology. It revolutionized dialysis for literally the whole world. This is Dr. Brescia, who then, after developing that, said he needed to move on to something I guess he thought had even more meaning. And so he came and

[175]

worked in the South Bronx with a group of nuns and established the medical program at Calvary that has grown into what it is today.

w.o.: Is it a Catholic thing?

c.c.: It may be rooted in faith because the mission of the institution to take care of individuals in their last days is really a compassionate mission. And it is a mission begun 110 years ago actually out of the work of widows of the New York City Fire Department who began a program in Manhattan which in the 1930s and 1940s moved up to the Bronx. The archdiocese of New York has been involved in this work for years. And through both the Sisters of Faith and archdiocesan individuals the mission has grown through its infancy to a true medical program as it exists today.

w.o.: Cardinal O'Connor used to say he does bedpans. Did O'Connor come to your joint?

c.c.: We have had all the cardinals over the last fifty to sixty years come and actively participate. Some have come to witness what goes on. Some have come to actually participate. Some had loved ones who have come and died with us.

w.o.: Doctor, Calvary is right over the line. We're in New Rochelle, but our ravings are also going worldwide at the moment. I was down at Calvary the other day, a friend of ours—a very famous and beloved one: Judge Andy O'Rourke, the former Westchester county executive—is in your care and keeping. And it's in kind of a drodsome section of the Bronx. Almost a factory section. I've got to tell you, your building on the outside is not the greatest architecture I've ever seen. But inside . . . it's a magical place. It's wonderful. . . .

c.c.: We're in the East Bronx literally across the street from the Weiler Division of Einstein near Jacobi Hospital. Those of us in the medical field look at it as "hospital row" in the Bronx.

w.o.: But there sits Calvary . . . sort of apart. The other ones seem like big medical centers. Calvary is sort of . . . I've never seen a building like that.

c.c.: And I think it is symbolic of what it represents. It represents a place that *is* different. It *is* unique. It has a very special and very identifiable place in the medical community.

w.o.: Doctor . . . do you ever see miracles? Did you ever attend a miracle or witness one?

c.c.: There's no question. Miracles come in a variety of different forms. Miracles arrive with individuals who come extremely ill and actually get well and go home. For weeks . . . and maybe for months.

w.o.: You've seen it?

c.c.: Absolutely. Miracles happen with families that have been fractured or estranged for years and at a tragic time in the life of the family they come together to witness a very difficult event. And the healing that occurs for families is nothing short of a miracle.

w.o.: But when they come together like that . . . is it for real? Do you believe it?

c.c.: My view on it is that it is the last chance we have . . . the last chance for a family to come together with a loved one. It really is a sacred time for them.

w.o.: Do people in your care and keeping, when they hear they've got to go to Calvary . . . is that like a death sentence?

c.c.: The difficulty with the name Calvary is . . . yes . . . it is associated with the idea of dying patients.

w.o.: You're a Roman, right?

c.c.: Yes.

w.o.: So . . . Calvary . . . what was that all about?

c.c.: The story of Calvary is the name of the hill where Jesus was crucified. It is a place of salvation. I think we've changed the concept of it being a place of death to where it is a place where someone comes that is a stepping stone to what comes next. I know Dr. Brescia likes to talk about it as entry into a special vestibule. In fact it is the waiting room . . . or vestibule of Heaven. And I think for many of our patients who have my belief . . . or may not have my belief . . . it is truly a place where they await a better life, a better time for themselves.

w.o.: You're the physician, you take care of them and make them comfortable. Do they tell you their mistakes, their sins, their errors, their transgressions? Do they try and make a priest out of you?

C.C.: Most people actually have a wonderful gift they give me. They give me their story. Some of that has to do with mistakes. Some of it has to do with transitions . . . and some has to do with great joy that has occurred throughout their life.

W.O.: There's a calmness about you. Do you ever get crazy and excited and speeded up? You have a peaceful face, a nice countenance. It feels good being around you.

C.C.: Well . . . I think that's the way it should be.

W.O.: Do you ever get speeded up?

C.C.: Every once in a while.

W.O.: How do you calm down?

C.C.: I actually go upstairs to the patient floor, sit down, have a discussion, observe a family, and realize the great blessings I have . . . not only to have the things—health, intellect—I have, but to realize what I'm able to give.

W.O.: Does it make you feel better to see someone worse off than you are?

C.C.: I'm not sure it's exactly that, Bill. I think more it is the honor of being able to make a difference at such a difficult time with people.

W.O.: Do you get the family involved with the care of your patients?

C.C.: That's an excellent question. The family is important to us. The question is how does that really happen? It really happens in two ways. One is that we strive to actually involve the family in much of the actual hands-on things in terms of care more than just educating families about what is going on . . . more than just explaining the time course that may go on. But we actively involve the family and invite them to involvement in what's going on . . . for choices of medications . . . and inviting families for activities. We actually have very extensive recreation therapy programs where patients who may be quite ill involve themselves in activities such as arts and crafts, Bingo, where families get to participate and realize it might be the last time a family sits down with a loved one in a usual and normal social situation. More importantly, we really do feel that the experience is not limited to the patient themselves. A patient may die. I have not seen resurrection yet. I may be wrong, but I know that families, as they watch them go through what they go through, die as well. The difference is that the *family* does resurrect. And so we feel it is important for us to be involved in that process of resurrection that goes on with the family as they live through the reality of losing a loved one.

w.o.: Do you find families, Dr. Comfort, who just can't handle the whole thing?

c.c.: I think it is an immense burden to put on any family to have to watch the death of a loved one. I don't think it is different watching a child die or a parent . . . whether that parent is thirty years old or ninety years old. It's a difficult event in a family's life, and it is certainly important to make sure it is as bearable an experience as possible.

w.o.: Dr. Comfort, what is a perfect death? You just slip away? Mario Cuomo said to me once . . . you just swoon. What's a perfect death?

c.c.: I'm not sure I can define it for you . . . I'm not sure I've experienced or watched a perfect death. I know I have watched a lot of different ways for death to occur. I think the most important part and one of the things we strive for is to recognize if they're suffering and to relieve that suffering because that is the mission we have. We're not going to change the time course. But we can make a significant difference in making sure the suffering is treated.

w.o.: How many people are suffering down in Calvary as we speak?

c.c.: We have 225 patients we're taking care of right now.

w.o.: How many are in there because of cancer?

c.c.: About 80 percent of the patients we're taking care of have a primary diagnosis of cancer.

w.o.: Do you take AIDS patients?

c.c.: We take other diagnoses so we take patients who have diagnoses such as AIDS, also end-stage cardiac disease or end-stage lung disease. The care of those patients is very similar to the kinds of care necessary for the treatment of cancer patients.

w.o.: Doctor, you said you will counsel with the family about the kind of medication. What if someone says . . . look, I know the hand I've been dealt, I'm here. But I would like to stay lucid. I'd like to think and be as productive as I can be lying here in this bed. I don't want you to zonk me out. You don't, in that case, just keep pumping them with feel-good stuff, do you?

C.C.: You know, it's interesting to look at that question because it's excellent. The purpose of the treatment we give is to maintain the integrity and dignity of the individual as long as it can be maintained. And that includes maintaining the awareness and thinking and the communicating capacity of that loved one. That time, as you know, is a special time for both patient and family. So it is extremely important to respect not just the wishes of the patient who might not want to have a grogginess or sedation related to medication, but realizing we strive for every patient to have good, meaningful time with loved ones.

W.O.: Do you ever see anybody come in there with a hip flask? Can you have a little cocktail?

C.C.: We actually have a "Friday Night Cocktail" and we have volunteers who go around on Friday night to the patient rooms. . . .

W.O.: You can have an Absolut?

C.C.: Those who have the doctor's permission to have a stiff one on Friday are offered that.

W.O.: Who started this? Frank Calamari, the boss man? Does he know you do this?

C.C.: It happened long before him, I'm sure.

W.O.: You know, I'm sort of figuring this out that Calvary is not such a heavy, heavy "what hangs over" place. Life goes on it seems. . . .

C.C.: This is where life continues. In fact, I've often thought the difficulty is not dying. The difficulty is the fear of what will happen as you lead up to dying. So our concept is very simple. Calvary is a place where the prognosis or event may occur, but it is also a place where we allow life to continue as long as it can continue and the meaningful things that can be done during that time are maintained.

W.O.: You know . . . you are more articulate than a lot of priests I know. Do you have guys with Roman collars walking along your halls?

C.C.: We actually have about twenty-five full-time pastoral care staff who take care of patients. Not only Roman collars, but we have a significant number of all religious persuasions.

w.o.: Do you have a rabbi on your staff?

c.c.: We have two.

w.o.: How about Muslims? Do you have any Muslim patients?

c.c.: In fact, we do. It's amazing to look at different ethnic groups and realize each of us as communities deals with life and with death differently. The practices of a Hindu . . . a Muslim . . . a Jewish individual . . . or a Catholic . . . there are some similarities. But there are some nuances, some differences in terms of both beliefs and the way individuals go through the experience of illness.

w.o.: What is the best thing a friend can do if somebody is at the end of his or her life? Do you say . . . "You're going to be all right"? "You're going to be out of here soon". . . ?

c.c.: We've learned . . . and it's been painful. But we've learned you don't make promises you can't keep. At a time when people are quite ill . . . and patients suffer, that is not the time for a promise to be made, and those of us in the medical profession often do that. Let me give you an example: If you had the misfortune of having to accompany a loved one to a doctor's office for a visit and bad news is given . . . the doctor leans over and says, "I'm sorry, sir . . . but I have to tell you you've got lung cancer" and you who are merely accompanying them are sad and begin to cry. It's not uncommon for the doctor to lean in and say, it will be all right. The problem is for you at that point and time and the meaning of that experience, to know and accept that it's not going to be all right. In fact, your life and the life of the loved one are changed forever. So, my advice for family and friends is that the most important thing you can do is to simply witness. To witness . . . that is to be there. Be a physical presence. Be an emotional presence. And a spiritual presence, not to have any expectation that magically you can make anything better. But that it is enough to actually witness the event.

w.o.: It would appear, I would opine, that you're doing the Lord's work. Are you a pretty religious guy?

c.c.: Not really . . . I have a belief system in making sure suffering is relieved. I have a belief system in making sure attention is paid to the needs of loved ones around a dying patient. But I make no firm promises regarding what comes thereafter. That is certainly an individual perspective.

w.o.: Nobody knows . . . ?

c.c.: No one knows.

w.o.: Dr. Comfort . . . do you tell people, "You've got three days" or "You've got a month"? Or "You've got six weeks"?

c.c.: Well, it's kind of interesting to look at the accuracy of physicians in determining prognosis.

w.o.: Can you tell?

c.c.: I can't. Having done this work for an extensive period of time, I can clearly identify decline in individuals so there is an expectation of dying let's say within a twenty-four-hour period of time. I think most physicians are pretty accurate with that. But past that, when you get to two weeks. Or you've got six weeks or six months . . . it's very, very difficult for the physician.

w.o.: But when they try and pin you down . . . what do you tell them? "How long have I got, Doc?" How many times have you been asked that?

c.c.: Probably thousands.

w.o.: What do you tell them?

c.c.: I tell them it could be a short period of time. It could be a long period of time. But I guarantee you, I'll be here with you through the whole process.

w.o.: You say you're not religious. I don't believe you. Not for a minute.

c.c.: Well, I think I'm spiritual. And I think Calvary is spiritual. And I think this is important because the patients we take care of and those we minister to, some may be Catholic, some Christian, some Jewish, some Hindu, some Muslim, and the common experience for that is not a particular religious belief, but it is the spiritual nature of what goes on.

w.o.: How do you get through to the patients the realization that they may never be leaving the hospital?

c.c.: That's a very, very good question. Let me take it from a couple of perspectives. One I don't think people have thought about is that sometimes the experience of advanced illness or severe illness is so difficult for the patient that it is a relief for them to know they will be taken care of and they will not suffer and the last thing on their mind is the idea of being home or being in a hospital. It is being taken care of. Secondly, and it is a sad kind of commentary on the way we take care of patients these days—and this isn't so much a medical issue, this is a social issue. As we decline, as we get sicker, many times it becomes impossible for the care of the patient at home because the way things go here in our country, the burden of the care falls upon family. And there are many, many people who don't have either involved families or a sophisticated enough structure where they can maintain themselves at home.

It's an amazing thing . . . when you think about one hundred years ago all of us would have said to that question—I've seen it. And I see it all the time. Because death and dying were a usual part of life. Now, it is something sequestered and something separated from our experience. I do teaching of medical students and residents, and I'll ask medical students . . . have you seen someone die? And they will tell me they never have.

w.o.: There's an old line . . . I used to attribute this to Jimmy Cannon, the great Hearst sportswriter, or the great Breslin himself. But it may have been Pete Hamill: Dying is something you have to do all by yourself. There are no cohorts, no accomplices, no *compadres* . . . it's a solo act.

c.c.: It is also a process. It is like birth, isn't it? Out you come and you're alone as you go through what is a difficult process. I don't remember the process myself. But it's clear the final goodbye . . . the final exit is an exit that has to be accomplished alone.

w.o.: Dr. Comfort . . . I asked you this in one form earlier but I want to have another whack at it. You've been at this seventeen years. You've got a couple of hundred patients in your care and keeping at any hour of the day or night. Have you become sort of inured to suffering, pain, and death? Do you ever go home and say . . . this was a really tough day? Or do you ever become attached to the patient and say I lost one of my favorites?

c.c.: I think we become attached to each of the patients because what happens is rather more than taking care of some 200 people or 225 people. We're taking care of this one person at a time and then this other person . . . and we're listening to that story. And we're experiencing that experience and it becomes *very* personal in terms of what goes on.

w.o.: John F. Kennedy Jr. once sat at that microphone quoting Mother Teresa: "You save them one by one by one . . ." But do they, I wonder, all go gentle into that good night? Or are some people just raging and fighting it off?

c.c.: There are some people who fight to the end. We fight with them. Because if it's important enough for them to fight, then it's important enough for us to stand by them in that last effort they make. Remember . . . it's how life continues. Not how I define how it continues. But it's how that life really does continue.

w.o.: So . . . you've got the fighters. Do you have the accepters?

c.c.: You've got both.

w.o.: Which are you going to be?

c.c.: I'm not sure . . . it will be interesting to see.

w.o.: Calvary Hospital in the Bronx. It's a great resource . . . and it's *ours*. Sooner or later.

Frank Gifford: "#16"

New York Giants legend Frank Gifford visited our studios many times. We had a friendship that went back many years, to the days when we hung out at Toots Shor's fabled saloon and I shared an office at the legendary WNEW with Frank's teammate and pal Kyle Rote.

Here are highlights from a WVOX interview with the great Gifford when he last visited the station a few months before his passing on August 9, 2015.

RE: HIGH SCHOOL

"I was a 'woodshop major' in Bakersfield High School when the coach, Homer Beatty, decided he would make a football player out of me."

ON HIS FIRST GAME IN HIGH SCHOOL

"I was standing out at Griffiths Stadium in Bakersfield that Friday night. It looked like the LA Coliseum to me. It was against Covina, and I was so scared. I don't even remember if we won the game."

"I never knew a rich kid who played football. If they weren't playing football back in Bakersfield, they would have been in the oil fields."

RE: COLLEGE

"I literally wound up on a 'Trojan horse' at USC."

RE: SIGNING BONUS

"My first contract with the New York Giants was $8,000. And my wife was in the hospital at the time. And I needed an extra $200 to get her out. I got Mara up $200. And that's how I got my signing bonus, from Wellington Mara: $200!"

RE: WELLINGTON MARA

"Wellington Mara delivered my first contract to me. Years later, when I went into the Pro Football Hall of Fame, he was my speaker. And when *he* went in, he asked me if I could speak for *him*."

RE: EARLY PRO FOOTBALL

"We were there when the Maras were struggling. They paid $2,500 for the Giants franchise. Wellington bought it because Tim Rooney's father—Art Rooney of the Pittsburgh Steelers fame—thought this would be a good deal.

"In 1953, my second year, we weren't even sure we were going to get paid. We heard they were going bankrupt, and I was wondering how I was going to get back to Los Angeles with my wife."

RE: THE 1958 CHAMPIONSHIP GAME

"It was the first game to be televised live across the country. The incredible, increasing audience was growing as we went into overtime for the first time ever. That was the real birth of pro football on television."

RE: HIS SON CODY PLAYING FOOTBALL

"I made a judgment that Cody was not going to play football at USC. He had committed to go to the film school there. He's 6'4" and 220 pounds, but I didn't want him to play."

RE: CONCUSSIONS

"Is there danger playing pro football? Yeah! And a lot of it! But driving to the game is probably a helluva lot worse than going out on the field."

RE: UNIONS (GIFFORD HELPED SET UP THE PLAYERS UNION)

"We were organizing because we were playing five exhibition games and not getting paid for them. Our first demand was for $25 a week and 'laundry money.' We had to clean our own uniforms.

"This is a great sport. It has problems. It has injuries, but it's a great sport. There should be some reasonability on either side to sit down and talk.

"I'm afraid future demands are going to get angry. And I think the NFL is headed in that direction. I wish they could reason it out."

RE: NEW GIANTS STADIUM

"There's nothing like going to a game at the new 'Giants' stadium, a beautiful facility—there is nothing better in the country. But Jerry Jones wouldn't like me saying that with the Cowboys."

William O'Shaughnessy on the Fred Dicker Radio Show

Fredric U. Dicker, the former state editor of the New York Post, *was for many years the controversial dean of the Albany press corps. In recent years, he's also hosted a daily radio show on WDGJ in the Capitol District, which is also carried on our own WVOX. The feisty Dicker, who is one of the brightest guys on air or in print, often turned the tables (and mic) on me. Here is one of our interviews from October 18, 2011.*

FRED DICKER: Our guest is a very well-known radio executive. He owns a powerful radio force in Westchester County, much more powerful than its 500 watts would suggest. He's an activist, writer, publisher, author of five books. He was recently talking about some remarkable "spontaneity" at the Columbus Day parade. Good morning, Brother Bill.

WILLIAM O'SHAUGHNESSY: I'm reporting today from Manhattan, Dicker.

F.D.: Is it true the March on Wall Street gang is heading for you, even now?

W.O.: No, I feel very safe because your shy, retiring colleague Cindy Adams dances overhead in my building, on the ceiling, near my bed, as the song goes.

F.D.: I know you're in that famous building down there. Let me just say that you're also the "Westchester Bureau Chief" of the *New York Post and* of this Talk 1300 radio show. I understand you attended the parade and saw the governor, Andrew Cuomo. You say the governor got quite a response.

W.O.: It was, as you know, a *big* weekend for parades. Columbus Day yesterday. And Sunday there was the Hispanic parade, and it was wonderful, perhaps even *more* fun and vibrant. But the

[188]

Columbus Day parade is always very *special*. And it stepped off on what I guess the Brits would call a perfectly brilliant Indian Summer day.

The parade moved up Fifth Avenue, and I thought I'd missed the governor. They had all the *carabinieri* and the nattily attired fire brigades direct from Italy, and the Italians, who love the uniforms, looked splendid. They wear them so well, and somebody told me last night at dinner that Armani designed many of those handsome uniforms.

And then came the governor.

Fred, I have seen, in that exact setting, Jack Kennedy, the great Nelson Rockefeller of sainted memory, and, of course, Mario Cuomo. I don't want to demean or lessen the moment and tell you Andrew "worked" the crowd. Only that there was a vast outpouring of love and respect and admiration for the governor, from *both* sides of the street. Andrew just seemed to warm to the crowd. And the *crowd* warmed to *him*. He looked terrific! He has so much charisma, it surprised even me. I mean, I've always liked Andrew because he is his father's *son*.

F.D.: Well, you were very close to Mario Cuomo.

W.O.: Well, I *admire* Mario. And I do to this day, to this very moment. And I've watched Andrew grow in wisdom and age. You, Fred, were really among the first to encourage Andrew and take him on his own. And every time I see him, he gets better.

F.D.: I always thought he was very able. I heard there were some "Andrew for President" cheers.

W.O.: I heard some of that. Yes. I also know he saw a white-haired Irishman and said, "Are *you* Italian?"

F.D.: How did you happen to be there, Bill? Do you go to a lot of the parades?

W.O.: You want the truth? I went there hoping to see him. I also have a lot of friends in that parade, from Westchester: the Casa Calabria, my friend Cavalieri Dom Procopio, and our county executive Rob Astorino.

F.D.: Have you had a chance to form an opinion about the Occupy Wall Street people?

W.O.: Fred, I'm watching it like your colleagues at the *Post* and Talk 1300. But I think Mayor Bloomberg is taking exactly the right tone; we're not going to stun gun you or mace you as long as you don't break any *laws*.

F.D.: Sleeping in a park breaks the law. Littering is breaking the law—and there's a lot of that. In general, they've been well behaved. But there have been some incidents of defecating on a police car. So it hasn't been totally benign.

W.O.: Fred, it's a very tough thing. They seem to be tapping into a general resentment about the greed of Wall Street and the vulgarity of those extravagant bonuses. I know that the great Jacob Javits once famously said, "You either *believe* in the genius of the free enterprise system or you *don't*."

F.D.: What is this "greed of Wall Street" stuff? I mean, what they are complaining about are the *subsidies* from Bush and Obama. Why accept the premise of greed in Wall Street? There is greed among public employees. There is greed everywhere. It's human nature. Is that to be condemned?

W.O.: Fred, you and our friends at the *Post* have more knowledge and depth on this. But Mario Cuomo once said to a young man—probably a hedge fund guy—"You've made all the money in the world, more than you'll ever need. Now what are you going to do?"

And Walter Nelson Thayer, the big eastern establishment Republican, my former father-in-law, was quoted in the *Times*: "New York is littered with guys whose only *goal* is to *make money*; they almost never do!"

But again back to Andrew Cuomo. Here's a guy, a smart guy, who could have just set out to make money. Instead, he was drawn to public service. Hallelujah!

F.D.: He did make some money in the private sector.

W.O.: Nothin' wrong with that, Dicker.

F.D.: Thanks, Brother Bill.

Alfred F. Kelly Jr.

President and CEO, Super Bowl XLVIII Host Company,
February 27, 2014.

———————

Alfred F. Kelly Jr., now president of Visa, headquartered in Purchase, ran *Super Bowl XLVIII* in 2014, the very first outdoor, cold-weather grid-iron classic in N.F.L. history. He was a former top executive of American Express and as a young man had a very important post in the Reagan White House. We spoke of his Catholic faith, his friendship with Cardinal Dolan, and his Westchester family. Kelly has been a class act in every season.

Although the legendary sportswriter Jimmy Cannon once called sports "the toys of a nation," football, which resembles sanctioned violence (our Westchester neighbor Commissioner Roger Goodell will forgive me), has appeal for many of our neighbors. One hundred and twelve million watched the extravaganza hosted by Kelly and his NY/NJ Super Bowl associates.

We were flattered that just a few weeks after the big event, he came by his hometown station for this interview. We talked of many things, besides football. Al Kelly is quite a guy, as you will see.

WILLIAM O'SHAUGHNESSY: Good morning, Westchester. It's what the Brits would call a "brilliant day" here in our home heath of Westchester. For the next several minutes while we're in your care and keeping, we have someone I've been looking forward to interviewing for a long time. You've read about him in the public press. This is his home heath as well, New Rochelle. He grew up around here. He's an Iona guy. He was an elder of Iona College. He has enormous influence around that campus because he raises a lot of money for them. But in recent years he had a career change.

You may have known him as the president of a small, tiny, little company called American Express—Amex, the huge credit-card company—where he served for many years as president with our New Rochelle neighbor Ken Chenault, husband of Kathryn Chenault. His name is Alfred F. Kelly Jr. And recently—you must know this—he's been running the Super Bowl. Al Kelly, are you glad you did it?

AL KELLY: Good morning, Bill. It's a pleasure to be with you and the folks of Westchester County. I'm *delighted* I did it. It was a wonderful event for this region. Considering the fact that Super Bowls have been played for almost five decades and one-sixteenth of the National Football League is in this region and calls this region home, in my mind it was high time this great game for American sports came to the greatest area in America, and I think we put on a terrific show. This region has so much to offer. It was really my pleasure to really play a bit of a "maestro" role in bringing tens of thousands of people together to make it a success. But we're really pleased with the way it went.

w.o.: *Was* it a success, Al Kelly?

A.K.: I do believe it was, Bill, on *all* accounts. It was the most-watched television show in television history.

w.o.: How many people?

A.K.: 111.5 million people. It beat the Super Bowl of three years ago when the Giants beat the Patriots by a few points. One of the reasons it did so well on television, despite the fact it wasn't a terribly competitive game, was because we were able to create an atmosphere where this really was—in this area—almost like either the Giants or Jets, or *both*, were playing in it. And the reality is we had a 51 share in this market, where a typical Super Bowl where the Giants or Jets are *not* in would get a 30 share. And that's because we got the region fired up about this great opportunity. There was a 21 percent increase in the number of credentialed media that followed this game: 6,400 credentialed media came to the Super Bowl and Super Bowl week. One of the things I looked at from the very beginning—as did the Tisch, Mara, and Johnson families—was that we wanted to take this platform of the Super Bowl and make sure we did some good for the community. Typically, a host committee would struggle to raise a million dollars for a single project. We have raised almost $12 million, and we have initiated or completed or have in progress over fifty projects on both sides of the Hudson River, all aimed at school-age youth and facilities they use after school, in the evenings, on the weekends, and in the summers. We did a playground in White Plains, a brand-new playground from scratch. We have done community-center renovations. We put new ball fields in place. And these are things, Bill, that are going to last for decades. And my hope is that people are going to say that in 2014 the Super Bowl was played here and this field, this community center, this playground we are enjoying today—five, ten, fifteen years later—came about because of the Super Bowl being here. That "legacy" element is the most gratifying work we've done.

w.o.: Alfred Kelly Jr., you're working for the Maras, and I'm reminded that Wellington Mara, of sainted memory, sat right at that very microphone, several times. And also the Tischs and Woody Johnson of the Jets. How's that different from working for a board of directors of Amex, where once you presided?

A.K.: Well, interestingly enough, this is a job where I don't think I've ever had more bosses. New York–New Jersey Host Company is a company. In addition to being CEO, I was chairman of a board that had eight members on it. The owners couldn't be members of it because we were a not-for-profit organization, and the Giants and Jets are *for*-profit organizations. So we actually had an advisory committee, where I met with the owners once a month.

w.o.: Were they easy to deal with?

A.K.: They were terrific. I have to say, they were perfect bosses. They were there when I needed them. They largely left me to do my thing. We called upon them tremendously as far as appearances. I had them at many breakfasts and cocktail parties, and unless they were traveling, they would never say no. I couldn't have asked for more. I knew the Maras, and I knew John Tisch a bit. I didn't know the rest of the Tisch family, and I didn't know Woody Johnson before I got into this, and they really have been a real pleasure to deal with. Interestingly enough, John Tisch and Woody Johnson, who were the co-chairs of this, were both born in New Jersey and today live in Manhattan. And for them to share a New York–New Jersey Super Bowl was important to them personally because this was their home area, and the fact they were able to show off their terrific new stadium to the world also gave them a real sense of pride. And it is a beautiful facility they've built.

W.O.: Alfred Kelly Jr., head of the Super Bowl, do you think there will ever be another one around here?

A.K.: Obviously, it's one of the smallest, elitist clubs in the world, the thirty-two owners of the National Football League. They determine where the Super Bowls go. And as of the current bylaws in the League, (a) it can only be in a region where there is an NFL franchise, and (b), Bill, there is this rule that the commissioner allowed a one-time pass on which a Super Bowl can only be held in a region where there's an average temperature in February of at least 55 degrees. So, obviously, that was waived, even though we got pretty darn close to 55 degrees on February 2nd.

W.O.: You were bailed out by the weatherman. What if we had a blizzard? Would you be scrambling now to explain the weather?

A.K.: Well, from the beginning, two things I knew I couldn't control were the weather and who was going to play in the game and thus determine the competitiveness of the game. Despite the fact that a lot of people paid a lot of attention to the weather, I never really worried about it per se. I just made sure we were prepared. We had great cooperation from Governor Christie and Governor Cuomo and Mayor Bloomberg and then Mayor de Blasio, who came in and was incredibly supportive in his early days in office. We have great assets in this region. We know how to clear snow. In fact, both governors and the mayor were prepared to prioritize where the snow removal happened based upon the day of the week in Super Bowl week and what events were happening and where they were happening. Truthfully, Bill, it would have taken the wrong storm at exactly the wrong time to impact the game because typically, even in a blizzard, we have a period of eight to ten hours where we're paralyzed. But after that you could start to get it cleared out. There have been a couple of times this winter where it started to snow at

11:00 in the morning and it snowed until 10:00 at night. Obviously, that kind of day would have been a problem. But I invited Cardinal Dolan, a good friend of my wife, Peggy, and me, about six months before, and I gave him the assignment of *praying* for good weather. Unfortunately, the cardinal ultimately couldn't come to the game, but I think that if he's ever up for sainthood, I'll be able to say that he had a miracle by creating the best day in 2014 to date, including today, which was February 2nd.

w.o.: I just got a note from him this week. His Eminence will claim credit for this; you know how he operates!

a.k.: And he *should*. I'm happy to give it to him!

w.o.: His name is Alfred F. Kelly Jr. He's a Westchester guy, lives in Rye with his wife, Peggy. Didn't you two fall in love right in our back yard here?

a.k.: We did. I grew up in the Crestwood section of Yonkers. Peggy grew up in Port Chester. I actually met her at her senior prom at Holy Child where she was—W.O.: Was she with somebody else?

a.k.: She *was* with somebody else! I was a year older, a freshman at Iona College after four years at Iona Prep. She was going to Iona College, so I was introduced to her at the prom, and six months later, in December of 1977, I took her to an Iona College basketball game and that was our first date; and we dated for seven years. And September of last year, we were married for thirty years, so we've been together quite a while.

w.o.: And you have a *few* children?

a.k.: We do; we have five children. Our two boys are graduates of Iona Prep. Our two girls are graduates of the School of the Holy Child, where I happen to be chairman of the Board of Trustees. And believe it or not, we have this incredible gift of a fourth-grader who is ten years younger than our fourth child and seventeen years younger than our oldest child, and she is an absolute gift from the good Lord, and she keeps us as young as can be. She is a fourth-grader at Resurrection School in Rye.

w.o.: Al Kelly Jr., you're what I used to call a "Castle Irishman." It's a term of admiration; it's not a pejorative term. You remind me of another son of Westchester, Jim Comey. *He's* got five kids. And what does Comey do? He's head of the FBI! Is this a Roman Catholic thing, you've got to have five kids? Kelly and Comey? Or the Plunketts!

A.K.: I don't know. I'm the oldest of seven. We never really set out, when we were engaged or in our early years of marriage, with a particular number of children in mind. It is what it is. There was no plan for us vis-à-vis children. But we have five terrific kids. The older four have gone to Boston College, and we've had four BC graduates. Father Lahey, their president, told me our fourth-grader is already accepted into the class of 2026!

W.O.: So your faith—the Catholic faith of the Roman Church—means a lot to you?

A.K.: It does. My parents still live in the Crestwood section of Yonkers. My dad goes to Mass every single day at Annunciation in Crestwood. I can't quite be that loyal. It does mean a lot to me. I'm very fond of our current cardinal, and he has me extraordinarily involved in the Board of Trustees of Saint Joseph's Seminary. I am on the Finance Council of the archdiocese of New York. I'm the vice president of the New York Catholic Foundation. So he's a hard guy to say no to. I have a lot of faith in him and a lot of faith in our Church. It is an important part of my life.

W.O.: Al Kelly, who better to ask: What do you think of the new pope? I can't get enough of the guy.

A.K.: I do think he's been an incredible breath of fresh air. One of the challenges the Church has is that it has lost a great deal of people. Not necessarily to other faiths or other churches, just the fact that they've lost them. I think they can be brought back, and I think Pope Francis has been a real evangelist, and I happen to think Cardinal Dolan has that similar personality. And quite frankly, Bill, not enough priests have this evangelistic personality and objective where they really need to understand [that] the Church is about the people, and we need to have the people there for the Church to be vibrant. I think that message the pope is sending is that we need people back and involved in the Church, and I think he's done a wonderful job of setting the tone in his first year as pope.

W.O.: Alfred Kelly, Mario Cuomo, father of our present governor, Andrew Cuomo, was rooting for your friend Cardinal Dolan to be

pope. Did you ever talk to the cardinal and say, "Did you want
the job?"

A.K.: Well, I think he, like many people in that position, would do
whatever you are asked, much like our incredible young women
and men who serve in the military. I've gotten a chance to witness
some of these people in this role of running the Super Bowl. These
people are incredibly selfless and do what they're needed to do
and go where they need to go, and I think people like Cardinal
Dolan will do what is necessary and what is right. And if the
wisdom of the other 125 cardinals would be that he should be the
pope, I think he would gladly embrace that. If the wisdom is that
he should be the head of the archdiocese of New York, he would
be happy doing that as well. That's one of the great things about
him: He's living in the moment.

W.O.: Alfred Kelly Jr., I don't want to patronize you, but you have
neighbors in Scarsdale, Bronxville, Rye, and Bedford, places with a
lot of "yuppie," hedge fund guys who *take* and give nothing back.
Do you and Peggy ever get kind of discouraged, when you look
around you, at the lack of manners, the lack of involvement? The
selfishness?

A.K.: We do what we do, and we don't look around at others or judge
other people. I think both of us feel extraordinarily blessed. I've had
success from a combination of hard work and good fortune, and
our big things are healthcare and Catholic education, and that's the
real core of our focus from a charity perspective, Bill. It's something
we believe: If we've had some good fortune, we should try to help
other people where we can.

W.O.: Second time I've mentioned him, but Mario Cuomo said he
prays for "sureness." Your Catholic faith—you've spoken eloquently
of it this morning—are you *sure* about all this?

A.K.: You have to have faith. Without it, it kind of leaves a void. Does
that mean our Church is perfect? It's far from it. And it has its
warts like every other or many other organizations do, and I think
one of the things Pope Francis is trying to do is deal with some of
those warts. When you look at the lack of men going into the
priesthood—I don't know what it's going to be like for my kids.

Who is going to say Mass on Sunday? I know there are many
more priests retiring every year than there are being ordained,
and obviously, it's just mathematics! So that certainly is a concern
for me.

w.o.: Did you ever think about being a priest?

A.K.: I never did, no. I don't know why. It is a calling, but it is not
something I've thought about.

w.o.: Al Kelly Jr., we've roamed far and wide. Let's get away from your
soul and your Church for the moment and your friend the cardinal
and go back to the Super Bowl, which you ran, in every telling and
in every account, brilliantly. What's next? You also ran that little
company American Express, which has been so good to me, in
every season. Aren't you also a director of Hershey and a big
insurance company?

A.K.: Well, I am not currently on the Hershey board anymore, but I am
on the board of Met Life, and recently, in January, I joined the
board of Visa in San Francisco, and I'm on the board of New York
Presbyterian Hospital, where I spend a fair amount of time. I think
it's a phenomenal facility and phenomenal organization. I don't
know what's next, Bill. I'm going to take the next six to eight weeks
and help them get things cleaned up and closed down, bills to pay,
reports to write, tax returns to file, audits to complete. And then I
want to take some time. I'm not looking to jump into anything. I
have to decide if I want to go back into a big corporate job or do a
portfolio of things. The thing I know for sure is I want to work full
time; it's just a matter of whether I piece together four or five or six
different things that role up to a full-time role. Or whether I take a
full-time role in corporate America. I also have to decide how
strongly I feel about going back into financial services, which is
kind of where I have the most experience. But it certainly has
become an incredibly regulated industry.

w.o.: Football, Al Kelly. I once had a conversation—again I summon
the name of Well Mara, of sainted memory. I once asked Mr. Mara,
"Isn't it really sanctioned violence?" You seem like a nice, gentle
guy. Are you uncomfortable when you see them get knocked
around and flattened on the field?

A.K.: These folks are in incredible shape. I've had the good fortune of watching a couple of N.F.L. games from the field, and from that angle and perspective, Bill, you really see how fast and tough the game is. I think it's one of the challenges, and Commissioner Goodell talked about it. One of the challenges for the league is how to make sure these young men who play the game are as protected as they can possibly be. But on the other hand, the roughness, the toughness of it is part of the attractiveness of the game. I have to say that although I'm a football fan, I'm probably a college basketball fan more than anything else. I didn't take this job because of this undying love for football—or even of sports—I took this job because of a love for this region of the country where I grew up and to see that this incredible, ultimate football game could be a catalyst for economic benefit, tourism, charitable legacy work for this region and galvanize people around the Super Bowl much more than just watching a football game. And that's what got me excited about this opportunity and has me feeling good about it now that it is over.

W.O.: When you were at the White House, what did you do for President Reagan?

A.K.: I was in charge of Information Technology for eight of the eleven agencies that comprise the Office of the President. So I had the desktops, which at the time were word-processing machines, and I was converting over to IBM PCs. I was there during the e-mail system profs, which got a lot of attention during the Iran-Contra affair, where John Poindexter and Bud McFarlane and ultimately Ollie North all had their—the history books will write that it is the first time people realized that, unlike phone calls that go away when they're over, e-mails don't disappear. What really was the first instance of an e-mail being a real zinger and capturing something that somebody did after the fact when the person would have thought it might have been private or might have gone away. It was an incredible time for me as a young person to have a job of that stature and be able to enjoy Washington, which is a wonderful city, a great place to live, and we enjoyed the three years we were down there.

w.o.: What did you think of Ronald Wilson Reagan?

a.k.: I can't say enough good things about him. Again, a guy who had vision, tried to pull people together of all kinds. We've talked about it, but it's true: He and Tip O'Neill could get in a room together— their politics were vastly different—but let's get stuff done. It's been so disappointing to me that President Obama and John Boehner can't get in a room and put stuff aside and say, "For the good of the country, let's just get things done!" I'd be hard pressed for anybody to be terribly impressed with the list—or lack of a list—of things that have gotten done, unfortunately, since President Obama became president. It's not all his fault. But it's a short piece of paper. It's not a chapter in a book. It's not even probably a full page in a chapter. That's because Washington has been really in a state of being paralyzed.

w.o.: What do you think about President Barack Obama?

AL KELLY: I did not vote for him, but when I watched him on election night and when I watched him on the first inauguration, I said, "You know what? This is going to be good for the country. He is going to be a real breath of fresh air. He's going to bring people together. He's going to galvanize people." I can't tell you how disappointed I've been. It's been anything but that. He's been a bit too divisive and hasn't really galvanized people. And unfortunately, president of the United States is a humongous job, and quite frankly, if you look at his résumé and his background, you wouldn't hire him for president of practically anything.

w.o.: You would not?

a.k.: You wouldn't, just on the merits of what he's got on his résumé!

w.o.: Could he have run the Super Bowl like Alfred Kelly Jr.?

a.k.: I don't want to get into that. I'm sure many people could have done a better job than I did. I'm happy with what I did, but I don't want to get into comparing who else could have done it.

w.o.: I don't want you to take this the wrong way, but as I think about all the information and computer stuff in your background, you don't look like a "computer geek"—yet you were running the damn White House.

The author and Jonathan
Bush, brother of President
George H.W. Bush and
father of William "Billy"
Bush . . . Jon is a great
favorite of me and mine.
Mario Cuomo was crazy
about him too.

Three wise men. *From left:* Father Joseph Cavoto, OFM; Father Kevin Mackln, OFM,
former president of Siena College and the College of Mount Saint Mary; and Governor
Mario Cuomo at one of my book parties.

A dance at Le Cirque with my brilliant and luminous daughter, Kate O'Shaughnessy Nulty.

"Try and cheer up, you guys!" *From left:* the author, Governor Mario Cuomo, and David Tucker O'Shaughnessy, president of WVOX and WVIP.

The author; Timothy Cardinal Dolan, archbishop of New York; and Father Chris Monturro, a beloved Westchester pastor.

Words to the wise from His Eminence, Timothy Cardinal Dolan, during a visit to WVOX.

Consigliere . . . Father and son discussing the great issues: Governor Mario Cuomo and Governor Andrew Cuomo.

New York radio star Mark Simone, who has a permanent gig emceeing my book parties. When I'm not listening to my own radio stations, I always tune in to Mark.

I sit across from the luminous Deborah Norville at our Board of Directors meetings of the Broadcasters of America Foundation. Deborah is one of our brightest and most valuable directors.

"The Black-Tie Gang." *From left:* Dr. Mehmet Oz, Lisa Oz, my pal Richard Ambrose Foreman, the author, and the great Gianni Russo, "Godfather" and cabaret star.

"You haven't been very nice to me, Mr. O'Shaughnessy." The author and Hillary Rodham Clinton at the West Street Grill.

"Nice hair!" Mega-road-builder and contractor Ray Oneglia of the mammoth O&G Industries (they built practically every road between here and Florida!) donned a "Bill O'Shaughnessy wig" as he tried to appropriate "my table" (number 21) at the West Street Grill.

One of Jimmy Breslin's sons sent me this photo of the great writer perusing my memoir of our friend Mario Cuomo. I idolized Breslin and savored his pen and pronouncements for many decades.

"La Liz." I was speaking at the prestigious Dutch Treat Luncheon Club about our Mario Cuomo memoir when in walked the great Liz Smith, doyenne of gossip columnists. She read me the riot act for seating her next to "three old crones" . . . instead of the president of a network who was also in attendance.

David Tucker O'Shaughnessy. He's now in his forties and even better-looking today. He's also a hell of a broadcaster.

The Chairman and the Chairman Emeritus. *From left:* Dan Mason, who ran CBS Radio, and Phil Lombardo, who runs Citadel Television and is chairman emeritus of the Broadcasters Foundation of America . . . two of the most generous broadcasters on the planet. They've raised millions for the hurting and almost forgotten in our tribe.

"Theeeeeee Yankees win!" The great John Sterling showed up at one of my talks and I brought him up to the microphone and persuaded him to give his immortal cry. The audience loved it. And I love Sterling.

From left: Andrea Bocelli, the magnificent international tenor; his beautiful wife, Veronica Berti; the author; and Marco Maccioni of Le Cirque. Bocelli is a lovely man and a great friend of the Maccioni family.

"Out and about of an evening!" *From left:* David Tucker O'Shaughnessy, president of WVOX and WVIP; and Gianni Russo, author of *Hollywood Godfather.*

"Brother Bill." Bill O'Reilly plugged my early books on Fox TV . . . and I tried to be there for him when life turned sad and difficult, as the powers that be turned on this great talent.

"It's only a number!" More than one hundred people showed up at the eightieth anniversary of my natal day at Le Serene, Larchmont, N.Y., including, *from left:* Richard Johnson, star feature columnist, *New York Post*; Sessa Von Richthofen; designer and philanthropist Kenneth Cole; powerful Congresswoman Nita Lowey; Maria Cuomo Cole, my "honorary daughter"; Stephen Lowey, prominent Westchester attorney; and Matilda Raffa Cuomo, founder of Mentoring USA.

My granddaughter Amelia Jane Nulty in a heart-to-heart with Matilda Cuomo, a very special lady.

Kenneth Cole with his mother-in-law, Matilda Raffa Cuomo. The famous designer calls her "MIL."

Two formidable women. Matilda Raffa Cuomo, wife of the late Governor Mario M. Cuomo and mother of New York state's present governor, Andrew M. Cuomo; and Congresswoman Nita Lowey, Chair of the powerful House Appropriations Committee.

The grandchildren and other family members. *From left:* Tucker Thomas Nulty, Amelia Jane Nulty, Kate Wharton O'Shaughnessy, Flynn Thayer Nulty, daughter-in-law Cara Ferrin O'Shaughnessy, son David Tucker O'Shaughnessy, Lily Anna O'Shaughnessy, and Isabel O'Shaughnessy.

The legend. I've always idolized Jimmy Breslin, Jimmy Cannon, Pete Hamill . . . and this guy, the great Gay Talese! Notice I stay very close to him . . . hoping some of his genius will rub off on me. He writes great books, so what's he doing with this one?

From my lips to Dan's ear.

The lady in red! Shy, modest, retiring Cindy Adams always finds time for my book parties. So does the great Dan Rather.

God forgive me, but I like this guy!

The governor and the ringmaster. Governor Mario M. Cuomo and maestro Sirio Maccioni of Le Cirque.

Sirio Maccioni, one of America's greatest restaurateurs. Mario Cuomo always thought he looks like John Wayne.

Great American actor, activist . . . and saint? Mario Cuomo always said he prays for "sureness." I'm not *sure* about a lot of things. But I'm *sure* my Westchester neighbor Ossie Davis was a saint.

A.K.: Well, you've got to remember, Bill, I have a 1980 computer science degree from Iona College, and today my ten-year-old runs rings around me. You wouldn't want me. . . .

W.O.: You're kidding?

A.K.: Oh, my gosh! It's changed. It's one of the most incredible things about the last thirty to forty years, the changes in technology. And the speed at which they are changing. It is truly amazing.

W.O.: Al Kelly, you're a man of so many parts. I have to ask what you think of this NSA spying on our European friends? It seems everything you do these days, the government is watching.

A.K.: Well, I think the government has to do its job of safeguarding us. I think it's one of the principal jobs of the federal government, to safeguard our borders and safeguard our liberty. And I'm not smart enough, Bill, to judge exactly what we ought to do to make sure we're safe. That said, I do think some spying, some active listening, probably has to play a role in that activity of protecting our freedom and protecting our way of life and protecting our borders. Whether it has gone too far is not really—I don't have enough information to make that judgment. I'm not sure there's really anybody in the private sector that does have enough information to make the judgment if we've really gone too far. I could tell you we'd all be very upset if the federal government wasn't doing the things necessary to protect our liberty, because at the end of the day, the thing that makes our country the great country it is, is that it is a true democracy, and we do live in true freedom where you have all kinds of states doing all kinds of things, but we all do coalesce as one country behind our freedom!

W.O.: Alfred F. Kelly, what does "F." stand for? I'll bet I can guess.

A.K.: Francis.

W.O.: You've been very generous to indulge my curiosity about you and my questions. I've admired you from afar for a long time. How old are you now?

A.K.: Fifty-five, Bill, a young fifty-five!

W.O.: But you're not finished yet, are you?

A.K.: No, I feel—I've got a ten-year-old. No, I'm not finished. I honestly think there will be at least two more chapters to my life. Probably three. I want to continue to have a very active corporate career over the next number of years, again in one job or in a portfolio of jobs. I've had a dream that, in my first stage of retirement, I'd go teach at the college or graduate-school level, and that remains a dream I would like to fulfill.

W.O.: What would you teach?

A.K.: I would probably teach a combination of management, leadership classes as well as product-marketing classes—not computer science classes! And the third chapter would be to travel, enjoying grandchildren, continuing to catch up with friends and those kinds of things.

W.O.: Let me beg another moment, Alfred Francis Kelly Jr. What makes a good *manager*? Who better to ask?

A.K.: Bill, I feel there's a huge difference being a good *manager* and a good *leader*. I think a good manager is somebody who makes the trains run on time and fixes problems and has good follow-up and runs good meetings. I think a leader ideally does those things, but a leader sets a *vision*. A leader makes sure their ego is in check and their most important job in the world is to get great people around them. A leader is somebody who is incredibly empathetic to their people and doesn't look at their people like an asset like a building or technology, but realizes their people are human beings and treats them as such. For me, the ultimate test of somebody being a good leader is if someone will follow them to the ends of the Earth and work for them and tell other people you should work for this person. Those are kind of the litmus tests of what I think are great leaders, and many of them are good managers. Some great leaders may not be as good on making the trains run on time, but they're smart enough to put people in place who do know how to make the trains run on time.

W.O.: Would you like Goodell's job?

A.K.: Roger has done a phenomenal job and has many, many great years ahead of him, and I root for him to do well for decades to come. I'll go do something else and let him do his job!

w.o.: One final, crazy question. You and Peggy courted at the
Beechmont, the local saloon. Do you ever go back?

a.k.: We haven't been back in a while, I have to confess. It's probably
been four or five years since we've been there. Bill, when we first
got married, we lived in Mount Vernon, and then we lived in two
different homes in New Rochelle, and when we lived in New
Rochelle, we would go there. But now we've been up in the
Harrison–Rye section of the county for almost seven years now.
So we don't necessarily come down. We come down a lot for Iona
College basketball games, but I haven't been to the Beechmont or
a lot of the New Rochelle hangouts I spent a lot of days and nights
at in my Iona College years.

Bill, thank you. It's been a pleasure to be with *you*.

w.o.: Alfred F. Kelly Jr. is his name. It will be interesting to see what's
next for this guy.

Gerald Shargel, Esq.

Gerald Shargel is one of the most famous criminal lawyers in America. In fact, The New Yorker *called him "maybe the finest practitioner of his generation." Several of his colleagues have* weekly *programs on* wvox, *including Matthew Mari, but if they were coming up the back stairs after me or mine . . . I would want the estimable Murray Richmond, Esq., based in "Da Bronx." He's known far and wide as "Don't worry, Murray," and, like Shargel, he's represented some very "colorful" characters. It's a fascinating calling, but everyone deserves a good defense. Murray Richmond once told me he loves murder trials . . . "because there's one less witness." Gerry Shargel has also represented his share of notorious defendants.*

WILLIAM O'SHAUGHNESSY: How did you get so damn well known— and survive—in the rough and tumble world of criminal law? You look like a college professor!

G.S.: It wasn't by plan but by happenstance. I started getting high-profile cases in the '70s, and I continued to get even more throughout the decade. And one thing leads to another. I'm not a planner. I went where my interests took me.

W.O.: Among your clients: John Gotti!

G.S.: John Gotti was a client, yes.

W.O.: And Sammy "The Bull" Gravano! How old are you?

G.S.: I'm sixty-nine and a half!

W.O.: You're pushing seventy, and no one's knocked you off yet?

G.S.: Not so far!

W.O.: Do you ever get afraid, a little fearful, of these guys you represent?

G.S.: I don't think about that. When there are unpleasant things one's concerned about, I think the best advice is to banish the thought.

W.O.: You've had 125 jury trials. What do you think about when you're addressing the jury?

G.S.: I like every minute of it. I like being up there. I like having the opportunity to address the jury. I like performing in public. I think any good trial lawyer has—and I'll be frank to admit this—a "Hey, look at me" personality. You can't be shy. It's not a profession for shrinking violets. There are many good lawyers who have never been in a courtroom. But I'm a courtroom lawyer. I'm a trial lawyer.

W.O.: For years you ran solo; you flew without a net, alone as a single practitioner. And now you're with a big, white shoe law firm. Why did you do that?

G.S.: I wanted to do something different. I think a large law firm with trial experience—we now have many highly experienced, highly regarded, highly competent trial lawyers to be able to have a wider net to bring more fire to the occasion. I think there is better opportunity to more ably represent clients.

W.O.: As I look across the microphone at you, Gerald Shargel, I've got some nerve questioning *you*.

G.S.: Good cross.

W.O.: When you pick a jury, Counselor Shargel, what do you look for? You're representing the defendant, and you obviously want somebody who is going to be inclined toward your views.

G.S.: I want someone who is going to listen to my arguments and not approach this with a closed mind and is not going to have some knee-jerk reaction for the government or the prosecutor. First, selecting the jury is the most difficult part of a criminal trial because you're not really in control. I carefully prepare my opening statement with what it is I'm going to say, or my cross examination or my closing argument to the jury. But there's a certain loss of control in jury selection because you don't know all that much no matter how careful the *voir dire* is, the probing of the jurors as to what their mindset is. It's still a crapshoot. Jury selection is not really jury selection, I have news for you. Jury selection is jury *deselection*. Because with the preemptory challenges we have, what you're doing is saying that person—that man or that woman—is not suitable for that case. Or I don't like the karma here. I don't like the reaction; I don't like the physiology of what I'm seeing, you know, hands that are crossed. You know, you better prove it mister or you're not getting our consideration. But who knows if I was right? You'll never know until the end whether I was right or wrong. So again, I call it jury "deselection," not jury selection.

W.O.: Gerald Shargel, counselor, famous criminal lawyer. Does it still work when you're called for jury duty and you say, "I hate everybody, fry him, kill him!" "You're dismissed!" Does that work?

G.S.: No. I can't give advice on what works to get people off a jury. I would hope people of goodwill and responsibility as citizens would serve. It was once said jury service is second only to military service in time of combat. Time of combat! And I think it's important. There are people who just want to say anything to get off the jury, but I'm more optimistic about people's good intentions.

W.O.: Questions you've always wanted to ask Gerald Shargel, famous criminal defense lawyer: If you know somebody is guilty, can you still defend them?

G.S.: If I know someone is guilty, I'm *required* to defend them and give them the best defense and put the government's case in the worst possible light, try to raise a reasonable doubt where it might not otherwise exist. And make it very, very difficult for the prosecution to win a conviction. If they don't win a conviction, it's because they didn't deserve it. The evidence wasn't sufficient, or bad choices were made by the prosecutor. And my job is to make it as hard as possible, as difficult as possible, and an authority no smaller than the Supreme Court of the United States has said there's an obligation to do that.

W.O.: Mr. Shargel, we've had some famous colleagues of yours at this microphone: Barry Ivan Slotnick, Murray Richman of "Don't worry, Murray" fame, Matthew Mari, on whose show you just appeared. These guys have great personalities. I'm crazy about the great Murray Richman. And his daughter, Stacey. Juries love them. And judges too. And Matthew Mari has had some real "wise guys" just like you. How important is it for the jury to *like* the lawyer?

G.S.: I think it's *very* important. You don't want to bore the jury. You don't want to be a lawyer who is up there thinking he or she is making points on cross-examination and then the jury doesn't understand what is going on. You have to be someone the jury has confidence in. You have to maintain credibility not only with the judge but with the jury as well. It's highly important.

W.O.: Are certain judges more inclined to the "wise guys" than others? Can you shop around and pick the judge?

G.S.: No, because in recent cases and statutes and rules, there's no judge shopping. There's what's called the "individual assignment system." Meaning that at the time of indictment, there's a wheel— like a Bingo wheel—it's spun. The clerk takes out a name and announces the name of the judge. And that's the judge, barring something very unusual, that will remain with the case for the duration.

W.O.: Have you ever gotten damn good and mad at the judge—His Honor or Her Honor?

G.S.: You know, to get mad or emotional about the judge is, in my view, unprofessional. I've been in front of very tough judges by reputation, very difficult judges. I think the caricature of the old, difficult judge is coming to an end. I think the judges that are being appointed, particularly in the federal system, the state system as well—are intellectually honest, and they go where the law takes them. Now some people complain and say the judge ruled on fifteen of our motions and all fifteen motions were denied!

W.O.: Did that ever happen to you?

G.S.: Sure. And we didn't get any relief from the judge. But you know what? It's not always the judge. It's the law. And when the judge is applying the law and applying the case law from higher courts, from appellate courts, the judge is just doing his or her job. I don't worry about who the judge is in the case. I'm not trying the case before the judge. I'm just thinking about one thing: what's the jury's reaction. Some lawyers take a lot of time, and they look at the judge or they look at the court stenographer or they look at the prosecutor or they look at the reporters in the first row. And the last place they look, if they ever look, is at the jury. If you want to know how you're doing, you just look over to the jury box, and you'll be able to tell.

W.O.: Gerald Shargel, did you ever want to be a judge yourself? Your Honor, Judge Shargel?

G.S.: Never. I wanted to be a law professor, and I did that. I wanted to be a trial lawyer, a criminal defense lawyer, and I did that. I never wanted to be a prosecutor, so I never did that. First of all, the people who select judges would have had no interest in *me*. I want to be fair and frank. And that's because I've represented so many high-profile organized-crime figures throughout my career. I've always had a very strong white-collar practice starting from the beginning that ran parallel to the organized-crime cases. In many cases, the organized-crime cases produced bigger headlines, and that's why I have the reputation I do. But did I ever want to be a judge? No! One, it could be very boring. Even though there's a lot of good advocacy, there's a lot of bad advocacy, unfortunately. I admire the judges who are so patient and bend over backward. The dopier the lawyer, the more bending over backward they do. And I applaud that. That's very decent. I don't know I could do that as calmly. Number one, there's the boredom factor, and I don't need people to call me "Judge." It's a hard job, you know. It's a very hard job to be a judge. If you do it right and you do it conscientiously, it's a tremendous amount of work. And judges carry huge caseloads. Particularly in civil cases. Law firms file briefs, and some judges, many judges, put limits on the number of pages you can have in a brief. But lawyers who are left to their own devices, instead of saying it in 25 pages, will say it in 125 pages. And you have to sit down and read that on a Sunday or a Saturday. Trial preparation, from a perspective of a lawyer, is darn hard. There's no question about it. I think judges work harder.

W.O.: Counselor Shargel—I almost called you Judge Shargel—how do you feel when the New York tabloids call you a "mob lawyer"? How does that feel?

G.S.: You know, you can't have this job, you can't do what I do and be thin-skinned or sensitive. I'm not sensitive, so I think I understand the press. I understand what interests them. I understand what doesn't interest them. I've gotten some fabulous press going back to the *New Yorker* article you quoted from, but that wasn't the beginning. I was admitted to practice in 1969. I have high-profile cases I tried two years after I was admitted. There was a man I represented who was charged with extorting the Mobil Oil Company as a strike breaker, and it was page two of the *Daily News*. I was twenty-nine.

W.O.: Do you ever become friends with some of these wise guys?

G.S.: Friends—I don't know—I've enjoyed the company of wise guys.

W.O.: Of an evening?

G.S.: Guys are guys. Some have great senses of humor. Or perhaps a bright interest in books, and I've discussed books with wise guys. I've discussed food with wise guys. I've told jokes with wise guys. I've ridiculed what needed to be ridiculed with wise guys. They are people just like anyone else.

W.O.: Are you saying they're just like thee and me?

G.S.: Maybe different when it comes to dispute resolution!

W.O.: Sir, one final question, and you're nice to suffer all my dumb queries. You're a law professor as well, Professor Shargel, at Brooklyn Law School. What do the kids, the wannabe lawyers who look in the mirror and see Clarence Darrow, what do they ask you, Professor?

G.S.: I have a large class, particularly when I teach "Evidence," I have over one hundred kids in my class, so it's a large lecture hall we're in, I think the people who enroll in my classes are interested in criminal law whether they're from the prosecutor's perspective or a defense lawyer. And I think that's why they choose me. We have some very good professors there who teach "Evidence." But that's what I bring to the table, the practical experience. It's an interesting and a very positive dynamic between me and the student body.

W.O.: Counselor Gerald Shargel: Every courtroom seems to have above the judge sitting up there the saying "In God We Trust." And they talk about *justice*. I'm not sure I know what the hell that means. What should someone expect when they go in there, into a courtroom?

[209]

G.S.: Well, what they should expect and what they should get—it doesn't happen all the time, the system is not perfect—is a fair trial. You know, it's often said you're not entitled to a perfect trial, you're entitled to a fair trial. Obviously, there's a difference. Not every trial is perfectly executed. But to get a fair ruling, to get an intellectually honest ruling from the court, to get a fair and dispassionate evaluation or assessment from the jury, is what you're to get. But not only that, I tell you something very interesting: 97 percent—and this was recognized quite recently by the United States Supreme Court, that's where I'm getting these statistics—97 percent of all cases of those indicted—across America—in every nook and every cranny, in every state and in every city, from Anchorage, Alaska, to Hawaii, 97 percent plead guilty, only 3 percent go to trial now. It used to be a trial practice. Now it's a plea-bargaining practice.

W.O.: Is that good or bad?

G.S.: I think it's bad in many ways, and here's why: You noted before that I've tried give or take 125 jury trials. No one can get that experience today. Not because of anything I did or said, but because 97 percent of your caseload results in pleas, and I know there are people who call themselves criminal defense lawyers, and every one of their cases resulted in guilty pleas. I'm not saying that's wrong, but it really has become a plea-bargaining process.

W.O.: How many of those 125 did you win? *The New Yorker* accused you of being the practitioner of your generation. How many did you win?

G.S.: My friend Alan Dershowitz commented on that very question, and it holds true for me. That criminal defense lawyers—and anyone who comes and tells you I'm a criminal-defense lawyer and I win all my cases, or I'm a criminal defense lawyer and I win 80 percent of my cases—well, I tell my clients to walk right out of the office; you're in the wrong place. Here's the deal. As Professor Dershowitz has said, a criminal defense lawyer is like a baseball player. If I could hit .380 or .390, I'm doing pretty good.

W.O.: Wow. Incidentally, Mariano Rivera is going to sit right across
that microphone soon, and I'm also going to ask him what his win/
loss record was. You won't tell?

G.S.: Maybe higher!

W.O.: Sir, thank you for joining us today, and thank you to your
colleague at the bar—Matthew Mari, himself a great one, as is our
good friend and radio colleague the legendary Murray Richman—
for bringing you to Westchester.

John Cahill

*Candidate for attorney general, state of New York. June 17, 2014.
Having left politics and his law firm, he is now chief of staff
to Cardinal Timothy Dolan of New York.*

John Cahill is like a breath of fresh air in the murky world of contemporary politics. Governor George Pataki's former chief of staff left me feeling better about politics, the potential of good, enlightened government, and even gave me a somewhat renewed confidence in a Republican Party that has lost its way. John Cahill, who speaks eloquently of a party that is more inclusive and compassionate, just might restore your faith in the political process and even in the confused and beleaguered Republican Party. We've argued for years that men and women of real quality, substance, and ability will not submit to the rigors of public service. And then every once in a while, along comes a John Cahill. We interviewed him when he was running for attorney general, a race he lost in the face of the Democrats' overwhelming registration advantage. He is now chief of staff to New York Cardinal Timothy Dolan.

WILLIAM O'SHAUGHNESSY: In our studio, live this very morning in June, is a man we've admired—I've got to tell you straight out—for a long time. He's a Republican—are you ready? And he's running for attorney general of the Empire State. He's a Yonkers, New York, guy, a child of Yonkers—"where true love conquers"—John Cahill.

JOHN CAHILL: Bill, it's great to be with you.

W.O.: You really ran the state of New York for a good, long time as George Elmer Pataki's secretary—which means chief of staff. You ran the damn place.

J.C.: Well, it was a job with a lot of responsibilities. It got me to know the state from Long Island to Buffalo, Bill. I have a real passion for the state. It's an amazing state with amazing people. Because of that background I have in government as his secretary and also previous to that as commissioner of the Department of Environmental Conservation, I'm anxious to get back into public service.

W.O.: "Secretary" doesn't mean the typing kind. Secretary means you run everything.

J.C.: "Secretary" means you do what the governor needs to get done. That includes typing if you have to. But really it's the highest appointed position in the state. All state agencies report in to the secretary to the governor. So your responsibilities run from the environment to healthcare to transportation. All of those state agencies out there run through the implementation of the governor's policies.

W.O.: John Cahill, you and former Governor Pataki have been together for a long time. How did you meet?

J.C.: Yes, it goes back to the days of practicing law with a mutual friend of ours—Mr. William Plunkett.

W.O.: "Brother Bill" Plunkett, Esquire.

J.C.: Yes, absolutely. Actually, Bill was very instrumental in convincing me to go to law school. I met him when I was coaching and teaching at Stepinac High School in White Plains, when I coached his oldest son, Ryan. And Bill convinced me to go to law school. He gave me a job as a summer intern. And the first case I tried at Plunkett & Jaffe was tried with Mr. Kevin Plunkett, his brother, and George Pataki, in upstate New York. George Pataki and I have been friends ever since.

W.O.: In every telling and by every account, John Cahill is a nice guy. You are greatly admired in your home heath. Why the hell do you want to mess with politics now?

J.C.: Well, never having run in politics before, but having been around government for a good twelve years, Bill, you see the difference it can make in people's lives. Government can be an instrument of good, or it can be an instrument of not so good. And I've seen the goodness of government. Whether it was working at DEC or our rebuilding efforts in Lower Manhattan, I believe in public service. And I believe my time in government and in the public sector has given me the qualifications and background to serve capably as the next New York state attorney general.

W.O.: What's going on in the state of New York? We only know what we see in the public press. It looks like a mess. Is it really as bad as it seems?

J.C.: Well, I think it really depends on where you go. I spent last week traveling much of upstate New York: Buffalo, Jamestown, Elmira, Corning—some great old towns in New York with wonderful people. And I must say there's a sense of concern and lack of confidence in the future. What I hear most, the biggest concern, is about jobs, and also the brain drain. Where are my children going to live? If they go off to college, do they come back? Is there going to be a future here for the next generation of New Yorkers? I believe there is, because New York is always going to be, as you mentioned, the Empire State. But we need to have government fighting for the needs of these people by having programs and policies and law enforcement that will build a future for New Yorkers, and that's my concern right now, Bill. There is a lot of concern in upstate New York about the future of the state and what it means for the next generation of New Yorkers.

W.O.: John Cahill, can anything, can anyone—even Cahill—save Binghamton or Utica or Batavia?

J.C.: Yes, I do believe they can, Bill. I think there are policies and opportunities in the state. One of the challenging issues the state is facing is on the issue of developing natural gases along the Southern Tier. Hydrofracking is a very controversial issue right now in the state. And as you travel the Southern Tier— Binghamton, Jamestown, Elmira—that is a really big issue. And having been commissioner of the Department of Environmental Conservation four years, and prior to that I served as their general counsel, I spent my entire life around environmental issues and energy issues. And I do believe it can be done safely. We shouldn't be drilling in the New York City watershed. We shouldn't be drilling in our state parks. But there are areas in the state—if properly regulated—that I believe my former agency is capable of regulating. And that would not only be an economic game-changer for the Southern Tier, but for all of New York state.

W.O.: There's a story in the *Wall Street Journal* this very morning, John Cahill, about all the little towns, hamlets, and villages that have actually banned fracking.

J.C.: Yes, and it's now before the Court of Appeals as to whether these towns and villages can act unilaterally to basically ban fracking. And if that was to happen, obviously, the opportunities for companies to come in is going to be severely limited. New York state has generally recognized in the past that energy mining, developing those resources, is pre-empted on the local level. So that's right now before the Court of Appeals, and that is going to be an important issue as to whether we do develop oil and gas in the Southern Tier.

W.O.: Well, you're not saying you know better than those local yokels?

J.C.: No, I'm not. I'm saying I think we need to have an overall state policy that certainly gives the locals the appropriate opportunity to participate in the decision-making process. Certainly, there would be a concern if with each town you had a patchwork around the state. And that would be a concern, Bill. But I think there is a process to make sure we get the locals on board, to get the counties on board. And if there's strong feeling that it's not the right place, no one should be forced to live with issues they don't want to live with. But at the same time, there are areas around the state, Bill, that very much are anxious to move forward appropriately and diligently on developing those resources.

W.O.: His name is John Cahill. He hails from Yonkers, right over the Cross County Parkway, that colorful, if sometimes beleaguered, city on the Hudson. And he's running and—surprise, surprise—as a Republican!

J.C.: Yes, I am. I've been a Republican my entire life, Bill. You say, "Why are you a Republican?" My parents are Irish immigrants; "How come you're not a Democrat?" Actually, my father was a Republican as well. We believe in opportunity. I do believe in an active government, but I don't believe in a dependent government or a government that forces dependency. And I think the government can have an awful lot to give people—as it's given me, a son of immigrants—an opportunity to achieve something in this world.

w.o.: So what kind of Republican are you, John Cahill? There was a story in *City and State* this week—a blog, a very good one—that there ain't no more Rockefeller Republicans.

J.C.: I guess I'm a Rockefeller Republican, a Pataki Republican.

w.o.: Is that one and the same?

J.C.: I would leave that to the Rockefellers and the Patakis. They have differences, but they have a lot of similarities, I expect. And I think it goes back to the idea that we're not anti-government. We do believe in a role for government. But we believe in the overriding sense and responsibility of opportunity and not dependency, Bill. And I think certainly that was Governor Pataki's mantra, and if I recall, Governor Rockefeller also had a lot to say about that as well. We're not like many of the other Republicans around the country who believe that government should have very little role in bettering the lives of its citizens.

w.o.: Do you remember when Louis Lefkowitz of sainted memory was attorney general?

J.C.: Yes, I'm old enough to remember Louis Lefkowitz. And you know, when I look at that office, Bill, he's somebody I certainly admire as an attorney general. He was known as the "people's lawyer." He was somebody who really served the interests of the people of the state and used that office not to aspire to higher office. He never ran for governor. He had a tough guy in front of him to run for governor!

w.o.: Rockefeller.

J.C.: Yes! Rockefeller. But he was dedicated to that notion of serving as the people's lawyer. And certainly, that is a model I would like to emulate again in the office of the attorney general.

w.o.: Out on the stump on the road, the rubber-chicken circuit, you've said again and again you want to be the people's lawyer. But aren't you also the *governor's* lawyer?

J.C.: Sure, you have a responsibility as the attorney general to serve as the lawyer for the executive and the executive agencies. That is an important component of serving as attorney general.

Absolutely, Bill. But the role of attorney general has broader responsibilities than just defending the governor or being the lawyer for the executive. It's also being an advocate for the people. The responsibility is clearly to defend the civil rights of the citizens of the state of New York. And that's why I've been such a strong advocate and, quite frankly, a critic of the current attorney general. When we have issues concerning the education of our children, which many of us do, it's a civil rights issue. I believe the attorney general should be more outspoken, more vocal, to be sure the children of the state are given a quality education, as our Constitution requires.

w.o.: John Cahill, I don't want to injure you, but the word in political circles is that the Democrat governor—Andrew Mark Cuomo— thinks you're a pretty good guy.

J.C.: Well, that's nice to hear.

w.o.: You're a Republican. He's a Democrat!

J.C.: You know what, I've always approached government and politics really nonpolitically, Bill. I mean, whether you're a Republican or a Democrat, we all have the responsibility to serve the interests of the people. That's the ideology, rather than being a Republican or a Democrat, I would take to the office of attorney general.

w.o.: Let's take some calls from our listeners for the Republican—are you also the Conservative candidate?

J.C.: Yes I am.

w.o.: John Cahill, your own party is a mess. The Republican Party. It almost doesn't exist anymore. Or does it?

J.C.: Oh, it does, Bill. I think there are different sectors of the Republican Party. But frankly, you're also seeing that in the Democratic Party. You saw that with the Working Family Party at their convention up in Albany two weeks ago, from the far left pressuring the governor on the endorsement. Listen, both political parties are going to have fringe elements pressing the issue. And many times, because they are so influential in the primary process, they can have a dramatic impact on elections. But I do believe in the Republican Party, with the right message and the right voice about being inclusive. One of the things the Republican Party has a problem with is being compassionate. At least projecting itself as compassionate, Bill.

W.O.: John Cahill, you mentioned state troopers, the state police. Weren't you just endorsed by the troopers?

J.C.: Yes, I was. I'm very proud my first political endorsement came from the New York State Police.

W.O.: So the next time I'm stopped going up 684, I'm going to have a Cahill bumper sticker.

J.C.: Bill, I think you know a lot of other people that can help you a lot more than I can. But I'd be proud to help you, Bill.

W.O.: That's a great endorsement, the troopers.

J.C.: Yes, I'm very proud. I worked with the state police both in the DEC and in the Governor's Office, and they are a tremendous group of men and women that risk their lives every day. I don't think anyone driving up the State Thruway at night, when they see a state trooper pulled over, they say, "Wow! That takes a lot of courage to do what they do every day to protect us."

W.O.: John Cahill, I still can't figure out something. You have a nice family, a beautiful blonde wife. And yet you're out and about. I see you constantly on Facebook in some cockamamie, obscure town that nobody's ever heard of. First of all, you went to Elmira, and you didn't go to the right place!

J.C.: Why is that?

W.O.: I told you, the chicken wings at Bernie Murray's! And Moretti's.

J.C.: I went to Louie's. It's a terrific place in Elmira.

W.O.: See, I'm a great advisor to Cahill. You really listen to me about chicken wings! When you're in these awful, far-flung places—that's *my* word, "awful"—you seem to like them.

J.C.: I love them. They're not awful. They're just wonderful people looking for a future for their towns and for their families. No different from my neighbors in Yonkers that are concerned if their kids are going to stay in the neighborhood. Are they going to be forced out because they need a job and can't afford the taxes here in New York and they'll have to move elsewhere? People have lived in these communities for generations. They want their communities to succeed. They want a government and an attorney general's office that is responsive to the needs of these communities.

w.o.: You mentioned earlier our mutual friend William Plunkett, Esq. He's had a great impact on all our lives.

J.C.: He has.

w.o.: He gets mad at me every time the New York tabloids quote me accusing Plunkett of being the most powerful man in New York state. He gets mad for about one minute!

J.C.: Yes, just a minute!

w.o.: So, I'm not surprised he likes you. We call him "Monsignor" Plunkett! I think he'd prefer "Cardinal." What about your Catholic faith? Is it important to you?

J.C.: Yes, it's real important to me, Bill. As you mentioned, I grew up in an Irish Catholic household. Went to Archbishop Stepinac. Fordham University. And actually, when I met Bill Plunkett, I was giving some serious thought to joining the seminary. I was teaching religion and coaching basketball, baseball, and soccer at Stepinac. It has remained an important element in my life until this day.

w.o.: Do you regret never becoming a priest?

J.C.: No. I have a wonderful wife and four beautiful kids. Bill was one of the ones who kind of steered me in that direction. Even though I decided to take a different path, my Catholic faith is and will always be an important part of my life.

w.o.: What do you think of your new pope, Francis?

J.C.: He's a hero. A *hero*. One thing that is remarkable is that you look at the leaders of the Catholic faith and when we really need a *dynamic* leader—which the Church desperately needed right now—we have this new pope. He's brought new energy, new excitement; he has just been a remarkable, remarkable leader. And Cardinal Dolan, whom I am a big fan of here in New York—once again, we have tremendous leadership in our faith.

w.o.: Cardinal Dolan—are you and Dolan pretty tight?

J.C.: Well, he's been very, very good to me. I serve on a couple of boards for the cardinal. So he has been very supportive. I think he's been a great leader of our faith. I was very close with Cardinal Egan as well. I was the governor's "ambassador" to the cardinal's office. I've enjoyed a relationship with our spiritual leaders here in New York for some time, Bill.

w.o.: How about ambassador to the Vatican? Wouldn't that be a great gig?

J.C.: I only have eyes for New York. That would be a great gig. But I only have eyes for Elmira probably more than the Vatican!

w.o.: Your Catholic faith—stick with it for a minute, John Cahill. Mario Cuomo said he prays for sureness. Sureness. Are you *sure* about your faith?

J.C.: I think all of us, whatever faith you believe in at points in your life, you question. I think it's good to question. We've been taught to question our faith. It makes you stronger in your faith once you help find the answers to what you're seeking. I do seek sureness. I guess I would say I pray for hope. I pray for opportunity more than I pray for sureness, Bill. Because I'm pretty sure, at this point in my life. I'm confident in my faith, but I really pray for the opportunities for other people, whether they're here in New York, that they be given a life of meaning and worth. That's why I want to get back into public service.

w.o.: Mr. Attorney General Cahill—I've already got you elected! You're the attorney general. Office in Albany. Office in New York. The court says you've got to close down an abortion clinic. Or you've got to keep one open. What do you do?

J.C.: You follow the laws of the state of New York, Bill. It's very clear. You leave your personal faith, your issues behind you when you take a constitutional oath to uphold the laws and the constitution of the state of New York. I recognized that when I got into this. I took that same oath when I served as secretary to the governor.

w.o.: The oath says what?

J.C.: You will uphold the laws of the state of New York, the constitutions of New York and of the United States.

w.o.: So help me . . .

J.C.: So help me God. I will do that as I have done. People might have criticized me for many things during my tenure in government, Bill. I don't think anyone would have questioned me for ever, ever violating the oath I took in serving out my public responsibility. And I would do the same again as attorney general.

w.o.: That job of secretary to the governor calls for "the hammer." Mr. No! Did you have a tough time being the tough guy?

j.c.: I think I tried to be tough in a fair way. I don't believe that in order to be tough you need to scream at people. But you need to give people a direct answer as to what they're seeking. I tried to represent the governor in that position. I don't think Governor Pataki was the type of guy who wanted people to be screamed at or yelled at. He was the type of guy who delivered, and if we couldn't do something, be direct and tell them exactly why and we'll move on. That's what I try to do. I didn't have a problem saying no to people, because by telling no, that was often in the best interest of the state.

w.o.: George Pataki—to this day, do we really know him? What kind of guy is he?

j.c.: A remarkable guy. He really is. I mean, he is a very regular sort of guy from Peekskill. A background in farming. At the same time, he has an amazing intellect. Yale, Columbia. His mind works at a different speed than anyone I've ever met. He is a very kind, decent, smart guy who loved to serve the state with great distinction in his twelve years. I'm happy to have him as a friend, and now I have him as a business partner as well, Bill.

w.o.: Do you think he still looks in the mirror and sees a president?

j.c.: I don't think there is anybody who served as governor of the state of New York who hasn't thought of being president. And I don't think there is anything wrong with that. When you're elected by what I would say is the most important state in the country, you should think about whether it's right with you personally to run for president. And once you have that one thought in your mind, you will have it for the rest of your life. So I think whether it's Andrew Cuomo, Mario Cuomo, George Pataki, Nelson Rockefeller, I think New Yorkers expect their governor to be of presidential timber.

w.o.: Someone said Nelson ran too hard for it, and Mario wouldn't run at all!

J.C.: It's a hard decision, running for president. It's hard enough traveling the state, Bill. Can you imagine going to Iowa, New Hampshire, and South Carolina, endlessly, for two years leading up to the presidential primaries and caucuses? That's a real demand on people's lives.

W.O.: Jimmy Breslin, the great writer, one of the great journalists of our time—I said to him, "Listen, I loved your stuff about Winston Churchill, Bobby Kennedy, Jack Kennedy. Why are you writing about these obscure guys?" He said, "*Who's* to write about?" So, John Cahill, is there anybody on the political scene or the national—or even international—who you think has the great stuff? Any heroes?

J.C.: You mentioned President Kennedy. We had his picture in my house, Bill, until the day my mom passed away. It was a center point of our lives. I'll never forget the day John F. Kennedy was assassinated. It was literally the first thing I remember in my life. I was four years old at the time and watching with my mother as she cried and we watched the funeral. Same thing with Bobby Kennedy. I remember my mom waking me up that morning, and she said, "Get down on your knees and say a prayer for Senator Kennedy." So the Kennedys, even though they were Democrats, they were Irish, and they were great politicians. They tried to change the world, which is extraordinarily admirable. And I think if you would look at the political map today, I still think there's the makings of political heroes. And I think we're all looking for people to look up to. I was a big Ronald Reagan fan in my formative days back when I was in college. But I'm still looking for that leader who is talking about compassion and care. Jeb Bush, I'm a big fan of his because he's open to Hispanics. He's open to expanding the breadth of the Republican Party, much as Governor George Pataki was. We need that type of leadership again, certainly in the party and in the country.

W.O.: Let's take another call.

CALLER: What do you think can be done about the rampant shootings in the schools, movie theaters, and the malls?

J.C.: Good question; an important question. We talk a lot about gun
   safety and gun violence, and we have the Safe Act that passed a few
   years ago, but we're not really talking enough about the mental-
   health crisis in this country. And I really worry that we are focused
   on guns, and I'm concerned about guns as well, although I have
   some issues with the Safe Act that was passed without any serious
   debate. We really need to do more on mental-health issues in our
   country, whether it is the young that are being exposed to violence
   and re-creating violence in these schools, which is creating horror
   around the country. So I think we really need to take a
   comprehensive approach to these issues of violence and gun
   violence. Certainly, tougher enforcement on illegal guns is
   important. But we can't lose sight of the fact that many of these
   people doing these horrible things show there really is a mental-
   health crisis in this country that we're not properly addressing.

W.O.: What's wrong with the Safe Act you don't like?

J.C.: The Safe Act—let's talk about how it was passed. It was passed in
   the middle of the night without any debate on the message and
   necessity. On an issue that is so important to so many people
   upstate, we need to have a serious debate on the issue, Bill.

W.O.: You mean, they like their guns?

J.C.: They do like their guns. They grew up in a culture of hunting and
   conservation. They are law-abiding citizens. These are not people
   who are violent. The law itself is flawed because it meant even
   police officers were carrying illegal weapons because it limited the
   magazine clip to seven clips, whereas most law enforcers carry ten
   clips. So there wasn't real serious thought put into the legislation,
   Bill. If we're going to look at gun control, we need to look at it as a
   comprehensive issue that addresses what we are trying to achieve,
   and that is to reduce violence in our schools. I think we can do
   better than we've done on the Safe Act.

W.O.: Whose fault was that about the only ten bullets?

J.C.: You have to put blame on everyone that had to do with the
   passage of the legislation. From the governor's office to the
   legislature. If we had a serious debate on an issue, weaknesses in

the bill such as that would have been pointed out. And we could have done something I think would have been more beneficial on gun violence along with mental-health issues.

W.O.: Caller, does that make sense?

CALLER: Yes, it does indeed.

J.C.: I recognize that Democrats and independents and Republicans—I have to reach out to all of those groups. And I certainly plan on doing that. I do not believe people of this state are monolithic voters, that they just go down and vote Democrat. You can just look at the election returns last year, for instance, on the comptroller's race: The comptroller got 47 percent while the governor candidate—Paladino—got 34 percent. People are willing—Democrats, independents—are willing to look at Republicans based upon what their message is and what they are going to offer the state. We have a long history of ticket-splitting in the state. People want to balance government in Albany. I think Democrats and independents will be there in November.

W.O.: Is your wife, Kim, OK with this?

J.C.: Yes, she's been great. She has supported me in all these crazy things I've done in my life.

W.O.: Did you walk in one day and say, "Guess what?"

J.C.: Well, this isn't as bad as when I went to Albany in 1995 when I had four kids under four years of age and was traveling back and forth to Albany, commuting. At least my kids are older now, and she has been my biggest supporter in life. She's more private than I am, Bill. But she has been 100 percent behind me. I wouldn't have done it without her.

W.O.: So, does Kim Cahill like the rubber-chicken dinners?

J.C.: She does. She loves meeting people. She loves talking to people. She is much more social than I am, thank God. So she's going to be a real asset to me on the campaign trail.

W.O.: I wish we had television, John Cahill. People could see the look of optimism and, to use your favorite word, *hope*. I see it on your face. Again, I've got to tell you, the thought occurs: This guy is *too* nice. We like rogues! We like Spitzer-types!

J.C.: No, listen. When I think about political heroes, one of the guys I really admired growing up was Jack Kemp as a Republican.

W.O.: Jack Kemp, the quarterback?

J.C.: The quarterback for the Buffalo Bills, a congressman.

W.O.: He was a nice guy.

J.C.: He was a wonderful man, a wonderful politician. And, as you mentioned, he was a nice guy with a vision about opportunity. About creating opportunity for those in the inner cities. He knew immigrants come to our shores, looking for hope, like my parents did. Let's leave parties aside; we need to be as a society more open and find ways to bring hope and opportunity to uplift people in our society. I think we can do that better from the attorney general's office. That would, obviously, be a priority of mine as an elected official.

W.O.: John, that's the second time you brought up immigrants. The paper this morning, the lead editorial in our beloved *New York Times*—do you have a chance to get their endorsement?

J.C.: You know, I'll certainly have a conversation with them. I'm going to be reaching out to everybody. I believe I do have a chance because of the message I have of inclusiveness and a different type of view/ideology toward government. But, you know, that will be up to the *New York Times*. I'm not counting on it, Bill. But I will certainly have a conversation with them.

W.O.: Speaking of immigrants, they say that 40,000 children have been picked up at the border and are now in custody. What the hell would you do with them?

J.C.: It's a really, really tough issue. We need to have laws in this country. We need to protect our borders. That's what defines a country, having borders. And clearly, the idea of forcing these kids out of their homelands onto U.S. shores is something that shouldn't be tolerated—frankly—on either side of the border.

W.O.: Who is forcing?

J.C.: The parents or the societies. Whether Mexican or from Central America coming up through Mexico and forcing these kids basically into the United States because they don't see that there's any hope in some of these countries. And I tell you, Bill, I've traveled to Central America, and you see the poverty in places like El Salvador. You understand why they're so desperate to get out of El Salvador and into this country. But that doesn't mean we don't need to secure our borders. But at the same time, we need to realize that these immigrants that are here, they're not going back. We need to bring them into our society, and we need to give them opportunities. I've been criticized for supporting the Dream Act, which would give tuition assistance to children of undocumented aliens. I don't believe in penalizing children because of the mistakes of their parents. I just really believe that society—*we* need to be more open, more inclusive. We need to absolutely secure our borders. That's what defines us as Americans. But these individuals that have been here for decades now, we need to find a way to bring them into our society.

W.O.: That's a very compassionate, generous, enlightened view. It ain't particularly a Republican view.

J.C.: Right. Maybe I'm not the typical Republican. I'll leave that up to others to define. When I think about being a Republican, it's about opportunity. Whether that is a child of an illegal immigrant or my child, I want to give them the same opportunity. That's what is going to make our country or our state better, by giving them the tools to succeed and having them as part of our society.

W.O.: John Cahill, I don't know if you can pull this off. But you've got a lot of people rooting for you. All of a sudden, I spend an hour with you and I feel better about politics. I feel better about the Republican Party. You're a damn breath of fresh air.

J.C.: Well, Bill, thank you. As the Mets used to say, "You gotta believe!" I can win this. And the polls may say something now, and then in June or July, that doesn't mean anything. What really means something is getting this message out across the state. I appreciate it. It's been fun being on with you. I think New York can do better. That's why I'm out there.

W.O.: Who is more difficult, O'Shaughnessy or Fred Dicker?

J.C.: That's not quite close.

W.O.: We carry him proudly, every afternoon at 4:00 on WVOX.

J.C.: I know. Fred and I go way back. We've had our conversations over the years, and listen, he's a tough journalist up in Albany. It's great to be on with you, Bill. You've been a good friend.

PART III
OF AN EVENING . . .

A Little Night Music

During my already long life, I've always been a sucker for a sentimental song. And one day I actually sat down and compiled a list of those absolutely essential and marvelous romantic songs that have accompanied the courting rites of several generations.

They're part of the canon of the great American songbook. Some are obscure and known only to musicians. Included in the list are several by Cole Porter, Rodgers and Hart, Harold Arlen, Johnny Mercer, Johnny Burke, Arthur Schwartz, Jimmy Van Heusen, and the Gershwins. There are also gems by my friends Matt Dennis and Sir Richard Rodney Bennett. All these melodic products of their genius have, I think, a certain sweetness to them. And you can understand—and feel—the words to these songs. We've tried to keep this kind of music alive over the years on Whitney Radio's regional stations in the New York metro area.

As you look through the list, I'm sure you'll find some of your own favorites included. And perhaps you will agree that most of them are best listened to while moving around a dance floor with a good-looking dame in your arms and a few shooters under your belt. And I wasn't going to tell you this, but if pressed, my own personal all-time favorites are "I've Got You Under My Skin," "I Get a Kick Out of You," "Polka Dots and Moonbeams," "Moonlight Becomes You," "Nancy (With the Laughing Face)," "It's Always You," and Love Is the Sweetest Thing."

And just one more: "Looking at You." ("I'm filled with the essence of the quintessence of joy. I hear poets telling of lovely Helen of Troy.") Here is my list of the "favorites":

"A Kiss to Build a Dream On"	"Again"
"A Nightingale Sang in Berkeley Square"	"All the Things You Are"
	"As Time Goes By"

[231]

"At Last"
"Autumn in New York"
"Begin the Beguine"
"Bewitched, Bothered and
 Bewildered"
"Blame It on My Youth"
"Blue Moon"
"Body and Soul"
"Change Partners"
"Cheek to Cheek"
"Down in the Depths on the
 Ninetieth Floor"
"Dream Dancing"
"Early Autumn"
"Embraceable You"
"Everything Happens to Me"
"Ev'ry Time We Say Goodbye"
"Fools Rush In"
"For All We Know"
"How About You?"
"How Did She Look?"
"I Can't Get Started"
"I Didn't Know What Time
 It Was"
"I Get a Kick Out of You"
"I Get Along without You Very
 Well"
"I Guess I'll Have to Change
 My Plan"
"I Love You Just the Way
 You Are"
"I Never Went Away from You"
"I Should Care"
"I'll Be Around"
"I'll Take Romance"
"I'll Remember April"

"I'm Old-Fashioned"
"I've Got a Crush on You"
"I've Got You Under My Skin"
"I've Never Been in Love
 Before"
"Impossible"
"Incurably Romantic"
"It Had to Be You"
"It Never Entered My Mind"
"It's Always You"
"Let's Fall in Love"
"Long Ago (and Far Away)"
"Looking at You"
"Love Is Here to Stay"
"Love Is the Sweetest Thing"
"Love Walked In"
"Maybe You'll Be There"
"Moonlight Becomes You"
"Moonlight in Vermont"
"My Romance"
"Nancy (with the Laughing
 Face)"
"Night and Day"
"On Green Dolphin Street"
"Polka Dots and Moonbeams"
"September in the Rain"
"She Dances Overhead"
"Smoke Gets in Your Eyes"
"Someone to Watch over Me"
"So Near and Yet So Far"
"Stars Fell on Alabama"
"Stella by Starlight"
"Stranger in Paradise"
"Sweet Caroline"
"Taking a Chance on Love"
"Time after Time"

"That's All"
"The Folks Who Live on the
    Hill"
"The More I See You"
"The Most Beautiful Girl in the
    World"
"The Nearness of You"
"The Night We Called It a Day"
"The Way You Look Tonight"
"The You and Me That Used
    to Be (Whatever Became
    of . . .)"
"Then I'll Be Tired of You"
"There Will Never Be Another
    You"
"There's a Small Hotel"
"These Foolish Things"
"They Can't Take That Away
    from Me"

"They Didn't Believe Me"
"This Could Be the Start of
    Something Big"
"This Is My Night to Dream"
"Too Late Now"
"Until the Real Thing Comes
    Along"
"Violets for Your Furs"
"Wait 'Til You See Her"
"What's New?"
"What Is There to Say?"
"Where Are You?"
"Where or When"
"Why Do I Love You?"
"Why Shouldn't I?"
"You Are Too Beautiful"
"You Make Me Feel So Young"
"You're My Everything"
"You've Changed"

The Best Interpreters
of the Great American Songbook

Frank Sinatra . . . Fred Astaire . . . Nat King Cole . . . Mabel Mercer . . .
Tony Bennett . . . Mel Tormé . . . Chet Baker . . . Ella Fitzgerald . . . Doris
Day . . . Bing Crosby . . . Louis Armstrong . . . Bobby Short . . . Hugh
Shannon . . . Rosemary Clooney . . . Tony Perkins . . . Vic Damone . . .
Skinnay Ennis . . . Charles Trenet . . . Norman Drubner . . . Blossom
Dearie . . . Jack Sheldon . . . Daryl Sherman . . . Ronny Whyte . . . Sylvia
Syms . . . Noel Coward . . . Richard Rodney Bennett . . . Robert Merrill . . .
Chuck Castleberry . . . Dean Martin . . . Gianni Russo . . . David Allyn
. . . Billie Holiday . . . Judy Garland . . . Murray Grand . . . Lady Gaga . . .
Sarah Vaughan . . . Steve Ross . . . KT Sullivan . . . Edith Piaf . . . Matt
Monroe . . . Mama Cass Elliot . . . Peggy Lee . . . Lena Horne . . . Eddie
Sessa . . . Billy Joel . . . Peter Mintun . . . Steve Lawrence . . . Eydie
Gormé. . . Andrea Bocelli . . . Neil Diamond . . . Rod Stewart . . . Ethel
Merman . . . Johnny Mercer . . . Matt Dennis . . . Charlie Cochran . . .
Tierney Sutton . . . John Pizzarelli . . . Michael Feinstein . . . Lee Wiley . . .
Charles Osgood . . . June Christy. . .

HOWEVER, I'M LESS THAN ENTHUSED BY . . .

Some who look on **Michael Bublé** and really know music, like
   Egidiana Maccioni, a gifted singer in her own right, see Michael
   as the second coming of the Great Sinatra. I don't.
Harry Connick, Jr., is a good-looking guy who may be terrific on
   stage. But I'm not convinced he can sing.
Steve Tyrell often emotes in the legendary Café Carlyle where, for
   many years, the regal and magnificent Bobby Short, of sainted

memory, dazzled the landed gentry. Tyrell's presence in that hallowed, exclusive venue is almost blasphemous. He's admittedly got a lot of admirers for his scratchy, gravelly voiced warbling. I'm not among them.

Jack Jones is a nice guy. I knew and interviewed his father and mother, both great singers. Jack has pipes almost as good as Damone's. But his choice of material, arrangements, and orchestrations has always been wanting.

And one more: **Barbra Streisand's** nasal, tonal, one-note voice is an "acquired taste" which I never acquired.

"A Real New York Evening . . ." Radio

Gianni Russo is a marvelous New York character who starred in The Godfather *as Carlo Rizzi, Michael Corleone's brother-in-law. He met his Maker via "Clemenza" on the way to the airport. Gianni, now in his seventies and still a very attractive fellow, is a cabaret performer in the New York area and author of* Hollywood Godfather, *a chronicle of his colorful life.*

Gianni Russo's dazzling dinner shows at the fabled Le Cirque are wonderful "New York evenings" with music, romance, style, great food, and beautiful people! He's the best entertainer around these days!

The beguiling and attractive *Godfather* star has been a class act in every season of his life—a crooner of romantic and achingly lovely songs. New York has not seen his like in a nightclub since Bobby Short or the late Hugh Shannon, the great café society saloon singers who wrote the book on pleasing well-heeled patrons by reaching out and drawing in an audience with timeless Cole Porter and Rodgers and Hart classics.

So many cabaret singers "emote" and "perform." It's all about *them.* Gianni Russo *entertains.*

[I was surprised to learn he's also quite a writer. His tome *Hollywood Godfather* was just published by St. Martin's Press, and it's a spectacular look back at the Golden Age of film and entertainment.]

On the Occasion of Sirio Maccioni's Eightieth Birthday

Sirio Maccioni reigned as America's greatest restaurateur for many decades. Remarks by William O'Shaughnessy, April 5, 2012, Le Cirque in New York City

---

Maestro . . . another distinguished member of your tribe (also with a considerable number of vowels in his name), Mario Cuomo, who himself will soon reach the milestone you have achieved this day, once said he prays for "sureness."

Well, I'm not sure of too many things in my own already long life. But of this I'm very sure: You . . . are . . . a . . . great man.

You have been a class act in every season of your life and we have repaired to your tables and to your care and keeping in every season of ours.

So keep going, Sirio . . . because we could not imagine New York—or our own drab lives—without you to paint color and style in all of it.

And so we congratulate you on this—the eightieth anniversary of your natal day.

And just one other thing: We love you.

All of us . . .

Sirio Maccioni of Le Cirque

A radio interview with Sirio and his son Marco, October 10, 2013.

WILLIAM O'SHAUGHNESSY: I'm getting hungry before we even start this interview. While in your care and keeping we're going to visit today with *the* most famous restaurateur in America. His name is Sirio Maccioni, the ringmaster of Le Cirque. And also with us in our Westchester studios is one of his sons and heirs, Marco Maccioni. Sirio, you and I have been friends for years.

SIRIO MACCIONI: Many, *many* years!

W.O.: Thus will you trust me to conduct myself properly?

S.M.: Absolutely. You always conduct yourself properly!

W.O.: First things first. Marco Eugenio Maccioni, since we last spoke, you've become a father.

MARCO MACCIONI: Yes, a very proud father. His name is Massimo Sirio.

W.O.: And that means Maestro Sirio is once again a grandfather.

M.M.: This is number five!

S.M.: His son is so beautiful. He's a beast, and I like him because he knows what he wants. And I hope he grows up like this.

W.O.: I've met him, an adorable kid, blonde hair. How old is he now?

M.M.: A year and nine months. His birthday is Christmas Day.

W.O.: Massimo Sirio Maccioni—how did you arrive at that name for the kid?

M.M.: Well, of course, to honor a certain someone. Massimo's personality, no coincidence, is very similar to that of an individual you and I have dealt with over the years. Only he's my old man.

W.O.: Young Massimo lights up a room; he owns the camera wherever he goes.

M.M.: He's a showman, that's for sure!

w.o.: Maestro Sirio Maccioni, you're in your eighty-second year. The clock ticks . . .

s.m.: Please don't talk about that. I ache. I have everything. Every malady. The only thing I like to do is walk with my sons. My wife doesn't beat me up anymore. But I hate to get old.

w.o.: You're being honored all over the planet. Everywhere I look, a food magazine or restaurant blog or newsletter or head of state— you're being honored in Paris, in Rome, in your hometown Montecatini in the hills of Tuscany, even in Dubai.

s.m.: I was also honored in Vegas!

w.o.: Did you lose any money while you were picking up those latest encomiums?

s.m.: No, I don't gamble. I hate gambling.

m.m.: My mom takes care of that!

w.o.: What do you mean?

m.m.: She's got a "golden arm" with the slots—let's just leave it right there. She likes the slots.

w.o.: Is it true your wife and mother of so many years, Egidiana Palmieri, was once a famous singer in Italy?

s.m.: *Very* famous! She's the one that introduced Italy to Julio Iglesias and the other guy who is still singing today in Vegas. And then one day she came home and said, "I don't sing anymore." I said, "You don't sing anymore? So you help with the soup." But she was a great singer.

w.o.: Is it true she gave up a $25,000 signing bonus to appear at Carnegie Hall to marry *you*?

s.m.: She did that after we were married. I thought it would be good for her to be a manager of me and the restaurant and the family, and I realized I had to start to sell soup again.

w.o.: Is that what you call your profession—the restaurant business— "selling soup"?

s.m.: That's what it *is*!

w.o.: Speaking of your wife, Egidiana—there's now another singer in the family: your dazzling daughter-in-law Sabrina Wender Maccioni.

s.m.: She's also very attractive.

w.o.: The girl can also sing. I've heard her. She can carry a tune.

S.M.: From now on, we have "Mondays with Music" at Le Cirque. And I would like her—only her—to be in charge. She knows more than anybody.

W.O.: You have music at the estimable and serene Le Cirque?

M.M.: Yes. In the wine lounge, the café.

W.O.: You now preside over many venues—they call it the Maccioni Restaurant Group. So "selling soup" has gotten pretty lucrative!

M.M.: No, there's just more of us. So Sirio has to sell more soup!

S.M.: We're still selling *soup*!

W.O.: Is your two-year-old son Massimo on the damn payroll?

M.M.: He does bring in the chicks.

W.O.: Like Sirio.

M.M.: Yes. And we share all the fun with my brother Mario, who has recently moved back to New York to assist us with the operation.

W.O.: How many sons are there?

M.M.: Mario is the eldest. I'm after Mario. And Mauro is responsible for Circo.

W.O.: Sirio, are they all good boys? Are they OK?

S.M.: They are all good boys. One different than the other, thank God! They start in the dining room. Especially with the ladies. Our patrons, the beautiful ladies, need to eat. They don't eat food. They just go, "Marco . . . Marco!" And Mario, he's, well, he's intelligent. But sometimes he should give up some intelligence and become more practical. And Mauro, he's the *beast*!

W.O.: The youngest one?

S.M.: Yes. A terror to the chefs. I keep telling him not to go into the kitchen while the chefs are busy. Talk to them the day after. You talk to a chef while he's busy, they don't even listen to you. But they are all doing well, my sons.

W.O.: I've seen them all in action, and the other two will forgive me— Marco is quite the most charming. He's the dining room dazzler— like his old man—I intuit.

S.M.: He *is* charming. Incidentally, while we're at it, it is not true I have an ego, or that I want to show off. Most of the time I could talk to the people we are fortunate to have as employees. I don't really like that. I think in a restaurant, you should not talk too much. You should know what your workers are doing, but not talk too much.

w.o.: Maestro Sirio Maccioni, there are so many things we want to ask the great restaurateur while you're here in Westchester. Didn't you also just receive another handsome honor, just two days ago?

m.m.: Yes, *Esquire* magazine's Hall of Fame. John Mariani, food writer, critic, author. He's someone who knows the New York food scene as well as the international scene. He presented it. He has been manning the food and culinary helm at *Esquire* for thirty years now, and Mr. Granger, his editor, is a wonderful person as well. Also a client.

w.o.: So you were all assumed into the *Esquire* magazine Hall of Fame?

m.m.: Sirio was; we were all just along for the ride.

s.m.: *No*, the *family*, the *family* was!

w.o.: Maestro Sirio, did you make a speech on the occasion?

s.m.: No. *He* [Marco] made a speech!

w.o.: Who is a better talker, father or son?

m.m.: Who's longer-winded, you mean?

s.m.: I like to tell the truth. Sometimes the truth hurts and takes time.

w.o.: Sirio, you and your sons, the Maccioni "family," as you like to call it, preside over the mighty Le Cirque in the Bloomberg Building on 58th Street. In the Bloomberg Courtyard. And also in Manhattan you'll find one of my favorites, Circo—over on 55th Street, off Sixth. And there you'll find a little guy—he weighs about 125 pounds, stripped, fighting wet—named Bruno Dussin, the maître d'.

s.m.: He knows what he's doing. Sometimes he's a pain the neck, but he knows what he's doing. Really, for me, he's one of the best assets we have.

w.o.: And your own name is also on Fifth Avenue, across from the entrance to the park. "Sirio," in the legendary Pierre.

s.m.: You know why? My first job when I came to this country was at the Pierre. I knew everybody—1955.

w.o.: What were you? A waiter? The maître d'?

s.m.: I was *nothing*—a cleaner!

M.M.: But soon after that, he worked at Delmonico's and then, eventually, at the fabled Colony, and he went back to the Pierre and was the manager of the Le Foret Club, where our dear friend Peter Duchin was musical director and pianist. That was in the Pierre too.

S.M.: I engaged, I signed, Peter Duchin. We actually had the first "disco" in New York. When Peter Duchin was playing, the people were packed to the walls until one o'clock in the morning. We had some of the most beautiful women staying at the Pierre, even more than today.

M.M.: Sirio started Le Cirque soon after that. But before that was the Colony, of course.

S.M.: I was twenty-three years old.

W.O.: Sirio, I've seen pictures of you in every season of your life surrounded by beautiful women.

S.M.: Very important, Mr. O'Shaughnessy.

W.O.: What's the secret of your charm?

S.M.: *Not having any* charm. That's the "secret." Not to tease, that you *have* charm.

W.O.: After eighty-two years, you can tell me.

S.M.: For example, lately we hired somebody who was working for us when he was really young. He was good. By mistake, he became an "owner" in his own mind, and now he's changed. I try to know what our clients want. You have to know when they want to talk, and you have to know when *you* have to stop talking.

W.O.: Sirio, at Le Cirque, you sit at your perch just inside the door, near the coatroom. And they say even at eighty-two, you miss nothing coming through the door in a low-cut dress or with a shapely leg. I've watched you of an evening.

M.M.: A good pair of legs never goes unnoticed!

W.O.: Marco, is it fair then to say your old man is something of a babe magnet, in every season?

M.M.: No. Say he is a "keeper" of the ladies! That was the success of Le Cirque over the years in that the power people—and that's no offense to anyone—but there was a time we didn't give the same importance to so-called professional females in this world who are now leading this country. But those power women were married to people leading this country, and they would come to Le Cirque, and he was their "keeper" and made sure they were well taken care of while everyone else—their husbands—[was] working.

W.O.: So how do you get a good table at a Maccioni restaurant, at the mighty Le Cirque?

M.M.: Make a reservation and become a client. That's it!

W.O.: Do you have to *look* a certain way?

M.M.: No, we've always had distinguished clientele. The reason we try to keep an elegant restaurant is out of respect to those ladies.

S.M.: Human nature, I still teach. You cannot like everybody. I *respect* everybody. But I don't *like* everybody. And the people you like, they must feel that you like them. And we like a lot of people. Most of them. Even the pope. I became a very close friend of the one that died.

W.O.: Is it true you once fed the Holy Father?

S.M.: Pope John Paul II; he's the one who named our HBO movie, the documentary, *A Table in Heaven*.

W.O.: How did they get that title? I know Sheila Nevins from the country. She's a smart dame.

S.M.: The Holy Father gave the title. He said you should call this film *A Table in Heaven*. We were talking about "reservations" when we fed him lunch at the Vatican nuncio's residence up on 72nd Street. The pope said, "Do you mean if I want to come back here to New York and go to Le Cirque, I have to call you for a reservation?" I said, "Don't worry, Holy Father, *you* can come anytime!" We were talking about reservations with him, and Cardinal O'Connor heard it. Although the cardinal was a completely different mentality, he was a great man too.

W.O.: But according to legend—and the documentary—you asked the Holy Father to make a "reservation" for *you*.

S.M.: Up there, upstairs!

W.O.: Upstairs, in heaven?

S.M.: He said, "Sirio, are we *sure*, are we sure we go '*up* there'?" He was really a great man.

W.O.: How do you like the new pope, Francis?

s.m.: He scares me. He's too good to be true.

w.o.: I can't get enough of him. I think he's great too.

s.m.: Last night, I was watching him speak. The *people* in the Vatican really tell the truth. The Church is great. I believe in the Church. You have to believe in something. If you don't—I, well, I have my own downfalls. I fail . . .

w.o.: We all do, Sirio.

s.m.: They don't like when I say that, my family. I desperately like my sons. I would like them to fight with me. Don't fight among yourselves. I love my wife. She's great. Too good to be true! You know who's becoming close to my wife? Mario's wife, the new wife. She's great. She's a good person. Also, you have to know how to take a difficult moment and difficult people—I have a lot of difficult people in my life—but I have become friends with these difficult people. I do it on purpose.

w.o.: Sirio, what's the secret of keeping someone happy, of an evening, in a restaurant?

s.m.: Knowing what you're doing, of course, is important. Don't talk too much! When people want to talk—the important people—they will let you know. For me, all the people that come into Le Cirque are important.

w.o.: In every season, you seem to get high-rollers like Donald Trump, Ron Perelman, Nancy Reagan, Jack Welch of GE.

s.m.: I can say I've become friends with some of the most "difficult" people in the world. And many were powerful too!

w.o.: Difficult?

m.m.: *Demanding.* Let's use that word.

s.m.: Powerful, yes. We even had the famous lawyer—in years gone by—Roy Cohn. *He* was difficult. But I would say to Mr. Cohn, "Come here anytime you want." He was even bringing his own tuna fish. But he was a most brilliant man. And those are the dangerous people—if they are against you. I never had one great man against me. Including all the presidents. I can say that Ronald Reagan would ask me, "Can I call you my friend?" I said, "Of course, Mr. President!" When we went to the inauguration in Washington, he said, "You guinea bastard, come over here and say hello!"

W.O.: President Reagan said that?

S.M.: I didn't know that he was the one who personally sent me the big, fancy, engraved invitation to his inaugural.

W.O.: He called you a "guinea bastard"?

S.M.: Yes! And speaking of which, two months ago I was in France with Albert of Monaco . . .

W.O.: The Crown Prince? Actually, I guess he runs the place now.

S.M.: There were 600 people there. He got up from the table with his girl and came over to my table. That was great. That's great, great.

W.O.: He was playing maître d'? The prince?

S.M.: Yes. And at the funeral of Malcolm Forbes at St. Bart's church here in New York, his sons said I knew their father better than they did. And the boys said, "Can you come to the church?" Well, we saw Nixon coming with the family. They said I had to talk to him because there wasn't room. "You are part of our family, Sirio. Can you talk to him?" So I went outside, and all the press in New York was there. "You bastard, you stay inside with the family and the high-rollers! Who do you think you are?" said the president.

W.O.: Nixon couldn't get in?

S.M.: I went to them and said to let him in. They didn't have the courage to say no to Nixon. So we took him inside.

W.O.: *You* got Nixon into Malcolm Forbes's funeral?

S.M.: Yes. There was another time when it was Malcolm Forbes's birthday in Morocco. We took the breakfast to the plane.

M.M.: We did the in-flight catering for the "Capitalist Tool" airplane that was flying out all the guests to La Mamounia in Morocco.

S.M.: Malcolm Forbes—I knew he had a plane that flew 80 people. But they said they had 600 for the trip! So they eventually had three planes flying. We worked all night, and they gave us a truck to go to the airport with the food.

W.O.: Maestro Sirio and your son and heir Marco Eugenio, it's nice to reminiscence about all these colorful people. A lot of them are gone now. Has it changed, the whole world around you?

S.M.: Unfortunately, my problem is sometimes I have to say what I want to say, and it's not politically correct. But for me I can say I was a friend of Nixon. He was a nice man. Politically, he did China

[245]

and everything. Let's stop there. Nixon was a very good man. Period. I would say to him, "Mr. President, would you like to go tell the chef what you would like to eat today?" He would go in the kitchen and tell the chef he wanted vichyssoise and rack of lamb and then chocolate soufflé. Can you imagine in the kitchen of a restaurant you would see the president of the United States give the order directly! It was great. But I could do that. I find myself saying terrible things, but I become nice if I have tell them something.

w.o.: Sirio, that was a time when all gentlemen wore ties and women were discreetly and stylishly "outfitted"—they didn't show too much shoulder or any cleavage.

s.m.: They were very elegant.

w.o.: Now I've seen people, even in your great restaurant, who walk in with blue jeans and with their belly buttons or backsides hanging out.

s.m.: We have two sides in Le Cirque now. The bar side, we're casual. But in the restaurant, No! People are very nice. They like that we insist on decorum. We have young people come in and after they are there they say, "Oh my God! Why do people say this is a difficult restaurant? We like it *because* everything is elegant." People like it elegant. It's a very good thing to do, besides good food.

w.o.: I've seen more young people come in; you treat them well.

m.m.: That's the misconception. Coming through the door of Le Cirque, most people think there is a certain "protocol"—which is true. But you yourself and anyone else who has come through that threshold are made to feel at home.

w.o.: Do you have to tip the maître d' to get a good table?

m.m.: Absolutely not! You tip *after* you've had your experience. Some of our regulars actually do because they have an established track record, but it's better not to.

s.m.: Let me say one thing. At one point we wanted to get away from people coming in with the $5.00 to the maître d'. I don't like that.

w.o.: $5.00?

m.m.: He's talking about 1974 when he opened! $5.00 doesn't get you a cappuccino now!

s.m.: People call me, and they say you cannot tell me not to give
  something to Mario Wainer, our great maître d', or to the doorman.
  This is *my* house, they think. $5.00, $10.00, $15.00. They take it as
  part of the show.

w.o.: What's an acceptable tip now?

m.m.: An acceptable tip is according to what you are spending. If a
  maître d' takes care of you—whether it's Le Cirque or any other
  restaurant—even the maître d' would appreciate something after
  the fact. They know they are being rewarded for something they
  have actually done.

w.o.: For service rendered.

m.m.: Yes, for service. If you get it *before*, then you're "sold." And if
  you can't maintain your word, then you've done a misdeed in
  their mind.

w.o.: Marco, have you ever had a *gavone*, someone come in and try to
  tip *you*? Someone said you never tip the owner!

m.m.: Oh yes. I politely decline, and if they insist, I tell them that once
  you're done, give it to my maître d', very discreetly letting them
  know I'm not the person.

s.m.: One time we decided we weren't going to let people tip. People
  would say, "Why are we not allowed to tip?" I would say, "After your
  lunch or dinner, you can do whatever you want. But don't do it
  when you come in." It's terrible. Most of the restaurants in New
  York—I hate that. You see the guy come in with the money in his
  hand, and the maître d' looks at the money, and then you go right
  in.

w.o.: Maestro, you honor us with your presence. How long do you
  think you can keep going? How long can you keep the music
  playing?

s.m.: I hope forever. I hate to get old. I have everything, every
  malady. But I have good sons. I have a good business. But I also
  know how to count. I know how to count. How many years do I
  have? It's terrible. Life is so great. I have a difficult life. But a great
  life. I had a tough beginning. My parents were killed. But I had a
  great grandmother.

W.O.: Sirio, you are one of the most honored men in your profession. Thank you for coming today and for bringing your son Marco, your memories, and your passion.

M.M.: Thank you, Your Excellency. That's what we call Mr. O'Shaughnessy!

W.O.: Marco, we went just a minute too long.

FYI: The great Le Cirque closed in 2017. And Circo was shuttered in 2018. But the Maccioni banner still waves in Vegas, Dubai, and India. The youngest son, Mauro, is struggling to open a New York flagship.

Saloon Songs from Toots Shor to Sirio Maccioni

Originally published in 1999 in AirWAVES,
Fordham University Press.

———————

I have always found great wisdom in saloons. As a young man I first knew the beguiling haze of an evening in Bernard "Toots" Shor's glorious establishment on 52nd Street in Manhattan. Toots had his "kids" back then. Frank Gifford and Kyle Rote were his favorites. But he also had a soft spot for an Irish radio-time salesman from Westchester.

At the Toots Shor bar one could learn many valuable lessons about times you never lived. The drinks were strong and the talk was of DiMaggio, Hemingway, Mark Hellinger, Runyon, Bill Corum, Eddie Arcaro, and Grantland Rice.

The conversation was vivid and dazzling. And on a good night you would encounter Howard Cosell; William Pierce Rogers, who had a day job as secretary of state; Bob Considine; James A. Farley and his tall, attractive son Jim; Paul Screvane; Jimmy Breslin; Jock Whitney; Walter Thayer; Hugh Carey; Howard Samuels; James Brady; John Lindsay; Sonny Werblin; Jack Whittaker; Jack O'Brien; Jackie Gleason; Edward Bennett Williams; and Ford Frick, who would stop in on his way home to Bronxville. Also the great Hearst sportswriter Jimmy Cannon. I idolized him. And everyone who ever had to approach a typewriter for a living has tried to copy him. One night Omar Bradley, a general of the armies, walked in with a circular cluster of *five* stars on the epaulets of his dress blues.

You would see the legendary John "Shipwreck" Kelly eating apple pie on a barstool while Toots ate kosher pickles washed down with diet Coke. On one such occasion, Toots paid Ship Kelly an extravagant compliment by identifying the two toughest guys he ever met . . . the ones you want next to you if you're "trapped in an alley!" Shipwreck

Kelly "with his bare fists" . . . or Sinatra "with a broken beer bottle in his right hand."

Other barroom philosophers included classy Bruce Snyder, an enduring and endearing presence at the invincible "21" Club. Bruce is keeper of the flame for "21" and guards the heritage and tradition of this grand old Lorelei of a saloon with a fierce devotion. He understands about generations and in-laws and always has a marvelous story to divert you when you are hurting or just plain exhausted.

Over the years, I've encountered some other prescient, sage observers across many nights in other towns . . . like Al and George Salerno of Salerno's Old Coach Inn in Tuckahoe. It is the first venue to which every Bronxville husband repairs to reflect on a busted marriage. The Salernos have heard it all. They listen with gentleness and generosity.

There have been other great saloonkeepers during the time of my careful research into these matters: General Richard Crabtree of the Kittle House qualifies. As does Joe Valeant of Bernie Murray's in upstate Elmira, who once advised me to sell a farm "due to the health of the owner . . . the owner's wife will *murder* him if he doesn't unload the damn thing!" just one example of his genius.

Joe Valeant has some competition from a steakhouse owner—Tommy Moretti, also of Elmira. And two brothers named Smith—John and Fran—and their Uncle Squeegie give good convo at Mangialardo's next to an old freight yard and rail head end of the Lehigh Valley railroad in the sad, bleak hills of Pennsylvania near the New York border, where Carl Hayden, the chancellor of the New York State Board of Regents, goes to drink and eat garlic pizza with his wife, Cindy; and Tom Mullen, the former mayor who prays for Mario Cuomo every morning at Mass in South Waverly.

And surely there are no more endearing souls than one encounters at Mario's of Arthur Avenue in the Little Italy–Belmont section of the Bronx. No matter how fast your world is spinning out of control . . . the Migliuccis—Mama Rose and her son Joseph—will restore your balance and equilibrium. The ingredient dispensed along with their drinks and Neapolitan food is called *Love*. Here you will see Lee Iacocca, Mario Biaggi, Bill Fugazy, some Yankees, and, maybe, Steinbrenner. Also a lot of Fordham professors and their students . . . plus a group of Westchester high-rollers in Jaguars, BMWs, and Range Rovers.

A darling man and real gentleman named Will Higgins presides over the historic King Cole Bar in the St. Regis Hotel, which is now in the care and keeping of master hotelier Richard Cotter. And Jimmy Neary still draws the likes of Jonathan Bush and Pat Barrett to his agreeable place on 57th Street. Journalist Neal Travis, a nice man in a murky profession, and his colorful sidekick Steve Dunleavy dispense wonderful witticisms and wild, irreverent observations about everything from their perch at Langan's in the theater district, while across town James Brady and Jack Rudin preside at the Four Seasons with its modern Miesian space also providing a great forum for the humorous antics of partners Julian Niccolini and Alex Von Bidder.

MAESTRO SIRIO

But the greatest of all barroom poets is Sirio Maccioni. Now when I recently encountered Billy Cunningham, the *Times*'s brilliant lensman, on his favorite corner, 57th and Fifth, the great society photographer who is Manhattan's pre-eminent chronicler of the rich, the famous, and stylish, advised me against comparing Toots Shor and Sirio Maccioni or even putting them in the same breath. Cunningham is a beloved icon of New York . . . and it may be a far stretch . . . but I still believe a saloon is a saloon, no matter the trappings or neighborhood. Thus Sirio.

Sitting on a barstool with Maestro Sirio at the Le Cirque restaurant is a thrilling adventure. Maccioni is a wise man, provocative, charming, and absolutely accurate in his marvelous commentary about life and people. Here then are some late-night *pronouncements* from the Magnificent Maccioni . . . who is America's greatest restaurateur. And bar keep. They were flung out into an empty dining room . . . late at night . . . when all the swells had gone home. Here then, retrieved from my notebook, are mementos of delightful evenings spent with the greatest of all contemporary saloonkeepers . . .

THE GOSPEL ACCORDING TO SIRIO

"I think there should be a moment in life when you do what you want to do."

"You should show that you respect people . . . but also show you can do without them."

"I resent stupidity. One must have rules. I have rules. One must always be 'correct.'"

"Ninety percent of the people are nice . . . too nice. If I would follow my instinct, I would be sued . . . I would open a restaurant for only attractive people . . . make that *nice* people."

"Donald Trump is a very nice person. I call him and within one minute he calls me back. I don't care about his problems with other people . . ."

"When you ask someone to build you a $3 million kitchen . . . they ask are you sure you need it. I never did all this to prove I am better than the other people in my business. We did it because it was something we had to do. We are working people. Physical work. Mental work. And not to be intrusive. That is what we are about."

"If something happens to me . . . just say: 'Sirio has said it all.' One life is not enough to prove yourself."

"I like women who are fun . . . who don't try to save the world . . . and men who are 'correct.'"

"There is an Italian saying: If you wake up in the morning and have no pain . . . you're dead!"

"When anybody can criticize a king or a president . . . then they are not a king. Or a president."

"In my short life, I have seen a fellow open a bottle of Dom Perignon when they killed Kennedy. Stupidity . . . just stupid."

"They say I put pressure on my sons to achieve. But I would never force anybody to be great in life."

"They ask me if I'm religious. Of course I am. But I hate people who only pray when they need something."

"When I was maître d' at the Colony . . . people didn't understand why I gave Warren Avis and Yanna the best table. They're *attractive.*"

"My wife Egidiana tells me when she came here she didn't know anybody. The only thing that mattered is she wanted to be with me."

"When I hear today that only twelve civilians were killed in the bombing in Iraq I got sick. I remember the bombs falling on us in my town. I have been under the bombs. My father, a civilian, died on his bicycle under the bombs. My grandfather saw it. He said let's go to church. He had unlimited respect for authority and uniforms. When he saw a uniform of any kind, he would bend. Twenty-seven percent had the courage to say we should not bomb. The Moroccans and the English 'liberated' us. They only raped 1,500. The Germans no one. They might *shoot* you!"

"My wife always says: If everybody takes care of their own little spot . . . everything would be O.K."

"I'm always scared. But for me to be scared is a point of strength. I don't believe in luck. If someone shoots you . . . you're unlucky."

"I tell my sons: Concentrate on the people. Don't spend time talking to the coat check girl or the bartender. Don't look outside on a day like this to see if it's raining or snowing. I tell them to look *inside*. The time you spend talking to the coat check girl is wasted forever."

"I'm reading a book *Europa Vivente*. It means Europe is still alive. A Florentine wrote it . . . a Florentine with a German father. He is trying to show the stupidity of democracy. The only problem with Mussolini is he was trying to please everybody. The greatness of Italy was in the Medici, the Borgias. They were assassins! But they alone created and encouraged art. But they were against the Italians. You put two Italians together and they can destroy anything!"

"The Italians always seem to need a tyrant to become great."

"The other night I was with the cardinal at the Knights of Malta dinner. I did not wear my sword and certainly not the cape because I look like Dracula. I was the only one at my table who was not Irish. They sang 'Danny Boy.' I said you are discriminating at this table. What about 'O, Solo Mio'? I hate that song! I didn't tell them that the first gift to me in America was given by Morton Downey. It was a record of 'Danny Boy.'"

"My sons lecture to me. You are in America, they say. You have to adjust. What is going to be with the next generation? There is no class, no style."

"Clinton is not the exception. There are so many stupid men."

"I am going to be one of the three voting judges of the Miss Universe Contest in Martinique the first week of May. Donald Trump asked me to take his place because he is so busy. He is also so smart. The first thing he did was ask my wife. She said it was very nice. It would be good for Sirio. And then she went off to Atlantic City with her Uncle Renato for the day and came home after midnight and woke me up to show me the 300 quarters she won!"

"I blame the basketball season on the players. My wife agrees. She went after Patrick Ewing at the restaurant. He is very nice, but she told him he was wrong and she will never to go another game. And she never will."

"New York has been very good to us . . . the press . . . Donald Trump . . . Mayor Giuliani . . . everybody. I never did all this to say I'm better than the others. It's something we had to do. We're working people. There is no such thing to be an artist. We work . . . the thing happens. It is about having an understanding of what people want when they come to your restaurant."

"When we fed the pope there were sixteen cardinals at the table. It was on 72nd Street at the papal nuncio's house. The pope is a good eater. He likes fish, he likes rice, he likes pasta. Archbishop Martino, a great, intelligent man, is the pope's ambassador, and so he can only be intelligent, was the host. We went, we cooked . . . with security from the United States, from Italy, from the Vatican. He is a good eater, the Holy Father. He ate risotto with porcini and he ate fish. My pastry chef Jacques Torres made a replica of the Vatican's Saint Peter's Basilica. The pope asked me if it was true we had a three-month wait list for a reservation. I said, 'Holy Father . . . why don't you come tonight.' The pope laughed and said tonight he was not going to have such a good dinner. Since the Holy Father was talking about 'reservations,' I asked Archbishop Martino what about a 'reservation' up in heaven. So the archbishop asked the Holy Father . . . don't you think it would be very nice to have a great restaurant in heaven? And the Holy Father looked at me and Cardinal O'Connor and said: 'Are we *sure* . . . are we sure we go *up there*?' The pope is amazing. He spoke to me in Italian, to my son in English, to the pastry chef in French, and to my executive chef Sottha Kuhnn in Thai. Then the Holy Father asked me if I was a good Christian . . . or just another Italian who only gets religious when he gets sick? You know in Italy we think because we have the pope . . . and it's a local call, we sometimes get a little casual and complacent."

"The philosophy of a restaurant is to make a place pleasant. Sometimes it is the people who create the problems. I think people should look correct. I'm not talking black tie. But in the middle of summer these people go out in a t-shirt that looks like they have come out of a shower . . . and then it is not right that they come to Le Cirque and want to sit next to a lady. New Yorkers are elegant people. We should teach the rest of the people. We should teach the world."

"I don't know why I have been chosen as one of the thirty most important men in New York. It is ridiculous. I just sell soup. I'm glad I'm well known in my country because everybody has to be what he is. You never talk bad about your country, your mother, your brother, your family. Here, I'm a guest. But in Italy I can have my say. Most of the political group there is a disgrace. A communist could be good, but it's bad when applied in the wrong way. Communism was bad in eastern Europe, so why try it in Italy? Thank God the Italians are not *with* anybody. They're *against* everybody!"

"They say I feed their egos as well as their stomach. But why do you buy a Versace suit instead of one that costs 60 percent less? It's a question of ego. Why do you go to your hairdresser who knows you? It's ego. It's also quality of life."

"Everybody should be equal when we start, when we are born. But then I don't believe in egalitarian any more. Everybody should start and go up. I tell my three sons if one gets up at 8 and one at 10 and one at 12 . . . the first one up should do better. It's a simple philosophy."

"People can't eat caviar and *foie gras* all the time. Sometimes they need hamburger . . . vulgar food . . . the things we grew up with . . . pig feet, tripe, boiled beef, lamb chop cooked with potato—lamb stew—roast chicken. And especially me . . . I'm not easy to please in a restaurant. But I will go when they have those dishes. We invented pasta primavera. In 1975. We were invited by the Canadian government to try new recipes for pigeon, lobster, and wild boar. But after three days, all this got boring. So it came my turn to cook. And I took everything I could find in the kitchen . . . all the vegetables . . . and we created pasta primavera."

"I notice that man is looking at your wife . . . but don't worry. He has had a lot of wine. But he is a gentleman and he is always correct. He has manners. But he can't help himself from looking."

"You're a man and automatically you're stupid. As a young boy in Italy I was crazy. I have always been stupid."

Q: But your greatness, a part of it, is that you're *Italian*.

A: Yes, but I'm alone!

More "Saloon Songs" (an Update)

Some of the old places in my previous saloon "tour" are shuttered now.
So I thought I would update my restaurant musings. It is 2017.

———————

Jerry Biggins at the original P. J. Clarke's glorious saloon is another bar-keep to whom I repair when I'm feeling few. He envelops you in his Celtic warmth, bonhomie, and *joie de vivre* during the day shift at this legendary drinking emporium and works his magic all the while dispatching gigantic hugs and even a kiss or two for his favorites, which include damn near everybody.

Sabrina "Sunny" Roper is a delightful and welcoming "roving" bar-maid who tends the taps with great style at several establishments in the Litchfield Hills, including the West Street Grill.

Incidentally, her father must have done something right because Sunny's sister is Samantha "Sam" Tilley, the widely praised chef and owner of Mockingbird in Bantam, Connecticut. Sam is a great cooker— and a great looker (pun intended).

And Michael DiLullo—who, with his wife, Fiorita, presides over the venerable Venetian, an old lorelei of a restaurant in Torrington, a faded Connecticut mill town—certainly makes my current and forever list. As a young man in New York, Michael worked with Sirio Maccioni. So he knows how to treat people.

A lot of high-rollers in western Connecticut favor the upscale Arethusa al Tavolo, another labor of love from Tony Yurgaitis and George Malkemus, who also own Arethusa Farm, the world-famous dairy farm south of Litchfield. FYI: In the city, Tony and George were also partners with the legendary shoe designer Manolo Blahnik. The duo has reinvigorated and enhanced the hamlet of Bantam, Connecticut, and the entire leafy region.

I also think very well of Mark Miller, the estimable major-domo at Lyford Cay's Yacht Club in the Bahamas. I knew Mark years ago as an altar boy at the local Roman Catholic church and watched him grow in wisdom and age as he now cossets and welcomes the landed gentry of that swell place.

Closer to home, John Cunningham, an Irish charmer who knows card tricks—and a lot more—is himself an "ace" as he presides at Woodland restaurant and bar, which sits cheek-by-jowl up the road a piece next to the exclusive Hotchkiss prep school in Lakeville, Connecticut. It has the look of a roadhouse in the far northwestern hills of rural Connecticut. If you blink, you'll miss the Woodland, a most agreeable, eminently comfortable pub-restaurant. Owner-chef Rob Peter's food is relentlessly creative and always satisfying. Another restaurateur in the Litchfield Hills once told me, "It's impossible to have a bad meal there." Although it's usually packed, the Woodland's legendary barkeep Cunningham will rescue you and wrap you in his care and keeping as he makes a place for you at the bar, which, the locals insist, is the best place to sit. Cunningham is a delightful man with a genius for hospitality. Thanks to his warmth and Rob Peter's food, the Woodland is my special favorite for Saturday lunch. The crowd is attractive. But they let me in anyway.

I'm also a great admirer of Franco Lazarri, who with his partner, Stefano Terzi, owns Vice Versa in Manhattan. They came out of the fabled San Domenico several years ago and really hit their stride over on the West Side off Eighth Avenue. But don't take my word for it. Ask the great Frank Bennack, boss (still) of the Hearst empire *and* New York–Presbyterian Hospital, New York's best medical center. Gotta give them a shout-out for getting me through seventy-eight years! (Now eighty-one!)

One of the greatest of contemporary maestros is the colorful James O'Shea, who runs the renowned West Street Grill on the village green up in the country, in Litchfield. He's a marvelous combination of feisty ebullience, effervescence, and Irish wit. And as we've observed him over the years, with all his bluster, there's really not a damn mean bone in his body. Mr. O'Shea, a charming son of the Old Sod, always rolls a great, fun show in every season with his partner, Charlie Kafferman.

While James is performing his edgy and provocative verbal high-wire act quite delightfully for the Grill's upscale patrons, Kafferman will keep you in touch and grounded with the wisdom and warmth of his considerable years. If you're lucky, you'll be there of an evening when some "untutored" or "out-of-control" patron dares send their fish or fowl back to the kitchen for "a little more fire," which James instantly takes as a most personal affront and lets them know it. But by the end of the evening, you'll also know you've been brilliantly entertained *and* well fed by the charming Irishman who has trained and mentored some of the most famous chefs in New England.

Julian Niccolini and his courtly, taciturn partner, Alex von Bidder, have relinquished the iconic and timeless space that once housed the Four Seasons restaurant in the Seagram Building. And all New York now hopefully awaits the Four Seasons' *new* incarnation a few blocks south at 280 Park Avenue. (Sadly, Julian has moved on as the result of a review in my beloved *New York Times* that was really an unfair attack on a talented restaurateur.)

And speaking of "legends" in the culinary firmament: Admirers and aficionados of the stately "21" rejoice in its recent rebirth and renewal. The ageless "Numbers" has been restored to its former glory by general manager Teddy Suric, and all is once again quite right with the world at "21"—thanks to Suric, a brilliant young restaurateur who brings his own great respect for the traditions of the hallowed New York landmark to our beloved "21."

Primola, a very agreeable place on the East Side, is presided over by Giuliano Zuliani, whose spectacular food and warm personality attract A-listers night after night.

I should also acknowledge that I've discovered, quite late in life, a marvelous place in what locals call the "outer" borough of Queens. We've had a lot of really wonderful evenings in the care and keeping of Tony Federici at Parkside in Corona. Its interior and customers are right out of the mind of Scorsese or Mario Puzo. And Tony's charisma and magic are always applauded and appreciated by a roomful of good fellows, attractive ladies, *and* assorted "Goodfellas." You gotta love it . . . if ya know what I mean. It's a favorite of Gianni Russo, Matthew Mari, Abramo Dispirito, and Ralph Campagnone. Also yours truly.

Harry Cipriani, in the stately old Sherry Netherland at 59th and Fifth, traces its lineage right back to Arrigo Cipriani's original Harry's Bar on the Venice waterfront near San Marco Square. The New York version is a magnet for society dames and an upscale Euro crowd. I go for late lunches or an occasional nightcap after black-tie charity dinners. No matter the hour, maître d' Sergio Vacca, who moves around the dining room like a Nijinsky or a Nureyev, makes sure all is right with your world as he escorts you to the care and keeping of star waiter Fernando or primo barman Luca. And occasionally you're also greeted by Maestro Arrigo's attractive grandsons Maggio and Ignazio. Cipriani is great fun at any hour and in any season.

At Milos on the West Side, you'll be greeted and dazzled by Bruno Dussin, the diminutive and graceful longtime *compadre* of the Maccioni family. The Greek seafood and European service are as good as the wines on offer. And the lobster pasta is even better than at the Mother Ship in Montreal, but don't tell Costas Spiliadis, the owner.

I've long been an admirer of Gerardo Bruno, the attractive dining room impresario who made San Pietro on East 54th Street an iconic spot.

Gerardo is one of the smartest and most intuitive guys in the hospitality business. He knows how to handle vice presidents (Dan Quayle), financiers (Ken Langone, Larry Fink, and Joe Parella), governors (Mario Cuomo, of sainted memory), bankers (Jamie Dimon and Vincent Tese), and mega-realtors and developers (Jerry Speyer and Katherine Farley). Also airline chieftains (Richard Anderson and Ed Bastian of Delta). *And* ex-wives! Why he's always been so good to me, I'll never know. After a rocky period following the passing of Gerardo's brother Antonio, San Pietro has climbed back up to its rightful place among the top rung of East Side venues. Lunch is still all "suits," however powerful and influential. But dinner is once again populated by attractive swells who come for Gerardo and his food.

Which brings me a little closer to home. In the village of Larchmont, Gerardo's brother Cosimo Bruno and his gifted nephew Gabriele Pepe recently opened another outpost of the Bruno brother's dynasty: Le Sirene. The food is drop-dead fabulous! And I'll probably get arguments, but I'll put Le Sirene's pasta with a simple, sublime tomato and basil up against *anything* in New York City . . . *or* Italy.

And all of New York celebrates the opening of Majorelle, next to the tony Lowell Hotel in the space where once the fabled Ouo Vadis reigned. Presiding in the dining room is the great restaurateur Charles Masson, formerly of his family's beloved La Grenouille. There's a hell of a lot of star power coming to 28 East 63rd Street these days. And Manhattan's Upper Crust is flocking to the place.

I've also discovered Provincetown—or P'town, as the locals call it— the lovely, lively little oasis of fun on the Cape. My first stop—for lunch— is always the Lobster Pot, run for years by Joy McNulty, an old family friend, and her son Shawn, a noted photographer. Sure, it's a "touristy" joint. But ignore the lines out the door and take the stairs to the second-floor bar where the barmaid Reema will make you feel like a "local." The food is quite good, and the wonderful drinks are world-class.

For dinner, it's always the Mews, owned by Ron Robin, a legendary Boston radio personality. The food and service are even worth the exhausting five-hour drive, believe me. And if you don't fall in love with Caroline Putnam—the tall, leggy, and beautiful dining room impresario, you're not paying attention. The Mews is an all-time favorite. By far the best on the Cape.

When you're putting together an evening for a client or a "friend" and it's just gotta be *right*, I still head for the mighty Le Cirque in the courtyard of the Bloomberg Building off 58th Street between Lex and Third. The incomparable and ageless Mario Wainer—"Your Excellency . . . welcome back!" (Is he talking to *me*? Yes, and what's not to like?)—still runs the dining room for Sirio and his attractive sons Mauro and Marco. President Trump and billionaire Ron Perelman are regulars. And so is Andrea Bocelli and his wife, Veronica Berti, friends of Sirio's.

And for a *really* fun, "let-your-hair-down" kind of night—close to home—it's Dan Rooney's Sports Pub at the Empire City Casino. There are two or three other quite good eateries at what I still call "Yonkers Raceway." But Dan Rooney's Sports Pub has the Rooney name *and* great food and drinks. It's another gift of the fabled and greatly revered Rooney family, presided over by Tim Rooney Sr., son of the Pittsburgh Steelers legendary owner Art Rooney of sainted memory. I *love* and respect the Rooney family. They are valued ornaments of Westchester and royalty of the sporting world. Dan Rooney's Sports Pub at Empire City is only one example of their genius and generosity. It's great, great fun of an evening. (MGM Resorts recently brought Empire City, and one hopes they will keep it up to Rooney standards.)

That I give the following estimable venues but a brief mention as I wind down this update should not at all be interpreted as anything less than unqualified admiration and enthusiasm for their powers and prowess and standing in the hospitality field and in my affections. Be assured that I have considerable regard and tremendous appreciation for the charms and attributes of the following:

The Kittle House is now run by John Crabtree, son and heir of General Richard Crabtree, one of the most colorful figures in the Golden Apple during the 1970s, 1980s, and 1990s. The Kittle is a hide-away and watering hole for ex-presidents. But don't hold the Clintons against them. My *mother* loved it too.

Winvian, the luxe and pricey resort in the Litchfield Hills run by the Smith family (of Webster Bank) gets five stars for Chris Eddy's creative and innovative cuisine. And the service and ambience orchestrated by Paolo Middei is first class too.

Posto 22, Joe Napolitano's place in downtown New Rochelle, is a magnet for politicos, City Hall types, and townies of every standing and stripe. It's a very agreeable place. As is the owner. My colleagues at the radio station love it.

This updated list with our current favorites wouldn't be complete without The Village in Litchfield. The secret ingredient therein is down-home hospitality. This near-perfect pub in the Litchfield Hills serves up burgers, shepherd's and chicken pot pie, heaping platters of batter-coated onion rings, spectacular fried oyster tacos, and hearty, warming chowders and soups. Their Arnold Palmers are world-class. And the wine list has some great finds at reasonable prices. But most townies and VIP visitors to tony Litchfield go for the proprietors Dave Vigeant and Greg Rapp, who, back in the day, were megastars on the basketball courts and baseball diamonds in these rarefied parts. They now star in their beloved Village with Greg's partner-wife, Denise, who really runs the place.

Everyone at the bar at Jimmy Neary's delightful saloon on East 57th Street still looks like Daniel Patrick Moynihan. It's a most civilized place favored by Hugh Carey's offspring and the estimable Jonathan Bush—Billy's father, George H.W.'s brother, and George W.'s uncle. Also Bloomberg staffers and Pat Barrett, the upstate millionaire who made a score with Avis. Proprietor Jimmy Neary is a treasure of New York, and his knockout daughter Una waits tables for her old man on weekends. During the week she's a senior exec at Goldman Sachs. The eighty-six-year-old marvelous Irishman-proprietor is always there. Long may he ever!

The Pioneer Saloon, a.k.a. "The Pio," in Ketchum–Sun Valley, Idaho, is maybe hands-down my all-time favorite. There is usually an hour (or more) wait for a table. But if you know owner Duffy Witmer, "Your table's ready. . . ." The Idaho baked potatoes are the size of Nerf footballs, and the slabs of roast beef thrown back on the grill are mind-blowing. As are the margaritas in huge bucket glasses. This special joint is a magnet for attractive folks of any age in any season.

And so I'll mercifully yield with these recollections of great watering holes and agreeable restaurants—some I discovered years ago as a young man and others in recent years as I approach senility. And as I do wind this down, allow me please only to toss a bouquet to the Fife and Drum, an old lorelei of a roadhouse in Kent, Connecticut. It was owned forever by Dolph Trayman, a darling man of some ninety-seven years who played the piano every night in this warm, welcoming place in the western hills of Connecticut. There was always pure magic in the air accompanied by the "saloon songs" Dolph Trayman coaxed out of his Steinway as his daughter Alyssa flambéed steaks tableside. And the very *best* part of the evening was watching the expression on the beautiful face of the maestro's wife, Audrey, as he played Rodgers and Hart and Cole Porter classics. As I said: a magical evening I discovered late in life. Sadly, we lost the great man early in 2017. But Dolph Trayman's music, and the "music" of "The Fife," linger. . . .

That's quite enough for 2017 and beyond.

Anybody got some TUMS?

"The Numbers"

A conversation with Teddy Suric, General Manager of "21."

————————

WILLIAM O'SHAUGHNESSY: The jockeys are back at "The Numbers" on 52nd Street. We're here in the iconic, hallowed halls of the fabled "21" Club in Manhattan because this is a big-deal day. With us is the managing director of the "21" Club, Teddy Suric. He's a restaurateur, highly respected in his profession. I've never seen you this excited.

TEDDY SURIC: Well, it's an exciting moment, Bill. This club has been here for eighty-five years. Anything you do in eighty-five years is really something special. Just the history within these walls and the way it all started with Jack and Charlie in 1929, and here we are at "21" in the twenty-first century!

W.O.: Teddy Suric, general manager of "21," this started as a saloon, a speakeasy.

T.S.: It's one of the oldest speakeasies in the country. The Prohibition-era wine room is still operational and very active. It's a special chef's table underground for twenty-two special people. It's available for lunch *and* dinner. Historically, when "21" opened—it opened up at 21 West 52nd Street—Jack and Charlie then purchased number 19 and then the building at number 17. They then combined the three homes into one. And that's where all the wine and liquor went, in the "Prohibition" room. They called it "21."

W.O.: Teddy Suric, major-domo of "21," there's a lot of colorful stuff, a lot of excitement out on 52nd Street tonight. Your *jockeys* are back!

T.S.: Huge for us! I think it's really huge for our fans as well, and bar patrons and clientele here in New York and all across the country. In fact, "21" is truly an international destination. After eighty-five years they had never been refurbished. In 1930 the Van Urk family donated a jockey back then. You see it was the "horsey" crowd that used to occupy the seats here, then and ever since. The rich and famous, you might say!

w.o.: Do you still get the rich and famous?

ts: Constantly.

w.o.: Are these *real* jockeys? I notice how you've had them placed on the front steps. They're no longer looking over their shoulders. Now you've got them full frontal—facing 52nd Street!

t.s.: They are *real* jockeys, Mr. O'Shaughnessy, almost lifelike statues thereof. They represent all the great breeders and stables. They're actually donated to "21" by the famous stables. The maker of these jockeys—you really can't find anyone like him anymore—was down in Virginia. The gentleman passed away nine years ago. But these jockeys were donated for "21"; they weren't purchased. And this year we have a *new* addition: the Triple Crown winner—American Pharaoh, by Zayat Stables. We added the Triple Crown winner for the first time in the past forty years.

w.o.: So all these rich guys, the horsemen, with their own racing silks, have their colors. And thus each one of these jockeys is attired differently.

t.s.: Six or seven months ago when I initiated the project, I reached out to the stables, and there were a couple of silks that were just wrong. And they were so happy I reached out to them because a lot of these—at least 80 percent—of these stables are still active. So they gave me the correct silks. I then ordered the jockeys to be taken "off property," and we carefully and lovingly refurbished them away from "21."

w.o.: As I listen to you, Teddy Suric, I'm reminded you've been a friend of ours for many years, all the way back to your Le Cirque days. Will you trust me to conduct myself properly, as I put this microphone before you?

t.s.: I will trust you for another one hundred years, Mr. O'!

w.o.: Teddy, I then can safely say that you're a pretty hot guy right now in your profession, in the restaurant business. You've reinvigorated this beloved old lorelei. It had not exactly fallen on hard times, but there was a bit of a "lull" hereabouts. And, if you'll forgive me, nobody was having any "fun."

T.S.: There was a "lull," I guess you could say. It's my second year here. I view it as kind of like "refurbishing" or "restoring"—or "revitalizing" is what I want to say—because the *bones* were still good. It's owned by a great company. And look—there are a lot of gentlemen out there who still want to wear a tie and have a nice martini. And a lot of lovely and attractive women who want to dress up.

W.O.: You said the racing guys, the rich guys who own horse farms in Virginia and Florida, used to put their backsides in your seats. Who does it now? Who do you get?

T.S.: Their grandchildren! Their sons, their daughters! On any given night we can have ten to fifteen famous clients, from athletes to politicians to actors in here. It's just another regular dining experience for them. And always special for us.

W.O.: Teddy Suric, whose *name* do you need to get into "21" these days? Sometimes people are a little "reluctant" to enter the threshold of a famous place like "21." How do you crash through the "Iron Gates"?

T.S.: I still have a greeter here named Shakir. He's been here for thirty-eight years, which is pretty remarkable in this business. And I've been in this business for my entire life. My cell phone is out there. You can call me or my right-hand man Aaron. Actually, the only "name" you need to get into "21" is *your* own.

W.O.: Teddy Suric, are you glad to have your damn jockeys back?

T.S.: I love it; the *Family* is back!

W.O.: Which is your favorite jockey?

T.S.: My favorite jockey is probably—I'll go with Secretariat!

W.O.: Once, I'm reminded, they had a charity in this very room up here on the second floor, and famous *designers* decorated a jockey with their colors. Like de la Renta did one. Cartier did one. I had a couple of them up in the country. But my ex got one.

T.S.: I do remember that occasion. It was for charity. I wasn't here at the time, but I read up on my history of the jockeys. And that was a great night. One of several.

W.O.: Why don't you do that again?

T.S.: We'll try. I'm trying to bring back a little bit of the good old times that used to make this place rock.

W.O.: How do you have to dress these days to get into this joint, this high-class saloon?

T.S.: A tie is *not* required. We relaxed the tie requirement in 2009. But a sports jacket is required. No jeans in the barroom. And in the lounge we actually relaxed it to "casual," but neat.

W.O.: Teddy, do you get a better table if you wear a tie?

T.S.: No comment!

W.O.: Thank you, Mr. General Manager. The place looks great. You've got 52nd Street buzzing tonight. Your beloved jockeys are back! It's a true New York night.

The One Night Stand of Charles Osgood

Charles Osgood, who hosted CBS Sunday Morning *for many years, has cut back somewhat on his broadcasting activities. He famously closed his Sunday morning show with "I'll see you on the radio." In addition to having a magnificent voice, he was a master of writing for the ear. Others who shared this unique talent were the legendary Paul Harvey . . . Charles Kuralt . . . and James Van Sickle of WNEW, my old alma mater of sainted memory. Osgood (whose real name is Charles Wood) was also a very generous benefactor of the Broadcasters Foundation of America. W.O. commentary, November 1, 2011.*

———————

Tourists gawked in the glare, the glitter, and the neon of Times Square, while a few blocks away at number 315 West 44th Street a man of culture and erudition sat at a piano in the great temple of jazz called Birdland.

His given name is Charles Osgood Wood. He is the last great writer of the English language to sit in front of a microphone. He does this every weekend on *CBS Sunday Morning* and during the week on the radio, which makes him a beloved icon of his profession. He is the Noel Coward of our tribe.

He is better at putting words and thoughts into graceful sentences and elegant paragraphs than Lowell Thomas, Eric Sevareid, James Van Sickle, Reid Collins, or the great Charles Kuralt of sainted memory, all of whom could paint pictures with the spoken word. Writing for the ear, they call it. And this particular practitioner of the dying art even does it in rhyme and meter.

But on this autumn night in the theater district of Manhattan, Charles Osgood wanted to make some real music. And so he came to Birdland for a charity gig with Vince Giordano and his entire Night-hawks Society Orchestra to back him up.

"Nijinsky is dancing in the hallways of Times Square to the sound of a kazoo," a lovely haunting line from the great Jimmy Cannon, kept coming back as you listened to Charles Osgood sit at a piano in this faded old jazz club and play his music into the New York night.

It was a benefit for one of Osgood's favorite charities, to which he has been devoted for years—the Broadcasters Foundation of America.

Not everybody in this calling makes the big salaries like Oprah, Imus, or Howard. And thus the Foundation assists those broadcasters who have fallen on hard times, most of them obscure sidemen in orchestras long dispersed.

The tunes he chose for his "One Night Stand" were marvelous old loreleis from the 1920s and 1930s, most of them, appropriately, show tunes from Broadway.

The seventy-nine-year-old poet-broadcaster crooned, "Young at Heart" after reminding his standing-room-only audience it was introduced by Jimmy Durante (and you thought it was Sinatra).

He then swung into a saloon song, "One for My Baby," with the marvelous line, perfect for the moment, "You'd never know it but Buddy, I'm a kind of poet." He sure is.

In addition to his enormous talent, and the Nighthawks orchestra, Osgood also brought with him the television anchorman Harry Smith. The follicle-ly challenged, bespectacled, and altogether delightful Smith actually played the damn tuba—quite well, in fact. "You wouldn't laugh if I had a violin," said Smith, as he ran the scale.

Then the elegantly attired Osgood brought forth a rising young CBS colleague, Mo Rocca, a sartorial disaster of a comedic genius who sang a witty and beguiling tune, "Rhode Island Is Famous for You," an intoxicating paean to the diminutive Ocean State made famous by the late Blossom Dearie. It was written by Arthur Schwartz (fabled father of deejay and musicologist Jonathan) and Howard Dietz and performed to this day by the luminous Christine Andreas.

Then Osgood sat again at the piano, adjusted his glasses on the bridge of his nose, and sang Johnny Mercer's "Moon River." "I'm off to see the world . . . there's such a lot of world to see. . . ." The song has been done too many times in too many venues. But never better than by the man with the bow tie hunched over a piano, whispering into a microphone this splendid autumn night in Manhattan.

He even called up his amanuensis Liz Powers, who belted out two numbers. And guess what? She can certainly do more than type and answer the phone. The kid can sing too.

Charles Osgood himself has written six books and thousands of rhymes and couplets. He has performed with the New York Pops and the Boston Pops, all since he came off the Fordham campus early in his seventy-nine years.

Toward the end of his graceful, lovely turn in the old, faded jazz club, he even paid tribute to Steve Jobs for caring "not just about the nuts and bolts, but also about the *beauty* of the thing."

Speaking of which, the next time one despairs after watching all the vacuous talking heads and bimbos—male *and* female—reading from teleprompters and staring into television cameras with teeth gleaming under perfectly coiffed "'dos," remember the graceful broadcaster who famously ends each television show, "I'll see you on the radio."

There still is someone.

Postscript: He won't at all approve of my telling you this. But after being informed of the night's "take," which was substantial and all of which went to the Broadcasters Foundation of America, the CBS icon handed over *another* check—his own—for *triple* the amount.

In case you haven't figured it out by now, he's a graceful guy. On the air. And for real.

PART IV
IN PRAISE OF "VIVID SOULS"

The Unforgettables

I am because of them . . .
—Bill O'Shaughnessy's great supporting cast

William Plunkett, Esquire, New York powerbroker, once accused me
of being "very good with eulogies." Now, as Plunkett has much influence
with the cardinals and archbishops of my Roman Catholic Church,
as well as with governors and the elders of our home heath,
I must take this as a compliment.

———————————

I've done eulogies in country churches and even great cathedrals for acquaintances, relatives, in-laws, outlaws, and the great and good of my profession.

All of which reminds me that dying is something you have to do all by yourself. There are no cohorts, no accomplices. It's a solo act. And thus I do not at all like standing up in a church, mosque, or synagogue to speak of the deceased at any time.

Of course, the greatest speaker on matters temporal and eternal during our time was Mario Cuomo of sainted memory, who was a failed baseball player with too many vowels in his name. And let it be known as well that his son and heir Andrew Mark Cuomo is also getting pretty good in front of a crowd as the curtain falls for the final time on us and our friends. His eulogies for his father and Jimmy Breslin were masterpieces of the genre. Speaking of which, the *ne plus ultra* example of eulogists was the fiftieth governor of New York, Charles Malcolm Wilson, the great Fordham orator who used to speak soaringly and longingly of "another and, we are sure, a better world." (Mario Cuomo used to say, with considerable admiration, great affection, and not a little envy, "In a debate Malcolm would beat you up in English . . . and finish you off in Latin!")

[273]

But if truth be told I much prefer to speak of the living. That's quite another matter. And although a Franciscan who is excellent with words that shake you and get your attention once told me, "God has pulled your file," I still refuse to retire or, God forbid, move to God's waiting room in Florida.

My portfolio as a community broadcaster in the New York suburbs has afforded me the privilege of interacting with many thousands of interesting, attractive, and luminous individuals during my fifty-six-year stewardship of WVOX, WRTN, WVIP, and our Whitney Global Media Publishing Group.

Over the years many extraordinary folks have entertained and enlightened our listeners as they sat before our microphones, and a great many have also counseled and encouraged me personally and professionally over the decades of my already long life.

And as I've just celebrated my eighty-first birthday, I get flashes of *déjà vu* as my mind drifts back over the years to all the vivid and multi-talented people of standing, stature, and influence I've encountered as a community broadcaster in Westchester. And so on one recent sleepless night, I made a huge list of these colorful characters.

Each was very special and altogether unique, and each really stood out against the often-dull landscape and everyday minutiae that occasionally attends every profession, even one as privileged, exciting, and, occasionally, as glamorous as mine. These spectacular women and men sure made a difference in my life. And I merely want to acknowledge them while precious time and lucidity still abide.

I've been instructed and taught by most of the 1,400 on this list and entertained and inspired by the others. I've also loved and been loved in return by a few of them. But be assured that I have real and lasting affection for all here mentioned. As Mario Cuomo might observe: There is even a kind of sweetness to each of them that they bestowed in varying degrees on my broadcasting and writing endeavors. So that, I guess, is really the overarching and consistent theme that runs through this compilation of those I've met along the way. They've been the real stars in my life. I am because of them.

(I realize you may have a somewhat difficult time applying the word "sweet" to everyone on this list. But although a few may be somewhat

of a "stretch" or, shall we say, a bit "colorful" . . . you'll just have to forgive me . . . for every individual here mentioned has actually been
altogether generous to, encouraging of, and supportive of me and mine
at one time or another.)

Many of the names here assembled will be known to you as they are
dear to me and mine. I've even been privileged to interview many of
these colorful, endearing souls on the radio.

But I really wanted to acknowledge—and thank them—before the
Supreme Editor writes a "30" after my name. I hope not any time soon.
So here they are. You might say I've been on "life support" for eighty-
one years because of them.

Please note that never once did I consult Whitney Global Media's
formidable Rolodex, or the voluminous archives presided over by
Cindy Hall Gallagher at our offices and studios in Westchester, which
contain highlights of the past six decades. I have relied only on my fading memory of these really extraordinary individuals we've actually
been privileged to know over so many years. Bowing to the always sage
advice and counsel of my friend, the legendary barroom philosopher
the Honorable Bernard "Toots" Shor, who once advised me to always
include an index in my books because "With our kinda friends . . . you
got to make it easy for them to find their own damn monikers!" . . . these
illustrious names, product of my nocturnal musings, are herewith rendered in neat alphabetical rows and tidy computer-generated columns
which was done in an instant with the pressing of a solitary button as
my only concession to modernity. But it took me eighty-one years to
compile the list.

—W.O.

Jack Abernethy . . . Bob Abplanalp . . . Bella Abzug . . . Nancy and
Michael Ackerman . . . Cindy Adams . . . Paul Adams . . . Gianni
Agnelli . . . Carlos Alberto . . . Nerul Alam . . . Anthony Alfano . . . Ethel
Albertson . . . J. Lester Albertson . . . Henry Alexander . . . Col Allan . . .
Steve Allen . . . Conroy Allison . . . David Allyn . . . Dr. Alphonse
Altorelli . . . Deborah Altorelli . . . Dr. Myles Altorelli . . . Briana Alvarez
. . . Edward Alvarez . . . Gregorio Alvarez . . . Miosotis Alvarez . . . Wini
and Joe Amaturo . . . Elliott Ames . . . Lynne Ames . . . Captain Joe

Anastasi . . . John Anderson . . . Walter Anderson . . . Sen. Warren
Anderson . . . Erin Andrews . . . Judge Daniel Angiolillo . . . J. J. Annable
. . . David Annakie . . . Albert Annunziata . . . Edson Arantes do
Nascimento "Pele" . . . Comm. Mike Armiento . . . Garner Ted
Armstrong . . . Louis "Satchmo" Armstrong . . . Ed Arrigoni . . . Isaac
Asimov . . . Dr. Laura and Michael Assaf, Esq. . . . Fred Astaire . . .
Eugene and Mike Athanasatos . . . Fr. Terry Attridge . . . Jim Austin . . .
Phil Austin . . . Peter Aziz . . .

Edward Larrabee Barnes . . . Judge Louis Barone . . . Tom Barrack
. . . David Barrett . . . Emily Barrett . . . J. Patrick Barrett . . . Bea Wain
and Andre Baruch . . . "Peg Leg" Bates . . . Special Agent Charles
Beaudoin . . . Larry Beaupre . . . Marty Beck . . . Franz Beckenbauer . . .
Keeling Beckford . . . Kathy Behrens . . . Judge Joe Bellacosa . . . Rocco
Bellantoni Jr. . . . Vin Bellew . . . Prof. Gerald Benjamin . . . Harvey
Bennett . . . Melissa and Paul Bennett . . . Sir Richard Rodney Bennett
. . . Tony Bennett . . . Kara Bennorth . . . Marty Berger . . . Sen. Max
Berking . . . Dr. Richard Berkoff . . . Hilda and Bill Berkowitz . . . Randy
Berlage . . . Henry Berman, Esq. . . . Federal Judge Richard M. Berman
. . . Arthur Bernacchia . . . George Bernacchia . . . Robin Curry
Bernacchia . . . Jason Bernbach . . . Justin Bernbach . . . Karen and
Judge Jeffrey Bernbach . . . Carl Bernstein . . . Phil Beuth . . . Alessandra
Biaggi . . . Rep. Mario Biaggi . . . Adamello Bianco . . . Jerry Biggins . . .
Joe Bilotta . . . Joe Binder . . . James K. Bishop . . . Joe Biscoglio . . .
Edward, James, John and Richard Blackburn . . . Sandra Blackwell . . .
Junior Blake . . . Elizabeth Blau . . . Robert Blau . . . Blend Blendo . . .
Sonny Bloch . . . Carol Bobrowsky . . . Lou Boccardi . . . Andrea Bocelli
. . . Veronica Berti Bocelli . . . John Bodnar . . . Warren Bodow . . . Lou
Borelli . . . Dr. Henry "Hank" Borkowski . . . Frank Boyle . . . Mayor
Adam Bradley . . . Ed Brady . . . James Brady . . . General of the Armies
Omar Bradley . . . Oscar Brand . . . Bonifacio Brass . . . Comm. Bill
Bratton . . . Paul Braun . . . Marty Bregman . . . Lynn and Dr. David
Breindel . . . Jimmy Breslin . . . Kevin, James, and Chris Breslin . . .
Colonel Paul Brier . . . Judge Charles Brieant . . . Stefano Briganti . . .
Ronald E. "Buzz" Brindle . . . Richard D. Brodsky . . . Claire Bronitt . . .
Lois Bronz . . . John Brophy . . . Pam Broughton . . . Gary Brown, Esq.
. . . Jim Brown . . . Les Brown . . . Bob Bruno . . . Cosimo Bruno . . .

Gerardo Bruno . . . Joe Bruno . . . Pat Buchanan . . . Jim Buck . . .
Richard Dimes Buckley . . . Josiah "Si" Bunting IV . . . Chef David Burke
. . . Trixie and David Burke . . . Bob Burlinson . . . Colin Burns Sr. . . .
Patricia and Barrett Burns . . . Peggy Burton . . . President George H.W.
Bush . . . Jonathan Bush . . . William "Billy" Bush . . . William Butcher
. . . Dr. Steven Butensky . . . Governor Brendan Byrne . . .

Elizabeth Cadoo . . . Frank Calamari . . . John Caldararo . . . Hilary
and Secretary Joe Califano . . . Bob Camman . . . James Campbell . . .
Todd Campbell . . . Jimmy Cannon . . . Joseph Wood Canzeri . . . Tricia
Novak Canzeri . . . Tony Capasso . . . Danny Capello . . . Gina Cappelli
. . . Kylie and Louis Cappelli . . . Nat Carbo . . . Judge Anthony Carbone
. . . Comm. Ed Carey . . . D. J. Carey . . . Gov. Hugh Leo Carey . . . Fr.
Michael Carnevale, OFM . . . Hoagy Carmichael Jr. . . . Michael Carney
. . . Robert Carravaggi . . . Comm. Patrick Carroll . . . Graydon Carter . . .
John Mack Carter . . . Dr. Frank Cartica . . . Lachlan Cartwright . . . Tom
Carvel . . . Cesare Casella . . . Senator Bob Casey . . . Kevin Casey . . .
Chuck Castleberry . . . Andrew Castellano . . . Margo and John
Catsimatidis . . . Fr. Joe Cavoto, OFM . . . Bill Cella . . . Maggie Cervantes
. . . Jack Cesario . . . Sue and Jim Champlin . . . Ken Chandler . . . Alan
Chartock . . . Mark Cheetham . . . Jody Chesnov . . . Dominic "Uncle
Junior" Chianese . . . Anthony Chiffolo . . . Giorgio Chinaglia . . . Tom
Chiusano . . . Hon. Stanley W. Church . . . Joe Cicio . . . Arrigo Cipriani
. . . Giuseppe Cipriani . . . Casper Citron . . . Bill Clark . . . James Mott
Clark Jr. . . . Mary Higgins Clark . . . Bobby Clarke . . . Jennifer and
Douglas Clement . . . President Bill Clinton . . . Hillary Rodham
Clinton . . . George Clooney . . . Rosemary Clooney . . . Tony Cobb . . .
Roy Marcus Cohn . . . Father Peter Colapietro . . . Supervisor Anthony
Colavita . . . Anthony J. Colavita Sr. . . . Kenneth Cole . . . Maria Cuomo
Cole . . . Ray Cole . . . Robert Coles . . . Michael Collins . . . David
Patrick Columbia . . . Dr. Christopher Comfort . . . Ralph Compagnone
. . . Frank Connelly, Esq. . . . Sir Sean Connery . . . John Connolly . . .
Fr. Mark Connolly . . . Katherine Wilson Conroy . . . Bob Considine . . .
Tom Constantine . . . Bob Conte . . . E. Virgil Conway . . . Burt Cooper
. . . Judge Matthew Cooper . . . FCC Comm. Michael Copps . . . Howard
Cosell . . . Richard Cotter . . . Aunt Joette Coulson . . . Jeff Coyle . . .
General Dick Crabtree . . . Guido Cribari . . . Walter Cronkite . . . Harry

Lillis "Bing" Crosby . . . Nathaniel Crosby . . . Judge Paul Crotty . . .
Johan Cruyff . . . Ellie Cucino . . . Matthew J. "Joe" Culligan . . . Jerry
Cummins . . . Bill Cunningham . . . Jim Cunningham . . . Chairman Pat
Cunningham . . . Gov. Andrew Mark Cuomo . . . Gov. Mario M. Cuomo
. . . Matilda Raffa Cuomo . . . Steve Cuozzo . . . Amb. Walter J.P. Curley
. . . Marianne Curnow . . . Paul J. Curran, Esq. . . . Bernard F. Curry Jr.
. . . Cynthia and Bernie Curry . . .

Sen. Alfonse D'Amato . . . Florence D'Ampiere . . . Kim and Bobby
D'Andrea . . . Sal D'Angelo . . . Hon. Marvin and Stacey Dames . . . Tony
Damiani . . . Michael Dandry . . . Judge Richard Daronco . . . Mayor
Ernie Davis . . . Evan Davis . . . Ossie Davis . . . Morton Dean . . . Mayor
Bill de Blasio . . . Ruby Dee . . . Max DeFabio . . . Nick DeJulio . . . Dixie
and Joep deKoning . . . George Delaney . . . C. Glover Delaney . . . Lt.
Gov. Alfred B. DelBello . . . Dee DelBello . . . Jerry DelColliano . . .
Michael DelGiudice . . . Carmen Dell'Orefice . . . Lauren and Armand
Della Monica . . . Cartha "Deke" DeLoach . . . Bill Deluca . . . Howard
DeMarco . . . Matt Dennis . . . Willard K. Denton . . . Andrea and
Richard Derwin . . . Matt Deutsch . . . Kevin Devaney Jr. . . . Robert
Deyber . . . Patti and Judge Tom Dickerson . . . Arthur Hill Diedrick . . .
Tara Stacom Diedrick . . . Frank DiGiacomo . . . Bernie Dilson . . . Terry
Dinan . . . Mayor David Dinkins . . . Congressman Joe Dioguardi . . .
Anthea Disney and Peter Howe . . . Abramo Dispirito . . . Richard K.
Doan . . . Rick Dobbis . . . Elly Doctorow . . . Tom Doherty . . . Charles
Dolan . . . Cardinal Timothy Dolan . . . Tom Dolan . . . Susan Dominus
. . . Angela Smith Domzal . . . "Radio" Chuck Donegan . . . David
Donovan . . . John Donnelly . . . Belle and Nick D'Onofrio . . . Marilyn
Doorley . . . Robert Royal Douglass . . . Maureen Dowd . . . John E.
"Jack" Dowling . . . Edward Reynolds Downe . . . Helen Downey . . .
Hugh A. Doyle . . . Peter Doyle . . . Vincent DePaul Draddy . . . Hon.
Anne Dranginis . . . Fadil Drenica . . . David Driscoll . . . Brother John
Driscoll . . . Sean Driscoll . . . Norman Drubner . . . Patricia Duff . . .
Hank Dullea . . . Steve Dunleavy . . . Senator John Dunne . . . Mark
Dunnett . . . Florence D'Urso . . . Speaker Perry Duryea . . .

Dick Ebersol . . . Fernanda Eberstadt . . . Frederick Eberstadt . . .
Cardinal Edward Egan . . . John Eggerton . . . Bill Eimicke . . .
Dr. Marc Sabin Eisenberg . . . Kevin Scott Elliott . . . Dwight M. Ellis

. . . Jack Ellsworth . . . Amb. Edward Eliot Elson . . . Frank Endress . . . Cong. Eliot Engel . . . Jean T. Ensign . . . Mary, Peter, and Ebie Ensign . . . Freddy Medora Plimpton Espy . . . Gov. Daniel Jackson Evans . . . Councilman Joe Evans . . .

Kate and John Fahey . . . John Fairchild . . . Jinx Falkenburg . . . Dr. Kevin Falvey . . . Robert Fanelli . . . Bill Fanning . . . Erica Farber . . . Somers Farkas . . . Erica Farber . . . Katherine Farley . . . James A. Farley . . . Pari Farood . . . Herman "Denny" Farrell . . . Mia Farrow . . . Joseph A. Fay . . . James Featherstonhaugh . . . Tony Federici . . . Paul Feiner . . . Frederic Fekkai . . . Lou Felicione . . . Giancarlo Ferro . . . Gene Klavan and Dee Finch . . . William M. "Bill" Fine . . . Suzi Finesilver . . . Pamela Fiori . . . Congressman Hamilton Fish . . . Hamilton Fish Jr. . . . Steve Fisher . . . Ed Fitzgerald . . . Irish Prime Minister Garrett FitzGerald . . . Jim Fitzgerald . . . Tina Flaherty . . . Ari Fleischer . . . Alan Flusser . . . Amb. William Flynn . . . Dr. Tom Fogarty . . . Ed Forbes . . . Trevor Forde . . . Richard Ambrose Foreman . . . Alex Forger . . . George Forstbauer . . . Arnold Forster . . . Michael Fosina . . . Mickey and Joe Fosina . . . John Fosina . . . Sir Norman Foster . . . Ray Fox . . . Abe Foxman . . . George Frank . . . Sidney Frank . . . Joe Franklin . . . Dr. Richard A.R. Fraser . . . Judge Samuel George Fredman . . . Louis B. Freeh . . . Judy Fremont . . . Richard French . . . Edward Owens Fritts . . . Marek Fuchs . . . City Manager C. Murray Fuerst . . . William Denis Fugazy . . . Allison Fulton . . . Bob Funking . . . Chris Furey . . .

Mario Gabelli . . . Danny Gagliardi . . . Judge Joe Gagliardi . . . Evan Galbraith . . . Kevin and Cindy Hall Gallagher . . . Dr. Hasan Garan . . . Cecile Garcia . . . Amb. Charles Gargano . . . Dessy Gargiulo . . . Hon. Frank J. Garito . . . Judy Garland . . . Pastor Richard Garner . . . James William Gaynor . . . Comm. Robert Gazzola . . . Hon. Herman Geist . . . Dr. Ira Gelb . . . Leon Geller . . . Jim and Sal Generoso . . . David Gentner . . . Rande Gerber . . . Edward "Ned" Gerrity . . . Arthur Geoghegan . . . Bill Gibbons . . . Bob Gibson . . . Dick Gidron . . . Frank Gifford . . . Louis P. Gigante . . . Robert (Bob Grant) Gigante . . . Phil Gilbert Jr. . . . Elizabeth Gildersleeve . . . Bennie Giles . . . Joan and Judge Charlie Gill . . . Congressman Ben Gilman . . . Jerry Gillman . . . Martin Ginsburg . . . Sen. Anthony B. Gioffre . . . Pete Giordano . . . Robert "Bob" Giuffra Jr., Esq. . . . Dave Girolamo . . . Daniel Glass . . .

Marty Glickman . . . Marla Golden . . . Judge Howard Goldfluss . . .
Marvin Goldfluss . . . Larry Goldstein . . . Terry Golway . . . Greg
Gonzalez . . . Sen. Charles Goodell . . . Senator Roy Goodman . . .
Dr. Marsha Gordon . . . Rob Gordon, Esq. . . . Shari Gordon, Esq. . . .
Dr. Ferris Gorra . . . Jack Gould . . . Milton Gould . . . John Gouveia . . .
Donald Graham . . . Katherine Graham . . . Murray Grand . . . Bob
Granger . . . Emily and Eugene Grant . . . Louie Grant . . . E. T. "Bud"
Gravette . . . General Alfred M. Gray, USMC . . . Vernon Gray . . . Jen
Graziano . . . Ralph Graves . . . Robert Gray, Esq. . . . Buddy Greco . . .
Bob Greene . . . Teddy Greene . . . Regina and Rainer Greeven . . . Dick
Gregory . . . Jamee and Peter Gregory . . . Armel Gren . . . Bill and Peter
Griffin . . . Richard Grudens . . . Tommy Guida . . . Tonny Guido . . .
Calla and Ralph Guild . . . Pranay Gupte . . . Bill Gurney . . .
    Evie Haas . . . Buddy Hackett . . . John Haidar . . . Sheila and Arthur
Haley . . . Stella Vinci Hall . . . Edward J. "Biff" Halloran . . . Jason P.W.
Halperin . . . Pete Hamill . . . Jeff Hanley . . . Ray Harding . . . Wade
Hargrove . . . Anne Harmon . . . John Harper . . . Gov. Averell Harriman
. . . B. J. Harrington . . . Bill Harrington . . . Michael Harrison . . . Kitty
Carlisle Hart . . . Graham Hastedt . . . Gordon Hastings . . . Carl T.
Hayden . . . Gabby Hayes . . . Guss Hayes . . . Brooke Hayward . . . Ted
Heath . . . Mark and Paul Hedberg . . . Commissioner Bill Hegarty . . .
Professor Rich Hendel . . . John Hennessy . . . Nat Hentoff . . . Ned
Hentz . . . Joyce Hergenhan . . . Scott Herman . . . Luis Hernandez . . .
Ramiro Hernandez . . . Amb. William vanden Heuvel . . . Al Hibbler . . .
David Hicks . . . Keegan Hicks . . . Nicole Hicks . . . Michael Higgins . . .
Louis Hillelson . . . Kris Hilpert . . . David Hinckley . . . Milton Hoffman
. . . Jim Hoge . . . Phil Hollis . . . Trooper Jim Holm . . . Napoleon
Holmes . . . Harold Holzer . . . Monsignor George Hommel . . .
Townsend "Tim" Hoopes . . . Todd Howe . . . Bishop Howard Hubbard
. . . Ed Hughes . . . Clement Hume . . . Judy Cascione Huntington . . .
Bobby Hutton . . . Joe Hutton . . . Paul Hutton . . . Bob Hyland . . .
    John Iannuzzi . . . Hon. Tim Idoni . . . Don Imus . . . Walter Isaacson
. . . Michael Israel . . .
    Adam Jacobson . . . Barbara Curry James . . . Sen. Jacob K. Javits . . .
Marian Borris Javits . . . Broadus "Speed" Johnson . . . President
Lyndon B. Johnson . . . Maricelly and Tom Johnson . . . Peter Johnson

... Robin Johnson ... Richard Johnson ... Bob Jones ... Jack Jones ...
Jerry Jones ... Shirley Jones ... Myron Joseph ... John M. Joyce ...
Mike Joyce ... Judy Juhring ...

Charlie Kafferman ... George S. Kalman ... Michael C.Y. Kang ...
Rick Kaplar ... Mel Karmazin ... Farooq Kathwari ... George S.
Kaufman ... William "Whitey" Kaufman ... Monsignor Charles
Kavanagh ... Pat Keegan ... Dick Kelliher ... John Kelly ... Nancy Q.
Keefe ... Irwin Kellner ... Cong. Jack Kemp ... Stanley Newcomb
Kenton ... Dr. John Keggi ... Alfred F. Kelly Jr. ... John "Shipwreck"
Kelly ... Judge Irving Kendall ... Bill Kennedy ... Brian Kennedy ...
John F. Kennedy Jr. ... President John Fitzgerald Kennedy ... Mary
Kerry Kennedy ... Senator Robert F. Kennedy ... William Kennedy ...
Hank Kensing ... Judge Susan Kettner ... Commissioner Doc Kiernan
... Corey Kilgannon ... Jim Killoran ... Destiny Kinal ... Larry King
... Doug Kingman ... Mike Kinosian ... Secretary of State Henry
Kissinger ... C. Samuel Kissinger ... Sam Klein ... Rikki Klieman ...
Chairman Arnold Klugman ... Costas Kondylis ... Hon. Oliver
Koppell ... Jack Kornsweet ... Bernie Koteen, Esq. ... Luciana
Klosterman ... Marcia Kramer ... Erwin Krasnow, Esq. ... Rainer K.
Kraus, Esq. ... Pete and Bob Kriendler ... Arthur "Jerry" Kremer ...
Emilia St. Amand Krimendahl ... Larry Kudlow ...

Bill Lacy ... Albert LaFarge ... Patti LaFontaine ... Brian Lamb ...
Bob Lape ... Julius LaRosa ... Marguerite Lascola ... Albert "Bunny"
Lasker ... Suzanne and John LaSorsa ... County Executive George
Latimer ... Jerry Lauren ... Jim Lemond ... Lenny Lauren ... Harry
Lavin ... Steve Lawrence and Eydie Gormé ... Rick Lazio ... Ron Leal
... Michael "Lionel" Lebron ... Attorney General Louis Lefkowitz ...
Wendy Vanderbilt Lehman ... Jane Lenihan ... Laura Accurso and
Scott Lennon ... Paul Lenok ... Mark Lerner ... Jack Lesniewski ...
Jacques LeSourd ... Ed Levine ... Susan and Dr. Jedd Levine ...
Comptroller Arthur Levitt ... Shim Lew ... Arthur Librett ... Charlie
Librett ... Prof. Mitchell Librett ... Rush Hudson Limbaugh III ...
Richard Littlejohn ... Mayor John Vliet Lindsay ... Walter Lipow ...
Penny Lipps ... Mario Vargas Llosa ... Cynthia Lobo, Esq. ... Jimmy
Lodato ... Amb. John L. Loeb Jr. ... Peter and John Loeb Sr. ... Sal
Lombardi ... Kim Lombardo ... Chairman Phil Lombardo ... John

Lomenzo . . . Michael Lomonaco . . . Father Paul Lostritto, OFM . . .
Jimmy Lopolito . . . Jim Lowe . . . E. Nobles Lowe . . . Steven and
Congresswoman Nita Lowey . . . Chairman William F. Luddy . . .
Wendy and Ambassador Bill Luers . . . Dan Lufkin . . . Mark
Lungariello . . . Dan Lynch . . .

   Peter Maas . . . Egidiana Maccioni . . . Marco Maccioni . . . Mario
Maccioni . . . Mauro Maccioni . . . Sabrina Wender Maccioni . . . Sirio
Maccioni . . . Leo MacCourtney . . . Fr. Kevin Mackin, OFM . . . Guru
Madeleine . . . Susan Magrino . . . David Mahoney . . . John Mainelli . . .
Patrick Maines . . . James Maisano, Esq. . . . Patrick Maitland . . . Tony
Malara . . . George Malkemus . . . Kit and Ed Mancuso . . . Nick Manero
. . . "Squeegie" Mangialardo . . . Archbishop Henry Mansell . . . Ann
Mara . . . John Mara . . . Wellington Mara . . . Matthew Mari . . . Tom
Margittai . . . John Mariani . . . John Marino . . . Bob Marrone . . . Alton
Marshall . . . Spencer Martin . . . Paolo Martino . . . Val and Nick
Mastronardi . . . Chris Matthews . . . Pastor Shirley Maxwell . . . Walter
Maxwell . . . Lowry Mays . . . Bill Mazer . . . Tim McAlpin . . . Bishop
James McCarthy . . . Gavin K. McBain . . . Mary Margaret McBride . . .
Charlie and Lynn McCabe . . . Kevin McCabe . . . Comptroller Carl
McCall . . . Charles F. McCarthy . . . Brother John McCarthy . . . Dr.
Richard McCarthy . . . Scott McCarty . . . Betsy McCaughey . . .
Suzannah McCorkle . . . Brian McCormick, Esq. . . . Malachy McCourt
. . . Bernie McCoy . . . David McCullough . . . Frank McCullough Sr. . . .
Frank McCullough Jr. . . . Bob McCurdy . . . Claudia McDonnell . . .
Susan Mara and John McDonnell . . . Bill McElveen . . . Cynthia
McFadden . . . Steve McFadden . . . Connie McGillicudy . . . J. Raymond
McGovern . . . Fr. Felix McGrath, OFM . . . Gene McGrath . . . Kevin
Barry McGrath, Esq. . . . Mary McGrory . . . Bryan McGuire . . . Bill
McKenna, Esq. . . . Renate and Thomas McKnight . . . Pat and Ed
McLaughlin . . . Hon. James "The Undertaker" McManus . . . Patrick
McMullan . . . Fr. Patrick McNamara . . . Fr. Joseph M. McShane, S.J. . . .
Bep McSweeney . . . Chairman Dennis Mehiel . . . Roland Meledandri
. . . Kim and Colonel Steve Mellekas . . . Mabel Mercer . . . Sandy Stark
and Jim Mersfelder . . . Herve Merlino . . . Judge Ben Mermelstein . . .
Robert Merrill . . . Jack Messmer . . . Congressman J. Edward Meyer . . .
Frank Miceli . . . Edwin Gilbert Michaelian . . . Randy Michaels . . .

Paolo Middei . . . Barbara and Joe Migliucci . . . Rose Bocchino and
Mario Migliucci . . . Bob Milano . . . Brett Miller . . . Cay and Stanley
Miller . . . Henry Miller, Esq. . . . Katherine Miller, Esq. . . . Marcia
Miller . . . Mark Miller . . . Clif Mills Jr . . . Philip Milner . . . Jackie and
Federal Judge Roger Miner . . . Peter Mintun . . . Shelby and Bill Modell
. . . Joseph Montabello . . . Louise Montclare . . . Fr. Chris Monturo . . .
Bill Mooney . . . Garry Moore . . . Walter Moore . . . Tom Moran . . .
Tommy Moretti . . . Hon. Robert Morgenthau . . . Bunny and Daniel
Morosani . . . Bev and Woody Mosch . . . Arthur H. "Red" Motley . . .
Senator Daniel Patrick Moynihan . . . Liz Moynihan . . . Carl Moxie . . .
Sidney P. Mudd . . . Tom Mullen . . . Federal Judge William Hughes
Mulligan . . . Bill Mulrow . . . Betty Ann Mummert . . . Trooper
President Tom Mungeer . . . Dan Murphy . . . Deborah and Declan
Murphy . . . Mark Murphy . . . Ted Murphy . . . John Murtagh, Esq. . . .
Ernie Muscarella . . . Stanley Frank Musial . . .

Fred Nachbaur . . . Richie Naclerio . . . Dawson B. "Tack" Nail . . .
Joe Napolitano . . . Jerry Nappi . . . Dennis "Dion" Nardone . . . Jackie
Neary Nash . . . Jimmy Neary . . . Una Neary . . . Beth Neuhoff . . .
Vanessa Neumann . . . H. D. "Bud" Neuwirth . . . Jack Newfield . . .
Dean Newman . . . Eric Newman . . . Amb. Edward Noonan Ney . . .
Julian Niccolini . . . Cristyne Nicholas . . . President Richard M. Nixon
. . . Dick Nolan . . . Chairman Jasper Nolan . . . Jimmy Noletti . . .
Margaret Noonan . . . Enrique Norten . . . Alex Norton . . . Deborah
Norville . . . Paul Noto . . . Harry Novik . . . Richard Novik . . . Amelia
Jane Nulty . . . Flynn Thayer Nulty . . . Tucker Thomas Nulty . . . Daniel
Nye . . . Dr. Joseph Nyre . . .

Jack O'Brian . . . Des O'Brien . . . Kate O'Brien . . . Monsignor Bill
O'Brien . . . Cardinal Edwin O'Brien . . . Father John O'Brien . . .
Kathleen Plunkett O'Connor . . . Justice Sandra Day O'Connor . . .
Madeline and Brian O'Donoghue . . . Paul O'Dwyer, Esq. . . . Fr. Joseph
O'Hare, S.J. . . . Michael "Buzzy" O'Keefe . . . Valerie Moore O'Keefe
. . . Mary O'Leary . . . Cathy and Greg Oneglia . . . Comm. James
O'Neill . . . Paddy O'Neill . . . William O'Neill, AIA . . . Sen. Suzi
Oppenheimer . . . Bill O'Reilly . . . William F.B. O'Reilly . . . Judge
Andrew P. O'Rourke . . . Grandma Alice O'Shaughnessy . . . Cara
Ferrin O'Shaughnessy . . . Catherine Tucker O'Shaughnessy . . .

David Tucker O'Shaughnessy . . . Isabel O'Shaughnessy . . . Jack O'Shaughnessy . . . John O'Shaughnessy . . . Julie O'Shaughnessy . . . Kate Wharton O'Shaughnessy . . . Lacey, Luna, Coco, Jack, Jesse, Runway, Babe, and Puppy Sam O'Shaughnessy . . . Laura O'Shaughnessy . . . Lily O'Shaughnessy . . . Matthew Thayer O'Shaughnessy . . . Nancy Curry O'Shaughnessy . . . William Mac O'Shaughnessy . . . James O'Shea . . . Sidney Offit . . . Stu Olds . . . Louisa and Francis Oneglia . . . Ellen and Ray Oneglia . . . Rod Oneglia and Michael Quadland . . . Charles Osgood . . . Giampaolo Ottazzi . . . Cong. Richard Ottinger . . . Lisa and Dr. Mehmet Oz . . .

Sen. Bob Packwood . . . Mayor Len Paduano . . . Babe Paley . . . William S. Paley . . . Steve Palm . . . Fabian Palomino . . . Anthony Paolercio . . . Joe Parella . . . Deborah Parenti . . . Diane Parette . . . Richie Parisi . . . Rev. Everett C. Parker . . . James O. Parsons . . . Vincent Pastore . . . Libby and Gov. George Pataki . . . Governor David Paterson . . . Nick Patrella . . . Hon. Leo Paul Jr. . . . Ken Paulson . . . Gregg Pavelle . . . Steve Pellettiere . . . Dr. Paul Pellicci . . . Speaker Nancy Pelosi . . . Gabriele Pepe . . . Gene Pepe . . . Joe Percoco . . . Joseph Perella . . . Ron Perelman . . . Mario Perillo . . . Bill Persky and Sam Denoff . . . Marco Perry . . . Joseph Persico . . . Frank Pesce . . . Secretary Pete Peterson . . . Mayor Augie Petrillo . . . Congressman Peter Peyser . . . Alex Philippidis . . . T. Boone Pickens . . . Drew Pickney . . . Deleon Pinto . . . Judge Jeanine Pirro . . . Sen. Joe Pisani . . . Kathy and Dr. Richard Pisano . . . Dave Piwowarski . . . George Plimpton . . . Caryl Donnelly Plunkett . . . Special Agent Ryan Plunkett . . . Rosemary and Kevin Plunkett . . . William Plunkett Jr. . . . Lisa Foderaro and Don Pollard . . . Leavitt Pope . . . Merna Popper . . . Mary Porcelli . . . Dr. Ken Porter . . . Nancy and Skyler Post . . . Tom Poster . . . Elizabeth Backman and Donn King Potter . . . Elissa Potts . . . Maury Povich . . . Bishop Wayne Powell . . . Fred Powers Jr. . . . Frederic B. Powers . . . Peter Powers . . . Gabe Pressman . . . Frances Preston . . . Patsy Preston . . . Gary Pretlow . . . Saverio Procario . . . Ralph Purdy . . . Caroline Putnam . . . Ward Quaal . . . Judge Kevin Quaranta . . . Jane Bryant Quinn . . . Peter Quinn . . .

Jennifer Raab . . . Ann-Christine Racette . . . Chris Raimo . . . Tiziana Raita . . . Federal Judge Jed Rakoff . . . Joe Rao . . . Tony Randall . . . Joe

Raposo . . . Denise and Greg Rapp . . . Assemblyman Clarence "Rapp" Rappelyea . . . Janet and Ken Raske . . . Dan Rather . . . Charlie "Pug" Ravenel . . . M. Paul Redd . . . Rex Reed . . . Ruth Reichl . . . Mary Louise Reid . . . Amb. Ogden Rogers Reid . . . Mary Clare Reilley . . . Joe Reilly . . . Phil Reisman . . . Elva Amparo Reynoso . . . Eric Rhoads . . . Stefano Ricci . . . Murray Richman, Esq. . . . Stacey Richman, Esq. . . . Jovan C. Richards . . . Reverend W. Franklyn Richardson . . . Robert Richnavsky . . . Matt Richter . . . Don Rickles . . . Judge David Rifas . . . Leonard Riggio . . . Volney "Turkey" Righter . . . Pierre Rinfret . . . Hon. Vinny Rippa . . . Lucille Ritacco . . . Geraldo Rivera . . . Mariano and Pastor Clara Rivera . . . Sam Roberts . . . Ron Robin . . . Dick Robinson . . . Col. Marty Rochelle . . . Margaretta Large Fitler Murphy "Happy" Rockefeller . . . Vice President Nelson Aldrich Rockefeller . . . Larry Rockefeller . . . Laurance Rockefeller . . . Rex Todd Rogers . . . Tommy Rogers . . . Secretary of State William Pierce Rogers . . . June and Tim Rooney Sr. . . . Janine Rose . . . Marlon Rosenbaum . . . Alan Rosenberg . . . Bob Rosencrans . . . A. M. "Abe" Rosenthal . . . Gladys Shelley and Irving Rosenthal . . . Flo Vizzi Rosse . . . Hal Rossiter . . . William Kyle Rote . . . Philip Roth . . . Phil Roura . . . Billy Rowe . . . Br. Darby Ruane . . . Dan Rubino . . . Jack Rudin . . . Christopher Ruddy . . . Michel Rudigoz . . . Joe Ruhl . . . Father Michael Ruminski . . . Dr. Natale Rusconi . . . Judge Alvin Richard Ruskin . . . Sylvia Besson Ruskin . . . Tim Russert . . . Gianni Russo . . . Maria and Constable Pete Russo . . . Ed Ryan . . .

Vincent Saele . . . Leonard Safir . . . Dr. Steven Safyer . . . Susan Saint James . . . Al and George Salerno . . . Bill Samuels . . . Howard Samuels . . . Dr. Irv Samuels . . . David Samson . . . Glen Sanatar . . . Lou Sandroni . . . Nick Sarames . . . Steve Savino . . . Jack Scarangella . . . Angela "Nudge" Scarano . . . Chuck Scarborough . . . Vinnie Scardino . . . Comm. Joe Schaller . . . Debbie Schechter . . . Faith Miller and Judge Alan Scheinkman . . . Judge Preston "Sandy" Scher . . . Stephen Schlesinger . . . Herb Schmertz . . . Edwin K. Schober . . . Louis Schwartz . . . Wally Schwartz . . . Andrew Jay Schwartzman . . . William "Kirby" Scollon . . . Senator Hugh Scott . . . Jim Scott . . . Justin Scott . . . City Council President Paul R. Screvane . . . Nancy and Dennis Scully . . . Sue and John Scully . . . Tom Sebring and Steve Vaughn . . . Ivan

Seidenberg . . . Bruno Selimaj . . . Nino Selimaj . . . Eddie Sessa . . .
Benito Sevarin . . . Jean Shafiroff . . . Hugh Shannon . . . Trish and Scott
Shannon . . . Mayor Tom Sharpe . . . Winston "Win" Sharples . . . Rev.
Al Sharpton . . . Jack Shaw . . . Eric Shawn . . . Lynn Shaw . . . Alan
Shayne . . . Wilfred Sheed . . . Judge Judy Sheindlin . . . Dr. Dan Sherber
. . . Lydia Sheremeta . . . Coach Allie Sherman . . . Daryl Sherman . . .
Bernard "Toots" Shor . . . Bobby Short . . . Harold Siegel, Esq. . . . Herb
Siegel . . . Francis Albert Sinatra . . . Peter Sinnott . . . Seymour Sinuk
. . . I. Philip Sipser . . . Luciano Siracusano III . . . Joe Sitrick . . . Dan
Slepian . . . Barry Slotnick, Esq. . . . Bobby Smillie . . . Emily Smith . . .
Francis and John Smith . . . Senator Gordon Smith . . . Jan Johnson
Smith . . . Liz Smith . . . Richard Norton Smith . . . Sally Bedell Smith . . .
Walter "Red" Smith . . . Tressa Goodwin and Tommy Smyth . . . Jeff
Smulyan . . . Dr. Allan Sniffen . . . Bruce and Marcia Snyder . . . Jane
Wharton Sockwell . . . Stephen Sorokoff . . . Domenico "Mimmo" Spano
. . . Mayor John Spencer . . . Phil Spencer . . . Jerry Speyer . . . Rob Speyer
. . . Robert "Bud" Spillane . . . General Joe Spinelli . . . John Spicer . . .
Michael Spicer . . . Bruce Springsteen . . . Rusty Staub . . . Andrew Stein
. . . Dennis Stein . . . George Steinbrenner . . . Gloria Steinem . . . Percy
Steinhart . . . Andrew Stengel, Esq. . . . Renee and Stuart Stengel, Esq.
. . . Bradley Stephens . . . Don Stevens . . . Martha Stewart . . . Judy
Stinchfield . . . Martin Stone . . . Roger Stone . . . Andy Stowers . . .
Murph Streger . . . Agatha Gasparini Strome . . . Charles Bowman
Strome . . . Ellen Sulzberger Straus . . . R. Peter Straus . . . Fr. John Sturm,
S.J. . . . Edward O. "Ned" Sullivan . . . John Van Buren Sullivan . . .
Bishop Joseph Sullivan . . . K. T. Sullivan . . . Arthur Ochs "Punch"
Sulzberger . . . Arthur Sulzberger Jr. . . . Susan and Bob Summer . . .
Frederic Sunderman . . . Teddy Suric . . . Paul Sutera . . . Percy Sutton
. . . John Cameron Swayze Jr. . . . Sy Syms . . . Sylvia Syms . . .

Sol, Larry, & Captain Rob Taishoff . . . Gay Talese . . . Joe Tardi . . .
Giuseppe Tarillo . . . Joan and Val Taubner . . . Eloise and James
Taussig II . . . Marlin R. Taylor . . . Tom Taylor . . . Sir John Templeton
. . . Steve Tenore . . . Stefano Terzi . . . Ann Wharton Thayer . . . Harry
M. Thayer . . . Jeanne Cooley Thayer . . . Thomas C. Thayer . . . Walter
Nelson Thayer . . . Lowell Thomas . . . Mayor Richard Thomas . . .

Andrew Thompson . . . Ellis Thompson . . . Jim Thompson . . . Adam
Tihany . . . Samantha "Sam" Tilley . . . Ron Tocci . . . Towle Tompkins
. . . Jerry Toner . . . Michael Tong . . . Melvin Howard Tormé . . . Jorge
Torres . . . Mary Tragale . . . Richard Neal Travis . . . Dolph Traymon . . .
Marietta Tree . . . Diane and John Trimper . . . President Donald J.
Trump . . . Maria Trusa . . . Diane Straus Tucker . . . Fr. Robert Tucker
. . . Peter Tufo . . . Mark Tulis . . . Tommy Tune . . . Dr. Laura Twedt . . .

Mayor Joe Vacarella . . . Comm. Paul Vacca . . . Attorney General
Dennis Vacco . . . Joe Valeant . . . Senator Guy Velella . . . Irma Becerra
Valencia . . . Charles Valenti . . . Jack Valenti . . . Jerry Valenti . . . John
Valenti . . . Cong. Lionel Van Deerlin . . . James Van Sickle . . . Alfred
Gwynne Vanderbilt . . . Wendy Vanderbilt . . . Paul Vandenburgh . . .
Captain Dan Venor . . . Mayor George Vergara . . . Carl Anthony
Vergari . . . John Verni, Esq. . . . Vito Verni . . . Davyne Verstandig . . .
Wendy and Royal "Mike" Victor . . . Dave Vigeant . . . Joe "Slick"
Vitulli . . . Floyd "Uncle Floyd" Vivino . . . Michael Vivolo . . . Sean
Vokhsoorzadeh . . . Alex Von Bidder . . . Bill Voute . . . Art Vuolo . . .
Ron Vuy . . .

Chief Judge Sol Wachtler . . . Phyllis Cerf Wagner . . . Mayor Robert
Wagner . . . Mario Wainer . . . Richard Wald . . . Elsie Maria Troija
Walter . . . John Ward . . . Stephen Warley . . . Ross Weale . . . Rosemary
Weaver . . . Will Weaver . . . John Weinberg . . . Sidney Weinberg . . .
Michael Weinstein . . . Charlie Weiss . . . Walter Weiss . . . Suzi and Jack
Welch . . . Deacon Charles Wendelken . . . Jordan Wertlieb . . . Donald
V. West . . . Lally Weymouth . . . Jack Whitaker . . . Bill White . . . Bruce J.
White . . . Ann Whitman . . . Amb. John Hay "Jock" Whitney . . .
Marylou Whitney . . . Ronny Whyte . . . Chuck Wilgus . . . William the
Doorman at Harry Cipriani . . . Brian Williams . . . William D. Williams
. . . Gov. Malcolm Wilson . . . Sloan Wilson . . . Robert Windeler . . .
Barbara Winston . . . Duffy Witmer . . . Rabbi Amiel Wohl . . . Fran
Wood . . . Hon. C. V. "Jim" Woolridge, OBE . . . Judge Bruce Wright . . .
Hon. Keith Wright . . .

David Yarnell . . . Mayor Clinton Young . . . Francis X. Young . . .
Leigh Curry Young . . . Whitney Moore Young Jr. . . . Susan and Jay
Youngling . . . Tony Yurgaitis . . .

Foreign Minister Mohammad Javad Zarif of Iran . . . Zahir Ziani . . . Beth Zander . . . Sam Zherka . . . Prophet Maixent Zogo . . . Susan and Art Zuckerman . . . Giuliano Zuliani.

So there it is. Enough reminiscing. As I look back over this list of those who shaped my life . . . it occurs to me, sadly and painfully, that many are long since gone to what Governor Wilson called "a better world."

And I'm often asked, who among the dearly departed do I miss the most? In response to which I always say, "Well, you mean besides Mario Cuomo . . . ?" And then I am overtaken with waves of sweet and vivid memories of Ossie Davis; my mother, Catherine; my brother Jack and my dad, William Mac O'Shaughnessy; Nancy Q. Keefe, the Westchester writer; Judge Alvin Richard Ruskin; the WNEW Make Believe Ballroom disc jockey William B. Williams; the saloonkeeper Toots Shor; Fred Astaire; a classy woman named Jean T. Ensign; Senator Jack Javits; New York Giants patriarch Wellington Mara; New York Mayor John V. Lindsay; a townie politician, Rocco Bellantoni Jr.; the cabaret singers Mabel Mercer, Hugh Shannon, and Bobby Short; an Armenian rug merchant, Edward G. Michaelian, who, as county executive, built our modern-day Westchester; and, of course, Francis Albert Sinatra and Nelson Aldrich Rockefeller. And I can't seem to forget my broadcasting mentors Martin Stone and John Van Buren Sullivan, *New York Post* columnist Richard Neal Travis, Cardinal John O'Connor, or the writers Jimmy Cannon and Jimmy Breslin. Also Caryl Donnelly Plunkett, Monsignor Terry Attridge, and Monsignor Ed Connors. Finally, a puppy named Luna belongs on this list and in my heart.

I'm greatly taken with a beautiful song, a hymn really: "Here I am Lord . . ." with a lovely, haunting line: "I hear you calling in the night."

These are the ones calling to me at night . . .

I often think of so many others of sainted memory. But these keep coming back to me . . . like a song.

A Different Kind of List

―――――――――

In the midst of winter . . . I found within myself an invincible summer.
—Albert Camus

I've always loved that quote. And now, as I sit at my desk on this January day, struggling to pull together my fifth book (another anthology), I shake off the cold-weather blues by reflecting on just how lucky I am.

I've written previously of the good fortune that has accompanied me in every season of my already long life, even during the domestic turmoil and chaos of recent years.

Happy Rockefeller once told me, "Good friends rally 'round when life turns sad and difficult." And Mario Cuomo advised me to "sweep away the rubble." But I can't discard my gratitude to some wonderful individuals whose encouragement and friendship sustained me during the travails of the past several years.

You will recognize a lot of familiar, if disparate, types among these good souls. But every single one of them went out of their way to do something nice for me and mine *at least once*. But I must admit I taxed the friendship of a great many on an almost daily basis.

As I consider my good fortune and tally up my blessings, there are, to be sure, some others. But *these* are the ones whose generosity I'll remember. They were wonderful as my marriage went south and chaos reigned.

I'm grateful for their kindness in any season.

And I don't forget:

Floyd Abrams . . . Cindy Adams . . . Roger Ailes . . . Ahmet Aloqui . . . Eleanor Alter, Esq. . . . Gregorio Alvarez . . . Joe Amaturo . . . Joe Apicella . . . David Aronson, Esq. . . . Michael Assaf . . . Rob Astorino . . . Fabio

Avendano . . . Vanessa Battle . . . Special Agent Charles Beaudoin . . . Judge Joseph Bellacosa . . . Kara Bennorth . . . Henry Berman . . . Judge Jeffrey Bernbach . . . Karen Dobbis Bernbach . . . Jerry Biggins . . . Robert Blau . . . Carol Bobrowsky . . . Hon. Oren Boynton . . . Dr. David Breindel . . . Gerardo Bruno . . . Colin Burns Sr. . . . Billy Bush . . . Jonathan Bush . . . Dr. Steven Butensky . . . John Cahill . . . Suzanne Calabrese . . . Kylie and Louis Cappelli . . . Judge Anthony Carbone . . . Father Michael Carnevale, OFM . . . Peter Carpenter . . . Commissioner Pat Carroll . . . John Catsimatidis . . . Lachlan Cartwright . . . Trooper Matt Cashman . . . Chuck Castleberry . . . Father Joe Cavoto, OFM . . . Guillaume Chamot-Rooke . . . Jody Chesnov . . . Jennifer and Douglas Clement . . . Kenneth Cole . . . Maria Cuomo Cole . . . David Patrick Columbia . . . Judge Matthew Cooper . . . Tim Corvo, Esq. . . . Jerry Cummins . . . Bill Cunningham . . . Jim Cunningham . . . Governor Andrew Mark Cuomo . . . Governor Mario M. Cuomo . . . Matilda Raffa Cuomo . . . Cynthia Foster Curry . . . Tony Damiani . . . Mayor Ernie Davis . . . Robert Davis . . . Lydia Devine, Esq. . . . Robert Deyber . . . Fred Dicker . . . Judge Tom Dickerson . . . Fiorita and Michael DiLullo . . . Joey DiMarco . . . Chief Lou DiMeglio . . . Abramo Dispirito . . . Timothy Cardinal Dolan . . . David Donovan . . . Jimmy the Doorman . . . Judge Ann Dranginis . . . Bruno Dussin . . . Dr. Fritz Ehlert . . . Dr. Marc Sabin Eisenberg . . . Kevin Scott Elliott . . . Lee Elman . . . Ambassador Edward Elliot Elson . . . Frank Endress . . . Judge Saralee Evans . . . Erica Farber . . . Michael Fasano, Esq. . . . Tony Federici . . . Steve Fisher . . . Dick Foreman . . . Joe Fosina . . . Justice Samuel George Fredman . . . Judy Fremont . . . Scott Fybush . . . Cindy Hall Gallagher . . . Leon Geller . . . Christine Gemelli . . . Jim Generoso . . . Simoni Gentile . . . Raul Geraldo . . . Edward "Ned" Gerritty . . . Gary Gerstein . . . Judge Charles Gill . . . Marla Golden . . . Marty Goldsmith . . . Terry Golway . . . Shari Gordon, Esq. . . . Jeff Greenberg . . . Regina and Rainer Greeven . . . Rich Guberti . . . Jo Hallingby . . . Ron Harris . . . Michael Harrison . . . Graham Hastedt . . . Donald Hayde, Esq. . . . Cynthia Hayes . . . John Hennessy . . . Nat Hentoff . . . Billy Herman, Esq. . . . Luis Hernandez . . . Maggie Hernandez . . . Debbie Hield . . . Trooper Jim Holm . . . Judy Huntington . . . Dennis Jackson . . . Billy Jacobs . . . Joan Jedell . . . Richard Johnson . . . Robert Johnson . . .

Thomas Johnson . . . Dr. Bob Jones . . . Charlie Kafferman . . . Larry Kaiser . . . Noel Kane . . . Mel Karmazin . . . Pat Keegan . . . Alfred Kelly Jr. . . . John Kelly . . . William Kennedy . . . Mike Kinosian . . . Hon. Henry Kissinger . . . Ralph Kragle . . . Erwin Krasnow, Esq. . . . Cappy LaBarbera . . . Senator George Latimer . . . Franco Lazzari . . . Mike Licalzi . . . Salvatore Lombardi . . . Philip Lombardo . . . Representative Nita Lowey . . . Egidiana Maccioni . . . Marco Maccioni . . . Mario Maccioni . . . Mauro Maccioni . . . Sirio Maccioni . . . Alec MacGillis . . . Kevin Mackin, OFM . . . Jane Mago, Esq. . . . Bob Mancuso, Esq. . . . Ed Mancuso . . . John Mara . . . Carl Marcucci . . . Charles Masson . . . Michaele McCarthy . . . Dr. Richard McCarthy . . . Brian McCormick, Esq. . . . Claudia McDonnell . . . Kevin Barry McGrath, Esq. . . . John McKenna . . . James R. McManus . . . Patrick McMullan . . . Father Joseph M. McShane, S.J. . . . Paolo Middei . . . Barbara and Joseph Migliucci . . . Faith Miller, Esq. . . . Judge Sondra Miller . . . Mark Miller . . . Suzi Mion . . . Dr. Sandy Mirabile . . . Jay Mitchell . . . Wendy Moger-Bross . . . Joe Mondello . . . Tom Mullen . . . Betty Ann Mummert . . . Dan Murphy . . . Deborah and Declan Murphy . . . Mark Murphy . . . Ryan Murphy . . . Ted Murphy . . . Fred Nachbaur . . . Joe Napolitano . . . Jimmy Neary . . . Ambassador Edward Noonan Ney . . . Judy Ney . . . Vu Nguyen . . . Julian Niccolini . . . Margaret Noonan . . . Deborah Norville and Karl Wellner . . . Ken Norwick, Esq. . . . Amelia Nulty . . . Flynn Nulty . . . Tucker Nulty . . . Dr. Joseph Nyre . . . Anita Oken . . . Ellen and Ray Oneglia . . . Father Joseph O'Hare, S.J. . . . Bill O'Neill . . . Cara Ferrin O'Shaughnessy . . . Coco O'Shaughnessy . . . David Tucker O'Shaughnessy . . . Isabel O'Shaughnessy . . . Julie Ascenzo O'Shaughnessy . . . Kate Wharton O'Shaughnessy . . . Lacey O'Shaughnessy . . . Lily O'Shaughnessy . . . Matthew Thayer O'Shaughnessy . . . James O'Shea . . . Phyllis Steves and Bob Partridge . . . Gregg Pavelle . . . Alina Pedroso . . . Dr. Paul Pellicci . . . Joe Percoco . . . Al Pirro, Esq. . . . Judge Jeanine Pirro . . . Kathy and Dr. Rich Pisano . . . Ray Planell . . . Caryl Donnelly Plunkett . . . Kevin Plunkett . . . William Plunkett . . . Postmaster Vincent Polacco . . . Mary Porcelli . . . Dr. Ken Porter . . . Assemblyman Gary Pretlow . . . Dominic Procopio . . . Doug Quinn . . . Denise and Greg Raap . . . Dan Rather . . . Ambassador Ogden Rogers Reid . . . Joe Reilly . . . Phil Reisman . . . Elva Amparo Reynoso . . . Eric Rhoads . . . Dan Ribicoff . . . Anthony

Riccardi . . . Murray Richman, Esq. . . . Judge Vincent Rippa . . . Col. Marty Rochelle . . . Joseph "Jim" Rocco . . . Tim Rooney Sr. . . . Cristina Rose . . . Janine Rose . . . Alan Rosenberg . . . Marjorie Rubin . . . Gianni Russo . . . Constable Pete Russo . . . Ed Ryan . . . Dr. Steven Safyer . . . Emilia St. Amand . . . Joao "Bamboo" Santos . . . Steve Savino . . . Mike Scully . . . Scott Shannon . . . Judge Judy Sheindlin . . . Judge Alan Scheinkman . . . Scott Shannon . . . Michele Silva Thomas, Esq. . . . John Sterling . . . Adele Suslak . . . Liz Bracken Thompson . . . Geoff Thompson . . . Mark Simone . . . Barry Slotnick, Esq. . . . Emily Smith . . . Jan Johnson Smith . . . Liz Smith . . . John Spicer . . . General Joe Spinelli . . . Rob Speyer . . . Renee and Stuart Stengel . . . Don Stevens . . . Gayle Stevenson . . . Chuck Strome . . . Howard Sturman . . . Arthur Ochs Sulzberger Jr. . . . Laurie and Rob Taishoff . . . Joan and Val Taubner . . . Tom Taylor . . . Steve Tenore . . . Ann Wharton Thayer . . . Janet and Wes Tilden . . . Jonathan Tisch . . . Father Robert Tucker . . . Irma Valencia . . . Jesus Valencia . . . Charles Valenti . . . John Valenti . . . Dave Vigeant . . . Sean Vokhshoorzadeh . . . Alex Von Bidder . . . Maria Von Nicolai . . . Ron Vuy . . . Mario Edwardo Wainer . . . Sabrina Wender . . . Ed Whitman . . . Bud Williamson . . . Rabbi Amiel Wohl . . . Greg Wright . . . Francis X. Young . . . Zahir Ziani . . . William Zimmerman . . . Guliano Zuliani . . . Todd Zuzullo.

Every one did something nice during a tough time.

I still love that "invincible summer" line. But before summer comes spring.

Pitchers and catchers report next week.

Vivid Women in Every Season

———————

In a previous volume I put together a list of "Vivid Souls" we've encountered over the years. But that assemblage was heavily skewed toward men. And I've been thinking for some time I ought to draw up a list of only those marvelous and unforgettable *women* who dazzled us with their style, intelligence, and even with their innate goodness during my already long life.

My readers and listeners will know many of these luminous women, especially those who've played on the national stage where my portfolio as a community broadcaster in the heart of the eastern establishment has afforded me opportunities to witness their magic. But I've also included those who operated out of the public spotlight, like my fourth-grade teacher Miss Elizabeth Cadoo, on whom I had an unrequited crush some sixty years ago at Bedford Elementary School. She was one classy dame in my nine-year-old eyes.

Of course my estimable mother, Catherine Tucker O'Shaughnessy, who kept the music playing for eighty-five years, is easily on the list. And so are those with whom I've had only a very casual or passing acquaintance. Many of these remarkable women I've seen only from afar. A few have returned the favor with a fleeting sidelong glance or even a slight furtive smile accompanied by a whispered greeting from across a crowded room. Some on this list I've loved. And been loved by in return.

All were vivid, unforgettable women who were class acts in every season. Some still are. And although many are gone now and no longer paint color into our drab lives, they surely had what the old men of the neighborhood called "staying power." So they stay. In my memory. And, a few of them, in my heart.

Many were "of a certain age" like Kitty Carlisle Hart, who was in her nineties when she left the stage. But as I'm also fast approaching "a certain age" myself as the eighty-first anniversary of my natal day looms; they keep coming back like a song . . . these special women. Unforgettable . . . in every way.

Laura Accurso . . . Cindy Adams . . . Elizabeth Adinolfi . . . Deborah Altorelli . . . Elva Amparo Augustina Alvarez . . . Miosotis Alvarez . . . Amelia St. Amand . . . Judy Fremont Arons . . . Brooke Astor . . . Heather Ball . . . Polly Bergen . . . Karen Bernbach . . . Alessandra Biaggi . . . Rae Bianco . . . Page Morton Black . . . Sandra Blackwell . . . Suzanne Blaicher . . . Barbara Taylor Bradford . . . Cornelia Bregman . . . Lois Bronz . . . Lucia Bruno . . . Connie Buckley . . . Anna Bulgari . . . Jodi Bush . . . Di Butensky . . . Elizabeth Cadoo . . . Trish Novak Canzeri . . . Wendy Carduner . . . Judy Ceruzzi . . . Maggie Cervantes . . . June Christy . . . Jennifer Clement . . . Elaine Wingate Conway . . . Maria Cuomo Cole . . . Lynn Crystal . . . Jane Cuozzo . . . Nancy Curry . . . Matilda Raffa Cuomo . . . Stacey Dames . . . Janet DeFiore . . . Dee DelBello . . . Regina Delfino . . . Carmen Dell'Orefice . . . Fiorita DiLullo . . . Arianna Dordit . . . Sue Doyle . . . Ann Dranginis. . . .

Fernanda Eberstadt . . . Jean Ensign . . . Lucille Falcone . . . Erica Farber . . . Katherine Farley . . . Geraldine Ferraro . . . Anne-Marie Fillipini . . . Suzi Finesilver . . . Miriam Imber Fredman . . . Francine LeFrak Friedberg . . . Frances Fusco . . . Cindy Hall Gallagher . . . Joan Gill . . . Karen Goodfellow . . . Ronnie Gouz . . . Emily Grant . . . Agnes Gund . . . Evie Haas . . . Jo Hallingby . . . Lynn Handler . . . Anne Harmon . . . Kitty Carlisle Hart . . . Gail Hilson . . . Marian Javits . . . Judith Kaye . . . Nancy Q. Keefe . . . Jane Hoey Kelly . . . Marie Kennedy . . . Laura Kowalski . . . Marguerite Lascola . . . Clare Lawrence . . . Mary Lindsay . . . Kim Lombardo . . . Iris Love . . . Nita Lowey. . . .

Egidiana Maccioni . . . Mary Marvin . . . Caryn McBride . . . Suzannah McCorkle . . . JoAnne McCormick . . . Claudia McDonnell . . . Renate McKnight . . . Mabel Mercer . . . Geneive Brown Metzger . . . Joyce Michaelian . . . Barbara Migliucci . . . Mama Rose Migliucci . . . Cay Miller . . . Faith Miller . . . Marcia Miller . . . Sondra Miller . . . Shelby Modell . . . Liz Moynihan . . . Kathy Mullen . . . Nora Murphy . . . Jackie Neary Nash . . . Roxanne Neilson . . . Beth Neuhoff . . . Judy Ney

... Lisa Niccolini ... Margaret Noonan ... Deborah Norville ... Kate Nulty. . . .

Kate O'Brien ... Kathleen Plunkett O'Connor ... Valerie Moore O'Keeffe ... Kim Olds ... Cara O'Shaughnessy ... Julie O'Shaughnessy ... Kelly O'Shaughnessy ... Margaret O'Shea ... Emilie O'Sullivan ... Anita Oken ... Ellen Oneglia ... Libby Pataki ... Nancy Pelosi ... Jeanine Pirro ... Kathy Pisano ... Caryl Plunkett ... Rosemary Plunkett ... Mary Porcelli ... Patsy Preston ... Lee Radziwill ... Jean Rather ... Mary Louise Reid ... Carol Reilly ... Happy Rockefeller ... Sabrina Sunny Roper ... Janine Rose ... Wendy Rosenberg ... Susan Rudin ... Maria Russo ... Elaine Sargent ... Diane Sawyer ... Angela Scarano ... Sue Scully ... Judy Sheindlin ... Daryl Sherman ... Michele Silva ... Emily Smith ... Jan Johnson Smith ... Liz Smith ... Jane Sockwell ... Brenda Resnick Spano ... Kathy Spicer ... Barbaralee Diamonstein-Spielvogel ... Sue Spina ... Susan St. James ... Andrea Stewart-Cousins ... Ellen Sulzberger Straus ... Marcy Syms. . . .

Kathy Taishoff ... Joan Taubner ... Ann Wharton Thayer ... Ruth Hassell Thompson ... Samantha "Sam" Tilley ... Tolly Travis ... Marietta Tree ... Catherine Tucker ... Wendy Vanderbilt ... Linda Vaughn ... Bonnie Verbitsky ... Sandra Von Bidder ... Shirin von Wulffen ... Sessa von Richthofen ... Barbara Walters ... Sabrina Wender ... Lally Weymouth ... Ann Whitman ... Margo Conway Wick ... Dotty Mack Williams ... Katherine Wilson ... Judy Woodruff ... Beth Zander ... Julia Zardoya.

LADIES IN WAITING

There are also in my life some vivid Dames "In-Waiting" ... my grand-daughters: Isabel Grace O'Shaughnessy, Lily Anna O'Shaughnessy, and Amelia Jane Nulty.

One day they'll be on some other kindly white-haired gentleman's list.

They're already on mine.

—W.O.

Notes for the Four Seasons Tribute Evening

I never get up in front of a crowd without notes. Here are some I relied on during a lovely evening at the Friars Club honoring Julian Niccolini and Alex von Bidder, impresarios of the iconic Four Seasons restaurant in Manhattan.

The evening got away from me and took a delightful turn when Larry King, the revered and beloved dean of the Friars Club, took over the questioning. He was so good, in fact, at the roving microphone, that I decided to just "let him run." But not before I said, "You know . . . you're pretty good at this. Have you ever thought of making a career of asking questions?" which brought the house down. Larry is still dean of the legendary Friars Club. And Robert De Niro has been elected abbot to replace the incomparable Jerry Lewis. The Friars Club, New York City, April 17, 2017.

––––––––––

We're very grateful to two of America's most famous and heralded restaurateurs for joining us on a sold-out evening: Shy, modest, retiring Julian Niccolini! And brilliant, taciturn Alex von Bidder, whom we first met at a home for the chronically suave!

How appropriate that we celebrate and honor the history, lineage, and tradition of a great, iconic venue here in the warmth and keeping of *another* New York treasure, our beloved Friars Club!

I mean it's just *perfect* that we are here in the Friars "Monastery" tonight with so many friends and patrons and admirers of the Four Seasons.

Allow me first some comments about the *previous* Four Seasons location.

We've all read in the public press that the new Seagram Building landlords may have made it somewhat "inhospitable" for this iconic restaurant venue. The way I see it, Mr. Rosen and Mr. Fuchs may have appropriated the brick-and-mortar and the bones of the place. But the lineage, the tradition, the history, and the very name itself go with Alex and Julian. And belongs with them. Rosen and Fuchs can never lay claim to any of that. The owners of the Seagram Building (and the Lever House) captured the shell. But the *heart* and *soul* of the Four Seasons still reside with these two marvelous and beloved characters!

So tonight we also salute, really, *two* New York icons.

The Friars Club: founded in 1904—103 years young. And the Four Seasons: founded in 1959—58 years young.

We remember, with fondness, the founders Joe Baum and Jerry Brody, who passed the torch to Tom Margittai, now living in retirement in Santa Fe, and Paul Kovi, gone to what Malcolm Wilson always called "another and, we are sure, a *better* world."

And then, in the seventies, the mantle was entrusted to Julian and Alex, in whose care and keeping this New York treasure has resided for forty years.

Some of those years were quite "colorful," Julian!

These proceedings are greatly enhanced by the presence of:

- Richard Johnson, one of the founders of "Page Six" and now a star feature columnist as "The Man Who Knows New York" for the *New York Post.* Julian has the world's record for mentions in the damn thing!
- Maestro Ralph Compagnone and his wife, Linda—"Mr. N.Y.," a tireless and creative promoter and visionary who put together this remarkable evening.
- Michael Guyre, major-domo and great leader of the Friars.
- Giuseppe Tarillo, the Friars' own dining room impresario.
- Shy, modest, retiring Bo Dietl, the next mayor of New York!
- Cesare Casella, another New York restaurant legend.
- Herman Geist, a Westchester icon and beloved Friar.

Q & A

- Julian and Alex, you're both, shall we say, a little "different." How the hell did you two get along for forty years?

- What was the most popular *dish*. I mean on the *menu*, Julian? Duck? Filet of sole?
- What happens if Pete Peterson and Vernon Jordan and Martha Stewart walk in at the same time? Or Edgar Bronfman, Henry Kissinger, and Jack Rudin?
- Is it getting harder and harder to maintain a quality, worthy, upscale restaurant in this day and age, and especially in Midtown?
- Will there be a *pool* in your new joint?
- Alex, is it *true* that a captain tripped one night in the pool room and dumped a whole filet of sole on a lady's dress, but part of it went in the *pool*, and you said, "Did you order the 'flying fish'?"
- Speaking of which, we thank the Friars' celebrated chef Anatole for *his* brilliant interpretations tonight of Four Seasons classics.
- What are some of the other iconic restaurant venues still afloat, still in the game? Which ones do *you* admire? You've mentioned "21" and La Grenouille.
- Better question: Where do *you* go on your nights off?
- Julian: a question for you. When Anthony Weiner was imploding, and you passed out two hundred wieners at lunch one day, with a dollop of mustard, did you really walk over to Vernon Jordan's table and say, "These are puny by your standards, Mr. Ambassador"? I mean, disgusting! Did you really do that?

Now some questions from our audience . . .

Westchester County Press
Ninetieth Anniversary

Remarks of William O'Shaughnessy at Reid Castle,
Manhattanville College, Purchase, N.Y. October 12, 2018.

First let me wish our beloved *Westchester County Press* congratulations on the ninetieth anniversary of your natal day. I should say your founding day.

I'm glad to see one of our most gifted talk show hosts—Michael Dandry—and so many other friends here tonight.

This is an historic occasion . . . one that bears testimony to the lasting relevance of a unique publication.

The *Westchester County Press* is a lot more than Westchester's most important and enduring black-owned weekly journal.

It's part of the history of our county . . . and thus part of our history.

The *County Press* has been around during all of my already long life. Indeed, when I came into this world kicking and screaming some eighty years ago (I'm still kicking and screaming!) the *Press* was already ten years old!

I never knew your founder, Dr. Alger Adams. But what a wonderful legacy and great gift he's left for all of Westchester regardless of ethnic background or color.

So I'm here in gratitude for what the *Westchester County Press* represents in our lives and in the life of Westchester.

And please forgive me . . . but this is also something of a bittersweet night for me . . . because I can't talk about the *Westchester County Press* without remembering the marvelous man who sustained and enriched it for so many years—the incomparable M. Paul Redd.

I think of him with every issue . . . and certainly during our Saint Patrick's Day community broadcasts during which he invariably did a star turn for many, many years . . . always relentlessly plugging his beloved *Westchester County Press* (and a few Democrats to go along with it!).

Paul Redd was one of the very first champions of our community radio stations . . . and I'll never forget it.

That's why I'm here. And that's why this damn paper is so very important to me and mine.

I should also acknowledge my great admiration for that absolutely extraordinary woman in whose care and keeping this essential journal now resides: your estimable president, publisher, and editor, Sandra Blackwell. Thanks to Sandra, the sweet music of Alger Adams and M. Paul Redd is still heard in the land. For Sandra, as with Paul and Dr. Adams before her . . . it's been a labor of love.

Finally, in the words of Mario Matthew Cuomo, the governor of New York of sainted memory (and he, I know, was a great admirer of Paul Redd and the *Press*) . . . the governor would say *"per cent' anni"*—for one hundred years!

And Sandra . . . we know you're going to make it!

Oh, and I almost forgot, I still . . . after all these years . . . I never found out who the hell Snoopy Allgood really is!

Richard Clark's Eightieth Birthday

Rick Clark was a dynamic, swashbuckling member of the American Yacht Club in Westchester for many years. He now winters in Jupiter, Florida, and, believe it or not, he turned eighty last year. The dashing Clark also has a home in Hyannisport, near the Kennedy compound. (His father, a local judge, was the Kennedy family lawyer.) Rick Clark has been a class act in every season. But I can't believe he's eighty. American Yacht Club, Rye, N.Y., November 10, 2017.

———————————

I do have some things I'd like to say about Richard McCourt Clark on this, the eightieth anniversary . . . of his natal day.

First of all, thank you Lauren and thank you Carolyn, for this spectacular party.

The greatest compliment I can give you both is that it is worthy of your illustrious father.

Eighty is quite significant, Rick. And I'll be there right behind you in but five months, God willing.

A Franciscan priest recently scared the hell out of me—and it should give you some pause as well—when he told me, "God has pulled your file. You're in mortar range." So we better make the most of this evening!

I've known Rick for many, many years. And I think it's very appropriate that we celebrate this evening at his beloved American Yacht Club.

This was a magical place in those days. I've raised two families on these hallowed premises. And when Rick and I first came on the scene, there was Garry Moore, Robin McNeil, Dick Pinkham, Bill Gibbons, Jim and Leggy Mertz, John and Sue Scully, Walter Thayer, Ambassador Ogden Rodgers Reid (who is now our greatly honored and universally revered most senior member), Wally Elton, Bill Keys, Federal Judge Charlie Brieant, and Tom Williams.

I didn't let on to any of these yachtsmen that I didn't know a damn thing about sailing.

But I first noticed Clark as the most glamorous *tennis player* in the history of the AYC.

He always had the best racket, the best tennis shoes, the best visor. And an overabundance of charm. And, of course, he always had the tightest tennis shorts! I mean the guy was perfect . . . he even tapered his *tennis* shorts! He was the envy of the strait-laced sailors in the joint, those who weren't insanely jealous of the guy because their wives were also greatly taken with Rick.

I understand he also cut quite a wide path thru Manursing . . . and up in Hyannisport as well. (The "intelligence" on Palm Beach is not yet in, but we're working on his exploits on the Gold Coast! And we'll have that information as soon as it is received.)

But back to tennis and his exploits here at the American Yacht Club. Although he made his mark on the fabled clay courts out here . . . he was never known as much of a *sailor*. Or *yachtsman*.

Until one day he—and Wally Carey (and I never knew what the hell you needed Wally Carey for. I could never figure him. And he would say he never figured *me* out!)—decided to borrow a sailboat and enter one of the club's most prestigious races. It may have been something like Rye to Fisher's or Block Island . . . something like that.

Like I said, it was a major sailing event, as more than fifty beautiful sailboats sailed off into the sunset one night. And guess what? Rick and Wally *won* the damn thing . . . much to the consternation and chagrin of the Dooie Isdale and Brad Sweeney types who ran the club in those days.

I will mercifully yield in but a moment. But I *also* want to recall one or two quick things you may *not* know about Rick Clark.

He's also quite a splendid human being. When an elder of this club ran into rough waters financially and was posted right outside by the desk where you came in, a great embarrassment for anyone . . . there, almost instantly, was Rick Clark raising funds among some of his friends to take care of the poor fellow's temporary indebtedness.

There's one more thing you may not know.

Rick Clark proposed and sponsored the *first* Jewish member of this legendary yacht club founded by New York financiers in 1883.

The man's name was Arthur Emil. He was a realtor, investor, and restaurateur. Among his holdings were Windows on the World which, as you know, was destroyed on 9/11.

And I can't forget, nor will he let me, that Clark discovered a failed baseball player named Mario Cuomo, of sainted memory, even before I did. And, over the years, I rarely had a conversation with the governor in which he didn't inquire after Rick. He usually said, "Did he put that company out of business yet?"

You all know as well that Rick has carved his initials on the walls of many hospitals between here and Boston over the years that have left him with a bionic brain and titanium knees. I'm not sure whatever else they replaced or adjusted!

Rick went through the airport recently en route to Palm Beach . . . and he had so many replacement parts going through security, they *closed the airport*! . . . in an abundance of caution!

But he survived all of it. And so we rejoice and say, Thank you God!

Rick, you've been a class act in every season.

Your most spectacular achievements were your beloved Susan and the incomparable Pat . . . and your adored Lauren and Carolyn . . . and of course Ricky and Alexandra, now grown, who are here tonight in this perfect venue.

When I first encountered them they were mere toddlers. I remember a lunch here at the Yacht Club in this very room. Rick was swanning about when the kids went missing. Finally, after a frantic search, we found them in the *floor vents* of the East Bar! Ricky had removed the grates. Look at them now! . . . with all your very best friends acquired in your first eighty years.

As Mario would say, "*keep going*" . . . !

For our sake as well as yours.

Because we can't imagine a world without you around to brighten our lives.

Judge Samuel Fredman's
Ninetieth-Birthday Celebration

Mr. Justice Samuel George Fredman was a big deal in Westchester. A very big deal. He was the preeminent matrimonial lawyer in these parts, head of the Westchester Jewish Conference, chairman of the Democratic Party, and a New York State Supreme Court justice. He was also, late in life, a radio talk show host, and his weekly program, "The Rabbi and the Judge," was widely heard and heralded. I had the privilege and honor of emceeing his ninetieth-birthday celebration at Knollwood Country Club, Elmsford, N.Y., on March 9, 2014, where His Honor mentioned and thanked more than 300 people there assembled. And he had an anecdote for every attendee. Here are my remarks about this beloved Westchester neighbor.

Welcome to a celebration of the ninetieth anniversary of the natal day of a Westchester legend: Sam the Man—Mr. Justice Samuel George Fredman!

This is indeed an historic occasion, so much so they even changed the clocks all over America for him last night!

You've left your hearth and home on this March 9th as another spring hovers on the horizon after a long, mean, drodsome winter. You came because you wanted to be with this amazing man who has meant so much in all our lives, not alone because you admire, respect, and revere him; but for many of us, we're here because we truly *love* the man.

Here assembled are his friends political, his friends judicial, his friends religious (we even have not one but *two* cantors who will perform later with a special song!).

And we really have—as you can see with only a cursory and very brief perusal of the lovely ballroom of this great Westchester country club—the White Plains Establishment!

I know White Plains. It's where all my divorce lawyers are!

Even a New Rochelle guy can recognize and not fail to be impressed by the standing and stature of those from your home heath who are here to celebrate with Sam.

There are so many of high estate from White Plains alone; I wonder who would get the headline in the *Journal News* if a bomb suddenly went off.

But come to think of it, I know we have Mayor Tom Roach and former mayors Al DelVecchio and Joe Delfino. If it were the *Journal News*, it would probably be *Adam Bradley*!

The other mayors (and Milton Hoffman) will forgive me!

Teilhard de Chardin, the great Jesuit philosopher-paleontologist, memorably wrote of the "diminishments' we all suffer. It's a great word: diminishments. Sam, as we observe you now with all your powers intact and very much on display with your friends tonight, we'd have to conclude that—somehow—you've managed to *conquer* all those "diminishments" and put them to exile.

I don't know how you manage to do it, Mr. Justice—in every season. As I approach senility, I'm reminded that Sirio Maccioni, the great ringmaster of Le Cirque, recently delightfully observed that Italians have a saying: "If you wake up in the morning and nothing aches, you're *dead*!" But Sirio is only eighty-one. So what the hell does *he* know!

I won't intrude for very long on your evening, but as I think about Sam Fredman and what he means to our county and state and his profession, I'm reminded of something said a long time ago, during a moment of reflection by a friend of his—a former governor, in fact— who has had a great impact on both our lives.

Mr. Cuomo once told me he prays for "sureness." For sureness.

And even as I approach seventy-six myself, I'm not *sure* about a lot of things.

But of only this am I sure: We are *sure* that you are a *great* man, Sam Fredman.

And when the history of our time in Westchester and New York state is written, compiled, and bound and preserved, *your* name will be writ large as one of our foremost leaders, as one of our legends.

And we thus have to put you right up there with the great Nelson Rockefeller and Ed Michaelian, Bill Luddy, and Nita Lowey, that extraordinary woman who graces us with her presence today. And Fredman belongs with Dick Daronco, WVOX's former Pelham Town correspondent; whose name adorns our courthouse; New Rochelle's Alvin Ruskin; and the Judges Gagliardi, William Butcher, Joe and Lee, and Malcolm Wilson, of sainted memory.

These are—and were—the giants of our time in the Golden Apple. And you are among them. Forever.

These proceedings are greatly enhanced by the presence of Westchester Democratic Chairman Reggie Lafayette, New York State Democratic Party treasurer David Alpert, Appellate Justice Mark Dillon, the great squire of Winged Foot (and Bedford) Mr. Justice Nick Colabella, and Nancy Colabella, his Irish wife. Also the dean of the Westchester press corps, Milt Hoffman; Court of Claims Madame Justice Terri Ruderman and her husband, Jerry Ruderman; also the Surrogate of Westchester and the pride of the FBI, Mr. Justice Anthony Scarpino. And a scion of a great Westchester family, Kevin Plunkett, who, as deputy county executive, is so highly respected, as is his boss, Rob Astorino. And, yes, Kevin is the brother of the estimable Bill Plunkett.

Sam's great friend, the former Chief Judge Frank Nicolai, is at a class reunion at the Coast Guard Academy. But we're so glad to have Aileen Nicolai and their daughter Dr. Angelique Nicolai!

Also Carolyn Abramowitz and Colonel Jeff Abramowitz, regimental commander at Fort Knox, Kentucky!

And Cantor Jack Mendelsohn and his wife, Cantor Freida Mendelsohn, with a special song for Sam. I wanted Irish bagpipes! We had them all ready to go! But Sam said, "Save that for the broadcast next Monday!"

I'm not sure if the cantors will perform in English or in Hebrew. If it's in Hebrew, I will *translate* for you! But go slow!

We have some very important speakers who will pay tribute to Mr. Justice Fredman.

But first I want to share with you a lovely, graceful note dispatched this week from the Chicago office by the managing partner of Sam's

1,100-member law firm, Wilson Elser, Daniel McMahon. He's Irish, with the "gift," so what do you expect? But listen to this, as it really captures Fredman:

> It's not often we get to wish someone a happy 90th birthday, let alone one of our colleagues at Wilson Elser. Sam Fredman has enjoyed a rich and storied career as a matrimonial attorney, a justice of the Supreme Court of the State of New York, and, most recently, a sought-after master arbitrator.
>
> Much to our delight, Sam chose to round out his career at Wilson Elser (unless we're but a *stepping stone!*) where for the past 12 years he has worked in our White Plains office as counsel and mentor to many grateful colleagues and clients.
>
> Sam's ability to bring together divergent parties and find common ground among their varied interests epitomizes his successful legal career. He brings these same talents to bear in his private life, where he has been a beloved and legendary figure in several educational, governmental and religious organizations in which he has played key leadership roles.
>
> A member of "The Greatest Generation," Sam served in the U.S. Army Air Force from 1943–1946 and saw action in the South Pacific and Japan—for which we thank him. Of course "greatest" aptly describes Sam on a number of levels, as those who daily benefit from his wisdom, wit and unwavering good cheer well know.
>
> —Daniel J. McMahon, Esq.

There's also a note that arrived at WVOX yesterday marked "Saturday Delivery" from a very special individual whom many of you know and we all admire. He was called by the *Boston Globe* "the great philosopher-statesman of the American nation." I have disrespectfully called him a "failed baseball player with too many vowels in his name."

Here's what he wrote for Sam. It's very brief. We also have a recording of it for you, Judge.

Sam:

I regret not being able to be present *in person* on this auspicious occasion when you are proving that *doing good* for others assures . . . longevity.

I'm *not* surprised . . . that you have manifested your high intelligence, your immense *generosity*, and your political expertise, all accompanied by your joyous love of life.

My toast to you is for continued good health and I make it in Italian . . . because in Italian it is very special. In Italian I say to you I wish *all* good things for you . . . per-cento anni . . . for 100 years, at least . . .

Keep going. Keep going, Sam . . . we love you.

Signed, simply, "Mario." Here's the original.

And finally, the *real* VIPs and those closest to Sam: his sons and heirs and his grandchildren: Neil Fredman and his wife, Michelle; Andy Fredman and his wife, Susan. And his grandchildren Daniel and his wife, Stephanie; Ariel and her husband, Perry Stuart; Joshua and *compadres* Jamie and Alie, who works in education with Eva Moscowitz.

Sam, we've had a lot of letters. And I just wanted to share one more that Cindy found in our archives at the station. It was a personal letter to you about a piece you did for the *Times* when David Brooks, their brilliant columnist, had suggested that his readers do a "Life Report." Here's my reaction to your submission:

Mr. Justice Sam:

I read your "Life Report" for David Brooks.

And while beautifully done with all your graceful style and marvelous wit . . . I hope you will forgive the observation that it does not nearly capture the greatness—and yes, the goodness— of the Sam Fredman we know and love.

I'm talking about the Sam Fredman who was a "nice man in a murky profession," which appellation I gave you so many years ago. Or the Sam Fredman the lowlifes and sharks in your matrimonial tribe used to derisively dismiss as a "settler" . . . a "conciliator" . . . a "compromiser." And it wasn't meant as a compliment.

I just don't think that comes through in the retrospective you prepared for Brooks.

Nor does the Sam Fredman who always steered his Democratic Party to champion hopeless, but worthy pursuits . . . as when a failed baseball player with too many vowels in his name who dared aspire to be governor had only a meager 9% in Westchester. But he had Fredman. Nita Lowey had 4% in her first race for Congress. But she had Fredman.

Actually, as I think about it . . . I may do my own "Life Report" one of these days. I'll have to stretch and scramble to come up with some commendable things *I've* done in *my* already long life.

But if there were a few worthy moments during my erratic stewardship of Bill O'Shaughnessy . . . they could not have been accomplished without you. Because I wouldn't have been able to do *anything* without the radio podium and broadcasting platform you helped protect, defend and save harmless in all the seasons of my life.

Yours is a beautiful piece. But you can do better by Fredman. You should enlarge and expand on it and make it into a *book*. A whole *chapter* should be devoted to how you advocated for Jewish causes over the years . . . without trampling on the free speech and opinions of others. And how you subtly and with gentle persuasion and compelling wisdom always kept me and mine firmly inclined to the *Jewish* view on matters domestic and international . . .

Now here is the Man of the Hour: Mr. Justice Sam Fredman, who has promised to keep it to an hour and a half.

Sam, if you forget everything said here tonight, all the encomiums and expressions of your worth and value to so many, remember *only* this: Collectively, and individually, we love you!

We should thank John Sarcone for using his influence to persuade Knollwood to take us in after this party became too big for another venue. You should know, in the intimacy of this grand ballroom, that this was to be a rather "restrained" affair with but a few of Sam's nearest and dearest. But, Sam being Sam, it grew and grew. And so we thank John Sarcone and Mauro Piccininni, the general manager, for our use of the hall. The *dinner* was spectacular! And the next time somebody takes a shot at "country club food," send them to Knollwood and Brother Piccininni!

HOPE Community Services Gala:
Honoring Frank Endress

I always try to make time for those organizations and events that, how-ever worthy, don't commend themselves to the society pages of my beloved New York Times. *Such an occasion was the HOPE Community Services Gala honoring a wonderful friend of our station, Frank Endress, a states-man of his profession. [He's an auto dealer.] Also honored was the LaSorsa family, which has car dealerships in Westchester and the Bronx. Beckwith Point, Westchester County, N.Y., Thursday, April 7, 2016.*

As this is the seventy-eighth anniversary of my natal day, I was feted at a lovely luncheon today at which I was somewhat reluctantly called upon for remarks as I approach senility. (You can't believe the "reluc-tant" part? Neither can I!)

Thus I won't intrude for very long on your evening. (You know you're in trouble when I say that!)

I come with gratitude for all you do, everyone here assembled, and with great admiration and tremendous respect for your honoree.

HOPE Community Services and those who run it 365 days a year are among the great unsung heroes of Westchester.

I've known and admired the work of Jim Henry; Brother Kevin Devlin, a Christian Brother who is so aptly designated; Dottie Meehan; Kathy Doscher; and Iris Fried for a long, long time.

I don't want to stray very far from the limited portfolio that has been assigned to me by Carol Troum, but I do want you to know that I am aware of the special privilege conveyed on me by the opportunity to thank this particular honoree on behalf of the 400 volunteers who operate HOPE's soup kitchen and daily fill those 600 grocery bags that contain 27 meals in each and every parcel.

I'm also aware that in presenting this award I have been given a very specific fiduciary responsibility to thank our honoree on behalf of the sixty homeless souls who are sheltered and protected—and made to feel loved—at your Homeless Resource Center.

You have chosen very well, ladies and gentlemen, by your designation of Frank Endress to receive HOPE's prestigious Commitment to Service Award.

I have admired Frank Endress and his work in our community for many years. Frank does his commerce and business successfully in a highly competitive profession. He's no shrinking violet. But he does his philanthropy and his civic beneficence very quietly and out of the limelight. And that's why we honor him.

This is the individual who saw to it that *every* child in New Rochelle had a backpack so they're not embarrassed to show up at school because their parents could not afford one.

Frank Endress did that. You may not know it, but *he did that.* You should also know that he's now working on yet another wonderful Frank Endress–inspired project to provide one hundred new bicycles this year for deserving minority youngsters in our community. I don't know if I'm authorized to tell you that or if it's even been announced. But Benito, your dedicated program coordinator, told me, Frank. And so I had to blab it.

For thirty-two years, HOPE Community Services has been a shining and brilliant example of the goodness and decency and generosity that reside in our battered and often misunderstood city.

And I don't want to be biblical about this, but *all* of you are doing the Lord's work by feeding the hungry and providing shelter for the homeless. And come to think of it, that *is* biblical.

For your *honoree*, ladies and gentlemen, it comes naturally and relentlessly and consistently, and it flows from his heart altogether generously and freely. It comes naturally.

And so it is a great honor—on *your* behalf—to present the HOPE Commitment to Service Award to the great Frank Endress.

And we're also well aware that his remarkable philanthropy would not be possible without the support, encouragement, and generous backing of a great company—New Rochelle Chevrolet and John LaSorsa and the great LaSorsa automotive family.

There are a lot of "takers" in our midst, corporations and individuals who *take* and put *nothing* back.

And then there are Frank Endress, the LaSorsa family, and their New Rochelle Chevrolet as dazzling exceptions to that rule.

Congratulations, sir.

Celebrating the 200th Anniversary
of the Christian Brothers

Over the years I've emceed hundreds of dinners at various venues in the New York area—including many in the legendary Grand Ballroom of the Waldorf Astoria. I was especially flattered to be at the microphone for the 200th anniversary gala saluting the Christian Brothers of Ireland, whose goodness is everywhere apparent in our home heath, at Iona College, Iona Prep, and Iona Grammar School.

Ladies and gentlemen, Bishop Nevins, friends of the Christian Brothers, we're here in this great ballroom on this perfectly brilliant October night to celebrate the 200th anniversary of the founding of the Christian Brothers.

I've been summoned, it seems, every twenty years to do this dinner.

This is a very special occasion.

We celebrate with great joy and gratitude the bicentennial of the Congregation of Christian Brothers. All of us here acknowledge the founding, 200 years ago, of the altogether unique, absolutely essential, and, even more, the still very *relevant* educational ministry and *mission* of the Christian Brothers, founded by Edmund Rice. Edmund Rice has been called "Blessed" by the Church of Rome, and his work and example have endured for 200 years.

Now, ladies and gentlemen, I have the pleasure to present to you the Blessed Edmund Rice Medal *honorees*. In celebration of the founding of the Congregation of Christian Brothers by Blessed Edmund Rice in 1802, the medal is presented to those men and women who reflect, in their personal and professional lives, the spirit and charisma of Brother Edmund.

Ladies and gentlemen, we come tonight in thanksgiving for the Brothers in our midst. All along the eastern seaboard, in Peru and the

Virgin Islands, on six continents, but essentially and most prominently in Westchester, the Bronx, and New Jersey for many years, and *especially* in New Rochelle.

New Rochelle went through a tough time for many years. And there in the center of the city, for many years we had only Iona College to sustain us

We also remember a legendary Christian Brother many of us love to this day, Jack Driscoll.

Tonight we honor the Brothers as educators and teachers. And it occurs to me that over the years, as they imparted knowledge and the wisdom that proceeds from it to our sons and grandsons, they also instruct all of us with their holiness, their fortitude, their devotion, and their commitment to the course set for them by Edmund Rice.

That's why we're here. Because who among us, in the intimacy of this grand ballroom, has not had occasion to be grateful to the Brothers? It seems they are with us throughout every season of our lives. That's why we've left our hearth and home and our families to be here on the occasion of their 200th birthday to celebrate their valuable, *relevant* ministry.

Thank you for the privilege of being with you on this wonderful night. And for the privilege of being witness to all the good the Christian Brothers have done in our lives.

—W.O.

A Community Celebration Honoring
Commissioner Patrick J. Carroll

*Remarks by William O'Shaughnessy and NYPD Commissioner
James O'Neill. The Surf Club, New Rochelle, N.Y., December 7, 2017.*

———————

WILLIAM O'SHAUGHNESSY

The glorious music as you came into the grand ballroom was by the *Godfather* star Gianni Russo. Thanks, pal, for being here and bringing your band of such talented musicians.

The proceedings are greatly enhanced by the presence tonight of the forty-third police commissioner of the City of New York. He's a national leader in neighborhood policing and has been a pioneer in police and community interaction and collaboration with the disparate and diverse communities served by the legendary NYPD. The commissioner is known abroad in the land as a dedicated and brilliant police *reformer*. Before becoming commissioner of the NYPD, he was commanding officer of Bill Bratton's office and played a key role in the restructuring of the headquarters of the NYPD. He then became chief of department, and he is now commissioner of the vaunted NYPD, a police force of *national* renown.

Please welcome New York City Police Commissioner James O'Neill.

COMMISSIONER JAMES O'NEILL

I always talk about what a great job we have, but without our families and without our friends and without the support you give us, we wouldn't be able to do these great jobs. You indeed have the hardest job, so once again, thank you for everything you do.

Pat, so now on to you. I've known Pat for about four years. I met him in San Francisco at a Major Cities Chief's conference. The minute I met him, I knew he was a man of integrity and a special person. Twenty-eight years in the NYPD; he was a CO of many precincts. They gave me a bio: they said you were the CO of the 75, the busiest and best precinct in New York City. Being the CO of the 44, I have a little problem with that; but then I said it's Pat's night, so I'm going to let it go!

Twenty-eight years in the NYPD, and then twenty-four years up here in Westchester: fifty-two years if I do my math real quickly. I just can't believe that you're quitting! It's only fifty-two years, c'mon!

What I'm going to present you with tonight is a statue that was commissioned by Mayor LaGuardia back in 1939, and it was supposed to be a representation of all the police officers killed in the line of duty. It's a statue of a police officer next to a child. And the child represents all the innocent people that the police officers protect each and every day. So, Pat, thank you for everything that you've done. Thank you for your fifty-two years!

WILLIAM O'SHAUGHNESSY

There's something about this unique city. It attracts talented and illustrious citizens in every season: Thomas Paine; Jacob Leisler; Eddie Foy and his kids, all seven of them; Lou Gehrig; Frankie Frisch; and two distinguished presidents of the National Urban League, Whitney Moore Young and Hugh Price, who lives here still. Also the great actress Frances Sternhagen and writer and playwright E. L. Doctorow.

And in recent years, our most beloved citizens were, of course, Ossie Davis and Ruby Dee. And we should never forget the genius of Norman Rockwell.

Each of *you* is also very special indeed. And don't forget that. And we're grateful for the gift of your presence tonight. Actually, everybody who's anybody is here tonight. Even the great *Don* Dominic Procopio is here (with his translator!) for his friend Commissioner Carrolli, Comisario Pasqualie Carolli! [applause]

Here's some good news: This will be a No-Proclamation Night! [applause] We got 'em. They're piled up over there, singing the praises of the commissioner. But we're not going to read them! [applause]

Which reminds us that over the years we've also been able to attract very superior *public servants*. Many of them assembled here tonight, including Mayor Noam Bramson and the high council of our city: Lou Trangucci, Al Tarantino, Jared Rice, Ivar Hyden, Barry Fertel, and Liz Fried; Judge Susan Kettner; Judge Anthony Carbone; Jim Generoso, who runs our City Court with such dedication; Bennie Giles, the chief clerk of the city; Westchester Commissioner of Jurors Dr. Betty Campbell; and Supreme Court Justice John Colangelo, New Rochelle's own.

At a recent meeting of your foundation, I was emboldened to suggest that before you can have an *enlightened* city, before you can have a *gracious* city, before you can have a city dedicated to the arts and higher learning and the finer things (as New Rochelle is), before any of *that* can occur and exist and thrive, you've got to have a *safe* community. And a *civil* community. You've *got* to have a *peaceful* community.

New Rochelle has had some great leaders as head of our fabled Police Department, which is known, by every account and in every telling, as one of the very best in New York state.

Our radio station goes all the way back to Ed Carey. And there was a handsome guy named Bill Hegarty from the Midwest, and New Rochelle's born and bred Commissioner Mike Armiento of sainted memory. Like I said, we've had some great leaders who carried our public-safety portfolio, among them Alex Toone, Howie DeMarco, Tony Murphy, and the great Commissioner Joe Schaller.

But tonight we salute you, sir, for the dedication of a lifetime in law enforcement.

And with almost 500 of your grateful neighbors here assembled, Pat Carroll, we will attempt to thank you for your stewardship and leadership of our Police Department for the past 24 years. We also thank your beloved Kathleen and your six children and fifteen of your eighteen grandchildren who are with us tonight and take such great pride in the accomplishments of their grandfather.

During your stewardship, Commissioner, you've presided over a peaceful city. And for that, *alone*, we *thank* you.

There have been no riots, there have been few protest marches. There have been no Crabtree fires. There have been no Neptune shootings. Our high school hasn't burned down during your tenure! *Peace* has reigned in our diverse community of 80,000 residents, thanks to you and the 165 men and women under your command.

And speaking of which: among your accomplishments, Commissioner, was the establishment of *our* version of the *Coast Guard*: The New Rochelle Harbor Patrol, whose flotilla now includes *five* worthy ships of the line and armed crews to protect our pristine nine-mile shoreline.

Physically and geographically, New Rochelle is a challenge. As members of the high council of our city here assembled will confirm, it's ten miles long, with those nine miles of shoreline resting cheek-by-jowl next to Long Island Sound. No *river* runs through it. But Federal Highway 95 sure does, and so does the Hutchinson River Parkway and the fabled heavily trafficked to this day U.S. Route 1, the Boston Post Road.

Pat, you got a *lot* done in the 24 years you've given us. In 1995 and '96 with the help and encouragement of the New Rochelle police unions— and Mike Ferrara is here tonight!—you made a decision to see to it that *every one* of your 165 officers was possessed of a college degree, and if they aspired to *higher* rank—lieutenant, captain, sergeant—they had to come bearing a *four*-year college degree!

And few will remember—but our News Department does—that Charlene Indelicato and Chuck Strome actually *found* Police Commissioner Carroll when we sent to "Central Casting" back in 1992 as our city was experiencing some of the "spillover" from the "Rodney King riots" in L.A., which were threatening to spread and engulf the whole damn nation. And so the very *first* thing the new commissioner did was commandeer twelve huge stratocruiser buses to take the protestors in our city down to Washington, D.C., the nation's capital, where they could vent and burn off some steam—*and*, while they were at it, to campaign for the Brady Bill.

That *really* happened. And it was a masterstroke. And we knew then and there that we had something *very* special in the person of Patrick Carroll.

I'll just take one more minute to tell you that before he came to our town, he commanded *three* precincts in the Great City, including one in East New York—probably the worst in the city in its day, next to Brownsville. And he also commanded the 79th Precinct in Bed-Stuy and the 108th in Sunnyside. Not one of them a walk in the park. I will disagree only on this one point with Commissioner O'Neill!

And as Commissioner O'Neill knows, and will confirm, Pat also commanded the fabled Critical Incident Unit. He brought all the lessons learned there and in his previous difficult commands to our home heath. And we're, all of us, sir, grateful for your enlightened service.

We did have a pretty "close call" when *two* different governors of New York were eyeing him for commander of the New York State Police. But he *stayed* with us, and for that, we're grateful.

We know you like it in Florida and Long Island, Commissioner, but don't get too comfortable in either venue, because we have *plans* that will require your presence. I don't think we are ready to announce it yet, but there is a scheme afoot to keep you very much involved with the city *and* the Police Foundation, which you really created and have inspired for such a long time.

Ladies and gentlemen: The rule of law is responsible for all that we are, my neighbors. It *forms* us and *defines* us. Everything we are proceeds from it. It has protected and sustained us for 241 years. The *law* is the miracle of what we are. The *law* that we entrusted to Patrick Carroll to interpret and uphold for the past 24 years.

That's what Pat Carroll and the women and men of his department have provided in such great abundance.

And so we *thank you* for that *and* the *dedication* of a lifetime.

We *thank* you for your judgment.

We *thank* you for your patience.

We *thank* you for your wisdom, your experience, your compassion, your integrity, and your intelligence. [applause]

What makes for a *great* peace officer, my neighbors, is not something learned on the NYPD shooting range down in the Bronx. It's learned in the community. And you and the men and women under your command have learned those lessons so well.

In certain parts of the country, your profession—what you do for a living—is called a *peace officer.*

And I hate to be "biblical," Pat. But *Blessed are the peacemakers!*

We're talking about you, sir.

And that's all I have to say on the subject. [applause]

PART V
EULOGIES: THE LAST WORD

Eulogy for John S. Pritchard III

This perfect eulogy was given by my pal of many years Joe Spinelli, who was a great friend of Mario Cuomo's. Spinelli spoke movingly and passionately about his fellow lawman John Pritchard on October 12, 2018.

Joseph Anthony Spinelli was part of a legendary three-man FBI squad with Pritchard and Louis Freeh (Spinelli became New York state's Inspector General under Mario Cuomo; Louis Freeh became a federal judge and director of the FBI). John Pritchard was not only a Special Agent in the Bureau, he also served as inspector general of the MTA and Police Commissioner in Mount Vernon, N.Y., during an illustrious career in law enforcement.

My name is Joe Spinelli, and I've known John for over forty years and had the privilege to be John's partner in the FBI for almost seven years.

Normally when I address a group in any forum I like to speak extemporaneously, but not today. I wrote my thoughts down today, because I did not want to omit anything.

When Anne requested I speak today I was honored. And yet I knew this would be difficult, because grief affects us all and does not discriminate.

I have never considered John to be just a friend. To do so would be an insult to both of us. John will always be my brother, and I loved and respected him as my brother. He was a gentle man and a true gentleman. He earned every accolade bestowed on him, and he gave all he had to be the best at what he did. And he achieved success despite the bias and prejudices he often faced as an African American. He did so by the simple eloquence of his example.

John visited me a few months ago in New York and we had dinner. He told me he wanted to say goodbye in person and we told each other how much we loved each other, and I'm thankful I got the chance to tell him how blessed I was to have him in my life.

John told me to please speak at his memorial service but was quick to admonish me to speak only about stories and events in which the statute of limitations has expired. Unfortunately, after over forty years together, I could come up with only three such stories that met that criterion.

In 1976, John was assigned as a new agent to our Criminal Squad that dealt with fugitives and organized crime. The first time John and I worked together, I had to serve a subpoena on an organized-crime member in the meatpacking district of New York City. Now this should have been a routine deal. We located the organized-crime figure, who was not happy at all to see us, and in the very next moment we found ourselves surrounded by six individuals all holding meat hooks! I looked at John and he smiled and said, "I'm not going anywhere." After I removed the barrel of my B57 from the bad guy's mouth, and all the meat hooks hit the floor . . . we successfully served our subpoena. From that day forward, John and I were partners.

In 1979, while riding in a Bureau car in New York City, over the radio came a call "91 new," which meant a bank robbery was in progress. We were two blocks away from the bank and responded. When we arrived at the bank, three African American men came running out of the bank. John and I immediately began pursuing them on foot. Before we got half a block, three white males came out of the bank and opened fire on us. *They* were the actual bank robbers. And as we took cover John looked at me and with that vintage Pritchard grin said, "You have to stop always blaming the black guys." We laughed out loud and then were fortunate to apprehend all three of the real bank robbers.

Finally, while I was New York State inspector general I began the Adopt-a-School Anti-Drug Program in Bushwick, Brooklyn. I would invite various individuals to present on Career Day to the entire school at assembly. John came and totally mesmerized these youngsters. While addressing them he grabbed my right hand and placed it next to his and asked them: "What is the difference between his hand and mine?" Immediately in unison, the students responded your hand is black and his is white. John shook his head no and said: "There is no difference. You see . . . Joe and I are brothers." I will never forget that moment and the reaction and message sent to those youngsters. I also will never forget how proud I was when John asked me to be Joe's godfather.

Thomas Paine once wrote: "*Reputation* is what men and women think of us; *character* is what God and Angels *know* of us. The greatest legacy one can pass on to one's children and grandchildren is not money or other material things accumulated in one's life, but rather a legacy of character and faith."

When I remember John, and I will for the rest of my life, I will remember his leadership, integrity, valor, and impeccable character. He always possessed the confidence to stand alone, the courage to make difficult decisions, and the empathy and compassion to be sensitive to all people. He never feared to choose right over wrong and truth over popularity. He taught me that there is never a wrong time to do what is right. And what you say and do in life defines who you are. And who you are . . . you are forever.

Each of us loved John because of this. So tonight when your knees hit the floor . . . please ask God to love him.

A wise man once wrote that the greatest of all journeys are those journeys that take you home. John is home now, at peace and waiting to one day be reunited with his beloved Anne and his children.

Rest in peace, my brother.

Henry Kissinger's Tribute to John McCain

Henry Kissinger, America's greatest diplomat and statesman, has been so generous to me and mine over the years. As I write this, the great man is ninety-five. He still dazzles people with his brilliance and erudition as when he struggled to his feet to speak for John McCain. Washington, D.C., September 1, 2018.

Our country has had the good fortune that at times of national trial a few great personalities have emerged to remind us of our essential unity and inspire us our sustaining values. John McCain was one of those gifts of destiny.

I met John for the first time in April 1973 at a White House reception for prisoners returned from captivity in Vietnam. He had been much on my mind during the negotiation to end the Vietnam War, oddly also because his father, then commander in chief of the Pacific command, when briefing the president answered references to his son by saying only, "I pray for him."

In the McCain family national service was its own reward that did not allow for special treatment. I thought of that when his Vietnamese captors during the final phase of negotiations offered to release John so that he could return with me on the official plane that had brought me to Hanoi. Against all odds, he thanked them for the offer but refused it. When we finally met, his greeting was both self-effacing and moving. "Thank you for saving my honor." He did not tell me then or ever that he had had an opportunity to be freed years earlier but had refused, a decision for which he had to endure additional periods of isolation and hardship. Nor did he ever speak of his captivity again during our near half-century of close friendship.

John's focus was on creating a better future. As a senator, he supported the restoration of relations with Vietnam, helped bring it about on a bipartisan basis in the Clinton administration, and became one of the advocates of reconciliation with his enemy. Honor is an intangible quality, not obligatory. It has no code. It reflects an inward compulsion, free of self-interest. It fulfills a cause, not a personal ambition. It represents what a society lives for beyond the necessities of the moment. Love makes life possible; honor and nobility. For John it was a way of life.

John returned to America divided over its presidency, divided over the war. Amidst all of the turmoil and civic unrest, divided over the best way to protect our country and over whether it should be respected for its power or its ideals. John came back from the war and declared this is a false choice. America owed it to itself to embrace both strengths and ideals in decades of congressional service, ultimately as chairman of the Senate Armed Services Committee, John was an exponent of an America strong enough to its purpose.

But John believed also in a compassionate America, guided by core principles for which American foreign policy must always stand. "With liberty and justice for all" is not an empty sentiment, he argued, it is the foundation of our national consciousness. To John, American advantages had universal applicability. I do not believe he said that there's an errant exception any more than there is a black exception or an Asian or Latin exception. He warned against temptation of withdrawal from the world. In this manner John McCain's name became synonymous with an America that reached out to oblige the powerful to be loyal and give hope to the oppressed.

John loved all these battles for decency and freedom. He was an engaged warrior fighting for his causes with a brilliance, with courage, and with humility. John was all about hope. In a commencement speech at Ohio Wesleyan University, John summed up the essence of his engagement of a lifetime. "No one of us, if they have character, leaves behind a wasted life." Like most people of my age, I feel a longing for what is lost and cannot be restored. If the happy and casual beauty of youth proves ephemeral, something better can endure and endure until our last moment on Earth, and that is the moment in our lives when we sacrifice for something greater than ourselves. Heroes inspire us by the matter-of-factness of their sacrifice and the elevation of the root vision.

The world will be lonelier without John McCain, his faith in America, and his instinctive sense of moral duty. None of us will ever forget how even in his parting John has bestowed on us a much-needed moment of unity and renewed faith in the possibilities of America. Henceforth, the country's honor is ours to sustain.

Philip Roth, Out and About of an Evening

William O'Shaughnessy's tribute, May 23, 2018.

Philip Roth has died. He was eighty-five, tall, trim, an attractive man who carried broad shoulders and a smoldering genius for the English language. And in his eighty-five years he wrote some thirty-two books that caused him to be accused by the *New York Times* of being "a giant of American letters" and "a pre-eminent figure in 20th century literature."

Dwight Garner, the *Times*'s graceful book critic, who can bang words around pretty well himself, called Roth "an archwizard whose best books eat into the mind like acid."

And Michael Chabon, the prolific American novelist and short story writer, said, "He was a giant, an artist as versatile and virtuoso as Sinatra and graceful and fireballing as Koufax." Philip Roth would have liked that.

I bought and collected a few of his books, but I never read one of them. I much prefer nonfiction and, as Roth himself once confessed, he did too.

I "knew" him mostly through our mutual patronage of and affection for the West Street Grill, the estimable country restaurant on the Village Green in tony Litchfield, which has been lovingly operated for almost thirty years by two marvelous and dear souls, Charlie Kafferman and James O'Shea. Philip Roth got there long before I darkened the door of the eatery. For years he was a member in good standing of "The Roundtable," a weekly private luncheon and lemon squeeze featuring the writers William Styron, John Updike, and Arthur Miller and the actor Richard Widmark.

In recent years Roth would dine at the Grill on Sunday nights with Mia Farrow, still a knockout at seventy-three. She would drive over from her Frog Hollow Farm in Bridgewater. And the great writer would journey down from his farmhouse in the woods of Warren, Connecticut.

And on one of these agreeable nights Charlie Kafferman steered me over to table 22 as I was about to sit at table 21, where my *compadre* Gregorio Alvarez and I were dining.

Here is a snippet of dialogue from that evening:

CHARLIE KAFFERMAN: Philip . . . Bill writes books too.

WILLIAM O'SHAUGHNESSY: Charlie, don't do this to me. I am not worthy to loose the strap of his sandal . . .

PHILP ROTH: I know him, Charlie . . . we talk baseball. You know Mia [Farrow]. We thought you were in radio. What kind of books do you write?

O'SHAUGHNESSY: Anthologies . . . but my new one is about Mario Cuomo and our friendship . . . I admired him.

ROTH: Well . . . so you do anthologies . . . about whom? Who do you write about?

O'SHAUGHNESSY: Oh, New York characters . . . Toots Shor . . . Nelson Rockefeller . . . Sirio Maccioni . . . John Lindsay . . . Cardinal O'Connor . . . characters . . .

ROTH: Oh, I see . . . you really write about all your friends! [laughter]

Here's another marvelous anecdote that comes out of our favorite restaurant in the Litchfield hills:

The great writer couldn't count the number or frequency of the literary awards bestowed on him or the encomiums showered on the canon of his prolific works. So one day Roth called his friend Charlie to beg a favor. "Charlie . . . I'm being given some big award up in Hartford by the governor and I just don't feel like schlepping up there. Could you 'represent' me and accept on my behalf . . . ?" So Kafferman and his West Street Grill partner James O'Shea journeyed to Hartford to accept the award, a two-foot-tall bronze with outstretched hands in a "winged victory" stance, from the governor's hands and lugged it back to the Grill where it sits to this day.

But the story doesn't end there. A few weeks later Roth was summoned to Washington to be honored as "America's Greatest Living Novelist" by President Barack Obama.

When Roth came in for dinner the next week, his friends at the restaurant inquired how the presidential award ceremony went, and he replied: "It went fine . . . but when I went up to receive the award . . . the president whispered, 'Where's Charlie?' He was really disappointed when he saw me!" (Roth swore it was a true story).

Someone once said he could have been a stand-up comic. When he wasn't out and about of an evening making people laugh, Philip Milton Roth published almost ninety books, including Hispanic and foreign editions of his American classics among which were *Goodbye Columbus . . . American Pastoral . . . Portnoy's Complaint . . . My Life as a Man.* And then in 2012 he closed down his computer and put a lid on his genius for all time to come.

"I was by this time no longer in possession of the mental vitality or the physical fitness needed to mount and sustain a large creative attack of any duration," he said. And he actually put a Post-it note on his computer: "The struggle with writing is done."

He also said, "Old age isn't a battle, old age is a massacre."

He inveighed against the "diminishments" which assault us as we confront old age. It's a marvelous word often used by Mario Cuomo and Father Pierre Teilhard de Chardin, the brilliant Jesuit philosopher-paleontologist.

And he said, "When I write, I'm alone. It's filled with fear and loneliness and anxiety and I never needed religion to save me."

He was a Jew, to be sure. But he hated to be called a "Jewish writer." "I am an American writer, if nothing else . . ." he once said. And like Mario Cuomo, he was denounced by his own. Cuomo was criticized and censured by auxiliary bishops. Roth was assailed by influential rabbis.

He was also a self-professed atheist who had a deep and abiding distrust of organized religion. But despite his strong feelings on the subject, he was a nice man in every season with an altogether attractive persona, who, in his eighty-five years, entertained millions and made them *think* . . . while causing some of us to laugh of an evening at his favorite watering hole.

He left us earlier this week with all those books I never read . . . his great good nature . . . and that marvelous sense of humor.

FOOTNOTE

Philip Roth was buried at Bard College in Annandale-on-the-Hudson on Memorial Day, May 28, 2018. Invitations to a reception at the residence of Leon Botstein, longtime president of Bard, went out a few days before the service on the college campus. Charles Kafferman and his West Street Grill partner James O'Shea were of course invited. But as their country restaurant was fully booked for the holiday weekend, they had to reluctantly decline. When a torn and conflicted Kafferman told Mia Farrow of his anguish about the decision to stay at their post, she texted: "Don't worry, Charlie. He won't be there either. And he'd much rather be at the Grill with you guys. Love, Mia."

I was not worthy to loose the strap of his sandal.

Governor Andrew Cuomo's Eulogy
for Jimmy Breslin

Church of the Blessed Sacrament, New York, N.Y., March 22, 2017.

———————

The Cuomo and the Breslin families grew up together in Queens. Mr. Breslin and my father had bonded over the Corona sixty-nine home-owners versus Mayor John Lindsay conflict. Obviously, they were with the homeowners. Together they were fighting City Hall—literally and metaphorically—and they would all their lives.

I was twelve at the time, and to me, Mr. Breslin was just plain scary. Mr. Breslin smoked a cigar, and he smelled like it. He had a gruff air and apparently had no time or love for little children.

With his broad chest, open collar, and full head of curly black hair, he looked like a lion with a flowing mane. Although I was frightened by Mr. Breslin, I couldn't help taunting him occasionally, the way a mouse would run through the paws of a lion.

I was too small to really engender his wrath. He would call the house multiple times a night, and I would imitate the way my father answered the phone with a simple, deep-throated "Yup."

That's all Mr. Breslin needed to start a diatribe. He would normally begin by cursing some politician and then continue for several min-utes, stringing together profanities and comments on parts of the human anatomy that I had never heard of before. He would pause for a breath, and I would say, "Oh, Mr. Breslin, you must want to talk to my father." This would incite the lion's rage, and he would say, "You little blank-blank" and just hang up.

He would come to the house and sit with my father at the kitchen table—a round, blue Formica table that was designed to look like mar-ble. They have only blue marble in Queens. I would sit down the hall

[333]

and listen. They would have a drink—and talk for hours, railing against the injustices in life and the failures of the system.

My father was a lion too—a different species without the mane or the colorful language, but a strong aggressive lion nonetheless, and together they would roar.

They were great crusaders for justice. Always on the side of the little guy. Dismissing the liberal elites and professional agitators, their true north was the common man. They were always looking to step into a fight against the bully. And they loved each other.

As they were two tough Queens guys, I'm sure they never actually said they loved each other. Queens men didn't say that to each other then, but they did, and they knew it.

There was a softer side to their relationship. Mr. Breslin in the quieter moments would talk about his family, and his face would change. His first wife, Rosemary, and how she was a saint; his daughters—Rosemary the superstar, the writer, my sister Maria's best friend; and Kelly, the enchantress. His boys, his sons—Kevin, James, Patrick, and Christopher. He talked with great pride and love in his voice, and listening to him speak, I hoped that my father had that same love for me.

My mother and Jimmy had a sweet, caring relationship. There was a vulnerability to Jimmy, and my mother, always the nurturer, was naturally drawn to him.

Jimmy met Ronnie Eldridge, a strong, brilliant woman and a political force in her own right, and the two married. I can only imagine being married to Mr. Breslin was more than a full-time job, and God bless Ronnie for all of the support and love. My mother believes Ronnie literally kept Jimmy alive for years, and with Ronnie came a bonus—Daniel, Emily, and Lucy. And they all brought him much joy.

If my father were here today, he would say Jimmy was an artist and his pen was to paper what Picasso's brush was to canvas. He would say Jimmy was never a *Newsday* reporter or *Daily News* employee—he was just Breslin, anywhere and everywhere. He would speak of his superb God-given gifts and selflessness in using them to do good. He would say Jimmy faced many hardships in life. That he came from a family of hardships and suffered much pain, early and later in life, losing both Rosemary and then Kelly.

But my father would say while a lesser man would have grown angry and bitter from the loss, Jimmy grew more empathetic and compassionate.

I hear Mr. Breslin's voice often. I hear his voice as governor. I recently commuted the sentence of a woman in Bedford Correctional after thirty-five years of imprisonment. It was clear she had committed a terrible crime. But after visiting her, it was also clear to me that she was a different person now. It was a hard political decision. I spoke to Ronnie, her fierce advocate, about it many times. I could hear Jimmy's voice saying, "She made a mistake—we all do. She learned, she paid the price, she spent her life in a cage, and she is now different. Jesus would pardon her. Who the hell made you better than Jesus?"

Mr. Breslin's life was a life well lived. We mourn today not for him but for ourselves—for his family's loss and our loss—because in truth in today's world we need his voice more than ever. A voice with power and credibility, who wrote stories from the street, not from a laptop. Who believed there was no truth worth telling that could be told in a tweet. Whose voice was authentic because he was authentic—he was New York—hardscrabble, brilliant, difficult, gifted, complicated, argumentative, accepting, and loving.

But as the spirit lives, his voice lives in all of us; and if we listen, we can hear him saying today, "What do they mean they are going to cut the taxes for the richest Americans and tell the poorest that we can't afford to give you health care? Who do they think they are—who made their lives more important than the rest of us?"

It's not over. Mr. Breslin's quest for social justice and integrity goes on. He is here today with his good friend Mario, and they are reading the papers—the hard copies—and railing at the outrage, disgusted by the political cowards, and ready to fight the good fight.

I say, "Roar, gentlemen, roar, let it echo down from the heavens, and we will hear you."

A Personal Tribute to Jimmy Breslin

March 20, 2017.

He was the DiMaggio of a profession that included Pete Hamill, Nat Hentoff, Gay Talese, Mike Barnicle, Wayne Barrett, Nancy Q. Keefe, Phil Reisman, Denis Hamill, Peter Maas, David Hinckley, Jack Newfield, McCandlish Phillips, Dennis Duggan, Richard Reeves, Sam Roberts, Terry Golway, Mike Lupica, Malachy McCourt, Michael Daly, Nick Pileggi, Meyer "Mike" Berger, and Jimmy Cannon of sainted memory who, as the Mother Lode, inspired damn near everyone here mentioned to write with passion, conviction, and honesty.

And, I'm sorry, but if we're talking here about those who can maneuver words like Nelson Riddle arranged notes and put them into actual graceful sentences and then insert them in elegant paragraphs that fill entire pages that move people, I suggest that one Mario M. Cuomo, although he went to work each day as a politician and possessed a business card that said, "Governor," has to be included in this fraternity too.

They were practitioners of a journalism that produced lean, strong, direct, muscular, unadorned, passionate, declarative, on-your-sleeve writing. *USA Today* called it "simple, but stirring prose." The *New York Times* referred to the product of Breslin's genius as "narrative nonfiction." By any name, it was *sui generis*: unique and able to be defined only in his own terms. So was he.

Breslin's *modus operandi*: After a sporting event or political race, don't go to the winner in the spotlight; find the loser. That's where the story is, at the locker room of the vanquished.

During my own fifty-eight years at the microphone of this community radio station, many friends have caused their sons and heirs and their daughters too to seek our advice and counsel, making them repair to a white-haired broadcaster completely lacking in wisdom or good judgment and possessed only of a good Rolodex.

So as I sat majestically and all-knowing in high council in my office: If a youngster wanted to spend his or her life in law enforcement, I would send them to Joseph Anthony Spinelli, who once headed an FBI SWAT team and participated in seven shootouts as a federal lawman. "Go see Spinelli." And if the kid was any good, Spinelli would ring up the director of the Federal Bureau of Investigation with instructions to "hire this guy."

If a youngster liked show biz or the theater, I would send them forthwith to Ossie Davis and Ruby Dee. And if government or public service was mentioned, I would ring up a failed baseball player with too many vowels in his name. And Mario Cuomo, of sainted memory, would get the kid's head filled with all sorts of crazy notions like "God didn't finish creating the universe; that's *your* job."

If, on occasion, a young man or woman mentioned newspapers, journalism, or broadcasting and seemed destined for the Columbia School of Journalism or the Newhouse School at Syracuse, I would reach over to my library and pull out a book, one of sixteen written by Jimmy Breslin. "Go home and read *this*; it's all I know. It's all *you* need to know. It's *everything* you need to know." Sometimes I would also thrust a Jimmy Cannon book across the desk.

Many years ago, before two busted marriages, I sat with the great Breslin at Costello's bar, which was near Grand Central and Saint Agnes Church, where suburban Catholics go with their sins if they are too lazy to take a subway ride to the Garden and walk to 31st Street where the generous and forgiving Franciscans assess only three Hail Marys for anything up to a homicide.

Anyway, Breslin and I sat on this one long-ago afternoon in the smoky now-gone Costello's midtown bar. Reaching way above my pay grade and for another Canadian Club, I told the greatest American journalist during our time that I loved his columns on Jack Kennedy and his brother Bobby, and certainly the magnificent one he dispatched from London, in England, which was my favorite: "The pigeons were on the statue of Lord Nelson in Trafalgar Square while a few blocks away, at Number 10 Downing Street, Sir Winston Spencer

Churchill lay dying. He was a man of beef and brandy and cigars and the last great statue of the English language."

I told the great Breslin that although I most certainly loved all the iconic columns describing the Kennedys and Mr. Churchill, he had recently taken to writing about guys named Ramon and José and Pedro, and I gently suggested he might return to the "mythic" figures abroad in the land. "Who's to write about?" said Breslin. And then he went out into the night to write of a Queens neighbor named Mario M. Cuomo.

They teach Breslin in "J" school at Columbia, NYU, Hofstra, and Ithaca. Professors often cite Breslin's legendary piece about the grave-digger who made $3.01 to dig a grave for John Fitzgerald Kennedy who, in an earlier sad November day some fifty-five years ago, had his brains blown out in Dallas, Texas.

It was a great piece of writing. But the Churchill piece stays with me because I am well aware that, with the encouragement or forbearance of the Jesuits, I have written some six books, anthologies that contain pages of sentences containing many words, not any of which would permit me to loose the strap on Jimmy Breslin's sandal.

He did to a typewriter and yellow legal pads, and later to a computer, what Michael Jordan did to a basketball and Sinatra did in a recording studio to Cole Porter lyrics.

He would take words and put them in strong, passionate, muscular sentences that caused Mario Cuomo to tell people, "Nobody can describe a scene like Breslin."

Jimmy Breslin's final, personal "30" comes at a most inopportune time. For it is 2017, and there is, abroad in the land, no Mario Cuomo to do Jimmy's eulogy. So I guess the graceful lines Dan Barry wrote in Monday's *New York Times* will have to do. These words leap out from among all the many written every day in our beloved *Times*, which exhausts itself trying to find ways to tell just how awful President Donald John Trump is. Here are those beautiful words said of Breslin in our most important newspaper, which survives him and will survive Trump.

Jimmy Breslin, the New York City newspaper columnist and best-selling author who levelled the powerful and elevated the powerless for more than 50 years with brick-hard words and a jagged-glass wit, died on Sunday in his home in Manhattan. He was 88, and until very recently was still pushing somebody's buttons with two-finger jabs at his keyboard. Love him or loathe him, none could deny Mr. Breslin's enduring impact on the craft of narrative nonfiction. At the same time, Mr. Breslin was unmatched in his attention to the poor and disenfranchised. If there is one hero in the Breslin canon, it is the single black mother, far removed from power, trying to make it through the week.

I can't do better this sad morning than Dan Barry, who had some help from Jim Dwyer and Richard Goldstein at the *Times.*

In the hours since James Earle Breslin left us, many other lovely, admiring pieces have been written in all the journals of the land about just how special Jimmy Breslin really was.

There were quite wonderful and graceful tributes from Jim Rutenberg, Jim Dwyer, Dan Barry, Sean Patrick Farrell, and Richard Goldstein of the *New York Times*; Kevin McCoy, John Bacon, and Adam Shell of *USA Today*; Jason Silverstein, Arthur Browne, and Josh Greenman of the *Daily News*; Christopher Bonanos of *New York* magazine; Verna Dobnik and David Bauder of AP; Joe Mahoney in upstate papers; Tom Allon of *City & State*; Michael "Lionel" Lebron, Phil Reisman, and Sarah Fagan Greenberg on Facebook; Paul Duggan of the *Washington Post*; Mark Moore and Joe Marino of the *New York Post*; and Debby Krenek and Michael O'Keeffe of *Newsday.*

But who, I wonder, will come into a funeral home or stand up in a Roman Catholic church this week to speak a eulogy of Jimmy Breslin? There really was only *one* equal to the sad task: Jimmy's old sparring partner and dear friend Mr. Cuomo, who himself departed on January 1, 2015.

So now, lacking the eloquence and presence of his friend, the "Gov," to define and celebrate Breslin, we are left with just these gracious remarks Mario put together for the sixtieth anniversary of Jimmy's career in journalism, organized by Pete Hamill.

I'm not eager to go out to events at night. Like a lot of other people, my day's work is sufficiently challenging to make me look forward to quiet evenings at home. It takes a really good reason to get me out, so when Pete Hamill called and told me that on December 7th there would be an event at night to honor Jimmy for his sixty years as a writer, I wanted to be sure it was real.

I asked Pete, "Does Jimmy know?" And he said, "Yeah, he's all for it."

At first it didn't sound right to me. Jimmy didn't even celebrate sixty years of *being alive*, so why would he be eager to celebrate sixty years as a writer?

Logic gave me a quick answer. Just being alive meant a lot less to Jimmy than being alive and *writing*.

That's the way it is with truly gifted people like him. Writers will remind you this evening of his Pulitzer and of a wall full of other significant honors over the years acknowledging his unique and vibrant writing skills. As a reporter he became the uncommon voice of the common man with his uncanny ability to find in newsworthy events details that made the events more meaningful to the people of New York's boroughs and millions of other people like them. Interviewing the gravedigger at John F. Kennedy's burial is a good example. The writers will remind you how he could make people smile, or laugh out loud when they bring back some of Jimmy's inimitable descriptions of hapless ballplayers, second-rate mobsters, and third-rate politicians, or reintroduce you to "Fat Thomas" and "Robert J. Allen."

There may even be a tear or two if someone chooses to read from "Short, Sweet Life of Edward Gutierrez," or parts of "World Without End, Amen."

But no matter how many bits of Breslin inspiration are shared this evening, they will amount to only light hints of the immense amount of great writing he has done in his uniquely long, productive, and heralded career. Think of it: He still works every day, writing or thinking about writing, and he has done it for sixty years—nearly 22,000 days and nights—except for the short hiatus when doctors were forced to drill a hole in his head to let out of his congested brain some of his unused lines. Then he wrote a book about it!

That's a lot of "Jim Breslin Writing" to cover in a single night of celebration. And the challenge is even greater because, as Pete has pointed out, there are really at "least two Jim Breslins." One "Breslin" is the public person: Writer, Raconteur, and Celebrity.

The other is the private guy from Queens when he's not on the stage or on the screen but is himself, on the phone or having an otherwise quiet dinner, explaining to you the world and it's various dysfunctionalities. And excoriating those who are responsible for the disorder, by creating it or by not doing enough to fix it . . . that often includes the people he's talking to at the moment.

That's when he's just "Jimmy," and that's the way I know him best and have for more than forty years.

I met him when I was a youngish lawyer trying to help sixty-nine barely middle-class homeowners in Corona, Queens, save their homes from a mayor who was about to condemn them to accommodate the builder of a huge housing complex.

They couldn't afford a big law firm, and I was neither prestigious nor politically influential, so the sixty-nine would probably have lost their homes if Jimmy hadn't gotten involved. He came to a meeting of the group, did some research, then wrote a long story and some short ones, and talked to some influential people at City Hall. He convinced them the mayor was wrong, and the sixty-nine stayed in their homes. That was Jimmy at his best, and it led to a friendship that has survived all the years since then. Good days and hard days. Days when we enjoyed some lucky breaks, and other days when we got hit by tragedies.

And most of the real tragedies were on Jimmy's side of the relationship. Heavy, heavy blows that would have left me and most people crippled and helpless.

But not Jimmy.

It had to be hard for him for sure, but Jimmy just kept writing. He had to! His world was too big, too complex, too filled with great characters. There were too many great stories that needed telling and retelling. And there were too many big problems that needed solving!

[341]

There still are! As there have been for sixty years: nearly 22,000 nights and days!

Almost every morning before he goes to his typewriter, he'll call one of his many friends to describe some of the problems: a war we should be ending, a healthcare bill we need to pass. I can hear him now, "Did you see the first page of the *Times*? Food stamps are back! Food stamps. And they say the recession is over! What are you doing about it? Write a damn letter! Call somebody—some big shot. You must know someone! Tell them about the abused immigrants and the abusive landlords, the crooked politicians and the bad priests."

Every morning, Jimmy has a bowl of oatmeal *and* his outrage.

And I suspect that's the way it will always be. He won't ever stop thinking about the world he lives in and writing about it.

Why?

Because way down deep, "Jimmy" is a believer.

He will argue with the priests of his Church, but he knows the God they are supposed to be working for has given him a personal gift. A gift that is given to only a few.

And he will not offend his God by not using that gift. And he *will* use it until there are no more stories to tell or problems to solve.

Thank you, Jimmy. Keep going!

He leaves a profession that is fast becoming a "Between you and I" industry, as he once called it, even before the bimbos—male *and* female—attempted to speak the English language from teleprompters in every television studio in the land.

One more memory of Breslin stays. It came out of an afternoon on the West Side when John Hay Whitney and Walter Nelson Thayer came to shut down for all time to come a magnificent newspaper called the *Herald Tribune*, which had been founded by Horace Greeley. As many at the "wake" for the paper crowded around Walter "Red" Smith, the *Trib*'s iconic sportswriter who sat on the edge of a desk with a shaky hand trying to light a cigarette, there was Breslin over in a corner with the cleaning women, trying to put together a story that survives in one of his books.

Breslin wrote sixteen, including:

Can't Anybody Here Play This Game?
World of Jimmy Breslin
World without End. Amen
Forsaking All Others
I Want to Thank My Brain for Remembering Me
Damon Runyon: A Life
The Short Sweet Dream of Eduardo Gutierrez
The Church That Forgot Christ
Branch Rickey
The Good Rat
The Gang That Couldn't Shoot Straight

But he once told me that *Christ in Concrete*, a long-out-of-print book by an obscure Long Island writer named Pietro DiDonato, was "the greatest novel ever written." Breslin would know.

Dying is something you have to do all by yourself.

It's a solo act. There are no accomplices, *compadres*, colleagues, or cohorts to accompany you. But James Earle Breslin *was* attended by several marvelous and unforgettable characters (some real, some imagined, all magnificent): Marvin the Torch, the loveable arsonist; Fat Thomas, the bumbling bookie; Klein, the love-struck lawyer; Un Occhio, the scary mob boss who ran a candy store and kept a wolf behind the counter; Jerry the Booster, the beloved shoplifter who could clean out a department store in fifteen minutes; Shelly, the bail bondsman who was a sucker for a sentimental song; and Pep Maguire, saloonkeeper in Queens.

So I idolized the guy. I'm not sure he returned the favor. At a dinner one night he announced, "Forget the swell way he dresses. You have to *like* O'Shaughnessy; he does so much for the poor of Mamaroneck!"

That's not so bad, I guess.

Our Neighbor Ruby Dee

June 12, 2014.

With the passing of Ruby Dee, the American theater has lost one of its most gifted and talented actors. And WVOX has lost a neighbor.

Ossie Davis and Ruby Dee—you have to take them together—were a beloved presence in our home heath.

When people think of New Rochelle, they think of Dick Van Dyke. But that was make-believe. Ossie and Ruby were for real. They were very real.

Over the years, she would walk Pinebrook Boulevard, taking her daily constitutional in every season, and she would cause "whiplash" for many a passing motorist: "Isn't that Ruby Dee?" And for many of her ninety-one years, it was.

Ossie and Ruby. As the African American Alfred Lunt and Lynne Fontanne of the modern American theater, they were royalty in that profession. But to all of us privileged to know and love them, they were "of the 'hood." Neighbors.

They performed in theaters, in television and radio studios, and on movie lots. But they did some of their best work out on the streets as citizen-activists.

A young Malcolm X used to sit in the living room of their big, sprawling house on Cortland Avenue and rage into the night about injustice and inequality. And a former police commissioner of this very city actually kept quite an active "subversive" file dedicated entirely to the most suspicious left-leaning "activist exploits" of the former Ruby Wallace and her equally dangerous husband, Ossie Davis.

They could have lived in any upscale, tony venue: Greenwich, Waccabuc, Manhasset, Bronxville, Scarsdale, Bedford, or Rye. But they lived all their days in New Rochelle, just a few blocks from our local community broadcasting station, which they supported all their days in every season.

When once I thanked Ossie for being so nice and so supportive of our local station, he said, "Ruby and I travel all over the world, making movies, and we go where there is an audience. When we're on the road, you watch our home. We have to be nice to you."

My mind drifts back many years to a political fundraiser we had at Le Cirque for Governor Mario Cuomo. A thousand dollars a ticket. When it was winding down and almost over, a car pulled up and delivered an exhausted-looking Ruby Dee and Ossie Davis. They had just come from Kennedy Airport after a long, bumpy transcontinental flight from Europe.

Ruby reached into her pocketbook and presented two checks for the Cuomo campaign. When I suggested they could just as easily have *mailed* them in, she said, "Not for him. Not for you. We wanted to deliver them in person."

There was another night at Le Cirque for dinner. When the main course arrived, I had my fork poised in hand, ready to dig in. Ruby said, "Not yet; a prayer first," and she had us clasp hands all round while she whispered a prayer for world peace. You do that at home, one would imagine. But she did it anywhere she damn well pleased.

Mario Cuomo used to say he prays for "sureness." I'm not sure about a lot of things. But of this I'm sure: Ossie Davis was a *saint*.

And now she's gone to meet him on a bigger, better, sweeter stage with no final curtain.

You have to give them equal billing.

Tribute to Ruby Dee by Harry Belafonte

The Riverside Church, New York City, September 20, 2014.

———————

How happy I am to spend today with you . . . to listen to and relish the wonderful things said about Ruby.

I've thought long and hard about what to say about Ruby for this sad moment. It was easy for me when I delivered the eulogy at the service for our beloved Ossie. I was able to stand here in this magnificent church and words easily came to me. But I had to sit quite alone on several occasions thinking and deliberating on what to say about our Ruby. She played such an important role in all of our lives.

When I first met her after coming out of my service for the United States Navy at the end of the Second World War . . . I was given two free tickets to see a play at the American Negro Theatre, an organization I had never heard of. Here I was almost twenty years old and looking for what to do with my life and wound up with a freebee to the A.N.T. to see what others were doing. So on that occasion I met Ruby and fell madly in love with her. And I was instantly aware of the fact that I was not the only one who had such an experience. A young man I met at the time became one of my closest friends in life, and Sidney Poitier also shared the same experience. He too had come to the A.N. T. for the first time and met Ruby, fell in love with her and he too discovered what I discovered . . . we had to stand in line with all the young men who were caught up with the beauty and charm and genius of Ruby Dee.

Not only was she exquisitely beautiful, but her intelligence, her gift, her art was really quite astounding and rewarding. But perhaps more than all of that was her *humanity*. Her deep commitment to fair play . . . to justice . . . to honor . . . to goodness. Wherever there was someone in need, especially if you were a person of color and especially if you were under the severest of experiences during the great "oppression" that represented life for many people of color . . . Ruby was always there to speak to justice . . . to speak to fair play . . . to speak to the needs of the endless number of people she met who needed to hear a voice of reason, a voice of caring. These qualities of Ruby led us all to be forever committed to who she was and what she did in life.

I think she was wise in not accepting that young fellow whose name was Sidney . . . and therefore she was also wise in not accepting me . . . or indeed in accepting a whole bunch of young dudes bouncing around the room trying to attract her attention and her affection. And you were struck with great wisdom by waiting for her, Ossie. *He* was the man! And we all had to, in the final analysis, attest to the fact that picking Ossie was an act of genius. And quite correct. They made an exemplary couple. Together they were the voices of our humanity. They were the paternal, maternal, fraternal . . . they were the family. They were the ones we could turn to for counsel, for wisdom.

And when it came to great art, watching them perform in any number of plays . . . any number of readings they would give . . . any number of hours they would spend at the Schomburg in Harlem where we all met and watched that institution grow into one of the great centers of study for black life.

Important for that process was the constant presence of Ossie and Ruby to give young people instruction and a sense of what the future held for them and what they could do. That's the kind of space in our lives that has been left because of their absence.

Yes . . . we're all sorry Ruby is gone. But I was glad I was able to see her just a few days before she passed away, still filled with spirit. A little bit more tame, a little bit more reflective. A little older.

But I saw in her the Way—when it becomes my turn—that I would like to go out. Peaceful . . . at ease with the world. Fulfilled with the idea I did the best I could while I was here . . . and to realize that the best I did wasn't too bad. That's how Ruby impacted us.

That's how we will all think of her. And I must say if there's a hereafter and if we are to be blessed for the things we did on Earth or that were somehow thought worthy of reward—I hope my hereafter is spent, once again, in the presence of Ruby and Ossie.

And if you go before me, Sidney . . . save a space. And if I go before you . . . I'll save one for you. But it will be good to know that all us old A.N.T.ers: alumni from the American Negro Theatre—which was the beginning of our renaissance on life—was spent in each other's company.

Ruby was no small part of that. And to you, Sidney . . . I'd like to say thank you for giving us a very rare opportunity to perform with the genius of Ruby Dee.

We love you Ruby . . . very much!

"A Death in the Family": Tim Russert

Commentary broadcast on WVOX and WVIP, June 16, 2008.

His father, Big Russ, immortalized in an endearing and bestselling book, collected garbage and trash from the hard, bleak streets of south Buffalo. And if you came out of that dwindling city in western New York as I did, you will recognize Tim Russert as a child of the neighborhood.

If you're listening to this in Yonkers (where true love conquers), the Bronx, or even in Peekskill or Mamaroneck, you will also feel a kinship with the television journalist who collapsed and died in a studio in Washington Friday afternoon. Timothy John Russert Jr. was the best of what we are as broadcasters. But he did not resemble anyone who ever lived in Scarsdale, Bronxville, Rye, Bedford, or Litchfield.

He was a reassuring, comforting presence you thought would always be there in our lives. And my own tribe, our entire profession, took this hard. Anyone who ever sat in front of a microphone or peered into a television camera feels an awful sadness that is deep and personal. Russert's passing, so unexpected and so sudden, was like a death in the family.

I knew him when he worked for Mario Cuomo. But I am entitled, if not entirely qualified, to get on the radio to tell you about Tim Russert because we also went to the same Canisius High School on Delaware Avenue, the big, broad boulevard that runs through one of the remaining nice sections of Buffalo even to this day.

And although we were in the care and keeping of the German Jesuits some ten years apart, Russert and I both got whacked upside the head by the same worn old leather prayer book belonging to the Reverend John Sturm, S.J., who took most seriously his title and high estate: Prefect of Discipline.

[349]

Father John was built like a fireplug. And although an equal opportunity disciplinarian, he made Timmy Russert his favorite charge almost from the minute he first encountered the personable Irish youngster from south Buffalo with the bright eyes and easy smile. That was back in the '60s and they have been friends ever since. Canisius has turned out federal judges named Crotty and Arcara, political power brokers like Joe Crangle, big car dealers, stellar athletes including a few Holy Cross and Notre Dame quarterbacks, and doctors and lawyers of great renown. The Jesuits spotted Russert's beguiling potential early on. Even then they knew.

He would go back to Buffalo over the years to see his father, and during summers better than this one Tim Russert would sit at Cole's bar in the Elmwood section to talk sports over a beer and a "beef on weck," Buffalo's legendary version of roast beef, a steamship round of which was personally carved by the bartender and then piled on a Kimmelweck roll covered with salt to be dipped in Heinz ketchup. The music in the air on those nights was provided by ancient tapes of Fred Klestine's old radio programs from the 1950s and '60s that survive to this day at Cole's.

They would order another Simon Pure beer or a Carling's ale and talk about the rich girls who went to "The Mount," a boarding school, and about Johnny Barnes, the old Canisius High football coach, and sometimes about Cornelius MacGillicudy, a favorite teacher who owned a bar in the Parkside section over near Delaware Park.

He never lost touch with the Jesuits. And just a few weeks ago, Father Sturm, now in his nineties, sent out invitations to a scholarship luncheon in his own honor with the obligatory picture of his protégé Tim Russert on the cover.

Before his dazzling work on television that made him famous, Tim labored in the service of the two brightest minds in public life during our time: those of Daniel Patrick Moynihan and the estimable Mario M. Cuomo.

Someone said yesterday on television: "He wasn't exactly a pretty boy." With his cheeks and jowls, Russert was the complete antithesis of all the hyper, vacuous "talking heads" and all the bimbos—male as well as female—who sit each day in those anchor chairs praying the teleprompter doesn't fail lest they be forced to utter something more profound than "absolutely!"

Only Chris Matthews was his equal in terms of depth and intelligence. And maybe Jon Meacham or Lawrence O'Donnell or Peggy Noonan. George Stephanopoulos can also hold his own in front of a camera (and in front of George Will). And classy Deborah Norville has a brain. While among the youngsters coming up, William "Billy" Bush and Chris Cuomo are bursting with intelligence and promise. Ditto Bill Geist's kid Willie. And David Gregory and Tucker Carlson are easy to take. Barbara Walters and Diane Sawyer are class acts in any season.

We've always liked Bob Scheiffer and Judy Woodruff. And how can you not like Mike Barnicle and Joe Scarborough (but not the girl with him, the one with the famous father, who talks over everybody). And I hope Larry King, like Paul Harvey on the radio, goes on forever. Plus I still take pleasure in our infrequent sightings of Rather and Brokaw.

Russert, however, operated on a level far beyond most of them. And he didn't need high-tech production values or fancy overhead lighting in an ultra-modern studio to enhance and amplify his unique genius. He was to network news what Mario Cuomo is to public discourse. And as the great Cuomo himself reminded us, "Tim never forgot where he came from and he never let us forget it either . . . and we loved him for it!"

He would summer on Nantucket and go to parties at Sally Quinn's in Washington. But Russert never denied his roots in Buffalo. There was a realness about him, a genuineness, on and off the air.

A few summers ago, Russert was the main speaker at an important conference of the New York State Broadcasters Association up at Bolton Landing on Lake George. After his talk he was persuaded by our mutual friend Joe Reilly, the head of the broadcasters in the Empire State, to linger and give out the Association's Awards for Excellence . . . even as an NBC plane waited on the tarmac at the nearby Glens Falls airport to rush him back to Washington.

There were many awards and citations in every category. But Russert was his usual generous self and so he stayed late into the night as the awards presentations wore on. And when it was announced that your own WVOX had won the designation for "Best Editorials in New

York State" (which we clearly did not deserve), Russert arched his eyebrows and the Irish eyes twinkled as my son David and I advanced to the front of the ballroom to receive our award.

As we posed for the cameras and the flashbulbs popped, Tim asked, *sotto voce*, "How's Mario? . . . how's Nancy? . . . how are the kids? . . . how's the station?" And now as my mind drifts back on this weekend after he died, I wonder if I remembered to inquire about his own welfare.

James O'Shea, who owns the West Street Grill, a high-class saloon in Litchfield, Connecticut (he much prefers the designation "fine dining establishment"), called while I was thinking about all this. According to O'Shea, "Russert possessed the genius of the Irish. Just say he was Irish. People will know what that means. He was Irish!" As O'Shea provides libation and sustenance for the likes of Philip Roth, Rex Reed, Jim Hoge, Bill vanden Heuvel, Rose Styron, George Clooney, Peter Duchin, and Brooke Hayward . . . I will bow to his wisdom. Russert did indeed have the genius of the Irish.

Nancy and I would see him around town of an evening, when he would come up from Washington to do some business at the NBC Universal mother ship at Rockefeller Center or if one of us had to emcee a dinner. And no matter how late the hour or how tired and rumpled he appeared, it was always the same: "How are the kids? . . . how are the stations doing? . . . how's the gov?"

NBC delayed the news of his passing and actually got scooped by the *New York Post* and the *Times* until someone from their shop was retrieved to go and inform his wife, Maureen Orth; their son, Luke; and his beloved father, Big Russ. But who, I wonder, had to knock on the door of the old priest in the Jesuit retirement house on Washington Street up in Buffalo to tell Father John Sturm, S.J., that Timmy Russert was gone?

I always thought Russert would have made a wonderful politician himself or a great teacher. Or even a priest. And with his sudden, untimely departure at fifty-eight, he probably taught us one more lesson learned from the old Jesuits: "You know not the hour . . . or the moment."

The newsman-journalist known as Tim Russert has been mourned by millions and eulogized in all the journals and periodicals in the land. But the most exquisite tribute, and probably the one he would have liked the most, came from Michelle Spuck, a waitress at Bantam Pizza in the Litchfield hills, who told a customer over the weekend, "I'm so sad about this . . . I never met him . . . but I knew him."

He died in front of a microphone.

—W.O.

Don Rickles and the Focaccia Kid at Le Cirque!

When Don Rickles departed for what former New York Governor Malcolm Wilson always referred to as "another, and we are sure, a *better* world," many hilarious moments from his razor-sharp repertoire flooded the airwaves.

Here's another from a long-ago evening at Le Cirque.

I was sitting with a pretty girl on a banquette when Maestro Sirio Maccioni moved the great Rickles and his wife right in next to us. And as we sat cheek-by-jowl, Rickles was trying hard to engage with just about anyone who would pay him a little attention in the swell, upscale New York eatery.

Enter the Focaccia Kid. It was a tradition at Le Cirque in those days to first offer a selection from the bread basket, and then, a while later, a young man bearing warm focaccia just out of the oven would appear at table, bowing slightly and saying only one word: "Focaccia?" The job was usually entrusted to an attractive young Chinese fellow. And this one night when the young man approached Rickles's table right next to us, the great comedian whispered, "Where are you from, my boy?"

The Focaccia Kid froze. Nobody had *ever*, in the long history of Le Cirque, asked him a question! Or was it even required that he speak to the patrons?

After surreptitiously checking to see that Sirio was not looking, the young Chinese fellow whispered back, "Beijing."

With that Rickles shouted for all the world to hear, "So am *I*! Do you want to buy a *bicycle*?"

The room exploded. And Rickles now owned the evening. And my date.

—W. O.

Frances W. Preston, "The Lady from Nashville"

W.O.'s Statesman Column for On the Air *magazine, Broadcasters Foundation of America.*

Frances Preston, the winsome southern girl who came up from Nashville to dazzle us all with her style and grace, passed away in June. In every season of her eighty-three years, her beguiling gap-tooth smile was accompanied always by a bright, fine mind, packed with exquisitely tuned executive smarts, all of which served her well as president and CEO of BMI for eighteen years.

"My hand used to shake at the end of the month when I had to make out the ASCAP and BMI checks for music licensing," said a fellow broadcaster when he heard the sad news. "But there were a lot fewer tremors when I had to cut that check for BMI."

Part of the reason was Frances Preston, the comely woman who glided easily between the two complementary and connected, but ultimately separate, worlds of music publishing and broadcasting. She fought like hell to protect the product of the genius and creativity of her composers, lyricists, and performers. And her influence was considerable in Nashville, New York, and Washington. Also in the lives and careers of Willie Nelson, Dolly Parton, Johnny Cash, Barry Manilow, Isaac Hayes, and hundreds of others. Kris Kristofferson called her the "songwriter's guardian angel."

Frances was the first nonperforming woman member in the fabled Friars Club in New York and its first female director. In that jocular, irreverent atmosphere, nobody made any jokes about this lady.

The BMI Building in Nashville and an entire wing at Vanderbilt Hospital in the South bear her name. And over the years, Frances raised millions for the T. J. Martell Foundation, one of the music industry's largest. Among her enthusiasms was our Broadcasters Foundation of America. And for years she fed and provided shelter and an agreeable venue for our board meetings and high councils at the old BMI head-quarters on 57th Street in Manhattan. She served us for many years as a director, and her gentle, yet firm, diplomacy helped us navigate some rough shoals and growing pains.

There have been many stellar and luminous women executives in broadcasting and the performing arts: Ellen Sulzberger Straus, Bernice Judis, Lady Bird Johnson, Oveta Culp Hobby, Kay Koplowitz, Dorothy Stimson Bullitt, Reggie Schuebel, Lucie Salhany, Irna Phillips, Agnes Nixon, Jane Cahill Pfeiffer, Carol Reilly, Frieda Hannock, Lucille Ball, Margita White, Katharine Graham, Cathy Hughes, Marian Stephenson, Ginny Hubbard Morris, our own Erica Farber, and, of course, Oprah. Frances Williams Preston, whom the *Times* called "the highest ranking woman in the music industry," was among them. She was a woman of music and song. But, in a very real sense, she was ours. And we broad-casters owned a piece of her too.

Del Bryant, Frances's polished, cerebral successor at BMI, he of great lineage himself in the music world, called her "a force of nature who put BMI on the culture map." And thus into our lives as well as our profession.

We last saw her in New York at the annual luncheon for Don West's Library of American Broadcasting as she was appropriately inducted into the company of the "Giants of Broadcasting." Slower of step and speech after a debilitating stroke, Frances, still a handsome woman with a commanding presence, spoke movingly, but briefly.

After the nostalgic luncheon, she departed the Grand Hyatt ball-room ever so slowly and haltingly on the arm of her son. But that great carriage and her trademark megawatt smile were still intact as the luncheon ended and the glare of the lights receded.

She went out like a lady. As always.

Kate O'Shaughnessy Nulty's Tribute to Mary Jane Wharton, Her Grandmother

I'm very proud of my daughter Kate O'Shaughnessy Nulty, who gave a wonderful eulogy at St. Thomas Church on Fifth Avenue for her legendary grandfather Walter Nelson Thayer, president of the dearly departed New York Herald Tribune, *and president of the Whitcom Investment Company. Her Grandpa was a pillar of the Republican Party and the eastern establishment.*

She also did this wonderful tribute to her grandmother Mary Jane Wharton for National Women's Day, March 8, 2017.

———————

Today I honor my maternal grandmother, Dr. Mary Jane Wharton.

She was a southern belle who went to Yale University in the 1930s and earned a Ph.D. in Zoology. She met and married a Yankee law student named Walter N. Thayer and moved to New York City to teach at the Brearley School for girls. When my mother was two, Walter asked for a divorce, which in the 1940s meant Janie had to relocate to Las Vegas for six weeks to establish residency to grant a divorce. My mother and Janie moved back to her home in Greensboro, North Carolina, and she devoted herself to raising my mother, another brilliant southern belle who is a beauty queen with an M.B.A.

I would spend the summers with Janie and her second husband, Pop, tending to her garden, learning to bake caramel cake and fry chicken, knitting, sewing, canning peaches from her six trees, eating tomato sandwiches, and feeling the deepest, most profound love I have ever known. When my own parents divorced, Janie moved back up north to care for me and my brother while my mother went back to graduate school. This was 1980, and my mom went to work on the train, wearing these silly silk-tie things. Janie spent those two years sewing doll clothes for my Barbies, singing to me, rubbing my back at night when I cried, and feeding us the most delicious southern food.

Grandma Jane, I am so grateful for all that you taught me, especially how to nurture, love, and serve others, and that it's OK to be a girl and to be smart. You lived well into your nineties (swearing at crossword puzzles, eating half a grapefruit a day, and a jigger of bourbon every night that kept you going), but not long enough to meet your great-granddaughter, Amelia Jane Wharton Nulty, who shares your love for all things domestic and is smart as a whip. I feel you with me, guiding me, every day; and when I miss you, I get out your KitchenAid book and whip up a caramel cake in your honor.

Nelson: A Child of the Neighborhood

January 27, 1979.

The phone rang after midnight. Joseph Wood Canzeri, president of the Greenrock Company, which runs the Rockefeller estates, was calling from Pocantico, in the hills above Tarrytown. "Billy, Nelson died last night."

It is bad timing. Saturday is a day for jeans, chores around the house, errands, trips to the dry cleaner and the greengrocer, and shopping at the A&P. It is not the sort of day I feel like getting on the radio to announce that Nelson Aldrich Rockefeller had died. He deserves better than our Saturday edition.

But last night Nelson Rockefeller collapsed at his office in New York. He was one of the neighbors' children. All night long, and into these early morning hours, the newspapers and the radio prepared bulletins and obituaries to tell you that this fabulous and zestful man's heart had stopped on him. In cold, clinical, medical language, he had a massive heart attack. It would have to be a slammer to take out this particular seventy-year-old man.

This weekend, there will be a great deal written and broadcast in the national media about Nelson Rockefeller. But if you want an objective, arm's-length report, you'd better tune elsewhere, for you'll not get an unbiased version here at his hometown radio station—or from me. We were with him at countless political dinners, dedications, functions—"events," as they called them. Over the years, we rode with him in airplanes, helicopters, and golf carts.

It started with Louis Lefkowitz and Jack Gilhooley, down at Ratner's on Delancey Street in New York City. It was outside the famous old Jewish delicatessen in a Puerto Rican neighborhood where I first discovered the great squire of Pocantico Hills. As the men from the

neighborhood looked on, this patrician—an aristocrat from Westchester—plowed into the crowd of Hispanic faces that were yelling,
"Senōr Rocky!"

For more than ten years, we followed Nelson as he dominated New
York state politics—settling garbage strikes, battling with John Lindsay,
building colleges and a great state university, pushing bond issues, and
building roads and expressways. He was always the best story of the
day—even just sitting up there on the dais at the Westchester Republican dinners at the old Commodore Hotel with the late Fred Powers and
telling his neighbors, "Good to see *you*! . . . Nice to see *you*! . . . Wow . . .
you look *faaabulous*!"

He loved to tell about the time old Boss Ward, the legendary Republican leader, put him on the Westchester Board of Health. And just last
Thursday, as Henry Kissinger spoke at this year's county dinner, I was
reminded of the time Fred Powers gave him a huge replica of the great
sword of Excalibur, which the Wilkinson Sword people had made up.
Nelson Rockefeller, like a kid, just loved it! "Are you suggesting I'm a
great *swordsman*?" he responded.

There were so many nights and speeches and trips, so many arrivals
at the county airport. The governor would come down out of his Gulfstream in the middle of the night—exhausted. He might finesse an
interview with the networks, but he never waved off a WVOX microphone. And when he left Albany, he gave us the last question at his final
press conference as governor. We used the occasion to inquire which of
his predecessors, of all those staring down at us in the Red Room, had
inspired him. Nelson said a lot of great men had been governor of New
York, but Teddy Roosevelt had really made an impact on him "as a
young boy."

And there was the time *Air Force Two* brought a tired vice president
home from a long trip around the world. As the national press and television camera crews clamored for interviews, the "governor," as we still
called him, made straight for the news crew from our local station.

On this terrible, sad morning, my mind also drifts back to the time
we accompanied him on a swing through the Deep South. David
Broder and I were finishing a drink with Nelson as *Air Force Two*, a

DC-9, hit the runway with a hell of an abrupt jolt—landing "hot," as the pilots call it—at Columbia, South Carolina. For a brief, nervous, fleeting moment, Broder and I were reminded of our own mortality. But Rockefeller never even winced. He winked, bounded down out of the plane to meet Strom Thurmond and about fifty southern belles in hoop skirts, and said, "Wow!"

On this same trip, down on Mobile Bay, Nelson Rockefeller even charmed old George Wallace and his lady, Cornelia. Eastern, patrician, aristocratic, wealthy, Yankee: Rockefeller wowed even the rednecks down South. We saw it; we felt it—and we remember.

Rockefeller could never, of course, make the great, formal speech in front of a television camera. But in a ballroom with a crowd, or one-on-one, he was superb when he was informal. In 1968, in Miami, he had just delivered an uninspired formal speech to the delegates to the Republican National Convention. He didn't come across. But then, after his formal presentation, he joined Walter Cronkite in the CBS broadcast booth for a more informal discussion. The great Cronkite was trying hard to be his usual, objective self when Nelson reached over, put his hand on Walter's arm, and said, "Just a minute, Walter. I'd like to thank you, sir, for all that you do. The way you conduct yourself is an inspiration to me and to our country!" An astonished, but flattered, Cronkite went over like a giant oak!

I will remember lots of moments with this neighbor of ours, but none more than the day just before Christmas 1974, when Nelson Rockefeller walked into the Oval Office to be sworn in as Vice President of the United States. America, which had just been through Watergate, felt good again about itself, having this extraordinary man at center stage for a while. I also remember President Gerald Ford's telling us, over drinks in the White House: "Don't worry, Bill. I agree with you. Nelson and I are a good team. He'll be on my ticket—and we're going to win." That, of course, was before Bo Calloway and the nasty, narrow southerners and the Rockefeller-haters started after him. Most men would sell their soul for the vice presidency or to sit in the Oval Office. But Rockefeller took himself *out* of it—with style and class, and with that sense of grace that came so naturally.

On this morning after he died last night in New York City, it is Nelson Rockefeller's sense of humor that keeps coming back to me. I heard him once say, "My lawyer just sued me!" I didn't understand, until Bobby Douglass, his counselor, explained that Louis Lefkowitz, the New York attorney general, had just brought suit against Mobil Oil.

He was in great, good form at his last public appearance here in the county at Purchase College, where he showed slides of his art collection to a very tony group—members of the Westchester Arts Council. As he quipped, joked, raised his eyebrows, and moved his blocky shoulders, his eyes twinkled.

It was vintage Rockefeller. As he greeted this staid, artsy crowd, an exceptionally well-endowed lady—falling out of a plenty revealing dress—came through the receiving line. Nelson's eyes lit up. Then, when he noticed that Joe Canzeri and I had also tuned in on the display, the governor threw a sly, mischievous wink to us—and to Happy, standing next to him—and said to the lady: "Wow! How are you? . . . Yes, sir! Good to *see* you!"

Nelson Rockefeller was a man of great enthusiasm. Although he could find humor in almost any situation, he had to have been hurt by that number done on him and his art reproductions by the reporter in the *Times* last month. And this weekend, I expect James Reston will write a sweet, affectionate column about him in the mighty *New York Times*—while Anthony Lewis, who shares the same page, will predictably find some way to tell us he never forgave Nelson for Attica.

Many Catholics, of course, will never understand Rockefeller's stand on abortion. Indeed, they have already declined to pray for him among the formal petitions on Sunday at Holy Family Church in New Rochelle. But in the same city, the Christian Brothers of Ireland will remember the soul of Nelson Rockefeller at a Mass for fathers and sons at Iona Grammar School.

There was a big, broad range to the life of Nelson Rockefeller. He was a high-roller who was as much at ease with the emperor of Japan and the shah as he was with Meade Esposito of Brooklyn or any Yonkers politician. As a wealthy man—as a Rockefeller—he had a lot of material things: Kykuit, the house at Pocantico; an apartment on Fifth Avenue; the place at Seal Harbor, in Maine; and his newest project in the desert near Brownsville, Texas. He would sit at "21" and jet off to Dorado for vacations or with Happy to visit an Italian princess named Letitia in Rome—but he also had great enthusiasm for some of the ordinary pleasures.

I discovered this the night we flew to Cleveland so Rockefeller could campaign for Governor Jim Rhodes. A busy tour had been arranged: television interviews, a visit to the publishers of the *Plain-Dealer*, and a rubber-chicken political dinner. Just before the supper, however, we stopped at a slightly run-down Sheraton Hotel, where anti-abortion picketers were screaming outside. The governor's hosts had provided him with the "presidential suite," high above street level where we might retreat for a brief rest stop before dinner. As we cased the room, the governor spotted a portable bar stocked with Dubonnet and milk, which suited *him* just fine. (I personally could have used a Canadian Club!) There also sat a gleaming silver tray of Oreo cookies, all grandly wrapped in cellophane and ribbon. "Wow," said the governor of New York. "Look at *that!*" And so there we were—sitting in our shirtsleeves, eating Oreo cookies, sipping Dubonnet and milk in the presidential suite—while picketers chanted on the street below. Today, the man has his name on tall buildings in Albany and New York, and has left around this state a lot of soaring architecture that will remind us and future generations of Nelson Rockefeller. But I will think of him every time I encounter enthusiasm and energy and optimism—and every time I see a kid eating an Oreo cookie.

As I sit here at this microphone, I can still hear and almost feel some of the rejection that met the man as he pursued his dreams across so many years, the rich man's son who could have been quite a glorious bum instead.

There will be a huge turnout at Riverside Church next week when the Rockefellers bury their most dazzling son. But as dying is something you have to do all by yourself; there were no crowds to cheer him last night on 55th Street. In countless radio editorials over the years I've tried to tell you what he has done for our state and for our nation—his accomplishments. They are many and known to you. You can read about them all weekend in the public press, and when you are old, you can see all of it in the history books. But this morning, I merely want to say that I am glad he was our neighbor—and friend. He lit up our lives.

Nelson, you were *faaabulous*!

William O'Shaughnessy's Tribute to Martin Beck

W.O. tribute to Martin Beck, fellow broadcaster, and reflections re: hometown, community broadcasters in New York state for The Broadcasters Foundation of America.

———————

Marty Beck was one of our great statesmen. He excelled in two careers. First, in the rep field as one of the founders of Katz. And then he was a shrewd, astute, and enlightened broadcaster here in the New York area and in several other markets across the country for decades.

But he will be remembered mostly for his brilliant contributions as a real diplomat in the high councils of our profession. Marty was one of the best presidents of our New York State Broadcasters Association. And he was surely one of the most illustrious and respected NAB (National Association of Broadcasters) Radio Board chairmen.

These entities and organizations always looked to Marty for his wisdom and warm, intelligent counsel on the critical issues of the day. He was very strong on free speech and First Amendment matters. And his great patience and agreeable personal style were key factors in persuading the NRBA (National Radio Broadcasters Association) to come into the NAB tent so that our industry could speak with one clear, unified voice.

Marty led the "delicate" negotiations with Sis Kaplan, Bernie Mann, and the other well-meaning elders of that breakaway radio organization. And as a result of his vision and foresight, NAB created our own radio show, whose very first sessions in Chicago in 1978 I had the privilege to chair.

He was also a key player in the decision to endow the New York State Broadcasters Association with the leadership of Joe Reilly some thirty years ago—which has benefited every broadcaster in the Empire State and beyond.

[365]

Marty was an early and consistent supporter of the Broadcasters Foundation of America. When we were struggling for recognition and badly needed funding, he was there with his generous purse.

For those of us who know him, he was a reminder of gentle sunlit days at the Otesaga in Cooperstown and the Gideon Putnam in Saratoga, when our profession was populated by marvelous, endearing characters.

This, of course, was all before Consolidation and before the local hometown radio stations over which community broadcasters presided fell to absentee owners and speculators, who then placed these vital instruments of communication in the care and keeping of "market managers" and M.B.A.s who operate out of airport lounges with their Palm Pilots, reporting to corporate masters a whole continent away.

Marty Beck lived through all of it. And he remembered all of it, when there were no BlackBerrys, iPhones, iPads, or iPods. But there was the camaraderie and warm friendship provided by Phil Spencer, Bob Peebles, Shel Storrier, Jim Delmonico, Leavitt Pope, Bev and Frank Harms, Cam Thompson, Al and Bob Lessner, Jim O'Grady, Rick Buckley, Pat Tocatlian, John Lynch and his son Chris, Oscar Wein and his son Rob, Jerry Gillman, Harry Thayer, Walter Maxwell, C. Glover Delaney, Curly Vadeboncoeur, Bill Warren, Paul Dunn, Ellen and R. Peter Straus and their son Eric, John and Jane Kelly, Si Goldman, Nick Verbitsky, Bill Hogan, Bill Cloutier, Larry Levitte, Bob Bernacki, John Hensel, Bob King, Andy Langston, Les Arries, Bill McKibben, Dick Novik, Jim Champlin, Phil Beuth, Bob Klose, and Warren Bodow—New York state broadcasters, many with national reputations.

The network guys were there too, and they were always a lot of fun and quick to slap a hundred dollar bill or a credit card on the bar: Wally Schwartz, Ed McLaughlin, George Williams, Dick Beesemyer, Bob McConnell, Bob Hosking, Dick Foreman, and Bob Mahlman. The brokers Frank Boyle, Keith Horton, and Dick Kozacko were omnipresent. And the elders of the national trade press Don West, Larry Taishoff, Jane Barton, Les Brown, and occasionally even Larry's illustrious father Sol Taishoff planned their summers to be there. Ellen Cody was the den mother. And, for a brief while, the legendary John Van Buren Sullivan of WNEW ran the Association. And an affable, beguiling Tony Malara from Watertown, New York, emceed all the dinners and banquets.

The great Nelson Rockefeller would swoop down on the eighteenth green of the Otesaga in a Wayfarer Ketch helicopter, which his family co-owned with Time, Inc. And at our podium in those halcyon days were Howard Samuels, Malcolm Wilson, Hugh Carey, Gloria Steinem, Ossie Davis, Ruby Dee, Geraldo Rivera, Cardinal O'Connor, Ogden Reid, Dan Rather, Mario Cuomo, Donald Trump, Liz Smith, Jimmy Breslin, Jack Javits, Ward Quaal, Mario Biaggi, Barbara Walters, Eddie Fritts, Frank Gifford, Wellington Mara, George Steinbrenner, Matilda Cuomo, Kenneth Cole, Happy Rockefeller, Pete Hamill, Harriet Van Horne, and the famous disc jockey William B. Williams.

And always, there was the reassuring presence of the graceful mandarin from Long Island who was respected and loved by our tribe. He was a gracious, magnetic guy whose charming smile lit up our lives. He left us on October 21, 2010.

Marty Beck was a class act in every season.

Tribute to Paul Hutton

File Paul Hutton under "great characters." He operated around Westchester for many years and spent his last days in Santa Fe, New Mexico. Here are my remarks at Gate of Heaven Cemetery, Hawthorne, N.Y., March 11, 2017.

Paul Hutton was a bright star in every season of a long, full life.

From the rarefied precincts of Westchester County, where he made an indelible mark and to which he now returns, all the way out to the great expanse and unlimited potential of his beloved New Mexico, Paul was a warm, agreeable soul who beckoned us with his generous persona.

He lit up the night in all sorts of venues, some of them—most of them—swellegant, elegant bistros and others "down home," but altogether welcoming and agreeable saloons, as long as they had a microphone and a piano player. Karaoke was all right with him too.

Paul Hutton was *sui generis*, unique and able to be defined *only* in his own terms.

And we loved him for that uniqueness and for that fierce, vivid individuality.

He left his mark on *everything*. His Westchester home—I think it was on Hathaway Road in tony, upscale Bronxville—is *still* known as "The Paul Hutton House," even though he moved out some fifteen years ago and a famous restaurateur now resides therein. But to the old men of the neighborhood, it's still "Paul Hutton's house." I know this because the poor fellow who lives there told me as much.

It is not a coincidence at all that Paul chose Santa Fe, a city of sophistication and culture in the great Southwest, home of the fabled Santa Fe Opera Company. A perfect stage for Winnie's remarkable talent. *And* for his.

He had some of the best years of his life with the incomparable Winnie Klotz, one of the legendary photographers of our time and a mythic figure in the operatic world.

As the official photographer of the Metropolitan Opera, she captured beautiful portraits—and that's what they were—that will be preserved forever in the archives of the Met and enshrined in the memories of opera lovers everywhere. Pavarotti, Domingo, Mario Lanza, our Westchester neighbor of sainted memory Bob Merrill, Maria Callas— she captured them all. They *were* works of art, just like Winnie.

In recent years, she captured *Paul*'s heart and imagination.

And Winnie: This is not the time or the place, but I'll bet you can still do your amazing, signature "Split," just as you used to do for Lou Walters at the Latin Quarter! Come to think of it: why not? Just one more, please, Winnie. For Paul.

Her own ageless dynamism added years to his life. And it's hard to imagine Paul—even now—without Winnie at his side.

For all his charisma and colorful persona, he was, at his core, a nice man and a very sweet soul with a relentless instinct to perform, to entertain and enlighten, to make people happy.

He should have had his own late-night show on television. And come to think of it, he did. And he did all this right up to the very end of his time among us.

As I said, he was a bright star in every season. And when Paul Hutton walked into a room—any room—you knew something important and joyful and pleasing was going to happen before your very eyes.

You *knew* he was there.

He was a marvelous showman. And he kept the music playing for a good, long time.

And we will all miss him.

Tribute to Peter Mustich, Townie

Peter Mustich was the quintessential Townie in our home heath.
Every community has one. He was ours. Broadcast June 27, 2011.

———————————

It was right there in the *Journal News* daily newspaper that Peter Mustich of New Rochelle, New York, had died. The key phrase being "of
New Rochelle."

That said it all about the man. All other details of his life and passing
are meaningless and irrelevant. For this Mustich was a Townie, and any
achievements, accomplishments, and milestones of his eighty-eight
years must yield to his relationship with his home heath.

Peter Mustich was "of New Rochelle" in every season of his long life.
But the venue of his days is not to be confused with the New Rochelle
of E. L. Doctorow, Cynthia Ozick, Teresa Brewer, Ossie Davis, Farook
Kathwari, Robert Merrill, Page Morton Black, Frances Sternhagen,
John Kluge, Norman Rockwell, Mariano Rivera, Dick Van Dyke, or Ken
Chenault, boss of American Express. We're not talking here about
Overlook Road or Premium Point either. Or about the Joyces or the
Powers family. The Swells.

Nor would you put him in Scarsdale, Bronxville, Bedford, or Rye.
10801 and 10804 were the ZIP codes where he got up each morning.
And among his enthusiasms were the Chamber of Commerce, the Elks
Club, the Lions, Holy Name Church, the Police Foundation, and this
local community radio station, where he would appear in our lobby
almost weekly with some importuning or pleading.

Peter Mustich was a Catholic, but he carried instincts taught by the
ancient Hebrews. He probably didn't even know the words *tzedakah* or
tikkun olam. But it came most naturally to him as he set about to build
up the community, to make it stronger, better, sweeter. He didn't need

some old rabbi to tell him, "God created the universe, but didn't complete it; that's *your* job." It was in him, a part of the man.

It seemed that he was around these parts forever. But Mustich did not go back as far as Lou Gehrig, Norman Rockwell, Frankie Frisch, or Eddie Foy and the Seven Little Foys, New Rochelle residents of fable and myth.

But he could absolutely tell you all about Teddy Greene, Alvin Ruskin, Alex Norton, Sam Kissinger, Hughie Doyle, Bob Cammann, Jack Kornsweet, Murray Fuerst, John Fosina, Darby Ruane, Sid Mudd, Jim Bishop, Jack Driscoll, Jack Dowling, the handsome plumber Marty Traugott, Dominic Procopio, Frank Connelly, Mickey and Joe Fosina, Bill Scollon, Art Geoghegan, Bill Sullivan, Amiel Wohl, Ben Mermelstein, Vinny Rippa, Ruth Kitchen, Lenny Paduano, Frank Garito, Arnie Klugman, I. B. Cohen, the Libretts, Harry and Bob Colwell, Dorothy Ann Kelly, Jim Maisano, Ogden Reid, Tommy O'Toole, George Vergara, Tim Idoni, Nick DeJulio, Rosemary McLaughlin, Evie Haas, Doc Kiernan, Rocco Bellantoni Jr., Joe Evans, Nick Donofrio, Stanley W. Church, Elmer Miller, Donny Zack, Mike Armiento, and P. J. O'Neil, keeper of the most glorious saloon. And, on information and belief, he even spent some time in Cesario's of an evening.

He was a joiner, a volunteer, a promoter, a drumbeater, a promulgator, and he always seemed to be coming up the street at the head of a parade. You will find none of these things in the New York papers.

But over this most perfect summer weekend just past, a Father Martin J. Biglin stood up in the Holy Name of Jesus Church to pray over Peter Mustich. Now this Biglin is a most rare and highly unusual person, who, when he puts on his Roman collar, is actually able to speak in entire graceful sentences and elegant paragraphs of the English language almost as well as most other priests of the Roman Catholic Church recite the ancient Latin.

"He always did unto the least of these," said the white-haired priest. And after quoting the carpenter's son, who was altogether perfect, he flung holy water on the casket of Peter Mustich, who spent eighty-eight years saying nice things about his neighbors, most of them obscure sidemen in orchestras long dispersed. But to Peter Mustich they were all A-listers.

Another Beloved Townie Open Line Caller

A WVOX commentary by William O'Shaughnessy,
broadcast August 2, 2012.

———————

Word came this morning of the passing of Inez Candrea. You will not read of her life in the *New York Times*. Around these parts she was known as the widow of Joe Candrea and mother-in-law of one Anthony Galletta. Mrs. Candrea was eighty, and I speak of her on this radio station because for so many of those eighty years she used WVOX as her own personal soapbox, as did her late husband.

And as we mourn Mrs. Candrea this day, our mind drifts back to her shy, modest, retiring husband, who was cut from the same outspoken cloth. And when he went to what Governor Malcolm Wilson would call "another, and we are sure, a better world" on December 21, 1999, we went into this studio and said these very words about the man:

"Joe Candrea was a Runyunesque figure. But instead of Broadway or The Great White Way, his canvas was our home heath. It was here in New Rochelle that Joe Candrea lived most of his years with great conviction.

"He confronted every proposition and civic issue with a relentless passion. Although his résumé said 'newspaper delivery man,' Joe Candrea could put power and energy into words that usually became majestic proclamations. His platform was behind this microphone, or on any street corner he could find.

"He possessed what most of us search for all our lives. There was a sureness to Joe Candrea's proposals and observations. He was the great articulator, the undiminished champion of the forgotten neighborhoods in the west end of our city.

"The politicians used to call it the old Fourth Ward. It is where Rocco Bellantoni once lived. And Tony and Sal Tocci and the Fosinas came from there. But in recent years there was only Joe Candrea to rage against injustices as they might be committed against his neighbors in the west end.

"New Rochelle was his mistress. And also his fortress. He felt about our city the way some men of his generation look upon the United States Marine Corps or the Notre Dame football team. Other callers and radio talk show hosts discuss with great erudition the cosmic issues of the day. Theirs is an international curiosity or a national inclination, but Joe Candrea's enthusiasms and passions extended only as far as the city limits. ZIP code 10801 was his territory, baby, and don't you forget it.

"He ran flat out and went straight for everything. There was no halfway station . . . no middle ground with the man . . . and never, ever a doubt about where he stood on civic issues, politicians, bureaucrats and other disreputable types.

"He was all about building up the damn neighborhood.

"Have I got it right, Joe?"

That was spoken for Joe Candrea, who, as I said, was the husband of one Inez Candrea, who left us early this morning at eighty.

There were other vivid Townie orators who used this WVOX broadcasting station over the years as their own personal soapboxes. Back in the '60s there was brilliant, cerebral David Kendig who drove them nuts at City Hall. And Lorraine Trotta, whose son Frank is now a bigtime lawyer in Greenwich and works with Lewis Lehrman who spent millions trying to become governor. Our roster of Townie callers in those days also included Bob Schaeffer, who called himself "The Neighborhood Watchdog" or was it "Junkyard Dog"? Memory fails. Bob weighed in on everything and everyone. So did Ken from Pelham and Frank from Connecticut who used to be Frank from Mount Vernon.

Every day on our "Open Line" programs they were there opining, arguing, debating, raging, cajoling, attacking, occasionally even flattering, and, on rare occasion, actually saying something nice about one of our neighbors.

Mario Cuomo once told me he prays for "sureness." Our callers never had that problem. They brought a rock-solid, unshakeable sureness to most of their pronouncements.

Other stations had Scott Shannon, Imus, or Howard Stern. We had Mitch from the north end and Bruce the Swimmer, a Libertarian who . . . lived . . . his . . . life . . . the . . . way . . . he . . . damn . . . well . . . pleased. And there was always, it seems, Mr. Cam, who demanded to be addressed just so. But I'll not leave this planet until I find out his regular, normal, human, given first name. He's gotta have one.

Day after day here on the radio there was Ann Witkowski, Peggy Godfrey, Mary Tedesco, and a brilliant William Kirby Scollon, who was descended from the Kirbys of Rye but became a New Rochelle "Townie" in good standing. He was a friend of Bill Mullen, no blushing violet he, who could also climb up on our soapbox. Right out here with Mullen would be Dave from Mamaroneck, Joanne, Alex from Greenburgh, and Michael Brown. They could all talk without shyness.

Some of our regular callers were possessed of great insight, and a few were even accompanied by a stunning intelligence concerning matters political. One of the most brilliant was Angela Scarano, who reveled in the moniker . . . "Noodge." She was. In the best possible way.

Also we recall Anthony Galletta, the Candrea son-in-law, Charlie from the west end, Lorraine Pierce, and don't forget Bob, her husband. And the late, great "Woody." That's all . . . just "Woody." There was a Rae Rega and an Isabel. And I have gone this far without mentioning the incomparable Carmine Saracino. And Mrs. Green.

Actually, some of these "frequent" callers were so good (and so frequent) we couldn't resist giving them their very own weekly shows: Colonel Marty Rochelle, the Yonkers legend who never met a judge he didn't like. Or a district attorney. And Mike Scully, the world traveler, who gets better every week. But I wish he'd let me "enlighten" him on the great issues. I'll bring him around. Like when Andrew Cuomo is sworn in . . . and Scully jumps off our 190-foot radio tower! And Lou Felicione, who opines about everything New Rochelle when he's not posting on Facebook. He has his very own show too. And Sam Spady.

Sometimes I've felt like taking a page from my friend—and mentor to us all—Bob Grant, who, when he couldn't abide it any more, would just scream into the microphone: "Get off my phone!" It was tempting, I should tell you. But then the advice we received so many years ago from Alvin Richard Ruskin would break through all the cacophony, noise, dialogue, and often disagreeable chatter.

Alvin Ruskin was mayor of New Rochelle back in the '60s before Nelson Rockefeller made him a judge. And one day he took me aside: "Your damn station is gaining a national reputation . . . the *Wall Street Journal* called you 'the quintessential community station in America' . . . and so on. And all that is well and good, O'Shaughnessy. But don't let it go to your head. And don't forget the Townies. They made you. They're the strength of your station . . . people with opinions."

Judge Ruskin was a wise man.

As I said . . . other stations had Imus, Scott Shannon, and Howard Stern.

We had Inez Candrea and Joe and all those other marvelous soap-box orators.

And with it all . . . there really was never a dull moment.

Have I got it right, Anthony . . . ?

Tribute to Rick Buckley, Beloved Broadcaster

August 1, 2011.

Rick Buckley came at you with great lineage. His father, Richard Dimes Buckley, owned the legendary WNEW of sainted memory all the way back in the days of Arde Bulova, John Jager, and Bernice Judis, before the food brokers from Washington, D.C., and Philadelphia descended on that mythic broadcasting station with their suits and diamond pinky rings. One of young Rick Buckley's first assignments was to pick out the records to be played on the "Make Believe Ballroom" program.

The Rick Buckley who slipped away from us on a warm, sultry summer Sunday was himself one of the giants of our tribe. Although Rick presided over a collection of stations in other states, including the estimable WDRC in Hartford, he will always be remembered as the permittee of the mighty WOR, an urban powerhouse known as one of America's "heritage" stations, which sends its signal throughout the Northeast from New York.

In every season, Buckley was in love with that notion, subscribed to in these parts, that a radio station achieves its highest calling when it resembles a platform, a forum, for the expression of many different viewpoints. And for many decades, while so much else was changing in the great city, WOR, residing firmly in Rick Buckley's enlightened and resolute stewardship, never did resemble a jukebox.

For decades, he kept this instrument of communication away from the speculators and absentee owners with a fierceness and relentless devotion that surprised even his friends. And they were legion. He saved it harmless even during the allurements and temptations of Consolidation.

Buckley carried himself with a shyness and a self-effacing wit that endeared him to so many of our colleagues. My son and heir David

Tucker O'Shaughnessy said on that sad Sunday afternoon just past, "Dad, he always pulled me aside to inquire how I was doing."

Rick lived like a country squire and had homes in Greenwich and Quogue and out in the desert in California. And he was quick, this Buckley, to grab a check in every circumstance and venue.

Just one month ago, Rick Buckley stood in the glow of the lights at The Sagamore in upstate New York before 600 of his colleagues there assembled by Joe Reilly to welcome him into the New York State Broadcasters Hall of Fame, as plaudits and encomiums rained down on the honorees. Brian Williams, Regis Philbin, wonderful Deborah Norville, my friend Joe Reilly, and others stepped up to the microphone. Norville was terrific. Williams did a dazzling turn. Reilly was superb. And Regis was . . . Regis. But the most touching, heartfelt response came off the lips and from the heart of Buckley.

And no one who heard it will ever forget the words he used to describe his love for the profession he distinguished for fifty years. And the enormous pride that was his as a result of WOR's independence, standing, and stature.

He also spoke movingly on that summer night on the shores of Lake George of his great love for his family, in whose care and keeping WOR is now entrusted. So there's a great sadness in our profession this August morning, a Monday. But nowhere is that sadness more profound than among those of us who served with Rick on the board of the Broadcasters Foundation of America. He was our treasurer, a member of the executive committee, and one of our strongest directors, who was unfailingly generous with his wisdom, his counsel, and his purse.

The Foundation's humanitarian mission of helping those for whom life has turned sad and difficult always resonated with and had an effect on Buckley. You could see it in his face as we would review the pleadings and importunings from those unfortunate souls who have fallen through the cracks.

He had a great family. And when Rick and his dazzling Connie—or his beautiful daughter Jen—entered the room at one of our events and high councils, you knew something good was coming at you.

He amplified the voices of the fabled Gambling family, Bob Grant, Mayor Bloomberg, Joan Hamburg, and Joey Reynolds. And in a profession populated by not a few swashbuckling—or, shall we just say, somewhat "colorful" front-office types—Buckley always surrounded himself with good, solid associates: Joe Bilotta, Jerry Crowley, Bob Bruno, Tom Ray, et al.

WOR, in its best moments, resembles one of the soapboxes favored by street-corner orators in London's fabled Hyde Park Square. While almost every other station in the great city was rocking and rolling, Rick Buckley used his franchise to amplify the disparate voices of his New York neighbors. Some of them were raucous, many were unsettling, and a few were even sweet. And Buckley made it very easy for all sorts and types of people to get on the radio.

As I said, he had absolutely no interest in presiding over a jukebox. Rather, he was powerfully and irresistibly drawn all the days of his life to *Vox Populi*, the real music of America. Not a bad legacy.

—W.O.

Tribute to Stu Olds, Beloved Broadcast Exec

As you know, we recently inaugurated a Statesman feature in the Broadcasters Foundation's *On the Air* publication to salute those pioneers who have done so much for our profession over the years. Many of them made their contributions way in the past, and we had to reach back through the mists of time to recall their accomplishments and milestones. Who knew or ever imagined when we began, however, that this space would one day speak of Stu Olds in the past tense, as a profound sadness descended on our profession with the passing of our dear, incomparable vice chairman on December 4, 2010.

All the industry newsletters, blogs, and websites were filled that sad winter morning with encomiums, reminiscences, and tributes to our graceful colleague and friend.

How remarkable and how absolutely wonderful, they all observed, that an ineffably *nice* guy, and a real gentleman, sat astride a huge, tough, no-nonsense commercial enterprise that deals in persuasion and numbers and hard-fought ratings. In a highly competitive world, Stu advocated for his stations. But never for himself. Perhaps that's what endeared him to so many. That and his relentlessly upbeat and positive demeanor.

In addition to his family, his golf game, a glass of wine, and a good cigar, we're also fortunate that one of his great passions was the Broadcasters Foundation of America, which he served as vice chairman and head of our "Angels" campaign, which has raised millions for the less fortunate in our tribe.

At our meetings and high councils, Stu's wisdom, foresight, judgment, and good nature always steered us to the lee of a safe harbor. So one can only observe that we've lost a graceful guy who was loved and respected by many.

As President Jim Thompson and Chairman Phil Lombardo will confirm, our foundation has received a stunning half-million dollars in memorial tributes and contributions in Stu's name. Unheard of and unprecedented, to be sure. But as we all know, Stu Olds was a *very* special—and altogether unique—individual.

The chairman has also recently announced plans for an annual golf event for Stu's friends at his beloved Knollwood Club in June.

And just a few weeks ago at the NAB in Las Vegas, our foundation presented the Lowry Mays Excellence in Broadcasting Award posthumously to Stu, which was accepted with grace and articulation and warmth by Kim Olds. There wasn't a dry eye in the place.

And at our last board meeting, which was hosted by Chairman Lombardo at the Columbus Club in New York City, the following motion closed our last business meeting for 2010:

> Mr. Chairman Lombardo . . . our work done for this day . . . may we request that we adjourn this final Meeting of the Board for 2010 . . . in tribute to . . . and in memory of . . . our beloved Vice Chairman Stu Olds.
>
> As everyone here assembled at this high council at year's end is aware, Stu loved this organization and was devoted to its noble mission in every season.
>
> His leadership, vision and dedication to our work enabled us to assist so many colleagues fallen on hard times all across the country.
>
> His passing is felt very deeply by everyone on this festive but sad occasion and by all those who loved him and feel the pain of his passing.
>
> And so we would ask, Mr. Chairman, that we set aside any and all other business which may come before us this day in his honor.
>
> We so move, Mr. Chairman and request that it be spread upon the Minutes and that a copy be sent forthwith to Kim Olds and his Family.

The motion was adopted unanimously on December 15, 2010. But the sadness remains. The work, however, which meant so much to Stu Olds, continues.

To assist. To assist. To assist.

FYI: To date more than $1 million has been donated in Stu Olds's name to the Broadcasters Foundation of America.

—W.O.

Tribute to Ward Quaal,
Broadcasting's Greatest Statesman

September 27, 2010.

———————————

The broadcasters of America have lost our greatest statesman.

Ward Quaal was also a seminal figure in the modernization of his beloved Broadcasters Foundation of America. He set the groundwork and provided the vision that led us into the dynamic development of the McLaughlin and Lombardo years.

I enjoyed an almost forty-year correspondence with him. He was a reliable and generous resource and an inexhaustible font of wisdom on all the great issues of the day. I was only one of thousands who consulted Ward on matters both professional and personal. On countless occasions over the years, we would hear his big, booming, sonorous, benevolent *basso profundo* voice on the telephone and at all our high councils.

No one ever spoke more powerfully or with greater eloquence on our precious First Amendment rights. All the rest of us, less gifted, appropriated, borrowed, purloined, plagiarized—actually we *stole*— from his vast store of knowledge and goodness on every fundamental free speech contretemps that erupted in the public discourse during the past four decades.

And, always, in every season, he was a man of great dignity, stature, and carriage. His advice and counsel were always given so freely and gently and generously. He advised presidents, powerful congressmen, and the solons of the Senate as well as the corporate panjandrums, mandarins, and elders of our profession. His advice was also sought by FCC chairmen, congressional committees, and three generations of broadcasters.

[382]

His enormous influence was felt far beyond even the mighty signal of WGN, the legendary midwestern powerhouse over which he presided for so many years.

A lifelong Republican, as a young man he introduced a struggling actress, Nancy Davis, to his friend Ronald Reagan, and years later Ward persuaded President Reagan to veto the so-called Fairness Doctrine.

His bright, fine mind generated a voluminous and graceful canon of missives, letters, encomiums, and advice freely given, which were produced by a dedicated office staff. At one time, Mr. Quaal had five secretaries just to handle his correspondence.

He was also a valued consultant to three generations of the Taishoff family, encouraging their essential and highly valuable work as our sentinels on the Potomac against government intrusion.

Ward Quaal's last gift to us was his encouragement to use his illustrious name for the Ward L. Quaal Pioneer Awards, enabling us to raise hundreds of thousands of dollars in contributions and donations from the generous purses of Stan Hubbard, Dennis Fitzsimmons, and the wonderful folks at the McCormick Foundation.

He informed our work and ennobled our profession. He never called it an industry.

And we were all his students.

William B. Williams's Hall of Fame Induction

———————

Chairman Ed Levine, Ernie Anastos, Joe Reilly, Brian Williams, Hall of Famer Regis Philbin . . . Deborah Norville, that was one of the most powerful moments we've witnessed in this room as you received the award named for our beloved Carol Reilly.

Dear friends and colleagues of so many years and so many seasons, as this is the first opportunity I've had to enjoy the privilege of your podium in quite some time, I want to first take a moment of personal privilege and tell all of you here assembled of my regret at not being able to join you for the induction of the *first* group admitted to the Hall some years ago. Your elders at the time, in their wisdom, chose to include an Irishman from Westchester when you first began the Hall. As many of you know, a great sadness overtook our family in 2005, and I was not able to be with you. So please permit me now, this evening, to thank you for that momentary lapse in good judgment and relaxation of your standards that enabled Bill O'Shaughnessy to darken the door of your hallowed Hall.

I want to speak about William B. Williams. David Hinckley, the great and gifted critic of the *New York Daily News*, in a gorgeous feature column this morning, said it all, much more gracefully and artfully than I am able.

I met William B. at one of those small cabarets that once flourished on Third Avenue in Manhattan. Of course, I had idolized him for many, many years. I remember the night so well. Matt Dennis, the great songwriter-singer who was one of Sinatra's favorites (and mine), was sitting at the piano in a little pencil spotlight as a midwinter blizzard descended on the great city that cold night.

Matt Dennis started with the verse to a lovely song that he himself had composed: "It was winter in Manhattan . . . falling snowflakes filled the air . . . the streets were covered with a film of ivory . . . but a simple little secret I heard about somewhere . . . changed the winter into summer . . . I bought you *Violets for Your Furs.*"

And then, from the banquette just behind me, I heard the unmistakable, rich, warm voice of the incomparable William B. Williams: "That's a gorgeous song, known only to songwriters and musicians." I introduced myself and went off into the night, vowing that one day I would work at WNEW, where he held forth with such style and grace.

Those were the days when WNEW, of sainted memory, was an oasis of taste on the AM dial. The number-one station today has—in its best moments—a 5.6 or 5.7 share. WNEW had a 26!

I did make it about a year later—thanks to the indulgence of the legendary general manager John Van Buren Sullivan—who brought me in as kind of an "ambassador without portfolio" (in other words, nobody ever knew what the hell I did!).

One thing I did, however, was to get myself invited to *lunch* at least four or five days a week with the great William B. Williams. I would tag along as part of his entourage, which much more prominently included Buddy Hackett, Bill Persky, Sam Denoff, David Yarnell, and, occasionally, Steve and Eydie.

Billy would take us to the Friars Club, Rocky Lee's, the Stage Deli, Toots Shor, and Basin Street East. And about every tenth day or so, we'd go to the coffee shop around the corner from WNEW at 46th and Fifth, and he'd let *me* pick up the check. (I was making about 125 bucks a week.)

He was the classiest man—and one of the nicest men—to ever stand in front of a microphone. His taste was impeccable. You could actually understand the words to the sweet songs he played. I'm talking Cole Porter, Rodgers and Hart, Jerome Kern, Harold Arlen, Johnny Burke . . .

He loved to tell the story of when he asked Louis Armstrong who was the greatest *girl* singer of all time. And Satchmo, after but a moment of reflection, said, "You mean, besides *Ella*?"

Edward Kennedy Ellington was the "Duke of Ellington." William Basie of Red Bank was "The Count of Basie." Nat King Cole was "Nathaniel." Mel Tormé was "Melvin Howard Tormé." And, as legend and the popular lexicon has it enshrined forever in our memory, Sinatra was the "Chairman of the Board."

William Bernard Breitbard was so much more than an entertainer or performer, and he walked the desperate, dangerous, dusty roads of Selma with Martin Luther King Jr. and squandered his talent across a thousand nights as master of ceremonies at all kinds of charitable functions. Sinatra called him "simply the most generous man I know."

He left us some twenty-five years ago, much too early at the age of sixty-three. Billy had been battling the cancer that killed him for a couple of years. And when he made a brief recovery during that siege and returned to the air, I did a piece that was published in *Variety* that included the line "An icon is properly restored." (I last saw him doing a remote from the lobby of the Waldorf Astoria.) I could see from the back of the room that we both had tears in our eyes . . . even as he was live on the air. I think we knew the clock was ticking.

I must tell you, in the intimacy of this room, it was somewhat bewildering to many of us that his genius had somehow eluded the elders of your Hall of Fame Committee—until now. But I'm so happy for this moment.

You have restored an icon, who, as I said, was about the classiest disc jockey we've had in this nation.

So I thank *you* on behalf of Billy's many friends who are still around. They are legion. And grateful.

I will send this memento of his designation by morning post to Dottie Williams, who is still as beautiful as ever, in Aventura, Florida, and to his son and heir Jeffrey.

William B.'s theme song was Henri René's "You Are the One."

I can still hear him say, "Hello, world!"

He was the One!

Tribute to Dawson B. "Tack" Nail

My kids were crazy about a wonderful man named "Tack" Nail, who was for many years one of the preeminent reporters on the communications beat in the nation's capital. March 29, 2011.

"Tack" Nail was a journalist and reporter the way the men of our fathers' time imagined them to be.

His beat was communications and television, the business thereof, its doings and deliberations. And his turf was the capital city of our nation, where he covered Congress, the regulatory authorities, and commissions like the FCC, and also those who resided in the White House itself for the past fifty years.

Tack Nail was unique. He looked like nothin' you ever saw: craggy, rumpled, disheveled; and his jowls were always in need of a shave. And, on information and belief, he enjoyed a cocktail of an evening. Or two. I was crazy about the man.

And as John Eggerton of *Broadcasting & Cable* observed, "He looked like a cross between Gabby Hayes and Abraham Lincoln." The brilliant Eggerton had it exactly right. Just perfect.

How appropriate then that a brainy *B & C* scribe had the best line as we mourn his passing, because for all those decades when Dawson B. Nail covered Washington, his only real competition came from the formidable Taishoff stable at *Broadcasting & Cable* over on DeSales Street.

That essential journal, long our sentinel on the Potomac, had the legendary Sol Taishoff himself, his son Larry of sainted memory, the estimable Don West—now president of the Library of American Broadcasting who was with Tack last week when he wrote "30" to his colorful life—and graceful, cerebral editors like Harry Jessell, Ed James, and Mark Miller. They have only Eggerton now to keep us honest.

All the while up against *B & C* and the national press, Tack Nail had only himself to report, write, and edit a slim newsletter he published, on mustard-colored paper, about an electronic medium that merely has the power to shape world events and influence the way we live.

He covered the business side of this pervasive and powerful industry from its infancy all the way up to the reality of reality shows. Where once he wrote of Tom Murphy, William S. Paley, Stan Hubbard, Leonard Goldenson, Jim Quello, Dick Wiley, Rupert Murdoch, Lowry Mays, Ward Quaal, and the Sarnoffs, he was left at the end only with business suits who preside over Charlie Sheen, Lindsay Lohan, and the Kardashians.

As the scribe and chronicler of this great communications force, he would often rage against the evils of Consolidation. And like his competitors and colleagues at *B & C*, he held broadcasters' feet to the fire on First Amendment and free speech matters. But there was no meanness or venom in the man. And his writings and reporting held no animosity toward even the conglomerateurs, absentee owners, and speculators who view a television station only as an instrument, a vehicle, and a conduit for importunings about products and goods and services few of us need and most can ill afford.

For all his offhanded, gnarly, un-PC, rough-edged demeanor and the southern twang, Tack could get through to any D.C. bureaucrat or solon of the Congress and always to any media mogul in whose care and keeping the powerful instruments of communication reside.

Today as we mourn Dawson B. Nail, we also mourn the passing of an era when once giants walked the land, when only he and the Taishoffs and Les Brown of *Variety* really covered our tribe. Today we are scrutinized by countless blogs, newsletters, and message boards. But nobody, no real live journalist as smart and dogged as Tack, is watching the profession.

I want to end by telling you also that my own *kids* always loved Tack Nail ever since they encountered him many years ago at one of Joe Reilly's high councils upstate. Or it may have been at NAB. My daughter, Kate, always lit up when she saw Mr. Nail, the kindly-looking man with the funny name. When I suggested to Kate that he was a very humorous fellow with a marvelous wit and widely known as a great character, she said, "Daddy, there's more there. I like him. He's a really good man."

And now as soon as I finish this piece, I have to go into the office of Kate's brother David Tucker O'Shaughnessy to tell him that Tack Nail died over the weekend. For the last thirty-some years, you see, David has carried around every day in his wallet a rare $2 bill given to him by Mr. Nail at one of those conventions. David, who is now president of these two radio stations, will reach into his pocket, I expect, and produce that wallet from which he'll gently remove the folded $2 bill. And if I know my son and heir, he'll wipe away a tear and tuck it safely back into his wallet when I tell him Tack Nail is gone.

Forgive the personal story about this marvelous character. But our profession—I know I'm supposed to call it an *industry*—can't lose too many more Ward Quaals, Stu Olds, Marty Becks, or Steve Labunskis only to be replaced by those "Make it happen"—"Doin' what it takes"—"Gettin' it done"—"Sounds like a plan" empty suits who sit in airport lounges tapping away at their BlackBerrys and iPads, communicating their ratings and financial results to corporate masters a whole continent away. They call themselves, these new mandarins of the trade, "market managers" and "chief revenue officers."

Tack Nail knew all of this. He wrote of it. And he did what he could to remind us that a television—or radio—station could elevate and energize a community and make it better and stronger and its people sweeter and kinder.

It must also be remembered that when he had filed his last stories for *Communications Daily*, Tack would somehow drag himself up to New York for board meetings of the old Broadcast Pioneers, which became the modern-day national charity known as the Broadcasters Foundation of America.

It meant a lot to Tack because it assists broadcasters and their families when the roof falls in and life turns sad and difficult.

Dawson B. "Tack" Nail heard that music too.

—W.O.

[389]

The Passing of Peggy Burton

I had a longtime crush—unrequited—on a woman around New York for many years named Peggy Burton. Here are my remarks at her memorial service in New York City, July 30, 2014.

———————

Permit me to inquire, is anyone the least bit surprised that Peggy had a daughter that *looked*—and *spoke*—like Linda?

Or a dazzling granddaughter like Tara?

Who among us is surprised?

Don't let these notes scare you. I intend to beg only two or three minutes, for Peggy.

Like many of you in this room, I make my living with words. In my case they usually occur awkwardly, inartfully, and imprecisely.

How then to describe your mother, Linda? She was serene, we know. She was elegant, to be sure. She was stylish. She was very glamorous, in every season of her eighty-seven years.

And Peggy Burton was—with apologies to all here assembled—the most dazzling and vivid member of the Dutch Treat, a luncheon club of great standing, stature, and influence in this town.

I must confess that, like every fellow member of the Dutch Treat family—even those like me of a certain age—I had an unrequited crush on your mother, as did most of our colleagues—at least those of us possessed of a discernible pulse and beating heart.

When I mentioned my feelings at our Annual Dinner at the Harvard Club—speaking of "words"—I looked at Sheldon Harnick, the great Broadway lyricist seated just in front of the podium and asked if "unrequited" was an appropriate word. He took one look at me and said, "It'll work!"

I thought I'd tell you this, Linda. And ladies and gentlemen, I don't care who *knows* it. But I think, Linda, I *think* your mother did.

And that's why she wisely kept me at a distance!

She knew we loved her.

I can tell you, in the intimacy of this room, that she did invite me over for lunch sometime during the last difficult year. And I will regret, to *my* last day, that we were never able to put it together.

But she went through it—the last year—and endured it all with her usual grace and reserve, never wanting to intrude on our lives or burden us with her travail.

The others can speak to her professional life in the corporate world as a legend of Madison Avenue and gifted filmmaker—careers that were accompanied by the same style and class (I have to use that word) and thoughtfulness and generosity and the great kindness she bestowed on us at those Dutch Treat luncheons on Tuesdays past . . . and, always, on all of us privileged to know her personally.

The headline from this memorial service, with apologies to the lovely presentations of Ray Fox, John Donnelly, K. T. Sullivan, and Alton James, has to go to Robert Kimball, who has spent a lifetime protecting and preserving Cole Porter's brilliant legacy and the canon of his work and lyrics. Mr. Kimball had quite the loveliest line of all: "Peggy had a natural charm."

And you, Linda, and your daughter, Tara Isabella, can speak to her *greatest* role in which she starred as a loving and devoted mother and grandmother, during every one of your own days and years with her, right up to the very moment she left you . . . and us.

Peggy was a classy dame, a *beautiful* woman.

And I liked her a hell of a lot!

—W.O.

Diane Gagliardi Collins Passes Away at Ninety

Diane Gagliardi Collins was a New Rochelle Townie. She came from a
great Westchester family. Her brothers were important judicial figures.
And the Gagliardis were all golf champions at Winged Foot.
William O'Shaughnessy's tribute, January 2011.

From Virginia comes the sad word that Diane Gagliardi Collins has passed away.

Diane Collins was part of the legendary Westchester Gagliardi political family, which exercised great influence in the county back in the '60s and '70s.

She was a county supervisor and the first woman on the County Board of Legislators, eventually serving as vice chairman.

The Gagliardis were also prominent in the world of golf. Her brother Lee was a federal judge, and another brother, Joe Gagliardi, was the presiding justice of the 9th Judicial District and in charge of all the courts in the Hudson Valley. They were the first Italian American members of the mighty Winged Foot Golf Club. And in 1974 the Gagliardis were named The Golf Family of the Year in New York state.

Diane Collins had a 10 handicap and played every day . . . well into her eighties. Her brothers were scratch golfers.

Mrs. Collins was married for many years to Bill Collins, an affable telephone company executive, who also served as Republican boss of New Rochelle, which is where their power base was. And for a while, Diane Collins also served as county clerk, the job Tim Idoni has now. Bill Collins passed away twenty-five years ago, and in recent years, Diane Collins lived with her sons spread out along the eastern seaboard . . . but always near a golf course.

—W.O.

John Mara's Eulogy for Ann T. Mara

The Mara family has been wonderful to me and mine over the years. Wellington Mara, the patriarch, honored me with the sobriquet "Coach" (I coached his "favorite" grandson, Tim McDonnell, in Little League baseball), and "moderated" some interesting dialogue between Mr. Mara and my friend Gov. Mario Cuomo on right-to-life issues. Mr. Mara's luminous life partner was the incomparable Ann Mara. Their son and heir John Mara, now president of the New York Giants, spoke for his mother in a packed St. Patrick's Cathedral in New York City on February 6, 2015.

———————————

Your Eminence Cardinal Dolan, Cardinal Egan, family and friends, thank you for being here to celebrate the life of our mother. Your support and friendship have meant the world to my family, and we are deeply appreciative.

I have to also thank and acknowledge all ten of my brothers and sisters for taking such good care of our mother since our father died more than nine years ago, especially my seven sisters. The care you gave her over the past two weeks was extraordinary, as only daughters can do. She was never alone for one minute. Most nights, two of you stayed all night with her in her hospital room. You held her hands, caressed her forehead, and constantly told her how much you loved her and were grateful for everything she had given us. Our father would have been so proud of you, as I am.

It was fitting that my mother chose Super Bowl Sunday to leave us. As embarrassed and uncomfortable as my father always felt about being the center of attention, that was *not* the case with my mother. When the doctors disconnected her from the ventilator this past Saturday around 10:30 A.M., they predicted she would last for maybe an hour or two. But nobody was going to tell *her* when it was time to go. It was the first time in her life when she was not in a hurry to get somewhere. We should have known she was not going to be yesterday's news. She was going out on Super Bowl Sunday for the whole world to see. It was also fitting that she lasted so long because she kept us all together in the same room for an entire day and night. Her children and grandchildren all in and out of her room, saying our goodbyes. We went from tears to laughter, to telling stories about her and about each other. And then finally to tears again. But we were together, loving and supporting one another the way she would have wanted. It was her final gift to us, yet another lesson in how to be a family.

My mother was very specific about her funeral arrangements. The wake had to be at Campbell's, and the funeral, of course, at St. Ignatius, this church where they met, where they were married, and where so much of our family history is . . . was so special to her. My parents were married here on February 10, 1954. I was born nine months and two-and-a-half weeks later. And yes, I did the math a long time ago!

My mom's Catholic faith was so important to her and shaped so much of her life. You have already heard how she went to Mass every day. She observed the sacraments so closely and expected her children to do the same. Just like my father before he died, I could always count on a phone call from Mom to remind me that it was a Holy Day of Obligation and I better get to Mass. My mother's hospital room over the past two weeks was a place of prayer, constantly visited by priests. I lost count of how many times she was anointed.

Although she followed the teachings of the Church closely, she sometimes played by her own rules. For as long as I can remember she parked in the same spot on the Resurrection Church driveway in Rye. She wasn't supposed to park there, of course, and eventually they put a sign "Thou shalt not park here." Well, that sign might just as well have said, "Reserved for Ann Mara," because she kept parking there right until she was hospitalized. I asked her about it, and she dismissed me by saying, "I've been parking there for years."

My mother had many endearing qualities. She was kind, loving, and compassionate. Patience, however, not so much. She supported many charities. With eleven children, forty-three grandkids, and sixteen great-grandchildren, she attended more baptisms, first communions, graduations, and school plays than anyone I will ever know. She never wanted to disappoint any of us.

She was never afraid to speak her mind, as I am sure many can personally attest. Several years ago we were playing in San Francisco, and before the game I escorted my mother to the owner's box. As I was getting ready to leave (we rarely sat together—for good reason), a security guard approached and said, "Speaker Nancy Pelosi would like to come in and say hello to Mrs. Mara." As fear ran through my entire body, in walks Speaker Pelosi, who goes right up to Mom and says, "Mrs. Mara, welcome to San Francisco." My mother thanked her and said what was really on her mind. "I just want you to know I'm a Republican, and I don't agree with most of your political views." I would tell you the rest of what she said, but I wasn't around to hear it. Frankly, I was too afraid, so I got out of there as fast as I could.

And, of course, she will forever be remembered for the encounter with Terry Bradshaw. It is difficult to put into words the paralyzing fear that ran through me, being on national TV and watching my mother charge the stage, with that determined look in her eyes, knowing there was nothing I could do to stop her. Many people would be embarrassed by the amount of attention she received. But not her. She became an overnight sensation and loved every minute of it. Fans sent her letters, cards, and gifts, including a pair of boxing gloves she proudly displayed in her home.

As many of you know, my mother delighted in telling everyone she was my boss. "You are just an employee, you know, and you can be replaced." She would sometimes heckle me if I was speaking at some event and she didn't particularly like what I was saying, "Don't forget, I'm your boss," she would yell from the audience. It got to the point that she would be asked to sign a football and she would sign, "Ann Mara, John's boss." In fact, maybe the last words she ever spoke to me were when I walked into her hospital room shortly after she was admitted. My sister Susan was with her and asked, "Mom, do you know who this is?" She looked up at me, her eyes barely open, and answered, "John, my employee."

Many people—and institutions—will feel the loss of my mother. Nobody I know attended more charity dinners and events than she did.

She felt it was her obligation to support all of these charities, and she did not want to disappoint anyone. And I'm reminded of Saks Fifth Avenue, which will undoubtedly announce a reduction in earnings in 2015! And there is Rocco, my mother's personal hairstylist, who gave her that Ann Mara trademark look. I think she would walk into Rocco's salon at five feet one inch and walk out at five feet nine inches! Nearly every week during the football season, Mom would call my assistant, Ann, and say, "I need two more tickets—for *Rocco*—please don't tell John." Mom, I knew . . . I knew.

Mom rarely missed a game. The team meant so much, and she lived and died with our successes and failures. I would sometimes try to convince her to stay home from a long road trip or a night game. "I can't," she would say, "the team would notice, and I don't want them to think I have given up on them." The sight of her holding up the Lombardi Trophy from Super Bowl XLVI, broken shoulder and all, with a big smile on her face, will live with us forever.

It was difficult to watch our mom deteriorate so quickly over her last two weeks. She was always so strong and feisty, and I thought she would outlive us all. She had every intention of going to the Super Bowl until that fateful day she slipped on the ice. As troubling as it was to watch her go through that, we tried to take comfort in realizing how fortunate we all were. My daughter, Lauren, kept saying to me, "Dad, do you realize how blessed we all are because of all that your father and mother had given us?"

The eleven of us (and our extended families) are so fortunate. Think about it. We had Ann and Wellington Mara as our parents. How much more blessed could anybody be than to have had the two most loving, caring, and supportive parents anyone could ask for. The ideal role models. Parents who gave us such a large and loving family, who loved us unconditionally, and had such strong faith. No amount of fame or fortune could compare with that.

There is a poem called "Her Journey's Just Begun" (by Rhonda Baker):

Don't think of her as gone away—
Her journey's just begun,

Life holds so many facets—
This earth is only one.
Just think of her as resting
From the sorrow and the tears.
In a place of warmth and comfort
Where there are no days and years.
Think how she must be wishing
That we could know today
How nothing but our sadness
Can really pass away.
And think of her as living
In the hearts of those she touched . . .
For nothing loved is ever lost—
And she was loved so much.

Thank you, Mom, for everything you gave us and taught us. You were the best mother and role model for all of us.

I may not have always shown it, but I was proud to be your employee. And I am even more proud to be your son.

Eulogy for Joseph A. Anastasi, "The Captain"

Captain Joe Anastasi of the New York State Police [Ret.] was assigned to an up-and-coming politician from Queens named Mario Cuomo when he was lieutenant governor of New York state. "Captain Joe" was a good-looking trooper who resembled the singer Vic Damone. We buried him up in Peekskill, whence he came. Church of the Assumption, Peekskill, N.Y., July 8, 2015.

May it please you, Father Higgins, pastor and shepherd of this historic Church of the Assumption, founded in 1859 and still to this day, under your leadership and guidance, a special and influential parish.

This is where Joe was baptized and confirmed, where he went to school. In this neighborhood, on these streets.

I will be mercifully brief. That instruction comes, mind you, not from Father Higgins but from two higher powers: Louise and Joe's sister, Marie!

How wonderful that his friends—past and present—turned out this morning to celebrate Joe Anastasi's life. I see judges (His Honor Jeff Bernbach), firemen, famous international lawyers (Peter Johnson, Esq.), great Westchester developers (Charles Valenti), Tom Mungeer, president ot the Troopers Foundation, and Joe's esteemed colleagues from the New York State Police as he now becomes enshrined in their fabled Long Gray Line after seventy-seven remarkable years.

We are also joined by Joe's beloved wife of thirty-five years—soft-spoken, shy, retiring Louise—and his infinitely wiser big sister, Marie, and her husband, Hick, who were always there for Joe in every season. As they are now as he comes home.

As I've said, I won't intrude for very long on your morning because there is actually very little I can add to your knowledge of the body of his work, or to the canon of his exploits and successes in the Troop or later in the security field or in matters of public safety, or to the world of sport, which he loved.

We're here—all of us—for Joe. And for Louise. And for Marie. And we're here for ourselves, because we need to be.

As a trooper and as a reliable and courageous wheelman for the Fire Department, Joe was a public servant the way the men of our fathers' time imagined them to be.

He was a bright, vivid, colorful guy in every season. And as we pray for Joe and savor his marvelous life, our minds drift back to different times. Times when we were all young. And we can't remember Joe without summoning up warm reminiscences of those who enjoyed his favor.

Preeminent among them, of course, was Mario Cuomo, of sainted memory, who left us on the first day of this year. They literally started together when Mario was lieutenant governor and Joe was Inspector Anastasi, soon to be Lieutenant Anastasi and ultimately to attain the high rank of captain.

I can tell you, because I heard it often from both of them, they were like brothers as they logged thousands of miles in that Troop car up and down the Thruway to Albany, the state capital.

And there was Joe "Willie" Namath and Bill Mathis of the New York Jets. Joe met them and formed a lasting friendship with both gridiron legends when they trained right up the road in Peekskill.

I still can't watch a Jets game without imagining that I see Joe on the sidelines, chatting it up with Mathis or whispering in Namath's ear. (They weren't talking about football, Father!)

In Joe's seventy-seven years he taught us so much, so many lessons—about friendship, about loyalty, about service, about being *in the arena*.

It is altogether appropriate, I think, that we are back here in Peekskill where Joe's attractive persona and his dynamism and generosity are the stuff of legend in this neighborhood and in this city.

From Assumption Grammar he went to Peekskill Military Academy and then the University of Miami. And over the years he also left his mark and made many friends in San Diego and Henderson, Nevada. But it was to *these* streets he always returned as the proud son of a

legendary police detective, Tony Anastasi, and an adoring, hardworking mother, Frances, who are themselves so fondly remembered in this
city on the Hudson.

The past few years, we know, were not so easy for Joe with his many
heart operations. I hate to be biblical about it, but I'm told the doctors
in the hospital out west, seeing his grit and determination to "Keep
Going," as Mario Cuomo instructed us, actually started referring to
Captain Joe as "Lazarus"!

And now the Anastasi family hopes you will join us for an early lunch
at the Piazza Roma right after Mass, where those of much greater articulation than I possess can tell you more intimate, sweeter stories of a
life well lived by a very generous man.

As I mercifully yield, I just want to say one thing to Louise and Marie:

We loved him too. Marvelous character that he was. And he *was* a
character.

Thank you for sharing Joe with us. And thank you for carrying on his
own instruction and example: to live life to the fullest and do the best
you can by those you meet, just like Captain Joe.

—W.O.

Eulogy for the Hon. Salvatore T. Generoso, "The Last Legend"

Sal Generoso was a Townie merchant. And a lot more. He ran the Mannerly Shop in downtown New Rochelle for several decades and served as chairman of the local Republican Party. His son James now runs our highly regarded city court. Saint Joseph's Church was packed over in the west end of the city for my eulogy. June 24, 2015.

May it please you, Father O'Halloran, pastor and shepherd of Saint Joseph's, still to this day a special and influential parish.

I will be mercifully brief. That instruction comes, mind you, not from Father O'Halloran, but from a Higher Power—Lindsay Generoso!

How wonderful that the elders of the town—past and present—turned out this morning to celebrate Sal Generoso's life. I see bank presidents, police commissioners, judges, academics. . . .

So many of standing and stature and high estate in our home heath are here assembled with his friends from the west end of our city, the neighborhood that he never left and to which he always returned from all his postings in public service and his exalted positions in civic affairs and municipal government.

He was a legend, perhaps the last to carry that appellation, and greatly respected at City Hall and in the world of politics. But he was *beloved* on these streets where he lived and loved with Jean, whom he now joins.

I won't intrude for very long on your morning, because there is actually very little I can add to your knowledge of the body of his work over ninety years, or to the canon of his exploits and successes in matters political and charitable.

We're here for Sal. And for Jimmy. And for Lindsay. And we're here for ourselves, because we need to be.

He was a politician the way the men of our fathers' time imagined them to be.

And as we pray for Sal and savor his marvelous life, our minds drift back to different times. Times when we were all young. And we can't remember Sal without summoning up warm reminiscences of those who enjoyed his favor:

Frank Garito, Joseph Raymond Pisani, Rocco Bellantoni Jr. ("Rocky Bal" or "Junior"), Alvin Richard Ruskin (the mayor and judge), state senator Tony Gioffre, Ogden Rogers Reid (a wonderful congressman and First Amendment champion who, incidentally, is ninety years old on this very day), Tommy Faso, Nelson Rockefeller, Dick Daronco of sainted memory (after whom our courthouse in White Plains is named), Carl Vergari, Malcolm Wilson, Lenny Paduano.

The Republican chairman even liked a few *Democrats*: Tim Idoni, and Mayor and Judge Vinny Rippa most certainly enjoyed his blessing and imprimatur.

His influence and benevolence were everywhere apparent. And all around us. I found something in the station's archives I once wrote about Sal, the *political* leader:

> I didn't always support the candidates who enjoyed his favor. But I can't think of any individual ever put forward during his stewardship who was *not* qualified for the position. Indeed, he often bravely stood alone against negative, reactionary elements to try to keep the party moving forward in a progressive, enlightened direction.

That was from 1991, twenty-four years ago. That's what we thought of him then. And that's what we think of him now at the end of an altogether exemplary life.

In Sal's ninety years he taught us so much, so many lessons: about friendship, about loyalty, about service, about being *in the arena*.

I will always be grateful that among his enthusiasms was a struggling radio station in the basement of the Pershing Square Building. But I quickly learned the town was really being run from down the street on North Avenue from a haberdashery, a men's clothing store—called The

Mannerly Shop. (I'm talking here of *real* influence. This was even *before* Dominic Procopio or Jimmy Generoso hit their stride!)

You've read of Sal's charitable work in the public press. His dynamism and generosity are the stuff of legend in this neighborhood and in our city. As I said, they were part of those lessons he taught us.

These are just a few of the many memories I wanted to share. Others, of far more articulation and grace than I possess—like Steve Tenore; devoted Harriet, his caregiver; and, of course, his beloved Lindsay— they can tell you better, more intimate, sweeter stories of a life well lived by a really generous man, as Father O'Halloran called him. The last few years, we know, were not easy for Sal. The great Dr. Pisano, I'm told, actually gave Sal the biblical name "Lazarus" as he fought his battles against infirmity in recent years.

And so as I mercifully yield, I just want to say one thing to the son and heir in whom Sal was so well pleased:

Jimmy, we loved him too.

Thank you for sharing Sal with us. And thank you for carrying on his instruction and example, which really was to all of us: to assist, to assist, to assist.

Caryl Donnelly Plunkett: An Appreciation

Caryl Plunkett was a bright star in the neighborhood—that is, West-chester, Litchfield, and Hilton Head Island. Her husband, William Plunkett Jr., was a mentor to former New York Governor George E. Pataki. And, like Ann Mara, she presided over a passel of children and grandchildren. I still receive requests for these remarks from September 11, 2015.

———————

I once received by U.S. postal service a letter from a William Plunkett, Esquire. As I usually do not open letters from practitioners or solicitors of the law, I did not rush to retrieve said missive from Plunkett, Esquire. "You'd better open it," said Cindy Hall Gallagher, amanuensis without whom my life would resemble a seven-car pileup.

Mercifully lacking any of the usual bad news conveyed by your typical lawyer's letter, inside the envelope was instead a very nice note from this Mr. Plunkett, Esquire complimenting us on a tribute we had broadcast over the radio airwaves. He called it a "eulogy."

Now as I do not like to do eulogies or even think about them, I quickly deposited the compliment in our very thin "nice letters" file, which in bulk, depth, and volume pales in comparison to our "not so nice letters" file, which after some fifty years is fairly bursting out of the file cabinets.

When he wrote his gracious note some years ago, I'm quite certain William Plunkett never anticipated that I would one day take pen in clumsy hand and sit over a pad with lines across it onto which I must now write words and later speak them into a radio microphone about the passing of one Caryl Donnelly Plunkett, who died earlier this week after some seventy years as the matriarch of a powerful and influential New York and Connecticut family. She was his wife, this Caryl Donnelly Plunkett.

All of this must be told on this particular radio station because Caryl and her husband, Bill Plunkett, barrister, lived together for many years in Tarrytown, in Sleepy Hollow country, where they were neighbors of the Rockefellers and patrons of Historic Hudson Valley and Phelps Hospital.

Our colleagues in the public press and especially our friends at "Page Six" always refer to Caryl Donnelly's surviving husband, Bill, as a "power broker" and "kingmaker." On the morning after the worst night of his life, when Mario Cuomo lost to George Pataki, Mario Cuomo was on the phone: "Do you know the Plunketts?"

Plunkett, you see, took a law firm once called Plunkett & Jaffe and built it into a legal and lobbying powerhouse with lines into the Executive Mansion and the New York state legislature in Albany. This occurred when one of his junior partners, George Elmer Pataki, became governor and another partner—the estimable John Cahill—started thinking about running for attorney general. It was also at this time that a daughter of Caryl Donnelly and William Plunkett advised governors of Connecticut on judgeships. One of the firm's clients owns a big chunk of Ground Zero real estate, and their children are making their mark in law enforcement, real estate, and high finance. And a son-in-law who practically ran the Justice Department in Washington, D.C., may one day be a governor of Connecticut. But this is about Caryl Donnelly Plunkett who left us just before the current, sad September weekend.

And if you lay the appellation "power broker" on her famous husband, you have to also acknowledge that Miss Donnelly was very much the power behind the kingmaker. They especially know of her standing and stature up in the Litchfield Hills of Connecticut, where this amazing Caryl Plunkett was identified as one of the fabled Donnelly girls of Bantam Lake, where the Plunketts summered each year before life turned sad and difficult as she battled the cancer that took her a few days ago.

A man named Jim Lamond walked out of Murphy's Pharmacy this morning with his fancy dog and the daily newspapers with tears in his eyes after being told of Caryl Donnelly's passing. And Mark Murphy, an affable, gregarious Townie who, with his sister Marla, runs this old-fashioned family drugstore, went suddenly silent. And Father Robert

Tucker, the charismatic, most colorful pastor of Saint Anthony's, the Roman Catholic church in the little town, was on the phone, requesting prayers for Mrs. Plunkett. In his most direct manner and completely typical way, the priest Tucker even directed an Irish broadcaster to weigh in with prayers.

"Look, I'm desperate. I've even got to ask *you*, O'Shaughnessy. This was a special person. Start praying." As Tucker is a "three Hail Marys for a homicide" priest and known in these parts as "The *God*-Father," I quickly mumbled some prayers, for all the good they will need to do.

Timothy Dolan, the cardinal archbishop of New York, will have more to say and do it much more artfully and gracefully than I am able at 1:30 Monday in the Cathedral of Saint Patrick in New York City.

It is almost certain he will speak of her influence "behind the scenes." I know, I know preachers have spoken for years about women who were "powers behind the throne." They struggle to find a way to exalt and memorialize a woman's standing and stature in marriages and in our midst. They do this with many words and elegant paragraphs. I don't struggle with this refrain. I have just two words to sum up the category: Caryl Plunkett.

A woman of my acquaintance from another robust, well-founded Westchester family once expressed to Caryl Donnelly bewilderment that the Plunkett offspring got along in such harmonious fashion and without any rivalry among their siblings. As the woman was of a tribe of brawlers and intriguers given to constant internecine warfare among brother and sisters, she was quite astonished by the reply: "Well, *we* just wouldn't *allow* them *not* to get along," using the royal "we," which meant, "*I* just wouldn't permit it." Miss Donnelly was pretty clear about things.

Cardinal Dolan will also speak to those assembled of the clout of the Plunkett family and of Caryl's personal dynamism, energy, effervescence, and radiance. "Radiant" is a good word for her. And radiant she was in every season. And Timothy Dolan will then look out in the great cathedral on Fifth Avenue and acknowledge her generosity of purse *and* spirit and recite how much she did for Catholic charities, hospitals, religious orders, and high schools in his care and keeping. This will take some time.

One can expect His Eminence will also speak of Caryl Plunkett's bravery and courage as she checked in and out of hospitals all up and down the east coast as she refused to yield to the killer that pursued her for almost ten years. At the Memorial Sloan Kettering Cancer Center where they daily battle this lethal stuff, she was known as "Lazarus." The priest Dolan, who slipped into Sloan Kettering earlier this week without staff and miter or the trappings of his high Roman office to whisper prayers into Caryl Plunkett's ear, won't have to work too hard to get this particular dame into heaven.

And then, on Tuesday, up in Litchfield, the aforementioned old country priest Robert Tucker will say final prayers over the woman as she is laid to rest.

She was a high-church lady who presided over a family that rivaled the Maras and Rooneys, and she was a Dame of Malta, the fabled international Roman Catholic charitable organization.

Mrs. Plunkett had homes in Westchester, Connecticut, the Carolinas, and Florida, and she was known on the Sleepy Hollow fairway overlooking the Hudson River. Such disparate types as Paul Tagliabue and Senator Lamar Alexander would take a Plunkett call in every season.

Caryl Donnelly Plunkett leaves two daughters, four sons, a whole posse of grandchildren. And that one husband.

The goodness and marvelous spirit of the woman will inspire them—and all of us—for a good long time.

I hate eulogies.

—W.O.

An Appreciation of Jim Delmonico
(1920–2012)

*Jim Delmonico was a dear man from upstate New York who
presided during the early days of the Broadcasters Foundation
of America, when it was known as the Broadcast Pioneers.
William O'Shaughnessy, January 23, 2012.*

———————

Jim Delmonico was a dear man and a respected member of our profession all the days of his life.

His remarkable leadership qualities were recognized early on when he ran some of the most important stations in our Empire State—the legendary "heritage" stations WGY and WRGB-TV—and when the elders of a tired, fading institution known as The Broadcast Pioneers made him our national president.

Legend has it that when Delmonico took over, the Pioneers organization was $19,000 in the red. He built it up by improving the quality of the board and by broadening and extending its outreach.

With an agreeable personality and a strong sense of mission, Delmonico got things on a firm, solid footing before turning the reins over to the midwestern broadcasting legend Ward L. Quaal, who succeeded him as chairman.

Ward Quaal brought on board a former ABC Radio Network chief and Rush Limbaugh discoverer Ed McLaughlin, and current Foundation chairman Phil Lombardo when the organization, which was founded by H. V. Kaltenborn, grew to be known as the Broadcasters Foundation of America. Today, as a respected and important national charity, the Foundation provides a safety net for down-and-out broadcasters who have fallen on hard times.

But it all started with the affable, gregarious upstater who steadied the ship during lean times. As a contemporary of C. Glover Delaney, E. R.

"Curly" Vadebonceur, Rick Buckley, Tony Malara, Martin Stone, Marty Beck, Les Arries, Harry Thayer, Paul Sidney, Bob Peebles, John Van Buren Sullivan, Leavitt Pope, Wally Schwartz, Phil Spencer, and Sy Goldman, he came out of the time when giants walked the land in our profession. And he outlived all of them. Jim was ninety-one when he left us.

Jim Delmonico became a broadcast legend in our state over the years and was a member of our Hall of Fame. But he did some of the best work of his life with his dynamic charitable efforts in our high councils in New York City.

He really was a pioneer.

—W.O.

The Incomparable "Joe Slick":
An Appreciation

A WVOX and WVIP commentary broadcast
February 27, 2012.

———————————

He was known far and wide as "Joe Slick." Somewhere, however, there exists a birth certificate from ninety-five years ago that tells you his real, given name was Joseph L. Vitulli Sr. By any name, he was the last colorful character of the west end of our town known as "the Fourth Ward."

Rocco Bellantoni Jr. ("Rocky Bal") is gone. So too are John Fosina, Tony and Sal Tocci, and Nick Donofrio. Only "Goombah Sal" Generoso and Dominic Procopio linger to remind us of New Rochelle as it was in the 1960s and '70s. This was all before the Portuguese and Mexicans came and, one is hard pressed not to observe, made it richer and better and even more vibrant.

The *Journal News* newspaper, which is still called the *Standard Star* in these parts, slapped the sidewalk this soft winter morning with a paid obit of Joe Slick's passing and tales of his exploits in the Great War. The rakish picture of Vitulli in the local daily newspaper is as classic as he was. Neither Mario Puzo nor Scorsese for all his Academy Awards could conjure up a better visage of this marvelous man.

His activities in places of death and heroism like the Battle of the Bulge earned him considerable honors given by a grateful nation: the Silver Star, a Bronze Star, the Purple Heart . . . just to name a few . . . and the French Croix De Guerre, which was bestowed for a little bit of business he did on the Germans at Verdun.

Joe Slick came back to New Rochelle and sixty-five years ago married a girl named Rose. Together they raised four kids, as a result of which Joe Slick presided over an extended family that includes doctors, lawyers, and realtors. Many of them now live in tony places like Bedford and Kent, New York.

Among his passions were the Republican Party, which he served as a major fundraiser. In this endeavor he had quite a bit of success as he caused many to reach into their pockets thinking all the while, "Who the hell can turn down Joe Slick?" Not many did.

His enthusiasms included Anthony B. Gioffre, the great old state senator from Port Chester, and Frank Joseph Garito, who looked like Dean Martin, came off a bulldozer, and made it all the way to the mayor's office in City Hall. He also had a wife named Rose.

Vitulli also loved Alvin Richard Ruskin, who was a dynamic liberal Republican mayor until Nelson Rockefeller made him a Supreme Court justice of the state of New York and put him into black robes sitting up in White Plains under an "In God We Trust" sign where he presided over nasty, contentious divorces driven by vitriol and vengeance.

He also put his blessing and imprimatur on Nelson Aldrich Rockefeller and Judge Richard Daronco of sainted memory. And I once heard him say many nice things about the father of Andrew Mark Cuomo. He also favored Malcolm Wilson, Joseph Raymond Pisani, Mario Biaggi, and Anthony J. Colavita Sr.

One day many years ago, I received a call at this local broadcasting station from "Commissioner" Vitulli. I was "encouraged" to address him by that appellation because of his work on the Waterfront Commission, which he took most seriously.

"I have a breaking news story for you, Mr. O'! My liquor store was just robbed. Could you please send somebody over to interview me. It just happened." As our reporters of the day were otherwise engaged, I decided to handle this "assignment" myself.

So, tape recorder and microphone at the ready, I mounted the steps of the Edgewood Liquor store over in that fabled area known as the Fourth Ward. As I put the microphone right up in front of his face, here is what Mr. Vitulli proceeded to say for the record. (We still have the tape somewhere in our archives.)

Well, you see Mr. O'Shaughnessy . . . I was standing right here behind the cash register when this perpetrator entered upon these particular premises . . . pointed a damn gun right at me and said: "Give me yo' money, Bro." (Right away you knew it was not an Irish kid!) I said: No problem. Then the perpetrator told me to take off my belt and drop my trou! That, Mr. O'Shaughnessy, was too much! I then proceeded to reach under the cash register and took out my own gun . . . the one I have for just such an unfortunate eventuality. Actually, I'm not supposed to have one, but the police commissioner kind of looks the other way, if ya know what I mean. When he saw my gun was bigger than his . . . that young "bro'" took off down the street. And because he had sneakers, those high top ones, I couldn't catch the S.O.B.

No attempt was ever again made to disrupt business at Edgewood Liquors since that day so long ago. It's a small story, one of many I know about Vitulli. But I do also recall a very clear message from the police chief asking that we not run that "damn tape" anymore.

As I think of Joe Vitulli, my mind drifts back to a New Rochelle that has all but disappeared. Most of the political business and ordinary commerce of the town in those days was done downtown at P. J. O'Neill's saloon on Lawton Street or at dear, departed Schrafft's on Main Street, where you could get a whole carafe with your whiskey sour or martini, or up in the north end at Cesario's bar, which later was run by Lou Saparito and his wife, Loretta, before they split.

But Joe Vitulli stayed pretty much to the streets of the west end where, with his brothers, he also owned a small oil company. None of their Edgewood Fuel trucks were ever bothered either.

I miss the old men of that neighborhood. The greatest compliment they could conjure up was to tell you someone "stays." This word was usually accompanied by the movement of a flat right hand, palm down, thrusting toward you, chest high. "He stays." Eloquence. Message delivered. You need an explanation?

Joe Slick had the back of this particular radio station. And this town, in every season. And for that he "stays."

They will pray for "Slick" at St. Joseph's Church in the neighborhood at 11 A.M. on Tuesday, February 28, another winter day on which our city instantly and irrevocably becomes lesser.

And fewer. And duller too.

—W.O.

John Scully: A Sailor and a Gentleman

September 15, 2012.

———————

It comes as no great surprise that John Watson Scully was a high church Anglican. I mean everyone at the American Yacht Club on Milton Point in Rye, New York, a most famous sailing club in the County of Westchester, when informed of the passing of this John Watson Scully, did not have to hesitate before pronouncing him a gentleman. It was not even necessary to read his obit in the *Times* and Gannett daily newspapers last week.

A gentleman he was. And that is now required to be carved by the stonemason and placed with him in the Anglican cemetery in Vero Beach, Florida, where he will go for all time to come.

John Scully was eighty-two. He came at you before hedge funds with their derivatives and well before yuppies invaded Westchester and his beloved Rye with their tasteless, out-of-scale McMansions which lumber oppressively behind wrought-iron electronic gates. As you look at Scully's life and way of operating, you also have to put him before iPads, cell phones, reality shows, Lady Gaga and the Kardashians, or politicians who talk of "crowd-sourced placemaking."

He was of the American Yacht Club of George Gibbons, Jim and Leggy Mertz, Ogden Rogers Reid, Rudy Schaefer, Walter Nelson Thayer, T. Garrison Morfit a.k.a Garry Moore, the Isdales, the Jamisons, Tinker Myles, George Bryant, the Mundingers, the Hibberds, Ann and Dr. Richard A.R. Fraser, Dick Pinkham, Wally Elton, Bill Ketcham, Rick Clark, Drake Sparkman, the Weins, Diana and Peter Gonzalez, and Judge Charles Brieant, whose name is on a federal courthouse in White Plains where once he sat in a black robe under an "In God We Trust" sign.

John Scully was, in every season, a cultured man who existed in our frantic "Between You and I" society where most flunk the interrogatory: "I'm fine . . ." and never mind the . . . "And how are you?"

Scully sold pension plans and retirement funds, which enabled him to shuttle between Vero Beach and his beloved Rye. And for the past sixteen years he battled the prostate cancer inside him with the relentless assistance and loving care of one Howard Scher of Sloan Kettering, which is the New York Yankees of cancer hospitals. And so Fleet Captain John Scully made it to his eighty-second year in order to bring his boat up from Florida for the very last time this summer.

A young John Watson Scully made his biggest score when he married a spectacular woman of great lineage in these parts named Suzanne Marechal, and together they raised a whole posse of little Scullys who were given impressive middle names of substance, carriage, and nobility that conveyed an aura of considerable heritage, provenance, and breeding.

These offspring of John and Sue Scully are now parents of yet another issue of little Scullys, each, of course, endowed with a formidable middle name, just as John Scully would have it.

He will be remembered next Monday, the 17th day of September, 2012, at precisely 1500 hours at the American Yacht Club where once he served as Fleet Captain. I don't think he ever made commodore or won any major sailing races. Thus no silver trophies adorned his mantle. Nor is his name carved in any wooden plaques above the yacht club bar. But few of the accomplished, actual winning yachtsmen there commemorated will be as fondly remembered by the sailing fraternity. Or by the people who pour the drinks, cook the food, wait on tables, and haul the boats at this iconic sailing place hard by Long Island Sound in our home heath.

It is also to be here noted that one John Scully associated his name with the application of the very first Jewish member of said legendary sailing organization. As memory serves, that particular individual was also proposed by a Richard M. Clark and has since preceded the Fleet Captain to a place where such designations, categories, and labels are no longer remarked upon. But Scully and Clark put up the first one.

The great philosophers, social commentators, and many of our statesmen speak often of a "coarsening of the culture." And Scully's departure surely gives them another chapter for their sad assumptions and bleak prognostications as they preserve the story of our times and lack of civility and manners.

But for eighty-two years there was a John Watson Scully.

—W.O.

A Tribute to "Colonel" Marty Rochelle

He knew the judges . . . . November 24, 2014.

———————

One of Westchester's most beguiling and colorful characters passed away over the weekend. Marty Rochelle left after seventy-eight years, and with his departure everything becomes duller, flatter, and less vibrant. The fun is taken right out of our humdrum, everyday existence here in the county.

He was out of Damon Runyon and Ring Lardner. Jimmy Cannon could also have written of him. To no one's surprise at all, "Colonel" Marty Rochelle, as he was known far and wide, came out of Yonkers, where true love conquers. I mean, he had to come from Yonkers. For you could never place him in Bedford or Rye or Pound Ridge for very long. And certainly never in Bronxville or Waccabuc.

At about 325 pounds, he was (no pun intended) *the* biggest bail bondsman on the entire eastern seaboard, which line of work brought Mr. Martin Rochelle into almost constant daily contact with criminals, crooks, and deadbeats just as soon as they were about to become "defendants." As the preeminent bail bondsman of his time, he did that for a living. He would bail them out. He would spring them. And in this endeavor, it helps if you know the judge.

Marty Rochelle *knew* the judge. *Every* judge. He also knew every law clerk, every secretary, every marshal who keeps order in every courtroom. The range and weight and depth of his Rolodex matched his ample girth.

And if you can believe it, he was a real, actual colonel in the Air National Guard (New York state really does have one), which is where the "Colonel" comes from. That's what our fellows at WVOX called him when he arrived, always several hours early, for his weekly radio program bearing two dozen Dunkin' Donuts—one dozen for himself, of course, and one for the studio engineers and staff. I know of this because—full disclosure—he always brought a butternut-covered donut *for me.* "Don't touch *that* one, it's for the boss!"

He would also come accompanied by the very latest behind-the-scenes political gossip, often mixed with rip-roaring tales of wrongdoing and skullduggery in just about every city hall in Westchester. He just knew of all these things.

But his specialty was the courthouse. And he knew every judge who ever donned a black robe to go up and sit in a courtroom under the "In God We Trust" sign. And there wasn't one jurist or magistrate who wouldn't come off the bench to take his call.

Recent years were not kind to this marvelous old character, who was in and out of many hospitals as he fought what Mario Cuomo and the great Jesuit philosopher Teilhard de Chardin call "the diminishments" we all suffer. It's a great word: diminishments. And yet despite those diminishments and infirmities, Marty Rochelle kept going. First with a cane. Then with a walker. He did his last few radio shows from a hospital room, propped up on a pillow, raging into the phone as usual. And I do seem to recall him calling out His Honor, the Chief Judge of the entire Court of Appeals, the highest judicial tribunal in our state, for some "error"—real or imagined—that didn't sit quite right with Colonel Marty. He could do this and get away with it because all the judges loved him.

And if they didn't actually "love" him, well, they knew that when they next had to submit to the nasty and altogether unpleasant rigors of reelection to keep their standing and high estate in the judicial system, the man who knows everybody would be right there to tell any and all who would listen just exactly what great judges he knew them to be.

Marty was also capable of delivering an extra line or two on the ballot come election day, which prowess also no doubt commended him to the favorable judgment of a most grateful magistrate or two over the years.

If you doubt the man had real clout and influence, I will leave you only with an actual scene from just last year at the White Plains Hospital, when one evening during visiting hours Marty's hospital room was filling up like a political convention. And according to several who were there assembled by his bedside on that very night, the head nurse burst in at one point and said, "You're only supposed to have

PART V. EULOGIES: THE LAST WORD

two visitors at any one time! There are ten people in the room; we can't have this!"

Colonel Marty looked up from his bed and said, very politely, "Ma'am, six of them are supreme court justices, two are county criminal court judges, and the other two are family court judges. Who do you want me to throw out?" The nurse retreated, and the "party" went on.

There will be many Marty Rochelle stories told at the Riverside Chapel in Mount Vernon on Wednesday and in every courthouse south of Albany. But the little "gathering" up in White Plains that night is my favorite.

The man had his "enthusiasms" during the seventy-eight years he pumped life and energy into his profession and Westchester itself. Among them were the casinos of Las Vegas, Atlantic City, Foxwoods, and the Bahamas, for he was a gamblin' man. But his favorite venue for games of chance of an evening was always Tim Rooney's Empire City right in Marty's home heath at Yonkers Raceway. "They're honest people, the Rooneys. You really have a shot there!"

Marty also loved Jeanine Pirro, and he never gave up on "Judge Jeanine" even after she dumped everyone in the old neighborhood and went on to Fox News to display her famous lips and toned arms, among her other attributes.

He also would not permit anyone to do injury to this community radio station or its inhabitants—even divorce lawyers. *Especially* divorce lawyers. And as my mind drifts back through the hundreds of conversations we had, usually over those damn fattening donuts, I can't recall his ever saying anything really mean or hurtful about any of those who inhabit the judicial world that he knew so well or the body politic.

We can't really afford to lose too many Marty Rochelle types around here.

Because, like I said, only dullness will prevail, everywhere.

I just hope Saint Peter likes Dunkin' Donuts.

But don't give him the butternut, Marty. Save that one for me.

—*W.O.*

[419]

Tribute to Ambassador Edward Noonan Ney

January 10, 2014.

———————

Edward Noonan Ney was the classiest ad man who ever climbed into a gray flannel suit.

He was the Fred Astaire of Madison Avenue and the most charming guy in the room.

He was the very antithesis of the *Mad Men* we see on television. Ed classed up the profession. He was chairman emeritus of Young and Rubicam and also U.S. Ambassador to Canada.

And my friend.

Tribute to Bob Grant

January 2, 2014.

We are all his students. And anyone who approaches a microphone on this sad day owes him.

He could be infuriating, caustic, and, often, outrageous. But he was an American original and a great champion and exemplar of free speech.

I know he's been lethal on the subject of the extraordinary individual I most admire in public life in America. And he once called me a "Stooge for Mario Cuomo." And that's when he was in a really *good* mood!

But Bob Grant was a gifted performer and a provocative social commentator. As the dean of talk show hosts, he was without peer in our profession.

I always thought the guy was like Lazarus in the Bible: You couldn't kill him!

—*W.O.*

"The Amazin'" Bill Mazer

October 24, 2013.

I first heard him on the radio in Buffalo, New York. And it was a privilege to amplify Bill Mazer's brilliant voice on WVOX for the last eight years of his long, "amazin'" broadcasting career.

Bill was knowledgeable about damn near everything. He could talk with eloquence and erudition on many subjects, from Joe DiMaggio and Henry Aaron to Sinatra, Toots Shor, Mario Cuomo, and our Westchester neighbor of sainted memory, Robert Merrill.

He had a way with words unequaled in our tribe and a voice of great resonance and timbre. And the state of Israel had no greater champion on the radio.

Jimmy Cannon called sports "the toys of a nation."

Mazer ennobled those toys.

—W.O.

Tribute to Governor Brendan Byrne

January 5, 2018.

Brendan Byrne, the former New Jersey governor who died this week at the age of ninety-three, was a delightful man with a marvelous sense of humor.

Each year he and our late New York Governor Hugh Leo Carey would give "The Governor's Report" at a boozy black-tie dinner at "21" arranged each year by The Skeeters, a group of sportsmen and pols.

Carey, a great raconteur, was always hilarious when it came time for the after-dinner repartee, but Governor Byrne could more than hold his own.

One year he told the crowd, "New Jersey, as you know, is very political. One year, long ago, we had a severe drought in the Garden State, and I got a call from the mayor of Woodbridge:

"Gov, you're doling out emergency water supplies, and I hear you're selling it to Paramus for a lot less than you're charging me!"

Byrne replied: "Relax, Carmine, I'm *diluting* his water."

"Oh, thank God, Gov. I knew you'd take care of me!"

At another Skeeters dinner, Byrne said he wanted to be buried in Hudson County: "So I can remain politically active!"

Another time: "I must be doing something right. A guy just waved at me with all five fingers!"

He was a marvelous man.

—W.O.

Page Morton Black, the "Chock full o'Nuts" Lady

W.O. remarks at Frank E. Campbell Chapel,
New York City, September 12, 2013.

———————————

Thank you, Robin Elliott, for gathering so many influential friends of an extraordinary woman.

Many of you knew her as a great philanthropist of national renown for her leadership of the Parkinson's Disease Foundation, which was founded by her beloved husband, William Black. Others remember Page as a gifted artist who could play and sing achingly romantic songs like an angel.

She lived for decades in a grand house in what the *Times* referred to as an "enclave" off the coast of New Rochelle. It was aptly named Premium Point.

It was from this redoubt that she conducted her own personal philanthropy and raised millions for national charitable causes.

And among her enthusiasms, I'm proud to recall, was WVOX, New Rochelle's community radio station. She would dispatch missives, suggestions (actually "directives") to me and mine, often about the great issues of the day. She backed the more enlightened politicians (when such existed) and she put her money where her heart was.

Like, for instance, during the broadcast celebrating the fiftieth anniversary of the natal day of WVOX. It was a very big day for us. And as I went into the studio, settled in behind the mike, and strapped on my earphones, I inquired of the engineer who the "sponsors" were. There was just one: Page Morton Black.

When I later asked why she was so nice to our little 500-watt flame-thrower of a radio station, Page said, "Many years ago the *Herald Tribune* gave me a flattering review. That was long before I met William

"Dad, stop it. I know you love me."

Towering figures in the public arena. Ambassador Ogden Rodgers Reid, former U.S. congressman, publisher of the *New York Herald Tribune* and First Amendment defender, discusses the great issues of the day with the incomparable Governor Mario M. Cuomo. I can't tell you how much I admire these two magnificent public servants.

Judge Andy O'Rourke, the popular former Westchester County executive, and Andy Spano, another former county executive, with Judge Jeanine, during her days on the Westchester bench, before she became a TV star.

Just nice people. The affable Jonathan Bush, brother and uncle of presidents; Ambassador Ogden Rodgers Reid; and Ruby Dee and Ossie Davis.

Former New York Governor Hugh L. Carey. I always admired his stand against the death penalty. He was a great governor and a New York treasure.

"Speak right into the microphone, Governor." Our Westchester neighbor, the dynamic Nelson A. Rockefeller, at the lectern, and, seated, Frederic B. Powers, chairman of the Westchester Republican Party, who was a great booster of our radio station in the early days.

Working the phones in my office. Mario Cuomo on the phone at the station before one of our interviews.

I bless the day we met. *From left:* the author; Matilda Raffa Cuomo, still First Lady of New York; and the fifty-second governor of New York, Mario M. Cuomo.

The author with John F. Kennedy Jr. (*left*), and Andrew Cuomo. They were plotting strategy to outflank the NIMBYs ("not in my backyard") in the heart of the eastern establishment and gain approval for local housing for the homeless.

Two icons of the Republic. A lion of the Senate, Jacob K. Javits, father of the War Powers Act (*left*), and my distinguished former father-in-law, Walter Nelson Thayer, a pillar of the eastern Republican establishment and president of the dearly departed *Herald Tribune* newspaper, who also ran Citizens for Eisenhower. (Richard Nixon once called him the "toughest and brightest son-of-a-bitch in this country.")

White-haired gentlemen! Legendary merchant prince Joe Cicio, whose illustrious career in merchandising and fashion included stints at Lord & Taylor, Macy's, and I. Magnin. His admirers also included Joan Rivers, Slim Keith, and Nancy Kissinger.

Julian Niccolini, the dazzlingly colorful dining room impresario and co-owner of the new Four Seasons restaurant on East 49th Street, spinning a tall tale before the WVOX microphone.

24/7! This spectacular middle-of-the-night photo was taken by Kevin Scott Elliot of two radio stations that never sleep.

The next generation. Amelia Jane Nulty, my granddaughter.

Still First Lady of New York, Matilda Raffa (Mrs. Mario) Cuomo and mother of Governor Andrew Cuomo.

In good hands. *Left to right*: New Rochelle Police Commissioner Patrick Carroll, the powerful Westchester "Don" Dominic Procopio, and my son Matthew Thayer O'Shaughnessy.

One lucky guy! *From left:* Flynn Nulty, Tucker Nulty, Kate O'Shaughnessy Nulty, the author, and Amelia Nulty, Ann Thayer, and David O'Shaughnessy.

Cool jacket, Grandpa! The author with grandson Flynn Nulty.

The affable and popular Andrew P. O'Rourke, former Westchester County executive who ran against Mario Cuomo for governor but helped Andrew Cuomo build housing for the homeless in Westchester.

Brilliant radio star Michael Scott Shannon, Maria Cuomo Cole, and designer-philanthropist Kenneth Cole.

Maria Cuomo Cole and designer-philanthropist Kenneth Cole.

The author in the early years.

GEORGE BUSH

Dear Bill,
Thanks for your book "More Rifts, Rants, and Raves".
I know I will enjoy the book. I know I have already savored both your warm message and your signature up front.
Life is good, Bill. Barbara ~ I are very happy having just survived 2 parachute jumps and a gala' 80ᵗʰ birthday celebration
Thanks so very much for both the book and your kind inscription —

P.S. Give my best to Mario Cuomo. I was touched by what he said about me on p 451

Most Sincerely
GB

WALKER'S POINT, POST OFFICE BOX 492, KENNEBUNKPORT, MAINE 04046
PHONE (207) 967-5800 / FAX (207) 967-0255

President George H.W. Bush never wrote his own biography. But he did publish a lovely collection of correspondence, *All the Best: My Life in Letters*. He sent many missives over the years—usually handwritten—to world leaders and others . . . including some to the author.

I treasure this note . . . and his friendship.

MARIO M. CUOMO
787 SEVENTH AVENUE
NEW YORK, NEW YORK 10019-6099
MMC

10/31/02

Bill,
There are some really great speeches in this collection.
And there is a speech I gave in 1984 that still accurately summarizes most of what I've been trying to say together for all these years. There aren't enough ways to say "thank you"
Mario

Martin F. Beck

Marty Beck was a respected and beloved fellow broadcaster in the New York area. This note expressing his regret at succumbing to the wave of Consolidation is telling. "Stuart" was his son, a U.S. ambassador.

10/18/03

BILL —

YOUR IRTS REMARKS WERE PURE BILL O'!

YOU'VE REMINDED ME AGAIN THAT I SHOULD NEVER HAD SOLD OUT TO THE MONSTERS AND INSTEAD HAD REMAINED POOR AND DEPRIVED.

KEEP IT UP, WILLIE — YOU'RE NON PAREIL.

STUART REMINDS ME HE MET YOU AT THE IRTS SEMINAR — AND WAS AS IMPRESSED!

HOPE YOU AND YOUR LADY ARE WELL

BEST,

Marty

Scholarly Commissioner Michael Copps was one of the brightest ever to serve on the FCC.

Michael J. Copps
Commissioner

Federal Communications Commission
Washington, D.C.

January 28, 2003

Mr. William O'Shaughnessy
Editor Director
Whitney Radio
One Broadcast Forum
New Rochelle, NY 10801

Dear Bill:

Thanks for your nice note of January 17. I thoroughly enjoyed listening to your eloquent statement at Columbia. If you just wouldn't be so bashful about saying what you really think!

Keep it up.

Warm regards,

Michael J. Copps

Mr. O + Mrs. N.C-O →
MERRY X-MAS AND THE
BEST WISHES FOR A GREAT
1994. I OFTEN *Peace on Earth* LOOK
BACK WITH GREAT FONDNESS
ON MY EXPERIENCE AT
WVOX / WRTN → THANKS
Your Friend,
Billy Bush

William "Billy" Bush never forgot where he started. This is one of many from a graceful young man. I'm rooting for a comeback.

MARIO CUOMO

Bill,   5/18/99

I read your presentation to Chris Colley.

It made me a little sad and even more guilt-ridden. You should be getting the awards and not just giving them. I've told you that before, and if you have any real respect for me, you'll begin believing it.

Keep writing. Keep speaking. Keep urging. Keep trying... the game is lost only when we stop.

Mario

This letter still resonates in my already long life. I shared it with my children and grandchildren.

Bill Clark is one of the most graceful and respected broadcasters in the nation. I treasure this letter, written when I left the NAB board in Washington . . . as usual with some remarks about free speech and the First Amendment.

shamrock BROADCASTING, inc.

Bill Clark
President, Radio Division

February 2, 1988

Mr. William O'Shaughnessy
WRTN/WVOX
One Broadcast Forum
New Rochelle, NY 10801

Dear Bill:

It may have been Shakespeare who wrote the words, "nothing so became his life as the leaving of it". It could be said about you that nothing so became your service to the NAB Board and through it to the profession we love as the leaving of it. I'm not referring to the fact of your leaving the board - quite the contrary. I'm speaking of your final, most eloquent, most elegant and certainly most brief address to the members. When the chips were down and the moment called for exactly the right combination of wisdom, counsel and humor, Bill O'Shaughnessy responded. And you were beautiful.

Thank you for all you have done for all of us, Bill. Thank you especially for those words to Eddie that perfectly said what needed to be said and heard. I'm not sure what we are going to do without you.

Your friend,

BC/Mc

1026 Battery Street
San Francisco
California 94111
(415) 788-5225

This book's cover illustration is by Robert Risko, celebrated caricaturist famous for his *Vanity Fair* and *New Yorker* celebrity portraits of notables in film, television, politics, and culture. And now with his vivid cover portrait of William O'Shaughnessy, Risko presents his witty and winsome take on an iconic broadcaster.

Ever upward. Engineers working on the WVOX radio tower in Westchester.

"Hmm . . . I'll have to think about that, O'Shaughnessy." The ever-thoughtful governor pondering the author's counsel.

Black. And you married the boss's daughter . . . didn't you marry Jock Whitney's daughter?"

I replied: "Not exactly, Mrs. Black. I married a wonderful girl named Ann Thayer, whose father, Walter Nelson Thayer, was president of the *Trib* . . ."

And she said: "Well, it was a great review anyway!"

Truth to tell, I'm not sure that speaks well of the station. But it does speak well of those qualities of loyalty, generosity, and friendship—as well as a long memory—which others have identified.

Her iconic red dress has also been mentioned. The first time I saw it was many years ago when a big limo pulled up to the station and a lady in red, *the* Lady in Red, got out and handed an envelope to our receptionist. "Here, Mr. O'Shaughnessy will know what to do with this . . ." It was a political contribution for a young aspiring Italian fellow—actually a failed baseball player with too many vowels in his name—Mario Cuomo.

I hope I don't do damage to her reputation by telling this story in front of all you Republicans. I'm a "Rockefeller-Catsimatidis Republican" myself. And it's nice to see John and Margo here. As well as Len Berman. And the legendary Sy Presten . . . great New Yorkers, as Page was.

And so we are here today to remember a Lady who touched so many for ninety-seven years. I will mercifully yield now with just one more small story about Page.

Several of her friends here assembled and all the obits mentioned the "Chock full o'Nuts" song. And every year on her birthday, we would play that damn jingle. And one year, after we had played it three times . . . she called up and asked if we had played it yet. The engineer said "Yes, Ma'am . . . three times." She said, "Well, I missed it this year . . . do you think you could indulge an old dame and play it just one more time?"

You can be sure we did.

So people will remember Page and that damn jingle for years to come.

And you'll remember her great philanthropy.

Have it as you will . . . I'll remember her as a neighbor.

Please don't hold it against her then . . . that she had a soft spot for failed baseball players . . . or Irish broadcasters.

She was a hell of a dame.

And her lovely music lingers. In every key. A generous, engaged, and thoughtful neighbor. In every chord. In every tempo.

And, as I said, in the neighborhood.

—W.O.

Brother Driscoll of Iona, Great Educator and More

September 22, 2010.

He died on one of those bright, perfectly brilliant September afternoons.

Gary Stern, the gifted religion editor of Gannett's *Journal News* newspaper, will write a graceful and elegant tribute to Brother John G. Driscoll tomorrow morning. And the sad folks at Iona College, where once he sat in the president's office with the heavy, old-fashioned brocade draperies and charmed fat cats and Castle Irish trustees, are even now cranking out papers filled with encomiums that bear testimony to Jack Driscoll's academic achievements and civic contributions.

Driscoll was not exactly what you might call a "brick and mortar" kind of guy. His legacy is not to be found in buildings you can reach out and touch or in gymnasiums, libraries, or science centers.

Brother Driscoll was a soulful, struggling, churning searcher all the days of his life. You would see him on his knees by the cold light of early dawn in the chapel on that campus, where you would also notice his fellow Christian Brothers—most of them tuned in to a higher power with a look of great sureness and absolute certainty on their saintly countenances.

And then you would see Driscoll in a black sweater up in the front row close to the altar. This particular Brother was always fidgeting and questioning and seeking and wondering right smack in front of the God he wrote and spoke so beautifully and lovingly about in every season.

Some of the hard-nosed trustees edged him aside two decades ago in favor of a tough, no-nonsense, edgy guy named Liguori (who promptly threw up that grotesque and forbidding Great Wall of Iona separating the college from the community). And then there followed a disappointing era during which Iona withdrew from said community. But, boy, did they ever set brick upon brick in a remarkable wave of uncontrolled expansion that showed little regard for the neighborhood.

I hate to tell you this because Driscoll, to his last breath, always loved Iona. And so will I. It's not that I have anything against "President" Liguori, who was once described to me as "a guy who studied Latin, but was missing the day they taught *quid pro quo*." Perfect!

Brother Driscoll then took his searching and questioning and goodness to Israel—which, of course, meant Jerusalem. Here he worked among the Jews, Arabs, and Christians for almost twenty years, during which his work was underwritten and supported by a wonderful man named Jack Rudin (who is himself ailing these days). Mr. Rudin, a Jew, the patriarch of the Rudin family real estate empire, never lost faith in Christian Brother Driscoll's essential goodness and bright, fine mind.

Driscoll once gave the most stunning description of Christmas I've ever heard:

> "You have sinned," said those who know the Law. "And you must pay."
>
> "It is time," said He who knows no time. "I am here. And you have been redeemed."

As I sit here in front of this microphone and try to imagine a world without Jack Driscoll, my mind drifts back to another morning in that chapel many, many years ago. Only this time I was doing the scrambling on *my* knees.

When I came out into the cold, wintry morning after offering up all sorts of prayers, petitions, and "deals" to that relentlessly forgiving carpenter's son, I noticed a "smile sign" on my steering wheel. From Driscoll.

I mention this because I knew—from Brother Jerry McCarthy and a few of the professors at Iona—that Driscoll was dying from an ugly, relentless form of cancer. And for the last several days, as I drove past the house where he lay, I wondered if somebody had remembered to put a smile sticker on his damn steering wheel before he went and took his goodness out of the world.

They'll say a lot of nice things about the man in the next few days and on Monday at Holy Family Church.

I can only attempt to tell you he was possessed of a monumental soul. Make that a *sweet* soul.

Rush Limbaugh III Tribute to Ed McLaughlin

My friend Edward F. McLaughlin was a legendary broadcast executive who presided over the ABC Radio Network during the days of the legendary Paul Harvey. And he discovered a fellow named Rush Limbaugh in Sacramento, California. But McLaughlin did some of his best work as chairman and later chairman emeritus of our Broadcasters Foundation of America, a remarkable organization which serves as a "foul-weather" friend and safety net for broadcasters who have fallen on hard times. Rush Limbaugh delivered these remarks on January 22, 2018, and put his money where his heart was with a very substantial donation in Ed's name.

————————

When we come back I want to indulge you, if you please, for some personal time. Because a man died last Thursday without whom this program would not exist and very likely conservative media as you know it today would not be what it is. His name was Ed McLaughlin, and Ed McLaughlin was the founder and the chairman of the Excellence in Broadcasting Network. Name of his company was actually PAM Media. Those are the initials of his beloved wife, Patricia. And it's been a long time since I've explained how this program began and how it made it. And there are many new people listening here who have not heard the story. For those of you who have, that's why I'm asking and begging your indulgence. And I must pay tribute to Ed.

Ed didn't intend any of this; don't misunderstand. He was one of us. But we were running a business. We were not engaging in politics when we started this program. But it wouldn't have happened without him, in more ways than one, and I would just like to tell you a little bit about him and how all this happened so that you who haven't heard can understand it, because to me, of course, it's a big thing. I was driving to play golf Saturday morning—in fact, played golf with Ron DeSantis, congressman, Florida, who is running for governor.

And this happens to me sometimes: I'm on the way up there. And I was—the route to this particular place takes you through shall we say less-than-affluent places. And each time I notice it, but today, Saturday, it really hit me how damn lucky I am and have been. I try to never, ever forget it. And I'm not being falsely humble here by saying "lucky." But the way we end up, all of us, as individuals, the way we end up in life, yeah, we have a lot to say about it ourselves, we do. But there's this sometimes intangible characteristic of good fortune or luck. Some people can't deal with it. They have success fear. Think it's undeserved, and therefore they sabotage their own success. Fortunately, I've never been that, but I understand it. If you look around and think, "My gosh, I'm not special. I don't deserve any of this." So you begin to undermine yourself. There are people that do that. I've never had that problem, but I also am constantly aware of just how lucky I have been. And that's why I never forget it.

And any time it's relevant, I give as much thanks to all of you in this audience as I can, because you are as much responsible for what happens here, the success of it, as anybody. Without you, it's an academic exercise and doesn't exist. But without Ed McLaughlin, it doesn't, either. So we'll take a brief time-out and come back. It won't take long, but I want to tell you a little bit about Ed and what it took to not just start this, but stick with it after we kicked it off.

Now, folks, Ed McLaughlin was a giant in the radio business for years. He was born in 1926. He ran one of the biggest and most important radio stations in the country, KGO in San Francisco. He built it into a decades-long era of leadership, being number one, top of the heap, staffed it with the best on-air talent that he could find. His career took him to the presidency of the ABC Radio Networks. There were many networks, and he was the head honcho of all of them. He was on the same executive suite as Roone Arledge on the TV side and any of the other noted and famous ABC executives. He was at ABC in its heyday, in its period of greatest accomplishment and achievement. He was right there making that a reality on the radio side for ABC. And then

[431]

ABC decided to merge with Capital Cities Communications. This merge resulted in many of the ABC executives' being, quote-unquote, "retired" so that Capital City executives could resume their positions 'cause Cap Cities was the purchasing entity. Ed McLaughlin, as his retirement package, was given whatever compensation, but more importantly, he was given two hours of satellite time from 12:00 noon to 2:00 Eastern.

Now, he was already syndicating Dr. Dean Edell. But he was given two additional hours as part of his retirement package, and he was free to do with those two hours whatever he wanted to do. The time he assumed control of those two hours, they were running a show—I forget who the host was, but they were on fifty-six radio stations, and the largest one was probably in a market not even in the top fifty. Daytime syndication of talk radio programming had simply not succeeded. That's why Ed took one of the biggest risks anybody ever took in radio.

I'm gonna stick with the CliffsNotes version of things here because to give you every fascinating-to-me detail about the beginning of this program, I could spend an hour, if not more. You have a giant in the radio business, Ed McLaughlin, who retires from TV, is given two hours of satellite time to fill as he wishes. That was part of his retirement package. He could have picked anybody. He could have chosen to do anything with these two hours. He could have played music. He could have done, you know, polka, he could have done Chinese opera. But he believed in the power of the spoken-word radio opinion; he believed it could win. Now, I mentioned the fact that I've been very lucky in life.

There are any number of people Ed McLaughlin could have chosen, any number of people Ed McLaughlin could have invested in. But I, fortunately, met some people along the way, after moving to Sacramento, that Ed McLaughlin knew and trusted implicitly. And when he was looking, unbeknownst to me—I don't know any of this is going on, but it's happening—unbeknownst to me, my name is on the list of people he should look into. So Ed came out to Sacramento and parked himself in for a week or two and listened. I didn't know anything about it. And then one day I got a phone call and was asked if I had any interest in meeting a man who was interested in syndicating me nationally. Now, there were a lot of hoops to jump through here. I had a contractual situation at KFBK in Sacramento that was another piece of good luck. It had an out for which this offer qualified, and that out was if I got a job offer from a station in a top-ten market, I could exit the contract to take it. But the key to that was—folks, it was much different then than it is now. There were no daytime syndicated radio programs that had any success, and by that I mean there were no big-time national advertisers. Nobody was investing money in programs like this. Back then in 1988 CNN was the only cable network. It was strictly the three broadcast networks and the newspapers, and that was it. And talk radio was a success at night. You had people doing business talk and personal relationship talk, had Larry King overnight, but it was all nighttime, but nothing in the daytime. Those that had been tried in the daytime hadn't succeeded. Everybody said, "Great effort, way to go," but it just was determined that radio was local, local, local. They didn't care, audiences in Sacramento, for example, didn't care what's going on in Oshkosh and vice versa. But Ed always believed—the Phil Donahue example. You think people who watch Donahue care where he is doing that show? You think it matters to people? And the answer was no.

The theory was that a good show could overcome all of these so-called restrictions, all these so-called formulas that were sacred, that couldn't be violated. So it took six months to put together the deal, and I was scared out of my gourd because I didn't think I had secured enough money to live distraction-free in New York. I needed to be distraction-free to be able to put everything I had into the program. But it was what it was. And then it began. And it took off. It took off faster and bigger than anybody had expected. It took off and exploded the way you dream about. We started with fifty-six radio stations, but we did not have a station in New York City. And without that, national advertisers are not even going to [*unintelligible*] listen to your sales call. You have to be on here in New York if you're going to have national advertisers. The first thing to do, then, was to find a way to be able to tell advertisers that their commercials would be heard in New York. And that's where Ed's experience and power and talent came in. Ed McLaughlin arranged for me to do a two-hour local show only in New York City, for which the compensation was advertising availabilities. We got five minutes in each of those two hours to sell, and we could add that two-hour show in New York to all the other fifty-six stations, and we could tell advertisers that we were on the air in New York. Then came the problem with actual advertising sales. We were using an agency to do this that just put us in the roster with all the other shows out there, nothing special about it, nothing to it. There was no attention being paid. Ed had to change that.

When this started expanding, Ed McLaughlin adapted to it; it became bigger than he ever thought it was gonna be. Remember, Ed is looking at this as—this was his retirement package. And it was exploding way beyond what anybody had staffed for, what anybody had planned for, and every step of the way, everything that was needed to keep it going, Ed McLaughlin provided. And every moment of controversy, when advertisers were complaining—Ed McLaughlin never wavered a single time. He never asked me to tone it down, to change things, to do whatever to accommodate this complaint or that complaint. Whenever we were on the verge of getting a major affiliate such as in Los Angeles or Detroit or Chicago, one of the greatest examples of Ed McLaughlin's brilliance and toughness and commitment—I'm not gonna mention the stations here because they're still up and running, there are people running them now, but that will be a distraction.

Big stations in Los Angeles called us and offered to pay us for the show, but it was not to air it. It's called shelving it. I'd never heard of this. I said, what is the point of paying for it and not airing it? Ed was tempted 'cause of the money, but—why?—what?—he says that's how they keep it out of the market, Rush. But I mean, why are they afraid of it? We're just now into our second or third—doesn't matter. They can see what's happening. They're willing to pay us for it and never air it. And he adamantly refused. It would have been easy to take the money, and we would have never been on the air in Los Angeles. Well, not never, but it would have been years. Another similar example was, I tell you, Pittsburgh; a station in Pittsburgh wanted to carry us on weekends. And at the time, you know, I'm eager to get this show on as many places as you can, and Ed said, you realize it will never leave weekends if you let them put this there. You realize they don't want it either. They want it on weekends to bury it, to make sure it doesn't end up anywhere else, but they don't want to carry it themselves. 'Cause look, folks, back then, syndicated radio in the daytime was just considered the worst mistake that could be made in a local market because of the local, local, local business, and nobody'd ever heard of me. And the show was controversial. Who wanted this? I don't know that this program would have made it if it hadn't been for the backbone of Ed McLaughlin and his knowledge of the business that helped me to avoid making some mistakes, business mistakes, from which then I learned immensely. So we held out. We did not sell the show to the guy in Los Angeles. We turned Pittsburgh down on weekends.

Then there were the controversies over, you know, "mean-spirited, extremist, not enough compassion." And it boggled Ed's mind. Now, this—some of this was new. I mean, Ed had dealt with controversy— San Francisco, KGO—but of a different kind. This was controversy generated by a conservative willing to go up against a liberal behemoth in the drive-by media, and their desire to silence and stuff any effective conservative voice they find, which they still do today. And he was perplexed by it. He said to me—he'd known me by this time for three years, two-and-a-half, three years. He came to me one day and said, "You love people. You love people." And it was—that simple little observation that he made helped me unlock a way of dealing with this. I didn't know how to deal with it. Hardly anybody else did, either. And many people today still don't. How do you deal with being defamed and lied about each and every day simply because of your political ideology?

Look. I could go on with all of this. Suffice it to say that after three years we were up to 500 radio stations. Everybody thinks that this program was made during the Clinton administration starting in 1993. We were—we have over 600 stations today. We were at 500 stations before Clinton was elected. That's how fast it grew. And then look what happened. You know, Sean Hannity was my first guest host. And he shortly—he had his own show. He shortly got his own national radio show, and then Ailes hired him at Fox to do *Hannity and Colmes*. My TV show was 1992 to 1996. That would not have happened without Ed's blessing. He could have told me, "No, I own you, you're radio only." But he didn't. He never restricted my ambitions or desires. Promoted them. So then Fox News starts in 1997. Then conservative websites started proliferating, and conservative blogs. Now there's an entire, huge, important, crucially relevant alternative media, conservative media, whatever you want to call it. And it would not have happened, certainly the way it has happened, if it hadn't been for Ed McLaughlin. You know, people credit me with this, but I couldn't have done any of this if it hadn't been for Ed McLaughlin.

Ed McLaughlin saved AM radio by investing in it and by continuing to believe in it and believing that content was king. But he was also— there aren't a whole lot of people—once you hit fifty, fifty-five, you're pretty set in your ways, think you know how things are done, you know what the young whippersnappers are doing, you know it isn't gonna work, they don't know it yet. But he remained completely adaptable and open about changes that were happening and how to get in front of them and capitalize on them. I could not have had—in fact, I actually think it was because he and his wife were just two individuals who owned the company rather than being a department of the massive corporate entity that allowed all of the freedom, that allowed all the creativity, the experimentation that permitted the risk, that withstood all of the attacks and the assaults, whereas maybe a corporate entity wouldn't have put up with it, too big a distraction. It was a combination of many things. They say luck is where preparation meets opportunity. Certainly. But there's a lot of luck in my meeting people who knew Ed McLaughlin. There's a lot of luck when I met Ed McLaughlin—I didn't realize what national syndication was. I had no idea. I've always told people I dreamed about success all those years, but it's nothing like I ever imagined it to be. So little of it is like I ever imagined it to be. And so I was unprepared for the growth and the evolution and how to maintain it and stay ahead of it. And it was all because of Ed McLaughlin and his commitment and his patience, his adaptability, his good nature.

The night we got Omaha, he called me, he was just as excited as he could be. It had taken us two months to get Omaha. And just at that time, things were happening when that happened, it was a reason to throw a party. Every one of those deals we closed at "21." That's what Ed did; the restaurant in New York, the 21 Club, that's where everything meaningful Ed McLaughlin ever did, was where the contract was signed. So was this one.

So that's the CliffsNotes version of how all this started and how it survived, many early attempts to prevent this from ever happening, and it's all because of Ed McLaughlin, who brought his own impeccable relationships and reputation to this business long before it started. But he was the guy, he was the broadcast guru and the radio greatness that I needed around me to learn from and be inspired by and protected by on a day-to-day basis, and he passed away in his late eighties on Thursday here in Palm Beach. Have to take a break. Back after this.

. .. By August 1st of 2008, the twentieth anniversary of this program, Ed McLaughlin had sold his founding portion of the program and had moved into semi-retirement. He spent a lot of time working on a foundation that helped people in radio who had fallen on hard times— broadcasting, in fact, had fallen on hard times—through the National Radio Broadcast, The Paley Center, I think it was, in New York. At any rate, he called. He was one of the people on the twentieth-anniversary program who phoned in congratulations, and I wanted you to be able to hear him, hear what he said to me on that day.

> Hey, Rush, this is Ed McLaughlin. Congratulations. It's been an incredible twenty years, and you deserve what you're getting today, all of these wonderful accolades. Actually, Rush, our anniversary goes back a little earlier by a few months, when we first met in San Francisco to talk about syndicating your program. You'll recall how important it was for us to acquire a New York affiliate, and fortunately for us, the program director of WABC recognized your talent, and we were off and running. Rush, I think we were all a little surprised by the effect you had on the radio audience. Always enjoyed listening to young listeners recalling how they discovered you and how much they learned from your show. Rush, you always said you'd keep doing radio as long as it was fun. So may it be fun for many years to come. My best.

That's Ed McLaughlin, who passed away on Thursday. That was August 1st of 2008. That comment about fortunately for us a program director at WABC recognized my talent, that's not quite true. Ed

McLaughlin had to tell them how good I was, and because of his experience running the ABC Radio Networks, he had a little leverage, and
he pulled it off.

*Rush Hudson Limbaugh III is a dear and generous individual as well
as a great communicator and broadcaster. Maybe the best we've ever
had. I'll have more to say about El Rushbo later in this book.*

PART VI
THE OBLIGATORY MARIO M. CUOMO SECTION IN EVERY BILL O'SHAUGHNESSY BOOK

"The Morning After": A Stunningly Candid Interview with Governor Andrew M. Cuomo

I once told a reporter for the New Republic: *"It's not easy being Mario Cuomo's son"* . . . *especially when an important newspaper, the* Boston Globe, *calls your father "the great philosopher-statesman of the American nation." Andrew Mark Cuomo has built a reputation as a hard-working and dynamic public servant who gets things done. But I've always thought there was a lot more to our current governor that he is often reluctant to reveal. In his best moments, the fifty-sixth governor of New York resembles his magnificent father of sainted memory. And in this revealing interview Andrew shows some of those Cuomo grace notes. November 7, 2018. See our endorsement of Governor Cuomo in Part VIII, "Airborne Endorsements."*

WILLIAM O'SHAUGHNESSY: Good morning and thank you again, ladies and gentlemen. While we're in your care and keeping . . . this is "The Morning After" on Westchester's legendary community station. We're glad you could join us. Phil Reisman and Matt Richter will be coming up soon. But now . . . now we welcome a very special guest to our microphone. Let's switch to Albany for that special guest . . . the governor of New York . . . Andrew Mark Cuomo. Andrew, congratulations!

GOVERNOR CUOMO: Thank you very much, Bill. Thank you. I appreciate it.

W.O.: Let me ask you something . . . why the hell are you working on this, the day after? Don't you take a day off?

A.C.: I like that "morning after" theory . . . it brings all kinds of things to mind. There are no days off in this job. There are no nights off. It's a totally different cadence than it was years ago. There's so many things that can happen at any given moment. You're always on edge. People don't give you a day off . . . they want to get their money's worth! They pay me a lot of money. [laughter]

W.O.: Andrew . . . Governor Cuomo . . . we endorsed you in a proud moment. In that endorsement we said you are your father's son. What would your father—of sainted memory—say on this, the morning after you ran the table. You really had a big night last night. What would your Dad—Mario Cuomo—say?

A.C.: Well, first Bill, just so it's easy, you can call me Andrew because I know you too long and too well. There will only be one Governor Cuomo for you, I know. And I respect that. My father would obviously be happy. You know, I missed him last night. I was with him on election night four years ago. And he was backstage and then we brought him onstage. I lifted his arm when the crowd was cheering, and I could feel the strength come back to his hand while I was holding up his arm. He turned to me and said . . . "What a crowd! What a crowd!" He was so excited to be there. And we then lost him on my inaugural day so I was very much thinking of him last night. He would have been very proud. Well, first, I really believe there was always part of him that just discounted the first name on the ballot and thought people were voting for the last name: Cuomo. So the victory was somewhat his.

But it was a great night not just electorally for me . . . I did better than I had done in my previous election, which was normally unheard of. But we also won the Senate, which is very important, and I worked very hard to make that happen, which allows me to get all sorts of things done that we haven't done before.

We had three congressional seats, which helped the Democrats get the Congress back, which I think is very important that we have a restraint on this president.

So . . . my victory was great. The Senate was great. The Congress was great. The turnout was great and we had worked for it all year. When I started the campaign in the beginning of the primary, Bill, it was all focused on the general election and communicating to Democrats all across the state and getting them energized—and independents and Republicans also. I don't really believe, and if you look at my numbers these were issues that affected New Yorkers generally, and values that affected New Yorkers generally. But I missed him tremendously last night.

And then we lost Drew Zambelli . . . which I am still in shock over, and you knew Drew. He was there from day one with my father and he was there literally the day before he passed . . . working on my campaign. So that also weighed heavily on the evening.

w.o.: Drew Zambelli was one of your senior counselors and one of your father's counselors. He lived up the road apiece in Eastchester. Governor, the geniuses in your office suggested some questions for me to ask you. I'm not going to use any of them. But will you trust me to ask you some dumb questions?

a.c.: Dumb questions . . . smart questions . . . whatever you feel like, Brother Bill.

w.o.: First of all, you received almost 3.4 million votes. I'm told that's more than any New York governor in history! This morning when you woke up—first of all, did you talk to your mother today? What did she say about last night?

a.c.: She was ecstatic! She was out there campaigning for me, Bill. You could not slow her down. She was doing events. She was doing senior citizen centers. And she loved it! She was excited. They were all there last night. My family was there. They were all there. She really enjoyed it.

w.o.: Governor, you won last night better than you won four years ago against Astorino. I think you picked up something like 59 percent. Were you ever a little worried about this?

a.c.: First, let's step back. The 3.4 million votes is the largest number of votes, I'm told, that a governor has ever gotten. That gives me two advantages. One is limited in scope, but very important. It allows me to say that I beat the record of your other hero Nelson Rockefeller, who held the record. It's a limited scope because it's only really relevant to you and me. [laughter]

w.o.: I still call myself a Rockefeller Republican!

a.c.: I know . . . and I have a little joy that I got more votes than your guy Rocky! But it also helps practically in governing. When you have a larger mandate—electorally—the other elected officials know you've literally come into government with a stronger hand. And having a larger victory helps you governmentally. I believe that. It's determinative. It does. I worked very hard for many candidates all across the state.

W.O.: You were pushing for the congressional seats and the Senate. And somebody told us you put $5 million into that.

A.C.: Yes . . . and even more. Because as I said, the whole effort from day one was geared toward last night. In other words, even during my primary election where normally you just focus on certain areas that are relevant in a primary. . . . From day one I started with a plan geared toward a statewide effort last night. What I was saying in the primary was the same thing I said in the general. Normally you say one message in the primary and one message in the general. I don't believe that's how it works . . . especially now. So I had the same message from day one.

W.O.: What message was that?

A.C.: First, talking about what we've done for the state. I don't care Democrat or Republican. I think this is a new age of politics. I think it's less theoretical. It's less abstract. People want to hear less "I think . . . or I believe . . . or I would like to see." They want to know what you've gotten done and what you will do and how you will do it because the credibility of politicians is down. So they want proof positive and I could go to people across this state . . . look them in the eye and say no governor has done what we have accomplished. Period!

W.O.: You worked especially hard, I'm reminded, for the Senate Democrats. Is our Westchester neighbor Andrea Stewart-Cousins finally—and I am crazy about that woman . . . she presented me with an award and she was so graceful I want her to do my eulogy— is she finally going to take over the damn Senate?

A.C.: She is going to be the Senate leader of New York. And I think she is magnificently suited for it. She represents Westchester County. She gets the complexity of the politics of New York. This is not a one-dimensional state politically. You have New York City politics. You have upstate . . . you have Long Island. And these are all different. Members of the legislature all too often only know their district. And we have districts in this state that are as conservative as any in the nation and others as liberal as any in the nation. But Senator Andrea Stewart-Cousins gets the complexity and the dimensions of the entire state. And I think her conference—the senators who won since they're now in the majority—they now represent the politics of the entire state. And she has what they call conference members—senators—with very conservative districts and very liberal districts. That balance is not easy. And Democrats have won the Senate before only to lose it the next term.

w.o.: Can you and Andrea hold it this time?

A.C.: I think so . . . I think so. Because I think she understands the complexity . . . and these elections were very intense and she was all over the state. And she feels it. And her conference is a sophisticated conference. The people who won . . . these were very smart candidates. They're sophisticated candidates. So they understand they have to represent their districts. They also understand that the conference has to represent the body politic statewide. They just went through seeing the national electorate pull back Trump which is what I believe they did when they elected a Democratic Congress.

They said this one party is going too far. And we want balance. And we want a check on Trump. And that's why the House flipped because they want restraint. So that pendulum can come back very quickly. And we saw that last night on the national level. And that's in very many ways the way of politics. You see that pendulum go back and forth. So if you want to maintain your position, you have to be very aware of all the dimensions. And I believe Andrea Stewart-Cousins, who I've worked with for years, but I've really worked with on an intimate level during these past few months— she "gets" that. And it is also the way we govern.

You know, Bill, I am a Democrat. But I used the expression from the very beginning that we're Democrats and Republicans—but we're New Yorkers first. And we act that way. I am aggressively "progressive." But I'm also aggressively pro–economic development for this state. And you look at both agendas which in the past were thought to be at odds, right? Well, Republicans want to grow the

[445]

economy . . . Democrats are just interested in social programs.
Well, we have accomplished more on the Democratic side than
you have ever seen. There's no other state that has done more for
the progressive agenda than we have: marriage equality . . . paid
family leave . . . $15 minimum wage, et cetera. And there is no
administration that has been as aggressive on economic
development and on fiscal measures: property tax cap. . . . We have
more jobs in this state today than ever before in the history of the
state of New York. We've cut the unemployment rate in about half.

w.o.: All right, sir, those are things that got you a big win last night. A
lot of people agree with you. Millions and millions of people voted
for Governor Andrew Mark Cuomo. What can they expect—you've
got four more years—what can they expect? The president said he
may "adjust his tone." Are you going to change anything the next
four years? Take as much time as you want on this . . .

a.c.: The basics are working as I just mentioned. We are going to be
the most aggressive state in terms of progressive measures. And the
most intelligent and progressive in terms of economic
development, et cetera. I'll put my economic record against any
Republican and I'll put my progressive record against any
Democrat. That will continue. There have been measures I could
not get done with a Republican Senate. I believe they were short-
sighted. I believe they acted parochially. But there were measures
they just would not do, Bill.

w.o.: You're talking about the Albany Senate?

a.c.: The Albany Senate . . . and I worked so hard for the Democratic
Senate because these are pieces I believe are essential to really
move the state forward. We need ethics reform and there is no
reason not to pass it. Legislative jobs should be full-time positions
with no outside income. We need to close financial loopholes they
call the "LLC Loophole." The woman's right to choose needs to be
protected. I know we disagree on it. You're entitled to your own
religious belief and moral belief and you could speak to your
spouse, significant other, or child and counsel them, however you
want. But I don't believe government has a right to impose its will
on a woman's right to choose.

There's voting reforms . . . it is so hard to vote in this state. It is a joke. I've gone through this with my daughters coming back from registering. Let people vote . . . early voting! Make it easier. Things like the Dream Act which is giving young immigrants more access to higher education. Why wouldn't you want to do that? There's more we can do on gun safety. I understand the Second Amendment and I understand how strong the NRA is . . . and I passed a Safe Act and the NRA took a pound of political flesh from me. But I believe we saved lives. And hunters still hunt and sportsmen still shoot and legal owners still have a gun. It's just the politics of it. They're afraid of the politics of it. That is not enough of a reason to run the risk of school shootings or mass murders the way we've seen them.

There's something called the Red Flag Bill . . . if a teacher or a family member knows a person may be emotionally disturbed, why wouldn't you give them recourse to try to get that person in a place of safety? Issues like that . . .

w.o.: Do you favor that, Governor?

A.C.: Yes . . . yes. And none of these things could get done with a Republican Senate. We can now get them done with a Democratic Senate. And they are significant. They are issues that frankly have bothered me and a lot of other New Yorkers for years. They are issues—but I am in some ways damned by my own success, Bill.

w.o.: How so?

A.C.: Because I've gotten legislation passed that nobody believed could get passed. Marriage equality . . . $15 [minimum wage] . . . these are big initiatives. So then they assume if you could pass that, you could pass anything! So anything that doesn't pass they blame me because they think I just didn't make enough of an effort. Which is wrong and absurd . . . but a reality.

So these are issues that have been around for years that I couldn't get done because being a governor is not a dictatorship . . . as I know all too well. You have to get that legislature to pass it.

w.o.: Excuse me . . . I'm laughing because some of your opponents think you're a pretty tough guy.

A.C.: I am a tough guy. Look . . . forget what I am genuinely, for real . . . because they don't even know who I am.

W.O.: I would agree with that!

A.C.: But as governor, you better be a tough guy or a tough gal. Otherwise you better get out of the job. There is nothing easy here. Nothing! When the phone rings in the middle of the night and they say they think they found a bomb in a subway, you better be tough. When you have to negotiate with two houses of the legislature and get them to a place where neither of them wants to be to close a budget . . . you better be tough. When you have a federal government that would put your state out of business with the SALT provision that would make our taxes higher than any other state . . . you better be tough! I don't want a governor or a person protecting my family and my safety who is not capable of being tough.

So yes, if you have to be tough . . . you have to be tough! You have to be tough to do the job well. "He's a tough person" . . . they don't even know who I am. They have no idea, but that's OK! In my role I think there is no doubt you have to have that capacity of strength. Otherwise you just can't do it. Not today. Not with the power and the forces against us. And the threats that are against us. This is a dangerous world.

W.O.: Governor Andrew Mark . . . I have accused you on the radio of knowing the levers and the minutiae of governance and government better than anyone in this country. Better than anyone. Better even than your father—of sainted memory. But you confuse people because you made a speech at a Jewish synagogue last week that was magnificently soaring. Your father could not have done better. Biden could not have done better. Why don't you show that more often? I mean—you're a tough guy, I'll give you that. But why don't you show that grace and those powers of articulation. You're getting to sound more and more like someone I've mentioned too many times in this interview . . . your father. But why don't you show that more often?

A.C.: First, I love the love that you have for my father. And he loved you. And you two had a really beautiful, special relationship for many, many years. In the good days and in the bad days . . . and talking to each other so many times. I wish I had a nickel for every conversation I overheard and the hours you both just spent talking on the phone. He valued your advice. And he loved your poetry. And he loved your sense of spirit and your art form. And you relished his. Now the Interfaith speech . . . the speech at the synagogue after the Pittsburgh massacre . . . is a speech I spent a lot of time on because I thought it was a profound moment for this state. . . .

w.o.: It was beautiful. There was magic in the air. Question . . . why don't you do that more? Why don't you show that side more?

a.c.: I think there's no doubt it's an important part of being governor. I think, Bill, that there is less of an appreciation of or an appetite for the rhetoric and for that asset today than there was when my father was governor. I think today's world and my job description [are] in many ways different than my father's. This is a more intense, more practical time. I think one of the problems that the Democratic Party has had is . . . I'm telling you . . . people have no patience for "This is what I think" . . . "This is what I believe" . . . "Here is my philosophy" and "Here's my beautiful use of language" . . . "Let me provoke you and motivate you". . . .

w.o.: And inspire you. . . .

a.c.: They want delivery. They want actuality. My daughters look at that device and they order something and it comes here tomorrow morning. They have no patience for anything else. They're reading tweets. They are not reading long newspaper articles anymore. I think that is part of it. It is also something my father relished and had the luxury, by the way, of spending a tremendous amount of time on—those speeches. Nobody writes a speech for me. I have people who help me. Nobody wrote a speech for my father—he had people who helped him. But that doesn't happen. When I tell you . . . I must have spent fifteen hours on the speech after the Pittsburgh synagogue massacre. That's not an exaggeration.

w.o.: It was beautiful . . . as I said, magic in the air. Governor, on this same subject and we've taxed our friendship by keeping you too long yet again.

On this morning after you had a big night. A big win—even more than your counselors had predicted. And surprise, surprise . . . on the morning after, they're talking about your running for president.

Who beats Donald Trump? The "doer" . . . the "results guy" that you are very proud of being, the "tough guy" . . . or the one who lifts us up and who inspires? What kind of Democrat would you send up against Donald John Trump?

A.C.: I think you offer a false choice, Brother Bill. You have to be both. You have to be both today. I do believe it's a more complex equation than during my father's time. You loved Nelson Rockefeller, Bill, and you loved his charisma and his charm. You loved my father's poetry. This is a much more demanding public than ever before. You need the inspiration and the articulation of a higher sense of purpose. If you are a national voice or a state voice . . . people want to hear the aspirational—I think that's very important. I think it was very important after the Pittsburgh synagogue, after Kentucky in this moment of division. I think President Trump is exactly wrong in his tone. I don't think he's trying to lift up. I think he's trying to pull down. So I think that is important. But that is not enough. They have to believe you will act surely and be able to produce because the problems are real. They are not theoretical problems anymore. "I can't pay a tuition bill. That is a very real problem for me . . ." they say.

W.O.: What do you mean?

A.C.: You know the old expression "You're not going to talk your way out of this"? . . . People's problems today are very real and practical. They don't want to hear just words. They want to hear the direction—the words—but they want to know there is actually a proof of product and delivery. And that's what I'm trying to balance. I'm trying to do both.

My father would say that in basketball you have to go to your left and your right. The great players could make a move either way. Now the body politic wants all of the above. It wants or needs motivation . . . the inspiration. But they also need to see a proof of concept so you have credibility and they want to see a difference in their life. "Help me today. Please! I need help today. Let me see it. Let me feel it." Take the city of Buffalo . . . fifty years of economic decline. Fifty years of politicians' saying I feel your pain, I feel your pain. I'm going to help. I have a plan. Fifty years and nothing changes. You go to Buffalo today, there's a totally different energy.

There's progress on the numbers. Build the airport. Fix the roads. Fix the train. Deliver and actually help me! I also want you to be a motivational, inspirational leader. But you need to do both. And that's why these positions are more complicated and harder than they have been in the past.

Democrats have issues. Yes . . . people are not just buying the rhetoric anymore. And by the way, the brand loyalty is down. Twenty years ago you were a Democrat because your parents were Democrats and you were in a Democratic neighborhood and you couldn't think about voting for anybody but a Democrat. Or you couldn't think about voting about anyone but a Republican! No . . . people are much less about the labels now. And they're going to vote the reality as they see it today.

I haven't gone through the election numbers from last night, but there are a lot of independents and Republicans and Republican women.

W.O.: Governor, forgive me . . . but why do I think I don't believe you? . . . I'm sure you know those election numbers like nobody else. [laughter]

A.C.: Well . . . I'm not as young as I used to be. Sleep is important and it was a late night last night by the time I finished. And the numbers don't really come in in detail. But we did well in areas I hadn't done well in before because I know people are less ingrained in their parochial political label and they will move and change their mind depending on the facts and they'll move from Democrat to Republican, et cetera. . . . much easier than they have in the past. So I try to do both aspects.

My father loved the articulation and he loved the advocacy. And he was brilliant at it. He didn't do it easily. But he loved doing it.

I have the same office in the Albany mansion that we actually built for him. I remember when we got to Albany, my mother was still home in Queens because the kids were in Queens. So just my father and I were in Albany for about the first year. And we move into this mansion—you've been there many times—it's not really a mansion, it's a great old house. But there are people around all the time. There would be tours and he would joke that you were afraid you would walk out in your boxer shorts and walk into a tour of the mansion. [laughter]

And he said he wanted one office built for him. Just twelve by twelve . . . a small space . . . where I can just put my books and I can lock the door and make sure nobody is going to walk in on me. And we built him this little office that I now use. But Bill, he could be in there for days working on a speech. I mean you wouldn't see him. He was like a monk transcribing ancient tablets and he loved it. I wish I had the luxury of being able to close the door for forty-eight hours. The job is just day to day more demanding all the time. . . .

w.o.: Andrew . . . with all due respect . . . hear me. Hear me. You can produce stuff as beautiful and as lovely and as moving as Mario. Now you heard it from me. I don't care if you do it in that little office or in Chappaqua, but you can do it.

Can I just beg one more minute? I want to ask you about Mayor Bill de Blasio. He used to work for you. That's where I met him, working for you. First of all he put up Cynthia Nixon to run against you. You engineered a crushing defeat. And last night in the general election you did even better. Can you and de Blasio ever become pals, buddies, best friends?

a.c.: You know, the relationship between a mayor and a governor is complicated. It institutionally is complicated. And everyone believes they know my relationship with the mayor the way my opponents think they know me. I've known the mayor for thirty years. I don't think anyone really understands our relationship as well as he does and I do. I consider him a friend. And we've done good work together and we'll do good work again together. We're working together now again on this Amazon project.

There are institutional differences. And there are political differences. I have, as we were just talking about, my idea of what an effective "Democratic progressive" is. He has his idea of what it means to be a Democratic progressive. So it doesn't mean we're not friends. It doesn't mean we can't work on things together. I represent New York City. He represents New York City. And we will have differences. And I don't think that's bad. I think, in some ways, because we know each other so well, we tend to be more outspoken about the differences. And I think this is also dated: Nelson Rockefeller and [John] Lindsay apparently hated each other—they wouldn't be in the same room, I'm told. And this is all folklore. But they didn't talk about it. Everything is more public now. Everything is more open now. And maybe because I know the mayor so well, we're both a little more open talking about it because it's not just an institutional relationship; he's not just the mayor and I'm not just the governor.

You know . . . it's Bill and it's Andrew. Maybe we're just more open and vocal about the differences we've had in the past. But yes, we have different political theories. And we have institutional differences. But we have a tremendous capacity to work together also. And that's what people—I think—don't see. I know him very well and he knows me. And when we are working on something together, it's quite effective. And that's a good thing. And when we have differences, I don't think it's so bad that people don't understand the differences and we talk it through.

W.O.: Governor, I don't know how to thank you for all the time you've given us at our Westchester station today. Is there anything you want to change in this discussion?

A.C.: No, I want to thank you for your support during the campaign . . . even though I'm third on the list to Mario Cuomo and Nelson Rockefeller. [laughter] And who I actually got more votes than in this last election as you know than Nelson Rockefeller . . . so I'll take number three on your list. A lot of great memories with WVOX. Remember the radio shows with John Kennedy Jr.

W.O.: I remember you two stuffing tuna fish sandwiches in your pockets.

A.C.: I was thinking about that the other day when I was driving past New Rochelle. John Kennedy Jr.—we did that call-in when I was starting HELP and he was on the board of HELP . . . so we have a lot of great memories. And you have been a tremendous service, not just to the community, but to the state, Bill. You really have. You've also been a great friend to all the Cuomos. And we love you.

W.O.: Governor, since we're the last community station in the region, one of our proudest boasts is that we're your "hometown radio station." You honor us with your presence on our airwaves and with your friendship. I've done editorials for fifty years and I don't ever think I ever said I love somebody . . . but it was a weak moment when we endorsed you and I blurted it out. We're grateful to you, sir.

Are you going to see your mother soon?

A.C.: Oh, yes . . . in the next couple of days.

W.O.: You going over for those scrambled eggs with potatoes?

A.C.: She loves to make it for me and I love to eat it.

W.O.: I asked her why do you like it so much. She said it's the way I slice the potatoes. [laughter]

A.C.: It all comes down to how you slice the potatoes, Bill.

Remarks of Gov. Andrew M. Cuomo
at Central Synagogue Interfaith Service

Following the deadliest assault on the Jewish community in U.S. history, Governor Andrew M. Cuomo delivered remarks at an interfaith prayer vigil at Central Synagogue in New York City October 30, 2018, with Rabbi Angela Buchdahl and other interfaith leaders including Cardinal Timothy Dolan, Reverend Amy Butler, Pastor Amandus Derr, and Rabbi Chaim Steinmetz. The governor also directed that flags on all state government buildings be flown at half-staff until sunset on Sunday, November 4, in honor of the victims of the shootings at the Tree of Life Synagogue in Pittsburgh and at a supermarket in Jeffersontown, Kentucky.

———————

Good evening to the elected officials, to the clergy, His Eminence, to all our friends who are here, especially on short notice in a sign of solidarity. We thank Rabbi Angela Buchdahl for those powerful comments. The rabbi was born in South Korea, to a Japanese-born Korean Buddhist mother and a father who was an American Ashkenazi Reform Jew. Her father's ancestors emigrated from Romania to the United States.

Rabbi Buchdahl is the first Asian American to be ordained as a cantor and as a rabbi in the world. My friends, that says it all—God bless America. Only in America. She is the first woman and the first Asian American to be the senior rabbi of Central Synagogue in its 175-year history. God bless the state of New York.

But we gather tonight on a somber moment, because this is a dark and frightening time in our nation. Our better angels are being overpowered. The character of America is being perverted. And yes, the power of hate is overtaking the power of love. We mourn and we embrace the families of the eleven victims in Pittsburgh and grieve with them. We mourn and grieve for the African American community in Kentucky. And, we suffer with those who endured the anxiety and threats of mail bombs last week.

But we would not be here tonight if these were isolated incidents. They are not. There is a frightening pattern developing on many levels of American society. Anti-Semitic incidents have increased 57 percent nationwide. Neo-Nazi groups have increased 22 percent in this country. Nativists and white supremacy groups are on the rise. At the demonstration in Charlottesville in August 2017, members of the Ku Klux Klan felt so empowered they didn't even need to wear hoods to hide their faces. The societal fabric of America is stressed and frayed. We gather this evening to pray and to marshal the voices of support and love as an antidote to the forces of division and hate.

Elie Wiesel said, "There may be times when we are powerless to prevent injustice, but there must never be a time when we fail to protest." As governor, I pray with you this evening. But as governor, I also state in the strongest terms that we are a nation of laws and we are a state that is a state of laws, and we have zero tolerance for discrimination or hate in the state of New York. Hate is not protected by our law, not in speech and not in action. Quite the opposite. And our state has the most aggressive hate crimes laws in the county and I announced today that we are doubling both our security efforts and our prevention efforts. You have my word as governor that we will stamp out the evil of discrimination wherever it rears its ugly head. The Jewish community is an important member of the family of New York and we will protect our family—all together, all united.

But I am afraid that enforcing the law, while an essential important step, is not the only step. Being prepared to fight the fire is necessary, but we must work to prevent the fires from starting in the first place. I feel as if we are standing in a field of dry grass with smoldering embers surrounding us. And a strong wind is shifting directions. We must stamp out the embers before they become flames and we must reduce the winds of hate that threaten the fields of peace.

There are those who now will wrap themselves in the flag of America and then go out and do violence in the name of America. But they could not be more wrong or more misguided. They do not begin to understand the character of America, and they disgrace the very flag they carry. Our Founding Fathers would be repulsed by these ignorant acts of violence.

In school, one of the first lessons we learn about America is when we are asked to raise our hands to the Pledge of Allegiance. I pledge allegiance to the flag of the United States of America, indivisible, with liberty and justice for all. Indivisible. With liberty and justice for all. Whatever your religion, whatever your race, whatever your creed, we are indivisible.

Our Founding Fathers anticipated that there would be differences because we were born as a collection across the globe. But we would have, as Jefferson said, "a decent respect" for the opinions of others. One of our Founders' first acts was to pass a law to make the motto on the seal of the United States, "E Pluribus Unum"—out of many, one. It set the tone of unity and commonality. The very same Founders didn't fear immigration; they embraced it. It was the British government's bid to block migration to the colonies that was among one of the reasons cited for the Revolution and the Declaration of Independence.

The tremendous right to practice your religion of freedom was a powerful magnet drawing many to America. The Pilgrims were separatists from the Church of England, the Huguenots settled the Hudson Valley, French Protestants fleeing persecution in Roman Catholic France, English Catholics under George Calvert colonized Maryland, Quakers in Pennsylvania, Jewish people in Rhode Island, seeking the religious freedom established by Roger Williams.

One year into his presidency, George Washington visited a synagogue in Newport, Rhode Island, as the First Amendment was being debated. To his Jewish hosts, Washington wrote a remarkable letter. He reasserted that the government of the United States, quote, "gives no sanction to bigotry, no assistance to persecution, and requires only that the people who live under the protection of the government conduct themselves as good citizens."

Washington quoted the Bible to remind them that, in effect, they had reached their Promised Land: "May the children of the stock of Abraham who dwell in this land continue to merit and enjoy the good will of the other inhabitants—while everyone shall sit in safety under his own vine and fig tree and there shall be none to make him afraid."

That was George Washington. There was no period that tested our unity more than the Civil War. And as the war closed, President Abraham

Lincoln pointed the nation to the future in his second inaugural address, saying: "With malice towards none; with charity for all; with firmness in the right, as God gives us to see the right, let us strive on to finish the work we are in; to bind up the nation's wounds—to achieve and cherish a just, and lasting peace."

Lincoln's invoking God is relevant and instructive. We are one nation under God. It is not just our government that instructs peace and tolerance, but our religious heritage as well. We are gathered in a house of worship today. Christianity teaches us tolerance. Matthew 25 instructs us Catholics to do for the least of our brothers. Judaism speaks to the concept of *tikkun olam*, to reach out and heal the breach, and the concept of *tzedakah* literally charity, but more broadly meaning the concept of social justice. Buddhism, Islam, virtually every religion speaks of tolerance, acceptance, and condemns violence.

The victims in Pittsburgh were engaged in a sacred Jewish naming ceremony of a newborn—a *bris*—celebrating the joy of a new life, only to perish in the face of hate. We will not let them die in vain. We must once again, in Lincoln's words, "bind up the nation's wounds." We must rise above our traditional political divisions. We must refrain from fanning the embers of hate before the flames are out of control. Our American values override our political, partisan differences. Intolerant voices of division must be condemned by all, and not episodically, but consistently. Not only for public consumption but genuinely with personal commitment. Political debate must honor Jefferson's mandate of civil discourse. Our political leaders must heed this wisdom today.

At this time of chaos, confusion, ignorance, and fear, this nation needs a light to follow. And let that light be the torch that is held by the great lady in our harbor. Let New York state once again serve this nation as an example to follow. That is the legacy of this great state: throughout history, a beacon of progressive values. We are home to 19 million people from every nation on the globe—New York state is the laboratory of the American experiment in democracy. We are not threatened by diversity; we celebrate diversity. Generations of immigrants stepped off ships and planes onto our shores. This state has thrived because we have no tolerance for discrimination. Not in our laws, and not in our spirit. We are a people of differences, but we have forged community through chords of commonality. This state exemplifies the best of the American spirit.

The rabbi asks us what we can do. Let us commit ourselves this evening to a constructive course of action. Let New Yorkers exemplify what it means to be a true American patriot. Let New York show this nation what the flag actually means. Let us lead forward in the way of darkness. Let us lead as a government, as a community, and let us lead as individual citizens. Let us lead this nation at this time of confusion by the power of our example. There is no place for hate in our state, and New York lives by the credo that the most powerful four-letter word is still "love." Thank you and God bless you.

Mario Cuomo: A Dream

———————

In my memoir *Mario Cuomo: Remembrances of a Remarkable Man*, which was so splendidly and lovingly put together by Fordham, the Jesuit university press in the city of New York and distributed by our own Whitney Media Publishing Group, we tried to focus on the *spiritual* component that always accompanied the governor. It was that *special* dimension that elevated Mario quite beyond other politicians and public figures during his marvelous and productive life, which instructs us still.

All this came rushing back to me in a *dream* I had earlier this week. And, so help me, it was as if Mario were actually talking directly to all of us. I remember him saying this: "I went from the almost to the Almighty."

Who else, I wonder, could have possibly put that lovely and perfect line in my head? *Mario* would have loved, and understood, it. And I know *you* will too.

Please don't think me crazy.

I *know* it was him.

Matilda Cuomo

New York State Mentoring Program, May 12, 2017.

―――――――――

WILLIAM O'SHAUGHNESSY: In our studio, live here in Westchester, is a very, very special woman. She's an old friend of this radio station. She's an icon of the state of New York. She's a former First Lady of the state of New York. And, in a way, she's still First Lady. She was Mrs. Mario Cuomo for many years, and now she's the mother of Governor Andrew Mark Cuomo. Please welcome Matilda Raffa Cuomo.

MATILDA CUOMO: It's good to be here with Bill O'Shaughnessy.

W.O.: We haven't seen you behind this microphone for some time.

M.C.: You're absolutely right. It's about time!

W.O.: Matilda Cuomo, I blew the socks off somebody in your press office who told me I have to be "careful" what I ask you!

M.C.: Why? We're old friends!

W.O.: We are, indeed. We've known you in every season. First, I have to tell you, you look terrific! I wish we had television!

M.C.: Thank you, Bill.

W.O.: I'm also going to tell you a secret. I blab everything with our audience. I've had a crush on you for a long time.

M.C.: Oh my goodness! I came on the show to hear *this*? [laughter]

W.O.: Mario is not so long gone that I dare say that.

M.C.: My son might be listening. [laughter]

W.O.: As always, it wasn't Mario I was afraid of, it was *Andrew*! My mind drifts back. I got a call once from Mario, of sainted memory. He said, "Brother Bill, I think I'm in trouble. Matilda is in Italy where, as you know, she travels like a visiting head-of-state for her Mentoring Program"—we're going to talk about that, because you started it up again. But this one day long ago you were in Lake

[461]

Como. Mario called, and he was concerned that there was a guy paying you "undue attention." He said, "There's a fellow with a crush on Matilda! I'm worried about this. He's a chubby boy! He sings. His name is Luciano Pavarotti."

M.C.: Ah, Luciano, may he rest in peace.

W.O.: Of course, I wanted to straighten Pavarotti out. I said to Mario, "Can you sing?" He said, "A little, but I can sure take him on the basketball court!"

M.C.: He was a masterful singer.

W.O.: We're not talking about Mario.

M.C.: No, I'm saying Luciano. *He* could sing.

W.O.: Matilda, thank you for coming by. You've had a busy schedule. You started up, again, with Andrew's encouragement—your son and heir who is our present governor—the state Mentoring Program. I call him the "Energizer Governor"! Does he ever stop?

M.C.: He doesn't. He seems to be just that! An Energizer bunny! He has so much to do, and he knows it. That's the point with him, and he has to *get it done*. That's the way he's always been.

W.O.: Matilda Raffa Cuomo, whose idea was it to reinvigorate and start up the Mentoring Program?

M.C.: Good question. Well, it was Andrew. I call him "my son, the governor." And in 2015 he actually found out from the Education Department that there are struggling, failing schools all around the state, from Buffalo all the way down to Suffolk County! So right away this he sees as a problem for the *governor*. And he takes it to heart. If the children don't stay in school and get educated, as you well know, Bill, we're all in big trouble because these children are going nowhere. And they get into a lot of trouble, drugs, everything. So we have to really stem the tide and make them understand the value of education. And this Mentoring Program does that.

W.O.: Matilda, Mrs. Cuomo, you are also head of the national group. It's called Mentoring USA.

M.C.: Well, this is the story. In 1982, Mario became governor, and by 1984 he found out the incarceration rate of young people in the prisons and told me to stop everything I had started as chairwoman of the Council of Children and Families. He said, "Matilda, this is more important. Get out of everything you started and help me with this. Think of something—a program—to help these children stay in school, as a mother, a grandmother." You know how Mario is, he gives you all the details! I said, "I know I'm a mother and a grandmother. . . ."

W.O.: And you started as a teacher.

M.C.: Yes, yes, I did. I was a teacher for three years.

W.O.: How old are these kids at risk right now?

M.C.: It varies. We can have them as old as being in third grade, from third grade on, when the teacher knows they're in trouble and need help. So the sooner, the better. Let me put it that way.

W.O.: So you've been visiting, Matilda Cuomo, with superintendents in our home heath, including Paul Feiner's group over in Greenburgh.

M.C.: Yes.

W.O.: What do you tell these guys?

M.C.: These "guys" were about seventy wonderful superintendents! Seventy in this one room. I was surprised to have that many. But that's a good sign because they wanted to be there to hear how they can make their children do better. They don't want to have failing, struggling schools if they have their mindset correct. So the fact is, I kidded them. I said I'm jealous of all of them here today because I wanted to be a superintendent. That was my goal in life! It's true. I wanted to be a school principal and make my parents proud, and then superintendent. That's the pinnacle for a teacher: superintendent!

W.O.: You only became a First Lady—and mother of yet another governor!

M.C.: That's destiny. I had no idea Mario would even get political at the time when I married him. So you see, I had *my* goals also, but it's amazing. *Life* is amazing. And the fact is, now we know where the children are. The schools are there to help with support. So what I discussed with them is this program that became known by Mario's time as the New York State Mentoring Program, and then by 1994 it was closed out completely by the next governor. Mario lost the election. I kid around and say the Italians don't vote. He lost by two points! That's what got him upset. That he lost by *two* points at the time. And the fact is, though, we had to do something else. So Andrew calls me, now working for President Clinton, with HUD—Housing and Urban Development. He said, "Mom, you can't lose that program, that unique program." I was fixing up the apartment and told him, "*Don't* fool around; tell me what you're saying." He said, "Mom, I have a *plan*!" When he says that, you gotta run because it means you're going to be stuck in a "project."

W.O.: This is Andrew, your son?

M.C.: That's it. He said it just like that. "We have to keep that program. It's unique; it's a wonderful program. It's nowhere else. It runs. It works." I knew that. He said again: "Ma, we call it 'Mentoring USA.' Go *national*—international—and Daddy can't stop you!" I loved that! That sounds great!

W.O.: When was this?

M.C.: This was in 1995. In '94 Mario lost the election. So in 1995 Andrew had me running the program again. He gave me a room in one of the HUD buildings, right near New York University.

W.O.: He used to be secretary of HUD in Washington, with Bill Clinton.

M.C.: Yes, exactly. And he gave me this room. He knew I had five volunteers to start because I have so many friends. I still have. I've been blessed with that. That's the best part of politics. And what happened is he gave us a downstairs room so that all we saw were legs passing by. The window was so subterranean. I said, "You can't do better than that as Secretary of HUD?" But he did, he did. Four years it took.

W.O.: He put his mother in the basement?

M.C.: Basement! Subterranean! Yes. Mother and all her helpers! But I did finally get moved up to the fourth floor.

W.O.: Have you forgiven him?

M.C.: No. I didn't want to be greedy. It was good enough he got the room for us to get us going.

W.O.: You mentioned that Mario lost by 2 percent. You haven't forgotten that, have you?

M.C.: That hurts.

W.O.: Mario once said you're not Italian. He said Matilda is not even Italian. He used to say, "She's Sicilian!"

M.C.: I don't forget! [laughter]

W.O.: It's now called again Mentoring . . .

M.C.: Mentoring USA is national *and* international. In fact, next week I go to Italy. And in Holland, Sylvia Simpson calls me from the Education Department. She wants the program. Brussels, in Belgium, wants the program. So that's all set. We're in Andalusia. Queen Sofia—many years ago when I was First Lady and she told me the need for the children to stay in school, I said, "I'm with you! I have the program," and I got her the program. So it's in Andalusia, Spain. It's in Morocco. It's also in England in many schools.

W.O.: I've got news for you, you're *still* the First Lady of New York! Matilda Cuomo, never mind Italy and Europe, where I've been told you're an even bigger celebrity than Mario was.

M.C.: It's because I speak Italian pretty well.

W.O.: There's a lot more to it than that. They *love* you! This I know, in every telling, that when you travel on the continent it's a big deal. And here at home, you had seventy superintendents there gathered that day. What do you want them to do?

M.C.: Well, many of them don't realize the program is ready to run. I have directors ready to help in all the counties to get the schools going with all the training. I have Brad DePietro. I have Keith Howard. These two young men are really spectacular. They do their work beautifully with great heart and understanding, with great acumen. It's one-to-one. It is again the only program like it around the country, if not the world. Now it is again reinstated in 2015 by the governor, my son, and he's not fooling around: "Right here again, at home, Mom! From Buffalo—forget everybody else." See, that's the way he is. Like the father of a family. *Family* first. What does the pope say, "*La Famiglia!*"

W.O.: Never mind the pope! Matilda Cuomo, the superintendents can only do so much. Who actually does the mentoring for the children at risk? First of all, are they high school kids or grammar school kids?

M.C.: Well, the children who need the mentoring can be from elementary school into high school as well.

w.o.: Who decides if they need the mentoring?

m.c.: The teachers. The teachers know. The youngsters are all classified as "struggling" or failing. "Struggling" meaning they are about to fail.

w.o.: What if someone wants to help Matilda Cuomo's Mentoring Program?

m.c.: Right now, there are the seventy superintendents we just saw here in Westchester. Under each superintendent, there are principals. Every principal, who I also meet with separately, they have ten schools, each principal.

w.o.: So the principal of the high school or middle school or elementary school, they each have kids who are a little troubled?

m.c.: Many of them don't live in an intact family. They have no one to listen to them. No one to talk to them. These are the kids that are really losing out. Drugs, problems. Problems that arise because they don't have someone—a mentor—to help them.

w.o.: Dear lady, where do you find the mentors?

m.c.: The mentors can be difficult to find today, more than ever. Because we find that a lot of companies are not as forthcoming with their volunteers as they used to be with the program, as a matter of fact. Maria, who is a director of Mentoring USA in New York City, concentrates on foster-care kids.

w.o.: Maria Cuomo Cole?

m.c.: Yes, my daughter, married to Kenneth Cole.

w.o.: *My* favorite daughter. She runs . . . ?

m.c.: She directs the whole program, Mentoring USA. And once a year you come, graciously, you do that for us, Bill, and she has a fundraiser. She's not with the state funding her.

w.o.: Maria Cuomo Cole is also running the wonderful entity Andrew founded right here, almost in this studio.

m.c.: HELP USA. HELP USA is also part of Mentoring USA. Those kids in HELP USA also get the program Mentoring USA.

w.o.: Why is it hard to get mentors?

m.c.: It's a lot of reasons. People are working today, and they don't have time. They don't have enough time for their own families.

What we do is we have a great model now. I thought, as a mother and a teacher, that if I get the high school students who are really great in academia, honor roll students who want to go to college and are geared for college. However, today it is very difficult to get into an Ivy League college without some kind of résumé. More than just your academics. Now, if you do a Mentoring Program for me as a mentor, one hour a week, just for one year for that one child, I will have a *letter* for you signed by the governor that will be so spectacular, I dare an Ivy League college not to take you! Because we also have, on the other side, kids who want to go to college but can't afford to get into them. Remember CUNY and SUNY are free!

W.O.: Are you telling me you only have to give *one* hour a week? Do you have to be a captain of industry? Or chairman of a bank, to mentor?

M.C.: No, these are ordinary people who have been retired from work and they have time. Just one hour.

W.O.: Can you be an Irish dunderhead like me? I got 28 in chemistry! You want *me* to mentor somebody?

M.C.: Yes, everybody! You would be wonderful! You're trained what to do with the child.

W.O.: Who trains the mentors?

M.C.: Oh, I have two great trainers, Brad DePietro and Keith Howard. They travel all over the state, and one is with me right now, Brad DePietro. And he's fantastic. They know all the essentials of what the training is supposed to give to this particular young person. And then the mentee is trained, completely different as the *receptor* of the mentoring. So they get their own training.

W.O.: How do they get together. Does the mentor go to the school or to the kid's home? Or meet on a park bench? What do you do?

M.C.: You said it so well. Mostly to the schools. Or if there's a recreational area in or around the school campus. They work that out. That's minor. We have to do it. They meet mostly in the classroom. And it's one-to-one. A very private kind of thing. One-to-one!

W.O.: I just got a flash of *déjà vu*! Remember the name Ely DelGado? Tell me about Ely.

M.C.: Oh, yes, Ely was *my* mentee, and she is a case in point. This girl wanted to leave school, and she was only about thirteen or fourteen and never smiled. In fact, she was really rude at times.

W.O.: You started with her when she was how old?

M.C.: Thirteen or fourteen!

W.O.: Now, are these her children in your brochure?

M.C.: Yes! She's married; she has two children. In fact, she just had another baby boy! I went to the shower, and she just had the baby right after the shower.

W.O.: She lucked out, Ely DelGado. How did she pick you?

M.C.: No, *I* lucked out because I learned so much from having her. She was a very unsociable person and very unhappy. She was told with a lie from her mother that her father died in Puerto Rico. And for that reason her mother took three little girls with Ely, the fourth, and came to this country. But she found out from her paternal grandmother it was a lie! The father was alive! ¡*Esta aqui y es muy Bueno*! "Not to worry." And she was upset. She said, "Who could lie to me like that?" It's called *sfogati*. I tell all the kids this word. You have to in life: *sfogati*. You've got to get it out. Because if not, you can get sick. Because really in your heart, if you have things that you are harboring, that you can't tell anybody, you can tell your mentor!

W.O.: So how old was Ely when you started?

M.C.: Thirteen!

W.O.: How old is she now?

M.C.: She's now almost forty!

W.O.: And you followed her all these years?

M.C.: Yes, I stayed with her! For a lot of reasons. I'm in Albany, conveniently. And she lived in that area. And now, she was great in math. That was my only weakness. I don't like math! I never really enjoyed that subject! So the fact is I found that was her acumen. She was great in math. I mean she would get 100s and 90s! She's got a special acumen for this math. I said I've got it made now! So, she now does the billing for all the doctors at Albany Medical Center! Right now. She's had the job for years. Since she got out of college. She got a scholarship to SUNY, and she got right into that job, on her own. They love her. They all tell me, the doctors when they see me in Albany, that she's a *genius*! And very reliable!

w.o.: It's called the New York State Mentoring Program. The mission is to create positive support of mentor relationships with a state-wide, school-based, unique one-to-one program to prevent students from dropping out of school. Does it work?

m.c.: It's working very well. Very well! Our main goal is to really get the mentors and to get that program running. So that's what we're doing. Working very hard.

w.o.: So, you never made it to superintendent, Matilda Raffa. You didn't even make it to principal.

m.c.: I told them today, all those superintendents, that I was very jealous of all of you. That's what I wanted to be, a superintendent! My father would have been so proud of me.

w.o.: You've had quite a life. Do you have any regrets? Besides not being a superintendent?

m.c.: No, I am very fortunate in the long run. I miss my husband, and I'm sorry God saw fit to take him away. So, that's the way it goes.

w.o.: Do you still talk to him?

m.c.: Yes, a lot, Bill.

w.o.: I've written a book about him, as you know. I miss him too. [pause] You don't know this, but there's another book coming out. Mine is called *Mario Cuomo. Remembrances of a Remarkable Man*. But I just learned yesterday—two days ago—that there's a new book—I love the title—by a professor at Lehigh University. Listen to this title: *American Cicero*. Wow!

m.c.: Wow is right.

w.o.: It was my hope that my book, which was a memoir of a friendship of thirty-eight years, would inspire other books, and they are starting. Why don't you write a book, Matilda Cuomo?

m.c.: I have a book. It's called *The Person Who Changed My Life*.

w.o.: But they are about other people. Why don't you write another one, a personal one?

m.c.: Well, this is a true story of people who tell you who their mentor was. Because you can't forget. Walter Cronkite told me to do the book when I met him. He said, "You have to do a book, Matilda,

[469]

and show the real people who benefited from having a mentor."
And he was right. It's a very good book.

W.O.: Are you able to talk to Andrew the way you used to converse
with Mario, of sainted memory?

M.C.: It's just that I don't have enough time with him. None of us do in
the family. He's always on the go! He's so busy. Even on weekends.
He's *called* to do this; people need him. So that's what he does.

W.O.: But I have heard, without telling any confidences, that Andrew,
when he wants to get away from it all, will come right to his mother
and sit on the terrace with you.

M.C.: He likes potato and egg omelets. A potato and egg omelet.
Nobody makes it like I do.

W.O.: How do you do that?

M.C.: Well, I dice the potatoes—he likes them that way. It's delicious!
It comes very well with parsley, fresh Italian parsley.

W.O.: You have five children?

M.C.: And fourteen grandchildren!

W.O.: Do you know all their birthdays?

M.C.: All thirteen girls and one boy. And you know his name. Mario
Cuomo!

W.O.: Is that a true story? That you had thirteen granddaughters
in a row.

M.C.: And then little Mario!

W.O.: Do you know, I got a call from Grandpa Mario. He said, "Brother
Bill, I think there's something going on. I think Chris—[Christopher
Cuomo from CNN]—is going to be the father of a boy!" How old is
young Mario now?

M.C.: He's twelve!

W.O.: Well, his grandfather was over the moon because Chris was
calling your daughters, was he not, saying, "Are there any good
girls' names that we haven't used yet with the thirteen?" And Mario
was smart. He said, "I think Chris is trying to throw us off track."
And when did you find out it was going to be a *boy*?

M.C.: She found out. She knew, Cristina knew, it was going to be a
boy. But after Mario, he now has Carolina. He has another girl. He
has two girls and a boy!

W.O.: Do you have any favorites?

M.C.: Oh, they're all favorites!

W.O.: How about that little boy, Mario Cuomo? What a name!

M.C.: You know, he holds his own, I have to tell you, with all those girls! He really is his own little man. He gets along with all of them. Especially with Madeline's little girl Tess. Tess is in the same school in the same grade. In two different classes, they put them.

W.O.: Grandma Cuomo, Matilda Raffa Cuomo, it's an honor. You honor us with your very presence. It was a thrill just to see you walk in the door. I talked to another admirer of yours just two days ago. He's back from Lourdes. The cardinal archbishop. You better watch out for *him*. He's got a crush on you too!

M.C.: That's nice to know!

W.O.: Good luck with the Mentoring Program. Is there a number? Here's a good number. 844-337-6304. Or can you call the local school and say, "I want to sign up for Mrs. Cuomo's Mentoring"?

M.C.: Sure, that would be wonderful! Just wonderful. We need mentors. Thank you, Bill.

W.O.: Dear lady, you honor us. Can I say, without getting into trouble with the governor, I love you.

M.C.: I love you too!

W.O.: Now I'm in trouble! [laughter]

William O'Shaughnessy Interview
with Mario Cuomo Re: Andy O'Rourke

I've written often about Andrew P. O'Rourke, the colorful and estimable Republican who served as Westchester County executive and wrote swash-buckling novels.

In a long, distinguished public career he also served as a New York State Supreme Court justice and an admiral in the State Naval Militia (who knew we had a naval militia!).

When the GOP persuaded the popular and good-natured O'Rourke to run for governor against Mario Cuomo, he famously toured the state with a cardboard cut-out of the governor that he "debated" in town after town. But Andy O'Rourke also used his considerable influence to assist Andrew Cuomo launch his highly praised transitional Housing for the Homeless (HELP) projects. (O'Rourke and Andrew met and bonded at a luncheon at "21" hosted by yours truly). Mario never forgot Andy O'Ro-urke's encouragement and kindness for his son. And when the beloved Westchester politician lay dying in Calvary Hospital in the Bronx a few years ago . . . Mario called his old adversary for a long farewell talk. We spoke about Judge O'Rourke on the radio when he left us in 2013.

—W.O.

WILLIAM O'SHAUGHNESSY: Governor Cuomo . . . an old opponent of yours has gone to another—and we're sure . . . a better world. Andy O'Rourke ran against you for governor.

MARIO CUOMO: Bill, it's very difficult to talk about Andy without sounding like you've made an effort to cover him as some kind of heroic figure. I really do think he is—was—and always will be . . . in my memory—a heroic figure . . . because he was such a powerful coming together of good things. His intelligence . . . his vision . . . his sense of humor . . . his sense of fairness . . . made all the political labels meaningless. Liberals are supposed to be Democrats and businesspeople are supposed to be Republicans . . . all of that.

It makes you feel once you meet and see what he is and see his goodness and his charm and see his intelligence . . . you say who needs categories, political categories? Just get the best human beings you can to serve you as public servants. He was a wonderful public servant because he was a wonderful human being. He's a great loss to Flora, his wife, and to his children.

W.O.: Governor Cuomo . . . do you remember when he was running for governor against you . . . and he had that cardboard cut-out of Mario Cuomo?

M.C.: Talk about sense of humor. Early in the campaign between Andy and me . . . we had always gotten together. But we had a small "disagreement" for a time which required on my end that I not debate until the very last moment and he—bright man that he was—thought of a way to deal with that. He had a cardboard cut-out made of me and it was a very good image of me . . . except it was considerably thinner than I was because it was just cardboard, and he debated the cardboard figure. Now . . . I didn't know that until I happened to be in Westchester on the first day he used it— didn't know it until the reporters came to me and said do you know Andy O'Rourke debated a cardboard figure of you . . . and I said, yes I know. I told them he's done it more than once and so far I'm told the cardboard figure won two out of three!

W.O.: But wasn't it because you were something like 1,000 points ahead and said I don't have to debate this guy?

M.C.: No . . . it wasn't that at all, O'Shaughnessy. He said something about Andrew I didn't like. And I decided to punish him . . . but he punished me by debating the cardboard figure. But then I put the cardboard figure on my side by saying he won two out of three!

W.O.: Governor Cuomo . . . Andy O'Rourke was a Republican. Mario Cuomo—as the world knows—is a Democrat. How did you two get together?

M.C.: Those are not real distinctions, Bill. And they shouldn't be. And I wish sometimes—frankly—I think one of the greatest errors made by our Founding Fathers was ignoring George Washington when he said two things. First, that you should never allow a single person to declare war. And so you should never start a war because the president of the United States asked for it. That's a ridiculous thing. It's ridiculous because the one person shouldn't be in a position where a bad judgment could be horrible for us. And he also said another thing. He said we should not have political parties. Why not? Because as soon as you commit yourself to leftists or rightists . . . to this kind of person or that kind of person . . . you choose up sides and you pit them against one another.

He said there should be no parties. And we didn't listen to that. And I think since he said that, we have had something like 176 parties. And the parties do exactly what he projected they would. And that is they would take a position which was contrary to the other side . . . because that's the way it is served up to us, our politics. And it's foolish. First of all, we don't stay true to the labels because there was a lot about Andy O'Rourke that wasn't classical Republican. And there was a lot about Mario Cuomo that wasn't classical Democrat. And so these silly labels—and they are silly labels. And who says so? George Washington. Too bad we didn't listen.

w.o.: Governor Cuomo . . . Andy O'Rourke helped your son build housing for the homeless here in Westchester when he was county executive. Do you remember those days? They both got ganged up on by the NIMBYs. . . .

m.c.: Yes . . . almost every time he did something notable . . . it was praiseworthy. What was a Republican in Westchester doing helping Andrew build housing for poor Democrats who were mainly the kind of people who lived in those humble homes he was building? But Andy (O'Rourke)—bright and intelligent person that he was— looked up over the labels constantly. If something was good he recognized it as good and he found something to do with it for our betterment. And that's what he did with Andrew and the housing projects. It got him no votes.

Got him the irritation of a lot of Republicans in your area. He would smile at that . . . make a joke and move on looking for another good thing to do.

W.O.: Governor . . . finally . . . I wonder if there is a lesson. Barack and Romney . . . Obama and Romney. Clearly they hated each other. O'Rourke and Cuomo ended up as friends. Any lessons there? Or has it gotten meaner? Nastier?

M.C.: Essentially you have to go back to George Washington again. Washington made it very clear in simple language. If you create parties . . . you are declaring that these two groups are different from one another and they should contend with one another. And you will not find your best answers by letting them fight with one another . . . lie about one another. And that's what we've been doing ever since the people ignored him when they wrote the Constitution.

W.O.: Governor Cuomo . . . I hear it in your voice. We've lost Andy O'Rourke here in Westchester. Opponent that he may have been . . . I think you kind of liked the guy.

M.C.: I liked him a whole lot. I admired him. And I should. Andrew— my Andrew—I'm sure will have nice things to say about him. Andrew O'Rourke and Andrew Cuomo. Andrew Cuomo in the last poll got at least as many votes as a Republican as he did as a Democrat. And it might even be that he got slightly more on the Republican line in the latest poll. Now why is that? It's because Andrew Cuomo has been acting like Andrew O'Rourke at his best. And I hope he keeps doing that.

W.O.: Politics is a nasty business that only occasionally gets an Andy O'Rourke . . . and a Mario Cuomo.

M.C.: O'Rourke was good, Bill. O'Rourke was really good. Mario Cuomo is not bad. But I tell you . . . that cardboard cut-out was a winner!

W.O.: You never forget, Mario. Thank you, sir.

Interview with Mario M. Cuomo

Re: Pope Benedict . . . the Catholic Church . . . his own life . . .
Ed Koch . . . Mariano Rivera. February 11, 2013

———————

"It would be wonderful if we could all get one more shot at it . . . to be given the opportunity to go back and do it over."

WILLIAM O'SHAUGHNESSY: No pope has given up the miter or the keys to the kingdom in 600 years . . . but it happened this week. Governor Mario Cuomo, you're a great student of things theological and you're a son of the Church . . . what do you think about the pope walking away from it and hanging it up?

MARIO CUOMO: What the pope did, it appears to me, was a practical, selfless, intelligent decision. He is a man who has worked very hard for a long time. He's now concluded that he doesn't have enough strength to do the job of being the most important person in the Catholic Church . . . at least when it comes to the group, the small group—the Curia—that makes the decisions about how we should deal with our religion and how we should keep it strong and how we can improve it. It takes a lot of strength.

He doesn't have that strength anymore. He has the desire, I'm sure. We witnessed that. But he did, it seems to me, the right thing. If you can't do the job, you have to step aside. Anything else would have been selfish and damaging.

W.O.: Governor, your friend of so many years Jimmy Breslin once wrote a book called *The Church That Forgot Christ*. And he went to great lengths to say there's a hierarchy and a church that now may not resemble what Jesus intended . . . how do you feel about that stuff?

M.C.: Well . . . when you say how do you feel about that stuff, that stuff is a huge, huge amount of law and religious law that guides us—those of us that are Catholic—in the way that we should live and it's a very difficult thing to try to sum it up in any tidy, neat, and convenient way. This probably is not well understood by people like me and other Catholics. We have to keep in mind that the Church—although it talks about infallibility—it has adopted a rule of ineffability, that rule of infallibility—which means we can't make a mistake if we're talking about our religion . . . we're not capable of making a mistake. That has been put to one side. That simply is not the working measure of the people who are making the rules. Infallibility was adopted at a time when the Church was already not well supported because it had proven itself vulnerable in a number of ways. To try to deal with that weakness, they suggested that this new rule—of course it's no longer a new rule— that when the pope chooses, because he believes it's a matter of very, very high importance, the pope chooses to say something, to make a doctrine, to make a ruling. And he does it with infallibility. It means he can't possibly be wrong.

Well, that struck a lot of people as not intelligent and not reasonable and, in fact, it has never been exercised specifically except, I think, with respect to the Virgin Mary and the question of whether or not she was assumed up to Heaven when she passed away. And that's the only issue on which infallibility has been promoted by the pope and the Church that makes the rules. Now . . . that's a very important thing because it means the Church is fallible. It means the Church can make a mistake.

W.O.: Are you saying the Church made a mistake with the Blessed Mother?

M.C.: No . . . I'm saying that it can make mistakes and it has made mistakes. And that's important because it's corrected a lot of mistakes. And if it can correct a lot of mistakes, that suggests that maybe more corrections are possible. At one time, you could not take any money for lending money to somebody . . . the interest bankers live with and a lot of other people that lend money. It was a sin to charge somebody for the use of money.

W.O.: What was that sin called?

M.C.: Usury . . . and . . . it was a major sin, let's put it that way. It was regarded as a very significant sin. And of course it's no longer the law of the Church. And there are other things the Church has changed its mind on. And made different rules for. There's a great book by an Irish Catholic judge who is a layman and has written a book on the Church's policy, three, four, or five of them. And how over the years the Church has accepted and even promoted the reality that it is capable of making mistakes. Usury is one of those issues. They made a big mistake—the Church—when they said it was a sin to charge interest. And certainly a whole lot of people are happy they didn't do that because there are a lot of people in this world who get a lot of money for lending money and they were very pleased with the idea of being able to do that and they didn't want to hear the Church saying it's a sin to charge interest.

W.O.: Governor, you've written lovingly and also critically—if gently— about the Church. You're not going to like it when I remind you of this, but when you were elected governor of New York three times by tremendous margins, a friend of yours said I think Mario really wants to be a cardinal. Forgive me, Governor . . . that really happened.

M.C.: No . . . no, that didn't happen, O'Shaughnessy. I could guess who it is that said that. But I'm not going to give you the name for fear that I'm shooting at the wrong target. No . . .

W.O.: Did you ever think about being a priest?

M.C.: No . . . let's stay with the governorship. I felt capable of being a competent governor before I decided to run. I had a lot of experience as a lay Catholic and that was useful in terms of being an active Catholic, I had a lot of experience doing that. And in terms of governing, I had four years as secretary of state in which I learned a whole lot about our government and traveled all over the state. And then I had four more years working with Hugh Carey as the lieutenant governor who would take his place if he would have to step away. I was well armed for the job. I was a lawyer before that and so I had the confidence I would be competent. OK? I never dreamt I would be more than that and when people started talking about me as a president, I could not say about myself what I could say about myself when I chose to attempt to be a governor. And that is I know I'm competent to do this. I did not have that same feeling about the presidency.

w.o.: But Mario Cuomo, excuse me, you've always been drawn relentlessly and consistently to the great cosmic and spiritual issues of the day. Somebody once said famously this guy is too good to be worried about how many Bob's Big Boys you should put on the Thruway. You've worked the territory that should be worked by cardinals and bishops. You know you have. You spoke famously on abortion. And you've tried to make some sense of it all. You sure you didn't go into the wrong business?

m.c.: No . . . not at all. If you're suggesting I should have become a priest, I've already confessed I wasn't good enough to be a president. I'm just as sure—or surer—that I'm not good enough to be a priest. Certainly not after I met Matilda.

w.o.: I'm not asking you to dump Matilda.

m.c.: The Church is a wonderful thing, Bill. The Church—when it stays close to Christ and what Christ said and what Christ believed and what Christ sought to teach all the rest of us—when the Church does that it's wonderful. Really wonderful. It can make the world better. And let's stay with the Church and what it represents in terms of religious belief. If you look very, very closely, the Roman Catholic Church is not very far separated from Judaism. The essence of Judaism is two simple principles that can be captured with two simple words: *tikkun olam* and *tzedakah*. *Tzedakah* is, roughly in Hebrew, charity . . . goodness in dealing with other people. Fairness. All of that. That's *tzedakah*. *Tikkun olam* is the Hebrew principle that says God made this world but didn't complete it. Your mission is to begin the work He began. And to correct some of the misdirections we have become guilty of. *Tzedakah* and *tikkun olam*. But those two principles are exactly what Christ taught. And as a matter of fact, there's a kind of dramatic evidence of this in the story about Christ on that night coming out of the synagogue and being confronted by people who are not friendly to Him and demanded to know from Him why it was other rabbis who were walking out and expressing astonishment at your intelligence and wisdom, et cetera. And what is it you said to these people in the synagogue? And He said simply . . .

w.o.: The Lord?

m.c.: Yes . . . this is Christ talking simply to the people in the synagogue, the rabbis particularly. He said: Look . . . this is the Whole Law. Love one another as you love yourself. That's *tikkun olam* and the *tzedakah* principle put together. Love one another as you love yourself for the love of Me for I am Truth. And what he was saying is I am God and you should rest on that principle and that principle calls upon you to be good to one another. To love one another. Well, if those two principles are the essence of Christ, then what distinguishes them from the Jews? Well, the Hebrews said exactly the *same* thing! One of the great rabbis said love one another as you would love yourself, for the love of God, because that's what God wants you to do. And everything else is commentary. I love that! Loving one another is all you need to do to be right with the religion, whether it's Judaism or Christianity. And if we could get that clearer in our minds, we wouldn't have spent all those years trying to blame every Jew for having killed Christ and for being the *massachristis* which were condemned in the Second Vatican Council.

The *massacristy* was a kind of slur on Jewish people to say they are the killers of Christ. In fact, they are not the killers of Christ. They didn't do the killing. But more than that, even as a matter of religious principle, they weren't the killers of Christ.

You know, you have all of that going for you. You had the possibility at one point, we will continue to refine, to study, and to discuss the relationship between the Christian principles and the Hebrew principles and get even closer together. When that happens, then the great issue of modern religion becomes . . . what do the rest of the world's religions say about a new religion that is the new Christianity and the old Judaism now making up the *new* religion.

Will they be frightened by it? Will they be attracted by it? There are more people out there that believe in the Koran and those things, than there are Jews and Christians. So . . . it's an exciting world we're living in if you judge it just by its religions. The kind of pope we need is the kind of pope who will say . . . it's time to look back on our history and to see we have failed in our mission because we simply have ignored opportunities. Like what? Well, wouldn't it be wonderful if women who we are so eager to make equal to men in all ways that are practical, wouldn't it be something if all the women who wanted to be priests could be priests? And all the women who want to be capable of conducting the Mass . . . then all the women would be the equal of all the men. How much stronger would that make us as a Christian nation?

W.O.: Governor, would you want to go to confession to a woman? It's hard enough telling a guy your sins!

M.C.: I'll take your word for it, Bill.

W.O.: At least for me . . .

M.C.: OK . . . let's leave it there, O'Shaughnessy.

W.O.: Governor, you're a politician. That's what you are. A governor . . . a politician.

M.C.: I'm a lawyer. That's what I am . . . a lawyer.

W.O.: A lawyer . . . but governors and politicians and lawyers are not supposed to talk about things like this. About *tikkun olam* and *tzedakah*. Soulful, religious, deep issues. . . .

M.C.: Why not?

W.O.: See . . . you prove my point. You've always been drawn to this stuff. So again I ask you . . .

M.C.: It's not stuff. It's the rules by which you lead your life.

W.O.: One of our callers is nominating *you* for pope and Mariano Rivera for vice pope. Will you serve if elected?

M.C.: No . . . but I tell you, I would love to see how he throws that one pitch . . . I mean, it's just one pitch this guy has . . . the cutter. And I hope he hasn't lost it to this year while he was sitting it out.

W.O.: The *Boston Globe* called you "the great philosopher-statesman of the American nation." Did you ever get the feeling you'd like to get in there and save your Church?

M.C.: No . . . no. I'm too weak to do a lot of the things I'd love to be able to do. It would be wonderful if we could all get one more shot at it. At one point be given the opportunity to go back and do it over. Imagine how much better you could do it. And that's the way we should feel about the Church now. We should feel the Church is invited to have a new day. A new week. A new month. A new era of the Church. If you could find the right person to lead it, then wonderful, wonderful things can happen to our religion and to the world that's affected by that religion.

W.O.: Governor . . . speaking of a final shot, you gave an exceptional interview with *New York* magazine about a sometimes friend, sometimes not so much a friend, Ed Koch. Would you like one final comment on the man?

M.C.: Final word on Ed Koch? I'll give you one final word . . . I wrote something . . . can I read it to you, Bill?

W.O.: We'd love to hear it, sir . . .

M.C.: Everyone who has ever sat in the magnificence of Temple Emmanuel cannot be unmoved by the dazzling and soaring beauty that surrounds them. Some of our great city's greatest citizens have chosen it as the platform for their last goodbyes as did Ed Koch on Monday, February 4, 2013. I knew Ed Koch for most of the quarter of a century that we both became involved in politics. During those years we had our ups and downs, but no politician I know ever equaled Koch's mastery of the media. All of it—television, radio, newspapers, public appearances. It made him, perhaps, the best known political leader in New York City's history. That was made clearer by the unprecedented media coverage his passing received. He deserved to be well known. Ed devoted his life to two great loves: the world of politics and his family. He spent his entire adult life in public service as a soldier, mayor, congressman, writer of books and columns and as one of the best-known mayors in our city's history. In the end he was more than a uniquely honored mayor. He was an institution that became an ineradicable part of our city's history, like the Statue of Liberty and the great bridges. New Yorkers will never stop answering his question, which was

"How am I doing?" And they'll answer it with their reply. You did good, Ed. You did good!

w.o.: Governor, I couldn't talk you into running for pope . . . but you've given us some great gifts as you always do. I'm glad you're a friend of this radio station, sir. Thank you.

m.c.: Thank you for having me once again, Brother Bill.

Dutch Treat Club Annual Dinner Presentation of the Gold Medal for Lifetime Achievement in the Arts for Governor Mario M. Cuomo

Remarks of William O'Shaughnessy,
The Harvard Club, New York City, May 5, 2014.

———————————

Fellow Dutch Treaters. I have never felt less worthy in my life.

We all make our living with words . . . that's certainly true for the brilliant Mark Russell and for a legendary lyricist like Sheldon Harnick.

And words are equally essential to the brilliance of Mark Nadler and Anita Gillette and Alan Schmuckler.

As for me, I'm afraid they usually emerge inartfully, awkwardly, and imprecisely.

So I feel most inadequate indeed to the task of presuming merely to thank you for your marvelous gesture in bestowing your prestigious Gold Medal on MARIO MATTHEW CUOMO . . . from whom words cascade with such grace and beauty and precision and power on all the great issues of the day.

The governor . . . who has graced our influential podium to kick off several seasons . . . deeply and dearly wishes he could join you. And recently, in a voice laden with emotion and regret, asked me to assure you of that.

He loves the Dutch Treat Club and he loves especially the "give and take" of the question and answer sessions that always followed his formal presentations. Every time he appeared I would get a call: "Can't we just do Q and A . . . they're so damn bright!" But Donnelly and Fox always insisted he pay for his lunch with a major address!

And speaking of which . . . I hope you'll allow me just a personal observation while we're on the subject: I don't think we've encountered—any of us—two nicer individuals than our two leaders: John Donnelly and Ray Fox!

Dutch Treat has a lot of luminous and vivid characters . . . many here assembled tonight . . . like our spectacular Peggy Burton, a class act in every season, on whom I've had an unrequited crush for twenty years!

Now I won't intrude for very long on your evening. You've struck your Gold Medal for the governor with the lovely—and accurate— phrase "Lifetime Achievement in the Arts."

I'll tell you who would have loved this night: Kitty Carlisle Hart, who for many of her ninety-six years, headed the New York State Council on the Arts. Mrs. Hart loved Mario Cuomo. For one thing, he never failed to reappoint her . . . or denied a request for funding! Maybe that's why she called him "Governor Darling!"

Come to think of it . . . I think she called Nelson Rockefeller . . . and Hugh Carey . . . the same thing. But Mario was her favorite!

When he heard of your generosity and the Arts Gold Medal . . . the governor dispatched an immediate e-mail touched with his marvelous wit: "I don't dance . . . I don't sing . . . what do you want of me, O'Shaughnessy?"

I've thought about this . . . and what we "want" . . . from him even in his eighty-second year. Especially in his eighty-second year.

We want him only to continue to be Mario Cuomo . . . to instruct us . . . to enrich the public discourse about us . . . to enlighten us . . . to inspire us.

And . . . to use his own favorite word: to make our world "sweeter" than it is.

You have chosen well. He's a great man. And, like I said at the beginning . . . I'm not worthy to loose the strap of his sandal . . .

He is surely one of the very greatest of our time . . . who has had a lot written and said about him . . . as when the *Boston Globe* called him "the great philosopher-statesman of the American nation."

So . . . a lot of recognition in his already long life . . . a lot of encomiums for this extraordinary man.

And now, by your generous hand: One more:

He now has a Dutch Treat Gold Medal . . . thanks to you.

Dutch Treat Club Luncheon

William O'Shaughnessy on Mario Cuomo: Remembrances
of a Remarkable Man, *Gramercy Park, The Player's Club,
New York City, (Election Day) November 8, 2016.*

John Donnelly: Our distinguished speaker is the great Bill O'Shaughnessy. Bill has been a member of the club for many years. He is a
broadcast journalist par excellence! And his approach to journalism,
resembling that of our beloved Liz Smith, who graces us with her
presence, is not "antagonistic" journalism. He interviews on his radio
stations rapscallions and all sorts of characters, forcing them to admit
to misdeeds that may abound. But he also draws out the better part of
people, even though there may be a lot of misdeeds, and that has
been his enlightened approach. The interviews have been little polished jewels. They are really quite good and totally different from
"gotcha" journalism, which can be very good if done by our friends
Hunter Thompson or Tom Wolfe and a rather large number of
practitioners.

Basically, O'Shaughnessy is a journalist. He has been head of the
Whitney radio stations in the New York area and owner for many, many
years.

His new book is *Mario Cuomo: Remembrances of a Remarkable
Man.* The governor was a remarkable man, as attested to via the public
record of many years. What was also remarkable was the friendship
that developed between them—O'Shaughnessy the journalist and
Cuomo the politician. That kind of friendship does not normally occur
in nature. There's basically an antagonistic element to it, almost like
landlord and tenant, or dog and cat, and lots of other examples. But
amazingly, the friendship endured and even prospered. It had, as we
shall hear, a number of different aspects, but a friendship in an area of

politics and journalism tends to be an alliance of convenience. And the friendships, if there are any, go sour fast, often with lots of recriminations. But that has never happened here. It's a little unusual also that it was in New York politics.

Interestingly, Theodore Roosevelt, when he was governor, had occasion to comment on the very same thing of which I speak, scandals and indictments. And he said of the state legislature that when the roll was called and the legislature stood up, they were not sure whether they should say, "Present" or "Not guilty!" [laughter] And that atmosphere, unfortunately, continues. But it may be because of the times—because it can be so bad that by a process of Darwinian selection some very great political leaders emerge out of all that, and Theodore Roosevelt was one, and Governor Mario Cuomo was surely another.

O'Shaughnessy's friendship with Governor Cuomo goes back to about 1977, when he interviewed the governor—who was then secretary of state. Being secretary of state is not exactly viewed as a stepping-stone to great things. But O'Shaughnessy did see greatness in Mr. Cuomo, particularly a greatness of spirit, even in that somewhat dead-end job at the time. But out of that blossomed a very deep friendship. And his new book is a memoir of that extraordinary friendship. It is certainly not a "tell-all" book. There is nothing "Page Six," or certainly nothing a gossip columnist would love to print.

You should know too that Mr. O'Shaughnessy had to endure, obviously as part of this friendship, endless good-natured kidding from the governor, particularly about his *hair* and his dress. The governor had a lot to say about those things. Some of it genuinely funny, actually. And that's all in the book. As I recall, one occurred at one of our luncheons. One of our members was talking with Governor Cuomo and, as O'Shaughnessy approached, said, "Look at him. He looks like a high-WASP Mafioso in that suit." The governor then said to O'Shaughnessy, "You know, she says you're a high WASP. Is that true?" So, this went on and on, but it's a great example of the depth of the friendship. O'Shaughnessy became "Brother Bill" to the governor. I give you Brother Bill O'Shaughnessy. [applause]

William O'Shaughnessy: John, will you do my damn eulogy? That was terrific. But please, not any time soon! [laughter]

[487]

First of all, thank you for coming, all of you Dutch Treaters and my friends. I take exception to only one thing you said, John. Don't put me in the same breath with Liz Smith. I'm not worthy to loose the strap of her brilliant and lovely sandal. [applause]

This is a great day. Election Day, 2016! Finally. And mercifully. I saw New Yorkers lined up to vote all the way down to 23rd Street. I'm sorry that so many of my friends showed up on Election Day to cancel out my one, lone absentee Republican vote, which I cast last week up in Litchfield. I know they've canceled me out. I can tell, because, they're all very "intelligent"—and prosperous looking. And educated! [laughter]

The Dutch Treat Club has been wonderful to me and mine for a long time, for many years. I'll say just a few things about the book, which has gotten praise very much beyond its due. I'm reminded that it's been a long time since I've been allowed to darken your door here at the prestigious Dutch Treat. The first time was up on Park Avenue when the great Lowell Thomas then looked out in the room. He was presiding. I was a twenty-nine-year-old Irish salesman trying to be a writer. He said in his magnificent stentorian voice, "He's the greatest speaker in the Outback!" My knees were already shaking when Mr. Thomas then looked out in the room and said, "Governor Lodge, I don't mean Australia. I mean *Westchester*—the Outback!"

I also remember as my mind drifts back to wonderful Dutch Treat luncheons of the past. I used to pick up my New Rochelle neighbor Robert Merrill of sainted memory and drive him to the city. And one day we're going across the Triborough Bridge and the driver—an impressionable young man—saw Mr. Merrill's World Series ring. He asked what position he played for the Yankees. And Robert Merrill— winking at me first to make sure it was OK—said, "Shortstop!" [laughter] We pulled up outside the building, and the young driver said, "I don't think that guy can make a double play! You sure he's their shortstop?" [laughter] Speaking of which, I would be happy just to hear once more the great John Sterling, the Voice of the Yankees, who joins us today. Vin Scully is the guy who got a lot of publicity recently when he retired. But the greatest sports announcer during my time—two of them, Mel Allen of sainted memory and the Great John Sterling, the Voice of the Yankees! [applause] John, come up and do just one "The

Yankees *wiiiiiin*!" Just once for us. We haven't heard it much this year! Listen to this voice.

John Sterling: You have no idea how far back I go with O'Shaughnessy. I just told this story to someone at my table, so I'm repeating it—old age, I think. When I was a kid, I knew I was going to be on the air on radio when I was nine or ten years old. I just knew it. So I had no problems growing up with a purpose in life. I have four kids, and I worry what are they going to do after I send them to these expensive colleges. Anyway, I was destined to be on the air, and I wanted to be on the great WNEW, the legendary AM station in New York. So I listened continually, and they had hired kind of a "gopher," a young kid named Bill O'Shaughnessy. He was mentioned all the time on the disc jockey shows. And boy, was I jealous. Anyway, this is why I am doing this Yankees victory chant, for Bill O'Shaughnessy. I never do this. I think it's ridiculous. People stop me all the time and ask if I'll do it. And I don't want to seem like a jerk. I figure when it's on the air, it's on the air! And that's OK.

William O'Shaughnessy: C'mon, Sterling, just one time!

John Sterling: There's two outs in the ninth, and there's a fly ball to center field, and Jake Ellsbury comes under it and makes the catch. And I say: "Ball game over! Yankees win! Theeeeeee Yankees Win!" [cheers and applause]

Bill, that was for you! [applause]

William O'Shaughnessy: Thank you, John. Ladies and gentlemen, that's the program for today! [laughter]

Listening to John Sterling, I'm reminded of the great Metropolitan Opera star Robert Merrill, another great baseball fan and one of our most revered members. I saw him one day around New Rochelle. He used to walk around, sometimes with his hair and sometimes without his hair. [laughter] And I said, "Robert, in the *Times* this morning..."—I don't know anything about opera; I see a few people who do here, and I'm not going to mess with you. [laughter] "... There's a big story on who is the greatest tenor." I said, "Are you a baritone?" He said, "I hope so!" [laughter] I said, "I just read the headline. Is it Luciano Pavarotti, or is it Placido Domingo? Who is the greatest tenor?" Without missing a beat, he said, "Sinatra!" [laughter and applause]

[489]

And then one more Bob Merrill story. I picked him up one day, and Marian met me at the car in the driveway and said, "Bill, he's on the phone with 'Frank.' He's giving Frank a little tune-up—a little voice lesson." So she said to go in, but I didn't want to get near this. This is high-church stuff. When he came out to the car, I asked Robert Merrill if that was really Sinatra. He said, "Of course, he calls me all the time for a little 'tune-up.' He goes: 'me me me.'" I asked him if he really coached the great Sinatra. He said, "Of course I did. We were on for twenty minutes!" I asked, what did Sinatra say? "What did he say? He said: You show off! And hung up!" [laughter]

There are so many who have graced this room and other venues before it. I remember Ralph Graves, the last editor of *Life*, and real journalists: Bob Windeler and Roy Rowan and Isaac Asimov.

And speaking of great writers—beyond those here assembled. It is my hope that journalists of far greater gifts will do more formal biographies of Mario. When he went to another and, we are sure, a better world, Terry Golway, Paul Grondahl, Phil Reisman, Mike Lupica, Ken Kurson, Michael Dandry, Wayne Barrett, Steve Cuozzo, Ken Auletta, Erica Orden, and Rick Hertzberg did beautiful and touching tributes. And the great Gay Talese, at dinner at "21" just before we went to press, gave me some great stuff, which I was able to get in the book.

One of the nicest tributes to the governor came from a man from Delaware: "I've been in politics since I was a twenty-nine-year-old kid, and the minute I saw Mario Cuomo, I knew he was better than I was." That was Joseph R. Biden Jr.

Now back to today's luncheon on this historic Election Day, which, I have a hunch, we'll remember for a long time.

And right here I have to confess in front of Liz Smith and Reisman and the other writers in the joint that I had a crush—an *unrequited* crush—on Peggy Burton for the longest time. She never knew about this. She knew that everyone here is more gifted of the mother tongue than I am, and as I've said, it's an honor to be in the same room with the luminous Liz Smith, an authentic living New York landmark. [applause]

Now, briefly, to my damn book, which John Donnelly has so graciously mentioned. Mario Cuomo gave us some of our greatest moments at the club. He always did it for John Donnelly—nobody can turn down an invitation from John, who is the heart, spirit, and soul of this club, along with Ray Fox and K. T. Sullivan. [applause] Mario actually tied Liz Smith for the greatest turnout at one of our meetings. There is a picture in the book of Mario addressing you—standing at this podium. He said he wanted a Q & A, "but O'Shaughnessy says you've got to pay for your lunch with a full speech." And he gave a magnificent one. He loved this club of so many accomplished minds.

You know, books are terrific. This is my sixth or seventh. And as is our custom, we had a spectacular launch at Le Cirque two weeks ago, to which we invited 80 people and 160 showed up. What I used to do at the parties for my other books—the anthologies—is I would say, here's the guy you came to see. Here's Mario Cuomo, and then I would put him on. And this year I couldn't do this. For the last book, *Vox Populi*, he was not well. He was feeling few and ailing, and his daughter Maria wrote a wonderful piece. Speaking of which, the Foreword to this new book was actually written by Mario Matthew Cuomo. It says some nice things about me. And I debated whether to include it. My Jesuit editors said to put it in. And as I was arguing about it, one of them said, "O'Shaughnessy, I edited a pope! It stays!" [laughter] So I said I was not going to mess with this guy!

Cardinal Dolan showed up at the book party. He knows what a poor, stumbling, staggering, weak, faltering Catholic I am. The current archbishop of New York, if you don't know, is a rock star! And Dan Rather, Jerry Speyer, Matilda Cuomo, Ken Auletta, Maria Cuomo Cole, and Sidney Offit, the great man of letters, were there. And Mario's son and heir, who with each passing day is starting to resemble his father of sainted memory.

At one of the earlier book parties, Mario was at the podium, and he looked out and saw Ken Auletta, the late Peter Maas, and Gay Talese. And he held up his hand with the Saint John's ring high in the air and said to the maître d': "Out; don't let them in. No *real* writers allowed. [laughter] They'll expose Bill O'Shaughnessy for the fraud he is." True story!

Ladies and gentlemen, I have to tell you, in the intimacy of this room, it was not an easy book to write. We all are seduced and beguiled and comforted by the illusion of permanence. I thought Mario was going to be around forever. We used to kid about who was going to do my eulogy, and I would say, "I'm taking names; you got to get in line for this." So it wasn't easy. I still have a difficult time putting him in the past tense.

I don't know how to describe this book. Call it a love letter, I guess. I'm a very fortunate author. Most writers would kill for what I'm about to tell you. I said to Cindy, "Do we have a good number for Leonard Riggio?"—the book baron, chairman and founder of Barnes & Noble, whom many of you know. A great man. She said, "What do you want to call him for?" I said, "I saw him at Cipriani a few months ago, and he said, 'You'll never finish the book, O'Shaughnessy. You're procrastinating.'"

I called, and the founder of Barnes & Noble answered the phone at his Park Avenue apartment and said, "It's a great book. I've got it right here in my den. And I'm going in and talk[ing] to our book buyer about it right now." Imagine how many writers would love to have that conversation? Leonard Riggio is a wonderful man. And he loved Mario too. And did a lot for him.

Sam Roberts has not reviewed it yet—neither has Dandry or Claudia McDonnell. [laughter] But probably the greatest endorsement I've already received is from a writer I've loved and admired all the days of my life—Jimmy Breslin. His son Kevin Breslin sent me a picture of his father—now eighty-six—reading the damn book in his den. I'll take that as a very good "review." [applause]

When I was writing it, I wouldn't even let the Cuomo family see it. The governor—I shouldn't tell you this—very gently sent word through one of his emissaries, who said, "Look, can we please at least get an early copy of the book?" Well, I adore the Cuomo family, but I resisted all the entreaties and importunings to do this. So I went directly to press with it. But you can be sure Andrew and his mother got the first copies of the book, which comes out next month.

Mario Cuomo was a maestro of the language. He wasn't afraid of the sibilant *S*. His phrasing was as good as Sinatra's. His father dug ditches in New Jersey. They called them trenches. Then he worked at that fabled grocery store in Queens. The Cuomos lived in the back of the store.

There was always an elegance about Mario. Mario's phrasing was great; I was so taken with it. Japan*ees*. No *z*. He arranged words like

Nelson Riddle arranged notes. He moved words around masterfully. So, there are some of his magnificent speeches in this book. I am not going to read from the book because I hate it when authors do that. I'm going to pray that you will read the book—we have one for everyone today, thanks to Kevin Elliott, the president of Whitney Media Publishing Group—I hope it will commend itself to your favorable judgment, and you will find it worthy of a place in your personal library.

There are conversations we had early in the morning and late at night. My friend Joe Reilly, the president of the New York State Broadcasters, is mentioned in a little vignette in the book. He's in a bar in Albany, and some of the guys from the executive chamber—Albany insiders—say to him, "You're a friend of the Westchester radio man who talks to the gov all the time. What the hell do they talk about?" And Reilly said, "Don't go there. These guys are 'out there.'" [laughter] "They talk about their sons, their souls, their daughters." And we did.

He famously said you govern in *prose*, but you campaign in poetry. We didn't do much of the prose. I didn't give a God damn, frankly, how many Bob's Big Boys he put on the Thruway. Or who was going to be the next commissioner of Labor! He was a very introspective, soulful guy. I don't even include his most famous speech, the one at the convention—"The Shining City on the Hill." But there's one in there almost forgotten until now—at the Omega Society, a group of seekers and strugglers. And Mario, late in life, always returned to this theme: *tze-dekah* and *tikkum olam*. One of them means—and I forget which one comes first—we're all in this together; we're all brothers and sisters. And the second one is that God created the universe but didn't complete it: That's *your* job.

And he was in love with the writings of the Jesuit paleontologist and philosopher Father Teilhard de Chardin, who wrote the *Divine Milieu*. There's a quote I didn't put in the book, which I just found the other day. "If we can ever learn to *love* one another, then for the second time in history, man will have discovered fire!" Mario was taken with stuff like this. And he hated when I called it "stuff."

I just will read one thing; and the musicians here assembled, I think you may enjoy this. It's called "Mario's Music." And because you are who you are, musicians and entertainers.

His favorite song was "Stranger in Paradise" as sung by his friend Tony Bennett, and he loved Johnny Burke's lyrics—and John Donnelly you'll know this—"Polka Dots and Moonbeams": "There were questions in the eyes of other dancers. There were questions. But my heart knew all the answers and perhaps a few things more. . . .".

He was also moved by Ray Noble's "Love Is the Sweetest Thing," later a great instrumental by Artie Shaw. "Love is the *sweetest* thing. . . ." And that was his favorite word. It's not a word that men are comfortable with. "Sweet." As in, you can make a community stronger, better—even *sweeter* than it is.

"What else on earth could ever bring such happiness to everything as love's old story . . . ?"

He liked two other songs from the Great American Songbook, lovely ballads favored by musicians, torch singers, and that dwindling breed of cabaret performers. One such was Jimmy Van Heusen and Johnny Burke's haunting "It's Always You." K. T. Sullivan will remember this: "Whenever it's early twilight I watch till a star breaks through. Funny, it's not a star I see. It's always you. Wherever you are you're near me."

The gorgeous and plaintive lyrics of these and other romantic songs favored by the governor, come to think of it, are, at first glance, merely romantic. But they would work as well in a *religious* context.

Maybe Mario was just drawn to the simplicity and sweetness of it all. As I recall, another achingly sensitive song that commended itself to his favorable judgment (and mine) was Rube Bloom and Sammy Gallop's beautiful "Maybe You'll Be There":

Each time I see a crowd of people
Just like a fool I stop and stare.
It's really not the proper thing to do,
But maybe you'll be there.
I go out walking after midnight [that's a great line]
Along the lonely thoroughfare
It's not the time or place to look for you
But maybe you'll be there. [applause]

Tony Bennett was a pal, and the governor wrote a gorgeous Introduction to Tony's art book. You know he paints under the name—Aldon James remembers it—"Benedetto." Here's what Mario said about Tony:

Ever since Tony began drawing chalk pictures on the sidewalks of Astoria, Queens, seventy-five years ago, he has painted—and sung—he says, "Because I have to. I've got to sing. I've got to paint." I've known Tony Bennett much longer than he has known me. I enjoyed listening to him sing "The Boulevard of Broken Dreams" on a jukebox in 1949. In 1954, I danced with Matilda to the strains of "Stranger in Paradise" on our honeymoon at the Condado Beach Hotel in San Juan.

He cannot tolerate discrimination, hypocrisy, or unfairness of any kind. Tony feels the world's pain and does all he can to soothe it, with music, with painting, with advocacy, and always with great love. Once Tony said to me [and this is where Mario can't resist being Mario] that sometimes when the sound of a standing ovation is ringing in his ears, or he receives another honor for one of his paintings, or he's sitting with Susan quietly enjoying a blissful moment, "I think to myself, [Mario's always stirring up trouble] "This is heaven." I asked him, "But then, what comes after heaven?" He said, "I can't even imagine; I'm just going to keep going like this for as long as I can." [applause]

I can't imagine either what comes after heaven [said Mario]. But I know this. What gives Tony's music the sweetness, the emotion, and the power that make it so moving—and what gives his painting the insight and sensibility that are so apparent—is not his throat, or his eye, or all his hard work. It's his heart. And his soul. Tony is a lover of all that is good and beautiful, and that makes him a great singer, painter, human being. John Keats got it right: "A thing of beauty is a joy forever: Its loveliness increases; it will never pass into nothingness." Never. "The Best Is Yet to Come." That's Tony Bennett. [applause]

Tony returned the compliment when he said recently, "I've sung for five presidents. But Mario Cuomo is the greatest man I ever met."

He was not the most popular Roman Catholic in America for a good, long time. There was an Irish auxiliary bishop—his name long forgotten. I'm sorry he was Irish. He "banned" Mario, for all intents and purposes, from appearing at Catholic schools and Catholic churches.

And I once asked an archbishop of the Holy Roman Church—a member of the hierarchy; he's now a cardinal. And I said, "Eminence"—although he was a bishop at the time—"what is it about Cuomo? Why are they so hostile, the hierarchy? Why are they nervous around him, uneasy?" He thought for a minute, this great churchman. "It's *not* his powers of articulation, his rhetorical gifts or powers of persuasion they fear, it's his *goodness.*" That tells me everything about the subject of my book.

I've also included, in its entirety, Andrew Cuomo's magnificent eulogy for his father. You only get to pray over your departed old man once, and you better get it right. Andrew did it beautifully—and powerfully.

Mario Matthew Cuomo gave me the gift of friendship. I only wish I could have given him one more podium, and one more springtime. [applause]

And you're nice to let me rattle on about a man I loved. There are some very good stories in here.

They all came from him. [applause]

Finally, I perhaps can't depart this podium without telling you how much we miss E. Nobles Lowe, who also left us recently. [applause] He too was a great man.

An Evanescent Supreme Court Nomination: The Gov. Mario M. Cuomo Story

By Joseph W. Bellacosa, July 17, 2018, originally published in the New York Law Journal.

Judge Joseph Bellacosa, who served on New York state's highest court, the Court of Appeals in Albany and was also dean of St. John's School of Law, was a lifelong friend and loved Mario Cuomo too,

An example from the early '90s offers some perspective on the subject of the looming confirmation battle of a Supreme Court nominee. The name of then-Governor Mario M. Cuomo was floated, and after a short tease, disappeared into a historical footnote. What happened?

Angst is brewing over the confirmation battle for the Justice Anthony Kennedy seat on the Supreme Court of the United States. An example from the early 90s offers some perspective on the subject. The name of then-Governor Mario M. Cuomo was floated, and after a short tease, disappeared into a historical footnote. What happened?

It was reliably reported that President Bill Clinton considered (some said, even offered) Cuomo the nomination to SCOTUS. Speculation ensued that Cuomo, if appointed, would become the jurisprudential equalizer to fellow Queens New York native, Justice Nino Scalia. Alas, the rousing intellectual debates around the super-secret Court conference table never came to be.

A recent book about the late Governor (*American Cicero* by Professor Saladin Ambar) confers the classical mantle of Cicero on him—in recognition of the oratorical skills that he projected nationally in heralded speeches in the 1980s at the Democratic National Convention in San Francisco and at Notre Dame University. To understand this Cuomo fellow in this SCOTUS context, Socrates and his pithy principle of "*Know Thyself*" is useful.

To set the stage, it is well to recall Cuomo's earlier dalliance of a run for the presidency in 1992. A national campaign would have necessitated his entrusting his message and ultimate success to many strangers. That was alien to his comfort zone, as he liked working close to his own nest and vest. He spoke often as a man who saw himself as the proud product of the neighborhood Mom & Pop shop. Make no mistake, he was also an ambitious man, confident about his God-given talents and strengths. Yet, his tightly tethered ambition was displayed when he ended another of his less-renowned speeches—his first Inaugural as Governor—by publicly promising his deceased and revered father that he would not be distracted by the *cérémonie* (the trappings of high office).

The unavoidable *modus operandi* to run for president was, thus, incompatible with the figure he saw reflected through his Socratic mirror. That realization probably would have convinced him to stay put on his New York home court turf, while the hilarious image of the plane idled away on the Albany Airport tarmac.

A POSSIBLE NOMINATION

That set the stage for the next dalliance—a possible nomination to the Supreme Court. This supreme capstone to Cuomo's public and lawyerly career seemed a perfect fit. Cuomo's mother's dream for him, as he often told the story, that he might become a judge, would also be fulfilled. Despite his tongue-in-cheek wisecrack about not wanting to top off his career hidden under a black robe, he held the judicial process in the highest regard. Privately, Cuomo also fantasized the debates he might have with the highly respected intelligence of his diametrically opposite number—Justice Antonin Scalia—two American-Italian immigrant success stories, wearing respective St. John's–Harvard "tee" shirts under their robes.

Socrates and the Know Thyself principle, however, popped up anew. An astute student of history, Cuomo would have weighed the temporal dynamic of confirmation. If he accepted the nomination, he would have been the first post–Robert Bork Senate *piñata*. Political party retribution hung heavily in the poisoned confirmation atmosphere—as it has ever since—skewing the process in a regrettable way. Cuomo enjoyed a feisty litigator reputation and intellectual debate about ideas, big and small. So, the trial combatant, the former law professor at St. John's highly skilled in the Socratic Teaching Method, faced a new crossroad. Should he enter the transmogrified confirmation ring, or once again stay put? This time he would be in control of his own destiny—no long-arm delegations to unknown others.

Occasionally caricatured as "Hamlet on the Hudson," Cuomo thus faced his "to be or not to be" moment. Picture it this way: The nominee, then and now, sits alone at the Senate confirmation hearing table, primed (and biting one's tongue, as it were) to reply respectfully and diplomatically by saying absolutely nothing of consequence. Every utterance on every issue to many Senate interlocutors (neither a Cicero nor a Socrates among them) would be counterintuitively interdicted—a Trappist-like silence.

Governor Mario Cuomo (full disclosure: A friend who appointed me to the New York State Court of Appeals in 1987) well knew his impatience for this kind of inane *kabuki*. Cuomo knew [that] his natural disposition as a person of combative rigor and intellectual integrity would not survive sitting there without blunt and serious ripostes. He probably grimaced at the Socratic and Hamletian reflections and decided to pass on the offered hemlock.

Joseph W. Bellacosa retired from his position as associate judge on the state Court of Appeals in 2000. He also served as dean of St. John's Law School.

Andrew Cuomo's Eulogy for Mario Cuomo

Over the years Mario did many wonderful eulogies for departed friends: Among them were lovely tributes to Bill Modell and for Modell's son Michael. He also spoke movingly and lovingly of his old Queens friend John Aiello and the columnist Jack Newfield. His remarks for his mother, Immaculata, which I've included earlier in its entirety, is a classic. He also had gracious and graceful words for Ed Koch, Malcolm Wilson, Andy O'Rourke, and Ted Kennedy that were carried on our radio stations.

But the most stunning and riveting eulogy during my time was delivered last year not by Mario, but by his son and heir Andrew Mark Cuomo, who did himself—and his father—proud. Although Mario famously said on many occasions that he wanted no eulogies, Andrew's tribute to his father was absolutely spectacular. It takes nothing away from Andrew— or from Mario—to observe that MMC. himself could not have done better, perhaps not even as well. Andrew's lips and heart and passion put Mario Cuomo right in front of every sad admirer of his late father there assembled in that huge, beautiful Jesuit church on January 6, 2015. Here is Andrew's tribute to his father.

───────────────

First let me begin by thanking the pastor and priests at St. Ignatius Loyola for their courtesy, hospitality, and this beautiful ceremony, especially Father Alex Witt and all the co-celebrants, on behalf of the Cuomo family and fourteen grandchildren—by which we defied all odds. Thirteen girls! And the boy was born just before Christmas to my brother, Christopher. My brother, Christopher, and Cristina named the boy Mario because some people will do anything to earn the praise of their father. There is no jealousy on my part, however.

We want to thank Columbia-Presbyterian for their really fantastic care of my father during these difficult months. Dr. Engel and Dr. Maurer were extraordinary. The health aides who took care of my father at home: Steve Crockett, Dan O'Conner, Tom, Fran, Sharon. For twenty-four hours a day, they were really magnificent and made his life much more pleasant and also looked out for the family. We thank his partners at Willkie, Farr and Gallagher. He practiced law for twenty years after public service, and he really enjoyed it. It was a beautiful partnership.

To his team. No administration, no government works without a team. And my father really had a fantastic team. They worked twenty-four hours a day, seven days a week, because that's the only way they knew how to work. Mary Tragale and Mary Porcelli, Michael DelGuidice, Jerry Crotty, Drew Zambelli, Tonio Burgos, John Howard, John Maggiore, Mary Ann Crotty, and my father's third "son," whom I sometimes think he loved the most, Joe Percoco. They did an extraordinary job with his funeral, and we want to thank them.

I want to thank President Clinton for being here and Senator Clinton. They both meant so much to my father for so long and we are all so proud, not only that you're here, but that you're New Yorkers. President Obama sent his remarks. Vice President Biden was here last night. Senator Gillibrand is here. Attorney General Eric Holder; U.S. Attorney Loretta Lynch, who soon we hope will be Attorney General of the United States. Mayor Bill de Blasio, whom my father and I were with the other day. Mayor Bloomberg, whom my father had tremendous respect for; Mayor Dinkins, who served with my father when the city and the state were in a very difficult time.

And the literally thousands of New Yorkers who showed up yesterday to pay tribute to my father at the wake—it was an amazing outpouring of support. Thousands of people standing outside in the cold. My father hasn't been in public service in twenty years. And he had gotten very quiet after public service. But people remembered to show up twenty years later. People from all walks of life, all across the state, whom he touched.

One day when I was at HUD I was talking to my father on the phone. He had given a big speech that day, and I called to ask how it went: Did he do it from notes, did he do it on cards, did he do it off the cuff? He said it was a very important speech so he wrote it out and read every word. He went on to explain his theory that you can't possibly deliver a speech extemporaneously that is as well done as a written speech. He then invoked Winston Churchill as a proponent of the reading-word-for-word theory of speech making.

Now you must understand the rules of engagement in debate with Mario Cuomo. Invoking an historical figure as a source—in this context—was more of a metaphor than a literal interpretation. It really meant Winston Churchill could have said, or should have said, or would have said, that reading was best. But my father's invoking the gravitas of Churchill meant he was truly serious about this point.

I explained I was uncomfortable reading a speech word for word because I needed to see the audience's reaction and adjust accordingly. He summarily dismissed my point and said that was all unnecessary. And he said who cares about what the audience wants to hear. It's not about what they want to hear, it's about what you need to say.

And that, my friends, was the essence of Mario Cuomo.

He was not interested in pleasing the audience: not in a speech, not in life. He believed what he believed, and the reaction of the audience or the powers that be or the popularity of his belief was irrelevant to him.

Mario Cuomo was at peace with who he was and how he saw the world. This gave him great strength and made him anything but a typical politician.

But then again, he wasn't really a politician at all. Mario Cuomo's politics were more a personal belief system than a traditional theory. It was who he was. Not what he did. In his early life, my father was never interested in politics. In general, he disrespected politicians and the political system. He never studied politics or joined a political club. He never campaigned for anyone, and his early life, until his late thirties, was all about becoming a lawyer and practicing law. Once in practice he became quickly bored with the typical corporate practice. My father was a humanist. He had strong feelings of right and wrong based on his religion, philosophy, and life experiences. He was very concerned with how people were treated, and that was the arena that drew him in. The bridge from law to politics arrived for him when he took on the representation of the homeowners in Corona, Queens, whose homes were being condemned by the city to build a ballfield. They were poor working families and couldn't possibly fight City Hall.

Poor, working-family ethnics. He took on their cause to right the injustice he saw. Central to understanding Mario Cuomo is that Mario Cuomo was from Queens.

For those not from New York: Queens is an "outer" borough, like Brooklyn, the Bronx, Staten Island. Interestingly, there is no borough referred to as the "inner borough," only outer boroughs: and that's probably the point. There are insiders and outsiders, and one defines the other. There are those from the other side of the tracks; there are those from the other side of town. An outer borough is where the working families lived: the tradesmen, the civil servants, the poor. Mario Cuomo was the son of Italian immigrants who were part of the unwashed masses, who came with great dreams but also with great needs. Who struggled but ultimately succeeded due to the support they received in this great state of New York.

Mario Cuomo's birthmark from the outer borough was deep, and he wore it with pride. He had a natural connection with the outsider looking in, the person fighting for inclusion, the underdog, the minority, the disenfranchised, the poor. He was always the son of an immigrant. He was always an outsider, and that was his edge.

His early days in politics were not awe-inspiring. He had an early aborted run for mayor in 1973. In 1974 he lost the Democratic primary to Mary Anne Krupsak. He ran for mayor in 1977, losing to Ed Koch. In 1978 he was elected lieutenant governor to Governor Carey.

While it is different now, the job of lieutenant governor was not all that taxing. Governor David Paterson said it best when describing his role as lieutenant governor. David said he would wake up, call the governor, and if the governor answered the phone, he would hang up and go back to sleep.

My father was living in the Hotel Wellington in Albany at the time, and I started law school there, and we were roommates. The typical schedule was my father was in Albany Monday, Monday night, Tuesday, Tuesday night, and would leave on Wednesday during session. Our third roommate was Fabian Palomino, my father's lifelong dear friend, whom he clerked with in the Court of Appeals. Fabian was from mixed origins. He called himself a "Heinz 57," part Italian, part Native American, part African American, part anything else. He was truly a unique and powerful man, and we would have dinner together on the nights they were in town.

My mother would send up care packages with my father on Monday, and all we had to do was warm up the prepared meals. My father insisted we sample every wine made in the state of New York, and we were soon connoisseurs of New York's best wines. Fabian, who was a portly fellow, wore a shirt with no sleeves, stretched over his belly tighter than a drumskin. He wore boxer shorts with dark dress socks over the calf. I assumed he had chronically cold calf muscles. My father, who was modest and always formal in attire, was perpetually frustrated with Fabian's dress. And he would say to Fabian, "Why can't you dress for dinner, Fabian?" And Fabian would say, "Out of respect for you, I have." He would say, "I wore my fancy boxers out of respect for you. I respect that you are the lieutenant governor and one heart attack away from having a real job." And then Fabian would laugh, and the laugh would make his belly shake, and my father, not loving being mocked, would smile, but slowly.

After dinner they would turn on the TV, and we would sit on the couch and watch television. We would watch a ballgame or the news, but it didn't really matter. The function of the TV was just to introduce a topic they could debate. And they could debate anything. An item on the news or a soap commercial, it didn't really matter. They debated to debate. They just loved it, and they were great at it. Eventually, the debate invariably turned to politics and government, and I could see my father refining and honing his own personal philosophy.

In 1982 my father ran against Ed Koch for governor. It was the impossible race that couldn't be won, but my father was ready and believed he was better suited to be governor than Ed Koch. The pollsters, with their charts demonstrating the impossibility of his pursuit, were unpersuasive. If my father thought he was fighting the right fight, it didn't matter whether we were going to win or lose. It was "the right thing to do." And there is one rule to live by, which is you always *do the right thing*.

Mario Cuomo did not fit neatly into any political category. He believed government had an affirmative obligation to help the excluded join the mainstream. He believed it was the country's founding premise and that more inclusion made the country a stronger country. Better education, better health care, economic opportunity and mobility helped the new immigrants progress and made the community stronger. Not to invest in the progress of others was a disservice to the whole. He believed in compassion for the sick and the needy. This was also the essence of Christianity and Jesus's teachings. But there were no giveaways. Responsibility and hard work were expected from all. He was not a spendthrift and came from a culture of fiscal responsibility. He was an executive and needed to balance a budget. He cut taxes and the workforce. When he took office the top tax rate in New York was 14 percent. When he left office twelve years later, it was 7 percent. The state workforce twelve years later was smaller than when he took office.

Mario Cuomo, intellectually, was all about subtlety and nuance. He was called The Great Liberal. He resisted the label. His philosophy defied a label, especially an undefined and nebulous one. My father called himself a "progressive pragmatist." Progressive values, but a pragmatic approach. He believed he needed to separate the two components, the goals and the means. His goal was progressive, but his means were pragmatic. I told him it was too complicated to communicate and no one would understand what he was saying. Frankly, I still don't understand what he was saying. But he said he didn't care and wouldn't be reduced by the shortcomings of others, including mine. My father was skeptical of people and organizations that profited from government, to whom government was a business, rather than an avocation. And he always focused on the goal of government rather than the means—the product, not the process—to help the people, the student, the parent, the citizens.

The truth is he didn't love the day-to-day management of government; the tedium and absurdity of the bureaucracy was mind-numbing for him. Nor did he appreciate the political back and forth with the posturing legislature. As governor, he was criticized by the right. As the icon of the left, he was criticized by the zealots on the left because his lofty rhetoric couldn't match the reality of his government programs.

At his core he was a philosopher and he was a poet, an advocate, and a crusader. Mario Cuomo was the keynote speaker for our better angels. He was there to make the case, to argue and convince, and in that purist mindset he could be a ferocious opponent and powerful ally.

And he was beautiful.

A speech never started with the words—it was about the principle, the idea and the passion, the righteousness, the injustice—and then came the words, arranged like fine pearls, each chosen for its individual beauty but also placed perfectly, fitting just so with the one that came before and the one that followed so there was a seamless flow, in logic and emotion, leading one ultimately to the inevitable conclusion—his conclusion—which was the point of the speech in the first place.

He was a religious man, and his relationship with the Church was important and complicated. His famous and influential speech at Notre Dame was done more for himself, to explain how he separated his personal views from his professional responsibilities. The public official fulfilling a constitutional responsibility was different but consistent with laymen's following Christ's teachings. He believed Jesus's teachings could be reduced to one word. And the word was Love. And love means acceptance, compassion, and support to help people. To do good. And that's what he wanted government to be. A force for good. His love was not a passive love, but an active love. Not tough love, but a strong love. The good fight was a fight for love, and it was a fight he was ready to wage.

In many ways my father's view on the Church was ahead of his time.

He was excited about our new Pope Francis and his enlightened perspective on Catholicism with an emphasis on inclusion and understanding. My father thought Pope Francis would agree that Jesus himself was probably from an outer borough.

My father loved Teilhard de Chardin, a French Jesuit who modeled service and a dedication to sustainable community as a way of life.

My father was a Lincoln scholar attracted by Lincoln's example of government as the pursuit of the great principles. He also appreciated that Lincoln was the triumph of substance over style and that his life exemplified the relative isolation of people in power.

We were a working-class family and proud of it. No fancy trips, no country clubs for us. He was the workingman's governor and remained loyal to the old neighborhood values always.

His grandchildren, my children, will speak of grandpa's sweetness. My father always had a "sweetness," but it grew over the years, much as a fine wine turns into a brandy.

I, however, remember his younger years, and "sweetness" is not the first word that comes to mind. Make no mistake, Mario Cuomo was a tenacious, competitive, incredibly strong man. He was impatient with the bureaucracy, unrelenting in the face of bigotry, uncompromising in remedying injustice. And he was really, really tough. It would have been malpractice not to be. These battles were for real consequences and made a difference to real people. And he was also competitive by nature. Whether in a campaign, fighting the legislature, or on a basketball court, you opposed him at your own risk and peril. I have the scars to prove it.

The basketball court remained the one place he could allow himself to be his fully aggressive self. Governors, you see, are supposed to comport themselves with dignity and decorum. The basketball court was his liberation. We had epic battles. He hated few things as much as a timid opponent on the court because you cheated him of a real contest.

We played in the State Police gym in Albany. He liked to play one-on-one because it was the purest form of competition. He was a solid 210 pounds and fast for a big man.

He would make faces at you, taunt you, talk constantly in a distracting and maddening banter designed to unnerve you. He would hit you in places the human body did not have anatomical defenses. The issue of calling fouls plagued us. We tried using state troopers as referees, but they were afraid of angering my father. With one wrong call they would wind up on a weigh station somewhere up on the Northway. We tried letting the trooper be anonymous so there was no fear of retaliation.

After I left Albany, the basketball competition became more institutionalized. My father started a basketball league with a number of teams. They had professional referees, and any disputes were settled by the commissioner. And my father served as the commissioner and also captain of one of the teams. At the end of the season there would be draft selections depending on the results. Some people accused my father of hiring state employees only for their basketball talents. He denied it. Well, at least let's say it didn't happen often. Basketball was my father's outlet, and it was always in good humor and always with good sportsmanship.

My father also loved to battle the press. They were like the opposing counsel in a courtroom. He thought if they could judge his actions and communicate that to the public then he had the right to challenge their facts and judgment. He was unmoved by his staff's passionate arguments that this was counterproductive. You don't fight with people who buy ink by the barrel, as the old saying goes. My father was undeterred. The press was too important to tolerate sloppiness or misinterpretation. The public deserved the truth, and the press did not have the right to distort it, certainly not with impunity. He railed against ivory tower pundits and reporters with an agenda. He had no problem calling a reporter at 7 A.M. to give them a critique of their article. Most often, it was fair to say the critique was not overly positive. I have evolved, and I would never call a reporter at 7 A.M. I wait until at least 9 A.M. But he also admired journalism done well, and he respected Jimmy Breslin, Pete Hamill, Jack Newfield, Murray Kempton and Mike Lupica, Mary McGrory, Marcia Kramer, all stars in the constellation of lives well lived.

He was humbled to be in public service and had disdain for those who demeaned it, with scandals or corruption, or cheap public relations stunts. It was a position of trust and deserved to be honored. Mario Cuomo served twelve years as governor with integrity. You can disagree with Mario Cuomo over those twelve years, but he never dishonored the state and he never dishonored his position.

In his private life he was exactly as he appeared in public life. He had a sixty-year love affair with his wife, Matilda. Not a storybook romance— no late-night kissing in the park, at least as far as we knew—but a real life partnership built on a foundation of mutual respect and tolerance. Commitment to Mario Cuomo was sacrosanct.

His children were everything to him. Although I may look the oldest, Margaret is actually the oldest and a source of great pride. He beamed when he said, "My daughter is a doctor." Maria, his artistic, altruistic delight. With Maria, he had the purest loving relationship. Madeline made him proud as a great mother and a tenacious attorney. Chris, talented, facile, and funny, could always make him laugh.

He loved his daughters-in-law, Sandy and Cristina, and his sons-in-law, with whom he had a special relationship: Kenneth, Howard, and Brian. They enjoyed a true father–son relationship with him. It was mutual, and they were adored.

He had a small group of friends: Jimmy Breslin, Vincent Tese, Fabian Palomino, Mike DelGuidice, Sandy Frucher, and Joe Percoco were his intimate world.

Over the years the press would love to give their dime-store psychoanalysis of our "complex" father and son relationship. It was all a lot of hooey. It is this simple: I was devoted to my father, from the time I was fifteen, joining him in every crusade. My dad was my hero, my best friend, my confidante, my mentor. We spoke almost every day, and his wisdom grew as I grew older. When it works, having a working partnership with your father adds an entirely new dimension to the father–son relationship. And for us, it worked. Politics is not an easy business. It shouldn't be. But we carried the same banner. I helped him become a success, and he helped me become a success, and we enjoyed deeply each other's victories, and we suffered the pain of each other's losses. My only regret is that I didn't return from Washington to help in his 1994 race. Whether or not I could have helped, I should have been there. It was the right thing to do, and I didn't do it.

I loved winning the governorship more for him than for myself. It was redemption for my father. Cuomo was elected governor—the first name was not all that relevant. It was a gift to have him with us this past election night. The doctors didn't want him to go, but I insisted, bringing him on the stage for one more fist pump. Holding up his hand, I felt his energy surge; his face brightened and his eyes shined as he gave us that great, satisfied smile one more time. He walked off the stage and said, "Wow, what a crowd that was!" It was the best medicine I could provide for Mario Cuomo that night.

He loved being governor and thought he could do four terms, and he valued that over anything else—even the Supreme Court. Why didn't he run for president? people ask. Because he didn't want to—he was where he thought God wanted him to be.

He was a man of principle—of honor, of duty, of service—and that defined his life. He had simple tastes, no expensive cars, no planes, no fancy homes. A weekend meal with family. Watching a baseball or basketball game with my father's running commentary, reading a good book, and just talking—but really talking—there was no small talk or superficiality with Mario Cuomo.

My father never lost his interest in public affairs. We would talk at 5 A.M., and he would have read all the papers and was ready to tell me everything I did wrong the day before. We would talk about the problems and how to find a way through the maze.

He was recently very troubled by the Washington "mess," as he would call it. He was concerned about the city. My father's 1984 convention speech was called "The Tale of Two Cities," and he was adamant about pointing out inequities and divisions in our society. But the goal was always to unify, never to divide. And the current factions in New York City were very disconcerting to him. He governed during Howard Beach and Bensonhurst and knew racial and class divisions are the New York City fault lines.

They say your father never leaves you. If you listen carefully, you will hear his voice. I believe that's true. But one doesn't need to listen that carefully or be his son to know what Mario Cuomo would say today: that it's time for this city to come together; it's time to stop the negative energy and keep moving forward. The positive course is to learn the lessons from past tragedies, to identify the necessary reforms, to improve our justice system, better safety for police officers, and to move this city forward.

And that's just what we will do, Dad. I promise you.

For Mario Cuomo, the purpose of life was clear: to help those in need and leave the world a better place (Matthew 25); *tikkun olam*, to heal the divide; *tzedakah*, to do justice. It's that simple and yet that profound. It's that easy, and yet that hard. By any measure, Mario Cuomo's voice inspired generations; his government initiatives helped millions live better lives. He left the world better than he found it. He was a leading opponent of the death penalty and proud of appointing the first African American to the Court of Appeals, of his Liberty Scholarship Programs, his pioneering child health insurance program, his leadership in AIDS treatment research.

New York is a better state thanks to Mario Cuomo.

The last few days as he was slipping I said to him, to give him something to look forward to, that he needed to stay strong for the inaugural because I wanted him to hold the Bible. And he asked, in a semiconscious state, "Which Bible?" Which only Mario Cuomo would ask. And I said the St. James Bible. He said the St. James Bible would be good for this purpose. I didn't follow up. A few weeks later he said he was too weak to hold the Bible, but he would be here. I stopped at his apartment, went to his bed, and said, "Dad, the inauguration is today. You want to come? You can hold the Bible, or you don't have to hold the Bible." There was no response. I said, "Well, let me know because there is a second event in Buffalo, and if you change your mind you can come to Buffalo." During that afternoon, my sister played the inaugural speech for him. He knew the Buffalo event was at 4:00. My father passed away at 5:15.

He was here. He waited. And then he quietly slipped out of the event and went home. Just as he always did. Because his job was done.

We believe the spirit lives, and I believe my father is not gone and that his spirit is with us—in Amanda's song, Michaela's charisma, Tess's dance, Christopher's laugh, and in every good deed I do.

I believe my father's spirit lives in the hope of a young boy sitting in a failing school who can't yet speak the language. His spirit lives in a young girl, pregnant and alone and in trouble. It lives in South Jamaica and the South Bronx. His spirit lives in those outsiders still living in the shadow of opportunity and striving to join the family of New York.

And Pop, you were right once again, and I was wrong: Tell Winston Churchill I now agree, I read every line, Pop, word for word, because it's not about what they want to hear. It's about what I wanted to say. And I said it, Pop.

Tell Officer Ramos and Officer Liu we miss them already, tell Fabian and Jack Newfield, Grandma and Grandpa, and Uncle Frank we love them.

I will listen for your voice. You taught us well. You inspired us. We know what we have to do, and we will do it. We will make this state a better state, and we will do it together.

On that, you have my word, as your son.

I love you, Pop, and always will.

Mario: This Is Personal

This piece was published as the Preface to Bill O'Shaughnessy's book
Mario Cuomo: Remembrances of a Remarkable Man.

Mario Matthew Cuomo left us after a magnificent life in his eighty-second year on the very first day of the new year, 2015. The fifty-second governor of New York was much more than the sum of his public papers preserved in the great Archives of the State of New York on Madison Avenue in Albany, or the more than 700 soaring and graceful speeches he gave on matters temporal and spiritual, or his eight books that have been translated into many languages and are part of private and public libraries all over the world. Mario Cuomo was much more than the sum of what he accomplished—he was an example for us to follow, and memories of his beautiful life will inspire and instruct us for many years to come.

He was a child of immigrants who grew up to be governor of what he called "the only state that matters." Mario was glib of tongue, agile of mind, and generous of heart. His admirers, and there were many all over the world, tried to install him in the White House as president of the United States. Failing that, they implored him to accept an appointment to the Supreme Court, the highest tribunal in the land, where he could continue his lifelong affair with "Our Lady of the Law." Declining all importunings and flattery, this gifted son of a Queens greengrocer who came to this country from an Italian hill town to dig ditches became instead the great philosopher-statesman of the American nation. As a public man he was also a preacher who made many of us wiser about love.

I will forever remember him because of all the gifts and good fortune bestowed on me. I was privileged to know the sweetness of his friendship for thirty-eight of my eighty years. His favorite word was "sweet"—as in, "You can make a community better, stronger . . . even sweeter . . . than it is." It is a designation and word most men are not comfortable with.

All our colleagues in the public press and every journal, blog, and magazine in the land noted his departure. Most who practice in our tribe "warehouse" these things known as obituaries. They have them preserved in computers and filing cabinets all ready to go, often to coincide with your last breath. So I know I'm late with all this, and far more gifted writers like Mike Lupica, E. J. Dionne, Terry Golway, Bob McManus, Wayne Barrett, Steve Cuozzo, Stephen Schlesinger, Jeffrey Toobin, Ken Kurson, David Shribman, Jeff Shesol, Ken Auletta, Mike Barnicle, Bob Hardt, Paul Grondahl, David Greenberg, Erica Orden, and Hendrik Hertzberg have already written lovely reminiscences that historians and the Cuomo family will collect and treasure. One of his daughters, Maria Cuomo Cole, has already begun to assemble all the graceful tributes to her father.

It must, however, be noted that one prominent journalist has not yet been heard from: the iconic Gay Talese, whose legendary *Esquire* essays "Frank Sinatra Has a Cold" and "The Silent Season of a Hero" about DiMaggio scream for yet a third Talese piece on another quite extraordinary Italian American from Queens whose contributions in the realm of public service were every bit as stellar as those provided by Sinatra in a recording studio and by Joe D. on a baseball diamond. Every time I see Talese around town of an evening or strolling Park Avenue in his fine clothes, I grab him by the pick stitching on his well-cut lapel: "You gotta do Mario!" Talese, a real writer of great gifts, is himself eighty-six, and however trim and fit he may be, his own clock is ticking. He writes now of bridges on Staten Island. Better he should write of one who built bridges . . . to our better nature.

As this book went to press I had the good fortune to be seated next to the great writer at a black-tie dinner at "21." He spoke movingly of Mario and how the governor was motivated and inspired by his roots:

Mario didn't run for president because he came from "village" people . . . like me. We're from the south—Calabria. That's like being from the South in this country. It's different. It's made up of villages. We're village people. We're not "national." We're all from southern Italy, our parents, our grandparents. We like to stay close to home and sleep in our own bed. Sinatra, Lady Gaga, DiMaggio, Tony Bennett, Talese. Mario Cuomo was the best of the village people, the most honorable. He was the Crown Jewel of Italian immigration. You always ask me why I didn't write about him. The truth is I didn't want to hurt him, I admire him so much. You said you make no pretense toward objectivity in your book. And you shouldn't. His father dug sewers. It's amazing what his father did. You guys are Irish. Your people could be cops [and] firemen and the wives could be nannies. You spoke the language. Italians had to dig ditches because we didn't speak the language. It makes Mario all the more amazing.

My colleagues in the public press rushed to their typewriters, computers, and yellow legal pads to note Mario's passing and assess and evaluate his stewardship of the eighty-two years he'd been given. One of the first off the mark with a tribute was Terry Golway. The brilliant Kean University professor, historian, author, and journalist who once served as a columnist and member of the editorial board of the *New York Times* and the *New York Observer* was always a special favorite of the governor's.

Here are some excerpts and lovely highlights from his appreciation:

Mario Cuomo became a political sensation through a medium thought to belong to another era: words. Beautiful, poetic, meaningful words, spoken in a strong, clear voice, with a cadence that turned even a clumsy phrase into a baroque masterpiece.

Embedded in all those beautiful words there was a palpable love of American possibilities. He was an Italian-speaking kid from Queens who become not just an orator but a philosopher whose texts will be read for as long as American political thought matters.

On January 1, 1983, after taking the oath as governor of New York on the first of the 4,380 days he would spend in residence on Eagle Street, Mario Cuomo spoke of "the idea of family, mutuality, the sharing of benefits and burdens for the good of all. No family that favored its strong children or that in the name of even-handedness failed to help its vulnerable ones would be worthy of the name."

Here was this man from Queens, all but saying that powerful people in the body politic were peddling lies. "It has become popular in some quarters," he said, "to argue that the principal function of government is to make instruments of war and to clear obstacles away from the strong. It is said the rest will happen automatically. The cream will rise to the top. Survival of the fittest may be a good working description of the process of evolution, but a government of humans should elevate itself to a higher order, one which tries to fill the cruel gaps left by chance, and by a wisdom we don't fully understand."

He came to the podium, waved, and then excused himself from "the poetry and temptation to deal in nice but vague rhetoric, the usual preliminaries."

Instead, he offered a polite but passionate assault on Ronald Reagan's America, his shining city on a hill: "A shining city is perhaps all the president sees from the portico of the White House and the veranda of his ranch, where everyone seems to be doing well," Cuomo said. "But there's another part to the shining city, where some people can't pay their mortgages, and most young people can't afford one; where students can't afford the education they need, and middle-class parents watch the dreams they hold for their children evaporate. . . . There is despair, Mr. President, in the faces you don't see, in the places you don't visit in your shining city. In fact, Mr. President, this nation is more a 'Tale of Two Cities' than a 'Shining City on a Hill.'"

Cuomo continued with phrase upon devastating phrase, pleading with the American people to see the poor and disenfranchised not as failures and losers, but fellow citizens.

Mario Cuomo's hold on the imagination of his fellow Democrats was all about soaring rhetoric and political poetry. But it was the governor himself who noted that politicians campaign in poetry but govern in prose. His principled stand against capital punishment—which he shared with his predecessor, Hugh Carey—won him accolades as did his nuanced defense of abortion rights, brilliantly argued in a speech at the University of Notre Dame in 1985.

Combined with his wonderful speeches, those two positions earned Cuomo a reputation as the Democratic Party's leading liberal spokesman at a time when liberalism was banished to the political wilderness.

Cuomo published a collection of his speeches, reminding so many of his supporters why they adored him. The volume was called *More Than Words*. It is a suitable epitaph for a politician who used words to inspire, to probe, to critique, and to provoke. Yes, he will be remembered best as an orator, but there was something more about him, something more than the pretty pictures he painted with the English language.

He was unafraid to challenge a comforting narrative with impertinent questions at a time when others preferred to simply go along and get along. That required more than words. That required ideas, courage, and intelligence.

Mario Cuomo had all three.

The reader can see and savor Golway's entire original piece at Politico.com, where his graceful essays now often appear.

I've hesitated until now because I could not summon the strength or find the desire to sit over a legal pad with a pen and then speak words into a microphone in a radio studio that place Mario Cuomo in the past tense. Everything that he was lingers. And will for years.

Even now I'm afraid it was a friendship I taxed too much with impatience; distractions about marital issues; tales of chaos around my hearth and home, much of it of my very own making; irreverence; and even, occasionally, impertinence. I mention impertinence because although we would occasionally "edit" each other's pronouncements and writing, I was constantly aware that I was not worthy to loose the strap of his sandal when use of the English language was at issue, and on many occasions I told him so. Yet undaunted by the prospect of adding anything of value or perspective to a pronouncement of the great man, I would usually attach a handwritten note to a working draft: "*You hold the bat like this, Mr. DiMaggio . . .*" Very few of my "suggestions" made it into the final transcript. Apply the impertinence to me anyway for even presuming to dare tweak a pronouncement of one of the greatest minds of our time. But now . . . now I sit alone.

Or am I alone . . . ?

Often late at night or early in the morning when he would be embarked on a lovely riff about one of the great issues of the day that was too good, too wise, too exquisite for my meager brain, I would plead with him to stop, please stop wasting the magnificent product of that bright, fine, beautiful mind on such an unworthy and untutored Irish dunderhead.

As the governor recognized very early on, almost at our first encounter, I'm not exactly a belletrist or writer of fine literary works known for their aesthetic qualities and originality of style and tone as he was. He was more alive to the world of ideas and to the study and lessons of history than most of us could ever hope to be.

At any rate, I cannot add to the official canon of his work or improve on the recitation of his many accomplishments as a mediator, a college professor, an author of eight books including *The Blue Spruce* for children, a Lincoln scholar, a diarist, an attorney in the service of what he called "Our Lady of the Law," and then as secretary of state, lieutenant governor, and governor of New York state, and even later as the most esteemed partner of the big, white shoe Manhattan law firm founded by Wendell Willkie. It is part of the popular lexicon, his public and legal career, and it resides now in the history books of a nation and in those voluminous archives in the state capital in Albany, while his mortal remains rest in St. John's Cemetery in Middle Village, Queens.

As a public orator, he was a man of his words. And in every season, for all his rhetorical gifts and power at the lectern, Mario was always searching for meaning and purpose, always looking toward the light, and never quite sure he had done enough to fulfill the moral obligations inherited from his father, Andrea, or his mother, Immaculata Giordano, or later from the Vincentians of St. John's. As Mario was fond of saying, "Every time I've done something that doesn't feel right, it's ended up not being right. I talk and talk and talk, and I haven't taught people in fifty years what my father taught me by example in one week!"

You can see—and feel—the yearning and struggling of a beautiful soul in *The Diaries of Mario M. Cuomo*, published by Random House in 1984:

> I've fought a thousand fights but not enough the good fight. I've not—truly enough—kept the faith. I've hurt people by bad example, even my own family.
>
> For whatever combination of genetic, environmental, and educational reasons, I have always found it easier to discern a challenge than to acknowledge success.
>
> I've always preferred privacy. Loneliness has never been the threat to me that the world has been. The more deeply I have become involved in opening myself, revealing myself, discussing myself, the more vulnerable I have felt.
>
> Why, then, am I in politics at all? I take power too seriously to be totally comfortable with it.
>
> Every day, a thousand lost opportunities: every day closer to the end. If only everything we did, we did in light of that, how differently we'd act. We would have so few regrets.
>
> But now I look back on nearly fifty years and I'm pained by the memory of so many hurts, so many mistakes, so many missed opportunities. So much weakness. It's a hard game, but "the game is only lost when we stop trying." So, on with the effort!

So for my part, I can really tell you only small things about the man, for I always thought of him as a teacher, albeit a great one, possessed of that beautiful soul that far outshone all his accomplishments in the public arena.

We spoke often of our souls, our sons, our daughters, and only occasionally did the great issues of the day, fleeting and temporal as they were over the years, intrude on his relentless searching and brilliant musings about matters eternal.

Our friend Joe Reilly told me of an evening at the bar of an Albany pub frequented by "political types." The affable, gregarious—and generous—Reilly was descended upon by some staffers from the executive chamber (the governor's office). One of them, after a cocktail or two, said, "Joe, we know you're a friend of O'Shaughnessy, the Westchester radio guy who's a big fan of the Gov. They seem to talk a lot on the phone early in the morning and late at night. What the hell do they talk about?"

Reilly said: "Don't go there; just don't go there. They talk about their sons and daughters and their souls. They're 'out there.'" Reilly then changed the subject. I mention this little vignette as relayed to me by my Irish friend because I want to make sure the reader understands that the governor, if you haven't already figured it out, mercifully spared me any of those complex and difficult issues that came under the heading of "prose"—those very complicated issues a governor has to deal with 24/7.

As I approach the ambiguities, confusion, and uncertainties of old age, l hope I've not succumbed to what Pete Hamill calls "the glib seductions of nostalgia." As I move into those ambiguities, my mind drifts back across many seasons of a unique friendship with a marvelous man who just happened to be a liberal icon of our American nation. It's been noticed, by more than a few of my friends, that I've always looked at the Cuomos, especially Mario, through rose-colored glasses. To which I have to plead, "Guilty." But that admission also puts me squarely in the same boat as the very first woman Chief Judge of the New York State Court of Appeals, Judith Kaye, who, when asked if she had any "objectivity" about one Mario Cuomo, answered, simply and honestly, "No."

The late Bob Grant, fiery and provocative dean of radio talk show hosts, who was lethal on the subject of Mario, accused me more than once of being a "stooge for Mario Cuomo" (which appellation never prevented the cranky old WOR and WABC star from generously plugging all four of my previous books). Incidentally, importuned by my friend Rick Buckley, who owned WOR, I tried mightily to persuade the governor to appear on Grant's final WOR show, to no avail. "I saved his job once at WMCA," said Mario about the fellow who practically made a career out of bashing him almost daily on the air. But I was never able to get them together. Still I liked Grant, cranky and acerbic though he was.

My feelings and great affection for Mario Cuomo, you should thus be advised, also place me in the very same pew with the late Jack Newfield and the crime writer Nick Pileggi. My mind drifts back to a late-night conversation at the Executive Mansion in Albany. William Kennedy, the novelist and Albany historian, was there too. And when the subject of Mario Matthew Cuomo came up, Pileggi (or it may have been New-field) said, "Hell . . . we've all gone over the edge on this guy . . . from objectivity to admiration and awe a long time ago." So I figure if tough, no-nonsense, unsentimental journalists like Newfield and Pileggi were not immune to Mario's charms . . . well, the hell with it. I'm sorry . . . I loved the man. And I'm not alone. A few months ago, in a public con-versation with *Vanity Fair*'s Michael Shnayerson up on the stage at the New York Public Library, the writer Ken Auletta of *New Yorker* fame almost teared up at the mention of Mario's name. M.C. has that effect. Still. The great Chris Matthews, without whom MSNBC would surely resemble a bowling alley, once urged caution upon young people who would idolize politicians. "Imperfection grows." But also, I'm per-suaded, do decency and goodness and thoughtfulness.

As I write this, we have just marked the third anniversary of the man's passing. I hope I've done justice to the memory of a great man. I'll let scholars and perhaps other journalists, commentators, and broadcast-ers aim for impartiality. I'll take a pass because I loved the man. I realize full well that subjectivity has a field day in all my recollections of Mario Cuomo. And I'm quite aware that objectivity is akin to the coin of the realm in the Republic of Letters. And as I don't aspire to standing or high estate in that rarefied realm, I'll not tolerate any criticism of my friend in these pages.

With these reminiscences, I'm not trying to make him an icon or, God forbid, a martyr of a long-ago age, or even a hero of a distant myth. It was especially clear to me that Mario tried to observe and adhere to in his personal life those lofty lessons about which he spoke so often. He often shared with friends the torment he encountered almost every morning when he would stride into the state capitol charged up to begin his day's work. "Should I stop and chat with the elderly man who sells newspapers or the blind shoeshine man and listen to their prob-lems and complaints . . . or should I breeze by and hurry upstairs to the governor's office where I can try to save thousands with a few phone calls and the sweep of my pen . . . ?" But in the next breath he would recall Mother Teresa's counsel as relayed to him by John F. Kennedy Jr.: "You save them one . . . by one . . . by one." Thus in this book I've attempted to show that Mario was a man who tried to live the lessons he preached.

He was, in every telling and by every account, a very *real* flesh-and-blood retail politician as well as a statesman and philosopher. And like Nelson Rockefeller, when Mario Cuomo walked into a room . . . you knew he was there.

"Quotable Quotes"—Reviews of *Mario Cuomo: Remembrances of a Remarkable Man*

"The book is powerful . . . and beautiful. My father loved Bill O'Shaughnessy. And they had so many good times. They loved to have those marvelous conversations for so many hours. Who was more philosophical . . . who was more melodic . . . who was more profound . . . who was deeper? There was a genuine, genuine love. My mother and my sisters watched it for many, many years. My father was an interesting combination of things and Bill has captured his notion of "sweet strength" beautifully. The book really touches my father's essence, that sweet strength. And, by the way, that is also the essence of my friend O'Shaughnessy."
—Governor Andrew M. Cuomo

"We've come to expect from Bill O'Shaughnessy a beautiful symphony of wit, wisdom, a perceptiveness and analysis of not only one's political actions and accomplishments . . . but also the character of the person. He hasn't let us down in this book. It's a winner and a joy to read. I have had a fascination with Mario Cuomo for a long time and O'Shaughnessy helped me understand and appreciate him even more. All you had to do is listen to Mario Cuomo's speeches. They were a matter of the heart and a matter of the soul. But I can't resist the observation that it has taken an Irishman to write so beautifully about Mario Cuomo. This book is very well done."
—Timothy Cardinal Dolan, Archbishop of New York

"Bill O'Shaughnessy is an *habitué* and chronicler of the New York scene. This is a book about a legend by another legend."
—Leonard Riggio, chairman, Barnes & Noble

"I've been in politics in this country since l was a twenty-nine-year-old kid, and the minute I saw Mario Cuomo, I knew he was better than I was . . ."
—Joe Biden, former vice president

"At some point, we're not going to get politicians like Mario Cuomo any more who are articulate and with substance. And that's one of the great things Bill O'Shaughnessy does with his latest book. He's leaving a paper trail for future generations to study and be inspired."
—Mark Simone, WOR

"Rarely has an intimate portrait of a relationship revealed so much about the talents and souls of both the narrator and subject. O'Shaughnessy has achieved just that. Engaging, enlightening and inspiring . . ."
—Sidney Offit, author; curator-emeritus, George Polk
    Journalism Awards

"O'Shaughnessy's *Mario Cuomo* reads as a tribute to statesmanship, vision, empathy, oratory, trustworthiness, gravitas and grace. Cuomo's words leap from the pages with themes of a 'higher calling.' The book begs the question, 'What happened to our national discourse?' and is filled with anecdotal insight into the governor, his friends, his day-to-day, his family and his lifestyle evolving into a tableau describing why he was admired by millions and loved by those closest to him."
—GOODREADS/Gordon Hastings

"The broadcaster William O'Shaughnessy's love letter to the former governor is both an unabashed tribute and a timely

reminder of the passion and inspirational positive thinking largely missing from today's loyal opposition. In one telling passage, the author Gay Talese explains why Mr. Cuomo decided against a presidential campaign: His family was from Calabria, a Southern Italian village of people who 'like to stay close to home and sleep in our own bed.' Mr. Talese told Mr. O'Shaughnessy: 'You guys are Irish. Your people could be cops, firemen, and the wives could be nannies. You spoke the language. Italians had to dig ditches because we didn't speak the language.' It makes Mario all the more amazing."
—Sam Roberts, the *New York Times*

"This poignant memoir portrays the spiritual journey of a man who played many roles: political leader, moral compass, orator, author, legal scholar, loving father and grandfather. He was, in O'Shaughnessy's words, one of the most articulate and graceful public men of the twentieth century. Much more than a simple memoir of a cherished friend, *Remembrances of a Remarkable Man* is a loving tribute to a political figure whose words and example continue to inform the conscience of our nation."
—*Brooklyn Daily Eagle*

"The 'bromance' between O'Shaughnessy and Cuomo began in 1977. The way he remembers it in his new book *Mario Cuomo* (Fordham University Press), O'Shaughnessy kept Cuomo waiting for 20 minutes. (He never let him forget it!) During the interview he asked Cuomo about his opposition to the death penalty. The two men's eyes met. Cuomo replied softly, 'Did God tell me to be against this? Look, even a Republican who doesn't wear socks can understand this: Vengeance doesn't work.' O'Shaughnessy was floored and so impressed with the passion, erudition and sensitivity of his guest, that after Cuomo had left the studio, the broadcaster called some Democratic friends and asked, 'Who is this guy . . . I mean who the hell is he?' For the next 38 years, O'Shaughnessy explored that question right up to the day his friend died on January 1, 2015, at the age of 82. And now in his fifth book, he has supplied a multitude of answers in personal reminiscences, anecdotes, speeches, radio interviews and letters. 'Call it a love letter!' And we will. For the author styles himself as a modern Boswell to the 'great man.'

A word that pops up several times is 'sweet.' When it comes to rock-ribbed loyalty toward friends, there really is no man sweeter than Bill O'Shaughnessy, whose community radio stations have served as free and open forums for more than a half century. When he writes of Cuomo's finer personality traits, he could just as easily be talking about himself.

Perhaps that's why Cuomo liked and trusted him. It wasn't just the O-Man's Irish charm that bonded the two. At WVOX and WVIP, Cuomo was given a platform to test his ideas and beliefs. Clearly, the two also shared principles of faith. They liked to talk about God, hope, freedom of expression, language, music, DiMaggio and Lincoln's appeal to the 'better angels of our nature.'

The book is . . . very . . . sweet."
—Phil Reisman, former Gannett feature columnist,
the *Journal News*

"A masterpiece about a remarkable American! Mario Cuomo would not only have expected the author's rich orchestration of language, he would certainly have cherished the graceful recounting of so many warm, personal anecdotes. As a word-smith, O'Shaughnessy is some kind of master, to be sure. . . ."
—Phil Beuth, pioneering co-founder, CapCities Broadcasting;
former senior ABC Television exec

"A touching remembrance of Cuomo's life, work and legacy. The author has assembled a wealth of previously unpublished material including stirring excerpts from Mr. Cuomo's inspirational speeches and the story behind why he refused entreaties to run for President."
—*The Biography Shelf*
Midwest Book Review
Library Bookwatch

"*Mario Cuomo* is a remarkable book written by a remarkable man. Bill O'Shaughnessy is very interesting, prominent in Westchester and political circles. He's a broadcaster, raconteur, Renaissance man and friend of the influential. While not exactly a young man anymore, he's working like one."
—Fred Dicker, *New York Post*; host, Talk 1300/WGDJ, Albany

"A memorably sensitive, informative and entertaining portrayal. O'Shaughnessy's prose is lively throughout, reading more like a snappy journalistic editorial than a scholarly rendering. The entire work is studded with speeches and aphoristic sayings—a testament to Governor Cuomo's sparkling rhetorical gifts, O'Shaughnessy is a gifted storyteller."
—*Kirkus Reviews*

"To borrow Mario Cuomo's favorite word: this is one of the sweetest books ever written. Has a painting recently made me feel this way? Has music? Mr. O'Shaughnessy's Cuomo book is mind expanding. And I might even steer my teenager to consider some of these big questions. Bless the author—and Mario Cuomo—for keeping the soulful issues alive. I hate to be lyrical, but I want to be a sweeter person myself because of this book."
—*Charles Barton Castleberry, photographer, critic, blogger, Santa Fe, New Mexico*

"William O'Shaughnessy's biography of Mario Cuomo is unusual because the writer did not just know his subject, he was also Cuomo's friend. If you're seeking an unbiased, warts and all assessment of Cuomo's life—you won't find it here. Instead, you'll savor many of the highlights of a notable politician's career. What you may not know about Cuomo—and something O'Shaughnessy does such a good job bringing out—is how Mario was so devoutly spiritual. He's right; Mario Cuomo was, indeed, a remarkable man."
—*Pacific Book Review*

"Bill O'Shaughnessy's Mario Cuomo book is by far the best thing he has ever written."
—Scott Shannon, legendary radio host and programmer, WCBS-FM

"O'Shaughnessy beautifully uses Cuomo's own words to show us his wit, intelligence, and spiritual side. Many speeches feature Cuomo's favorite themes: searching for something larger than ourselves and loving thy neighbor. The author, a Rockefeller Republican, and Mario Cuomo, a liberal Democrat icon, discuss every topic from the death penalty to their faith. A strong introduction to Cuomo, as well as entertaining."
—*blueink Review*

"Bill O'Shaughnessy's ability to use words the way master artists use watercolors is startling. He has really captured the very essence of a special New Yorker. And the author is himself in that column."
—O. Aldon James, National Arts Club

"This new book about the poetry and prose of Mario Cuomo is by his language-gifted friend O'Shaughnessy and every word, chapter and sentence is in brutal conflict with the state of U.S. national politics in the here and now. It's a direct line to the life, career, speeches and writings of a skilled wordsmith on the Public Stage."
—Michael Dandry, columnist, *Westchester County Press*

"If you're looking for a straight biography of Mario Cuomo, then you must look elsewhere. And if you're looking for a hierography, making the man into a candidate for sainthood, this is not that either. Nor is it strictly a political biography, a study in statecraft, or any kind of historical document. The Mario Cuomo we see here is a man dedicated to his family, the law and his faith, a man whose mind is always asking questions, probing for answers,

going beyond the simplistic, easy way. He was a man who spoke with a natural and reasoned eloquence that on occasion caused others to recall his hero, Abraham Lincoln. In conversation he could be as humorous and as self-deprecating as—well—as Abraham Lincoln."
—*The Country and Abroad Magazine*

"O'Shaughnessy has put together a book that veers away from the typical biographical format in order to reveal the heart of his friend. Since Cuomo was esteemed as both a writer and orator, the author has chosen to let his subject speak for himself. The white-haired radio host, who is famous for his own gift of gab, uses his considerable skills to the full extent as he shares a variety of personal vignettes about Cuomo, seeing sides of the man only someone close to him would notice. Through O'Shaughnessy's insightful writing, we get an insider's view of the politician, lawyer, and author as a person and not just a celebrity. Much has been written about Mario Cuomo over the years, and in all likelihood, there will be even more articles and biographies to come. Yet few will be able to portray him quite like O'Shaughnessy does. Mr. O'Shaughnessy's writing, is filtered through the lens of friendship and unabashed love."
—The *US Review of Books*

"A highly acclaimed, very personal memoir. As a politician climbs Disraeli's "Greasy Pole" of politics, it is easy, even common, for friendships to go overboard along the way. Yet the personal friendship of the journalist O'Shaughnessy, an 'Establishment' Rockefeller Republican, and Cuomo, an up-from-the-streets liberal Democrat, endured, like two oak trees with roots intertwined. Cuomo's life and accomplishments are part of the public record, but O'Shaughnessy gives us a deeply personal portrait of one of the most articulate and graceful public men of the twentieth century, sorely missed in the current political season."
—*Bulletin*, Dutch Treat Luncheon Club

"A love letter wrapped into an elaborate scrapbook that touches lightly on Cuomo's significant political achievements while spending the bulk of this engaging work on Mr. Cuomo's contemplative side. The concept of 'never forgetting the "little man"' is the driving theme of O'Shaughnessy's riveting memoir. The Governor saw American immigrants, both then and now, not as a 'melting pot' but as a 'mosaic.' Cuomo chose his words wisely, using his speeches 'to inspire, to probe, to critique, and to provoke' via an array of full orations so readers can experience the power of this iconic wordsmith. Truly a work of love, the book is nothing less than inspiring."
—*Publisher Daily Reviews*

"Bill O'Shaughnessy, the broadcasting legend and prolific author, is perhaps too humble when it comes to his ability at a computer keyboard or, as he prefers, moving words around on a legal pad before they're set in print. But he has proven, yet again, that he can write a book as hard to put down as a fast-paced whodunit. *Mario Cuomo* is a heartfelt tribute to the late New York governor. But it is more than that; it is a look into Cuomo's mind and soul . . . an appreciation of the intellectual and spiritual gifts Cuomo had, and how he used them to benefit others. It's a touching recollection of Cuomo's life as a family man, a friend, and a commentator on life, love, friendship, the law, politics and citizenship. Because the author is an Irishman, it is filled with stories that make a reader say, 'I want to remember that.' When O'Shaughnessy says his writing is 'not worthy' of the remarkable 38-year friendship he shared with Cuomo, he's wrong. Don't buy that stuff. Buy the book instead and read it, savor it, and you will see why."
—Claudia McDonnell, feature columnist, *Catholic New York*

"When I sat down with the Cuomo book I was determined to read it with care because of the importance of the subject. Well, I read it twice from cover to cover, taking time to digest every detail and thought expressed. That's how rich I found the book.

It's a fine work, a tribute to an extraordinary man and a thoughtful, insightful explanation of what made Mario Cuomo so damn special."
—Dan Lynch, columnist, broadcaster, educator

"The broadcaster William O'Shaughnessy's love letter is both an unabashed tribute and a timely reminder of the passion and inspirational positive thinking largely missing from today's loyal opposition, It makes Mario Cuomo all the more amazing!"
—Sam Roberts, BOOKSHELF, the *New York Times*

"New York is in Bill O'Shaughnessy's debt for his gracious, eloquent appreciation of the best of us . . . and best in us."
—Professor Gerald Benjamin, The Benjamin Center,
    SUNY New Paltz

"I have admired Bill O'Shaughnessy's writings for a good number of years. As I am to the left of Karl Marx, we probably don't agree on damn near anything in the whole wide world. But his writing is always generous, decent and open-minded. He has gone out among the Republicans like a missionary for intellectual activity and tried to elevate their senses and sensibilities to the glories of words, to poetry, to language and to their heritage. He has been a perennial presence in this State for a long time as an accomplished broadcaster."
—Malachy McCourt, writer, broadcaster, author, saloonkeeper,
    member in good standing of the great McCourt family of
    letters

A Note on Mario Cuomo and Teilhard de Chardin

"Mario Cuomo is an admirer of the great Jesuit philosopher-paleontologist Teilhard de Chardin, who wrote *The Divine Milieu.*"

As I was walking in the brilliant Manhattan sunshine earlier this week, feeling, I must admit, somewhat "few" . . . even though it was a stunningly beautiful day, I came upon more of Teilhard's wisdom posted on the outside of a Protestant church.

Some day after mastering the winds, the waves, and gravity . . .
we shall harness for God the energy of love.
　And then for the second time in history, we will have
discovered fire.
—Teilhard de Chardin

I thought I'd publish it for you and a few other wordsmiths I know. I wish I could write like that. . . .

—W.O.

Mario Cuomo's Omega Society Speech:
A Meditation on Ultimate Values

So many readers and listeners who have indulged my enthusiasms over the years know of my great admiration for Mario M. Cuomo. Thus I'm often greeted with an inquiry about his present activities.

I answer them this way. He practices law at the prestigious New York law firm Willkie Farr and Gallagher. He continues to write and takes more than a passing interest in the career of his son and heir Andrew M. Cuomo.

Meanwhile, the gifted man the Boston Globe *called "the great philosopher-statesman of the American nation" often departs from the confines of his ivory tower law firm in midtown Manhattan to give the thought-provoking speeches for which he is known.*

This one before The Omega Society, a group of "thinkers and seekers" is one of Cuomo's best. Better even than his iconic speech at the Democratic Convention.

GOVERNOR MARIO M. CUOMO AT THE OMEGA SOCIETY:
A MEDITATION ON ULTIMATE VALUES

When I was asked to give the closing remarks tonight, I hesitated because of the intelligent, distinguished and articulate individuals slated to appear before me.

The representative of Omega insisted, "Your input as a three-term Governor could be especially relevant given the frightening implications of 9/11."

So, I agreed to try.

Actually, I once offered similar observations at a conference titled, "Who or What is God?"

I addressed the question then, as I do now, as an ordinary New Yorker from Queens, who grew up in a poor and middle-class neighborhood with asphalt streets and stickball, and earned a living, somewhat improbably, in the demanding world of politics.

I struggle to maintain my belief in God as a Catholic raised with simple Sunday Mass practitioners, far from the high intellectual traditions of Talmudic scholars, elegant Episcopalian homilists, or abstruse Jesuit teachers.

The simple folk of South Jamaica, Queens, came from tenements and attached houses and perceived the world as a cosmic basic-training course, filled by God with obstacles and traps for the unworthy. The prevailing moral standard was easily learned: "If you liked it, it was probably a sin; if you liked it a lot, it was probably a mortal sin."

The believers saw themselves as "the poor, banished children of Eve, mourning and weeping in this vale of tears," until by some combination of grace and good works, and luck, they escaped final damnation.

For many, their sense of God was reflected in their own collective experience as the poor and wounded.

God seemed to have a cold voice when—on Beaver Road, next to a cemetery across the street from St. Monica's Catholic Church—a famous ex-jockey, one of the homeless winos, froze to death while sleeping in a large wooden crate.

Maybe, others in America felt content with their world. But for most of the people in my old neighborhood, it was hard to see God's goodness in the pathetic faces pleading with my father for bread at our small grocery store, until the next relief check came in.

It grew harder still during the Second World War, when a gold star in a window announced the death of someone's son.

It was hard to believe in God after Hiroshima, too.

Others reveled in the cultural liberation of the sixties, but for most of our neighborhood, the sadness of that time was memorialized by Simon and Garfunkel, "Where have you gone, Joe DiMaggio; our nation turns its lonely eyes to you. What's that you say, Mrs. Robinson? Joltin' Joe has left and gone away."

No more John F. Kennedy, no more Martin Luther King. No more Bobby Kennedy. Nothing to believe in. Nothing to grab hold of. Nothing to uplift us.

People weren't asking, "Who is God?" They were asking, "Is there a God?"

Many asked the same question after 9/11; after a preemptive war in Iraq killed more than 40,000 human beings, most of them innocent civilians; and after Rwanda and the grotesquely lethal tsunami.

Many ask the same question today when a child dies in a crib. Many resign themselves to a world with no answers to the biggest questions.

For some of us, however, the burden becomes intolerable; the absurdity of a world without explanation pushes us to find a rationale, an excuse, anything to escape the despair, something larger than ourselves to believe in.

We yearn for more than a God of prohibition, guilt, and punishment. More than John Calvin's chilling conclusion that God loves Jacob but hates Esau. For us, it must be a God of the New Testament, of mercy, peace, and hope. In the end, to make any sense, it must be a God of love!

Mostly, we want a God because the accumulation of material goods and the constant seeking to satisfy our petty appetites, for a flash of ecstasy or popularity or even temporary fame, is just a desperate, frantic attempt to fill the shrinking interval between birth and death!

In my old neighborhood, despite the doubts, the simple and sincere theology of the pre–Vatican II Catholic Church and the prodding of uneducated parents were still respected. Probably because there was no viable alternative.

In the fifties, some of us were presented with the enlightened vision and profound wisdom of an extraordinary man.

A scientist, a paleontologist. A person who understood evolution. A soldier who knew the inexplicable evil of the battlefield. A scholar who studied the ages. A philosopher, a theologian, a believer. And a great priest.

Teilhard de Chardin heard our lament, and he answered us. He reoriented our theology and rewrote its language, linking it, inseparably, with science. His wonderful book, *The Divine Milieu*, dedicated to "those who love the world," made negativism a sin.

Teilhard glorified the world, and everything in it. He taught us to love and respect ourselves as the pinnacle of God's creation. He taught us how the whole universe, even the pain and imperfection, is sacred. He taught us in powerful, cogent, and persuasive prose, and in soaring poetry.

He integrated his extensive knowledge of evolution with his religious understanding of the "Divine Milieu." He envisioned a vibrant human future: "We are all foot soldiers in the struggle to unify the human spirit . . .".

"Faith," he said, "is not a call to escape the world but to embrace it." Creation is not an elaborate testing ground with moral obstacles, but an invitation to join in the work of restoration; a voice urging us to improve the world by our individual and collective efforts, making it kinder, safer, and more loving. Repairing the wounded world helps it move upward to the "Pleroma," St. Paul's word for the consummation of human life.

The Omega Point, when the level of consciousness and civility eventually converges, elevates us to the highest level of morality. A new universe, a peerless one; one we could help create by our own behavior.

Teilhard's vision challenges the imagination, but it has achieved sufficient plausibility among celebrated intellectuals like Robert Wright, a scientist and declared agnostic.

Some of Teilhard's fundamental principles are clear to all rational human beings whatever their level of formal education. They are called "natural theology" or "natural law" because they can be ascertained solely through observing the world around us.

Without books, instruction, or revelation, three things should strike us about our place in the world.

First, the greatest gift is our very existence.

Second, we are each unique elements of creation, deserving respect and dignity.

Third, we work together to protect and enhance the life we share.

The Hebrews spread these ideas as the foundation of their monotheistic belief. The principle of *tzedakah* involves treating one another as brothers and sisters from the same great source of life. And the tenet of *tikkun olam* instructs us to join together in repairing the world.

Rabbi Hillel merged these two ideas as the foundation of the whole law. "All the rest," he said, "is commentary."

Jesus did likewise for Christians, saying, essentially, "The whole law is that you should love one another as you love yourself for the love of truth, and the truth is God made the world but did not complete it; you are to be collaborators in creation."

I don't know any religion that rejects these ideals.

If politicians today are looking for guidance from religion, they must apply the ancient truth used by primitive people to ward off their enemies and wild beasts, to find food and shelter, to raise their children in safety, and eventually to raise up a civilization: We're all in this together, like a family, interconnected and interdependent, and we cannot afford to revert to a world of us against them.

It is the one indispensable idea to realizing our full potential as a people; to sharing the wealth of our economy; to relieving the economic and political oppression all over the world; and to rescuing millions of Africans from the ravages of AIDS and the barbarism of warlords.

Each of us must choose whether we will change the world for the better. The brilliant, agnostic Chief Justice Oliver Wendell Holmes echoed Teilhard's call for vigorous involvement but added a warning. He said, "As life is action and passion, we are required to share the passion and action of our time, at the peril of being judged not to have lived."

Teilhard would have augmented Holmes's remarks with his promise of glory: "The day will come when, after harnessing the wind, the mind, the tides and gravity, we shall harness for God the energies of love, and on that day, for the second time in the history of man, we will have discovered fire."

I wish I could record people's favorite music. In Teilhard's vision, I hear Beethoven's wonderful message in his Ninth Symphony, with its unforgettable ending.

Beethoven saw the world as a family. Listen to it again. It begins dark and threatening; disaster and confusion loom from clashes of the will, misunderstanding and alienation. It then moves into the frenetic hunt for meaning, seeking an answer to comfort and reassure humanity.

Then, in the final movement, it swiftly presents again the initial picture of disunity and discord, only to dissolve into the "Ode to Joy," using the words of Friedrich Von Schiller's poem, ending in "ecstatic jubilation," the chorus rejoicing at the convergence of the world's people through maturity, brotherhood, and love!

Simple, and simply wonderful!

So, "Who or What is God?"

I have grown old enough to understand the vanity of trying to define the infinite and eternal. But I'm not required to eliminate any possibilities by the limits of my intellect either.

In the end, I can choose to believe and call it "faith" if I must, if that promises me meaningfulness.

So, it may not be easy to understand Teilhard or why God commits us to the endless task of improving the world around us, with fulfillment an eternity away.

But it's better than the anguish of futility. Better than the emptiness of despair.

And capable of bringing meaning to our most modest and clumsy efforts.

That's a useful consolation for any of us still struggling to believe.

April 2005, Sheraton New York, New York City.

PART VII
THE EXTRAORDINARY BUSH FAMILY

Our listeners know of my admiration of—and great affection for—the Cuomo family—including Governor Mario M. Cuomo, of sainted memory . . . my beloved Matilda Raffa Cuomo, and my dear and constant friend Maria Cuomo Cole and also the gifted present governor of New York state, Andrew Mark Cuomo.

But I also have considerable regard for the Bush family. I have admired President George H.W. Bush and his son and heir President George W. Bush for many years. But my favorite Bush is President H.W.'s brother Jonathan Bush, a very graceful fellow (who was also a favorite of Mario Cuomo's). Jonathan is the father of William "Billy" Bush, a very talented young man whose career we were privileged to launch on WVOX and WVIP. He's a very attractive young man who was done wrong by the elders of NBC who were out to embarrass President Trump. Thus this brief section on the extraordinary Bush family.

George W. Bush's Eulogy for His Father, President George H.W. Bush

---

Distinguished guests, including our presidents and first ladies, government officials, foreign dignitaries, and friends, Jeb, Neil, Marvin, Doro, and I, and our families, thank you all for being here.

I once heard it said of man that "The idea is to die young as late as possible."

At age eighty-five, a favorite pastime of George H.W. Bush was firing up his boat, the *Fidelity*, and opening up the three 300-horsepower engines to fly—joyfully fly—across the Atlantic, with Secret Service boats straining to keep up.

At ninety, George H.W. Bush parachuted out of an aircraft and landed on the grounds of St. Ann's by the Sea in Kennebunkport, Maine—the church where his mom was married and where he'd worshiped often. Mother liked to say he chose the location just in case the chute didn't open.

In his nineties, he took great delight when his closest pal, James A. Baker, smuggled a bottle of Grey Goose vodka into his hospital room. Apparently, it paired well with the steak Baker had delivered from Morton's.

To his very last days, Dad's life was instructive. As he aged, he taught us how to grow old with dignity, humor, and kindness—and, when the Good Lord finally called, how to meet Him with courage and with joy in the promise of what lies ahead.

One reason Dad knew how to die young is that he almost did it— twice. When he was a teenager, a staph infection nearly took his life. A few years later he was alone in the Pacific on a life raft, praying that his rescuers would find him before the enemy did.

God answered those prayers. It turned out He had other plans for George H.W. Bush. For Dad's part, I think those brushes with death made him cherish the gift of life. And he vowed to live every day to the fullest.

Dad was always busy—a man in constant motion—but never too busy to share his love of life with those around him. He taught us to love the outdoors. He loved watching dogs flush a covey. He loved landing the elusive striper. And once confined to a wheelchair, he seemed happiest sitting in his favorite perch on the back porch at Walker's Point contemplating the majesty of the Atlantic. The horizons he saw were bright and hopeful. He was a genuinely optimistic man. And that optimism guided his children and made each of us believe that anything was possible.

He continually broadened his horizons with daring decisions. He was a patriot. After high school, he put college on hold and became a Navy fighter pilot as World War II broke out. Like many of his generation, he never talked about his service until his time as a public figure forced his hand. We learned of the attack on Chichi Jima, the mission completed, the shoot-down. We learned of the deaths of his crewmates, whom he thought about throughout his entire life. And we learned of his rescue.

And then, another audacious decision: he moved his young family from the comforts of the East Coast to Odessa, Texas. He and Mom adjusted to their arid surroundings quickly. He was a tolerant man. After all, he was kind and neighborly to the women with whom he, Mom, and I shared a bathroom in our small duplex—even after he learned their profession: ladies of the night.

Dad could relate to people from all walks of life. He was an empathetic man. He valued character over pedigree. And he was no cynic. He looked for the good in each person—and usually found it.

Dad taught us that public service is noble and necessary; that one can serve with integrity and hold true to the important values, like faith and family. He strongly believed that it was important to give back to the community and country in which one lived. He recognized that serving others enriched the giver's soul. To us, his was the brightest of a thousand points of light.

In victory, he shared credit. When he lost, he shouldered the blame. He accepted that failure is part of living a full life but taught us never to be defined by failure. He showed us how setbacks can strengthen.

None of his disappointments could compare with one of life's greatest tragedies, the loss of a young child. Jeb and I were too young to remember the pain and agony he and Mom felt when our three-year-old sister died. We only learned later that Dad, a man of quiet faith, prayed for her daily. He was sustained by the love of the Almighty and the real and enduring love of our mom. Dad always believed that one day he would hug his precious Robin again.

He loved to laugh, especially at himself. He could tease and needle, but never out of malice. He placed great value on a good joke. That's why he chose [Alan] Simpson to speak. On e-mail, he had a circle of friends with whom he shared or received the latest jokes. His grading system for the quality of the joke was classic George Bush. The rare 7s and 8s were considered huge winners—most of them off-color.

George Bush knew how to be a true and loyal friend. He honored and nurtured his many friendships with his generous and giving soul. There exist thousands of handwritten notes encouraging, or sympathizing, or thanking his friends and acquaintances.

He had an enormous capacity to give of himself. Many a person would tell you that Dad became a mentor and a father figure in their life. He listened and he consoled. He was their friend. I think of Don Rhodes, Taylor Blanton, Jim Nantz, Arnold Schwarzenegger, and perhaps the unlikeliest of all, the man who defeated him, Bill Clinton. My siblings and I refer to the guys in this group as "brothers from other mothers."

He taught us that a day was not meant to be wasted. He played golf at a legendary pace. I always wondered why he insisted on speed golf. He was a good golfer.

Well, here's my conclusion: He played fast so that he could move on to the next event, to enjoy the rest of the day, to expend his enormous energy, to live it all. He was born with just two settings: full throttle, then sleep.

He taught us what it means to be a wonderful father, grandfather, and great-grandfather. He was firm in his principles and supportive as we began to seek our own ways. He encouraged and comforted, but never steered. We tested his patience—I know I did—but he always responded with the great gift of unconditional love.

Last Friday, when I was told he had minutes to live, I called him. The guy who answered the phone said, "I think he can hear you, but hasn't said anything most of the day. I said, "Dad, I love you, and you've been a wonderful father." And the last words he would ever say on Earth were "I love you, too."

To us, he was close to perfect. But, not totally perfect. His short game was lousy. He wasn't exactly Fred Astaire on the dance floor. The man couldn't stomach vegetables, especially broccoli. And by the way, he passed these genetic defects along to us.

Finally, every day of his seventy-three years of marriage, Dad taught us all what it means to be a great husband. He married his sweetheart. He adored her. He laughed and cried with her. He was dedicated to her totally.

In his old age, Dad enjoyed watching police show reruns, volume on high, all the while holding Mom's hand. After Mom died, Dad was strong, but all he really wanted to do was to hold Mom's hand, again.

Of course, Dad taught me another special lesson. He showed me what it means to be a president who serves with integrity, leads with courage, and acts with love in his heart for the citizens of our country. When the history books are written, they will say that George H.W. Bush was a great president of the United States—a diplomat of unmatched skill, a Commander-in-Chief of formidable accomplishment, and a gentleman who executed the duties of his office with dignity and honor.

In his Inaugural Address, the forty-first president of the United States said this: "We cannot hope only to leave our children a bigger car, a bigger bank account. We must hope to give them a sense of what it means to be a loyal friend, a loving parent, a citizen who leaves his home, his neighborhood, and town better than he found it. What do we want the men and women who work with us to say when we are no longer there? That we were more driven to succeed than anyone around us? Or that we stopped to ask if a sick child had gotten better, and stayed a moment there to trade a word of friendship?"

Well, Dad—we're going remember you for exactly that and so much more.

And we're going to miss you. Your decency, sincerity, and kind soul will stay with us forever. So, through our tears, let us see the blessings of knowing and loving you—a great and noble man, and the best father a son or daughter could have.

And in our grief, let us smile, knowing that Dad is hugging Robin and holding Mom's hand again.

Whitney Global Media Endorsement:
George H.W. Bush for President, 1992

The passing this year of former President George H.W. Bush inspired us to go back to the archives for this 1992 endorsement.

———————

This is an endorsement for president of the United States of America with which our two eastern establishment broadcasting stations now attempt to "save" the Republic from Governor Bill "Slick Willy" Clinton. By this fine, selfless act of sheer patriotism, I hereby and forever alienate Nancy Q. Keefe, star feature columnist of the powerful Gannett Suburban Newspapers, and her editor Lawrence "Excellence in Journalism" Beaupre. This will also bring symptoms of cardiac arrest to several other admirers of these splendid radio stations, such as Pete Hamill, Lars-Erik Nelson, Mary McGrory, Jimmy Breslin, Michael Kramer, Jeffrey V. Bernbach, Justice Samuel George Fredman, Nita Lowey, the Honorable John Marino, Dennis Mehiel, Ken Auletta, Messrs. Arthur Ochs Sulzberger Senior and Junior, and one Joseph Spinelli, survivor of seven FBI shootouts. Our courage will not go unnoticed by Frederic Dicker, state editor of the *New York Post*, or Marc Humbert of the mighty Associated Press. There is, however, absolutely no telling what his boss Louis Boccardi will have to say when this reaches the world headquarters of the AP in Rockefeller Center.

We are for George Bush.

You can, all of you, just forget the 16 percent lead now possessed by William Jefferson Clinton. I am used to these odds. In 1982 Mario M. Cuomo was down 38 percent to Koch the mayor. Cuomo's bright, fine mind and his magnificent tongue had nothing to do with that episode. And, incidentally, it is yet another myth that Andrew Mark Cuomo was somehow responsible for his father's come-from-behind victory. This is nonsense. It was only my editorials, which have more circulation by mail than by air, that saved my beloved New York state from Koch. I will now proceed to save an entire nation.

I begin by reminding you that the same pollsters, pundits, and prognosticators, some of whom I have chosen to identify above, are the same highly placed and intelligent individuals who insisted you install Michael and Kitty Dukakis in the White House four years ago, and the very same folks who have forgotten those 22 percent interest rates, those helicopters crashing in the desert. Not to mention the oil problem and our making nice with the rocket scientist who ran the corner gas station as well as his genius brother-in-law who dispensed extra gasoline cans at the True Value hardware store to enable us to hoard three gallons of super unleaded premium petrol while Jimmy Carter, Bert Lance, and Hamilton Jordan ran the country in such splendid fashion.

All of which means that it is one thing to be very important in Plains, Georgia, or Little Rock, Arkansas. It is quite another to be stellar in Washington, D.C., where one might be called at any moment to order a nuclear strike or be required to conduct a civilized conversation with François Mitterand, Helmut Kohl, or Boris Yeltsin.

THE PRESIDENT

There is a word flying around the Westchester and Fairfield counties' cocktail parties. You hear it on the North Shore too. The word is "gravitas." It means substance and weight, and it is one more reason I am for George Bush. Bush is a man of substance, depth, breeding, and intelligence, with a keen understanding of geopolitical matters. And, yes, he is a gentleman who has shown great patience and grandness of spirit during this bleak, mean campaign in which the president has been subjected to much worse than the routine pummeling our nation feels compelled to heap on its sovereign every four years. President Bush has endured a torrent of derision and ridicule unheard of even in a society not renowned for civil discourse.

Let's set the record straight. George Bush should not be blamed for the instability in the international fiscal and monetary circles. It is worldwide, and that global tide that lifts all boats also lowers all boats as it recedes. In the face of this recession, the president has had the courage to reject any radical "instant fix" by holding to the sensible notion that "no one thing got us into this, and no one thing is going to get us out." Bravo, Mr. President!

The Japanese and the Germans work harder, smarter, and longer. And the Mexicans and Chinese work cheaper. But the United States, in President Bush, has a world-class strategist who understands global realities and is determined to get us back on a competitive footing. It can't be done with Governor Clinton's slogans or glibness or with Ross Perot's populist "kick ass" rhetoric and entertaining *bon mots*.

ROSS PEROT

As for Perot, we can't do better than Michael Kramer in *Time* magazine, who exquisitely dubbed him "a paranoid hoisted by his own self-regard." He does, however, roll a good show, and the "Joe Six-Pack" crowd is having a whopping good time watching this breathtaking intrusion of ego and money into presidential politics. OK, Ross, we know who you are now, we heard you, Ross, now pipe down Ross, please! Actually, in a funny way, I could almost take the mischievous, jug-eared, diminutive, cock-of-the-walk Texan over the eager striver from Arkansas. Both of them aspire to the highest office in the land without having acquired the depth of knowledge or the breadth of experience possessed, in great abundance, by President Bush.

SLICK WILLY

Mike McAlary of the *Post* got it about right when he called Bill Clinton "a disingenuous bore." Or is the word "unctuous"? In the first debate, Slick Willy stood in the hot television lights and imagined he was Jack Kennedy: "A new vision . . . a new tomorrow . . . a new beginning . . . a new era . . . let's get this country moving again. . . ." Ad nauseam. The right forefinger, bolstered by the thumb, went out and chopped the air, and I recalled the words of the Pulitzer Prize journalist from Arkansas, Paul Greenberg, who has covered Clinton for decades: "At the core, at the center, there is nothing."

Notice there is one word his advocates and surrogates never use to describe him. The word is "inspiring." "Dazzlingly competent," "youthful," even "dynamic," but never "inspiring." And so he crisscrosses the nation, reciting clichés and slogans in parrotlike fashion. "Unctuous" is a good epithet for this man who would bring down a president. And "slickness"—which may be consistent with political adroitness, but it doesn't inspire. Sadly, but ultimately, Bill Clinton comes across as something smaller than what we want in our leader.

It's about music, the music that's made when your heart comes together with your intellect. Bill Clinton is energetic and resilient, but he does not inspire confidence. He makes no music. And as frantically as our colleagues in the national press wave their batons, there is no sweetness to the sound of Bill Clinton. He is dancing to the sound of a kazoo. It is harsh and shrill and self-centered. The Democratic Party, which once offered such towering figures as FDR, Lyndon Johnson, Adlai Stevenson, Harry Truman, and Jack Kennedy, had just one chance to make us forget Carter, Mondale, McGovern, and Dukakis. Only the governor of New York could have brought worth, substance, stature, dignity, meaning, passion, and eloquence to the Democratic cause. Instead, the Democratic Party of the United States has again put up two "suits" with eager red ties and upwardly mobile wives.

THE HILLARY FACTOR

Since we cannot have a sheer, pure, natural force known as Matilda Raffa Cuomo in the White House, I will gladly continue Barbara Pierce Bush as First Lady. Barbara Bush has served this country with a marvelous and becoming serenity, gracious bearing, and gallant dignity. She is much to be preferred to Hillary Clinton, who runs together in the minds of many observers with Anita Hill, Geraldine Ferraro, Linda Ellerbee, and Suzi Oppenheimer, better known in these parts as "Senator Suzi." You either buy their act and believe the stuff they're selling, or you don't. We don't. They have only ambition in common. We simply can't detect any of the grace Nancy Q. Keefe and other pundits find in them. And Hillary Clinton, standing off to the side of a podium, nodding mock-serious approval, while Slick Willy spouts pure "wisdom" into a microphone, just doesn't ring true. But she sure is eager. And like her husband, she is ambitious.

I have always been suspicious of that marvelous phrase uttered by so many well-intentioned parents, "Even then I knew"—as in "my son

Billy (or Albert) would be president" or "my daughter Hillary (or Tipper) would be First Lady." It has to do with destiny, I guess. And with sons in eager red ties and suits that make them look like regional managers of Kmart. And with daughters who discuss grand ideas with Barbara Walters or on "Good Morning America." Dear Marshall McLuhan, what is happening to this country? And to all of us? I mean, I like Larry King! He's a friend!

THE JEWISH PROBLEM

Since I had to be dissuaded (by local rabbis) from flying the Israeli flag over these radio stations during the Six Day War, I guess I'm entitled to respectfully suggest that a Connecticut Yankee WASP, George Herbert Walker Bush, and James Baker, with the cowboy boots, have done more to ensure the safety and integrity of Israel than any two others on the face of the Earth. Israel got the loan guarantees—and a lot more—thanks to two damn shrewd poker players who had to get the Arab representatives to the table in the first place in order to begin the long, arduous journey toward peace. The president gets appropriately high marks as the warrior-leader of Desert Storm. But it is as a peacemaker and global statesman that George Bush truly deserves to be remembered.

And so, after some more meaningless debates and television journalism and Rush Limbaugh and "Larry King Live" and symbols and slogans and rhetoric and posturing, the nation gets to elect a president. We've got a pretty good fellow in there right now. Maybe even a great one. WVOX and WRTN endorse President George Bush for president.

P.S. If you're still not persuaded, try to imagine a Democratic president in Washington alongside our wonderful Democratic Congress. OK, I'll stop. I don't mean to get anyone crazy.

November 1992

Thank You Letter from "41"

GEORGE BUSH

February 22, 1993

Dear Bill,

Thanks for sending me a copy of your radio editorial
with your wonderful endorsement. I really appreciate it.
Jonathan told me of the great effort you put out during
the campaign. For that, I send my profound thanks.

Barbara and I are settling nicely here in Houston. We
will always be grateful for the privilege we had to serve
the American people. Again, thanks for your support.
With best wishes,

Sincerely,

There truly is a life, a good life after public service —

G

Mr. William O'Shaughnessy
Whitney Radio
One Broadcast Forum
New Rochelle, New York 10801

George W. Bush for President, 2000

Another endorsement from the archives.

For eight years Bill Clinton and Al Gore have led a nation that has become rich and powerful but stands for nothing. And now William Jefferson Clinton, he of majestic name only, is hoping you will pass his battered baton to Albert Gore Jr.

And the Democratic Party of our parents' time—from the days of Franklin D. Roosevelt, Al Smith, Adlai Stevenson, Jack and Bobby Kennedy, and Hubert Humphrey, to the magnificent brilliance and soaring passion of Mario Cuomo—that party has now become an amorphous, pragmatic, cynical, hollow shell of its former self, adorned only with a centrist label that resembles the mantra of every spoiled and selfish dot-com millionaire: "Gettin' it done! Doin' whatever it takes! Make it happen!"

And we feel lousy about ourselves and our country.

Albert Gore is the quintessential product and embodiment of these times. He has embellished and reinvented himself so often he has become a Doctor Spock–like chameleon who climbs up on every stage, no matter the venue, to present himself with meaningless, empty slogans and always with the chant, "Ah want to fight for you (whoever happens to be in the audience on any given day)!" He has no grace, no rhythm, no music. He is a man who *wants to get elected*. And he attempts to divide with his demagogic calls to class warfare.

The vice president was raised in privilege—almost, it seems, born and bred to grow up and one day assume his "rightful place" as president of the United States. George W. Bush is a man with *another* sort of "mission." The Texas governor has, with patience and even, occasionally, with considerable bravery, forced us to think about loftier things, those timeless virtues that have been ignored and almost forgotten in the go-go Clinton-Gore years.

The editorial writers of the day, our colleagues in the press, labor valiantly to have us stick to the *issues*, and concentrate *only* on where the candidates stand. But the issues evolve and change. And the so-called "issues" of this mean election season will recede and disappear as our nation confronts new challenges not yet seen or imagined—from within and without. It has always been thus in the roiling history of our Republic. So no matter what the pundits and talking heads tell us, we are left, then, with only the matter of *character*. And *values*. And the "vision" thing both candidates are trying to develop.

The difference is that George W. Bush brings a remarkable *conviction* to his pronouncements. There is a *center* to the fellow, a core. He *stands* for something.

After a shaky start, Governor Bush has grown in wisdom on the campaign trail. We see it every day. And as we watch his hopeful, positive demeanor (marred *only* by his bewildering enthusiasm for the damned death penalty!), we are reminded that George W Bush is the son of one of the most decent and classy men ever to serve as president. (He also has a pretty formidable mother, who is one of the most respected women in America!) For many of us, that he is his father's son (and his mother's too) would be reason enough to recommend him. But George W. Bush brings more than good bloodlines to this race. He approaches us with a *realness* that can't be imagined by Vice President Gore or manufactured by his handlers.

We're for George W. Bush. For we would rather have a president whose actions are informed by the counsel of Dick Cheney, Colin Powell, John McCain, and Condoleezza Rice than by James Carville, Paul Begala, Harold Ickes, or Susan Estrich. (Secretary Cheney, especially, has been a *spectacular* pick as a running mate, while Senator Lieberman has been preachy, all-knowing, holier-than-thou and not a little bit "pragmatic" himself.)

Longtime listeners to these stations, who have indulged and suffered our enthusiasms for so many years, will recall our telling you, on countless occasions, that Nelson Aldrich Rockefeller and Mario M. Cuomo would have made splendid presidents. They never made it. But we hope George W. Bush does. He's got Cuomo's conviction and passion and Rockefeller's dynamism. And he's a *gentleman* who will restore, almost instantly, dignity and stature to the presidency.

In this, perhaps the closest presidential election of our lifetime, we commend to your favorable judgment the Republican candidate: George W. Bush of Texas. We endorse Governor Bush because he takes us beyond the "issues" to a higher place.

November 2000

Billy Bush Deserves a Second Chance

May 24, 2017. As I recalled in my book Mario Cuomo: Remembrances of a Remarkable Man, *even the former governor of New York was greatly taken with young Mr. Bush and the way he carried himself years ago. Here's an excerpt.*

The governor had considerable admiration for the Bush family. And vice versa. I vividly recall a summer meeting of the New York State Broadcasters Association at the fabled Gideon Putnam, an historic old lorelei of a hotel in Saratoga Springs. William "Billy" Bush, who spent the summer with us as a news intern at our Westchester community stations, "covered" the upstate confab, with broadcasters from all over the state, at which the governor was the featured speaker. After Mario's formal remarks, he opened it up for a Q & A session.

The very first question came from the attractive young man in the back of the room: "Mr. Governor, my name is William 'Billy' Bush. I am an associate of your friend Mr. O'Shaughnessy. I'd like to ask you *why* must it always be 'us' against 'them' in the public discourse?"

The room hushed and waited for Mario's response to the excellent philosophical question, which was right over the heart of the plate for Mario Cuomo. "Well, I can tell from the elegance of your question that you are indeed a Bush. . . ." And then Mario hit it out of the park with a beautiful ten-minute reply.

After the conference was over, I received a call in my car going down the Hudson River Valley. "Who was that attractive young man; is he really a Bush?" Mario asked. When I explained that Billy was the son of Jonathan Bush, Mario said, "Oh, I like his father very much. He's the one with the great personality, the one all the other Bushes wish they were like."

Billy Bush is an absolutely wonderful young man, a graceful fellow with sterling manners. But for one unfortunate and memorable lapse, he's always been a perfect gentleman.

He started as an intern with our suburban Westchester station WVOX right out of Colby College in 1994.

Despite the "Access Hollywood" incident, Billy Bush has been a class act in every season of his life.

He brings to everything he does—*on* and *off* the air—a generous helping of born-and-bred *bonhomie*, gregarious ebullience, *joie de vivre*, and effervescence. He has always been accompanied by a lot of pep and gracious enthusiasm in everything he does.

He's also a fine journalist with good instincts who lights up a television studio. And as we've observed him over the years, there's not a mean damn bone in his body.

As the world knows, he is also a nephew of a former president of the United States (George H.W. Bush), a cousin of another (George W. Bush), and a grandson of a U.S. senator (Prescott Bush). Interesting that he's never "played" or bragged on any of that.

His father is the estimable Jonathan Bush, whom Mario Cuomo once described as "the Bush all the others would like to be."

In an era of vapid, vacuous, boring, tedious, unexciting talking heads, bimbos, and poseurs glued to teleprompters, we still think Billy Bush is a bright, shining star with great potential and a great future. Because he's *real!*

And it is our hope that the elders of the television networks will not hold the temporary vulgarity of his frat-boy episode with Donald Trump against him.

William "Billy" Bush has clearly done a lot of sincere soul-searching with respect to the feelings of women. And he remains the gentleman he was brought up to be.

To choke off this young man's career would be unfortunate . . . nay, inexcusable.

He deserves a second chance.

—*W.O.*

Phil Reisman: In Defense of Billy Bush

This October 14, 2016, column by the great writer Phil Reisman is reprinted from the Journal News, *Gannett's Westchester paper.*

If Donald Trump's X-rated disquisition on how to conquer the opposite sex amounted to nothing more than "locker room banter," then it's also true that Billy Bush played the fawning toady to the Big Man on Campus.

Basking in the reflected glory of Trump's Day-Glo tan, Bush giggled obsequiously. He ogled: "Yeah, those legs, all I can see is the legs."

Immature and embarrassing? Yes—especially for a man who was thirty-three years old at the time. He unwittingly acted like a kid who kisses up to a bully to avoid getting ridiculed in the shower, or stuffed into a locker.

But that's as raunchy as Bush got. He didn't say anything on tape that couldn't be heard by virgin ears. And let's face it, if he had behaved that way in the company of anyone but Trump, no one would even give a damn.

This was in 2005, too. That's a lifetime ago—before Twitter, before the iPhone, before the Great Recession and before Obama.

And the crowning irony of all is that it happened long before Trump made himself a permanent blood enemy of the Bush clan by derailing cousin Jeb "low energy" Bush's bid for the Republican nomination.

And yet, Billy Bush is getting the business. Oh, is he ever. Any day now, he will get the official word that he's been fired from his job as a host on NBC's "Today" show—a haven of cutthroats. (Think Matt Lauer.) Bush is getting whacked eleven years after committing what was essentially a non-crime.

Why? It's because in this endless presidential cycle of thin-skinned identity politics, media-enforced political correctness, and scorched-

Earth campaigning, there is no statute of limitations for the least offense.

Billy Bush is a martyr of the popular, dumbed-down culture. He appears to be nothing worse than an innocuous, somewhat shallow guy who is paying for the sins of our stupidity.

William O'Shaughnessy, the colorful president and editorial director of WVOX radio in New Rochelle, believes Bush is collateral damage, caught in the cross-hairs of a nasty election.

Bush worked as a WVOX intern in the summer of 1994. O'Shaughnessy claims he "discovered" him.

In a radio commentary last week, he effusively praised his former protégé.

"Billy Bush has been a class act in every season of his life," O'Shaughnessy gushed. "He brings to everything he does—on and off the air—a generous helping of born-and-bred *bonhomie*, ebullience, *joie de vivre* and effervescence."

He remembered how the young Bush once impressed Gov. Mario Cuomo during an interview.

"Well," Cuomo said, "I can tell from the elegance of your question that you are indeed a Bush."

It should be stated here that O'Shaughnessy is loyal to a fault. Many times, I've heard him say, "I always root for the defendant." Whenever a high-profile political type gets convicted for something, he invariably will write a letter to the judge attesting to the felon's good character.

His defense of Billy Bush sounds like one of those letters. "There's not a mean damn bone in his body."

O'Shaughnessy said Bush shouldn't be blamed "for being caught up in the vulgarity of Donald Trump's locker room, frat boy episode. To choke off this young man's budding career would be unfortunate . . . nay, inexcusable."

I'll take O'Shaughnessy's word for it.

"Great on Imus": A Letter from Jonathan Bush

This letter from the brother of President George H.W. Bush, uncle of President George W. Bush, and father of Billy Bush references our piece on Don Imus in the first chapter.

———————————

Dear Bill.

Great on Imus. What bothered me was the full-fledged exit by his "friends." None stood up for him. What happened to "Let him that is without guilt among you cast the first stone"?

It was a shocking display of men (and some women) at their worst.

Imus gave joy to millions of people stuck in their cars driving to work. It was a dreadful day for our country when he was fired.

Enclosed please find a letter to the editor of the *New York Times*. Undoubtedly they will not print it.

All the best.

Sincerely,

Jonathan.

Jonathan Bush's Letter on Imus to CBS Radio

Dear Editors.

Much has been written and much said about the firing of Don Imus. After the recent appearance of Hillary Clinton at Rutgers, opportunistically pandering away, if a little late, about rising up against those who might disparage minorities or women, I felt compelled to speak up. So here goes.

About ten years ago my company moved from New York to New Haven, and I commenced the daily grind of a forty minute morning drive to work. In that first year I turned my radio to Don Imus and have listened to him at least two or three days a week ever since. Occasionally I would switch to Bloomberg or satellite radio, but wound up listening to Imus more than the others. At times I found his show funny; at other times I would turn off the radio violently as he talked to politicians that did not exactly share my point of view. The show offered a welcomed escape to the caged listener. From laugh-out-loud funny skits to serious political discussions with the likes of Tim Russert, Brian Williams or David Gregory, to interviews with politicians such as John McCain, Joe Biden, Joe Lieberman, James Carville, Mary Matalin, to authors of books, to country and western singers, no show presented an attention getting format remotely close to "Imus in the Morning." Through it all the mercurial Imus rode with effortless charisma, guiding the program with a sure hand and a deft instinct for humor. His long suffering support staff beginning with Charles McCord, honed in their roles by years of experience, stood ever at the ready to bail the chief out if he had gone too far.

Part of the shtick centered around Imus' fecklessness, such as a recent episode which focused on an invitation to Imus from

Brian Williams to join him on a trip to Iraq. Naturally the cast of characters took up a dialogue around the idea that Imus was afraid to go. Imus, in a sense, was playing the role of everyman but with one exception, Imus' equivocating was delightfully funny.

Appearance on the program could often prove a boon to authors whose books he pushed, to politicians looking for votes or notoriety, to singers, even to a previously unknown retired NY city cop and now shameless, self-promoting clown named Bo Dietl.

Occasionally Imus, speaking probably ten million words a year or more, would stray close to the line of decency. But listeners didn't particularly care. They tuned in to hear Imus' wit, Imus' charm, Imus' intransigence, Imus' melodic baritone voice, in short Imus, warts and all.

Now on Thursday April 5th Imus, in a brief snippet of humor, let slip a demeaning phrase. He referred jokingly to the Rutgers women's basketball team as nappy headed hos. Could any sensible person think he meant this disparagingly? Of course not. However, he immediately apologized, subsequently almost falling over backward apologizing, even going on the radio show of one of the nation's leading mountebanks, the Reverend Al Sharpton. (As an aside has anyone yet heard Sharpton apologize for his hand in the deplorable Tawana Brawley affair?)

So what happened? NBC turned off the cameras on MSNBC. Then CBS suspended him for two weeks. Then, knuckling under to pressure from a few big advertisers, themselves afraid of losing African American customers through a threatened boycott by Sharpton and the Reverend Jesse Jackson, Les Moonves of CBS cancelled the entire show. Poof! Gone.

One thing amazes me that in a country which prides itself on free speech, a gifted performer who brightens the lives of millions of listeners every morning could be snuffed out in an instant.

Of course cowardice gained the victory. Cowardice by Mr. Moonves for knuckling under and the cowardice of the advertisers who feared a boycott if they continued to sponsor Imus. However, far worse seems the cowardice of all those who fed at his table only to abandon him when the tables turned against him.

Where were those men and women whose voices should have spoken out against that firing such as:

Senator Chris Dodd of Connecticut, who announced his candidacy for President of the United States on the Imus show, former Congressman Harold Ford, Jr., of Tennessee, whose candidacy for the U.S. Senate Imus backed enthusiastically, Senator John Kerry, a frequent guest and backed by Imus for the Presidency [who] knows full well that Imus is no bigot, but yet he kept silent, or Frank Rich of the *New York Times*, who relished his appearances on Imus, but then wrote a mea culpa article seeking forgiveness for befriending Imus.

On his program Imus frequently used the term weasel to refer to those [about whom] for one reason or another he was being critical. Little did he know that the term would apply to all those people who toadied up to him, who leapt at the opportunity of appearing on his program only to run from him when their support was called for.

There exists one vast constituency who would gladly speak up for Imus had they but a voice so to do, namely, the millions of listeners who have been denied the joy of hearing "Imus in the Morning" and are wondering what happened to the idea "Let him that is without guilt among you cast the first stone."

Sincerely,

Jonathan Bush

Jon: A magnificent letter. Who, I wonder, will speak so brilliantly in defense of your son and heir who got caught up in NBC's desire to hurt Trump.

—W.O.

PART VIII
AIRBORNE ENDORSEMENTS

WVOX is one of the very few radio stations that still editorialize on the great issues of the day and endorse national, local, and regional candidates. There are plenty of "jukeboxes" on the radio dial, presided over by our colleagues who have never subscribed to the theory that a radio station achieves its highest calling when it resembles a platform, or soapbox, where many different voices are heard in the land. Here are a few editorials of the air from the Whitney Global Media archives, including some of our recent findings and pronouncements.

Governor Andrew Cuomo for Governor

A WVOX editorial of the air, broadcast November 1, 2018.

He is Mario Cuomo's son.

And in his best moments, he resembles his magnificent and graceful father.

That being said . . . no one knows the minutiae of governance or the complicated levers of government like Andrew Cuomo. Not even his father of sainted memory.

Sure, Andrew knows how to play the powerbrokers and the union warlords. He knows how to fist-bump and chest-pump and back-slap better than anyone.

But for those who think he doesn't yet possess the rhetorical skills of his father, or Joe Biden for that matter, they should have heard Andrew speak passionately and movingly at the Central Synagogue in Manhattan earlier this week.

Indeed, there was soaring eloquence in the air despite the solemn occasion. We were almost tempted to observe: There was Mario in the air at the podium.

So much for those who dismiss the governor as a mere "mechanic."

His mother, the estimable and greatly respected—and I would say quite universally beloved—Matilda Raffa Cuomo, calls Andrew "The Energizer Governor." And we can't do better than that.

In his first two terms, Andrew has rung up an impressive list of solid accomplishments: gun control, the strongest in the nation; minimum wage; gay marriage; property tax caps . . . long-needed improvements to bridges and airports. He's also doing his level best on the subways; no easy task with Mayor de Blasio's ambition in the way. And the governor deserves great credit for pushing to eliminate all the wasteful overlap in services among the thousands of redundant local jurisdictions.

He's also made every move humanly possible to improve the diminishing fortunes of upstate New York—everything short of murdering the damn weathermen who prescribe those brutal, freezing, snow-covered winters west of Albany. If there were a way to fix the drodsome weather, you can be sure Andrew would find it.

He's not at all perfect. Although he has carried forth his father's and Hugh Leo Carey's revulsion and disdain for the death penalty, we're not crazy about where he is on the other, fundamental and essential right to life issues: i.e. the awful abortion question. But one can only hope that he shares his father's personal revulsion for the killing of innocents, despite his reluctance to impose his religious beliefs on others.

A great deal of attention has been paid by our colleagues in the public press to a few who may have disappointed the governor and let him down.

But he's also had some very intelligent and able counselors on his quest for good and effective government: the classy William Mulrow, Michael DelGuidice, Steven Cohen, Joe Spinelli, John Marino, Rick Cotton, Alphonso David, and the late Andrew Zambelli.

We've been quoted in national journals saying, "It's not easy being Mario Cuomo's son." It's not at all easy when a prominent newspaper—the *Boston Globe*—calls your father "the great philosopher-statesman of the American nation." Nor is it easy when a family friend, Tony Bennett, the last of the great romantic crooners, tells his audiences, "I've sung for five presidents of the United States . . . Mario Cuomo is the greatest man I ever met." I mean that's heavy, very heavy stuff to lay on a young man who is in the "family business."

And then you have Joe Biden, who is a politician the way the men of our fathers' time imagined them to be: "I've been in politics since I was twenty-nine. But the minute I saw Mario Cuomo . . . I knew he was better than I was."

So he is a son and heir of Mario Cuomo, and in his best moments Andrew resembles his father of sainted memory.

Listeners to these radio stations know of our enthusiasm and admiration for President Trump. While none can deny Andrew's use of the bully pulpit which attends the governor of New York, one can only hope Andrew will continue to devote his remarkable creativity and energy and his considerable talents to the $168 billion enterprise over which he now presides and focus on the welfare of the 20 million souls in his daily care and keeping.

We cringe when we see him marching in patriotic parades in Chappaqua with Bill and Hillary Clinton. And it doesn't exactly win points when the Governor seems always to be accompanied by so many outriders and security people at every event. And the glib, booster-like slogans plastered on the podium often distract from the message and the worthwhile things he is trying to achieve.

And it's perhaps a small thing, but to his great credit Andrew ordered that his own name not greet motorists on the many highways and byways leading into the Empire State. Every other governor before him couldn't resist those "Welcome to New York State (fill in the name), Governor."

We know little of his Republican opponent Marc Molinaro, who certainly didn't hit it out of the ballpark when he had the opportunity to debate the Governor provided by our friends Marcia Kramer and Rich Lamb of WCBS-TV.

Indeed Stephanie Miner, the former mayor of Syracuse who, for a time, also headed the state Democratic Party, has been quite the most impressive among those others who aspire to lead our state.

Andrew is who he is. Everybody knows he's dynamic and driven. But our recent interview with the governor showed him to also be a brilliant, introspective, and altogether thoughtful fellow . . . qualities he often seems reluctant to reveal.

To get a grip on what Andrew is really about, read the piece posted on Thursday by the *Times*'s gifted political writer Shane Goldmacher, himself a great student of the Cuomos *père et fils*.

He may not have Nelson Rockefeller's charisma and ease with retail politicking, or his father's graceful brilliance and beautiful soul, but no one has ever worked harder as governor. No one. Period. No one.

In our far-ranging recent interview, we asked the governor if he wanted to be loved or respected. With the facile brain inherited from his father, he quickly replied, "I want to be loved by those I respect."

In case you haven't figured it out, our stations have tremendous respect for Governor Andrew Mark Cuomo.

[567]

And, God forgive me . . . I'm afraid we do love him as well.

Thus our Whitney Global Media radio stations WVOX and WVIP enthusiastically and with great confidence—and affection—endorse the Democratic candidate: Governor Andrew Cuomo for governor of New York.

He's a damn hard worker.

And he's Mario Cuomo's son.

Alessandra Biaggi for State Senate

Alessandra Biaggi's grandfather Mario Biaggi was one of the most decorated police officers in the history of the NYPD . . . and a U.S. congressman. Before he got tangled up in a nasty bit of business called the Wedtech scandal, he was a great pal of the legendary Speaker of the House Tip O'Neill and a charismatic figure who is beloved to this day in Riverdale and the Bronx. Mario would be very proud of his granddaughter, who has recently become a New York state senator. A WVOX editorial of the air broadcast September 5, 2018.

In a dreary and nasty political season, Alessandra Biaggi stands out as a refreshing and very welcome breath of fresh air.

The granddaughter of the late Mario Biaggi of sainted memory is running an enlightened, inspiring—and very effective—campaign for the Democratic nomination in the 24th State Senate District against the controversial Senator Jeffrey Klein.

The odd-shaped 24th District includes a lot of the Bronx and a chunk of Westchester, and we've thus known Jeff Klein for a long, long time. He used to come around almost every day early in his career until . . . he cut a slick deal with the elders in Albany and led five or six disgruntled, rogue Democrats into a questionable scheme in which the IDC (Independent Democratic Conference) made their infamous "power-sharing" deal with Senate Republicans, the sole purpose of which was to accrue personal power and influence for Mr. Klein.

However, with pressure at last from the governor, this cozy and nefarious compact has now fallen apart as Senate Democrats rallied to the legitimate and authentic leadership of Westchester's own State Senator Andrea Stewart-Cousins.

Now that Jeff Klein has lost his once-powerful perch in the leadership . . . good government types in the district are hoping Biaggi can

[569]

finally put an end to Senator Klein's self-serving and less than stellar career.

And so now our friends in Westchester and the Bronx can render the final *coup de grâce* by voting next Thursday, September 13th, for a gifted, dynamic, committed—and really quite wonderful—challenger, Alessandra Biaggi.

In the New York area's roiling political waters there have emerged several candidates waving the banner of so-called Progressivism. But Alessandra Biaggi, with her sensible, centrist approach to the great issues of the day, has steered clear of the way-out fringe loonies abroad in the land.

And while some candidates and challengers are entranced by national issues and Trump-bashing . . . Biaggi has appropriately kept a laser-like focus on state issues within the purview of the Senate to which she aspires.

To be clear, she's bright, she's creative and very dynamic. But she ain't "way out there." Alessandra Biaggi will make a great New York state senator.

WVOX and WVIP proudly endorse her candidacy.

Julie Killian for State Senate

A WVOX editorial of the air broadcast April 18, 2018,
by William O'Shaughnessy.

———————

Julie Killian versus Shelley Mayer. Someone on Facebook said this week that they're *both* nice women. Of that we have no doubt. But how then to explain the catfight between Julie Killian and Shelley Mayer? Granted, the race to succeed the estimable George Latimer in the state Senate is a matter of considerable importance, not alone here in Westchester, but in New York state as well. But it's gotten downright nasty.

Here's how *we* see it shaping up: First, let's take a look at the Democratic candidate, Assemblywoman Shelley Mayer of Yonkers. We tried hard to like her, but Shelley Mayer doesn't have any of the grace notes of George Latimer.

During her brief but undistinguished tenure in the Assembly, the legislature's lower house, Shelley Mayer has been almost invisible in our Sound Shore communities and in southern Westchester in general, save her home base in Yonkers, to which she clings.

In this current shouting match, she has predictably trotted out the old Democrat warhorses for their obligatory blessing and imprimatur. But her campaign is completely controlled by paid hired guns from Brooklyn, some of whom labored on behalf of such Democrat "all stars" as the hapless David Paterson, who succeeded the "stunningly magnificent" Eliot Spitzer for another brief, chaotic interlude before Andrew Mark Cuomo restored some professionalism, intelligence, and ability to the governance of our state. And we're reminded that one of Shelley Mayer's current handlers at one time also touted the charms of two other stellar candidates: the disgraced State senator Malcolm Smith *and* Comptroller Alan Hevesi, another star in that troubled Democratic firmament in Albany. As the distinguished Senator Smith currently resides in the federal penitentiary in Lewisburg, Pennsylvania, he was temporarily unable to join the long list of Mayer boosters who are now speaking for her.

As you know, this seat in the state Senate, which is really *your* seat in the state Senate, was held for many years by "Senator Suzi"—Suzi Oppenheimer. And no Republican, no matter how endowed or possessed of purse and resources, was able to break the Democratic Party's grip on *your* Senate seat. Over the years, the fading GOP here in the Golden Apple did field some pretty attractive and even extraordinary candidates, like John Verni of Mamaroneck, an absolutely terrific fellow, and the well-intentioned (and well-heeled) Bob Cohen from Scarsdale, who impressed a lot of people but could not overcome the Democratic majority in Westchester. The Republicans also put up a couple of rich guys from Rye who weren't ready for prime time.

Which brings us to now. And we're tasked with finding someone to take the place of the graceful and articulate Mr. Latimer, our county executive, and in whom we are so well pleased.

The choice you make could also affect the balance of power in Albany.

We're for Julie Killian, who really proved her mettle during that debate staged last week by our *Journal News* friends at the College of New Rochelle. The lady from Rye did *very* well indeed, while Shelley Mayer was scripted and predictable as she recited from the Democratic playbook, never once straying from its ultraliberal orthodoxy. Clearly, Ms. Mayer is one lady who paints by the numbers.

Mrs. Killian, on the other hand, showed herself to be eminently and refreshingly "real" by bringing genuine conviction and passion to the discussion.

Listen to what this brave lady—the Republican candidate—had to say on the critical, fundamental abortion issue:

I don't support partial birth abortion and abortion up to the ninth month performed by non-doctors, or "infanticide" abortion. It's hard to even think of this, but if a baby is born live, they're able to kill it. There's a reason that has not passed yet in our state government. And I think it's horrible, it's horrible. I do not support those things. I am for access to quality healthcare for everybody. But I am *not* for these things. I don't even want to talk about it because I find it reprehensible.

Boom! Good for you, Julie Killian!
Listen now to her Democratic opponent, Shelley Mayer:

Well, I'm not sure what bill my opponent is talking about. The Reproductive Health Act takes the provisions guaranteed under *Roe v. Wade*. Nothing more, nothing greater than the current constitutional protections that apply to abortion. We don't have an "abortion law." We have a law, the criminal law. And it moves the relevant provisions that "mirror" *Roe v. Wade* [again *Roe v. Wade*!] into the public health law. Just like any other health procedure, it is defined under the public health law.

Brilliant. Spoken like a lawyer! But never once did Assemblywoman Mayer add to her enthusiasm for and embrace of *Roe v. Wade*, a cruel finding that elevated lethal violence against the most vulnerable of human bodies. Its byproduct is vulgar, violent, and, as a growing number of people are now beginning to realize, really akin to permission for murder. The slaughter of the innocents.

It's fine to wave the banner and wax enthusiastic about *Roe v. Wade* if you wish, but then, we think, you've got to pause, reflect, take a deep breath, and say—straight out—just how horrible and absolutely terrible abortion really is.

Julie Killian *did* that, bravely and powerfully and sincerely. We admire her guts and courage.

Why do we focus now on the awful and unsettling abortion issue? Only because that exchange during the recent debate, which was completely missed by our colleagues in the public press, captures, in the case of Julie Killian, how a candidate *thinks* and *feels*. Or in the case of Shelley Mayer, how she *recites*, devoid of feeling. Or compassion.

[573]

For over fifty years we've covered *both* sides of the abortion question, letting countless individuals get on the radio and have at you with their sad pro-abortion views. (But as I approach senility, I'm wondering if there exists any more important issue than life itself.)

Life in every instance.

Julie Killian gets it.

Then there was the bombshell story last week in the *Daily News* by respected veteran Albany bureau chief Ken Lovett, covering two full pages and revealing that while serving as counsel to the senate Democrats, Shelley Mayer did little beyond "passing on" harassment complaints from at least two female workers in the legislature. Even Mayer said, "I should have done more." We can't resist the observation that Killian would have raised holy hell in that situation.

Shelley Mayer's Brooklyn handlers are also laboring mightily to tarnish Killian with President Trump. (We think the president is a lot more popular than the polls suggest.) But this race to succeed George Latimer is *not* for a seat in the House of Representatives. It's all about Albany. And *our* state government. And it's all about our own back yard.

Much has been written about the "Good Old Boys" culture in Albany. What we're saying today, perhaps inartfully, awkwardly, and imprecisely, is that we don't think Westchester wants to send, with all due respect, a "Good Old Girl" who has been around the tainted and tarnished corridors of power back up to Albany yet again to accommodate those "Good Old Boys" in the state Senate.

But we *do* want, we urgently suggest, a woman of independence, bravery, and good common sense who *thinks* for herself.

It's clear that Julie Killian is the enlightened choice for the Latimer seat.

She's fresh, fearless, and altogether very "real" and not at all afraid to say what she thinks and believes in her heart of hearts.

The Republican candidate doesn't need talking points crafted by political handlers in Brooklyn. She's got a real mind. And we'd much prefer Mrs. Killian than someone slavishly devoted to that Democratic playbook.

In this contentious race, the Republican thinks for herself, while the Democrat paints by the numbers.

We're for Killian.

This is a Whitney Global Media editorial of the qir. This is William O'Shaughnessy.

FYI: Shelley Meyer won. Killian lost.

George Latimer for Westchester County Executive

George Latimer, who presently serves as county executive of Westchester, is an extraordinary political figure. He was chairman of the Westchester County Board and a New York state senator, and, with it all, he always finds the time to be our WVOX "Sound Shore Correspondent." When Latimer defeated his Republican predecessor as county executive, he walked in the door of our station and his first words were, "How does it feel to have a county executive in the family?" George Latimer is a very gifted, graceful, and articulate public servant. His postings on Facebook in recent years are beautifully crafted and often with soaring eloquence. The hope is that he can also find the time to pull together a collection of his musings and observations. Broadcast November 2, 2017.

——————————

Our colleagues at Gannett's *Journal News*, Westchester's important daily newspaper, have found in favor of George Latimer to be our next county executive.

Their editorial endorsement is a well-constructed and exquisitely reasoned treatise on both candidates in the contentious and nasty county race.

The paper argues that with all his mistakes and flaws—and they are considerable—Senator Latimer, the Democrat, is much to be preferred over the incumbent, Rob Astorino, the Republican, who also has the endorsement of the Conservative Party. As you know, if you've been reading the public press and listening to WVOX, the Astorino machine has hit George Latimer with everything but the proverbial kitchen sink. Some of it justified.

Our take, however, on Senator Latimer is that he is one of the hardest-working and most dedicated public servants we've encountered in over fifty years as your local station. Only Greenburgh's peripatetic Paul

Feiner can match Latimer for being everywhere apparent and constantly at the people's business, 24/7.

At the risk of being biblical, Latimer reminds us often of Saint Paul in the Bible who, it is said, advised converts to the early Christian faith, "What doth it matter if everyone else is fine . . . and *you* are not all right . . . ?" Paul's instruction was clearly a message to ancient Latimer-types who are driven to do good for all the other people, their neighbors, but often neglect themselves. Which brings us to the present-day George Latimer. It is obvious he needs to spend some time tending to himself. In other words, Senator George needs to, every once in a while, take some time out from doing the *mitzvahs* and kindnesses of his public life to tend to his own damn household (no pun intended).

Much has been made of Latimer's transportation problems. It's no excuse, but he doesn't have drivers and bodyguards to convey him here and there as Astorino commands in abundance (after vowing to cut back on "security"—read "perks").

Gannett is right. Latimer is a rumpled but hardworking and altogether dedicated fellow.

Having been a former chairman of the county board—and in every telling and account, a very good one—he knows the levers and potential of county government. And when we speak of superior county board chairmen, the great and estimable Herman Geist is in that class with Latimer, and so too was Andy O'Rourke and New Rochelle's brilliant Stephen Tenore.

In this mean-spirited race, Mr. Latimer is also up against an ultraconservative billionaire and his daughter's purse, who are reported to have put one million bucks on the line to reelect Mr. Astorino and defeat the Democrat.

It's no secret abroad in the land that Rob Astorino wants to be governor, and his heart and soul are clearly in another run for Albany.

We don't always agree with the local Gannett elders. But in this important race, we are in 100 percent agreement with the *Journal News* and their thoughtful editorial. George Latimer is *much* to be preferred as our next county executive.

Rob Astorino, in his best moments, is a nice, agreeable, and affable fellow, and we were proud to endorse him over our own New Rochelle Mayor Noam Bramson, the stunningly brilliant and precocious but tone-deaf mayor of New Rochelle who is ultra-fluent in the jargon and municipal-speak of government rules and regs, but you wouldn't want to ask him for a favor for your brother-in-law or a neighbor who is hurting. You may recall, we "endorsed" Noam for the U.S. Congress in the last county exec's race because that's where Bramson has *his* sights set, still to this day.

On the occasion of the last county executive contest, we opted for Astorino. He has many good qualities. And very much to his credit is his relationship with the Plunketts. The estimable William Plunkett is an advisor, as he is to many. And his brother Kevin is Rob's hardworking deputy county executive. He also found something for the highly regarded former Supreme Court Justice Daniel Angiolillo when the Cuomo office cut him loose after a distinguished career on the appellate bench. He's also been loyal, many think to a fault, to his former colleagues at the dearly departed White Plains radio station before it gave up the ghost and mantle of a community station.

He also enjoys, as we do, the friendship of Timothy Cardinal Dolan, archbishop of New York. But make no mistake, Senator Latimer is the better choice in *this* race.

Nobody quite knows where Astorino is on Playland, Westchester parks, or the county airport.

It really is a question of priorities, instincts, and inclination. While Rob Astorino spends a lot of time "auditioning" for New York City radio stations, here every morning without fail for the past thirty-something years has been the voice of George Latimer, calling attention to community meetings and local events. It tells you something.

Incidentally, we've also learned just this week that Astorino's campaign quietly slipped over $21,000 to WOR for "advertising," which means that somebody at least knows the meaning of the Latin phrase *quid pro quo*.

During the fifty-plus years of our stewardship, WVOX has usually found our way to the side of gifted and able local Republican candidates: the incomparable Nelson Rockefeller, Malcolm Wilson, Andy

O'Rourke, Edwin Gilbert Michaelian, Anthony J. Colavita, Alvin Richard Ruskin et al., while saving our enthusiasm on the state and national scene for Jack and Robert Kennedy, Daniel Patrick Moynihan, Mario Matthew Cuomo of sainted memory, and his dynamic son and heir, Andrew Mark Cuomo, the "Energizer Governor."

We've clearly favored Republicans on the local scene close to home. But in this critical county election of 2017, we confidently endorse the Democrat: Senator George Latimer for county executive.

We believe he'll make a great one with his accessibility, stamina, willingness to listen to ordinary people, and very good and generous heart.

Plus, when it comes to government and governance, he's damn smart.

We suggest he begin to apply those smarts to his personal life and the minutiae of everyday living that we all have to deal with.

This is an editorial of the air. This is Bill O'Shaughnessy.

Rob Astorino for County Executive

Robert Astorino, who preceded the estimable George Latimer as West-chester county executive, was a conservative Republican and a favorite of our friend Cardinal Timothy Dolan, whom I greatly admire. Astorino, as you may recall, ran for governor of New York some years ago against Andrew Cuomo. He carried almost all the upstate, rural counties. But Andrew prevailed. Previously we backed Astorino for county executive when he ran against our New Rochelle mayor Noam Bramson. Broadcast October 29, 2013.

———————

Despite what you've heard, we are endorsing Noam Bramson—for *Congress*!

We're sorry. But Noam Bramson has been running a "*congressional campaign*" from the get-go. Young Mr. Bramson, I tell you, has all the Kennedy-esque moves. All the gestures. The pace. The cadence. The rhythm. All the Harvard elocution. He's *got* the moves.

But downtown New Rochelle, with rare exception (a few good restaurants, an art gallery, a couple of jewelry stores), is essentially all "dollar" stores and a for-profit college owned by out-of-towners. For, you see, Mayor Bramson has practically turned over most of our faded and beleaguered downtown to Monroe College and the Jerome family's *for-profit* empire. *And* he's trying to jam that ill-conceived Echo Bay so-called "development" down everyone's throat. But the concerned, sensible residents of his city are asking what the hell Forest City Ratner has ever done for New Rochelle! We can answer that: absolutely *nothing*!

We've been at the people's business for fifty years, ladies and gentlemen, covering politics and government here in Westchester, and we've had Mayor Bramson at this microphone often during his tenure as our part-time mayor. He's articulate. He talks a very good game of policy-speak. But he's gone missing during his recent bewildering "congressional campaign."

Noam Bramson is precocious. He's brilliant. And he lets everyone know it. He's a policy wonk very much at ease with the jargon of governance and lingo of textbook public policy.

But the Westchester county executive is supposed to run the damn county parks, the county parkways, the county police. And preside over the $1.7 billion county budget. Mr. Astorino does that all with great skill and sound judgment.

Our friends at the *Journal News* have blessed Mr. Bramson's lofty aspirations, saying he offers a "holistic" approach. With all due respect, I'm not sure what the hell that means (we're sure our friend Phil Reisman, their star feature columnist, didn't write that holy "holistic" headline!). Have it as you will, we believe Rob Astorino offers a sensible, prudent, commonsense approach to regional, local government.

Mr. Bramson has shoveled hundreds of thousands of dollars down to Washington, D.C., consultants and political gurus in the state of Virginia. But he has almost completely ignored local media—the local newspapers and, indeed, our local radio stations. There's no question he's shooting for the big time. He's really running for *Congress*. And it was ever thus.

Indeed, Mr. Bramson has even ignored the elders of his own Democratic Party in Westchester. No, as I said, I think our mayor is shooting for bigger fish. He wants to go *national*. We don't think he's at all interested in this job of Westchester county executive.

We go all the way back in this county to Edwin Gilbert Michaelian, the legendary county executive of sainted memory. The county office building is named after Mr. Michaelian. He was a wonderful man. And a great county executive. So too was Andy O'Rourke, whom we lost just recently after a long, distinguished career in public service. Rob Astorino is cut from the same bipartisan, sensible cloth as Michaelian and O'Rourke.

Astorino is also astute and smart enough to repair to the wise counsel of some very intelligent individuals who *know* Westchester well, such as his deputy Kevin Plunkett and Kevin's estimable brother William Plunkett, as well as John Cahill, who, indeed, *ran* the state of

New York at one time as chief of staff to a former governor. Whereas Mr. Bramson seems to have wrapped himself in the bosom of those paid-gun political strategists from Arlington, Virginia, and Washington, D.C., who see big things for him. But the bottom line is: Noam Bramson is *not a good fit* for this job.

We're sorry, but *guns* and *abortion* are national issues. And so is *gay marriage*. And while we're at it, it's *one* thing to say you're pro-choice. Everybody should be pro-choice. A state can't legislate where it has no power, that is, in a woman's body. *But* in the very next breath, we think you've got to say how horrible and vulgar and violent *abortion* is. We haven't heard that from Noam Bramson.

On his record, on the issues that should count in this race, Mr. Astorino has been, in fact, a very brave and able executive. He's taken bold and, at the same time, prudent, sensible steps to curb the excesses and sweep away the rubble of the Spano years. And he's done it all thoughtfully and carefully and fairly.

The battered and discredited national GOP in Washington can certainly take a lesson from our enlightened Republican county executive. He's reached across the aisle and actually cooperated with (God forbid) *Democrats*.

Astorino has worked especially well with our Westchester neighbor Governor Andrew Cuomo, in whom we are so well pleased. And, in case anyone failed to notice, the governor, in what was supposed to be a huge, momentous endorsement of Mayor Bramson last weekend, opted instead to just do a perfunctory "shout-out" to Rockland and Westchester Democratic candidates in general.

And say what you will about wily Bill Clinton, he's not stupid. And Bill Clinton's so-called "endorsement" of Mr. Bramson was along the same lines. (Anyway, we *think* he endorsed Mr. Bramson. It's "rumored" that he did, anyway.) But notice that no members of the press were allowed to witness the grand event. Not *one*. In fact, the media were summarily *banned* from the proceedings (something that was very pointedly noted by News 12's great Janine Rose during the recent debate).

Now, despite the outstanding job he's *been* doing, Astorino has some formidable obstacles. He's got registration numbers against him. Westchester, in case you haven't noticed, is *heavily* Democratic. He's

[582]

most likely got my beloved *New York Times* against him. He's certainly got our friends at "Mother Gannett"—the *Journal News*—against him. And to his great credit, he's got shy, modest, retiring Senator Chuck Schumer against him.

Rob Astorino has also had a lot of endorsements. But he's going to have *one more*. We're very pleased to announce this morning that WVOX and WVIP are endorsing Mr. Astorino, the very able and dedicated Republican and Conservative candidate for county executive of Westchester.

We're glad to stand with Mr. Astorino.

Judge Daniel Angiolillo

*We not only endorsed candidates on the airwaves. I have often taken
to the hustings to share my enthusiasms for several candidates.
Here's a speech I did for a wonderful judge named Daniel Angiolillo,
running for justice, Appellate Division, New York State Supreme Court.
The Avalon, New Rochelle, N.Y., October 1, 2013.*

First of all, permit me to thank you for the gift of your presence as well
as the generosity of your purse.

So many of you, as I look around the room, have been admirers and
supporters of the judge for a long, long time, and I won't intrude for
very long on your evening.

We've come on this beautiful Indian summer night because we need
something to believe in. To hold on to. And to be guided by.

Something wiser than our own quick personal impulses, and something sweeter than the taste of a political victory.

Our presence here tonight is a tribute not only to a gifted and able
jurist, but it is a tribute as well, I think, to what one of the most graceful
and articulate of your profession—Mario Cuomo—calls "Our Lady of
the Law."

As the lawyers here assembled know, the Constitution, our more
than a 200-year-old legacy of law and justice, has been the foundation,
the rock on which we have built all that is good about America. For
more than 200 years, "Our Lady of the Law" has proven stronger than
the errors or sins or omissions of her acolytes, which is what lawyers
are, and has made us better than we would have been.

But you know all of these things. They teach them in law school. And
you practice them every day as officers of the court.

But you also know and are aware that the law does not apply to every
single case or circumstance or even, perhaps, to every day and age. So

judges must take a wonderful instrument, the Constitution—or statute or precedent—and try to lay it over and apply it to each case. They must try to fit it to reality.

To work well, the law, in the care and keeping of a judge, has to have the restraint that comes with fairness, and it also must have tension to move and bend and be compassionate—firm, but flexible—to deal with each new circumstance.

What qualities, then, should we have a right to expect from the men and women we raise up from among us to interpret and define that rule of law?

They must have:

- Experience.
- Intelligence.
- Integrity.
- Wisdom.
- And compassion.

So where do you find people with such qualities? Where must a governor who appoints them or those who elect them find such people? Not in every lawyer. Or in every judge.

To whom, then, do you entrust the power to restructure families? To take a business or restructure our purse. Who maintains this rule of law? What protects it? Not a rifle or a bayonet or a prison cell. Only, only a good mind, accompanied by the precious, sound instinct of a judge who is both wise *and* good.

We found such an individual (albeit with too many vowels in his name) fourteen years ago.

And so here we are now in 2013 with another opportunity to reaffirm our confidence in and admiration for an appellate judge with a collegial, compassionate, and loving touch, with a gentle heart to interpret the law, but with a firmness and power to apply it.

So, as I mercifully yield, I would ask again: Where do you find these qualities? Not in every lawyer, or even in every judge.

But we found all of it and *more* in the compassionate and caring heart of Mr. Justice Daniel Angiolillo.

And we must continue his brilliant service, *despite* the registration numbers, *despite* the political winds.

There is no Republican or Democratic way to interpret or dispense justice.

We've got to reelect Mr. Justice Dan Angiolillo!

FYI: Judge Angiolillo, running as a Republican
in heavily Democratic Westchester, lost.

Ernie Davis for Mayor

Mount Vernon is sui generis, *truly unique and able to be defined only in its own terms. It sits cheek-by-jowl with Bronxville, one of the wealthiest and most influential towns on the eastern seaboard. But it's not been immune to the problems that plague cities everywhere. It's also been a launching pad for the likes of Denzel Washington, P. Diddy, the great Herman Geist, who, in his nineties, is still a formidable presence in our county. Over the years Mount Vernon has also had some very colorful politicos, including the flamboyant Mayor Joe Vaccarella. The doings and deliberations in Mount Vernon City Hall have often drawn the attention of federal authorities. And Ernie Davis earned their attention during his stewardship of the beleaguered city. But he was always one of our favorites. Broadcast November 4, 2011.*

The city of Mount Vernon and its people have always been very special to WVOX. And we take a keen interest in the doings and deliberations of that beleaguered and often misunderstood municipality.

The landlocked city, which sits cheek-by-jowl between Yonkers and New Rochelle and those upscale enclaves of Pelham and Bronxville, has had colorful, vivid leaders over the years. We remember, with great affection, "Mayor Joe" Vaccarella, Augie Petrillo, Tom Sharpe, and other mythic figures who once inhabited City Hall in Mount Vernon.

But then, a few decades ago, this great city began a long, inexorable slide into urban chaos and decay. *Until,* that is, the people of Mount Vernon raised up from their midst Ernie Davis.

Mayor Davis is articulate. He is thoughtful. And we probably do him damage among his enemies by observing that he is—to this day—a man of great dignity and style who brought a magnificent bearing and carriage to the office of mayor.

[587]

And now in 2011 Ernie Davis is the Lazarus of Westchester politics. His innate decency and undeniable love for often-ignored Mount Vernon have given him another chance to place his vision and dreams in the service of Mount Vernon's disparate and deserving residents.

We've always liked the soft-spoken and altogether sincere man who now aspires to a second term. The articulate Mr. Davis has risen above all the division and acrimony that usually accompany politics in his beloved city. He runs this time as a healer. And a conciliator.

And he runs personally untarnished and untouched by all those from within—and from without—who tried to bring Mount Vernon down during his first term and, indeed, are still at it in this nasty campaign.

Mayor Davis is respected and admired far beyond the city limits of Mount Vernon. But he also has great "street creds" on every block and in all the dazzlingly diverse neighborhoods of that magnificent, misunderstood city bursting with potential.

And it should tell you something that even former Mayor Clinton Young, who was vanquished by Ernie Davis in the Democratic primary, is backing his old opponent—which speaks well of Mayor Davis, as well as of Mayor Young, who turns out to be a class act.

Having won the Democratic primary, Mayor Davis is now faced with a candidate put forward by the Conservative Party: Maureen Walker, who has done a reasonably credible job as comptroller. She's good at the books and numbers. However, for the much bigger and infinitely more demanding job of mayor, there is no prudent choice but His Honor Mayor Ernie Davis.

The graceful, soft-spoken man has always had a love affair with his city.

Let's hope it's lovelier the second time around.

We endorse the Democrat with confidence, enthusiasm, and even real affection for the decent, caring, good man he has always been and remains.

This is a WVOX editorial of the air. This is William O'Shaughnessy.

P.S. He won. And . . . he's running again in 2019 . . .
only to be knocked off the ballot!

Stay the Course with Mayor Bradley

January 7, 2011.

Embattled White Plains Mayor Adam Bradley has been pilloried and castigated in the public press. And much of it is fed by the personally ambitious Democrats on the White Plains City Council, many of whom see a "future mayor" when they look in the mirror in the morning.

Despite his well-publicized matrimonial woes, Adam Bradley has not given any indication whatsoever that he is not up to the task of governing his important Westchester city.

The highly regarded and greatly revered retired Supreme Court Justice Samuel George Fredman, himself a former chairman of the Democratic City Committee, who also served as Democratic county chairman, has spoken passionately in defense of Mayor Bradley's absolute right to remain at his post until his personal domestic issues are behind him.

This whole contretemps is a perfect example of our theory of long standing that men and women of ability and quality will not submit to the rigors of public service. And this issue, about his divorce, however unpleasant and contentious it may be, would be treated as a "garden variety" matrimonial matter if Mayor Bradley were in any other kind of endeavor or career.

No one knows the absolute truth of what happened in the Bradley household. No one—the judge included (albeit a very good jurist she is)—knows who is lying. And Mayor Bradley certainly deserves the opportunity to have his case play out via the appellate process.

Indeed, with all the carping and backstabbing that have been visited on Adam Bradley by members of his own political tribe, he has diligently and sincerely—and effectively—applied himself to the people's business without any noticeable letup.

We don't believe a man's political career should be destroyed by the self-serving ambition of the Democratic members of the City Council (or by our own colleagues in the public press!).

And everyone else should just stay the hell out of this mess until it can be proven beyond a reasonable doubt that Mayor Adam Bradley is unable to govern.

So far we haven't seen that. In fact, he has applied himself to his municipal duties with vigor, determination, and an optimistic demeanor—as well as a good heart.

We certainly agree with Mr. Justice Fredman—a man of great probity who, at eighty-six, is, in every telling, a gray eminence and statesman of our Westchester community—that the attempted "public hanging" of Adam Bradley tarnishes and diminishes the image of the entire city as well as a political party.

The duly elected mayor is entitled to all the legal remedies available to him, even in the face of the character assassination to which he has been subjected.

Indeed, our own Republican "leanings and inclinations" are well known to one and all. But the vitriol being heaped on Mayor Bradley by those bearing a political agenda should concern everyone interested in fair play.

The whole, unhappy matter is in the courts, where it should play out and remain.

And the mayor should remain in City Hall, where he is doing an exemplary job.

"Duly elected" is the key.

Adam Bradley has since left politics and now hosts
a weekly WVOX radio program dealing with civic issues.

PART IX
A MAN OF LETTERS

In addition to keeping WVOX and WVIP afloat as the last independent radio stations in the New York area . . . I spend a great deal of time on another of my enthusiasms, the Broadcasters Foundation of America, our profession's national charity, which assists the hurting and almost forgotten in our own tribe.

I am chairman of the Foundation's Guardian Fund, and, sadly, our vital work does not always resonate with many in our profession, who have been amply rewarded by our industry. Many of them just don't get the notion of "giving back." But then there are some, as John Meacham observed as President George H.W. Bush's memorial service, who are "instinctively generous." At the risk of embarrassing him . . . one such altogether generous broadcasting colleague is the incomparable Rush Hudson Limbaugh III. He's been so good to our unique mission . . . I've almost run out of ways to thank the great man. But I tried in the following notes. I've also taken pen in hand on many other topics, some of which are recorded here, along with some eloquent and graceful notes we've received over the years.

Letter to Rush Limbaugh

March 1, 2018

Dear Rush,

We all make our living with words (none of us as artfully, gracefully, or powerfully as Rush Limbaugh). But how do I find the words to properly thank you for your magnificent expression of friendship for Ed McLaughlin?

All of us who have been associated with the Broadcasters Foundation of America for many years are grateful to you beyond the reach of mere words. So I just wanted to presume, as chairman of the Foundation's Guardian Fund, to thank you for your spectacular beneficence in honor and memory of Ed.

Ed was relentlessly supportive of our work and humanitarian mission for several decades, giving of his time, enthusiasm, and the generosity of his purse . . . and so too is his beloved and wonderful Pat.

Incidentally, I'm dictating this note en route to my home in Litchfield while listening to El Rushbo on WOR (today with a marvelous riff on sea turtles and their whacko protectors!) . . . and I was wondering just how many among the millions of other folks listening to Rush Limbaugh right now have any idea what a generous and good soul you are in addition to being the great communicator.

Thank you, Rush, on behalf of those hurting and almost forgotten colleagues—past and present—the Foundation helps all over the country.

We're also fortunate and grateful that we enjoy the blessing and imprimatur of your associates and friends Kraig Kitchen and our esteemed director Julie Talbott.

We thank you. And The Great McLaughlin thanks you from another, and we are sure, a better world . . .

Yours,
Bill

Letter to Rush Limbaugh

March 26, 2018

Dear Rush Hudson Limbaugh III:

You magnificent bastard!

How in the world do we even presume to properly thank you yet again for your relentlessly generous beneficence to the Broadcasters Foundation of America!

What else can we do but bless the day our late chairman emeritus Ed McLaughlin of sainted memory met the great Rush Limbaugh. That we'll do and when we address our Creator tonight we'll be remembering, with considerable gratitude, America's Greatest Communicator. We can also absolutely assure you that a lot of the hurting and almost forgotten among your broadcasting colleagues will directly benefit from your spectacular generosity to the Foundation.

I almost wish we could do a "Lazarus" on Ed so he could thank you as well. But I'm persuaded that McLaughlin already knows of your great kindness to the national charity that meant so much to him and Pat.

Although our mission of providing a "safety net" for our radio and television colleagues is eminently worthy and usually so urgent and vital . . . our work as a "Foul Weather Friend" to broadcasters who have been laid low by sudden illness and life's vicissitudes does not always resonate with many in our profession who have over the years been quite amply rewarded by our industry. But many of them just don't get the idea of "giving back." That's why you are so very special and dear to all of us.

And as we attempt to thank you yet again, Rush . . . we should also properly acknowledge our director Julie Talbott and Kraig Kitchen, those two brilliant souls who are so devoted to your interests as well as to the humanitarian work and noble mission of the Broadcasters Foundation.

We're indeed fortunate to enjoy Kraig and Julie's blessing and imprimatur. But, most of all, we thank you, Rush.

And like I said in my previous letter . . . I wonder how many of your millions of listeners, fans, and admirers really know what a generous, loving, and good fellow you are. . . .

We sure do.

Yours,

Bill

Letter from Rush Limbaugh to William O'Shaughnessy

April 19, 2018

———————————

Dear Bill,

Thanks very much, that is one heckuva letter and I greatly appreciate it. It is great to receive such compliments from someone who actually knows the business of broadcasting and understands. Heck, you define it in so many ways.

One of the (very few) unfortunate things in all of this is the lack of general reporting and understanding of the obstacles Ed had overcome to make this enterprise a success. We had to do things none of us expected to have to do, including find ways around a general ad agency ban from the get-go, just because I was conservative (controversial). It took fortitude to stick with it and keep pushing for Top 20 clearances.

I don't know if you know, but George Green, then of KABC, offered to buy the show and shelve it. He was afraid of Ed, not me. Nobody knew who I was when all this started. Ed refused his offer and off we were to KFI some months later.

Anyway, thanks again for your letter. I feel like I know you even though we haven't met. You were constantly in "Page Six" and else-where, galivanting around and getting the radio business publicity. They love you still. As do all those you are working to help and assist.

Thanks for letting me be a small part of it.

All the best,

Rush Limbaugh

Letter to Rush Limbaugh

April 23, 2018

Dear Rush:

Thank you for that very gracious—and altogether beautiful—note about the Broadcasters Foundation of which you have become its greatest and most valued benefactor.

I'm afraid you've exaggerated my own meager involvement in its noble mission. But, of course, I really do appreciate the kind words from The Great Limbaugh.

Your other thoughtful and prescient comments about the work of the Foundation itself, which enjoys your blessing and imprimatur, also prompted the thought that so many of our fellow broadcasters take from our profession . . . and give nothing back.

I attribute it to the sad fact that many of our colleagues never really "learned" philanthropy . . . or developed an "instinct" for it. It's rather like a shortstop, I guess, who can't go to his left in baseball. And, I also have a hunch that many broadcasters never really learned the "concept" of generosity at home. Sadly, maybe it started there.

But then . . . then there are some, as Jon Meacham observed at Barbara Bush's memorial service, who are "instinctively generous."

During my work with the Foundation over the last ten years, Rush, I'm learning who are the givers (and, sadly, who are the takers).

You, sir, are a brilliant, vivid, and shining example of those who are possessed of that rare and loving generosity of spirit.

And so was Ed McLaughlin.

But you already know the song . . . and you sing it brilliantly.

As I've tried to tell you in my previous notes, so awkwardly, inartfully, and imprecisely—we love you for it.

Yours,

Bill

The Holy Roman Catholic Church:
Letter to Michael "Lionel" Lebron

Michael Lebron, a.k.a. Lionel, is a multimedia phenom, a radio star, provocative blogger, and delightful contrarian. I like the guy but don't always agree with him. August 21, 2018.

———————

Dear Lionel:

As you are well aware . . . I'm a huge fan and admirer of yours.

I delight in—and savor—many/most of your delightful and prescient contrarian views. And it is a pleasure to amplify your brilliant voice on the radio. Plus I very much like you and Lynn.

Now comes The However. I think you make a considerable mistake by trashing the Holy Roman Catholic Church. This from a poor, stumbling, staggering, faltering, weak Catholic.

But I'm with the great Mario Cuomo of sainted memory who begged us to believe the Church is not its flawed predator priests or the bishops, cardinals, vicars, deans, and metropolitans far removed from the poor and cloaked in their scarlet finery and trappings of gilt, satin, and gold.

"Christ is the Church," reminded the failed baseball player from Queens. "Christ."

Mario was fascinated that "Catholics are able to cling to their faith, notwithstanding the many serious sins of the Church's priests and popes over its 2,000-year history."

Christ told Peter he was to be the rock on which Christ would build his church. But he also pointed out to Peter that despite his bestowal of that awesome and unique responsibility, Peter would—on his very first night of service—commit three serious sins by denying Christ three times.

[598]

Christ was letting Peter—and all the rest of Christendom—know that for all the years to come, the Church would be charged with the mission of spreading Christ's word, but its members would be vulnerable human beings who may sin seven times a day.

In fact, Christ is our religion, not the Church.

And that's why Catholics are behaving rationally, as well as loyally, when they continue to believe.

I also beg you to believe, my brilliant friend, that the wonderful Jesuit pope that you call "Bergoglio," who took the name Francis is a magnificent, very real gift to all of us . . . even though he struggles as we all do.

I got no problem with you going after the Clintons, Lionel.

But, I beg you, cut the Holy Roman Church some slack with your fertile brain and articulate tongue.

Yours,

Bill

A Note from Dan Rather

February 15, 2018, New York City

———————

Dear Bill,

Just a quick note to say thank you to you, my old friend, for all that you broadcast and wrote in connection with my Westchester book appearance.

My appreciation runs deep.

Cheers and courage,

Dan

Facebook Note from Kate O'Shaughnessy Nulty

This Facebook posting from my daughter
Kate O'Shaughnessy Nulty meant a lot to me.
More than all the others I've received.

—————————

Kate O'Shaughnessy is with William O'Shaughnessy.
April 6, 2017

Happy Birthday to my sweet daddy . . . .for all the pomp and circum-stance, blue blazers, Belgian loafers, and heads you turn . . . there are thousands of people in this world whose lives are better because of your generosity, powerful words, and sweetness of spirit. . . . Jesuit priests, governors, fruit vendors, doormen, waitresses, students, judges, restau-rateurs, mobsters, homeless, and one daughter. You light up a room, daddy, but your brightest light shines deep in my heart. I love you!

In Defense of Le Cirque: Letter to Pete Wells

Pete Wells is the powerful restaurant critic for my beloved
New York Times. *September 20, 2012.*

———————

Dear Pete:

I'm a Pete Wells fan.

But I do have some concerns and a few urgent thoughts about your Le Cirque piece.

My very first reaction was to wonder how the hell you could do this to Sirio Maccioni. And I even started to dash off a letter to Arthur Sulzberger asking the publisher of my beloved *Times* the same question I put to you. Indeed, I've often seen your own publisher in Sirio's care and keeping and he always seemed to be enjoying himself . . . as did his father before him.

However, after several more readings of your review, I realized that you did indeed endeavor to be respectful of this great man. Sirio is not only the most graceful and attractive individual in his profession, he is also the most generous and inspiring.

I was also pleased to note that you bestowed on the Le Cirque captains, waiters, and staff the approval they rightly deserve. But I have to note that you quite missed the glamour and vibe of the place and the fun to be had of an evening at Sirio's beckoning tables. And I'm afraid I found, in general, a lack of respect for Le Cirque itself as a beloved, enduring, and endearing New York institution.

We can argue over stars. I would have given them at least two even if I had written your particular piece. But I must share with you my very real disappointment that a professional journalist and critic of your stature and standing would lay off on one of your "companions" that devastating, bleak, cutting—and not a little mean-spirited—

observation: "They've given up." That one deeply hurt all of Sirio's friends and admirers.

And it surely had to have disappointed not only Sirio, but his wife, Egidiana, and their sons as well who work so damn hard to provide an agreeable and welcoming venue for—as you have pointed out—all comers.

They really are wonderful people, Pete. And although I too had my own "issues" with the current chef, I don't believe the Maccioni family deserved the savage pummeling you gave them . . . or the humiliation of losing two stars by your hand.

FYI: I stopped in for a quick drink just last night and to see if I could detect any "damage" to the place. Eighty-year-old Maestro Sirio was as always beautifully attired and sitting by the coatroom signing copies of the new Le Cirque cookbook and missing nothing in a low-cut dress or with shapely legs coming through the door. He was also dictating to his new amanuensis—a spectacular blond woman (who, I'm told, is an authentic baroness).

A vivid and immensely popular New York character named Gianni Russo, one of the stars of *The Godfather*, was swanning about the place fielding compliments on his sold-out turn the night before in Le Cirque's Wine Bar lounge, which was packed with not a few Park Avenue dames with blueing in their hair and also some very "interesting" and colorful Las Vegas, bada-bing types (and it's probably better if I don't tell you any more about their background or lineage).

Russo does his crooner act featuring Cole Porter, Rodgers and Hart, and Johnny Mercer songs once every month with four marvelous musicians in black tie, and all of them of a certain age.

And, as occurs most every night, with it all, everybody was having fun in a perfectly luxe setting. So, in addition to the greatness and goodness of Sirio, that, I think is really what you missed in your review. Sure, there may be better, more exquisite, pristine offerings of food to be had abroad in the land. But in most other venues of the type, nobody is having any damn fun at their serious tables.

And, to be sure, there are some tired old loreleis around still hanging on to faded reputations. Sadly, many now resemble sidemen in orchestras long dispersed. But Le Cirque is still a vibrant, exciting, and altogether unique venue. Is it then the "charm" of Le Cirque you missed? Or perhaps the "charisma" of the place?

Anyway, The Great Sirio remains a beloved—and universally respected—icon of the profession you usually cover with such grace and brilliance. And Le Cirque itself remains *sui generis*.

I'm only sorry a bright guy and gifted writer like you didn't pick up on its music.

But one day, like Ruth Reichl, maybe you will.

We all hope so . . .

Yours,

William O'Shaughnessy

Letter to Pete Wells Regarding the New Four Seasons

December 5, 2018

Dear Pete:

As you know, I'm a huge fan of Pete Wells, who writes so brilliantly in my beloved *Times*, which has been so good to me and mine.

Here is my "review" of your Four Seasons review. . . .

You bestowed some really nice—and entirely justified and accurate—accolades on the food, the service, the ambiance, the desserts, the bar, the lineage, the bathrooms, the wine collection—and even the damn cotton candy towers which my grandchildren love.

But you missed the point entirely about Julian Niccolini.

Most people I know go to the Four Seasons precisely because of Julian, a delightful dining room maestro who entertains and performs while we do our commerce and courting at his agreeable tables.

As you well know, there are any number of serious, humorless "heavy-heavy, what hangs over" dining rooms abroad in the city where the one thing not on offer is a sense of just plain FUN!

The late Tom Margittai, one of Julian's predecessors at the Four Seasons, who was recently recalled by Sam Roberts in a lovely and graceful piece last week, once told me: "People think I'm in the food or hospitality profession. But I'm not. I'm in the real estate business. I rent you—for two hours—beautiful space and graceful architecture as a setting for you to do your commerce or courting."

Julian and his cool, calm, and serene partner Alex add personality, color, and contrast to the classic ambience provided by the architecture. (The Four Seasons is still the one venue in New York where the folks at the next table can't hear what the hell you're saying . . . or whispering).

So apparently some of your friends don't hear Julian's unique music.

But a hell of a lot of mine do.

We see him as quite an altogether dazzling dining room impresario and as a brilliant purveyor of generous hospitality . . . and lots of FUN.

Yours,

William O'Shaughnessy

P.S. Given your gracious and enthusiastic comments in the second half of today's review, sans the irrelevance about Julian, the place clearly deserves a second or even a third star.

—W.O.

Admiring John Sterling: Letter to Scott Herman

I've always liked John Sterling, the voice of the New York Yankees,
who often finds himself under siege from New York sports writers
(who I've often suspected are more than a little bit jealous that
John Sterling enjoys his fabled podium). This one I wrote directly
to one of his bosses at CBS Radio. May 23, 2011.

———————————

Dear Scott,

I'm hoping you won't mind if I prevail on our friendship of so many years to tell you only of my great admiration for John Sterling.

I must confess this note is prompted by those recent columns of Phil Mushnick, who is a *very* nice guy personally (he even, in a weak moment, attended my last book party). But it seems all too obvious that John Sterling's genius has eluded The Great Mushnick. However, Sterling's charms and greatness are not at all lost to me. Or to his legion of fans who are crazy about the Yankees announcer.

Actually, I discovered Sterling kind of late in life. I loved Mel Allen, who used to drive down from Greenwich and hang around our radio station in his last years. I also loved Jimmy Cannon (without whom there would not have been a Pete Hamill or Breslin, let alone an O'Shaughnessy, a hack writer to be sure—my four books are blazing testimony to my own lack of grace and articulation in print and on the air!). But I'm afraid my interest in baseball and the Yankees waned over the years. (I know it's heresy to say this . . . but I never got excited about the whole Mattingly–Munson era of sainted memory. Until one day I listened to Sterling, who literally brought me back to baseball and to my beloved Yankees.)

Sterling made the game exciting once again with his vivid, colorful descriptions. He raised the players up and put them back on their unique (I almost used the word "mythic") pedestal where they belong.

What I'm trying to say—so inartfully and awkwardly—is that Sterling elevates and ennobles your/our Yankees . . . even during their rare, occasional flashes of ordinariness.

The Yankees are *sui generis*. So too is John Sterling. And, God help me, I'm also greatly taken by Suzyn Waldman, who has conquered my ridiculous prejudice against women sports jocks . . . which goes all the way back to the early Martin Stone days at the original WVIP when he would inveigh against "girls" sports announcers. I like Waldman too. And I like the dynamic between them.

I'm delivering all this directly to your door, Scott, because Mushnick says it's WCBS's call. I thus hope you'll keep Sterling as the voice of the Yankees for many years to come. And I hope too that you, Steve Swenson, and Dan Mason will forgive me for meddling in your affairs. (I sure wouldn't want anyone to tell me how the hell to run WVOX or WVIP.)

And finally, I can't close a letter to Scott Herman without telling you again how grateful we all are for your consistent and relentlessly generous support of the Broadcasters Foundation of America.

We wish there were a few thousand more like Scott Herman. But alas . . . like John Sterling . . . I'm afraid he's altogether unique.

Yours,
William O'Shaughnessy

"A Westchester Legend":
Letter from Samuel G. Fredman

I treasure this note from a Westchester legend,
Mr. Justice Samuel George Fredman. March 28, 2014.

My Dear Wonderful Bill:

As if it wasn't going to be difficult enough to try to prepare an adequate thank you letter to cover the multitude of kindnesses you bestowed upon me prior to and during the course of my birthday celebration, where you must know you absolutely excelled in your role as emcee, you have now compounded the nature of the task by adding to it the dissemination of the same birthday remarks to what must be your closest 1,000 admirers. It seems over the past few days that everyone who is anyone in Westchester County has been familiarized with the details of the Party (I can and do capitalize it), thus getting me into a lot of trouble with a lot of people who didn't make the A list; it now takes on the aspects of being comparable to having been in the audience which heard the Gettysburg Address or Marilyn Monroe's Madison Square Garden paean to JFK.

Being referred to as a "Westchester Legend" to the extent of being put on a pedestal with folks such as Nelson Rockefeller and including Malcolm Wilson and Ed Michaelian and Bill Luddy, amongst those who you also hold in such high esteem, is a tonic, a privilege, a compliment of the highest order, and may even be a test of your sanity.

I like being called a great man. I have never strived to be great—I want to be regarded as decent, honorable, involved, caring, imbued in the faith of our fathers with a love for this great country which gave me and my ancestors a chance to live challenged only by what you do, not who you are, in a way that makes it appear that my children, and perhaps their children, etc., etc. will have that same opportunity.

I have been referred to during the course of these last few weeks as a judge, a teacher, and, most of all, as a friend. That's how I feel about you!

So with thanks to you and all the Whitney Broadcasting family, of course inclusive of your boys, your superb Cindy and Don, as well as others, let me not gild the lily any further.

You have my thanks and appreciation. Your big heart and broad smile and winning ways engulf me, and I am more than just a happy camper.

Most sincerely yours,
Samuel G. Fredman

Re: William B. Williams and Rick Buckley: Letter from Dick Robinson

Dick Robinson is a broadcasting legend who founded the famous Connecticut School of Broadcasting and now owns a radio station in the Palm Beach area, where he plays selections from the Great American Songbook. He's also a well-known philanthropist on the Gold Coast. Here is one of his effusive and much too generous letters. August 5, 2011.

———————————

Dear Bill,

Recently, I asked Joanie to write you a note about your wonderful testimonial to William B. Williams and his induction into the New York State Broadcasters Hall of Fame. It was so beautifully and thoughtfully written as you provided an inside peek into your intro and tag-along life with the not-so-make-believe William B. Williams. I was so wrapped up in reading your piece that I found myself traveling back to the yesteryears when our lives were intertwined in the medium of radio that we loved, lived, devoured, and breathed. Your reference to David Hinckley was right on. His portraiture of William B. was glowing. He writes so keenly and purposefully. I loved reading both upfront and personal takes on the Make Believe Ballroom man!

But alas, before Joanie set words to processor, an unimaginable fall of a radio behemoth occurred, and that took my breath away. Hearing about Rick's death hit me so hard because that thought is one that never crossed my mind. How could Richard D. Buckley be dead? It is still unfathomable to me. (I flash back to 1972 when Rick's dad passed away. I had worked with Richard Dimes Buckley since 1960, and he was one of my mentors.)

Once more, you glowingly and personally wrote a passage on the passing of a great one. You so easily told the story of a man who truly loved radio for what it was and who kept it that way. He made his dad proud. You, William O'Shaughnessy, are a radio raconteur with no match.

My memory lane of Rick is dotted with all kinds of remembrances: fond, silly, daring, funny, serious. We did it all. The old days when Rick would travel and party with us in Lake Tahoe, Vegas, NYC, California, and, of course, home base at WDRC were always special, and I am so glad I knew him and was able to keep our communication lines flowing. If only his fate was make believe.

Take care of yourself and those who mean the most to you. There are no make-goods.

Sincerely,

Dick Robinson

Letter to William O'Shaughnessy from Ralph Graves

*Ralph Graves, a dear man, was the last editor of Life magazine
and an elder of the influential Dutch Treat Luncheon Club
in New York City.*

———————————

Dear Bill,

I am honored beyond words to be included in your list of Great Ones. However, as a writer you will understand that I, as a writer, am never quite beyond words. So this will be a long but, I hope, interesting letter.

First of all, my thanks for the very signal honor of what you rightly call your imprimatur. I believe there are 572 of us—difficult to count them with all the ellipses, but I don't think I'm off by more than a digit or two. Of course there are many I don't know at all, and of course there are many I know only by reputation, whom I envy you the privilege of knowing personally.

There are forty-one that I do know personally, including me and Cindy (your Cindy, not Cindy Adams). A few comments on a few of them may entertain you.

I met Louis Armstrong only once, fifty years ago, in a Chicago cabaret where he was touring with a small group and the plump, jolly singer Velma Middleton, built like Ella Fitzgerald but with a much funnier personality. I still remember their duet "Get your blueberry bucket, baby, and come out to the woods. We may not find any berries, but we'll come back feeling good." While I was *Life* editor, I ran a wonderful article about Armstrong, with a gatefold cover shot by Philippe Halsman.

I never met DiMaggio, but my first wife and baby son did. The son was just able to walk when DiMaggio, striding along Fifth Avenue, stumbled over him and knocked him down. Joe D. said nothing but picked him up, set him on his feet and walked on.

I edited Winston Churchill's four-volume *History of the English Speaking Peoples* for *Life*, many, many installments. Churchill, quite elderly at the time, said, "Lovely, lovely."

I had the pleasure of awarding the Dutch Treat Gold Medal for lifetime achievement in the arts to Kitty Carlisle, Liz Smith, and David McCullough. As you know, Mario and Liz are neck-and-neck for the all-time lunch attendance record.

Before JFK became president, *Life* bought the pre-publication rights to excerpt his *Profiles in Courage*. For some complicated scheduling reason, we had to run some other articles and ran out of pre-publication time. As an assistant articles editor I was given the chore of calling up Senator Kennedy to tell him we were not going to run his article, though of course he could keep the fee. I have never, never heard a colder, angrier voice.

I am so glad that you included Giuliani and Lindsay and Koch.

I never got to meet Sinatra, but during *Life*'s last year I ran several of his ringside photographs of the first Ali–Frazier fight (the greatest sports event I have ever attended in person). On the cover I billed "Cover Photograph by Frank Sinatra," which infuriated all the staff photographers who had never received such a billing. I would do it again because I thought it was so different and would probably sell magazines.

Punch Sulzberger was a hell of a lot better publisher than his son.

Lowell Thomas was a Dutch Treat president, and as you may or may not have read in one of the yearbooks, he was once chastised for talking too long at the president's podium before introducing the speaker. He apologized and said, "At my age, everything I say reminds me of something else."

If I were doing my own list, the top figures would be Maria Callas, Charles Lindbergh, and the 1930s novelist Michael Arlen, the wittiest conversationalist I ever met. Details on request.

Meantime, thanks again for the bouquet, and congratulations to my co-celebrant Cindy Gallagher.

I hope to see you at the Dutch Treat when we come back in April. Meantime, best regards as always.

Ralph

PART X
THE GREAT ISSUES

Abortion and the Death Penalty:

Life in Every Instance

Timothy Cardinal Dolan: Reclaim the Truth of the Human Person

Remarks at the John Cardinal O'Connor Lecture at Georgetown University, January 2019.

———————

It is an honor and a joy to be with you this morning.

Especially do I savor this chance to salute a towering prophet in our beloved nation's pursuit of the civil rights of the baby in the womb, John Cardinal O'Connor, after whom this lecture is entitled.

Just last Monday we celebrated his ninety-ninth birthday, but he remains ever-young and timeless, especially for his daring pro-life witness.

On the sidewalks of New York I encounter women and men whose eyes moisten and whose throats lump as they recall stories for me, his unworthy successor. Hundreds of cops will show me his picture enshrined on the inside of their uniform hats; waiters or bartenders will recall a word of spiritual encouragement he gave them; only recently did I have breakfast with a philanthropist who recalled an invitation to breakfast from His Eminence. At the time, the philanthropist tells me, he was living an immoral, scandalous life. As breakfast began he brashly told the cardinal, "I know you only invited me to ask for money. How much do you want?" Cardinal O'Connor looked him in the eye and calmly replied, "Keep your money. I want your soul!" To this day this prominent benefactor could not relate the story without choking up, for that Christ-like rejoinder from John Joseph O'Connor was the spark to his conversion.

Then there was the twenty-two-year-old senior at Fordham—the premier Jesuit university in America (Father McShane, its president, told me would give my niece a scholarship if I said that here at

Georgetown) who introduced himself as "John Joseph," telling me his mom was considering aborting him until she heard the cardinal speak tenderly and compellingly about the sanctity of pre-born life. Thus did he bear the cardinal's name.

> If all the marches, all the prayers, all the vigils, the lectures, articles, debates, and encyclicals saved but one tiny, fragile life, would not the Lord of Life say to us, "Well done, good and faithful servant. For you not only fed me and clothed me, encouraged and consoled, visited me in prison and welcomed me a stranger. You saved my life."

So he wrote only months before brain cancer took him nineteen years ago.

It is humbling to be with you, genuine confessors of the faith, courageous apostles who year-after-year in the capital of the nation built to serve a republic founded on certain inalienable rights, with life put first, a nation so big in power, might, influence, prestige, and cash . . . stand-up for a tiny, fragile, helpless, innocent infant in the intended sanctuary of the mother's womb.

Just two years ago, I had the privilege of addressing the Rose Dinner, and I commented how the world paused to recall that, at the center of history, at the very moment B.C. became A.D., stands a pregnant woman, that brave woman of Nazareth, who exclaimed to her cousin, Elizabeth, both of them with what we would term a "problem pregnancy," "My soul proclaims the greatness of the Lord . . . for He has looked with favor on his lowly servant. . . . He has cast down the mighty from their thrones, and has lifted up the lowly."

The "mighty" may mock, as they do from academia, Hollywood, media, Congress, and the courtroom, but we today acclaim "the power of one. . . ."

"Even the smallest can change the course of history," to quote Tolkien, as we salute "the power of one" . . . one baby in the womb of His mother, born at Bethlehem . . . and the civil rights of the tiniest today, the baby in the womb, to "life, liberty, and the pursuit of happiness."

I look out in admiration this evening at a hall of "ones" who have become one, inspired by one woman who believed the one true God lifted her up to give a human nature to one who would be called the Son of God. The "power of one."

When we more seasoned adults have the cherished chance to speak to those younger, as I do this morning, we're usually expected to urge them not to repeat our past mistakes. One such that I made in college was to ignore philosophy, to concentrate not on wisdom and normative ideas but on more "practical" courses. I regret I did not take philosophy more seriously. Oh, I've since tried to compensate by reading the classics of philosophy, but I still regret that eclipse of philosophy in my own academic formation.

To be sure, I wish I were better versed in the wisdom of Aristotle, Plato, Augustine, Bonaventure, and Thomas Aquinas; but I also wish I had better comprehended the empiricism of Comte, the utilitarianism of Bentham, and the pragmatism of Mill and James.

Because ideas have consequences. Those philosophers we thought irrelevant, both those who gave us the moral, political, economic, and spiritual coherence we call "civilization" . . . and those who were dismantling it . . . were expounding ideas that would shape what we today think of the true nature of a human person.

We think of a Charles Darwin, whose theory of evolution was sadly reduced to a social strategy of "survival of the fittest," leading to a victory of the most lethal, where the weakest were left behind in a grand march of progress; of Friedrich Nietzsche's "death of God," with its emphasis on regeneration through destruction, and a celebration of the will to power.

Of Ludwig Feuerbach's subjectivism, that God is a mere projection of ourselves, that we individually define the good, with no objective truth to protect others.

Of Karl Marx's materialism, that the spiritual is only an illusion, that economics is the new code to understanding history and the human person, that ethics and belief needed to be steamrolled by the will of the proletariat.

Of a utilitarianism of Jeremy Bentham and John Stuart Mill, that reduces the valuable to the useful, of a pragmatism that claims the worthwhile is only what works for us.

Behold what the British historian Owen Chadwick calls the "secularization of the Western mind, with the biblical understanding of the human person, and of good and evil, on the run." Behold the "dictatorship of relativism" Pope Benedict grieved; behold a Senate hearing that could question the suitability of an acclaimed jurist for a higher appointment because "dogma rings loudly in her," or another candidate feared as an extremist because he belongs to the Knights of Columbus! Or a third-term governor who insists that those questioning abortion on demand, paid for by all, up to the moment of birth, are retrogrades holding back progressivism; behold the "throwaway culture" regretted by Pope Francis.

George Weigel posits that Pope St. John Paul believed that every problem we today face comes from a faulty understanding of the human person, what he called a "flawed anthropology." Is it any wonder St. John Paul, himself a philosopher, would commence the project to reclaim the truth of the dignity of the human person and the sacredness of human life, as revealed by God, evident in our nature, discoverable by enlightened reason, a project advanced by his successors, Benedict XVI and Francis, a project of which we are a part, as this flawed understanding of the human person reached a tragic but logical outcome in *Roe v. Wade*.

For if you believe that what is true is only what can be verified in a laboratory; that what is good is only what is useful, functional, and productive; that what is beautiful is only what I want, what I need, what I find convenient, what I consider helpful to reach my goals; that the divine is no longer "Thee" but "me," well, it is no surprise that an innocent baby in the womb could be deemed useless and inconvenient, that Grandma dying slowly yet naturally would be thought a burden and annoyance, that a refugee would be caricatured as a rapist and a terrorist.

To reclaim the truth of the human person, with its liberating and uplifting logical corollary of human dignity and the sacredness of all life, let me hold up the example of a man who displayed the "power of one," Detective Steven McDonald, whom all of New York mourned as we buried him from St. Patrick's Cathedral just two years ago.

In September 1986, Steven, a handsome, strapping twenty-nine year-old third-generation New York cop, was shot three times in the back by a fifteen-year-old boy who had stolen a bike in Central Park.

When finally removed from ICU after three months, he was paralyzed from the neck down, never again able to breathe, eat, drink, or move on his own. His first public words, proclaimed by his wife, Patty, since Steven could only whisper, were addressed to his assailant, "I forgive you!"

Three bullets did not kill his body; those three words showed that neither would [they] kill his soul. When his assailant went before the parole board, guess who testified on his behalf? When the shooter admitted he had no place to stay if he were granted parole, it was Stephen and his wife, Patty, who spoke up, "He can live with us."

In the eyes of a purely pragmatic, utilitarian, empirical, economically driven world, Steven McDonald was useless, unproductive, inconvenient, a burden to himself, his family, to society.

To a world tempted to believe religion an opiate, and faith a superstition, Steven showed a hope and love which he insisted only came from a soul in daily union with Jesus, nurtured by prayer, the Eucharist, confession, devotion to the Mother of Jesus, and the fortification of his Catholic faith.

Behold the "power of one." Behold the consequences of ideas translated into beliefs, grounded in faith; behold a life many today would consider a waste, an inconvenience, a burden, transformed into an icon of reconciliation and love.

As Detective McDonald often remarked, "The value of life depends not on what you have or what you can do, but on who you are: a child of God, made in His image, destined for eternity, put here for a purpose, an identity made the stronger the more it is tested."

Cardinal O'Connor wrote, "Each one of us is an unrepeatable act of God, each one brought into being for a specific purpose, a purpose that will not be carried out by anybody else. It is this person's mission. This makes every human being, at every inch of life's journey, sacred and inviolable."

[621]

Am I being too theological, too spiritual, too "Catholic"? Martin Luther King—whose birthday the nation will observe Monday—would tell me, "No, Timothy, you are not."

Cardinal O'Connor again: "We have to keep an appreciation of being, of the fact that we are. All being is made in the image and likeness of God. Today there seems a contempt for being, a preference for having and doing. The genuine reason we have this pro-life movement is because we have an awesome sense of the sacredness of being, which cannot be trumped by the exigencies of having and doing."

His pro-life credentials, like those of the Reverend King, did not exclude a burning solicitude for the sick, the poor, the underpaid laborer, the immigrant, the dying, the person on death row, the minorities, or the oppressed.

But he would insist that, if we get it wrong in ignoring the civil rights of the pre-born, we'll sure have a tough time promoting the others, because we'd be hypocrites.

Pope Francis would agree. In his letter to the Pontifical Academy for Life just two weeks ago, the Holy Father describes what he calls "the paradox of 'progress.'"

How can those who consider themselves "progressive," or "humanists," advance a cause that would trample the right to life of the baby in the womb? "How can an act that suppresses an innocent and helpless life as it blossoms in the womb be thought therapeutic, civil, or simply humane?" This is hardly progress. A genuine progressivism always advocates for the weakest, the most vulnerable, those with no one to defend them. A sincere progressive, in our American tradition, would accompany and support a pregnant woman and advocate for the baby.

Pope Francis has often expressed anxiety that, the older we get, the more fatigued we become in what St. Paul calls "fighting the good fight." Weariness sets in. . . .

Such can be the case for those of us who have been fighting for the human rights of the pre-born baby since January 22, 1973. The antidote Pope Francis prescribes is You!

As he said to the youth in Rio de Janeiro, "Do us a favor; do your duty! Keep the dream alive."

The journalist David Brooks holds that a humane, prosperous, vibrant culture has to have both memory and dreams.

John Cardinal O'Connor had a dream; I have one; so do you. Mine might fade a bit at times. Not this morning. Not as I look out at you.

For as the prophet Habakkuk encourages, "For the dream awaits its appointed time. It hastens to the end—it will not let us down if it seems slow, Await. It will surely come. I will not disappoint."

The Greatest Issue, Abortion:
A WVOX Commentary

Just as the evil we call abortion is not new, neither is the outcry against it. Far from it. Back in 190 A.D., in the ancient city of Carthage, the writer and scholar Quintus Septimus Tertullian said, "To prevent birth is only a quicker way of committing murder. He is a man who is to be a man. The fruit is always there in the seed."

Tertullian was not alone in expressing his horror. Ishmael Ben Elisha, a rabbi, cried out in the second century against abortion and the slaughter of children yet unborn: "It is a capital crime to destroy an embryo in the womb."

And once in the United States of America, Terence Cooke, a cardinal archbishop, warned, "Once innocent life at any stage is placed at the mercy of others, a vicious principle has been legalized. Thereafter, it may be decided that life is to be denied the defective, the aged, the incorrigible, and granted only to the strong, the beautiful and the intelligent."

Thus, centuries apart, a Carthaginian, a rabbi, and an American cardinal were not deceived.

He is a man who is to be a man.

Long after our bond issues are passed or rejected and long after our bridges and tunnels are built or rejected, our nation may be judged on its embrace of this horror we call abortion.

—*W.O.*

The Death Penalty

*The good Pope Francis also reminds us: There's no humane
way of killing another person.*

———————

Pope Francis made a clear denunciation of the death penalty and even
of sentences to life imprisonment: "Today the death penalty is inadmissible, no matter how serious the crime of the condemned."

The Holy Father cited scripture and the Church's teaching regarding
human dignity. "Human life is sacred because from its beginning, from
the *first* instant of conception, it is fruit of the creative action of God,
and from that moment, man, the only creature God loves for itself, is
the object of personal love on the part of God."

States kill in various ways, both by action and by omission: "by
action when they apply the death penalty, when they take their peoples
to war or when they carry out extra-judicial or summary executions.
They can also kill by omission, when they do not guarantee to their
peoples access to the essential means for life."

"Life, especially human life, belongs to God alone" [the pope con-
tinued]. "Not even the murderer loses his personal dignity and
God himself makes himself its guarantor. As Saint Ambrose
teaches, God did not want to punish Cain for the murder, as He
wants the repentance of the sinner, not his death.

When the death penalty is applied, persons are killed not for
present aggression, but for harm caused in the past. It is applied to
persons whose capacity to harm is not present but has already been
neutralized, and who find themselves deprived of their freedom.

Today the death penalty is inadmissible, no matter how serious the crime of the condemned. It is an offense against the
inviolability of life and the dignity of the human person that
contradicts God's plan for man and society.

The Death Penalty

Governor Mario Cuomo was passionately opposed to the death penalty all the days of his life. Many political watchers believe he paid a price for his opposition. This piece, from October 2, 2011, explains his deeply held view.

I have studied the death penalty for more than half my lifetime. I have debated it hundreds of times. I have heard all the arguments, analyzed all the evidence I could find, measured public opinion when it was opposed to the practice, when it was indifferent, and when it was passionately in favor. Always I have concluded the death penalty is wrong because it lowers us all; it is a surrender to the worst that is in us; it uses a power—the official power to kill by execution—that has never elevated a society, never brought back a life, never inspired anything but hate.

And it has killed many innocent people.

This is a serious moral problem for every U.S. governor who presides over executions—whether in Georgia, Texas, or even, theoretically, New York. All states should do as the bold few have done and officially outlaw this form of punishment.

For twelve years as governor, I prevented the death penalty from becoming law in New York by my vetoes. But for all that time, there was a disconcertingly strong preference for the death penalty in the general public.

New York returned to the death penalty shortly after I was defeated by a Republican candidate; the state's highest court has effectively prevented the law from being applied—but New York continues to have the law on its books with no signs of a movement to remove it.

That law is a stain on our conscience. The forty-six executions in the United States in 2008 were, I believe, an abomination.

People have a right to demand a civilized level of law and peace. They have a right to expect it, and when at times it appears to them that a murder has been particularly egregious, it is not surprising that the public anger is great and demands some psychic satisfaction.

I understand that. I have felt the anger myself, more than once. Like too many other citizens, I know what it is to be violated and even to have one's closest family violated through despicable criminal behavior. Even today, I tremble at the thought of how I might react to a killer who took the life of someone in my own family. I know that I might not be able to suppress my anger or put down a desire for revenge, but I also know this society should strive for something better than what it feels at its weakest moments.

There is absolutely no good reason to believe that using death as a punishment today is any better an answer now than it was in the past—when New York state had it, used it, regretted it, and discarded it.

Experts throughout the nation have come out strongly against the death penalty after hundreds of years of lawyers' cumulative experiences and studies revealed that the death penalty is ineffective as a deterrent.

Some of history's most notorious murders occurred in the face of existing death penalty statutes.

Psychiatrists will tell you there is reason to believe that some madmen—for example, Ted Bundy—may even be tempted to murder because of a perverse desire to challenge the ultimate penalty.

It is also unfairly applied.

Notwithstanding the executions of mass killers like Timothy McVeigh, capital punishment appears to threaten white drug dealers, white rapists, and white killers less frequently than those of other races. Of the last eighteen people in New York state to be executed (ending in 1963), thirteen were black and one was Hispanic. That racial makeup seems an extraordinary improbability for a system operating with any kind of objectivity and consistency.

Because death penalty proponents have no other way to defend this policy, they cling unabashedly to the blunt simplicity of the ancient impulse that has always spurred the call for death: the desire for revenge. That was the bottom line of many debates on the floor of the state Senate and Assembly, to which I listened with great care during my tenure as governor. It came down to "an eye for an eye, a tooth for a tooth."

If we adopted this maxim, where would it end? "You kill my son; I kill yours." "You rape my daughter; I rape yours." "You mutilate my body; I mutilate yours." And we would pursue this course, despite the lack of any reason to believe it will protect us even if it is clear that occasionally the victim of our official barbarism will be innocent.

It is believed that at least twenty-three people were wrongfully executed in the United States during the twentieth century. Twenty-three innocent people killed by the official workings of the state, but it is not called murder.

According to the Innocence Project, 17 people have been proven innocent—exonerated by DNA testing—after serving time on death row. These people were convicted in 11 different states. They served a combined 209 years in prison. And government was prepared to end their lives.

Tragically, New York holds the record for the greatest number of innocents put to death over the years. According to some, New York leads all states with at least six (perhaps more) wrongful executions since 1905.

Yet proponents of the death penalty continue to assume that the criminal justice system will not make a mistake, or they simply don't care. As was shown by the recent Troy Davis execution in Georgia, where shaky witness testimony and a lack of physical evidence were considered insufficient to create "reasonable doubt," too many people seem unconcerned about the overly ambitious prosecutor, the sloppy detective, the incompetent defense counsel, the witness with an axe to grind, the judge who keeps courthouse conviction box scores.

But these imperfections—as well as the horrible and irreversible injustice they can produce—are inevitable. In this country, a defendant is convicted on proof beyond a reasonable doubt—not proof that can be known with absolute certainty. There's no such thing as absolute certainty in our law.

We need to continue to do the things that will control crime by making the apprehension and punishment of criminals more effective and more precise. We need adequate police and prisons and alternatives to incarceration. We should also have a tough, effective punishment for deliberate murder. There is a punishment that is much better than the death penalty: one that juries will not be reluctant to impose; one that is so menacing to a potential killer that it could actually deter; one that does not require us to be infallible so as to avoid taking an innocent life; and one that does not require us to stoop to the level of the killers.

There is a penalty that is—for those who insist on measuring this question in terms of financial cost—millions of dollars less expensive than the death penalty: true life imprisonment, with no possibility of parole under any circumstances.

True life imprisonment is a more effective deterrent than capital punishment. To most inmates, the thought of living a whole lifetime behind bars, only to die in a cell, is worse than the quick, final termination of the electric chair or lethal injection.

I've heard this sentiment personally at least three times in my life. The second time, it came from a man on the way to his execution in Oklahoma. He was serving a life sentence for murder in New York at the same time that Oklahoma was eager to take him from New York so they could execute him for a murder he had committed in Oklahoma. I refused to release him so that he could be executed in Oklahoma, but then the governor who replaced me in 1995 was able to get New York to adopt the death penalty—and to prove New York really approved of death as a punishment, he released the inmate from prison and sent him to Oklahoma, where he was promptly executed.

On the night before he died, he left a note that was published in the *New York Post* that said, "Tell Governor Cuomo I would rather be executed than to serve life behind bars."

Because the death penalty was so popular during the time I served as governor, I was often asked why I spoke out so forcefully against it although the voters very much favored it. I tried to explain that I pushed this issue into the center of public dialogue because I believed the stakes went far beyond the death penalty itself. Capital punishment raises important questions about how, as a society, we view human beings. I believed as governor, and I still believe, that the practice of and support for capital punishment is corrosive; that it is bad for a democratic citizenry and that it had to be objected to and so I did then, and I do now and will continue to for as long as it and I exist, because I believe we should be better than what we are in our weakest moments.

—*Mario M. Cuomo*

Las Vegas Shooting: Another "Thoughts and Prayers" Day

A WVOX commentary, October 2, 2017.

"Thoughts and prayers." We tote out the phrase and cling to it with a fierceness as we apply it to the victims after every tragedy, every shooting, every bombing. It has become banal, hoary, and hackneyed from overuse.

And so here we are again on a Monday, October 2, 2017, with another "thoughts and prayers" day that comes at us from a glitzy, hedonist town out in the Nevada desert called Las Vegas, the Baghdad of North America.

It is a place where dentists, deputy sheriffs, plumbers, electrical contractors, doctors, judges, matrimonial lawyers, John Deere dealers, politicians, even broadcasters, and—ahem—gun manufacturers go each year to get away from their wives. They call this annual rite a "convention," where they meet in high council for a few hours each day before succumbing to all the earthly pleasures of this remarkable city that grew up around a big, broad, sprawling boulevard they call "The Strip."

Slot machines line the concourse leading to and from jet planes parked on the tarmac. And a van advertising a shooting gallery for sawed-off, automatic, repeating guns is parked even now outside the vast Las Vegas Convention Center to greet visitors to this lovely city, which once sent Harry Reid to the Senate of the United States.

This time it was several of those automatic weapons that dispatched death and destruction from the thirty-second-floor windows of the Mandalay Bay Hotel, spewing it among 22,000 helpless people there assembled for a concert. The said individual behind the weapons with a scrambled-egg mind didn't let up on the trigger as he murdered 59

[631]

and wounded almost 550 with one of his beautiful repeating guns that pumped murder into the desert night air.

And on our televisions once again there is praise for the first responders, the police, the doctors and nurses, and calls for an end to all this by banning instruments designed for killing.

They will blame this carnage on the make-believe violence that plays nightly across television screens and in movie theaters. They will also target the politicians and especially President Donald John Trump who is so hated by the Democrats and the Deep State establishment for trying to do the right thing by the nation he inherited from a well-intended but ineffective college law professor and Chicago community organizer.

This time it was a shooter. But it could have been a bomber or a glassy-eyed, deranged driver behind the wheel of a huge careening truck mowing down innocents out for an evening stroll. Banning guns and weapons won't stop it. The guns are already out there, under mattresses in house trailers and wrapped in towels in five-floor walk-ups in the Bronx, Harlem, and Chicago. And, implausibly, in luxury thirty-second-floor hotel suites in Las Vegas. There will be rioting in the streets if we try to take them and damn near a civil war. These hidden guns are everywhere and await only a prompt and a caress from one of life's losers boiling with rage.

And those who want guns only in the hands of law-enforcement officers forget it was a former NYPD cop who left his house trailer in New Jersey to murder federal Judge Richard Daronco as he tended a rosebush in his back yard on Monterey Avenue in Pelham here in Westchester just a few years ago. Judge Daronco's name is on our courthouse in White Plains as a reminder.

Call for gun control all you will. But the halls of Congress have no wisdom on the awful dilemma that resides so close to our home as well as in foreign capitals abroad.

And how about the vengeance known as capital punishment, the death penalty, which has never saved one life or prevented one murder? As Hugh Leo Carey and Mario Matthew Cuomo warned us, it diminishes us as a people and makes the state no better than the perpetrator, the killer.

60 Minutes had a stunning piece Sunday night about the cosmos and the intergalactic world trillions of miles out in space, which made us feel small and insignificant, if not in awe of the Creator's magnificent handiwork, all this startling and breathtaking information coming to us courtesy of the revived Hubble Telescope.

But on this blood-drenched Monday you can just forget about those planets and stars that exist millions—nay trillions—of miles out in the solar system. For here in this very country, the great United States of America, we are shooting the *Bejesus* out of each other.

I wish we had a Mario Cuomo to explain this killing, which comes so easily and so often to us, and the rage behind it. The holy men from all walks and persuasions will try in the next several days. The Jesuits will advocate for reason, while the Franciscans will come at you with love. And the rabbis will recommend that we rebuild the universe and remind us we are all brothers and sisters. They will use words from the ancient Hebrew like *tzedekah* and *tikkun olam*.

But I'm not sure "thoughts and prayers" works on this stuff. It may help with the fury and force of a hurricane or a *tsunami*. But not in the roiling, scrambled-egg mind of a madman bursting with loneliness, fury, and hatred.

For once I have no answer. . . .

– *W.O.*

The New Killing Season

Commentary by William O'Shaughnessy, October 2, 2012.

First they took the rabbits and squirrels. That was easy. Then they went after the deer with rifle shot and bow and arrow, which was just plain fun. And they even took their sons into the quiet, dense, dark forest to teach them how to stalk and kill using just the right amount of "Kentucky windage" on muzzle and scope.

Next they set about ravaging woodland and forest. There was much money to be made in the timber from out-of-state loggers who brutally cut and culled the tall trees which grew up from the rich soil underfoot through hundreds of bleak, lonely winters across upstate New York.

And now in 2012 yet another predator beckons and threatens once more to violate the Earth as the desperate stewards of the burdened land succumb and yield to the blandishments and enticements of surrogates of these new speculators who sing the siren song of the natural-gas industry in the name of hydraulic fracturing.

Their allurements are considerable and irresistible to landowners and farmers who, when dining in the entire southern tier, really need make only two decisions at their favorite local restaurant. Just two, as the bored waitress inquires: "Do you want 'veal parm' . . . or 'chicken parm'?" And one more: "'Sprinkled blue' . . . or 'plain'?" Salad, that is.

Then they ride the dusty backroads with their beer bellies stuffed into Ram pickup trucks outfitted with gun racks and powerful spotlights with which to stun deer before shooting them dumb and done as they forage for food in the sparse, mean winter landscape. Opening day of hunting season is a most sacred stop on the calendar of their lonely days and drab existence as the killing season begins.

In once-verdant fields where fleet, sleek quarter horses and stout, elegant Morgans grazed in the summer sun, ugly drilling contraptions now penetrate and violate the land and pump their deadly cocktail into the Earth almost a mile below. The horses, most of them, disappeared when it was realized that they were worth more at the local rendering station than competing for a ribbon at a horse show in Elmira.

But they are not stupid, these people who exist north of Poughkeepsie and west of Binghamton. And in their back-country wisdom they know they'd best grab on to the fragile lifeline dangled by the energy companies from Oklahoma and Texas to further pillage the weary and exhausted land by injecting vulgar and dangerous chemicals hundreds of feet down into the Earth. This latest obscenity carries a glib but ugly nickname: fracking. It is something akin to raping or pillaging the neighborhood.

It has already begun, these back-country folks know, just over the line in Pennsylvania, where towns like Sayre, Towanda, and Mansfield sit near the border astride the Marcellus Shale. The area is known, on the other side of the line, for purposes of tourism, as the Endless Mountains. They are anything but.

But our poor, hardscrabble New Yorkers can smell the beguiling scent of money just over that state line. It is altogether more powerful and alluring than the smell of sulfurous, toxic chemicals fouling the water supply and causing flames to leap out of kitchen faucets and toilets in those Endless Mountains where once the Pooles and Talada clans raised their inbred families in house trailers and ramshackle hovels. My grandfather was a Talada so I can tell of these things.

Andrew Mark Cuomo, our brilliant, dynamic, and stunningly effective new governor, has pledged to restore some prosperity—and hope—to this troubled area of our state.

The governor has always had an exquisite feel for the region, and if anybody can pull a Lazarus up there, Andrew can.

We just hope fracking isn't part and parcel of the state's effort to renew the sad, beleaguered land of my birth.

—W.O.

Comments from "The Deplorables"

Vox Populi

Early morning notes and jottings taken in a coffee shop up in the country (Connecticut) over a three-month period in the summer and early fall of 2017. There was actually very little criticism of President Donald Trump to be heard . . . except from occasional disgruntled folks who predictably called him "crazy, Hitler-like," etc. But these direct comments reflect the vast body of sentiment and approval that exists among ordinary citizens for the president. Everybody knows I'm a fan . . . but even I was surprised! Again, I ask the question: Is it possible The Deplorables know something we don't . . . ?

"The Dems pick on everything he does. . . . They just hate the guy. I think it's jealousy."

"Sometimes his mouth gets him in trouble. But I think he's of good heart and trying to do the right thing. He's trying, damn it!"

"Ya know, I think I understand what they mean about that 'Deep State' stuff. It's just another word for the Washington establishment. They're all against him and protecting their asses. They ain't foolin' anybody."

"He ought to think a little before he speaks—or tweets—but he's done more down there than any other president."

"The Congress shouldn't just be opposing him. They should try to make it easy for him to do what he's gotta do."

"I can't watch MSNBC anymore. Rush calls it 'PMSNBC.' Even Chris Matthews has signed on the Bash Trump Bandwagon. He used to be an O.K. guy. Now . . . forget it!"

"Every time I think the *New York Times* will run out of ways to attack and say bad things about Trump . . . they prove me wrong. I mean, I know the Times is important and a big fucking deal. But they're not being fair to this president at all."

"Every one of my friends is for the guy. Is it possible the people, the 'normal,' human people, know more about this than the elite, know-it-alls? I always say: Trust the people. Doesn't that make sense to you?"

"He's shaking things up . . . and it's about time. It had gone too far with Obama, although he was not a bad guy. Just not such a dynamic president."

"You got CNN, MSNBC, the mighty *New York Times* and, I guess, the *Washington Post*, saying shitty things about the president. They should ask every cop, every soldier, every plumber, every fireman, every electrician . . . the normal, regular people. They 'get it.' They like him. The big muckety-mucks are missing something."

"The guy is shaking up both the Republicans and the Democrats . . . and who can blame him? They both stink."

"I can't really explain it. I just like the president. What he said about North Korea is so true. We've been slipping them money and kisses behind the scenes for years."

"What they say about him is really disgusting. I mean, c'mon . . . gimme a break! Give him a break!"

"It's a tough job. You couldn't pay me to take the job. But I'll tell you what: They ought to just shut the fuck up . . . and let him do his job."

"I like the Mara family. But I'm very much with Trump on the NFL. The Dallas Cowboys guy got it right. These players are spoiled rotten!"

"He's reaching out to the Democrats. If you recall, Obama had no time for the Republicans. Proves that Trump is smart. You'll see . . ."

"There are too many yahoos in the Republican Party. Donald is right to chart his own course. Who needs this sorry bunch of Republicans!"

"Look at the markets, the economy. The 'Smart Money' knows. The Trumpster or somebody around him must be doin' somethin' right."

"If they are dumb enough to try to impeach or indict this guy . . . there will be rioting in the streets. Mark my words!"

"They're wasting my money—and yours—with this Russia crap. Who cares? He didn't beat Hillary because of Putin!"

"And I'll tell you somethin' else, Mr. O . . . the guy Mark Simone on WOR [oops, sometimes I listen to them] calls the Clintons a 'Criminal Enterprise' . . . a very big one . . . I mean international. Donald called them to task on that. Damn straight he did! And he's right on."

The 137 Real Reasons Why
Hillary Lost and Trump Won

———————

It wasn't the Russians. Here are the real reasons . . .

- Debbie Wasserman Schultz
- Barack Obama
- Barbara Boxer
- Anthony Weiner
- Elizabeth Warren
- One-sided, anti-Trump punditry from the commentariat and media
- Rachel Maddow
- Joe Biden didn't run
- Rupert Murdoch
- NATO
- Chuck Schumer
- Obamacare
- Rush Hudson Limbaugh III
- Rahm Emanuel
- The Federal Bureau of Investigation
- Valerie Jarrett
- Planned Parenthood
- Eric Holder
- Melania Trump
- Fox News
- Political "correctness"
- The abortion culture
- Bernie Sanders
- The ubiquitous Donald Trump "Make America Great Again" hat

- Middle East policy (or lack thereof)
- Rhona Graff
- An overreaching, out-of-control federal government
- The *New York Times*
- Brexit
- Amy Schumer
- Obama national security advisors John Brennan, James Clapper, and Michael Hayden's attacking Trump and trying to assist Hillary
- Chris Hayes
- Urban chaos and rioting
- Colin Kaepernick
- Bill Clinton, Inc.
- The Clinton Foundation
- Mark Simone
- Open borders
- George F. Will
- *Roe v. Wade*
- Lanny Davis
- A sluggish economy
- David Corn of *Mother Jones*
- Fake news! CNN, MSNBC, the *Times* and *Washington Post*, *The New Yorker*, *New York* magazine
- Sidney Blumenthal
- Know-it-all pollsters and pundits
- Harry Reid
- The United Nations
- Joe Conason
- Mr. and Mrs. Khizr Khan
- Nancy Pelosi
- Whoopi Goldberg
- The battle cry "Make America Great Again"
- Hillary's private e-mail server
- New York state Senator Jeff Klein
- Jennifer Granholm
- The Clinton lifestyle, surrounded by Secret Service (for life!)
- The VA (U.S. Department of Veterans Affairs)

- Barack Obama's hip "street-rap" campaign rhetoric
- Sarah Silverman
- A sense of disconnect from government
- Michelle Obama
- Too many on the public tit!
- Donna Brazile
- Government waste and fraud
- Jared Kushner
- Local, state, and federal bureaucrats
- Cher
- *The View*
- David Brooks
- A confusing and weak foreign policy: Iran, Syria, Libya, North Korea, etc.
- Joe Scarborough
- Pensions chocking local government
- Bill O'Shaughnessy
- The thought of Bill Clinton careening around the White House again
- Lack of support for "Made in the USA"
- The Supreme Court . . . going forward
- Jeanine Pirro
- Obama's lack of support for Israel
- Gary Johnson
- The *New York Post*
- Steve Bannon
- Disrespect of Bibi Netanyahu
- Ann Coulter
- Martha's Vineyard vacations
- Lack of support for our military, veterans, and law enforcement
- Huma Abedin
- ISIS
- Mika Brzezinski
- Common Core
- Obama's whispering to Medvedev: "Tell Vlad I'll have more 'flexibility' after the election"

- WVOX
- Kellyanne Conway
- The America First movement
- The political and cultural establishments
- Miley Cyrus
- Deteriorating downtowns
- Larry Kudlow
- An impressive Mike Pence!
- Anti-Catholic mindset
- The Deep State
- Hillary's walk in the woods
- Joy Behar
- The one-sided and vitriolic coverage by the *Daily News* and other papers
- A deteriorating infrastructure!
- The sluggish recovery from the recession
- Al Sharpton
- Henry Kissinger
- Ivanka Trump
- Lack of respect for the national anthem
- The arrogance of the elite and "educated"
- Lawrence O'Donnell
- Concern over Nino Scalia's successor(s)
- The plight of the poor
- Newsmax
- Ruth Bader Ginsburg
- Incarceration rates for African American males
- Terry McAuliffe
- The "basket of deplorables"
- Chelsea's salary and $10 million apartment
- Rudy Giuliani
- Black Lives Matter
- Frank Bruni, a wonderful writer, who ran out of ways to tell us how evil Trump is
- The Clinton Foundation's foreign entanglements
- Bill Weld

- NFL's "take a knee" problem
- Every cop, fireman, tradesman, electrician, plumber, butcher, truck driver, landscaper, greengrocer, fishmonger, heavy equipment operator, subway conductor, baker, sausage maker, school crossing guard, garage mechanic, bartender, and taxi driver in America
- Hillary's and Bill's speaking fees
- Donny Deutch
- Hillary Rodham Clinton herself
- Benghazi
- Chris Ruddy
- Chelsea Handler
- Mario Cuomo, who wasn't around to instruct, to inspire, to enlighten
- The genius and political smarts of Donald J. Trump
- Trump's being very "real" and accessible
- Chris Cuomo: "The Democrats lost because they were talking about transgender bathrooms . . . and Trump was talking about jobs"

—W.O.

"Those People"

Friday, July 31, 2015.

———————

Donald Trump's unfortunate remarks about Mexicans took us back a few months to a very unsettling piece in the Westchester daily newspaper about some dedicated, hardworking employees of the American Yacht Club in Rye who were let go following a surprise visit to the club by Homeland Security. Most of them were Mexicans who have been in this country for a good, long time.

I know many of these employees who were foreign-born, and their sad story really set me to thinking about all the essential contributions immigrants—"legal" or otherwise—make in our lives.

But it must first be here noted that Barack H. Obama, the particular individual who is the current president of the United States of America, has deported more aliens than any previous inhabitant of the White House. And be advised as well that in certain rarefied parts of Westchester and in our better neighborhoods, they are referred to as "those people."

Here is what "those people" do for us just to earn a living. They cook our meals, set our tables, wash our dishes, scrub our floors, haul away our trash and garbage, weed our gardens, plant our flowers, cut our grass in the spring, rake our leaves in the fall, shovel our sidewalks and plow our driveways in the winter, iron our shirts, wash our laundry, clean our toilets, style our hair, cut our toenails and buff our fingernails, babysit and pick up after our kids (and our pets), walk our dogs, fumigate our houses, tote our bales, shine our shoes, sell us lottery tickets, drive our school buses, sow and harvest our fields, grow our vegetables, muck out our stalls, cobble our shoes, tend our vineyards, sweep our streets, paint our fences, pick up our litter, gas up and wash and fix our cars, repair our roofs, shoe our horses, carry our heavy leather golf bags across hot Westchester fairways, manicure the greens at our fancy country clubs, haul boats at our yacht clubs, hoist our banners and club burgees, move our furniture, play in our orchestras, mend our clothes, sew our buttons, empty our bedpans, push our wheelchairs, dig our graves, flip our pizzas, butter and *schmear* our bagels, stir our cocktails and pour our drinks, make our beds, park our cars, stack our plates, bus our tables . . .

In addition to the above-mentioned "services" they daily provide, "those people" also enrich our culture and our lives.

All of which brings a stunning flash of *déjà vu.*

Because we've been there.

And done that—when it was the Irish and Italians who attended to all these most necessary things.

It was not too long ago.

Down-Home Democracy in the Land of Thomas Paine

November 2013.

Thomas Paine would have loved this.

One after another, they approached the podium at City Hall to scream into the night. It was another "Citizens to Be Heard" session before the high council of our city. And it was democracy at its finest as assorted skeptics, gadflies, watchdogs, contrarians, cynics, doubters, naysayers, negativists, misanthropes, alarmists, outliers, pessimists, troublemakers, and *pot*-stirrers (I had another word ready to go here) raged in all their sureness at the controversial out-of-town developer Forest City Ratner.

There were, granted, a great many authentic "colorful characters" shouting into the microphone this cold winter night as the developer's ill-conceived plan for Echo Bay was beaten down. And some screamers, to be sure, were certifiably off the wall. Others, however, were accompanied by a remarkable and undeniable sincerity and a becoming concern for the neighborhood, the "public good."

Through it all, the young, slim Mayor Bramson was unfailingly gracious. But even his undeniable brilliance and Harvard courtliness were no match for the fury that came up from these New Rochelle residents, concerned citizens all, whose love for their damn city was stronger than Bramson's fluency and ease with the jargon and buzzwords of municipal governance.

The Thomas Paines-in-the Ass won the night.

The old rabble-rouser would have been proud.

This is, after all, New Rochelle.

—*W.O.*

Fifty Years after President Kennedy Was Assassinated

I'm doing a guest shot on my pal Phil Reisman's Gannett television show this week via the *Journal News* lohud.com to talk about the fiftieth anniversary of the assassination of President Kennedy.

November 22nd has now come around fifty times as a stain on the calendar of our years since that terrible day in Dallas.

And even though we've since learned that President Kennedy was more than a little "human" and perhaps not so perfect as our young eyes had hoped and imagined, his killing and loss to America still stings, sears, and burns.

The hurt has lingered in our lives over all those fifty years since he was murdered. And still we feel it. Especially . . . especially if you're Irish.

For when John Kennedy got to the White House, we weren't "micks" anymore. He was a child of the neighborhood who meant a lot to me. And mine.

Even now.

And my flashes of *déjà vu* always end with a riderless black horse and a caisson rolling down Pennsylvania Avenue behind it.

—W.O.

ACKNOWLEDGMENTS

I'm grateful, beyond my ability to express it, to Fordham University Press, the great Jesuit publishing house in the City of New York which once again bestowed its blessing and imprimatur on this volume, which bears the imprint of our Whitney Global Media Publishing Group. The Press has earned an international reputation for scholarship—which I hope I have not damaged or diminished.

Fordham's former publishing director, Saverio Procario, an old Rockefeller Republican, was my friend and early mentor for many years. During his tenure as director, the Press grew in stature and influence and now publishes more than eighty relevant and valuable books each year. I was first introduced to Fordham University Press when I came across a marvelous book of powerful speeches by the legendary federal judge William Hughes Mulligan.

Mr. Procario's unique genius was complemented by his successors and their talented associates. And by four other great souls at the Press to whom I'm indebted for their extraordinary interest in all five of my books: Margaret Noonan is the great definer and protector of the Press (when she's not rooting for that other magnificent New York institution, her beloved Yankees), and Kate O'Brien, who uses her considerable influence with booksellers and the media to find shelf space for my books all over the country; but first we had to produce the five books that bear my poor name and Fordham's prestigious imprimatur, and for their production and design I am privileged to rely on the creativity and judgment of Mark Lerner, who knows all the levers and secrets of publishing. I'm especially grateful to Mark, and to Fordham's brilliant publishing director, Fred Nachbaur. I liked Fred instantly when I came bearing my earlier manuscripts, and this new book would not have had a chance without his blessing, imprimatur, and encouragement. Fred is an emerging and rising star in publishing. I'm grateful as well to his talented associates, including the patient and forgiving managing editor, Eric Newman, and editor and rights & permissions manager Will Cerbone.

[649]

RADIO ACTIVE

The late and estimable saloonkeeper Mr. Bernard "Toots" Shor once advised me that "With your kind of friends . . . you gotta have a damn *index* so they can find their brilliant names!" Thus, I'm again grateful to Jennifer Rushing-Schurr on this essential account.

All Fordham's worthy and scholarly publishing activities and literary efforts are informed by the example and vision of two extraordinary educators: Father Joseph O'Hare, S.J., a legendary Jesuit educator, who is universally admired for his public service in New York City as well as for his academic leadership, and Father Joseph M. McShane, S.J., a dedicated, dynamic, and, if he will permit me, a saintly man, as well as a great educator and administrator.

As with my all my previous books, Anthony Chiffolo, a dear man who writes prayer books and has actually edited popes, was helpful on this volume as well.

But for this anthology, I am most indebted to Douglas P. Clement, the great editor, critic, superb journalist, country squire, and scholar who came rushing in like the cavalry from his redoubt in the Litchfield Hills to rescue my sixth book. I am thus rendered eternally grateful to young Mr. Clement and to his wife, Jennifer Hartmann Clement, and their children, Paul and Avery Jane, for sharing their talented husband and father with me so he could make some sense of my clumsy writing efforts. Doug also took valuable time away from consulting several white shoe law firms in the New York area. And, of course, he is forever revered for his stewardship of the iconic *Litchfield County Times*, during the halcyon period when it reigned as one of America's most prestigious weekly newspapers.

For the cover design of this book, I have again relied on the genius of Professor Rich Hendel, who actually wrote the industry bible on book design.

And I'm tremendously grateful to the legendary Robert Risko, the world-renowned illustrator whose work has adorned many *Vanity Fair* covers. Although I'm not a worthy subject for his rare talent, I am in awe of Risko's stunning genius and his work on the cover.

And, closer to home, once again I also must thank the incomparable Cindy Hall Gallagher of Whitney Global Media, my dear friend, amanuensis, and confidant of forty years, without whom my life would resemble a seven-car pile-up. It should tell you something that when my friends—Mario Cuomo most prominently included—would ring up our Westchester radio stations, they usually ask for *Cindy*, and most are quite disappointed when I pick up the phone.

Cindy has been my friend, confidant, and Executive Everything for 42 years. As an amanuensis and personal assistant, she has no equal. Dwight Eisenhower and, later, Nelson Rockefeller enjoyed the devoted service of the legendary Mrs. Ann Whitman to run their offices and lives. And Mario Cuomo, during the various seasons of his life, relied on Mary Tragale, Pam Broughton, and the estimable Mary Porcelli. As great as all these women are, they can't at all compare to Mrs. Gallagher. Cindy's intuitive powers and wise judgment inform everything I do. And my family shares my admiration of and affection for this marvelous woman who has devoted herself to me and mine for four decades.

My professional life as a community broadcaster also relies heavily on the dedication, creativity, and brilliance of several colleagues. The influential contributions of Kevin Scott Elliott are everywhere apparent in my life. His genius and loyalty are gifts I treasure. Kevin is not alone in terms of devotion and dedication. Don Stevens, our senior vice president and chief of staff, is essential to the success and longevity of the last two independent community stations in the New York area. Speaking of which, WVOX and WVIP are also fortunate to enjoy the talent and wisdom of Judy Fremont, president of our Stations Division and about a two-handicap golfer. She's also a woman of culture and the theater. Why she hangs with me, I'll never know. All my efforts—including this book—rely as well on Maggie Cervantes, who is a star in the office *and* on the air as co-host of *Momentos Latino*.

One absolutely essential reason our local stations have survived and prevailed despite all the social and technological challenges swirling around our profession is my son David Tucker O'Shaughnessy, now our president. He's a rising star in our industry. And I am a proud—and admiring—father.

David's mother, Ann Wharton Thayer; his brother, Matthew O'Shaughnessy; and his sister, Kate Warton O'Shaughnessy—who serve as directors of our enterprises—will confirm David's standing and stature in our lives. And David himself will second my admiration for Gregg Pavelle, Richard Littlejohn, Irma Becerra, Ahmet Alloqi, Joe Giambona, Mike Belusczak, and Ralph Kragle.

And two more: Judge Jeffrey Bernbach and his estimable wife, Karen, have been fierce advocates and defenders of these stations—and my stewardship thereof—for many years. Judge Bernbach is a gifted public servant who served in the administrations of both Mario and Andrew Cuomo. But he's always found time to watch over me and mine.

And for reasons they must know, everything I do—on the air or in print—is with the forbearance, encouragement, and protection of Michael Assaf, Jody Chesnov, Jeff Coyle, Glen Sanatar, Charlie Kafferman, James O'Shea, Erwin Krasnow, and my *compadre* Gregorio Alvarez. Those who know this eminently decent, loving, and gentle Dominican will agree that many of the lovely qualities I found in my late friend Mario Cuomo also exist in great abundance in Gregorio. I am capable of no greater praise for him.

As the permittee of WVOX and WVIP, which, as of the spring of 2019 are just about the last remaining independent stations in the New York area and are now also the *only* local community stations in Westchester, I'm thus immensely grateful to several other talented folks who help us keep these two stations relevant and away from the speculators, predators, and absentee owners who have descended on our profession since Consolidation began in the 1980s. Those generous souls, who over the years have "adopted" and bought into the unique mission and independence of our radio stations, include William Plunkett, Jeff Bernbach, Michael Assaf, Governor Andrew Cuomo, Joe Reilly, General Joe Spinelli, the late Alan Rosenberg, Jim Generoso, Norman Drubner, Jesus Valencia, Tervor Forde, Colonel Steve Mellekas, Steve Tenore, Adam Friedlander, Tony Federici, Tom Mungeer, Matilda Raffa Cuomo, Dr. Emancia Neil, Father Chris Monturo, Jim Killoran, Reverend Richard Garner, Jerry Nappi, Marty Goldsmith, Martin Stone, Frank Connelly Jr., Kathleen Plunkett O'Connor, Elva Amparo Reynoso, Michelle Thompson, June and Tim Rooney, Gianni Russo, Tommy Smyth, Gem Morrison, Teddy Suric, George Latimer, Treasa Goodwin-Smyth, Andrea-Stewart Cousins, Julian Niccolini, Mary Clare Reilly, Floyd Vivino, Alex Von Bidder, Joe Napolitano, Adam Friedlander,

Junior Blake, Chuck Strome, Dr. Gil Lederman, Keeling Beckford, Commissioner Patrick Carroll, Donald Vernon, Commissioner Joe Schaller, Professor Maixent Zogo, Andrew Gerardi, Judge Anthony Carbone, Bep McSweeney, "Don" Dominic Procopio, Chief Andy Sandor, Steve Pellettiere, Kevin Barry McGrath, Charles Valenti, Maria Cuomo Cole, Judge David Rifas, Garfield "Chin" Bourne, Sergio Maccioni, Jennifer Graziano, Herman Geist, Katherine Miller, Esq., Bobby Hutton, Leighton Wilson, Shari Gordon, Esq., Bobby Clarke, Jeff Schwartz, Dr. Ronald Hoffman, Sean Driscoll, Professor Mike Damergis, Dr. Dan Miller, Steve Fendrich, Conroy Allison, David Ridder Driscoll, John Verni, Judge Susan Kettner, Joe D'Aloisio, Jeff Hanley, Ed Mancuso, Dan Rubino, Carrie Crawford, Taryn Duffy, Jennifer Rampersaud, Shirley Maxwell, Judge Matthew Cooper, Dr. Marsha Gordon, Major Arthur Goodale, John Harper, Guru Madeleine, Michael Israel, Sergio Vacca, Captain Rob Taishoff, John Valenti, Carl Whyte, Bud Williamson, Erin Murphy, Billy DeLuca, Glenroy Walker, Frank Endress, Frank Miceli, David Hinckley, Patrick Maitland, Joe Tardi, Joe Amaturo, Ellen and Ray Oneglia, Jim Cunningham, Kara Comblo, Deb Rizzi, Barbara Kram, Chris Chin, Gabriele Pepe, Wilfred Roberts, David Gentner, Dennis Jackson, Tony Cobb, David Donovan, Nat Carbo, Rocco Bellantoni Jr., Bahamas Minister Marvin Dames, Carl Moxie, Colonel Marty Rochelle, Lindsay Salandra, Brian Figeroux, Rev. Bertram Maxwell, Deborah and Declan Murphy, Donald V. West, Mara Gibbs, Alvin Richard Ruskin, Clif Mills Jr., Anthony Ellis, William O'Neill, Clement Hume, David Josey, Jean Ensign, John Van Buren Sullivan, Lindon Brown, Michael Fosina, Erwin Krasnow, Cosimo Bruno, Kara Bennorth, Wayne Powe, Jules Cohen, Fran Sisco, Michael Fiumara, Dr. Victor Sternberg, Steve Savino, Gina Revel, Joseph Ruhl, Noel Stevens, Renate and Thomas McKnight, Avril Francis, John Eggerton, Judge Ann Dranginis, Angela Ciminello, Antoinette Osborne, Chief Judge Alan Scheinkman, Jonathan Bush, Fiorita and Michael DiLullo, Gerardo Bruno, Susan and Art Zuckerman, Murray Richman, Esq., William "Billy" Bush, David Annakie, Sam Tilley and Dave Vigeant, Richard Ambrose Foreman, Dr. Russell McLeod, Bradford Bernstein, Esq., Mark Habeeb, Harry Jessell, Father Joe Cavoto O.F.M., Franco Lazzari, Albert Smith, Joan and Judge Charlier Gill, Dennis Nardone, William Harrington, B. J. Harrington,

Father Robert Tucker, Phil Lombardo, Charles Barton Castleberry, Steve Savino III, Joe Cicio, Bernie Koteen, and the late Rainer Kraus.

Teilhard de Chardin, the great Jesuit philosopher and paleontologist, wrote of the "diminishments" we all suffer as we get older. I've been very fortunate during my already long life to have encountered some terrific medical practitioners who help me confront those diminishments. I've written previously of my great admiration for Dr. Richard Rocco Pisano, who, with his wife, Kathy, runs a thriving "mom-and-pop" medical office. He still makes house calls and does a lot of *pro bono* work in the wilds of Westchester. In an age when a lot of doctors are in it strictly for the bucks, that alone should recommend the guy. When you're scrambling and in trouble, you couldn't have a brighter, more caring fellow on the case. Thank God, I've only had to "scramble" a few times in my eighty-one years. And as I sit here at my desk early on a winter morning in 2019, I am also aware of my debt to Dr. Marc Eisenberg, Dr. Paul Pellicci, Dr. Steven Butensky, Dr. Kevin Falvey, Dr. David Breindel, Dr. Hank Borkowski, Dr. Fritz Ehlert, Dr. Kenneth Porter, and Dr. John Keggi.

And speaking of great physicians, healers really, I've also discovered—somewhat late in life—the great Altorelli family . . . including the patriarch, Dr. Alphonse Altorelli, and his spectacular wife, Deborah Slatcher, who runs their practice in New Preston, Connecticut, which now includes their daughter Dr. Nicole Altorelli, who graduated first in her class at Yale Medical School, and the Altorellis' young son and heir Dr. Myles Altorelli, perhaps the finest chiropractor in the country, who has recently started a medical spa at the same location in New Preston. Henry Kissinger repairs to their care and keeping. And so do all the elders of the Litchfield Hills.

I also have great admiration for a certifiable legend at New York–Presbyterian: Dr. Hassan Garan, the estimable heart specialist who lectures all over the world but somehow finds time to keep me in the game.

I'm reminded that my illustrious Connecticut neighbor, the great man of letters Philip Roth, wrote "30" to his writing endeavors and hung up his spikes in his mid-eighties when he was "no longer in possession of the physical strength or mental acuity and fitness needed to mount and sustain a large creative endeavor." (He actually put a Post-it note on his computer: "The struggle with writing is done.") I am often tempted to bestow the same damn sentiment toward my yellow legal pad. But as long as you'll indulge me, I'll stick with it a bit longer.

I would also beg an author's privilege to tell you of my tremendous pride in my own children: Matthew Thayer O'Shaughnessy; David Tucker O'Shaughnessy and his wife, Cara Ferrin O'Shaughnessy; and my spectacular daughter, Kate O'Shaughnessy Nulty. *And* my grandchildren Tucker, Flynn, and Amelia Nulty and Isabel and Lily O'Shaughnessy.

Finally, in all my endeavors, I was instructed and inspired for thirty-eight years by the goodness, friendship, and example of Mario Matthew Cuomo. I loved the man. And I attempted to express those feelings in my surprisingly well-received—quite beyond its due—memoir *Mario Cuomo: Remembrances of a Remarkable Man* . . . thanks, also, in no small measure, to the encouragement of the great titan of publishing, the incomparable bookseller and philanthropist Leonard Riggio, founder of Barnes & Noble, who loved Mario too.

INDEX

"21" Club, 43, 250, 259, 423, 472, 490; McLaughlin and, 436; Suric and, 264–67

Abedin, Huma, 641
Abernethy, Jack, 275
abortion, 524, 639; Cuomo (Andrew) on, 446, 566; Cuomo (Mario) on, 517; Dolan on, 617–23; Killian on, 572–73; Mayer on, 573; Sullivan on, 168
Abplanalp, Bob, 275
Abramowitz, Jeff and Carolyn, 306
Abrams, Floyd, xviii, 26–31, 53, 72, 79–81, 289
Abzug, Bella, 275
Accurso, Laura, 281, 294
Ackerman, Michael, 275
Ackerman, Nancy, 275
Adams, Alger, 299–300
Adams, Cindy, xv, 188, 275, 289, 294
Adams, Paul, 275, 300
Adinolfi, Elizabeth, 294
advertising: editorial, 69–70; Ney and, 420
Africa, Rockefeller and, 119
African Americans: Dee and Davis and, 344–48; Jeffersontown, KY, supermarket shootings and, 455; and *Westchester County Press*, 299–300
afterlife, Cuomo (Mario) on, 495
age: Bush (G. H. W.) and, 541; Kelly on, 201; Kissinger on, 327; Maccioni on, 239, 247; Martinelli and, 137, 145–46; O'Shaughnessy on, 258, 301, 520; Roth on, 331; Shargel on, 204; Teilhard de Chardin on, 305, 331, 418, 654
Agnelli, Gianni, 276
Aiello, John, 500
Ailes, Roger, 85–87, 289, 435
Alam, Nerul, 275
Alberto, Carlos, 275
Albert of Monaco, 245
Albertson, Ethel, 275
Albertson, J. Lester, 275
Aldrich, Nelson, 122
Alexander, Henry, 275
Alexander, Lamar, 407
Alex from Greenburgh (caller), 374

Alfano, Anthony, 275
Ali, Muhammad, 614
Allan, Col, 275
Allen, Mel, 488, 607
Allen, Steve, 275
Allgood, Snoopy, 117, 300
Allison, Conroy, 275, 653
Allon, Tom, 339
Alloqi, Ahmet, 289, 652
Allyn, David, 275
Alpert, David, 306
Alter, Eleanor, 289
Altorelli, Alphonse, 275, 654
Altorelli, Deborah, 275, 294
Altorelli, Myles, 275, 654
Altorelli, Nicole, 654
Alvarez, Briana, 275
Alvarez, Edward, 275
Alvarez, Elva Amparo Augustina, 294
Alvarez, Gregorio, 275, 289, 652
Alvarez, Miosotis, 275, 294
Amaturo, Joe, 275, 289, 653
Amaturo, Wini, 275
Ambar, Saladin, 497
Ambrose, saint, 625
American Broadcasting Cos. v. Aereo, Inc., 30
American Civil Liberties Union, 57
American Express, 191, 198
American Negro Theatre, 346–48
American values, Cuomo (Andrew) on, 456–57
American Yacht Club, 301–3, 414–15
Ames, Elliott, 275
Ames, Lynne, 275
Anastasi, Joe, 275–76, 398–400
Anastasi, Louise, 398
Anastasi, Tony and Frances, 400
Anastos, Ernie, 384
Anatole, chef, 298
Anderson, John, 276
Anderson, Richard, 260
Anderson, Terry, 76
Anderson, Walter, 276
Anderson, Warren, 276
Andreas, Christine, 269

Andrews, Erin, 276
Angiolillo, Daniel, 276, 578; endorsement for, 584–86
Annable, J. J., 276
Annakie, David, 276, 653
Annunziata, Albert, 276
Apicella, Joe, 289
Apple, R. W. "Johnny," 135
Arantes do Nascimento, Edson "Pele," 276
Arcara, Richard J., 350
Arledge, Roone, 431
Arlen, Harold, 385
Arlen, Michael, 614
Armiento, Mike, 318, 371
Armstrong, Louis, 276, 385, 613
Arons, Judy Fremont, 294
Aronson, David, 289
Arries, Les, 366, 409
Arrigoni, Ed, 276
art, Lostritto on, 157, 159
Asimov, Isaac, 276, 490
Assaf, Laura, 276
Assaf, Michael, 76, 276, 289, 652
Astaire, Fred, 276, 288
Astor, Brooke, 294
Astorino, Rob, 120, 189, 289, 306, 576–78, 580–83
Athanasatos, Eugene and Mike, 276
atheism, Roth and, 331–32
Attridge, Terry, 276, 288
Auletta, Ken, xv, 490–91, 514, 521, 546
Austin, Jim, 276
Austin, Phil, 276
Avendano, Fabio, 289–90
Avis, Warren and Yanna, 252
Aziz, Peter, 276
Aziz, Tariq, 165

Backman, Elizabeth, 284
Bacon, John, 339
Baker, Bobby, 108
Baker, James, 541, 550
Baker, Rhonda, 396–97
Baker, Susan, 60
Ball, Heather, 294
Ball, Lucille, 356
Bannon, Steve, 641
Barnes, Edward Larabee, 276
Barnes, Johnny, 350
Barnicle, Mike, 336, 351, 514
Barone, Louis, 276

Barrack, Tom, 276
Barrett, David, 276
Barrett, Emily, 276
Barrett, Pat, 251, 263, 276
Barrett, Wayne, 336, 490, 514
Barry, Dan, 338–39
Barton, Charles, 53
Barton, Jane, 366
Baruch, Andre, 276
Basie, Count, 386
basketball, Cuomo family and, 507–8
Bastian, Ed, 260
Bates, "Peg Leg," 276
Battle, Vanessa, 290
Bauder, David, 339
Baum, Joe, 297
Bazelon, David, 53
Beatty, Homer, 185
Beaudoin, Charles, 276, 290
Beaupre, Larry, 276
Beaupre, Lawrence, 546
Becerra, Irma, 652
Beck, Glenn, 71
Beck, Marty, 276, 365–67, 389, 409
Beckenbauer, Franz, 276
Beckford, Keeling, 276, 653
Beesemyer, Dick, 366
Beethoven, Ludwig von, 537–38
Begala, Paul, 553
Behar, Joy, 642
Behrens, Kathy, 276
Belafonte, Harry, 346–48
Belkin, Lisa, 137
Bellacosa, Joseph W., 53, 276, 290, 497–99
Bellantoni, Rocco, Jr., 276, 288, 371–72, 402, 410, 653
Bellew, Vin, 140, 276
Bellini, Giovanni, 157
Belusczak, Mike, 652
Belushi, Billy, 142
Belushi, Jim, 137, 142
Benedict XVI, pope, 476, 620
Ben Elisha, Ishmael, 524
Benjamin, Gerald, 276, 531
Bennack, Frank, 258
Bennett, Harvey, 276
Bennett, Melissa and Paul, 276
Bennett, Richard Rodney, 276
Bennett, Susan, 495
Bennett, Tony, 276, 494–95, 515, 566
Bennorth, Kara, 276, 290, 653

Bentham, Jeremy, 620
Bergen, Polly, 294
Berger, Marty, 276
Berger, Meyer "Mike," 336
Bergoglio, Jorge Mario. *See* Francis, pope
Berking, Max, 276
Berkoff, Richard, 276
Berkowitz, Hilda and Bill, 276
Berlage, Randy, 276
Berman, Henry, 276, 290
Berman, Len, 425
Berman, Richard M., 276
Bernacchia, Arthur, 276
Bernacchia, George, 276
Bernacchia, Jason, 276
Bernacchia, Justin, 276
Bernacchia, Karen and Jeffrey, 276
Bernacchia, Robin Curry, 276
Bernacki, Bob, 366
Bernbach, Jeffrey, 8, 53, 76, 290, 398, 546, 652
Bernbach, Karen, 290, 294, 652
Berns, Charlie, 264
Bernstein, Bradford, 653
Bernstein, Carl, 276
Berti, Veronica, 261, 276
Beuth, Phil, 276, 366, 526
Bevel, Gina, 653
Biaggi, Alessandra, 276, 294, 569–70
Biaggi, Mario, 250, 276, 367, 411, 569
Bianco, Adamello, 276
Bianco, Rae, 294
Biden, Joseph, 145, 448, 490, 501, 524, 560, 565–66, 639
Biggins, Jerry, 257, 276, 290
Biglin, Martin J., 371
Bilotta, Joe, 276, 378
Binder, Joe, 276
Biscoglio, Joe, 276
Bishop, James, 276, 371
Black, Page Morton, 294, 424–26
Black, William, 424
Blackburn, Edward, James, John and Richard, 276
Blackwell, Sandra, 276, 294, 300
Blaicher, Suzanne, 294
Blake, Junior, 276, 653
Blanton, Taylor, 543
Blau, Elizabeth, 276
Blau, Robert, 276, 290
Blendo, Blend, 276
Bloch, Sonny, 276

Bloom, Lisa, 8
Bloom, Rube, 494
Bloomberg, Michael, 190, 194, 377, 501
blueink Review, on Cuomo biography, 528
Blumenthal, Sidney, 640
Bobrowsky, Carol, 276, 290
Boccardi, Louis, 53, 76, 276, 546
Bocchino, Rose, 283
Bocelli, Andrea, 261, 276
Bodnar, John, 276
Bodow, Warren, 276, 366
Boehner, John, 200
Bonanos, Christopher, 339
Bono, 25, 67
Borelli, Lou, 276
Borkowski, Hank, 276, 654
Botstein, Leon, 332
Bourne, Garfield "Chin," 653
Boxer, Barbara, 639
Boyle, Frank, 276, 366
Boynton, Oren, 290
Bradford, Barbara Taylor, xv, 294
Bradley, Adam, 276, 305, 589–90
Bradley, Omar, 249, 276
Bradshaw, Terry, 395
Brady, Ed, 276
Brady, James, 249, 251, 276
Bramson, Noam, 317, 578, 580–82, 646
Brand, Oscar, 276
Brandeis, Louis, 28, 77
Brass, Bonifacio, 276
Bratton, Bill, 276
Braun, Paul, 276
Brawley, Tawana, 561
Brazile, Donna, 641
Bregman, Cornelia, 294
Bregman, Marty, 276
Breindel, David, 276, 290, 654
Breindel, Lynn, 276
Brennan, John, 640
Brennan, William, 77, 79–80
Brescia, Michael, 175–77
Breslin, James and Chris, 276, 334
Breslin, Jimmy, xvii, 161, 183, 222, 249, 273, 276, 288, 336–43, 367, 476, 492, 508–9, 546, 607
Breslin, Kelly, 334
Breslin, Kevin, 276, 334, 492
Breslin, Patrick, 334
Breslin, Rosemary, 334
Brexit, 640

Brieant, Charles, 75, 276, 301, 414
Brier, Paul, 276
Briganti, Stefano, 276
Brindle, Ronald E. "Buzz," 276
Broadcasters Foundation of America, 73, 87, 366, 608; Buckley and, 377; Guardian Fund, xviii, 591, 593–97; McLaughlin and, 430; Nail and, 389; Olds and, 379–81; Osgood and, 269–70; Preston and, 356; Quaal and, 382
broadcasting: Buckley and, 376–78; Fairness Doctrine and, 46–56, 62–68; issue advertising and, 69–70; McLaughlin and, 430–39; Olds and, 379–81; Quaal and, 382–83
Broadcasting and Cable, 66, 73, 387–88
Broadcast Pioneers, 408–9. *See also* Broadcasters Foundation of America
Broder, David, 360–61
Brodsky, Richard D., 276
Brody, Jerry, 297
Brokaw, Tom, 351
Bronitt, Claire, 276
Bronz, Lois, 276, 294
Brooke, Ed, 128
Brooklyn Daily Eagle, on Cuomo biography, 525
Brooks, David, 308, 623, 641
Brophy, John, 276
Broughton, Pam, 276
Brown, Gary, 276
Brown, Jim, 276
Brown, Les, 53, 73, 276, 366, 388
Brown, Lindon, 653
Brown, Michael, 374
Brownback, Sam, 67
Browne, Arthur, 339
Bruni, Frank, 642
Bruno, Antonio, 260
Bruno, Bob, 276, 378
Bruno, Cosimo, 260, 276, 653
Bruno, Gerardo, 260, 277, 290, 653
Bruno, Joe, 277
Bruno, Lucia, 294
Bryant, Del, 356
Bryant, George, 414
Brzezinski, Mika, 351, 641
Bublé, Michael, 234
Buchanan, Pat, 277
Buchdahl, Angela, 455
Buck, Jim, 277

Buckley, Connie, 294, 377
Buckley, James, 128
Buckley, Jen, 377
Buckley, Richard Dimes, 277, 376, 611
Buckley, Rick, 366, 376–78, 409, 520, 611–12
Buffalo, NY, 349–50, 450
Bulgari, Anna, 294
Bullitt, Dorothy Stimson, 356
Bulova, Arde, 376
Bunting, Josiah "Si" IV, 277
Bunzell, Reed, 75
Burgos, Tonio, 501
Burke, David, 277
Burke, Johnny, 385, 494
Burke, Trixie, 277
Burlinson, Bob, 277
Burns, Barrett and Patricia, 277
Burns, Colin, Sr., 277, 290
Burton, Peggy, 277, 390–91, 485, 490
Bush, Barbara, 540–41, 544, 549, 553, 597
Bush, George H. W., 277, 539, 551, 553, 556, 591; endorsement for president, 546–50; eulogy by G. W. Bush, 541–45
Bush, George W., 33, 37, 539, 556; endorsement for president, 552–54; eulogy for G. H. W. Bush, 541–45; Sullivan on, 165
Bush, Jeb, 144, 222, 543
Bush, Jodi, 294
Bush, Jonathan, 251, 263, 277, 290, 539, 555–56, 653; and Don Imus, 559–62
Bush, Prescott, 556
Bush, Robin, 543
Bush, William "Billy," 11, 71, 277, 290, 351, 539, 653; and Mario Cuomo, 555–56; Reisman on, 557–58
Butcher, William, 277, 306
Butensky, Di, 294
Butensky, Steven, 277, 290, 654
Butler, Amy, 455
Byrd, Robert, 58
Byrne, Brendan, 277, 423

Cadoo, Elizabeth, 277, 293–94
Cahill, John, 212–27, 290, 405, 581
Cahill, Kim, 218–19, 224
Calabrese, Suzanne, 290
Calabria family, 189
Calamari, Frank, 174–75, 277
Caldararo, John, 277
Califano, Hillary and Joe, 277
Callas, Maria, 369, 614

Calloway, Bo, 361
Calvary Hospital, 174–84
Calvin, John, 535
Cam, Mr., 374
Cammann, Bob, 277, 371
Campbell, Betty, 318
Campbell, James, 277
Campbell, Todd, 277
Camus, Albert, 79, 289
Canada, Mohl on, 101–2
Candrea, Inez, 372–75
Candrea, Joe, 372–73
Cannon, Jimmy, 183, 191, 249, 269, 277, 288,
    336, 422, 607
Canzeri, Joe, 124, 277, 359, 362
Canzeri, Tricia Novak, 277, 294
Capasso, Tony, 277
Capello, Danny, 277
capital punishment. *See* death penalty
Cappelli, Gina, 277
Cappelli, Kylie and Louis, 277, 290
Caravaggi, Robert, 277
Carbo, Nat, 277, 653
Carbone, Anthony, 277, 290, 318, 653
Carduner, Wendy, 294
Carey, D. J., 277
Carey, Ed, 277, 318
Carey, Hugh Leo, 249, 277, 367, 423, 478, 485,
    503, 516, 566, 632
Carey, Wally, 302
Carlin, George, 53, 76
Carlson, Tucker, 351
Carmichael, Hoagy, Jr., 277
Carnegie, Jim, 53
Carnevale, Michael, 147–48, 277, 290
Carney, Michael, 277
Carolli, Pasqualie, 317
Carpenter, Peter, 290
Carroll, Kathleen, 318
Carroll, Patrick J., 277, 290, 316–20, 653
Carrozzo (priest), 148, 158
Carter, Graydon, 277
Carter, Jimmy, 133, 547
Carter, John Mack, 277
Cartica, Frank, 277
Cartwright, Lachlan, 277, 290
Carvel, Tom, 277
Carville, James, 553, 560
Casella, Cesare, 277, 297
Casey, Bob, 277
Casey, Kevin, 75, 277

Cash, Johnny, 355
Cashman, Matt, 290
Castellano, Andrew, 277
Castleberry, Charles Barton, 277, 290, 527,
    654
Catholic Church: Breslin and, 342; Cahill
    and, 219–20; Comfort and, 176; Cuomo
    (Mario) and, 298–99, 476–82, 496, 506;
    Dolan and, 170–73; Kelly and, 196–98;
    Lionel and, 298–99; Lostritto and, 147–60;
    Maccioni and, 244; Mara (Ann) and, 394;
    Mustich and, 371; Rockefeller and, 362;
    Sullivan and, 161–69
Catsimatidis, John, 277, 290, 425
Catsimatidis, Margo, 277, 425
Cavoto, Joe, 147–48, 277, 290, 653
Cella, Bill, 277
censorship, 62–68; Abrams on, 79; Grant
    and, 15–17; Hastings on, 41; Imus episode
    and, 12–14; Limbaugh episode and,
    18–20; O'Reilly episode and, 8–11; Stone
    on, 108
Central Synagogue interfaith service,
    Andrew Cuomo remarks at, 455–59, 565
Cerbone, Will, 649
Ceruzzi, Judy, 294
Cervantes, Maggie, 277, 294, 651
Cesario, Jack, 277
Chabon, Michael, 329
Chadwick, Owen, 620
Chamot-Rooke, Guillaume, 290
Champlin, Jim, 277, 366
Champlin, Sue, 277
Chandler, Ken, 277
Charlie from the West End (caller), 374
Chartock, Alan, 277
Cheetham, Mark, 277
Chenault, Katherine and Ken, 192
Cheney, Dick, 135–36, 553
Cher, 641
Chesnov, Jody, 277, 290, 652
Chianese, Dominic "Uncle Junior," 277
Chiang Kai-shek, 129
Chiffolo, Anthony, 277, 650
Chin, Chris, 653
Chinaglia, Giorgio, 277
Chiusano, Tom, 277
Chong, Rachelle, 53
Christian Brothers, 314–15, 362, 427–29
Christie, Chris, 111, 194
Christmas, Driscoll on, 428

Christy, June, 294
Church, Stanley W., 277, 371
Churchill, Winston, 337–38, 502, 614
Cicio, Joe, 277, 654
Ciminello, Angela, 653
Cimino, Jack, 175
Cipriani, Arrigo, 260, 277
Cipriani, Giuseppe, 277
Circo, 240–41, 248
Citron, Casper, 277
civics education, Abrams on, 27
civility, versus free speech, 10, 19, 65
civil liberties, 57–61; Kelly on, 201; limits of, 59–60
Clapper, James, 640
Clark, Bill, 53, 277
Clark, James Mott, Jr., 277
Clark, Mary Higgins, 277
Clark, Richard, 301–3, 414–15
Clarke, Bobby, 277, 653
Clean Energy Standard, 98–99
Clear Channel, 75
Clement, Avery Jane, 650
Clement, D. Paul, 1–2, 277, 290, 650
Clement, Jennifer, 277, 290, 294, 650
Clement, Paul, 650
climate change, Lostritto on, 154
Clinton, Bill, 37, 74, 277, 464, 497, 501, 567, 582, 640–41, 643; and Bush family, 543, 546, 548–49, 552
Clinton, Chelsea, 642
Clinton, Hillary, 277, 501, 549–50, 560, 567; loss by, 639–43; Martinelli on, 145; Stone on, 111–12
Clooney, George, 277
Clooney, Rosemary, 277
Cloutier, Bill, 366
Cobb, Tony, 277, 653
Cody, Ellen, 366
Cofer, John, 107
Cohen, Bob, 572
Cohen, I. B., 371
Cohen, Jules, 653
Cohen, Steven, 566
Cohn, Roy, 244, 277
Colabella, Nancy, 306
Colabella, Nick, 306
Colangelo, John, 318
Colapietro, Mike, 109
Colapietro, Peter, 277
Colavita, Anthony, 277, 579

Colavita, Anthony, Sr., 277, 411
Cole, Kenneth, 277, 290, 367, 466, 509
Cole, Maria Cuomo, xv–xvi, 277, 290, 294, 466, 491, 508, 514, 653
Cole, Ray, 277
Coles, Robert, 277
Collins, Bill, 392
Collins, Diane Gagliardi, 392
Collins, Michael, 277
Collins, Reid, 268
Columbia, David Patrick, 277, 290
Columbus Day parade, 188–89
Colwell, Bob, 371
Colwell, Harry, 371
Comblo, Kara, 653
Comey, Jim, 88, 195–96
Comfort, Christopher, 174–84, 277
Communications Daily, 387–89
communism, Maccioni on, 255
Compagnone, Linda, 297
Compagnone, Ralph, 259, 277, 297
compassion: Cahill on, 218, 222; Comfort on, 183–84; McCain and, 327
Conason, Joe, 640
Confession, Lostritto on, 151, 159
Connelly, Frank, 277, 371, 652
Connery, Sean, 277
Connick, Harry, Jr., 234
Connolly, John, 277
Connolly, Mark, 277
Connors, Edward, 288
Conroy, Katherine Wilson, 277
Conservative Party, 128, 576, 588
Considine, Bob, 249, 277
Constantine, Tom, 277
Constitution, 584–85; Abrams on, 30. See also First Amendment
Conte, Bob, 277
Conway, E. Virgil, 277
Conway, Elaine Wingate, 294
Conway, Kellyanne, 642
Cooke, Terence Cardinal, 524
Coolidge, Calvin, 133
Cooper, Burt, 277
Cooper, Matthew, 277, 290, 653
Copps, Michael, 67, 277
copyright, Abrams on, 30
Corn, David, 640
Corn-Revere, Robert, 53
corporate censorship, xviii, 47–48, 71; Grant on, 15–17; Imus episode and, 12–14;

Limbaugh episode and, 18–20; O'Reilly episode and, 8–11
corporations, and issue advertising, 69–70
corruption, Reid on, 34
Corvo, Tim, 290
Cosell, Howard, 249, 277
Cotter, Richard, 251, 277
Cotton, Rick, 566
Coulson, Joette, 277
Coulter, Ann, 71, 641
Council of American Ambassadors, 44
The Country and Abroad Magazine, on Cuomo biography, 528–29
Coward, Noel, 66
Coyle, Jeff, 277, 652
Crabtree, John, 262
Crabtree, Richard, 250, 277
Crangle, Joe, 350
Crawford, Carrie, 653
Cribari, Guido, 277
Crigler, John, 53
criminal justice system, Breslin and, 335
criminal law, Shargel on, 204–11
Crockett, Steve, 501
Cronkite, Walter, xv, 33–34, 45, 53–54, 75, 277, 361, 469–70
Crosby, Harry Lillis "Bing," 277–78
Crosby, Nathaniel, 278
Crotty, Jerry, 350, 501
Crotty, Mary Ann, 501
Crotty, Paul, 278
Crowley, Jerry, 378
Cruyff, Johan, 278
Cruz, Ted, 111
Crystal, Lynn, 294
Cucino, Ellie, 278
Culligan, Matthew J. "Joe," 278
Cummins, Jerry, 270, 290
Cunningham, Bill, 278, 251, 290
Cunningham, Jim, 278, 290, 653
Cunningham, John, 258
Cunningham, Pat, 278
Cuomo, Andrea, 518
Cuomo, Andrew Mark, 188–90, 273, 278, 290, 411, 491, 546, 571, 579, 652; on biography of Mario, 523; and Bramson, 582; Cahill and, 217; Central Synagogue Interfaith Service address, 455–59, 565; on economy, 446, 450–51, 635; election as governor, 441–54; endorsement for governor, 565–68; eulogy for Mario, 496,

500–12; Kelly on, 194; Matilda on, 461–62, 464, 470; Mohl and, 95; and O'Rourke, 472; and Rockefeller, 120; Stone on, 112
Cuomo, Carolina Regina, 470
Cuomo, Chris, 351, 470, 509, 643
Cuomo, Christopher, 39, 500
Cuomo, Cristina, 39–40, 470, 500, 509
Cuomo, Immaculata, 500, 518
Cuomo, Madeline, 283, 508–9
Cuomo, Margaret, 508
Cuomo, Mario (younger), 39–40, 470–71, 500
Cuomo, Mario Matthew, 189, 260, 273, 278, 288, 290, 367, 513–22, 552, 579, 585, 651, 655; and Anastasi, 399; and Andrew, 442, 448–49, 451–52, 509, 565–66, 568; and Billy Bush, 553–54, 558; and Black, 425; and Breslin, 338–42; on broadcasting, 62, 72; and Catholic Church, 298–99, 476–82, 496, 506; character of, 496; on civility, 65; and Clark, 303; death of, 514; on death penalty, 626–30, 632; and Dee, 345; and Dolan, 173, 196; dream of, 460; election of, 546–47; eulogy by Andrew, 496, 500–12; and family, 470, 508–9; and Franciscans, 147–48, 151–52, 159; and Fredman, 307–9; on freedom of speech, 47, 53, 76; Grant and, 17, 421; and Graves, 614; interviews with, 35–40, 472–83; Lifetime Achievement in the Arts Medal presentation, 484–85; and Lindsay, 333–34; and Mara, 393; and Martinelli, 144, 146; and Matilda, 461–65, 469, 479, 495, 508; and Mullen, 250; O'Shaughnessy biography of, 486–96, 523–31; O'Shaughnessy friendship with, xv–xix, 17, 57–58, 186–87, 196, 469, 517–21; and Plunkett, 405; and presidency, 56, 221; quoted, 139–40, 171, 179, 190, 197, 220, 237, 274, 289, 300, 305, 337, 373, 400, 418, 514; and Roosevelt, 59; and Russert, 351; and Stone, 110, 114; and Sullivan, 161–62, 164–65; and Supreme Court, 497–99; and Talese, 514–15; tributes to, 514, 517, 521; and writing, 336
Cuomo, Matilda Raffa, 39, 278, 290, 294, 334, 367, 461–71, 479, 491, 495, 508, 652; and Andrew, 443, 454, 565
Cuomo, Sandy, 509
Cuozzo, Jane, 294
Cuozzo, Steve, 490, 514
Curran, Paul J., 278

Curry, Bernard F., Jr., 278
Curry, Cynthia, 278
Curry, Cynthia Foster, 278, 290
Curry, Nancy, 294
Cyrus, Miley, 642

D'Aloisio, Joe, 653
Daly, Michael, 336
D'Amato, Alfonse, 278
Damergis, Mike, 653
Dames, Marvin, 278, 653
Dames, Stacey, 278, 294
Damiani, Tony, 278, 290
D'Ampiere, Florence, 278
D'Andrea, Kim and Bobby, 278
Dandry, Michael, 117, 278, 299, 490, 492; on Cuomo biography, 528; on Rockefeller, 122, 133–35
D'Angelo, Sal, 278
Danzig, Fred, 53
Daronco, Richard, 278, 306, 402, 411, 632
Darwin, Charles, 619
Dave from Mamaroneck (caller), 374
David, Alphonso, 566
Davis, Ernie, 278, 290, 587–88
Davis, Evan, 278
Davis, Lanny, 640
Davis, Ossie, 53, 58, 76, 278, 288, 317, 337, 367; and Dee, 344–48
Davis, Robert, 290
Davis, Troy, 628
Dawson, Mimi Weyforth, 53
Dean, Morton, 278
Dearie, Blossom, 269
death: Comfort on, 174–84; Cuomo (Mario) on, 535; Dee and, 347; Dolan on, 170–71; Jesuits and, 352; Rockefeller and, 124–25
death penalty, 632; Bush (G.W.) and, 553; Cuomo (Andrew) and, 566; Cuomo (Mario) and, 40, 516–17, 626–30; Pope Francis on, 625
de Blasio, Bill, 194, 278, 501, 565; Cuomo (Andrew) on, 452–53
Dee, Ruby, 53, 278, 317, 337, 344–45, 367
DeFabio, Max, 278
DeFiore, Janet, 294
DeJulio, Nick, 278, 371
deKoning, Dixie and Joep, 278
Delaney, C. Glover, 278, 366, 408
Delaney, George, 278
DelBello, Alfred B., 278

DelBello, Dee, 278, 294
DelColliano, Jerry, 75, 278
Delfino, Joe, 305
Delfino, Regina, 294
DelGado, Ely, 467–69
DelGuidice, Michael, 278, 501, 509, 566
Della Monica, Lauren and Armand, 278
Dell'Orefice, Carmen, 278, 294
Delmonico, Jim, 366, 408–9
DeLoach, Cartha "Deke," 278
Deluca, Bill, 278, 653
DelVecchio, Al, 305
DeMarco, Howard, 278, 318
Democratic National Convention keynote speech (Mario Cuomo), 493, 516
Democratic Party: Cahill on, 217; Cuomo (Andrew) and, 445–47, 449, 451; Mayer and, 571–75; WVOX and, 578–79
De Niro, Robert, 296
Dennis, Matt, 278, 384–85
Dennis, Patricia Diaz, 53
Denoff, Sam, 284, 385
Denton, Willard K., 278
DePietro, Brad, 465, 467
Derr, Amandus, 455
Dershowitz, Alan, 86, 210
Derwin, Andrea and Richard, 278
DeSantis, Ron, 431
desegregation, Martinelli and, 137, 141
Despirito, Abramo, 259
Deutch, Donny, 643
Deutsch, Matt, 278
Devaney, Kevin, Jr., 278
Devine, Lydia, 290
Devlin, Kevin, 311
Deyber, Robert, 278, 290
Diamonstein-Spielvogel, Barbaralee, 295
Dicker, Fred, 188–90, 290, 546; Cahill on, 226–27; on Cuomo biography, 527
Dickerson, Patti, 278
Dickerson, Tom, 278, 290
Diddy, P., 587
DiDonato, Pietro, 343
Diedrick, Arthur Hill, 278
Diedrick, Tara Stacom, 278
Dietl, Bo, 297, 561
Dietz, Howard, 269
DiGiacomo, Frank, 278
Dillon, Mark, 306
Dilson, Bernie, 278
DiLullo, Fiorita, 257, 290, 294, 653

DiLullo, Michael, 257, 290, 653
DiMaggio, Joe, 514–15, 613
DiMarco, Joey, 290
DiMeglio, Lou, 290
Dimon, Jamie, 260
Dinan, Terry, 278
Dinkins, David, 278, 501
Dioguardi, Joe, 278
Dionne, E. J., 514
Disney, Anthea, 278
Dispirito, Abramo, 278, 290
Disraeli, Benjamin, 130
Doan, Richard K., 278
Dobbis, Rick, 278
Dobnik, Verna, 339
Doctorow, E. L., 317
Doctorow, Elly, 278
Dodd, Chris, 562
Doherty, Tom, 278
Dolan, Charles, 278
Dolan, Timothy Cardinal, 148, 155, 278, 290, 393, 406, 455, 471, 491; Cahill on, 219; on Cuomo biography, 523; interview with, 170–73; Kelly on, 195–97; and Latimer, 578; on values, 617–23
Dolan, Tom, 278
Dole, Bob, 128, 131
Doll, Bob, 53
Domingo, Placido, 369, 489
Dominus, Susan, 278
Domzal, Angela Smith, 278
Donahue, Phil, 433
Donegan, "Radio" Chuck, 278
Donnelly, John, 278, 391, 484–87, 490–91, 494
D'Onofrio, Belle, 278
D'Onofrio, Nick, 278, 371, 410
Donovan, David, 74, 278, 290, 653
Doorley, Marilyn, 278
Dordit, Arianna, 294
Doscher, Kathy, 311
Douglas, William O., 53, 63, 77
Douglass, Robert, 278, 362
Dowd, Maureen, 278
Dowling, John E. "Jack," 278, 371
Downe, Edward Reynolds, 278
Downey, Helen, 278
Downey, Morton, 253
Doyle, Hugh A., 278, 371
Doyle, P. J., 257
Doyle, Peter, 278
Doyle, Sue, 294

Draddy, Vincent DePaul, 278
Dranginis, Ann, 278, 290, 294, 653
Dream Act: Cahill on, 226; Cuomo (Andrew) on, 447
Drenica, Fadil, 278
Drinan, Robert, 53
Driscoll, David, 278, 653
Driscoll, Jack, 315, 371
Driscoll, John, 278, 427–29
Driscoll, Sean, 278, 653
Drubner, Norman, 278, 652
Duchin, Peter, 242
Duff, Patricia, 278
Duffy, Taryn, 653
Duggan, Dennis, 336
Duggan, Paul, 339
Dukakis, Michael and Kitty, 547
Dullea, Hank, 278
Dunleavy, Steve, 251, 278
Dunn, Paul, 366
Dunne, John, 278
Dunnett, Mark, 278
Durante, Jimmy, 269
D'Urso, Florence, 278
Duryea, Perry, 278
Dussin, Bruno, 241, 260, 290
Dutch Treat Club, 390–91; Bulletin, on Cuomo biography, 529; Graves and, 613–14; Lifetime Achievement Medal presentation, 484–85; luncheon for Cuomo biography, 486–96
Dwyer, Jim, 339
Dylan, Bob, 64

Ebersol, Dick, 278
Eberstadt, Fernanda, 278, 294
Eberstadt, Frederick, 278
economic issues: Cahill on, 214; and Clinton loss, 640; Cuomo (Andrew) on, 446, 450–51, 635; Rockefeller on, 130–31
Eddy, Chris, 262
Edell, Dean, 432
editorial advertising, 69–70
education: Abrams on, 27; Cuomo (Matilda) on, 461–71; Rockefeller on, 129; Shargel on, 209
Egan, Edward Cardinal, 166–67, 219–20, 278, 393
Eggerton, John, 53, 73, 278, 387, 653
Ehlert, Fritz, 290, 654
Eimicke, Bill, 278

Eisenberg, Marc, 278, 290, 654
Eisenhower, Dwight D., 120
Eldridge, Ronnie, 334
Ellerbee, Linda, 549
Ellington, Duke, 386
Elliott, Kevin, 278, 290, 493, 651
Ellis, Anthony, 653
Ellis, Dwight M., 278
Ellsworth, Jack, 279
Elman, Lee, 290
Elson, Edward E., 279, 290
Elton, Wally, 301, 414
Emanuel, Rahm, 639
Emil, Arthur, 303
employment, Cahill on, 214
endorsements: Angiolillo for appellate jus-
    tice, 584–86; Astorino for county
    executive, 580–83; Biaggi for state senate,
    569–70; Bradley for mayor, 589–90; Bush
    (G. H. W.) for president, 546–50; Bush
    (G. W.) for president, 552–54; Cuomo
    (Andrew) for governor, 565–68; Davis for
    mayor, 587–88; Killian for state senate,
    571–75; Latimer for county executive,
    576–79
Endress, Frank, 279, 290, 311–13, 653
energy: Cahill on, 214; Mohl on, 93–104
Engel (doctor), 500
Engel, Eliot, 279
Ensign, Jean, 279, 288, 294, 653
Ensign, Mary, Peter, and Ebie, 279
Entergy, 93–104
equality, Maccioni on, 255
Esposito, Meade, 121
Espy, Freddy Medora Plimpton, 279
Estes, Billy Sol, 108, 110
Estrich, Susan, 553
eulogies, 168–69, 273; for Joe Anastasi, 398–
    400; for Marty Beck, 365–67; for Page
    Morton Black, 424–26; for Jimmy Breslin,
    336–43; for Jimmy Breslin (by Andrew
    Cuomo), 333–35; for Rick Buckley, 376–
    78; for Peggy Burton, 390–91; for Brendan
    Byrne, 423; for Joe Candrea, 372–73; for
    Diane Gagliardi Collins, 392; for Ruby
    Dee, 344–45; for Ruby Dee (by Harry
    Belafonte), 346–48; for Jim Delmonico,
    408–9; for John Driscoll, 427–29; for Sal
    Generoso, 401–3; for Bob Grant, 421; for
    Paul Hutton, 368–69; for Ed Koch (by

Mario Cuomo), 482–83; for Ann Mara (by
    John Mara), 393–97; for Bill Mazer, 422;
    for John McCain (by Henry Kissinger),
    326–28; for Ed McLaughlin (by Rush
    Limbaugh), 430–38; for Peter Mustich,
    370–71; for Tack Nail, 387–89; for Edward
    Noonan Ney, 420; for Stu Olds, 379–81;
    for Caryl Donnelly Plunkett, 404–7; for
    Frances Preston, 355–56; for John
    Pritchard (by Joe Spinelli), 323–25; for
    Ward Quaal, 382–83; for Don Rickles, 354;
    for Marty Rochelle, 417–19; for Nelson
    Rockefeller, 359–64; for Philip Roth, 329–
    32; for Tim Russert, 349–53; for John
    Scully, 414–16; for Joe Slick, 410–13; for
    Mary Jane Wharton (by Kate O'Shaugh-
    nessy Nulty), 357–58
Europe, Maccioni on, 253
Evans, Daniel Jackson, 279
Evans, Joe, 279, 371
Evans, Saralee, 290
Ewing, Patrick, 254

Fahey, John and Kate, 279
Fairchild, John, 279
Fairness Doctrine, 21, 35–36, 46–56, 77, 81,
    383
faith: Cahill on, 220; Cuomo (Mario) on, 538;
    Dolan on, 170; Kelly on, 197
Falcone, Lucille, 294
Falkenburg, Jinx, 279
Falvey, Kevin, 279, 654
family: Comfort on, 177–79, 183; Cuomo
    (Mario) and, 470, 508–9; Cuomo
    (Matilda) on, 465; Kelly on, 195–96
Fanelli, Robert, 279
Fanning, Bill, 279
Farber, Erica, 279, 290, 294, 356
Farkas, Somers, 279
Farley, James A., 249, 279
Farley, Jim, 249
Farley, Katherine, 260, 279, 294
Farood, Pari, 279
Farrell, Herman "Denny," 279
Farrell, Sean Patrick, 339
Farrow, Mia, 279, 329–30, 332
Fasano, Michael, 290
fashion: Maccioni on, 246, 255; Stone on,
    112–13; Suric on, 267
Faso, Tommy, 402

Fay, Joseph A., 279
fear, Maccioni on, 253
Featherstonhaugh, James, 279
Federal Bureau of Investigation (FBI), 323, 639
Federal Communications Commission (FCC), 46, 50–51, 62–64, 67; Goldfluss on, 24–25; on issue advertising, 70; Maines on, 21; Rehr and, 35
Federici, Tony, 259, 279, 290, 652
Feiner, Paul, 279, 463, 576–77
Fekkai, Frederic, 279
Felicione, Lou, 279, 374
Fendrich, Steve, 653
Ferrara, Mike, 319
Ferraro, Geraldine, 294, 549
Ferro, Giancarlo, 279
Fertel, Barry, 317
Feuerbach, Ludwig, 619
Figeroux, Brian, 653
Fillipini, Anne-Marie, 294
Finch, Dee, 279
Fine, William M. "Bill," 279
Finesilver, Suzi, 279, 294
Fink, Larry, 260
Fiori, Pamela, 279
Fiorina, Carly, 144
First Amendment, xviii, 3–81; Abrams and, 26–31; Cuomo discussion on, 32–42; defenders of, 53, 72–81; Fairness Doctrine and, 21, 35, 36, 46–56, 77, 81; Maines and, 21–23; Nail and, 388; Quaal and, 302; Reid and, 45; terrorism and, 57–61; Valenti and, 5–7. See also freedom of speech
First National Bank of Boston v. Bellotti, 70
Fish, Hamilton, 279
Fish, Hamilton, Jr., 279
Fisher, Steve, 279, 290
Fitzgerald, Ed, 279
Fitzgerald, Ella, 385
FitzGerald, Garrett, 279
Fitzgerald, Jim, 279
Fitzsimmons, Dennis, 383
Fiumara, Michael, 653
Flaherty, Tina, 279
Fleischer, Ari, 279
Fluke, Sandra, 18–19
Flusser, Alan, 279
Flynn, William, 279

Foderaro, Lisa, 284
Fogarty, Tom, 279
football: Gifford and, 185–87; Kelly and, 192–95, 198–99
Forbes, Ed, 279
Forbes, Malcolm, 245
Ford, Gerald, 109, 122, 133, 136, 361
Ford, Harold, Jr., 562
Forde, Trevor, 279, 652
Fordham University Press, 649
Foreman, Richard, 279, 290, 366, 653
Forger, Alex, 279
Forstbauer, George, 279
Forster, Arnold, 279
Fosina, Joe, 279, 290, 371
Fosina, John, 279, 371, 410
Fosina, Michael, 279, 653
Fosina, Mickey, 279, 371
Fosina family, 372
Foster, Norman, 279
Four Seasons Restaurant, 251, 259, 296–98
Fourteenth Amendment, 60
Fox, Ray, 279, 391, 484–85, 491
Foxman, Abe, 279
Foy, Eddie, 317
fracking, 634–35; Cahill on, 214–15; Mohl on, 100
Fran (aide), 501
Francis, pope, 147–48, 172, 506, 599, 620, 622; Cahill on, 219; on death penalty, 625; Kelly on, 196–97; Maccioni on, 243–44
Francis, Avril, 653
Franciscans, Lostritto and, 147–60
Franciscans Deliver, 147–49, 156–58
Francis of Assisi, saint, 147–50, 152; prayer of, 160
Frank, George, 279
Frank, Sidney, 279
Frank from Connecticut (fka Mount Vernon; caller), 373
Franklin, Benjamin, 66
Franklin, Joe, 279
Fraser, Ann, 414
Fraser, Richard A. R., 279, 414
Frazier, Joe, 614
Fredman, Andy and Susan, 308
Fredman, Daniel and Stephanie, 308
Fredman, Joshua, Jamie, and Alie, 308
Fredman, Miriam Imber, 294
Fredman, Neil and Michelle, 308

Fredman, Samuel George, 142, 279, 290, 546; and Bradley, 589–90; ninetieth birthday, 304–10, 609–10

freedom of speech, xviii, 5, 49, 64, 66, 68, 70; Abrams on, 26, 30; Bush (Jonathan) on, 561; defending terrible things, 3, 55–56, 65, 68; Grant and, 421; Killory on, 51; Maines on, 21, 23, 51–52. *See also* censorship; First Amendment

Freeh, Louis B., 279, 323

Fremont, Judy, 279, 290, 651

French, Richard, 279

Friars Club, 296–97, 355

Frick, Ford, 249

Fried, Iris, 311

Fried, Liz, 317–18

Friedberg, Francine LeFrak, 294

Friedlander, Adam, 652

Friendly, Fred, 53

Frisch, Frankie, 317

Fritts, Edward, 279, 367

Frucher, Sandy, 509

Fuchs, Marek, 279

Fuchs, Michael, 296–97

Fuerst, C. Murray, 279, 371

Fugazy, William, 250

Fulton, Allison, 279

Funking, Bob, 279

Furey, Chris, 279

Fusco, Frances, 294

Fybush, Scott, 290

Gabelli, Mario, 279

Gagliardi, Danny, 279

Gagliardi, Joe, 279, 306, 392

Gagliardi, Lee, 392

Galbraith, Evan, 279

Gallagher, Cindy Hall, 275, 279, 290, 294, 308, 404, 492, 610, 613–14, 650–51

Gallagher, Kevin, 279

Galletta, Anthony, 372, 374

Gallop, Sammy, 494

Galway, Terry, 515–17

gambling: Maccioni and, 239; Rochelle and, 419

Gambling family, 377

Gannett Company, 75

Garan, Hasan, 279, 654

Garcia, Cecile, 279

Gargano, Charles, 279

Gargiulo, Dessy, 279

Garito, Frank, 279, 371, 402, 411

Garland, Judy, 279

Garner, Dwight, 329

Garner, Richard, 279, 652

gatekeepers: Cuomo (Mario) on, 39; Hastings on, 38, 41

Gaynor, James William, 279

Gazzola, Robert, 279

Gehrig, Lou, 317

Geist, Herman, 142, 279, 297, 577, 587, 653

Geist, Willie, 351

Gelb, Ira, 279

Geller, Leon, 279, 290

Gemelli, Christine, 290

gender issues, O'Reilly and, 8–11

Generoso, Jean, 401

Generoso, Jim, 279, 290, 318, 401, 403, 652

Generoso, Lindsay, 403

Generoso, Sal, 279, 401–3

Gentile, Simoni, 290

Gentner, David, 279, 653

Geoghegan, Arthur, 279, 371

Geraldo, Raul, 290

Gerardi, Andrew, 653

Gerber, Rande, 279

Gerritty, Edward "Ned," 279, 290

Gerstein, Gary, 290

Giambona, Joe, 652

Gibbons, Bill, 279, 301

Gibbons, George, 414

Gibbs, Mara, 653

Gibson, Bob, 279

Gidron, Dick, 279

Gifford, Cody, 186

Gifford, Frank, 185–87, 249, 279, 367

Gigante, Louis P., 279

Gigante, Robert, 279

Gilbert, Phil, Jr., 279

Gildersleeve, Elizabeth, 279

Giles, Bennie, 279, 318

Gilhooley, Jack, 359

Gill, Charlie, 279, 290, 653

Gill, Joan, 279, 294, 653

Gillette, Anita, 484

Gillibrand, Kirsten, 501

Gillman, Jerry, 73, 279, 366

Gillman, Sasha, 73

Gilman, Ben, 279

Ginsburg, Martin, 279

Ginsburg, Ruth Bader, 642

Gioffre, Anthony, 279, 402, 411

Giordano, Pete, 279
Giordano, Vince, 268
Girolamo, Dave, 279
Giuffra, Robert "Bob," Jr., 279
Giuliani, Rudy, 254, 614, 642
Glass, Daniel, 279
Gleason, Jackie, 249
Glickman, Marty, 280
God: Cuomo (Mario) on, 533–38; Lostritto on, 153–54, 160
Godfrey, Peggy, 374
Goldberg, Whoopi, 640
Golden, Marla, 280, 290
Golden Rule, 60–61
Goldenson, Leonard, 388
Goldfluss, Howard, 24–25, 280
Goldfluss, Marvin, 280
Goldmacher, Shane, 567
Goldman, Si, 366, 409
Goldsmith, Marty, 290, 652
Goldstein, Larry, 280
Goldstein, Richard, 339
Goldwater, Barry, 128–29
Golway, Terry, 280, 290, 336, 490, 514
Gonzalez, Diana and Peter, 414
Gonzalez, Greg, 280
Goodale, Arthur, 653
Goodell, Charles, 280
Goodell, Roger, 191, 199, 202
Goodfellow, Karen, 294
Goodman, Julian, 53
Goodman, Roy, 280
Goodwin, Tressa, 286, 652
Gordon, Marsha, 280, 653
Gordon, Rob, 280
Gordon, Shari, 280, 290, 653
Gore, Al, 552–53
Gore, Tipper, 60
Gormé, Eydie, 281, 385
Gorra, Ferris, 280
Gotti, John, 204
Gould, Jack, 73, 280
Gould, Milton, 280
Gouveia, John, 280
Gouz, Ronnie, 294
government: Cahill on, 213–16; Cuomo (Mario) and, 504–6; Rockefeller and, 120, 131
governorship: Cuomo (Andrew) and, 448, 565–68; Cuomo (Mario) and, 478–79, 509
Graff, Rhona, 640

Graham, Donald, 280
Graham, Katherine, 280, 356
Grand, Murray, 280
Granger, Bob, 280
Granger, David, 241
Granholm, Jennifer, 640
Grant, Bob, 13–17, 53, 76, 279, 374, 377, 421, 520
Grant, Emily, 280, 294
Grant, Eugene, 280
Grant, Louie, 280
Gravano, Sammy "The Bull," 204
Graves, Ralph, 280, 490, 613–14
Gravette, E. T. "Bud," 280
Gray, Alfred M., 280
Gray, Robert, 280
Gray, Vernon, 280
Graziano, Jennifer, 280, 653
Greco, Buddy, 280
Greeley, Horace, 33, 43, 54, 74, 342
Green, George, 596
Green, Mrs., 374
Greenberg, David, 514
Greenberg, Jeff, 290
Greenberg, Paul, 548
Greenberg, Sarah Fagan, 339
Greene, Bob, 280
Greene, Teddy, 280, 371
Greenman, Josh, 339
Greeven, Rainer and Regina, 280, 290
Gregory, David, 351, 560
Gregory, Dick, 76, 280
Gregory, Jamee and Peter, 280
Gren, Armel, 280
Griffin, Bill and Peter, 280
Grondahl, Paul, 490, 514
Grudens, Richard, 280
Guberti, Rich, 290
Guida, Tommy, 280
Guido, Tonny, 280
Guild, Calla and Ralph, 280
Gund, Agnes, 294
gun violence: Cahill on, 222–23; Cuomo (Andrew) on, 447, 455–59; Las Vegas shooting, 631–33
Gupte, Pranay, 280
Gurfein, Murray, 78
Gurney, Bill, 280
Guyre, Michael, 297

Haas, Evie, 280, 294, 371
Habeeb, Mark, 653

Hackett, Buddy, 280, 385
Haidar, John, 280
Haley, Sheila and Arthur, 280
Hall, Stella Vinci, 280
Halleck, Charlie, 34
Hallingby, Jo, 290, 294
Halloran, Edward J. "Biff," 280
Halperin, Jason P. W., 280
Halsman, Philippe, 613
Hamburg, Joan, 377
Hamill, Denis, 336
Hamill, Pete, xvii, 183, 280, 336, 339–40, 367,
    508, 520, 546, 607
Hamilton, Alexander, 79
Handler, Chelsea, 643
Handler, Lynn, 294
Hanley, Jeff, 280, 653
Hannity, Sean, 53, 71, 435
Hannock, Frieda, 356
Harding, Ray, 280
Hardt, Bob, 514
Hargrove, Wade, 280
Haring, Bernard, 165–66
Harmon, Anne, 280, 294
Harms, Bev and Frank, 366
Harnick, Sheldon, 390, 484
Harper, John, 53, 280, 653
Harriet (aide), 403
Harriman, Averell, 123, 130, 280
Harrington, B. J., 280, 653
Harrington, William, 280, 653
Harris, Ron, 290
Harrison, Michael, 53, 74, 280, 290
Hart, Kitty Carlisle, 280, 294, 485, 614
Hart, Lorenz, 385, 603
Harvey, Paul, xvii, 268, 351
Hastedt, Graham, 280, 290
Hastings, Gordon, 33, 38–39, 41, 280, 524
hate crimes laws, Cuomo (Andrew) on, 456
Hayde, Donald, 290
Hayden, Carl, 250, 280
Hayden, Cindy, 250
Hayden, Michael, 640
Hayes, Chris, 640
Hayes, Cynthia, 290
Hayes, Gabby, 280
Hayes, Guss, 280
Hayes, Isaac, 355
Hayward, Brooke, 280
health care: Comfort on, 183; Rockefeller
    on, 129

Heath, Ted, 280
Hedberg, Mark and Paul, 280
Hegarty, Bill, 280, 318
HELP USA, 466, 472, 474
Hendel, Rich, 280, 650
Hennessy, John, 280, 290
Henry, Jim, 311
Hensel, John, 366
Hentoff, Nat, 53, 73, 77, 280, 290, 336
Hentz, Ned, 280
Hergenhan, Joyce, 280
Herman, Billy, 290
Herman, Scott, 280, 607–8
Hernandez, Luis, 280, 290
Hernandez, Maggie, 290
Hernandez, Ramiro, 280
Hertzberg, Hendrik, 490, 514
Hevesi, Alan, 572
Hibberd family, 414
Hibbler, Al, 280
Hicks, David, 280
Hicks, Keegan, 280
Hicks, Nicole, 280
Hield, Debbie, 290
Higgins (priest), 398
Higgins, Michael, 280
Higgins, Will, 251
Hill, Anita, 549
Hillel, rabbi, 537
Hillelson, Louis, 280
Hilpert, Kris, 280
Hilson, Gail, 294
Hinckley, David, 53, 74, 280, 336, 384, 611, 653
Hinman, George, 120
Hobby, Oveta Culp, 356
Hoffer, Eric, 49
Hoffman, Milton, 280, 305–6
Hoffman, Ronald, 653
Hogan, Bill, 366
Hoge, Jim, 280
Holder, Eric, 501, 639
Hollis, Phil, 280
Holm, Jim, 280, 290
Holmes, Napoleon, 280
Holmes, Oliver Wendell, 28, 69, 77, 537
Holzer, Harold, 280
Hommel, George, 280
Hoopes, Townsend "Tim," 280
Hoover, J. Edgar, 106
hope: Dolan on, 170–71; McCain and, 327
HOPE Community Services Gala, 311–13

Horowitz, David, 88
Horton, Keith, 366
Hosking, Bob, 366
Howard, John, 501
Howard, Keith, 465, 467
Howe, Peter, 278
Howe, Todd, 280
Hruska, Roman, 53
Hubbard, Howard, 280
Hubbard, Stanley, 75, 383, 388
Hughes, Cathy, 356
Hughes, Ed, 280
Humbert, Marc, 546
Hume, Clement, 280, 653
Humphrey, Hubert, 122, 552
Huntington, Judy, 280, 290
Hussein, Saddam, 165
Hutton, Bobby, 280, 653
Hutton, Joe, 280
Hutton, Paul, 280, 368–69
Hyden, Ivar, 317
Hyland, Bob, 280

Iacocca, Lee, 250
Iannuzzi, John, 280
Ickes, Harold, 553
Idoni, Tim, 280, 371, 392, 402
Iglesias, Julio, 239
immigrants, 640; Cahill on, 215–16, 225–26;
    Trump and, 644–45
Imus, Don, 12–14, 71, 76, 280; Bush (Billy) on,
    559–62; Grant on, 15–17; Maines on, 21
indecency, 63–64, 66; Reid on, 34–35
Indelicato, Charlene, 319
Indian Point, 93–99, 101
infallibility, Cuomo (Mario) on, 477
infrastructure: and Clinton loss, 642; Rocke-
    feller and, 131
Innocence Project, 628
Iona College, 315; Driscoll and, 427–29; Kelly
    and, 191, 195
Iran-Contra affair, 199
Iraq war: Cuomo (Mario) on, 535; Sullivan
    on, 164–65
Irish Americans: Dolan and, 523; Kennedy
    and, 647; Russert and, 352; Talese and,
    515
Isaacson, Walter, 280
Isabel (caller), 374
Isdale, Dooie, 302
Isdale family, 414

Israel: Bush (G. H. W.) and, 550; and Clinton
    loss, 641; Driscoll and, 428; Mazer and,
    422; Reid and, 44
Israel, Michael, 280, 653
issue advertising, 69–70
Italian Americans: Cuomo (Matilda) and,
    463, 465; Gagliardi family and, 392;
    Maccioni on, 256; Talese on, 515
Italy, Maccioni on, 253–55

Jackson, Dennis, 53, 74, 290, 653
Jackson, Janet, 24–25, 67
Jackson, Jesse, 16, 561
Jacobs, Billy, 290
Jacobson, Adam, 280
Jager, John, 376
James, Alton, 391
James, Barbara Curry, 280
James, Ed, 387
James, Letitia, 11
James, O. Aldon, 528
Jamison family, 414
Jarrett, Valerie, 639
Javits, Jacob K., 53, 59–60, 190, 280, 288, 367
Javits, Marian, 280, 294
Jedell, Joan, 290
Jefferson, Thomas, 26, 79–81, 457
Jeffersontown, KY, supermarket shootings,
    455
Jessell, Harry, 53, 74, 387, 653
Jesuits, 159, 349–50, 352
Jews: Bush (G. H. W.) and, 550; Central
    Synagogue interfaith service, Andrew
    Cuomo speech, 455–59; Clark and, 303;
    Cuomo (Mario) and, 480; Roth and, 331;
    Scully and, 415
Jimmy (doorman), 290
Joanne (caller), 374
Jobs, Steve, 270
John Paul II, pope, 165–66, 620; Maccioni on,
    243, 254–55
Johnson, Broaddus "Speed," 280
Johnson, Gary, 641
Johnson, Lady Bird, 356
Johnson, Lyndon B., 105–8, 110, 113, 119, 280
Johnson, Maricelly, 280
Johnson, Peter, 280, 398
Johnson, Peter, Jr., 159
Johnson, Richard, xv, 281, 290, 297
Johnson, Robert, 290
Johnson, Robin, 281

Johnson, Thomas, 108, 280, 291
Johnson, Woody, 193–94
Jones, Bob, 281, 291
Jones, Jack, 235, 281
Jones, Jerry, 187, 281
Jones, Shirley, 281
Jordan (priest), 148
Jordan, Hamilton, 547
Jordan, Vernon, 298
Joseph, Myron, 281
Josey, David, 653
journalism: Breslin and, 336–38, 340–42;
    Cuomo (Mario) and, 508; Donnelly and,
    486; Maines and, 21–23; Nail and, 387–89;
    Russert and, 349–53
Joyce, James, 66
Joyce, John M., 281
Joyce, Mike, 281
Jude, saint, 173
Judge, Mychal, 147–48, 155–56
judges: Rochelle and, 417–19; Shargel on,
    207–8
Judis, Bernice, 356, 376
Juhring, Judy, 281
juries, Shargel on, 205–7

Kaepernick, Colin, 640
Kafferman, Charlie, 258–59, 281, 291, 329–32,
    652
Kaiser, Larry, 291
Kalman, George S., 281
Kaltenborn, H. V., 408
Kane, Noel, 291
Kang, Michael C. Y., 281
Kaplan, Sis, 365
Kaplar, Rick, 53, 281
Karmazin, Mel, 53, 281, 291
Kasowitz, Marc E., 8
Kathwari, Farooq, 281
Kaufman, George S., 281
Kaufman, William "Whitey," 281
Kavanagh, Charles, 281
Kaye, Judith, 294, 520
Keats, John, 495
Keefe, Nancy Q., 281, 288, 294, 336, 546
Keegan, Pat, 281, 291
Keggi, John, 281, 654
Kelliher, Dick, 281
Kellner, Irwin, 281
Kelly, Alfred, Jr., 191–203, 281, 291
Kelly, Dorothy Ann, 371

Kelly, Jane, 294, 366
Kelly, John, 281, 291, 366
Kelly, John "Shipwreck," 249–50, 281
Kelly, Megyn, 9, 143
Kelly, Peggy, 195, 203
Kelly, William, 291
Kemp, Jack, 225, 281
Kempton, Murray, 508
Ken from Pelham (caller), 373
Kendall, Irving, 281
Kendig, David, 373
Kennedy, Anthony, 497
Kennedy, Bill, 281
Kennedy, Brian, 281
Kennedy, Edward, 500
Kennedy, John F., 281, 534, 552, 579, 647;
    Breslin and, 337–38; Cahill on, 222;
    Graves on, 614; Stone on, 105–7, 110–11
Kennedy, John F., Jr., 184, 281, 453, 522
Kennedy, Marie, 294
Kennedy, Mary Kerry, 281
Kennedy, Robert F., 106, 110, 222, 281, 534,
    552, 579
Kennedy, William, 281, 521
Kensing, Hank, 281
Kenton, Stanley Newcomb, 281
Kern, Jerome, 385
Kerry, John, 562
Ketcham, Bill, 414
Kettner, Susan, 281, 318, 653
Keys, Bill, 301
Khan, Khizr, 640
Kiernan, Doc, 281, 371
Kilgannon, Corey, 281
Killian, Julie, 571–75
Killoran, Jim, 281, 652
Killory, Diane, 51, 53
Kimball, Robert, 391
Kinal, Destiny, 281
King, Bob, 366
King, John Wells, 53
King, Larry, 281, 296, 351, 550
King, Martin Luther, Jr., 386, 534, 622
King, Nancy, 117–18, 120, 122, 130
Kingman, Doug, 281
Kinosian, Mike, 75, 281, 291
Kirkus Reviews, on Cuomo biography, 527
Kissinger, Henry, 1, 125, 281, 291, 360, 642,
    654; on McCain, 326–28
Kissinger, Sam, 281, 371
Kitchen, Kraig, 593–95

Kitchen, Ruth, 371
Klavan, Gene, 279
Klein, Jeff, 569–70, 640
Klein, Sam, 281
Klestine, Fred, 350
Klieman, Rikki, 281
Klose, Bob, 366
Klosterman, Luciana, 281
Klotz, Winnie, 368–69
Klugman, Arnie, 371
Klugman, Arnold, 281
Knoll, Steve, 53
Know Thyself principle, Cuomo (Mario) and, 497–99
Koch, Edward I., 482–83, 500, 503–4, 614
Koch brothers, 96
Kondylis, Costas, 281
Koplowitz, Kay, 356
Koppell, Oliver, 281
Kornsweet, Jack, 281, 371
Koteen, Bernie, 281, 654
Kovi, Paul, 297
Kowalski, Laura, 294
Kozacko, Dick, 366
Kragle, Ralph, 291, 652
Kram, Barbara, 653
Kramer, Marcia, 281, 508, 567
Kramer, Michael, 546, 548
Krasnow, Erwin, 53, 73, 281, 291, 652–53
Kraus, Rainer, 53, 281, 654
Kreindler, Jack, 264
Kremer, Arthur "Jerry," 281
Krenck, Debby, 339
Kriendler, Bob, 281
Kriendler, Pete, 281
Krimendahl, Emilia St. Amand, 281, 292, 294
Kristofferson, Kris, 355
Krupsak, Mary Anne, 503
Kudlow, Larry, 281, 642
Kuhnn, Sottha, 264
Kuralt, Charles, xvii, 268
Kurson, Ken, 490, 514
Kushner, Jared, 641

LaBarbera, Cappy, 291
labor, Gifford on, 186–87
Labunski, Steve, 389
Lacy, Bill, 281
Lady Gaga, 515
LaFarge, Albert, 281
Lafayette, Reggie, 306

LaFontaine, Patti, 281
LaGuardia, Fiorello, 317
Lamb, Brian, 281
Lamb, Rich, 567
Lamond, Jim, 405
Lance, Bert, 547
Langone, Ken, 260
Langston, Andy, 366
Lanvin, Harry, 281
Lanza, Mario, 369
Lape, Bob, 281
LaRosa, Julius, 281
Lascola, Marguerite, 281, 294
Lasker, Albert "Bunny," 281
LaSorsa, Suzanne and John, 281
LaSorsa family, 311–13
Las Vegas: Maccioni on, 239; shooting, 631–33
Latimer, George, 281, 291, 571–72, 652; endorsement for county executive, 576–79
Lauer, Matt, 557
Lauren, Jerry, 281
Lauren, Lenny, 281
law: Angiolillo and, 584–86; Cahill on, 212–27; Shargel on, 204–11
Law, Bernard Cardinal, 164
Lawrence, Clare, 294
Lawrence, Steve, 281, 385
Lazarri, Franco, 258
Lazio, Rick, 281
Lazzari, Franco, 291, 653
leadership, Kelly on, 202
League of Women Voters, 57
Leahy, Patrick, 53
Leahy, William, 196
Leal, Ron, 281
Lebron, Michael "Lionel," 9–10, 281, 339, 598–99
Le Cirque, 236–48, 251, 261, 491; Rickles at, 354; Wells and, 602–6
Lederman, Gil, 653
Lefkowitz, Louis, 123–24, 216, 281, 359, 362
Lehman, Wendy Vanderbilt, 281
Lehrman, Lewis, 373
Leisler, Jacob, 317
Lemond, Jim, 281
Lenihan, Jane, 281
Lennon, Scott, 281
Lenok, Paul, 281
Lerner, Mark, 281, 649

Lesniewski, Jack, 281
LeSourd, Jacques, 281
Lessner, Al and Bob, 366
Levine, Ed, 281, 384
Levine, Susan and Jedd, 281
Levitt, Arthur, 281
Levitte, Larry, 366
Lew, Shim, 281
Lewis, C. S., xviii
LGBT issues, 582; Cuomo (Andrew) and, 565; Lostritto on, 155–56
libel laws, Abrams on, 29
Library Bookwatch, on Cuomo biography, 526
Library of American Broadcasting, 73, 356
Librett, Arthur, 281
Librett, Charlie, 281
Librett, Mitchell, 281
Librett family, 371
Licalzi, Mike, 291
Lieberman, Joe, 553, 560
Liguori, Jim, 427–28
Limbaugh, Rush, 2, 18–20, 53, 71, 281, 408, 591, 639; and McLaughlin, 430–38, 593–97
Lincoln, Abraham, 59, 81, 457–58, 506
Lindbergh, Charles, 614
Lindsay, John V., 34, 122–23, 249, 281, 288, 333, 614
Lindsay, Mary, 294
Lionel (Michael Lebron), 9–10, 281, 339, 598–99
Lipow, Walter, 281
Lipps, Penny, 281
Litchfield County Times, 650
Littlejohn, Richard, 281, 652
lobbying, 33–34
Lobo, Cynthia, 281
Lodato, Jimmy, 281
Loeb, John L., 281
Loeb, Peter and John, Sr., 281
Lombardi, Sal, 281, 291
Lombardo, Kim, 281, 294
Lombardo, Phil, 33, 281, 291, 380, 408, 654
Lomenzo, John, 281–82
Lomonaco, Michael, 282
Long Island Railroad, 131
Lopolito, Jimmy, 282
Lostritto, Paul, 147–60, 282
love: Cuomo (Mario) on, xvii; Teilhard on, 493, 532, 537
Love, Iris, 294

Lovett, Ken, 574
Lowe, E. Nobles, 282, 496
Lowe, Jim, 282
Lowey, Nita, 282, 291, 294, 306, 309, 546
Lowey, Steven, 282
Luddy, William, 142, 282, 306, 609
Luers, Wendy and Bill, 282
Lufkin, Dan, 282
Lungiarello, Mark, 282
Lupica, Mike, 336, 490, 508, 514
Lynch, Dan, 282, 530–31
Lynch, John and Chris, 366
Lynch, Loretta, 501

Maas, Peter, xv, 282, 336, 491
Maccioni, Egidiana, 234, 239, 244, 252–54, 282, 291, 294, 603
Maccioni, Marco, 238, 241, 261, 282, 291
Maccioni, Mario, 240, 282, 291
Maccioni, Massimo Sirio, 238, 240
Maccioni, Mauro, 240, 261, 282, 291
Maccioni, Sabrina Wender, 239–40, 282, 292, 295
Maccioni, Sergio, 653
Maccioni, Sirio, 237–48, 251–56, 261, 282, 291, 305, 354, 602–4
MacCourtney, Leo, 282
MacGillis, Alec, 291
Mackin, Kevin, 147–48, 282, 291
Maddow, Rachel, 639
Madeleine, Guru, 282, 653
Madison, James, 46, 77–78
Maggiore, John, 501
Mago, Jane, 75, 291
Magrino, Susan, 282
Mahlman, Bob, 366
Mahoney, David, 282
Mahoney, Joe, 339
Maier, Howard, 509
Mainelli, John, 282
Maines, Patrick, 1, 21–23, 51–53, 73, 282
Maisano, James, 282, 371
Maitland, Patrick, 282, 653
Malara, Anthony, 282, 367, 409
Malkemus, George, 257, 282
management, Kelly on, 202
Mancuso, Bob, 291
Mancuso, Ed, 282, 291, 653
Mancuso, Kit, 282
Manero, Nick, 282
Mangialardo, Squeegie, 282

Manilow, Barry, 355
Mann, Bernie, 365
manners, 197. *See also* civility
Mansell, Henry, 282
Mara, Ann, 282, 393–97
Mara, John, 282, 291, 393–97
Mara, Susan, 282
Mara, Wellington, 185–86, 193, 198, 282, 288, 367, 393, 396
Marcello, Carlos, 106
Marcucci, Carl, 53, 75, 291
Margittai, Tom, 282, 297, 605
Mari, Matthew, 206, 211, 259, 282
Mariani, John, 241, 282
Marino, Joe, 339
Marino, John, 282, 546, 566
marriage: Martinelli on, 138; for priests, Lostritto on, 155
Marrone, Bob, 282
Marshack, Megan, 125–26
Marshall, Al, 125
Marshall, Alton, 282
Marshall, Henry, 108
Martell (T. J.) Foundation, 355–56
Martin, Spencer, 282
Martinelli, Angelo, 137–46
Martinelli, Carol, 138, 146
Martinelli, Ralph, 139–40
Martinelli, Ralph, Jr., 137–38
Martinez (commentor), 61
Martino, Paolo, 282
Martino, Renato, 254
Marvin, Mary, 294
Marx, Karl, 619
Mary Magdelene, saint, 157
Mason, Dan, 608
Masson, Charles, 261, 291
Mastronardi, Nick and Val, 282
Matalin, Mary, 560
Mathis, Bill, 399
Matthews, Chris, 282, 351, 521, 636
Maurer (doctor), 500
Maxwell, Bertram, 653
Maxwell, Shirley, 282, 653
Maxwell, Walter, 282, 366
May, Walter, 53
Mayer, Shelley, 571–72, 574
Mays, Lowry, 75, 282, 388
Mazer, Bill, 282, 422
McAlpin, Tim, 282
McAuliffe, Terry, 642

McBain, Gavin K., 282
McBride, Caryn, 294
McBride, Mary Margaret, 282
McCabe, Charlie and Lynn, 282
McCabe, Kevin, 282
McCain, John, 143, 326–28, 553, 560
McCall, Carl, 282
McCarthy, Charles F., 282
McCarthy, James, 162, 282
McCarthy, Jerry, 428
McCarthy, John, 282
McCarthy, Michael, 291
McCarthy, Richard, 282, 291
McCarty, Scott, 282
McCaughey, Betsy, 282
McConnell, Bob, 366
McCord, Charles, 560
McCorkle, Susannah, 282, 294
McCormick, Brian, 282, 291
McCormick, JoAnne, 294
McCormick Foundation, 383
McCourt, Malachy, 282, 336, 531
McCoy, Bernie, 282
McCoy, Kevin, 339
McCullough, David, 282, 614
McCullough, Frank, Jr., 282
McCullough, Frank, Sr., 282
McCurdy, Bob, 282
McDonald, Patty, 621
McDonald, Steven, 621
McDonnell, Claudia, 282, 291, 294, 492, 530
McDonnell, John, 282
McDonnell, Tim Mara, 393
McElveen, Bill, 53, 282
McFadden, Cynthia, 282
McFadden, Steve, 282
McFarlane, Bud, 199
McGillicuddy, Connie, 282
McGovern, J. Raymond, 282
McGrath (priest), 148
McGrath, Felix, 282
McGrath, Gene, 282
McGrath, Kevin Barry, 282, 291, 653
McGrory, Mary, 508, 546
McKenna, John, 291
McKibben, Bill, 366
McKnight, Renate, 282, 294, 653
McKnight, Thomas, 282, 653
McLaughlin, Ed, 282, 366, 408, 593–94, 596–97; Limbaugh on, 430–38
McLaughlin, Pat, 282, 594

McLaughlin, Rosemary, 371
McLeod, Russell, 653
McMahon, Daniel J., 307
McManus, Bob, 514
McManus, James, 282, 291
McMullan, Patrick, 282, 291
McNamara, Patrick, 282
McNeil, Robert, 53
McNeil, Robin, 301
McNulty, Joy, 261
McShane, Joseph, 282, 291, 617, 650
McSweeney, Bep, 282, 653
McVeigh, Timothy, 61
Meacham, Jon, 351, 591, 597
Meade, George, 122
meaning, Cuomo (Mario) on, 533–38
media: and Clinton loss, 639–40, 642;
    Cuomo (Mario) and, 508, 514–15; and
    Fairness Doctrine, 46–56; Maines and,
    20–22; McLaughlin and, 430–39; Rather
    and, 90–91; Rockefeller and, 125–26;
    Trump supporters on, 636–37
Media Institute, xviii
Meehan, Dottie, 311
Mehiel, Dennis, 282, 546
Meledandri, Roland, 282
Mellekas, Kim, 282
Mellekas, Steve, 282, 652
Mendelsohn, Jack and Frieda, 306
mental-health issues, Cahill on, 223
Mentoring Program, Matilda Cuomo and,
    461–71
Mercer, Johnny, 269, 603
Mercer, Mabel, 282, 288, 294
Mercer family, 577
Merlino, Herve, 282
Mermelstein, Ben, 282, 371
Merrill, Robert, 282, 369, 488–90
Mersfelder, Jim, 282
Mertz, Jim and Leggy, 301, 414
Messmer, Jack, 53, 75, 282
#MeToo movement, 8–11
Metzger, Geneive Brown, 294
Meyer, J. Edward, 282
Meyer, John, 168
Meyers, Michael, 60
Miceli, Frank, 282, 653
Michaelian, Edwin G., 129, 142, 282, 288, 306,
    579, 581, 609
Michaelian, Joyce, 294
Michaels, Randy, 282

Michelangelo, 157
Middei, Paolo, 262, 283, 291
Middle East, Reid on, 44
Middleton, Velma, 613
Migliucci, Barbara, 283, 291, 294
Migliucci, Joseph, 250, 283, 291
Migliucci, Mama Rose, 250, 294
Migliucci, Mario, 283
Milano, Bob, 283
Mill, John Stuart, 58, 620
Miller, Arthur, 329
Miller, Brett, 283
Miller, Cay, 283, 294
Miller, Dan, 653
Miller, Elmer, 371
Miller, Faith, 285, 291, 294
Miller, Henry, 283
Miller, Katherine, 283, 653
Miller, Marcia, 283, 294
Miller, Mark, 75, 258, 283, 291, 387
Miller, Sondra, 291, 294
Miller, Stanley, 283
Mills, Clif, Jr., 283, 653
Milner, Philip, 283
Miner, Jackie and Roger, 283
Miner, Stephanie, 567
Mintun, Peter, 283
Mion, Suzi, 291
Mirabile, Sandy, 291
miracles, Comfort on, 177
Mitchell, Andrea, 11
Mitchell, Jay, 53, 75, 291
Modell, Bill, 283, 500
Modell, Michael, 500
Modell, Shelby, 283, 294
Moger-Bross, Wendy, 291
Mohl, Bill, 93–104
Molinaro, Marc, 567
Mondello, Joe, 291
Montabello, Joseph, 283
Montclare, Louise, 283
Monturo, Chris, 283, 652
Mooney, Bill, 283
Moonves, Les, 561
Moore, Garry, 283, 301, 414
Moore, Mark, 339
Moore, Michael, 38
Moore, Walter, 283
morality, Cuomo (Mario) on, 518, 533–38
Moran, Tom, 283
Moretti, Tommy, 250, 283

Morgenthau, Robert, 283
Morosani, Bunny and Daniel, 283
Morris, Ginny Hubbard, 356
Morrison, Gem, 652
Morrow, Hugh, 119, 125–26
Mosch, Bev and Woody, 283
Moscowitz, Eva, 308
Moses, Robert, 121
Motley, Arthur H. "Red," 283
Mount Vernon, NY, 587–88
Moxie, Carl, 283, 653
Moynihan, Daniel Patrick, 53, 72, 80, 283, 579
Moynihan, Liz, 283, 294
Mudd, Sidney, 283, 371
Mueller, Robert, 89
Mullen, Bill, 374
Mullen, Kathy, 294
Mullen, Tom, 250, 283, 291
Mulligan, William Hughes, 140–42, 283, 649
Mulrow, William, 283, 566
Mummert, Betty Ann, 283, 291
Mundinger family, 414
Mungeer, Tom, 283, 398, 652
Murdoch, Rupert, 35–37, 388, 639
Murphy, Dan, 118, 283, 291
Murphy, Deborah and Declan, 283, 291, 653
Murphy, Erin, 653
Murphy, Mark, 283, 291, 405
Murphy, Marla, 405
Murphy, Nora, 294
Murphy, Ryan, 291
Murphy, Ted, 283, 291
Murphy, Tom, 388
Murphy, Tony, 318
Murtagh, John, 283
Muscarella, Ernie, 283
Mushnick, Phil, 607
Mustal, Stanley Frank, 283
music, 231–35; Black and, 424–26; Cuomo (Mario) and, 493–95, 537–38; Hutton and, 368–69; Maccioni and, 239–40; Osgood and, 268–70; Williams and, 384–86
Mustich, Peter, 370–71
Myles, Tinker, 414

Nachbaur, Fred, 283, 291, 649
Naclerio, Richie, 283
Nadler, Mark, 484
Nail, Dawson "Tack," 75, 283, 387–89
Namath, Joe "Willie," 399
Nantz, Jim, 543

Napolitano, Joe, 262, 283, 291, 652
Nappi, Jerry, 283, 652
Nardone, Dennis, 283, 653
Nash, Jackie Neary, 283, 294
Nash, Ogden, 66
National Association of Broadcasters, 48, 52, 365
National Radio Broadcasters Association, 365
National Security Agency, Kelly on, 201
NATO, 639
natural law, Cuomo (Mario) on, 536
Neary, Jimmy, 251, 263, 283, 291
Neary, Una, 263, 283
negativism, Teilhard on, 535
Neil, Emancia, 652
Neilson, Roxanne, 294
Nelson, Lars-Erik, 546
Nelson, Willie, 355
Netanyahu, Benjamin, 641
Neuharth, Al, 73
Neuhoff, Beth, 283, 294
Neumann, Vanessa, 283
Neuwirth, H. D. "Bud," 283
Nevins, John, 314
Nevins, Sheila, 243
Newfield, Jack, 283, 336, 500, 508, 520–21
Newman, Dean, 283
Newman, Eric, 283, 649
New Rochelle, NY, 646; Bramson and, 580; Candrea and, 372–73; Carroll and, 318–20; Collins and, 392; Generoso and, 401; Harbor Patrol, 319; Kelly and, 203; Mustich and, 370–71; Vitulli and, 411–12
Newseum, 73
Newsmax, 85–89
New York Herald Tribune, 33, 43, 54, 74, 342
New York State: Cahill on, 214, 218–19; Cuomo (Andrew) on, 455–59; Cuomo (Mario) on, 513; Independent Democratic Conference, 569; Mohl on, 95–96; state senate races, 569–75; State Supreme Court, 584–86
New York State Broadcasters Association, 351–52, 365, 377
New York Times: and Breslin, 338–39; and Cahill, 225; and Clinton loss, 640; and Niccolini, 259
New York Times Co. v. Sullivan, 79
Ney, Edward Noonan, 283, 291, 420
Ney, Judy, 291, 294

Nguyen, Vu, 291
Niccolini, Julian, 251, 259, 283, 291, 296–97, 605–6, 652
Niccolini, Lisa, 295
Nicholas, Cristyne, 283
Nicolai, Aileen, 306
Nicolai, Angelique, 306
Nicolai, Frank, 306
Nietzsche, Friedrich, 619
Nixon, Agnes, 356
Nixon, Cynthia, 452
Nixon, Richard, 67, 74, 119, 129, 283; Maccioni on, 245–46; Stone on, 106, 109, 114
Noble, Ray, 494
Nolan, Dick, 283
Nolan, Jasper, 283
Noletti, Jimmy, 283
Noonan, Margaret, 283, 291, 295, 351, 649
Norten, Enrique, 283
North, Ollie, 199
Norton, Alex, 283, 371
Norville, Deborah, 283, 291, 295, 351, 377, 384
Norwick, Ken, 75, 291
nostalgia, O'Shaughnessy on, 520
Noto, Paul, 283
Notre Dame speech (Mario Cuomo), 497, 506, 517
Novik, Dick, 366
Novik, Harry, 283
Novik, Richard, 283
NRA, Cuomo (Andrew) on, 447
nuclear power, Mohl on, 93–104
Nulty, Amelia Jane, 283, 291, 295, 358, 655
Nulty, Flynn Thayer, 283, 291, 655
Nulty, Kate O'Shaughnessy, 295, 357–58, 601, 655
Nulty, Tucker Thomas, 283, 291, 655
Nye, Daniel, 283
Nyre, Joseph, 283, 291

Obama, Barack, 501, 637, 639, 641, 644; Ailes and, 85; Kelly and, 200; Martinelli and, 145; Roth and, 331; Smith and, 130, 133; Stone and, 110
Obama, Michelle, 641
O'Brian, Jack, 283
O'Brien, Bill, 283
O'Brien, Des, 283
O'Brien, Edwin, 283
O'Brien, Jack, 249
O'Brien, John, 283

O'Brien, Kate, 283, 295, 649
obscenity, 64, 67; Abrams on, 29; Cuomo discussion on, 32–42; Goldfluss on, 24–25; Reid on, 78; Rockefeller and, 131–32. *See also* First Amendment
Occupy Wall Street, 189–90
O'Conner, Dan, 501
O'Connor, John Cardinal, 141–42, 162, 167, 176, 288, 367; Dolan on, 617–23; Maccioni on, 243, 254
O'Connor, John J., 73
O'Connor, Kathleen Plunkett, 283, 295, 652
O'Connor, Sandra Day, 283
O'Donnell, Lawrence, 351, 642
O'Donoghue, Brian, 283, 509
O'Dwyer, Paul, 283
Offit, Sidney, 284, 491, 524
O'Grady, Jim, 366
O'Halloran (priest), 401, 403
O'Hare, Joseph, 283, 291, 650
O'Keeffe, Michael, 283, 339
O'Keeffe, Valerie Moore, 283, 295
Oken, Anita, 291, 295
Olds, Kim, 295, 380
Olds, Stu, 284, 379–81, 389
O'Leary, Mary, 283
Omega Point, Teilhard on, 536
Omega Society speech (Mario Cuomo), 533–38
Oneglia, Cathy and Greg, 283
Oneglia, Ellen, 284, 291, 295, 653
Oneglia, Louisa and Francis, 284
Oneglia, Ray, 284, 291, 653
Oneglia, Rod, 284
O'Neil, P. J., 371
O'Neill, James, 283, 316–18
O'Neill, Paddy, 283
O'Neill, Tip, 200, 569
O'Neill, William, 283, 291, 653
Opie and Anthony episode, 38, 65, 71
Oppenheimer, Suzi, 283, 549, 572
Oprah, 356
Orden, Erica, 490, 514
O'Reilly, Bill, 8–11, 71, 283
O'Reilly, William F. B., 283
organized crime: Pritchard and, 324; Shargel on, 204, 208–9
O'Rourke, Andrew, 176, 283, 472–75, 500, 577–79, 581
Orth, Maureen, 352
Orwell, George, 77

Osborne, Antoinette, 653
Osgood, Charles, xvii, 268–70, 284
O'Shaughnessy, Alice, 283
O'Shaughnessy, Cara Ferrin, 283, 291, 295, 655
O'Shaughnessy, Catherine Tucker, 283, 288, 293
O'Shaughnessy, Coco, 284, 291
O'Shaughnessy, David Tucker, 284, 352, 651, 655; and Buckley, 376–77; and Nail, 389
O'Shaughnessy, Isabel Grace, 284, 295, 655
O'Shaughnessy, Jack, 284, 288
O'Shaughnessy, Jesse, Runway, Babe, and Puppy Sam, 284
O'Shaughnessy, John, 284
O'Shaughnessy, Julie, 284, 291, 295
O'Shaughnessy, Kate Wharton, 284, 291, 388–89, 651
O'Shaughnessy, Kelly, 295
O'Shaughnessy, Lacey, 284, 291
O'Shaughnessy, Laura, 284
O'Shaughnessy, Lily Anna, 284, 291, 295, 655
O'Shaughnessy, Luna, 284, 288
O'Shaughnessy, Matthew Thayer, 284, 291, 651, 655
O'Shaughnessy, Nancy Curry, 284, 352
O'Shaughnessy, William: biography of Mario Cuomo, 486–96, 523–31; correspondence, 551, 591–614; Donnelly on, 486–87; friendship with Mario Cuomo, xv–xix, 17, 57–58, 186–87, 196, 469, 517–21; friends of, 273–95, 613–14
O'Shaughnessy, William Mac, 284, 288
O'Shea, James, 258–59, 284, 291, 329, 332, 352, 652
O'Shea, Margaret, 295
O'Sullivan, Emilie, 295
Oswald, Lee Harvey, 106–7
O'Toole, Tommy, 371
Ottazzi, Giampaolo, 284
Ottinger, Richard, 284
Oz, Lisa and Mehmet, 284

Pacifica, 55
Pacific Book Review, on Cuomo biography, 527
Packwood, Bob, 53, 74, 284
Paduano, Lenny, 284, 371, 402
Paine, Thomas, 77–78, 317, 325, 646
Paladino, Carl, 224
Paley, Babe, 284

Paley, William S., 44, 53–55, 74–75, 284, 388
palliative care, 174–75, 179–80
Palm, Steve, 284
Palm Beach, Ruddy on, 86–87
Palomino, Fabian, 284, 503–4, 509
Paolercio, Anthony, 284
Parella, Joe, 260, 284
Parenti, Deborah, 284
parenting, and censorship, 36–37, 40, 67
Parette, Diane, 284
Parisi, Richie, 284
Parker, Everett C., 284
Parkinson, A. J., 40
Parsons, James O., 284
partisanship, Cuomo (Mario) on, 473–75
Parton, Dolly, 355
Partridge, Bob, 291
pasta primavera, 255
Pastore, Vincent, 284
Pataki, George, 139, 143–45, 284, 405; Cahill and, 212–13, 216, 221
Pataki, Libby, 284, 295
Paterson, David, 284, 503, 571
Patrella, Nick, 284
Patrick, Dennis, 50, 53
Paul, saint, 536, 577
Paul, Leo, Jr., 284
Paul, Rand, 111
Paulson, Ken, 73, 284
Pavarotti, Luciano, 369, 462, 489
Pavelle, Gregg, 284, 291, 652
Paz, Tito Gainza, 54, 75
Pedroso, Alina, 291
Peebles, Bob, 366, 409
Pellettiere, Steve, 284, 653
Pellicci, Paul, 284, 291, 654
Pelosi, Nancy, 46, 56, 284, 295, 395, 640
Pence, Mike, 642
Pepe, Gabriele, 260, 284, 653
Pepe, Gene, 284
Percoco, Joe, 284, 291, 501, 509
Perella, Joseph, 284
Perelman, Ron, 261, 284
Perillo, Mario, 284
Perot, Ross, 548
Perry, Marco, 284
Persico, Joseph, 284
Persky, Bill, 284, 385
Pesce, Frank, 284
Peter, saint, 167, 170
Peter, Rob, 258

Peterson, Pete, 284
Petrillo, Augie, 284, 587
Peyser, Peter, 284
Pfeiffer, Jane Cahill, 356
Philbin, Regis, 377, 384
Philippidis, Alex, 284
Phillips, Irna, 356
Phillips, McCandlish, 336
Piccininni, Mauro, 310
Pickens, T. Boone, 284
Pickney, Drew, 284
Pierce, Lorraine and Bob, 374
Pierre Hotel, 241–42
Pileggi, Nick, 336, 521
Pinkham, Dick, 301, 414
Pinto, Deleon, 284
Pirro, Al, 291
Pirro, Jeanine, 10, 284, 291, 295, 419, 641
Pisani, Joe, 284, 402, 411
Pisano, Kathy, 284, 291, 295, 654
Pisano, Richard, 284, 291, 403, 654
Piwowarski, Dave, 284
Planell, Ray, 291
Planned Parenthood, 639
Plimpton, George, 284
Plunkett, Caryl Donnelly, 284, 288, 291, 295,
    404–7
Plunkett, Kevin, 213, 284, 291, 306, 578, 581
Plunkett, Rosemary, 284, 295
Plunkett, Ryan, 213, 284
Plunkett, William, 213, 219, 273, 291, 306, 404–
    5, 578, 581, 652
Plunkett, William, Jr., 284
Poindexter, John, 199
Poitier, Sidney, 346–48
Polacco, Vincent, 291
police: Anastasi and, 398; Cahill and, 218;
    Carroll and, 318–20; O'Neill and, 316
political correctness, 78, 639; Reisman on,
    557–58
politics: Cahill on, 213, 222, 225; Cuomo
    (Andrew) on, 444–45, 448, 450; Cuomo
    (Mario) on, 502, 509, 515–16; Cuomo
    (Matilda) on, 464; Dolan on, 173; Marti-
    nelli on, 140–45; O'Rourke and, 473;
    Rockefeller and, 118, 360; Sullivan on,
    162. See also endorsements
Pollard, Don, 284
Pope, Leavitt, 284, 366, 409
Popkin, Arlene, 60
Popper, Merna, 284

Porcelli, Mary, 284, 291, 295, 501
Porter, Cole, 66, 385, 391, 603
Porter, Ken, 284, 291
Porter, Kenneth, 654
Post, Nancy and Skyler, 284
Poster, Tom, 284
Potter, Donn King, 284
Potts, Elissa, 284
poverty: Breslin and, 339; Lostritto on, 152
Povich, Maury, 284
Powe, Wayne, 653
Powell, Colin, 165, 553
Powell, Lucas A., Jr., 63–64
Powell, Wayne, 284
Powers, Frederic B., 284, 360
Powers, Frederic B., Jr., 284
Powers, Liz, 270
Powers, Peter, 284
pragmatism: Cuomo (Andrew) and, 444,
    449–50; Cuomo (Mario) and, 505
prayer: Dee and, 345; Lostritto on, 154; of
    St. Francis, 160; Sullivan on, 167; Tucker
    on, 406
preaching, Lostritto on, 157–58
presidency: Bush (G. H. W.) and, 546–50;
    Cuomo (Mario) and, 498, 509–10
press. See media
Pressman, Gabe, 284
Presten, Sy, 425
Preston, Frances, 284, 355–56
Preston, Patsy, 284, 295
Pretlow, Gary, 284, 291
Prezioso, Sal, 142–43
Price, Hugh, 317
priesthood, Lostritto on, 155
principles, Cuomo (Mario) on, 533–38
Pritchard, John S. III, 323–25
privacy, Rockefeller and, 125–26
Procario, Saverio, 284, 649
Procopio, Dominic, 189, 291, 317, 371, 410,
    653
profanity, 63, 66–67
progressivism: Cuomo (Andrew) and, 445–
    46; Cuomo (Mario) and, 505
Proxmire, William, 53
public service: Bush (G. H. W.) and, 542;
    Cuomo (Mario) and, 508
Publisher Daily Reviews, on Cuomo biogra-
    phy, 530
Purdy, Ralph, 284
Putnam, Caroline, 261, 284

Quaal, Ward, 53, 73, 77, 284, 367, 382-83, 388-89, 408
Quadland, Michael, 284
Quaranta, Kevin, 284
Quayle, Dan, 260
Queens, NY, 259, 333-34, 495, 503
Quello, Jim, 53, 388
Quinn, Doug, 291
Quinn, Jane Bryant, 284
Quinn, Peter, 284
Quinn, Sally, 351

Raab, Jennifer, 284
Raap, Denise and Greg, 262, 285, 291
race issues: death penalty and, 627; Imus and, 12-13; Spinelli on, 324-25
Racette, Ann-Christine, 284
radio, Rehr on, 41
Radziwill, Lee, 295
Raimon, Chris, 284
Raita, Tiziana, 284
Rakoff, Jef, 284
Rampersaud, Jennifer, 653
Randall, Tony, 284
Rao, Joe, 284
Raposo, Joe, 284-85
Rappelyea, Clarence "Rapp," 285
Raske, Janet and Ken, 285
Rather, Dan, xv, 53, 81, 90-92, 285, 291, 351, 367, 491, 600
Rather, Jean, 295
Ravenel, Charlie "Pug," 285
Ray, Tom, 378
Reagan, Nancy, 383
Reagan, Ronald, 53, 77, 383; Cahill on, 222; Kelly and, 199-200; Maccioni on, 244-45
Redd, M. Paul, 285, 299-300
Red Flag Bill, 447
Red Lion v. FCC, 55, 70
Reed, Rex, 285
Reeves, Richard, 336
Rega, Rae, 374
Rehr, David, 32-36, 39-42
Reichl, Ruth, 285, 604
Reid, Harry, 631, 640
Reid, Mary Louise, 43, 285, 295
Reid, Ogden Rogers, 53-54, 75, 78, 142, 285, 291, 301, 367, 371, 402, 414; interviews with, 33-36, 43-45
Reilley, Mary Clare, 285
Reilly, Carol, 295, 356, 384

Reilly, Joe, 53, 74, 285, 291, 351, 365, 377, 384, 493, 519-20, 652
Reilly, Mary Clare, 652
Reisman, Phil, xv, 19, 285, 291, 336, 339, 490, 581, 647; on Billy Bush, 557-58; on Cuomo biography, 525-26; on Rockefeller, 117-18, 122, 130, 134
religion: Comfort on, 180-82; Dolan on, 172; Lostritto on, 153; Maccioni on, 252; Martinelli on, 138-39
religious liberty, Cuomo (Andrew) on, 455-59
René, Henri, 386
Republican Party: Cahill and, 212, 215-18, 226; Cuomo (Andrew) and, 445-47; Killian and, 571-75; Martinelli and, 143-44; Smith and, 128-30; Trump supporters and, 637; WVOX and, 578-79
responsibility, Hastings on, 38
restaurants, 249-63; Le Cirque, 237-48, 251
Reynolds, Joey, 377
Reynoso, Elva Amparo, 285, 291, 652
rhetoric: Cuomo (Andrew) and, 448-49, 565; Cuomo (Mario) and, 497, 501-2, 506, 511, 516, 518
Rhoads, Eric, 53, 75, 285, 291
Rhodes, Don, 543
Rhodes, Jim, 363
Ribicoff, Dan, 291
Riccardi, Anthony, 291-92
Ricci, Stefano, 285
Rice, Condoleezza, 553
Rice, Edmund, 314-15
Rice, Jared, 317
Rich, Frank, 562
Richards, Jovan C., 285
Richardson, W. Franklyn, 285
Richman, Murray, 204, 206, 211, 285, 292, 653
Richman, Stacey, 206, 205
Richnavsky, Robert, 285
Richter, Matt, 285
Rickles, Don, 285, 354
Riddle, Nelson, 493
Rifas, David, 285, 653
Riggio, Leonard, 92, 285, 492, 524, 655
Righter, Volney "Turkey," 285
Rinfret, Pierre, 285
Rippa, Vinny, 285, 292, 371, 402
Risko, Robert, 650
Ritacco, Lucille, 285
Rivera, Clara, 285

Rivera, Geraldo, 285, 367
Rivera, Mariano, 285, 481
Rizzi, Deb, 653
Roach, Tom, 305
Roberts, Sam, 285, 336, 492, 605; on Cuomo biography, 524–25, 531
Roberts, Wilfred, 653
Robin, Ron, 261, 285
Robinson, Cari, 60
Robinson, Dick, 285, 611–12
Rocca, Mo, 269
Rocco (hairdresser), 396
Rocco, Joseph "Jim," 292
Rochelle, Marty, 285, 292, 374, 417–19, 653
Rockefeller, Abby Aldrich, 122, 127
Rockefeller, Happy, 124–27, 129, 285, 289, 295, 362, 367
Rockefeller, Larry, 285
Rockefeller, Laurance, 136, 285
Rockefeller, Mary Todhunter Clark, 117
Rockefeller, Nelson, 110, 142, 216, 221, 285, 288, 306, 367, 402, 411, 485, 522, 553–54, 567, 578, 609; Cuomo (Andrew) on, 443; death of, 124–25, 359–64; Smith on, 115–36
Rockefeller, Nelson, Jr., 128
Rockwell, Norman, 317
Rodgers, Richard, 385, 603
Roe v. Wade, 573, 640
Rogers, Rex Todd, 285
Rogers, Tommy, 285
Rogers, William Pierce, 249, 285
Romney, George, 119
Rooney, Art, 186, 261
Rooney, June, 285, 652
Rooney, Tim, 261, 285, 292, 419, 652
Roosevelt, Franklin Delano, 59, 552; Rockefeller and, 118, 120, 130
Roosevelt, Theodore, 487; Rockefeller and, 116, 118, 130, 360
Roper, Sabrina "Sunny," 257, 295
Rose, Cristina, 292
Rose, Janine, 285, 292, 295, 582
Rosen, Aby, 296–97
Rosenbaum, Marlon, 285
Rosenberg, Alan, 285, 292, 652
Rosenberg, Wendy, 295
Rosencrans, Bob, 285
Rosenthal, A. M., 53, 285
Rosenthal, Irving, 285
Rosse, Flo Vizzi, 285
Rossiter, Hal, 285

Rote, (William) Kyle, 249, 285
Roth, Philip, 285, 329–32, 654–55
Roura, Phil, 285
Rowan, Roy, 490
Rowe, Billy, 285
Ruane, Darby, 285, 371
Rubin, Marjorie, 292
Rubino, Dan, 285, 653
Rubio, Marco, 144
Ruby, Jack, 106
Ruddy, Chris, 85–89, 285, 643
Ruderman, Jerry, 306
Ruderman, Terri, 306
Rudigoz, Michel, 285
Rudin, Jack, 251, 285, 428
Rudin, Susan, 295
Ruhl, Joe, 285
Ruhl, Joseph, 653
Ruminski, Michael, 285
Rumsfeld, Donald, 135–36
Rusconi, Natale, 285
Ruskin, Alvin Richard, 285, 288, 306, 371, 375, 402, 411, 579, 653
Ruskin, Sylvia Besson, 285
Russell, Mark, 484
Russert, Big Russ, 349–50, 352
Russert, Luke, 352
Russert, Tim, 285, 349–53, 560
Russo, Gianni, 236, 259, 285, 292, 316, 603, 652
Russo, Maria, 285, 295
Russo, Pete, 285, 292
Rutenberg, Jim, 339
Rwanda, Cuomo (Mario) on, 535
Ryan, Ed, 75, 285, 292

Saele, Vincent, 285
Safe Act: Cahill on, 223–24; Cuomo (Andrew) on, 447
Safir, Leonard, 285
Safyer, Steven, 285, 292
St. Amand, Emilia, 281, 292, 294
Saint Francis Breadline, 147–49, 156–58
St. James, Susan, 285, 295
Salandra, Lindsay, 653
Salerno, Al and George, 250, 285
Salhany, Lucie, 356
Samson, David, 285
Samuels, Bill, 285
Samuels, Howard, 249, 285, 367
Samuels, Irv, 285

Sanatar, Glen, 285, 652
Sand, Leonard, 141
Sanders, Bernie, 639
Sandor, Andy, 653
Sandroni, Lou, 285
Sandy, Hurricane, 149, 154
Sanford, Bruce, 53, 75
Santos, Joao "Bamboo," 292
Saracino, Carmine, 374
Sarames, Nick, 285
Sarcone, John, 309–10
Sargent, Elaine, 295
Sarnoff family, 388
Savino, Steve, 285, 292, 653
Savino, Steve III, 654
Sawyer, Diane, 295, 351
Saxe, Frank, 53, 75
Scalia, Antonin, 497–98
Scarangella, Jack, 285
Scarano, Angela "Nudge," 285, 295, 374
Scarborough, Chuck, 285
Scarborough, Joe, 351, 641
Scardino, Vinnie, 285
Scarpino, Anthony, 306
Schaefer, Bob, 373
Schaefer, Rudy, 414
Schaller, Joe, 285, 318, 653
Schechter, Debbie, 285
Scheinkman, Alan, 285, 292, 653
Scher, Howard, 415
Scher, Preston "Sandy," 285
Schieffer, Bob, 351
Schiller, Friedrich von, 538
Schlesinger, Arthur, xv, 133
Schlesinger, Stephen, 285, 514
Schmertz, Herb, 69, 285
Schmuckler, Alan, 484
Schober, Edwin K., 285
Schuebel, Reggie, 356
Schultz, Debbie Wasserman, 639
Schumer, Amy, 640
Schumer, Chuck, 583, 639
Schwartz, Arthur, 269
Schwartz, Jeff, 653
Schwartz, Jonathan, 269
Schwartz, Larry, 120
Schwartz, Louis, 285
Schwartz, Wally, 285, 366, 409
Schwartzman, Andrew Jay, 285
Schwarzenegger, Arnold, 543
Scollon, William Kirby, 285, 371, 374

Scott, Hugh, 285
Scott, Jim, 285
Scott, Justin, 285
Screvane, Paul, 249, 285
Scully, John, 285, 301, 414–16
Scully, Mike, 292, 374
Scully, Nancy and Dennis, 285
Scully, Sue, 285, 295, 301, 415
Scully, Vin, 488
Sebring, Tom, 285
Seidenberg, Ivan, 285–86
Selimaj, Bruno, 286
Selimaj, Nino, 286
September 11, 2001, 59, 155, 533, 535
Sessa, Eddie, 286
Sevareid, Eric, 49, 53, 268
Sevarin, Benito, 286
Shafiroff, Jean, 286
Shakespeare, William, 66
Shannon, Hugh, 236, 286, 288
Shannon, Scott, 76, 286, 292, 528
Shannon, Trish, 286
Shargel, Gerald, 204–11
Sharon (aide), 501
Sharpe, Tom, 286, 587
Sharples, Winston "Win," 286
Sharpton, Al, 16, 286, 561, 642
Shaw, Artie, 494
Shaw, Jack, 286
Shaw, Lynn, 286
Shawn, Eric, 286
Shayne, Alan, 286
Shear, Stanley, 57
Sheed, Wilfred, 286
Scheindlin, Judy, 286, 292, 295
Shell, Adam, 339
Shelley, Gladys, 285
Sherber, Dan, 286
Sheremata, Lydia, 286
Sherman, Allie, 286
Sherman, Daryl, 286, 295
Shesol, Jeff, 514
Shnayerson, Michael, 521
Shor, Toots, 249, 275, 286, 288, 650
Short, Bobby, 234, 236, 286, 288
Shribman, David, 514
Sidney, Paul, 409
Siegel, Harold, 286
Siegel, Herb, 286
Siegel, Norman, 60, 74
Siegenthaler, John, 74

Silva, Michele, 292, 295
Silverman, Sarah, 641
Silverstein, Jason, 339
Simon and Garfunkel, 534
Simone, Mark, 292, 524, 638, 640
Simpson, Alan, 543
Simpson, Sylvia, 465
Sinatra, Frank, 250, 286, 288, 384, 386, 489–90, 514–15, 614
singers, 234–35; Hutton, 368; Maccioni on, 239–40; Osgood, 268–70
Sinnott, Peter, 286
Sinuk, Seymour, 286
Sipser, I. Philip, 286
Siracusano, Luciano III, 286
Sisco, Fran, 653
Sitrick, Joe, 286
skepticism, Lostritto on, 153
Slatcher, Deborah, 654
Slepian, Dan, 286
Slick, Joe, 287, 410–13
Slotnick, Barry, 206, 286, 292
Smillie, Bobby, 286
Smith, Al, 552
Smith, Albert, 653
Smith, Emily, xv, 286, 292, 295
Smith, Fran, 250, 286
Smith, Gordon, 286
Smith, Harry, 269
Smith, Jan Johnson, 286, 292, 295
Smith, John, 250, 286
Smith, Liz, xv, 286, 292, 295, 367, 486, 488, 490–91, 614
Smith, Malcolm, 571–72
Smith, Richard Norton, 115–36, 286
Smith, Sally Bedell, 286
Smith, Squeegie, 250
Smith, Walter "Red," 286, 342
Smulyan, Jeff, 286
Smyth, Tommy, 286, 652
Sniffen, Allan, 286
Snyder, Bruce, 250, 286
Snyder, Marcia, 286
social issues: Cuomo (Andrew) on, 446; Cuomo (Matilda) on, 466; Kelly on, 197
social media, Cuomo (Andrew) on, 449
Sockwell, Jane Wharton, 286, 295
Socrates, 497–99
Sorokoff, Stephen, 286
Spady, Sam, 374
Spallone, Henry, 140, 142

Spano, Brenda Resnick, 295
Spano, Domenico "Mimmo," 286
Spano, Josephine, 146
Spano, Len, 146
Spano, Michael, 146
Sparkman, Drake, 414
speech, freedom of. See freedom of speech
Spencer, John, 286
Spencer, Phil, 286, 366, 409
Speyer, Jerry, 260, 286, 491
Speyer, Rob, 286, 292
Spicer, John, 286, 292
Spicer, Kathy, 295
Spicer, Michael, 286
Spiliadis, Costas, 260
Spillane, Robert "Bud," 286
Spina, Sue, 295
Spinelli, Joe, 286, 292, 337, 546, 566, 652; on Pritchard, 323–25
Spitzer, Eliot, 571
Springsteen, Bruce, 286
Spuck, Michelle, 352
Staggers, Harley O., 33–34, 44–45, 54, 75
Stanton, Frank, 33–34, 44, 53–54, 75
Stark, Sandy, 282
State University of New York, Rockefeller and, 131
Staub, Rusty, 286
Stein, Andrew, 286
Stein, Dennis, 286
Steinbrenner, George, 250, 286, 367
Steinem, Gloria, 286, 367
Steinhart, Percy, 286
Steinmetz, Chaim, 455
Stengel, Andrew, 286
Stengel, Renee and Stuart, 286, 292
Stephanopolous, George, 351
Stephens, Bradley, 286
Stephens, Don, 286
Stephens, Martha, 286
Stephenson, Marian, 356
Sterling, John, 292, 488–89, 607–8
Stern, Gary, 427
Stern, Howard, 31, 53, 60, 67, 71, 76
Sternberg, Victor, 653
Sternhagen, Frances, 317
Stevens, Don, 53, 292, 651
Stevens, Noel, 653
Stevenson, Adlai, 552
Stevenson, Gayle, 292
Steves, Phyllis, 291

Stewart, Potter, 25, 29, 37, 53, 55
Stewart-Cousins, Andrea, 295, 444–45, 569, 652
Stinchfield, Judy, 286
Stone, Martin, 53, 286, 288, 409, 608, 652
Stone, Roger, 105–14, 286
Storrier, Shel, 366
Stowers, Andy, 286
Strang, Marie and Hick, 398
Straus, Ellen Sulzberger, 286, 295, 356
Straus, Eric, 366
Straus, R. Peter, 286, 366
Streger, Murph, 286
Strome, Agatha Gasparini, 286
Strome, Chuck, 286, 292, 319, 653
Stuart, Ariel and Perry, 308
Sturm, John, 286, 349–50, 352
Sturman, Howard, 292
Styron, William, 329
subways, Sullivan on, 163
Sullivan, Bill, 371
Sullivan, Edward O. "Ned," 286
Sullivan, John Van Buren, 53, 286, 288, 366–67, 385, 409, 653
Sullivan, Joseph, 161–69, 286
Sullivan, K. T., 286, 391, 491, 494
Sulzberger, Arthur O., Jr., 75, 286, 292, 546, 602
Sulzberger, Arthur O., Sr. "Punch," 53, 75, 286, 546, 614
Summer, Susan and Bob, 286
Sunderman, Frederic, 286
Super Bowl, Kelly and, 192–95
Supreme Court, 70; Abrams on, 28, 30; and Clinton loss, 642; Cuomo and, 37, 497–99
sureness, 139, 171, 197, 237, 305, 345, 373; Cahill on, 220
Suric, Teddy, 259, 264–67, 286, 652
Suslak, Adele, 292
Sutera, Paul, 206
Sutton, Percy, 286
Swayze, John Cameron, Jr., 286
Sweeney, Brad, 302
sweetness, xvii, 274, 485, 507, 514
Swenson, Steve, 608
Syms, Marcy, 295
Syms, Sy, 286
Syms, Sylvia, 286

Tagliabue, Paul, 407
Taishoff, Kathy, 295

Taishoff, Laurie, 292
Taishoff, Lawrence, 3, 12, 53, 66, 73, 286, 366, 387
Taishoff, Rob, 12, 73, 286, 292, 653
Taishoff, Sol, 12, 53, 73, 80, 286, 366, 387
Talbott, Julie, 593–95
Talese, Gay, xv, 286, 336, 490–91, 514–15
Talkers, 74
Tarantino, Al, 317
Tardi, Joe, 286, 653
Tarillo, Giuseppe, 286, 297
Taubner, Joan, 286, 292, 295
Taubner, Val, 286, 292
Taussig, Eloise and James II, 286
tax issues, Rockefeller on, 130–31
Taylor, Marlin R., 286
Taylor, Tom, 53, 75, 286, 292
Tea Party, Smith on, 128
technology, Kelly on, 200–201
Tedesco, Mary, 374
Teilhard de Chardin, Pierre, 305, 493, 654; Cuomo (Mario) on, 506, 535–36; quoted, 305, 331, 418, 532, 537, 654
Templeton, John, 286
Tenore, Steve, 286, 292, 403, 577, 652
Teresa of Calcutta, Mother, 184, 522
terrorism, and civil liberties, 57–61
Tertullian, 524
Terzi, Stefano, 258, 286
Tese, Vincent, 260, 509
Thayer, Ann Wharton, 286, 292, 295, 425, 651
Thayer, Harry, 286, 366, 409
Thayer, Jeanne Cooley, 286
Thayer, Thomas C., 286
Thayer, Walter Nelson, 53, 74, 190, 249, 286, 301, 342, 357, 414, 425
Thomas, Lowell, 268, 286, 488, 614
Thomas, Richard, 286
Thompson, Andrew, 207
Thompson, Cam, 366
Thompson, Ellis, 287
Thompson, Geoff, 292
Thompson, Jim, 287, 380
Thompson, Liz Bracken, 292
Thompson, Michelle, 652
Thompson, Ruth Hassell, 295
Thurmond, Strom, 361
Tihany, Adam, 287
tikkun olam, 60, 458, 479–80, 493, 510, 536–37
Tilden, Janet and Wes, 292
Tilley, Samantha "Sam," 257, 287, 295, 653

tipping, Maccioni on, 247
Tisch, John, 193–94
Tisch, Jonathan, 292
Tocatlian, Pat, 366
Tocci, Ron, 287
Tocci, Tony and Sal, 273, 410
Tolkien, J. R. R., 618
Tom (aide), 501
Tompkins, Towle, 287
Toner, Jerry, 287
Tong, Michael, 287
Toobin, Jeffrey, 514
Toone, Alex, 318
Tormé, Mel, 287, 386
Torres, Jorge, 287
Tragale, Mary, 287, 501
Trangucci, Lou, 317
Traugott, Marty, 371
Travis, Neal, 53, 251, 287–88
Travis, Tolly, 295
Trayman, Alyssa, 263
Trayman, Audrey, 263
Trayman, Dolph, 263, 287
Tree, Marietta, 287, 295
Tree of Life Synagogue shooting, Andrew
    Cuomo remarks following, 455–59
Trimper, Diane and John, 287
Trotta, Frank, 373
Trotta, Lorraine, 373
Troum, Carol, 311
Trump, Donald, 71, 261, 287, 338, 367, 556–
    57, 566, 574, 632; and Ailes, 85; and
    Clinton loss, 643; Cuomo (Andrew) on,
    445, 450; and immigrants, 644–45; Mac-
    cioni on, 252–54; Martinelli on, 143–44;
    O'Reilly episode and, 8, 11; Rather on,
    91–92; Ruddy on, 86–88; supporters of,
    636–38
Trump, Ivanka, 642
Trump, Melania, 639
Trusa, Maria, 287
Tucker, Catherine, 295
Tucker, Diane Straus, 287
Tucker, Robert, 287, 292, 405–7, 654
Tufo, Peter, 287
Tulis, Mark, 287
Tune, Tommy, 287
Twedt, Laura, 287
Two Cities speech (Mario Cuomo), 493, 516
Tyrell, Steve, 234–35
tzedekah, 60, 458, 479–80, 493, 510, 536–37

United Nations, 640
United States: Dolan on, 172; McCain and,
    327; Rather on, 90, 92
United States of America v. Schwimmer, 77
University of Maryland Library of American
    Broadcasting, 73
Updike, John, 329
Upton, Fred, 67
US Review of Books, on Cuomo biography,
    529
usury, Cuomo (Mario) on, 477–78

Vacca, Paul, 287
Vacca, Sergio, 260, 653
Vaccarella, Joe, 287, 587
Vacco, Dennis, 287
Vadeboncoeur, Curly, 366, 408–9
Valeant, Joe, 250, 287
Valencia, Irma, 287, 292
Valencia, Jesus, 292, 652
Valenti, Charles, 287, 292, 398, 653
Valenti, Jack, 5–7, 49–50, 287
Valenti, Jerry, 287
Valenti, John, 287, 292, 653
Valenti, Tom, 261
values: Bush (G. H. W.) and, 544; Cuomo
    (Mario) on, 533–38; Dolan on, 617–23
Van Deerlin, Lionel, 53, 74, 287
Vandenburgh, Paul, 287
vanden Heuvel, William, 280
Vanderbilt, Alfred Gwynne, 287
Vanderbilt, Wendy, 287, 295
Van Heusen, Jimmy, 494
Van Horne, Harriet, 367
Van Sickle, James, 268, 287
Van Urk family, 265
Vargas Llosa, Mario, 281
Vaughn, Linda, 295
Vaughn, Steve, 285
Velella, Guy, 287
Venor, Dan, 287
Verbitsky, Bonnie, 295
Verbitsky, Nick, 366
Vergara, George, 287, 371
Vergari, Carl, 287, 402
Verni, John, 287, 572, 653
Verni, Vito, 287
Vernon, Donald, 653
Verstandig, Davyne, 287
Victor, Wendy and Royal "Mike," 287
Vigeant, Dave, 262, 287, 292, 653

Vincentians, 518
violence, Cuomo (Mario) on, 40
Vitulli, Joseph L., Sr., 287, 410–13
Vitulli, Rose, 410
Vivino, Floyd, 287, 652
Vivolo, Michael, 287
Vokhshoorzadeh, Sean, 287, 292
Von Bidder, Alex, 251, 259, 287, 292, 296–97,
   605, 652
Von Bidder, Sandra, 295
Von Nicolai, Maria, 292
von Richtofen, Sessa, 295
von Wulffen, Shirin, 295
voting reforms, Cuomo (Andrew) on, 447
Voute, Bill, 287
Vuolo, Art, 287
Vuy, Ron, 287, 292

Wachtler, Sol, 287
Wagner, Phyllis Cerf, 287
Wagner, Robert, 287
Wain, Bea, 276
Wainer, Mario, 247, 261, 287, 292
Wald, Richard, 287
Waldman, Suzyn, 608
Walker, Glenroy, 653
Walker, Maureen, 588
Walker, Scott, 111
Wallace, George and Cornelia, 361
Wallace, Malcolm, 105, 107–8
Walter, Elsie Maria Troija, 287
Walters, Barbara, 295, 351, 367
Walters, Lou, 369
war: and civil liberties, 59–60; Maccioni on,
   252–53
Ward, John, 287
Ward, William "Boss," 360
Warley, Stephen, 287
Warren, Bill, 366
Warren, Elizabeth, 639
Washington, Denzel, 587
Washington, George, 457, 473–75
Wasicsko, Nick, 140–41
Weale, Ross, 287
Weaver, Rosemary, 287
Weaver, Will, 287
Weigel, George, 620
Wein, Oscar and Rob, 366
Weinberg, John, 287
Weinberg, Sidney, 287
Weiner, Anthony, 298, 639

Wein family, 414
Weinstein, Michael, 287
Weinstein brothers, 38
Weiss, Charlie, 287
Weiss, Walter, 287
Welch, Suzy and Jack, 287
Weld, William, 642
Wellner, Karl, 291
Wells, Pete, 602–6
Wendelken, Charles, 287
Wender, Sabrina, 239–40, 282, 292, 295
Werblin, Sonny, 249
Wertlieb, Jordan, 287
West, Donald, 53, 73, 287, 356, 366, 387, 653
Westchester, NY: county executive races,
   576–83; Martinelli and, 140; Mohl and,
   102
Westchester County Press, 299–300
Weymouth, Lally, 287, 295
Wharton, Mary Jane, 357–58
Whitaker, Jack, 287
White, Bill, 287
White, Bruce J., 287
White, Margita, 356
White Plains, NY, 304–5; Bradley for mayor,
   589–90
Whitman, Ann, 120, 287, 295
Whitman, Ed, 292
Whitney, John Hay "Jock," 53, 74, 249, 287,
   342
Whitney, Marylou, 287
Whittaker, Jack, 249
Whyte, Carl, 653
Whyte, Ronny, 287
Wick, Margo Conway, 295
Widmark, Richard, 329
Wiesel, Elie, 456
Wiley, Dick, 388
Wilgus, Chuck, 287
Will, George, 351, 640
William (doorman), 287
Williams, Brian, 287, 377, 384, 560–61
Williams, Dotty Mack, 295
Williams, Edward Bennett, 249
Williams, George, 366
Williams, Tom, 301
Williams, William B., 287–88, 367, 384–86,
   611–12
Williamson, Bud, 292, 653
Willkie, Wendell, 518
Wilson, Katherine, 295

Wilson, Leighton, 653
Wilson, Malcolm, 273, 287, 306, 367, 402, 411, 500, 578, 609; Martinelli and, 140, 142; quoted, xv, 124, 131, 288, 297, 372
Wilson, Sloan, 287
Windeler, Robert, 287, 490
Winer, Lawrence, 53
Winged Foot Golf Club, 306, 392
Winston, Barbara, 287
Witkowski, Ann, 374
Witmer, Duffy, 263, 287
Witt, Alex, 500
WNEW, 385
Wohl, Amiel, 287, 292, 371
women priests, Cuomo (Mario) on, 481
Wood, Charles. *See* Osgood, Charles
Wood, Fran, 287
Woodruff, Judy, 295, 351
Woody (caller), 374
Woolridge, C. V. "Jim," 287
WOR, 376–78, 578, 593
Working Family Party, 217
World War II: Bush (G. H. W.) and, 541–42; Cuomo (Mario) and, 534
Wright, Bruce, 287
Wright, Greg, 292
Wright, Keith, 287
Wright, Robert, 536
writing: Breslin and, 336–42; Cuomo (Mario) and, 517–18; Roth and, 329, 331; Smith on, 134
WVIP, xvii, 652

WVOX, xvii, 41, 351–52, 652; Black and, 424; callers, 372–75; Cuomo (Andrew) on, 453; Reid on, 45; Rockefeller and, 360; and September 11, 2001, 59

X, Malcolm, 344

Yarborough, Ralph, 113
Yarnell, David, 287, 385
Yonkers, Martinelli and, 137, 141–42, 146
Young, Clinton, 287
Young, Francis X., 287, 292
Young, Leigh Curry, 287
Young, Whitney Moore, 287, 317
Youngblood, Rufus, 113
Youngling, Susan and Jay, 287
Yurgaitis, Tony, 257, 287

Zack, Donny, 371
Zambelli, Drew, 443, 501, 566
Zander, Beth, 288, 295
Zardoya, Julia, 295
Zarif, Mohammad Javad, 288
Zenger, John Peter, 57, 78–79
zero tolerance, Sullivan on, 167
Zherka, Sam, 288
Ziani, Zahir, 288, 292
Zimmerman, William, 292
Zogo, Maixent, 288, 653
Zuckerman, Susan and Art, 288, 653
Zuliani, Giuliano, 259, 288, 292
Zuzullo, Todd, 292